Presidential Leadership

The Vortex of Power

Bert A. Rockman

Purdue University

Richard W. Waterman

University of Kentucky

New York   Oxford
OXFORD UNIVERSITY PRESS
2008

Oxford University Press, Inc., publishes works that further Oxford
University's objective of excellence in research, scholarship, and education.

Oxford   New York
Auckland   Cape Town   Dar es Salaam   Hong Kong   Karachi
Kuala Lumpur   Madrid   Melbourne   Mexico City   Nairobi
New Delhi   Shanghai   Taipei   Toronto

With offices in
Argentina   Austria   Brazil   Chile   Czech Republic   France   Greece
Guatemala   Hungary   Italy   Japan   Poland   Portugal   Singapore
South Korea   Switzerland   Thailand   Turkey   Ukraine   Vietnam

Copyright © 2008 by Oxford University Press, Inc.

Published by Oxford University Press, Inc.
198 Madison Avenue, New York, New York 10016
http://www.oup.com

Oxford is a registered trademark of Oxford University Press

ISBN 978-0-19-533251-3

Printing number: 9 8 7 6 5 4 3 2 1

Printed in the United States of America on acid-free paper

Contents

Acknowledgments

The authors would like to thank the following reviewers for their useful comments and suggestions: Bruce Altschuler, SUNY–Oswego; Lara M. Brown, CSU Channel Islands; David A. Crocket, Trinity University; Chris Dolan, University of Central Florida; Andrew Dowdle, University of Arkansas; Daniel Ponder, University of Colorado–Colorado Springs; Anna Marie Schuh, Roosevelt University; Greg Shaw, Illinois Wesleyan University; Robert Spitzer, SUNY–Cortland; Charles Walcott, Virginia Polytechnic Institute; and J. Mark Wrighton, University of New Hampshire. ✦

Chapter 1

What Is Presidential Leadership?

Richard W. Waterman and Bert A. Rockman

In the business world leadership is often equated with the proverbial bottom line. Executives who lead companies with successful products and positive balance sheets generally are considered to be successful leaders. The same, however, cannot be said for presidential leadership. If we measure presidential success by the nation's economic performance, then Calvin Coolidge would be among our greatest presidents, while Franklin Roosevelt would be among our worst. Yet historians consistently rank Coolidge in the "below average" category while Roosevelt ranks in the "great" category.

Furthermore, if we associate successful presidential leadership with another common benchmark, popularity, then Calvin Coolidge and Dwight Eisenhower would be among our greatest leaders, but Abraham Lincoln would not. On the other hand, if we only value a president's ability to function as crisis manager, then Abraham Lincoln and Franklin Roosevelt would be our greatest leaders, but Theodore Roosevelt would not. Yet many polls of historians rank Teddy Roosevelt as a "great" or "near great" president.

Before we can analyze the determinants of presidential leadership, it is therefore important to answer a basic question: what do we mean by the term presidential leadership? It is clear that in asking this question we believe that some individuals are more capable of exhibiting leadership ability than others. But what criteria are most important? Is it the ability to bargain and compromise with other policy actors, good communication skills, an ability to deal with foreign policy crises, acumen in decisionmaking, or sound management capabilities? In each case, how important is personal skill? Is successful leadership merely a matter of being in the right place at the right time (during good economic times or during a crisis when presidents are best able to show their personal abilities)? Or is it possible that there are so many obstacles to successful presidential leadership that few presidents are able to govern successfully, no matter how skillful they may be?

This book examines the concept of presidential leadership from a variety of different perspectives. In so doing, our goal is to provide new insights into the meaning and role of presidential leadership.

The Great Presidents

In 2000, historians, political pundits, and politicians were asked to rank the 41 men who had served as President of the United States. The poll results are presented in Table 1.1. As expected, Abraham Lincoln, Franklin Roosevelt, George Washington, Theodore Roosevelt, and Thomas Jefferson are ranked among the nation's greatest presidents. But also ranked among the top 10 presidents are Lyndon Johnson, Dwight Eisenhower, Harry Truman, John Kennedy, and Woodrow Wilson. Many scholars argue that while Johnson had extraordinary legislative successes (particularly related to civil rights) he also led the nation into a protracted and ultimately disastrous war in Vietnam. Eisenhower's reputation has improved in recent decades, yet many scholars consider him to be a passive and unimaginative president. Truman's scholarly reputation also has been in ascendancy in recent decades, yet he left office with one of the lowest approval ratings ever recorded, the nation mired in a war in Korea, and allegations of corruption in his administration. As for Kennedy, scholars have noted that other than the 1962 Missile Crisis he had relatively few substantive accomplishments. And while Wilson undoubtedly had a profound influence on the development of the presidency, he also suffered one of most renowned presidential defeats in American political history, the Senate's rejection of the Treaty of Versailles.

Table 1.1   2000 Ranking of Presidents

1. Lincoln	15. McKinley	29. Garfield
2. F. Roosevelt	16. J. Adams	30. Van Buren
3. Washington	17. Cleveland	31. B. Harrison
4. T. Roosevelt	18. Madison	32. Arthur
5. Truman	19. J. Q. Adams	33. Grant
6. Wilson	20. G. H. W. Bush	34. Hoover
7. Jefferson	21. Clinton	35. Fillmore
8. Kennedy	22. Carter	36. Tyler
9. Eisenhower	23. Ford	37. W. H. Harrison
10. L. Johnson	24. Taft	38. Harding
11. Reagan	25. Nixon	39. Pierce
12. Polk	26. Hayes	40. A. Johnson
13. Jackson	27. Coolidge	41. Buchanan
14. Monroe	28. Taylor	

Source: Waterman (2003, 71).

Given their notable failures and limitations, why were these men considered to be among our greatest presidents? Part of the answer is the methodology employed by the 2000 survey. Presidents were ranked in 10 leadership categories: "public persuasion, crisis leadership, economic management, moral authority, international relations, administrative skill, relations with Congress, vision/setting the agenda, pursuit of equal justice for all, and performance within [the] context of their times." While these leadership qualities reflect what the public and other politicians expect from presidents today, these qualities were not always at the forefront of presidential leadership.

For instance, it is true that presidents today are expected to persuade the public, but this was not always the case. In fact, the Founding Fathers feared demagogues and most nineteenth-century presidents seldom spoke publicly, particularly on policy matters (Tulis 1987). Crisis leadership is certainly more prevalent today than it was before the twentieth century. Presidents were not expected to be active economic managers until Congress opened this door with the passage of the Budget and Accounting Act of 1921 (Sundquist 1983). While one can argue that moral authority always has been a main component of the presidential office, prior to the Spanish-American War in 1898 few presidents played a major role in international relations. Likewise, administrative skill was not necessary because the administrative state was relatively diminutive until the 1930s (Arnold 1986). Early presidents also were not expected to lead Congress. Rather, throughout most of the nineteenth century a passive executive coexisted with an activist legislative branch (Sundquist 1983). These expectations are different today. Presidents now are expected to take the lead in setting the policy agenda. Thus, on at least seven of the ten leadership qualities considered in the 2000 poll, expectations of presidential performance changed over time. As a result, the more activist presidents of the twentieth century received high rankings in the 2000 poll.

Changing expectations of presidential leadership are therefore an important criterion when we consider the question of presidential leadership. Still, it is possible that all of our so-called great presidents had certain leadership qualities or skills that made them more effective presidents. Alternatively, it is possible that they governed in difficult times that demanded higher levels of presidential leadership. To better understand this point we need to examine how scholars define the concept of presidential leadership.

Presidential Leadership in Historical Time

What makes a great president? As Burns (1965, 121) writes, "The President must be more than administrative chief or party leader. He must exert great leadership in behalf of the whole nation." If a president is not perceived as exerting such leadership then he or she is deemed as average or below average, or even a failure. Neustadt (1980, 3) notes, "In the United States we like to 'rate' a President. We measure him as 'weak' or 'strong' and call what we are measuring his 'leadership.'" Yet the difficulty for presidents is that while "we all make judgments about presidential leadership, we often base our judgments upon images of [the presidential] office that are far removed from reality." As Lowi (1985) observes, because we expect more from our presidents than they are capable of delivering, the potential for presidential failure is exacerbated. Given this dynamic, how can presidents be successful leaders?

In his classic work, Laski (1940, 36) contends, "The president must never be ahead of his time; he achieves the maximum unity by moving to objectives that are expected as well as desired." But if presidents are never ahead of their time, how can they be expected to lead rather than to follow public and elite opinion in a desired direction? One answer is provided by Skowronek (1993), who argues that presidential leadership exists in three cycles of political time: reconstruction, articulation, and disjunction. Presidents who govern during periods of reconstruction govern when expectations encourage broader presidential leadership and policy accomplishment, with a new governing coalition constructed to assist presidents in this process. During periods of articulation, presidents find themselves articulating (or rearticulating) the reconstruction president's theme. Hence, while achievement is possible, it is not as easily facilitated as it would be in a period of reconstruction. During periods of disjuncture, presidents find themselves defending the ideas of now discredited political regimes. Expectations have changed, but the presidents' policies and governing approach have not. As such, these presidents find themselves swimming against the prevailing political tide. This disjuncture provides a basis for a new president to articulate a new political vision, thus constructing a new coalition. A new period of reconstruction is therefore established. For example, Andrew Jackson was a president of reconstruction, James K. Polk of articulation, and Franklin Pierce of disjuncture. The Pierce and Buchanan presidencies thus opened the door for the construction of a new political coalition that began with Abraham Lincoln.

Thus, for presidents to take Laski's advice and not get ahead of their time, they would have to be aware of the expectations associated with the type of leadership that they can exert. Presidents of reconstruction would have the greatest leeway, while those of disjuncture would have the least. The model suggests, however, that there is relatively little that a president of disjuncture can do to provide real leadership. As such, Skowronek provides a model of incentives and constraints for presidential leadership, with incentives for leadership highest in periods of reconstruction and lowest in periods of disjuncture. He does not, however, tell us how presidents lead during either of these cyclical periods (that is, are all presidents of reconstruction destined to be successful leaders, or can disjuncture presidents overcome the constraints they face?).

Skowronek's description of four periods of political time further confounds the leadership equation. He identifies four governing periods during which presidential power emerged: the patrician period (1789–1832), the partisan period (1832–1900), the pluralist period (1900–1972), and the plebiscitary period (1972–present). During the first of these periods, "the presidency operated most directly through interpersonal relations among elites in the governing community, and the incumbent's most important political resource was his personal reputation within the nation's relatively closed society of notables" (Skowronek 1993, 52). During the partisan period, "the presidency attained an organized political foundation in a national coalition of local party machines" with presidents "acting politically as unabashed representatives of their party organization" (ibid., 54). During the pluralist period, "America rose to world power, the national economy became interdependent, and economic interests organized nationally. The presidency in this period gained new responsibilities for national affairs through an expanding bureaucratic establishment" (ibid.). Finally, in the current period of plebiscitary politics, presidents are no longer selected by the parties but rather by "candidate-centered primary campaigns." In addition, "independent candidate-centered organizations elect the party nominee; and a White House–based public relations machine manages the incumbent's political strategy" (ibid.).

These four periods of political history/time therefore further define the incentives and constraints of the presidential office. During the first period, interpersonal skill (as exhibited by George Washington and Thomas Jefferson, who dined with legislators in an attempt to advance their political views) was at a premium. Presidents such as John Adams and James Madison, who were less skillful in this regard, proved to be less effective leaders. During the second period, with the political party at the foundation of presidential leadership, presidents such as Andrew Jackson and Abraham Lincoln, who were at the forefront in founding national partisan movements, had definite political advantages over other presidents. During the pluralist period, as America rose to the status of a world power with a more centralized economy, a larger administrative presidential office emerged and with it a greater potential for strong presidential leadership. Expectations of presidential leadership also increased, but with a greater focus on the economy, and foreign policy presidents also at times became the captive of forces that often were beyond their immediate control (e.g., depressions and international crises). Those who governed in good economic times or were successful in confronting foreign policy crises were viewed as successful leaders. This dynamic continues during the plebiscitary period, though now the constant campaign aspect of this political time has exacerbated political conflict, with resulting charges of policy gridlock. Presidents also have less reliable political allies, because they run their own campaigns and coalitions often shift from issue to issue (Seligman and Covington 1989). At times their electoral incentives are different from even those of their own partisans in Congress. Hence, the ability to bargain and compromise may be less effective today than it once was, placing a premium on the need for presidents to go over the heads of elected officials and directly to the public (see Kernell 1997), if, that is, the public is willing to listen (Edwards 2003).

Skowronek's focus on four periods of political time therefore suggests that presidential leadership has not been a constant over time. Different characteristics provided the basis for presidential leadership throughout our history. Jefferson's interpersonal skills may have better fit with his time than they would today. Jackson's and Lincoln's party-building activities may have been more useful in the early to mid-1800s. Franklin Roosevelt's, John Kennedy's, and Ronald Reagan's ability to communicate directly with the public is a more valued skill in the pluralist and especially plebiscitary periods. Thus, not only are presidents constrained if they happen to be unfortunate enough to govern in periods of articulation and even more so of disjuncture, but they also must be sure that their personal skills match well with the expectations of each period of political time. Lincoln's great oratorical skills may have brought him national notice and indirectly helped him secure the White House in 1860 (Goodwin 2005), but they were of less use to him once he became president because presidents were not expected to speak publicly, not even before Congress. Fortunately, Lincoln had other political skills that allowed him to be an effective president, skills that were conducive to his time in office.

The Skowronek model therefore suggests that the qualities we seek in our leaders are a moving target. Other than obvious factors such as corruption and gross incompetence, there is no one set of leadership characteristics that distinguishes great leaders from bad ones. Rather, finding qualities that are conducive to the expectations of one's time are of critical importance.

Changing Expectations of Presidential Leadership

Skowronek's work raises a fundamental question: at certain times in political history, should we expect the president to lead at all? It is

certainly unreasonable for us to expect much from a president of disjuncture, for example, but we should always expect a great deal from
a president of reconstruction and, given the differential expectations,
should we expect most nineteenth-century presidents to be mere
clerks, faithfully administering or executing the will of the Congress
and the public? Are we unreasonable in expecting more from presidents such as Franklin Pierce, Rutherford Hayes, Chester A. Arthur,
and Grover Cleveland than presidents in the succeeding century? For
if we are attentive to the differential expectations of political time, we
must acknowledge that most nineteenth-century presidents followed
a clerkship or magisterial model, seldom taking the lead on policy
matters, whether foreign or domestic. Leadership was not expected
from 1600 Pennsylvania Avenue and thus most often it was not
provided.

Likewise, should we evaluate the presidents of the twentieth century with a different standard? With the dawn of the twentieth century both elite and public expectations of the presidential office
changed. Particularly from Theodore Roosevelt's time onward, presidents began to justify and employ a more activist presidential role. As
they did so, the public and political elites came to look with greater
frequency to the White House for policy direction and new initiatives.
"The changes that evolved during the twentieth century have created
new demands on presidents that, as a consequence, have generated
new roles and obligations for them and new criteria by which they
are judged. These new roles and criteria have, in turn, affected perceptions of leadership. . . ." As a result, the "president is expected to
be a chief policy maker and to exercise a wide range of powers" (Edwards and Wayne 1999, 11–12).

During the first half of the twentieth century, particularly during the presidencies of Theodore Roosevelt, Woodrow Wilson, and
Franklin Roosevelt, the presidency developed a new leadership esprit.
This altered the focus of scholarly studies from a preoccupation with
the powers of the presidential office to the characteristics and personal skills of the person inside the White House. That is, while biog-
raphies of presidents were always available, most scholarly works on
the presidency, even beyond the first half of the twentieth century, focused on the *institution* of the presidency (*its functions and roles*)
rather than on presidential leadership (for example, Corwin 1984;
Rossiter 1956). In fact, a primary concern with presidential leadership is a relatively modern development, one reflecting the idea that
the presidency, not Congress, should be the fulcrum of our governmental system. This reflects a broader change in expectations of the
presidency. We now expect our presidents to provide active and continuing leadership in both foreign and domestic policy. Consequently,
more so than ever, it is important for us to know what leadership
entails.

Defining Leadership

Yet, while we have come to expect leadership from our presidents, a precise definition of the characteristics of leadership has yet to emerge, though there have been several attempts to do so. For example, Burns (1965, 197–203) identifies five types of presidential leadership. "The most typical and customary type of leadership," he notes, "is the fashioning of innovations following a change of administration." A second kind of "leadership is the establishment of a precedent in such a way that it becomes a permanent fixture of the Presidency." Third is a "decisive interpretation of events at a time of crisis when traditional doctrine has been shaken and people are willing to turn to new ideas." Fourth is leadership "capable of changing the basic goals in mid-passage, by reorganizing the coalition supporting the President." While the latter is difficult to do, the fifth type "is the most exacting of all." It is "the effort not only to reshape the alignment of group interests behind one's party and administration, but to reshape the institutional framework within which the political leader seeks to realize his goals." This type of leadership is difficult "because the very institutional arrangements a leader might wish to change, operate against the feasibility of such change."

All five of Burns's criteria have one characteristic in common. They all require the president to do something affirmative, that is, to make changes to the status quo. Neustadt (1980, 3–4) agrees, arguing that governmental action is the basis for leadership.

> Although governmental action may not be the whole of leadership, all else is nurtured by it and gains meaning from it. Yet if we treat the Presidency as the President, we cannot measure him as though he were the government. Not action as an outcome but his impact on the outcomes is the measure of the man. His strength or weakness, then, turns on his personal capacity to influence the conduct of the men who make up government. His influence becomes the mark of leadership.

For Neustadt (1980, 4) influence is power and presidential power is the power to persuade. The president's ability to bargain and compromise with members of Congress and other elites is at the heart of leadership. Those presidents who can effectively develop and employ this ability are most likely to be deemed successful leaders because they are more likely to effectuate the changes that Burns recommends in his definition of leadership.

But power is not necessarily inherent in the presidential office. As Hargrove and Nelson (1984, 87) write, "Presidents are not powerful by virtue of being president. Constitutional, cultural, and political forces empower a president at some times and on some issues. . . ." As a result, "political 'skill' is crucial to leadership." The problem is that while individual "presidents can make a difference . . . different kinds of presidencies face different strategic problems, and the political resources available to them vary" (see also Rose 1991; Lammers and Genovese 2000). In other words, not all presidents have the same opportunities to be effective leaders. Consequently, when we consider what presidential leadership entails we cannot merely identify characteristics or objectives that presidents seek to advance. We must also examine the resources available to them and the impediments they face.

Unfortunately, as Neustadt concludes, the resources available to the presidency are limited. The founders did not intend for the presidency to be the most powerful branch of our governmental system. They anticipated that the legislative branch would be dominant. Presidential power therefore evolved not because of a constitutional mandate, but because of a variety of contextual factors (e.g., the industrial revolution centralized the national economy, thus creating a greater need for executive leadership, as did America's more activist role in foreign affairs). As a result, the public came to expect leadership from the presidency (Waterman 2007).

Thus, leadership involves more than the mere willingness of presidents to lead the nation. It also involves their capability to do so. As most scholars argue that the presidency has few tangible resources available to it (e.g., Buchanan 1978; R. Rose 1991; G. Rose 1997; Genovese 2003), it is not surprising that few presidents are deemed successful leaders and that presidents in turn have responded by developing new unilateral techniques (or resources) of presidential leadership (Howell 2003).

Presidents also have developed a closer relationship with the public, even at times going over the heads of the lawmakers in an attempt to influence public opinion (Kernell 1997). In an attempt to deal with ever growing public expectations, presidents also have turned the presidency into a public relations and image machine that often confuses substance with symbolism (Cohen 1997; Waterman, Wright, and St. Clair 1999). Thus, in place of leadership we often are presented with rhetoric and spectacle. These developments further confuse our notions of what constitutes real leadership and what *merely appears to be leadership*. Given these developments it is imperative that we have a clearer sense of what presidential leadership entails. That is the task of this book.

The Outline of the Book

In this book we address the question "what is presidential leadership?" from a variety of different perspectives. In Chapter 2, Jeffrey Fine and Richard Waterman synthesize the literature and develop a new model of presidential leadership. Their model identifies three basic characteristics of leadership: presidential skill, the resources available to presidents (e.g., the amount of leverage presidents have available to them), and the outcomes that result from presidential attempts at leadership. The model is designed to show that just because a president achieves a positive outcome he or she is not necessarily a successful leader. Some lucky presidents find themselves in the right place at the right time (e.g., the economy is healthy and the nation is at peace), though they exhibit little leadership ability. On the other hand, some skilled presidents find themselves in the unenviable position of being in the wrong place at the wrong time. In sum, leadership requires personal skill, but skill is not enough. Nor can we measure success merely by examining outcomes. We must consider both of these factors, along with the resources available to a president, in order to properly evaluate his or her leadership ability.

With this leadership framework in mind, the next three chapters then examine factors related to how presidents bargain and interact with other governmental institutions. These chapters address the question: do presidents have the capacity to lead, and if so under which conditions? Presidential leadership often involves getting other policy actors to support or do what the president wants. Among these policy actors, the Congress is the most prominent. An important component of presidential leadership is therefore the ability to secure congressional approval for the president's legislative program, which in Chapter 3 Cameron and Park define as a "comprehensive set of requests for new or modified laws. . . ." In securing approval for their program, presidents confront major obstacles, including a greater propensity for divided government (where at least one house of Congress is not controlled by the party of the president). This often results in high levels of gridlock. Under these circumstances presidents have less leverage to be successful leaders.

As Cameron and Park demonstrate, presidential success in dealing with Congress, then, is *contingent* on these and other political factors, which in turn define whether opportunities exist for policy action. When do presidents have the greatest leverage to act? According to Cameron and Park, presidential influence is contingent on congressional policy preferences, as well as the salience that members have toward an issue. It also depends on how much political cost legislators are willing to invest in writing new legislation. If they can pass a bill written by the president that they agree with, or at least one that is close to their preferred policy position/preferences without having to invest valuable time writing the legislation, they will have more time for constituency service, campaigning, raising campaign funds, and other activities. However, the more the president's policy position differs from the median (or middle member) of Congress, or when the level of congressional salience increases and they care more about existing differences between the president's position and their own, it becomes more difficult for presidents to secure the passage of legislation they prefer.

In Chapter 4, Epstein, Kristensen, and O'Halloran also examine gridlock, but they do so from a different perspective. They critique Keith Krehbiel's theory of gridlock. Gridlock is a well-recognized impediment to presidential success with Congress. Krehbiel (1998) developed a measure of what he called the "gridlock interval" or region, which reflects differences in ideology between the president and members of Congress (see also Brady and Volden 2006). The larger the interval, the less success presidents are expected to have with Congress. This means that presidents have limited potential to bargain with members of Congress. Epstein, Kristensen, and O'Halloran improve on Krehbiel's measure and then demonstrate that while the gridlock interval is not related to the number of laws passed by Congress, it is related to how much discretion Congress is likely to delegate to the executive. They also provide a new theoretical framework for understanding the idea of conditional presidential leadership. They find that presidential leadership is conditional on factors external to the presidency. Thus, one can extrapolate, while presidents can exert leadership, they should not be expected to do so with equal success at all times.

While Chapters 3 and 4 examine the conditions under which presidential leadership of Congress is most likely to succeed, in Chapter 5 Howell and Kriner present an alternative to Neustadt's bargaining model. They examine the concept of "power without persuasion," or the propensity of presidents of both political parties to use their *unilateral powers* to secure the policies they prefer; essentially, a means whereby presidents attempt to create their own political leverage to influence political outcomes. Presidents can employ executive orders, proclamations, and other tools of the unilateral presidency to advance their goals. But how successful is this strategy? Howell and Kriner address this question by exploring four case studies from the presidency of George W. Bush. While these case studies demonstrate the potential limitations of the unilateral presidency approach, they also reveal that in many situations presidents can greatly increase their leverage over Congress. Hence, while presidents cannot ignore the need to bargain and work with Congress, it is no longer the only game in town for presidents.

The theme from the first five chapters is that presidential leadership is contingent or conditional on presidential leverage. Presidents are more likely to be successful in promoting their policy agenda when they have greater leverage than at other times. This is so even when presidents employ their unilateral powers. But while they may have leverage, presidents also face considerable constraints or impediments when they try to lead Congress. What alternatives do they have? In his seminal book, Kernell (1997) argues that the political environment that Richard Neustadt described in 1960 is now more polarized and less amenable to the politics of bargaining and compromise. He therefore articulates an alternative leadership strategy where presidents "go public" in an attempt to go over the heads of members of Congress. Although Kernell finds that the going public strategy has not always been successful, he provides a number of case studies demonstrating how presidents have come to rely on this approach in order to increase their chances of securing congressional support for their policies.

In Chapter 6, George Edwards directly addresses Kernell's strategy. Edwards first examines the various impediments to presidential leadership, such as the system of checks and balances, a trend in recent decades toward increased ideological polarization of the two parties in Congress, and the decline of the president's coattail effect. As a result of these impediments, Edwards notes that presidents have turned to the strategy of "going public" and the "permanent campaign." In stark contrast to Kernell, however, Edwards argues that this strategy is ineffective and even counterproductive. With references to polling data, he finds, "The reality of the president's predicament is that no matter how skilled the White House may be, the president is unlikely to be consistently successful in leading either the public or Congress. Only the presence of contextual conditions that encourage deference to the president, such as occurred in Franklin Roosevelt's first term, are likely to provide the president the opportunity to dominate the policy-making process." In short, Edwards finds that the potential for successful presidential leadership depends on factors that are often outside of the president's direct control.

As noted, Edwards argues that the strategies of going public and the permanent campaign are not effective. In Chapter 7, Jeffrey Cohen provides an explanation why these strategies do not work. His focus is the president and the media. Cohen describes how the media has been transformed over time, from its golden age of the 1950s, 1960s, and 1970s when the public received most of its news from the three network news broadcasts (and from newspapers). These accounts tended to be overwhelmingly positive or neutral in the coverage of the presidency. When coverage was negative, however, particularly during the presidencies of Lyndon Johnson and Richard Nixon, Cohen contends that the press played a powerful role in affecting public perceptions of the presidency.

This relationship between the public and the press changed over time. With the advent of cable television, the public had more choices, not only regarding news broadcasts, but entertainment versus news. News cycles also changed, from a focus on the 30-minute network broadcasts to 24/7 coverage by CNN and other cable networks. As the media environment evolved, four trends became apparent: (1) the news media became more competitive and decentralized,

(2) reporting styles changed as news content became softer and more negative, (3) the public came to rely less on newspapers and more on television, and (4) public evaluations of the news media declined. Cohen argues that,

> To a degree, this news environment insulates the president from news, which helps explain Clinton's popularity rise in 1998 despite bad news. But this news environment also impedes the president's ability to lead the mass public. As a result, the president's governing style has changed. Instead of focusing his efforts on leading the nation, presidents spend more time targeting select constituencies. This narrow "going public" style reinforces the polarization in the political system, while also alienating the broad middle from American politics.

Consequently, as does Edwards, Cohen finds that the strategy of going public has its limits and may not provide presidents with increased influence.

If "going public" is not an effective leadership strategy, as Edwards and Cohen argue, then how can presidents lead Congress? As Cameron and Park and then Epstein, Kristensen, and O'Halloran argue, presidential leadership of Congress is contingent or conditional, with occasional opportunities for action. Left unclear, however, is what presidents themselves bring to the table to make things happen. What is the value of presidential skill? Are presidents dependent on factors beyond their control?

In Chapter 8, Fleisher, Bond, and Wood address these questions. Through a quantitative analysis of the determinants of presidential success with Congress they find that the political environment, particularly the level of support or opposition the president faces in Congress (e.g., whether the president's party controls Congress, the level of polarization), is a more important determinant than personal presidential skill. The battle for presidential leadership, once again, is portrayed as one between impediments and leverage. When presidents have more leverage at their disposal, they are more likely to prevail politically.

Political impediments come in different forms. While the relationship between the president and Congress is of central importance to a president's reputation, presidents also face constraints when they interact with other policy actors, such as the courts. Traditionally, the courts are described as showing considerable deference to the executive branch. In Chapter 9, Forrest Maltzman counters this judicial acquiescence thesis. He demonstrates that in recent decades, in cases where presidential administrations have filed *amicus curiae* or "friend of the court" briefs, they have been less successful. Maltzman also challenges the idea that presidents are able to use their appointment power to remake the courts. He demonstrates that the length of time that it takes for the Senate to confirm appointments has increased. In addition, the ideological distance between the president and members of the opposition party explains a concomitant decline in confirmation rates.

Consequently, the increasing ideological polarization that is occurring in Congress and between the president and Congress, and the fact that more ideologically charged issues are reaching the policy agenda, not only have implications for how presidents interact with the legislative branch, they also affect presidential success rates with the courts. This finding is important, for it suggests that as presidential leverage declines with Congress, it has additional ripple effects. In short, the impediments to presidential success are significant and growing.

If impediments are prevalent and affect the president's ability to get things done, what then can presidents do about it? One solution offered in the literature is that presidents can make greater use of their institutional resources to achieve their political goals. Moe (1985) argues that presidents have politicized the institutional presidency (consisting of executive branch officials who most often serve within the Executive Office of the President, or EOP). He says that presidents are now interested in securing "responsive competence" from these officials (that is, greater loyalty to the president) and less "neutral competence" where officials provide expertise in a nonpartisan fashion. Nathan (1983) sees this greater reliance on loyalty as necessary for greater presidential control of the executive branch agencies.

But this strategy of relying on White House staffers and other EOP agencies also has been criticized as promoting increased centralization, a general thickening of government, and a loss of presidential control (see Hess 1988; Light 1995). In addition, there is a concern that an increased reliance on loyalty over competence may threaten presidential control of the bureaucracy (Waterman 1989).

In Chapter 10, Lewis contributes to this debate in an innovative way. He describes how presidents have incentives to increase their control over the executive branch. In so doing, they are most likely to increase its size, by adding new personnel. While reorganizations do eliminate some EOP units, the general trend is toward a thickening of the presidential staff and office. This tendency can not only create inefficiencies in government, but also actually can undermine presidential attempts to control their own executive branch. The irony, then, is that in their attempts to increase their leverage over the political process, presidents may unwittingly be creating further impediments. Extrapolating from Lewis's findings, when presidents redesign the EOP they should be interested in the potential long-term consequences of their actions.

From a focus on leverage and the impediments to presidential leadership, the next chapters focus on the skills that presidents themselves bring with them to the White House. Much of the presidential literature focuses on the relevance of presidential skill. Yet, of the three characteristics of presidential leadership identified by Fine and Waterman in Chapter 2, skill is the most difficult to measure, particularly systematically over time. One way to examine skill is to look at how individual presidents have governed. Many biographical studies take this approach, identifying the individual skills that each president possesses, or alternatively his shortcomings. But while this approach provides considerable historical and anecdotal information on the presidency, it does not provide a systematic way of thinking about presidential leadership. To do that we need a well-developed framework for understanding how and why individual skill matters.

In Chapter 11, Fred Greenstein examines two of the most commonly cited models explaining presidential behavior: James David Barber's typology of presidential psychological motivations and Richard Neustadt's model of presidential leadership. Greenstein provides a description and a critique of both models. In an addendum, Waterman then further elaborates on the problems of thinking systematically about presidential skill.

Richard Neustadt's theory of presidential power is also Matthew Dickinson's theme in Chapter 12. Dickinson provides a cogent and detailed examination of Neustadt's thesis. He provides a discussion of the genesis of Neustadt's ideas, how they developed and evolved through various versions of his book, *Presidential Power,* and how research over time has addressed the book's fundamental ideas. Particular attention is given to two countertheories of the presidency: Samuel Kernell's "going public" model and Stephen Skowronek's model of the presidency over political time. Dickinson, then, addresses both the importance of presidential skill, as well as examining a number of major theories of the presidency.

Finally, before we sum up in the final chapter, in Chapter 13 Bert Rockman examines how presidents decide. How can we assess the normative elements of presidential leadership and decisionmaking, and why they are important? How do presidents differ as decisionmakers?

While the overall theme of the book is presidential leadership, the combined work presented here provides answers to some basic questions:

- What is presidential leadership?
- Does presidential skill matter?
- How important is presidential leverage?
- When are presidents more likely to have leverage?
- What are the impediments to presidential leadership?

- Is the president's leverage sufficient to offset these impediments?

- Given the relationship between leverage and impediments, are our expectations of presidential leadership realistic or unrealistic?

- Given the high level of impediments in our governmental system, how can presidents be more effective leaders? That is, how can presidents succeed?

- What do we mean by presidential success?

Before we can begin to address these basic questions we first need to understand what presidential leadership entails. That is the task of the next chapter.

References

Arnold, Peri. 1986. *Making the Managerial Presidency: Comprehensive Reorganization Planning 1905–1980.* Princeton: Princeton University Press.

Brady, David, and Craig Volden. 2006. *Revolving Gridlock: Politics and Policy from Jimmy Carter to George W. Bush.* Boulder, CO: Westview Press.

Buchanan, Bruce. 1978. *The Presidential Experience: What the Office Does to the Man.* Englewood Cliffs, NJ: Prentice-Hall.

Burns, James MacGregor. 1965. *Presidential Government: The Crucible of Leadership.* New York: Avon Books.

Cohen, Jeffrey C. 1997. *Presidential Responsiveness and Public Policy-Making: The Publics and the Policies that Presidents Choose.* Ann Arbor: University of Michigan Press.

Corwin, Edward C. 1984. *The President: Office and Powers, 1787–1884.* New York: New York University Press.

Edwards, George C. 2003. *On Deaf Ears: The Limits of the Bully Pulpit.* New Haven, CT: Yale University Press.

Edwards, George C., and Stephen J. Wayne. 1999. *Presidential Leadership: Politics and Policy Making.* New York: Wadsworth Publishing.

Genovese, Michael A. 2003. *The Presidential Dilemma: Leadership in the American System.* New York: Longman Publishers.

Goodwin, Doris Kearns. 2005. *Team of Rivals: The Political Genius of Abraham Lincoln.* New York: Simon and Schuster.

Hargrove, Erwin C., and Michael Nelson. 1984. *Presidents, Politics, and Policy.* New York: Knopf Publishers.

Hess, Stephen. 1988. *Organizing the Presidency.* Washington, DC: Brookings Institution.

Howell, William G. 2003. *Power Without Persuasion: The Politics of Direct Presidential Action.* Princeton, NJ: Princeton University Press.

Kernell, Samuel. 1997. *Going Public: New Strategies of Presidential Leadership.* Washington, DC: Congressional Quarterly Press.

Krehbiel, Keith. 1998. *Pivotal Politics: A Theory of U.S. Law Making.* Chicago: University of Chicago Press.

Lammers, William W., and Michael A. Genovese. 2000. *The President and Domestic Policy: Comparing Leadership Styles, FDR to Clinton.* Washington, DC: Congressional Quarterly Press.

Laski, Harold J. 1940. *The American Presidency.* New York: Harper and Brothers Publishing.

Light, Paul. 1995. *Thickening Government: Federal Hierarchy and the Diffusion of Accountability.* Washington, DC: Brookings Institution.

Lowi, Theodore J. 1985. *The Personal Presidency: Power Invested Promise Unfulfilled.* Ithaca, NY: Cornell University Press.

Moe, Terry M. 1985. "The Politicized Presidency." In *New Directions in American Politics*. Edited by John Chub and Paul E. Peterson. Washington, DC: Brookings Institution.

Nathan, Richard P. 1983. *The Administrative Presidency*. New York: John Wiley and Sons.

Neustadt, Richard E. 1960/1980. *Presidential Power: The Politics of Leadership From FDR to Carter*. New York: Wiley and Sons.

Rose, Gary L. 1997. *The American Presidency Under Siege*. Albany: State University of New York Press.

Rose, Richard. 1991. *The Post-Modern Presidency: The White House Meets the World*. Chatham, NJ: Chatham House Publishers.

Rossiter, Clinton. 1956. *The American Presidency*. New York: Harcourt Brace.

Seligman, Lester G., and Cary R. Covington. 1989. *The Coalitional Presidency*. Chicago: The Dorsey Press.

Skowronek, Stephen. 1993. *The Politics Presidents Make: Leadership From John Adams to George Bush*. Cambridge, MA: Harvard University Press.

Sundquist, James L. 1983. *The Decline and Resurgence of Congress*. Washington, DC: Congressional Quarterly Press.

Tulis, Jeffrey K. 1987. *The Rhetorical Presidency*. Princeton, NJ: Princeton University Press.

Waterman, Richard W. 1989. *Presidential Influence and the Administrative State*. Knoxville, TN: University of Tennessee Press.

———. 2003/2007. *The Changing American Presidency: New Perspectives on Presidential Power*. Cincinnati: Atomic Dog Publishers.

Waterman, Richard W., Robert Wright, and Gilbert St. Clair. 1999. *The Image-Is-Everything Presidency*. Boulder, CO: Westview. ✦

Chapter 2

A New Model of Presidential Leadership

Controlling the Bureaucracy

Jeffrey A. Fine and Richard W. Waterman

Many books and articles have been written on the subject of presidential leadership. While almost everyone believes that presidents should be good leaders, there is considerable disagreement regarding what constitutes good leadership. In part this disagreement exists because there is no real consensus on what presidential leadership itself entails. In other words, what do we mean by the term *presidential leadership?*

Some common characteristics of leadership are often discussed by observers of the presidency, such as the idea that presidents should have the ability to persuade other political actors (e.g., members of Congress) to do what the president prefers. Yet even here there is disagreement, with some suggesting that persuasion is a less feasible leadership option in a political system characterized by constant campaigns and policy gridlock.

Pundits and scholars also often argue that leadership is associated with certain personal presidential characteristics: presidents should be strong, charismatic, rhetorically skilled, and so on. Yet, under which circumstances are these personal skills most effective? Do all presidents need to have rhetorical skills or be charismatic? Do all presidents need to have extensive knowledge (e.g., of foreign affairs) or prior governmental experience to be successful? We can debate the values of each of these characteristics, but even two individuals who share common characteristics may not exhibit the same leadership ability. Abraham Lincoln had little experience with Washington politics (one term in the House of Representatives) and is widely considered to be a success. Jimmy Carter had limited experience as well, but is often viewed as a failed president. Thus, a discussion of the characteristics of presidential leadership only takes us

We would like to thank Bert Rockman for his useful comments on this manuscript, as well as the faculty at Purdue University's Department of Political Science for comments during a seminar at which an earlier draft of this chapter was presented.

so far in terms of understanding the underlying concept. How then can we come to a better appreciation of what presidential leadership entails?

In this chapter, Jeffrey A. Fine and Richard W. Waterman argue that we need to develop a more systematic approach to the study of presidential leadership in order to better understand the concept. They argue that all presidents do not confront the same circumstances when they arrive in Washington. Different characteristics of presidential leadership are likely to vary from president to president (and even within presidencies). Hence, we should not entirely base our evaluation of whether or not a president is a successful leader purely on the success of his political outcomes. Some presidents may be in no-win situations, in which they exhibit considerable political skill, but have no real ability to influence the final outcomes. Other presidents may be passive and inadequate, yet because of events beyond their control, positive outcomes may be achieved. To consider the first president to be a failed leader and the second to be a successful leader, the authors contend, is to confuse outcomes with leadership.

As an alternative, the authors identify three distinct constructs related to presidential leadership: (1) political skill, (2) the leverage or tools/resources that presidents possess in office, and (3) the ultimate policy or political outcome. They argue that we need to examine and understand variations in each of these three constructs or variables in order to understand how presidential leadership operates. They then use a number of examples related to presidential attempts to control the bureaucracy to illustrate their model. The purpose of this chapter is to provide the groundwork for a discussion of how the concept of presidential leadership can be defined and measured.

✦ ✦ ✦

During the 1980s, President Ronald Reagan appointed individuals who shared his political philosophy of smaller government and less regulation to positions throughout the bureaucracy. For example, he appointed Anne Gorsuch Burford as Administrator of the Environmental Protection Agency (EPA). The president also proposed, and Congress enacted, major cuts in that agency's budget. A reorganization that eliminated the EPA's enforcement office also was undertaken. As a result, at least temporarily, the overall level of EPA enforcement and compliance activity declined significantly. While this outcome was consistent with the president's political goals, is it really an example of presidential leadership?

If we look at it from a subjective perspective, and if you believe in smaller government and less regulation, then the outcome achieved was certainly amenable. But if you believe that Reagan subverted environmental laws and therefore did not take care that the laws were faithfully executed, one can conclude that Reagan's policies represented a failure of presidential leadership. Does this example prove that presidential leadership is in the eye of the beholder and nothing more? If so, then the term *presidential leadership* is of limited utility.

While subjective interpretations of leadership certainly are a valid consideration, it also is important to think more objectively about the concept of presidential leadership. Yet, in order to do so we first must develop a clearer idea of what we mean by the term. In this chapter we argue that three constructs are related to presidential leadership: personal presidential skill, political leverage, and political outcomes. With these constructs as our main focus, we introduce and discuss a new model of presidential leadership. As an example, we then examine bureaucratic politics to demonstrate how this model can be applied to real world situations.

What Is Leadership?

In his classic study *Presidential Power*, Richard Neustadt (1960) drew a distinction between presidential "powers" (those formally allocated to the president via the Constitution) and presidential "power" (the power to persuade). His work has guided the study of the presidency for nearly a half a decade. Yet while there is some divergence of opinion regarding Neustadt's thesis (see Kernell 1986; Howell 2003), scholars agree on one key point: *presidents should be effective leaders.* They should lead the public, Congress, and other political actors to achieve positive results. When they do so we consider them to be successful leaders, and when they do not we rate them as failures. But the term *leadership* begs a simple question: does it matter where presidents lead? Even though leadership does not necessarily have to be positive (the first lemming over a cliff is a leader), the term is typically used in a positive way: that is, leadership has come to mean *good leadership.* But it is at least theoretically possible to think of cases where good leadership results in a positive outcome, as well as those where good leadership does not. Likewise, it is possible for a poor leader, through fortuitous circumstances, to end up with positive results. If we call each instance an example of good leadership are we really talking about leadership at all, or is something else involved?

To answer this question let's take an example. It can be argued that the president has little real leverage over the state of the economy. The chairman of the Federal Reserve Board has a more direct impact. Yet we know that the public traditionally evaluates presidential performance of this key dimension. A good economy leads to higher approval ratings and contributes to reelection success, and vice versa. If, however, presidents have limited leverage to influence the state of the economy, should they be given credit for a good economy or the blame for a bad one? Likewise, hypothetically speaking, if the leadership of Al Qaeda were to collapse tomorrow due to bureaucratic in-fighting, would this be evidence that the president was an effective leader or merely evidence that he or she was lucky? While any admin-istration would no doubt take credit for this accomplishment, there may be no tangible connection between the president's policies and the favorable outcome.

It is likely, then, that leadership is more than the ability to achieve a favorable political outcome. But if the outcome is not synonymous with leadership, then how do we define it? When discussing what constituted obscenity and pornography in the 1960s, Supreme Court Justice Potter Stewart said that he did not know how to define ob-scenity, but that he knew it when he saw it. Due to its subjective na-ture, are we left with no other alternative than to follow Justice Stewart's dictum with respect to leadership? We think not.

Conceptually, presidential leadership can be defined as getting an-other political actor or actors to do what you want them to do, even to get them to believe that what they are doing is in their own best in-terest. As such, leadership is not necessarily either the stick or the carrot, but rather a more subtle method of affecting the behavior of another. In this sense one can argue that a "leader" does not need to coax or cajole to get others to follow. He or she inspires others to fol-low. Thus, the ability to *persuade* others and convince them to do what you want them to do is at a premium. Neustadt's (1960) notion of presidential "power" therefore is tapping into this conceptualiza-tion of presidential leadership. The power to persuade is vital to pres-idential leadership for it suggests that a president desires an outcome and systematically seeks to achieve it. While persuasion as leadership is attractive on a conceptual level, it is extremely difficult to actually measure this definition of leadership, since it requires us to know what other political actors (e.g., members of Congress) think, how their thinking changed, and the methods that were used to effectuate that change, as well as the methods that did not promote a change in opinion. Thus, while conceptually it may be a useful definition, meth-odologically it leaves much to be desired. What then can we do to rec-tify the definitional problem?

A New Model of Presidential Leadership

Neustadt (2002) urged the subfield of presidential studies to come together and agree upon a common set of definitions for key con-cepts, so that we may move on toward testing them. In taking this im-portant step, we think many presidential scholars mix various concepts together when they discuss leadership. Rather than talking about one concept they are discussing three different ones that Neustadt himself identified. We therefore conceptualize leadership as being part of a triad of variables: personal presidential skill, leverage, and political outcomes.[1] As Hargrove and Nelson (1984, 87) note,

> Presidents are not powerful by virtue of being president. . . . Political "skill" is crucial to leadership. Individual presidents can make a difference. Nonetheless, different kinds of presidencies face different strategic problems, and the political resources available to them vary.

It is this variation that is often lost in discussions of presidential leadership. Generally, it is assumed that certain personal qualities (e.g., strength, integrity, honesty, decisiveness, experience in foreign affairs, knowledge of Washington politics, likeability, charisma, sensitivity to the concerns of others, rhetorical skill, and so on) are required to be a good leader. Less attention is paid, however, to whether all of these personal qualities are always required for presidential leadership or when these skills might be of more or less utility.

Different qualities and different circumstances suggest that context matters. Some personal skills may be more important at one time in history than at another. For example, different presidents face different political circumstances when they enter office, and even the same president will likely see political circumstances change during his or her tenure in office. One president also may possess a different amount of political leverage than another and political leverage may change (often radically) during a president's term (e.g., a president's approval ratings may fall or his partisans in Congress may lose reelection contests in large numbers). For all of these reasons, then, it is important to consider variations in the level of presidential political skill and resources (or what presidential scholars often call *leverage*).

Finally, in addition to securing reelection and other political goals, presumably presidents also are interested in policy outcomes. This may be a planned agenda or a domestic or foreign policy crisis. How successful one perceives presidents to be in responding to and managing these policy outcomes is often an important determinant of historical evaluations of presidential success or failure. Thus, what Hargrove and Nelson call making "a difference" is the outcome that presidents are interested in effecting (or what is technically called the *dependent variable*). This can be anything from lower levels of EPA enforcement, to congressional passage of legislation, to the war with Iraq, or any number of other political outcomes.[2]

Skill (which technically is considered to be the independent variable) represents what the president wants (his political intentions) and his personal ability to achieve it. According to Hargrove and Nelson (1984, 87) there are four types of skill. *Strategic skill* "includes the ability to formulate coherent policy goals that match the historical situation and to develop strategies for their attainment that are based on the political resources that are available or can be developed." The second is *"skill at presenting oneself and one's ideas to the public* through rhetoric and drama." The third is *"tactical capacity* to construct coalitions or power holders to secure agreement on particular questions." The final skill is *"managing authority* for policy formulation and administration."

Leverage (an intervening variable between skill and the outcome) represents the tools, resources, and political capital available to the president to accomplish his or her political objective (e.g., the outcome). These tools can involve factors external to the White House such as the number of supporters a president has in Congress, the existing state of the economy, whether the nation is at war or peace, the nation's political mood, and the international political climate. It also can involve tools (constitutional and otherwise) that presidents have available to them, including the appointment power, the veto power, the mechanisms of the institutional presidency, and so on. Presidential skill is therefore an important determinant of policy outcomes. But skill is not enough. Presidents also must have the political leverage to turn their political goals and ambitions into real accomplishments.

To put this in simpler terms, we often confuse leadership with an outcome, yet as any baseball fan will tell you, there are good baseball managers with bad teams and bad baseball managers with good teams. It is often not difficult for the discerning fan to distinguish between the two. The fact that your team loses more games than it wins may have more to do with the quality of the players or your team's payroll than the quality of the manager's leadership. In this case the manager may be highly skilled, but does not have the talent on the field that he needs to win. Thus, it is possible to envision a situation where you have good leadership but a bad outcome. It also is possible to have bad leadership and a good outcome; that is, a bad manager, talented players, and lots of victories. Hence, a first step at understanding what is meant by leadership requires us to separate out two concepts: the personal skill of the leader and the desired outcome.

As noted in our example, there is an intervening variable between skill and the outcome: in this case, the quality of the team. If you take a bad team and add better ball players, then the manager will have more *leverage* over the outcome of the game. Now his strategic moves, such as removing a starting pitcher and going to the bullpen early, may pay off and result in a victory. By adding the capability to influence the outcome, the manager is better able to translate his leadership skill into a desired outcome. Thus, following this example, our model is:

$$\text{Skill} \longrightarrow \text{Leverage} \longrightarrow \text{Outcome}$$

The baseball example provides the basis for an understanding of how these three components are related. It also shows us how we can measure them. We can measure whether the team wins, the quality of the players' performances, and, while it is no doubt more subjective, what the manager contributed to the success of the team. If the manager does not know how to use a bullpen, for example, this would be evidence of limited skill.

Since not everyone is a sports fan, let's take our model back to the world of presidential politics. In a hypothetical case, a president inherits a bad economy in deep recession. She does not have many tools at her disposal to influence the outcome and as a result she is unpopular and ultimately is not reelected. Conventional wisdom would suggest that this president failed as a leader. We would argue her ability to influence the outcome was limited. Thus, whatever the level of her skill, a desired outcome was unlikely. Hence, this case is not necessarily evidence of poor leadership, but perhaps of a president in the wrong place at the wrong time. Likewise, if she had inherited a strong economy and had limited knowledge of economic matters, this would not suggest that she was a good leader, only a fortuitous one. Thus, in determining whether presidential leadership exists we need to not only look at the outcome but also to understand *how and why* the outcome occurred.

Our model provides a theoretical basis for considering a variety of political possibilities. For example, if we just consider the relationship between skill and outcomes there are four distinct possibilities:

- Case A: A president displays personal political skill and there is a successful policy or political outcome.

- Case B: A president displays no skill and there is a successful outcome.

- Case C: A president displays skill and there is an unsuccessful outcome.

- Case D: A president displays no skill and there is an unsuccessful outcome.

These four distinct cases are important. While Cases A and B both result in a successful outcome, and many of us might assume that each president succeeded, in one case a president had skill and in the other he or she had none. Again, an example helps us to understand this point. If we had a Democratic president and firm Democratic control of both chambers of Congress, then there is a high likelihood that the president would be able to convince Congress to pass legislation that he or she favors, regardless of the president's persuasive abilities. A good example of this is Lyndon Johnson versus Jimmy Carter. Johnson was the consummate political insider who knew how to persuade members of Congress (an example of Case A). Carter was a political outsider who often rubbed members of his own Democratic party the wrong way (Case B). Both, however, were reasonably successful in getting their legislation enacted by Congress, but not because both men were equally skilled in legislative bargaining. Rather, both had large Democratic majorities to work with—that is, both had considerable political leverage. Of course, Johnson's success rate with Congress was higher than Carter's, but he also had larger Democratic majorities, especially in the years between his ascension to the presidency (1963) and the 1966 midterm elections. He also had a legislative agenda better primed to build on these majorities than did Carter.

These examples show that if we examine leadership and outcomes without considering the intervening variable, leverage, we can develop a skewed impression of the ability of presidents to lead. If we look at the outcome only, at first glance, both Carter and Johnson seem to have been successful with Congress. Yet, a closer analysis demonstrates a different story.

Cases C and D also are vastly different. If a president is a Democrat and Congress is firmly controlled by Republicans, then it is unlikely (or at least less likely) that a bill the president favors will be enacted. A president without legislative skill also may not be capable of achieving his or her legislative goals. While political skill is not irrelevant, the outcome in the two cases could be very much the same. Consequently, a president who has great skill at working with Congress may have a poor legislative record, while a president without much skill might have a similar record.

Another example is the economy. If presidents really have limited leverage over the outcome, then if the economy is strong the result likely will fall into one of two categories in our model: Cases A or B. Likewise, if there is a weak economy the result is likely to be Case C or D. Ultimately, presidential ability will have little to do with the outcome. Thus, we may be too generous if we argue that Eisenhower or Clinton was a great leader because the 1950s and 1990s were prosperous economic times and too negative if we assert that Carter or Ford was an unsuccessful president because he governed during times of high inflation, unemployment, and interest rates. The historical times in which each president governed and the state of the economy are both factors that would have to be considered as intervening variables. As well, leaders governing in more pacific and prosperous times may have fewer opportunities to make their mark than those governing during times of greater change.

What then happens when we include leverage in the analysis? We now have eight possibilities. To make them more easily recognizable we provide names for each. The typology is presented below and in Table 2.1. The presence of skill, leverage, or a successful political outcome is represented in the figure by a plus sign (+), while an absence of these qualities is represented by a minus sign (–).

Table 2.1   A Typology of Presidential Leadership Models

	Skill	Leverage	Successful Outcome
Ideal Leadership	+	+	+
Indiana Jones	+	−	+
Pseudo-Leadership	−	+	+
The Right Place at the Right Time	−	−	+
The No-Win Situation	+	+	−
The Wrong Place at the Wrong Time	+	−	−
Incompetent President	−	+	−
Undistinguished President	−	−	−

- **The Ideal Leadership Model:** The president displays skill, has considerable leverage at his or her disposal, and there is a successful outcome. This is most consistent with the preferred outcome in Neustadt's model of presidential power and leadership. Examples here are generally provided from the presidency of Franklin Delano Roosevelt, who used extraordinary political skill, combined with extraordinary leverage deriving from the twin crises of the Depression and World War II, to fashion first a series of New Deal policies and then a successful war effort.

- **The Indiana Jones Model:** The president displays skill, but has no or only limited leverage, and yet there is a successful outcome. In this case, things look really bad for our hero! We know the president is gifted, but given the situation there is just *no way* he or she can possibly prevail. *But somehow, the president does.* Sometimes, skill and a bit of good luck have a way of producing happy endings for presidents. They shouldn't have won, heck they shouldn't even have come close to winning, but they did.

- **The Pseudo-Leadership Model:** The president displays no skill, has leverage, and there is a successful outcome. This is more likely with passive presidents, such as Eisenhower, where leaders in Congress help to pass important legislation. Meanwhile, the president pays relatively little attention to the issue but gets credit for the outcome anyway. In these cases, scholars and pundits sometimes confuse the outcome with presidential leadership and an ability to persuade. This is a mistake because *there is no leadership;* that is, the president demonstrated no skill. This is an important case to contrast with the ideal model, because it shows how positive results can occur without presidential persuasion or skill.

- **The Right Place at the Right Time Model:** The president displays no skill, has no leverage, but there is a successful outcome.

This is a case of pure good fortune. Calvin Coolidge's good economy and his resulting high popularity are examples of this case. To call this presidential leadership is a real bastardization of the term. The best that can be said is that some presidents are lucky, some are not: these are the lucky ones!

- **The No-Win Situation Model:** The president displays skill, has leverage, and there is an unsuccessful outcome. This is the contrast to the case above. Had Johnson shown greater skill in foreign affairs, the Vietnam War may have represented this type of case. Even with leverage at his disposal (that is, initial strong public support for the war and large Democratic majorities in both houses of Congress), the outcome was unlikely to be successful. Illustrating this point, the recently released Johnson tapes show him agonizing as he realizes that if he goes to war there is little chance of victory. If on the other hand he does not he will be blamed for losing Vietnam (as Truman was accused of losing China). Sometimes presidents are put into these situations. Even the most skilled presidents cannot prevail under this no-win scenario.

- **The Wrong Place at the Wrong Time Model:** The president displays skill, has no leverage, and there is an unsuccessful outcome. This is often the case with the economy. The president has little leverage to influence the state of the economy. With high inflation, high interest rates, an OPEC crisis, or other similar problems even a highly skilled president may find it virtually impossible to do anything other than wait for better economic times. By the time they have arrived, however, the president likely has lost his or her bid for reelection and is rated by pundits as a failure. Like the no-win scenario above, this is obviously a very bad leadership situation for any president.

- **The Incompetent President Model:** The president displays no skill, but has leverage, and there is an unsuccessful outcome. This is a case where a president misuses his or her leverage. An example of this is George H. W. Bush and the Family Leave Bill. He vetoed the bill, though it later proved to be one of Bill Clinton's most popular achievements. By using his veto (his political leverage) he misread public opinion, gave his political opponent an issue in the fall election (which Bush then lost), and ultimately the bill was enacted by his successor anyway. This is clearly a case of bad presidential leadership.

- **The Undistinguished President Model:** The president displays no skill, has no leverage, and there is an unsuccessful outcome. This model is descriptive of many forgettable nineteenth-century presidents, though probably the best example is poor Herbert

Hoover, who governed from 1929–1933. He displayed little political skill in dealing with the Depression, had very little leverage to
deal with its negative effects (in part because the dominant political philosophy of the day to which he adhered ruled out many
government solutions to the problem), and the outcome was the
worst economic crisis in our nation's history. We can also include
presidents like Franklin Pierce, James Buchanan, and Ulysses
Grant in this category.

Our model thus provides variation across eight distinct cases of potential presidential leadership. To demonstrate how important these
differences are let's look at an example that is ongoing as we write
this chapter. In 2003, President George W. Bush officially made the
decision to go to war in Iraq. There is evidence that the president
showed considerable political skill, particularly in securing the support of both Congress and the United Nations. At the same time, he
also was accused of selectively using information from the national
security bureaucracy (he listened to neoconservatives from the Defense Department who shared his policy viewpoint and ignored more
temperate voices from the State Department and the Central Intelligence Agency). This unwillingness to consider all bureaucratic options (e.g., expertise) is evidence that he may have displayed limited
policy skill; that is, the ability to ask hard questions before taking action. And limited policy skill can affect future political credibility.
While there is therefore debate regarding how much skill he exhibited, there is no doubt whatsoever that Bush had considerable political leverage following the September 11th terrorist attacks, as
evidenced by his 90 percent approval rating and strong united support from both parties in Congress. As for the outcome, as we write
this chapter Iraq could end up with a democratic government or a
civil war. Hence, this ongoing situation raises a number of different
possible leadership outcomes. If one accepts that Bush's leadership in
going to war demonstrated political skill, then this could be either an
example of an Ideal Leadership Model: the president displays skill,
has leverage, and there is ultimately a successful outcome (e.g., a
democratic Iraq); or a No-Win Situation Model: the president has
skill, has leverage, but there is an unsuccessful outcome (e.g., civil
war). If one believes that Bush did not display skill because he did not
consider the advice of all of his experts before making a decision,
then this could be either a Pseudo-Leadership Model: the president
displays no skill, has leverage, and yet there is a successful outcome;
or the Incompetent President Model: the president displays no skill,
has leverage, and the outcome is unsuccessful. Since this is an ongoing example, we will have to wait for the historical record for a final
determination, but even at this point we can safely eliminate four
possible leadership models (all those involving no leverage in going to

war). Still, our model demonstrates four ways George W. Bush's leadership in Iraq ultimately will be perceived.[3]

As this example demonstrates, the distinctions between cases in our model are important. Another example is provided when we use Carter and his relationship with Congress to represent the Pseudo-Leadership Model and Clinton to represent the Indiana Jones Model. If we look only at the ranking that presidential scholars use most often to evaluate presidential success with Congress, published by the *Congressional Quarterly,* Carter's average success rate during his presidency far exceeds Clinton's. This would lead us to believe that Carter had far more skill in dealing with Congress than Clinton. But the circumstances for each president were radically different. Carter governed with Democratic majorities in both the House and the Senate throughout his four years in the White House. Clinton had Democratic majorities for only his first two years in office. For his last six years, Republicans controlled both the House and the Senate. Thus, the outcome variable (presidential success with Congress) is greatly affected by the intervening variable leverage.

When we realize that Clinton had a disastrous relationship with congressional Republicans (as evidenced by his impeachment) and that he also had limited leverage (Republicans were in firm control of Congress), it is remarkable that he had any success at all. Yet, as Cameron (2000) notes, Clinton skillfully used the leverage that he did have, his veto bargaining power and his high approval ratings, to block Republican efforts to pass legislation he opposed. He even on rare occasions forced them to enact legislation that was closer to his own policy preferences than those of the Republican majority. Thus, while his leverage was limited, and his successes much more modest than those of Carter, he did have some important legislative successes (welfare reform and portable health care coverage, as well as a series of victories in budgetary battles). As this example demonstrates, we can draw false conclusions about leadership if we merely compare a measure of presidential success rates without first placing it in context. To properly evaluate these presidents we need to examine how much influence each president had, as well as his skill and the outcome. Leverage is important for it can shed new light on the level of presidential skill.

Our model thus shows that leadership involves three, not one, basic constructs. But how do we actually measure each of them? One factor that is useful in measuring skill is the president's policy intent. Rudalevige (2002, 131) writes,

> Most observers would agree with the statement that a skilled president is more likely to succeed than an unskilled one. Defining any of the terms in that sentence, though, elicits controversy. What constitutes

skill? What makes one a "better" leader? Are these definitions themselves conditional on environmental attributes separable from the president himself?

Indeed, measuring the level of a president's skill is not an easy task. At a minimum, however, presidents must indicate an intention to lead before we can give them credit for exerting leadership skill. With regard to Congress, they publicly can identify the legislation they favor, perhaps identify it in the State of the Union Address, make phone calls to legislators to twist their arms, or make speeches to the public advocating certain policies. As Rudalevige does in his study of centralization and its effects on presidential success with Congress, we can determine if presidents are signaling their intent and then examine the various measures they have taken to follow through on it.

Measuring leverage generally is an easier task. With regard to Congress we can determine if a president governed in a time of divided government, the extent of the gridlock interval, whether the president faced an adversarial ideological relationship with members of Congress, and the breakdown of seats by each party in Congress (see Fine and Waterman 2004). As Cameron (2000) demonstrates, one can consider the potential threat of a presidential veto. Time factors such as whether it is the beginning of a president's first term and the size of the president's electoral victory also provide measures of presidential leverage (Pfiffner 1988). Finally, with regard to outcomes, congressional votes can be analyzed to see if a president actually received the desired political outcome (see Fleisher, Bond, and Wood in this volume; also Bond and Fleisher 1990).

We recognize that it is not always easy to develop measures for these three concepts and there even are debates in the scholarly literature regarding how much leverage presidents actually possess. For example, Kernell (1986) argues that presidents have followed a strategy of "going public" because they lack the leverage to bargain and compromise with Congress, while Edwards (2003) contends that the public is deaf to appeals from the bully pulpit. Finally, there are likely to be subjective debates about outcomes. Some may argue that the war in Iraq is a success because Saddam Hussein was deposed and millions of Iraqis are free, while others see it as a quagmire with an unimaginable loss of life. Still, by separating leadership into three distinct concepts and providing more variation in terms of how political outcomes are achieved, we believe the model provides a sounder basis for understanding the nature of presidential leadership. To illustrate this point we now turn to an examination of how presidents attempt to influence the bureaucracy. We choose this area because there is a wide array of empirical literature on this subject upon which to draw for illustrative purposes.

The Bureaucracy and Presidential Leadership

Early research on the bureaucracy asserted that there should be no politics in administration, a notion often referred to as the "politics-administration dichotomy" (Wilson 1885/1981). The question today is not whether but how political actors such as the president and the Congress can control the behavior of bureaucrats. If we look only at the Constitution for guidance, it is Congress, not the president, which has the clearest delegation of authority over the bureaucracy (see Arnold 1986, 7). Through the "necessary and proper" clause, it can create and abolish bureaucratic units. Presidents do this too, but via extraconstitutional executive orders. Congress also can allocate funds, set bureaucratic authority through statutes, and provide continuous oversight. The Senate also has a role in presidential appointments, through the confirmation process. To put this in different terms, constitutionally speaking, it appears that the founders gave the members of Congress greater leverage to deal with the bureaucracy. Yet while scholars have examined whether Congress can control the bureaucracy (e.g., Weingast and Moran 1983) they seldom use terms such as congressional leadership. Instead, they tend to talk about oversight, with at least a presumption that leadership (or a lack thereof) resides elsewhere.

Today the presumption among many scholars is that the president should lead the bureaucracy, though this has not always been the case (see Dodd and Schott 1979; Noll 1971). Nathan (1983) argues that presidents should play an active role, while much subsequent empirical research established that presidents, especially since Richard Nixon, actually can control the bureaucracy (Moe 1982, 1985; Wood and Waterman 1991; Wood and Anderson 1993).

For example, after his 2004 reelection, President Bush used the president's appointment power to make substantial changes in his cabinet and in his appointments to other agencies. Under his new head of the Central Intelligence Agency, Porter Goss, a major transformation occurred in the agency's personnel. Those individuals who were perceived to have politically opposed the president were removed from office. It was a clear demonstration of presidential power. While some Democratic members of Congress criticized these personnel moves at the CIA, no one questioned their constitutionality. No one argued that the president did not have the authority to put his own team in place or to remake the agency in his political image. Instead, it was expected that the president would lead, even if there were disagreements regarding where he was leading the CIA. Consequently, we should be able to use presidential-bureaucratic politics to illustrate our model.

How can presidents lead the bureaucracy? According to our model, in order for successful leadership to occur there must at least be evidence that the president effected a particular outcome or output in a manner that is consistent with the president's political philosophy and policy predisposition. In the case we cited at the beginning of this chapter, Reagan was initially able to promote his policy of less regulation and smaller government by inducing the Environmental Protection Agency to reduce the level of its enforcement and compliance activity. While individuals may disagree with this outcome on a subjective level, it was the outcome that was preferred by the Reagan administration. Yet, Reagan's success was short-lived, engendering a political backlash from Congress, the EPA, and the environmental community. Thus, Reagan's efforts to control the EPA ultimately were not successful (Wood 1988) and therefore represent a long-term failure of presidential leadership. On the other hand, in other agencies Reagan was more successful at using the same approach to control the bureaucracy (Moe 1985; Wood and Waterman 1991). It is therefore important to examine the tools of leverage that he employed and how he employed them (his skill) to evaluate Reagan's leadership.

Skill

Declining enforcement and compliance rates could result from a reduction in the sources of pollution or to a variety of other possible explanations. If a president did not seek to alter policy outcomes then we argue it is not evidence of presidential leadership, even if the outcome is the one preferred by the president. In the case of the EPA, however, there is evidence that Reagan articulated a clear antiregulatory agenda, and that he actively implemented a strategy to control the bureaucracy (see Waterman 1989). In other words, Reagan clearly expressed an intent to achieve a particular bureaucratic outcome and designed a method to achieve that goal.

The primary method used was the appointment power. Presidents have the constitutional authority to nominate officials, but how they use this power relates to their skill. They can choose individuals who are loyal to the president and their programs. As Weko (1995) notes, for most of our nation's history presidents did not use the appointment power in this way. Rather they allowed party officials, cabinet members, and others (often through the process of senatorial courtesy) to dominate the appointment process. As a result, many appointees did not reflect the president's policy interests. Indeed, often appointees undercut the president's political interests.

Over time, presidents came to rely on loyalty and, particularly from Richard Nixon's presidency onward, invented new organizational mechanisms that helped them to stack the bureaucracy with

loyal individuals. In so doing, however, presidents did not always consider the competence of their appointees. As a result, presidents often
put potential political landmines in place. The Watergate scandal and
the Iran-Contra Affair were in large part the result of overly zealous
loyalists who ended up subverting the presidents' political interests,
rather than promoting them. Thus, the quality or competence of appointees relates to presidential skill. The selection process determines
whether an appointee shares the president's political goals and can
ably carry them out.

Another consideration is, who does the president pay attention to?
In the case of the current war in Iraq, George W. Bush's willingness to
listen to a small group of neoconservatives inside his administration
and to ignore much of the other advice he received from so-called experts has been criticized by critics of the war. Some have argued that
he would have been better served by listening to Secretary of State
Colin Powell rather than to Secretary of Defense Donald Rumsfeld or
neoconservatives such as Deputy Secretary of Defense Paul Wolfowitz. As this case suggests, it is not sufficient for a president to appoint individuals, even experts. Does the president listen to a wide
group or limit his or her advice to a small and cohesive cohort?
Hence, another dimension of presidential skill is how a president
uses his appointees. This is a major point of concern for presidential
scholars. They note that as we move away from expertise toward a
greater reliance on loyalty, presidents are losing an important resource that appointees can provide (see for example Hess 1988).

Obviously, how presidents use the appointment process is but one
example of presidential skill in relation to the bureaucracy. There are
many others. The important point is that we can examine presidential skill in relation to the outcome of bureaucratic politics by examining how presidents attempt to influence the bureaucracy.

Leverage

Presidents have numerous tools, resources, and political capital at
their disposal to influence bureaucratic behavior. As Mayer aptly
notes, "Presidents may not be able to say 'do this, do that' and then sit
back and wait, but they do have the ability to create, adapt, and modify institutions and organizational processes in ways that maximize
the chances that policy and political outputs will match their own
preferences" (2001, 109). Research has borne out this statement,
demonstrating that presidents can effectively control bureaucratic
behavior and policy outputs (see Moe 1982, 1985; Wood and Waterman 1991, 1993, 1994).

Of the various tools or leverage that presidents can employ in their
attempts to control the bureaucracy the most prominent is the constitutionally allotted appointment power (see Nathan 1983). While the

president's appointment power is broad, it is not unconstrained: that is, the president's political leverage is constrained by Congress. As the Constitution prescribes, appointments are to be made subject to the "Advice and Consent of the Senate." Although the Senate rejects relatively few presidential appointees, this does not mean that the confirmation process is perfunctory or irrelevant. The Senate plays an active role in the confirmation process (Mackenzie 1981; King and Riddlesperger 1987), though as Deering (1987) warns, the Senate's role has been far from systematic with a great deal of variation between congressional committees regarding the amount of time and effort devoted to the confirmation process. Why is there variation?

Fisher (1981, 40) notes, "The Senate's responsibility for confirming presidential nominees, although fixed firmly in the Constitution, remains unsettled in its application." In fact, "for the most part" the Senate "has acted cautiously, uncertain of the scope of its own constitutional power." While Fisher contends that the "source of this uncertainty is not the Constitution," it is clear that the Senate's role in the confirmation process is not clearly delineated, thus leaving open the possibility of considerable flexibility in the implementation of the confirmation phase.

Since the Senate rejected Ronald Reagan's appointment of Robert Bork to the U.S. Supreme Court in 1987, the confirmation process has become more political and confrontational. Still, at the same time presidents have derived even greater power to appoint individuals by avoiding the Senate's "Advice and Consent" role entirely. Presidents Clinton and G. W. Bush made recess appointments, allowing them to avoid the confirmation process for limited periods of time. Furthermore, the establishment by Congress of the Executive Office of the President (EOP) and the growth since 1939 of the White House staff provide presidents with considerable leverage by increasing the number of important executive positions that can be made without Senate confirmation.

Despite its constitutional potential to control the scope of the president's appointment power, Congress grants presidents considerable latitude. Thus, from the perspective of our model, the appointment power provides an important source of potential political leverage. Knowing this, presidents can choose to employ it to advance their political agendas.

Another tool of presidential leverage is the ability to shape the budget of bureaucratic agencies. Much like the appointment power, the president and the Congress share this tool. While the president proposes a budget and sends it to Capitol Hill, the federal budget is subject to final passage by the Congress. Thus, whether or not Congress is controlled by the party of the president is an important point. When the president's party controls Congress it is easier for him or her to get the budget he or she prefers. If not, as Cameron (2000) discusses, presidents can, and do, use the veto or the threat of a veto to influence the final budget passed in the legislature. After funds are approved by Congress, the president also has some ability to redistribute funds allocated in the budget, both within an agency and even across agencies (Fisher 1975).

While much of the literature on presidential control of the bureaucracy focuses on the more conventional tools of presidential leverage discussed above, recent work has examined the ability of the president unilaterally to affect bureaucratic outcomes through the use of executive orders (e.g., Mayer 1999, 2001; Howell 2003). These executive orders are used by presidents to expand the power of the office, as presidents can manipulate the structure and province of bureaucratic agencies. Mayer (2001, 109) writes,

> Presidents, especially in the 20th century, have used executive orders both to create and to gain control of institutions that are now crucial to presidential leadership. By creating new organizations, expanding the scope and powers of existing institutions, and unilaterally altering crucial administrative procedures, presidents have been remarkably successful in gaining control of the government's institutional apparatus, outmaneuvering Congress, and only rarely being blocked by the courts.

Mayer's work demonstrates the various ways in which executive orders can be used as an arm of the institutional presidency. The literature on executive orders also notes that this tool is sometimes used to circumvent the legislative check. In these instances, Congress is often compelled to pass new and more specific legislation, the Courts are called upon to challenge the constitutionality of the executive order (which is extremely rare), or this unilateral tactic goes unchecked and the president wins for the time being.

Countervailing Leverage

While presidents thus have several tools of presidential leverage (and we should note that we have not enunciated all of them here), in understanding presidential control of the bureaucracy we must also consider how much leverage other political actors have. Presidential leverage can be constrained if other political actors can exert countervailing power. As noted, the appointment power is constrained by senatorial "advice and consent" and Congress shares control over the budget. While Congress's impact on appointments is limited to confirmation, its impact on the budget can be seen as outweighing that of the president.

Obviously one of the primary means of congressional leverage is in its lawmaking province. As the policy that bureaucrats are charged with implementing is passed by the Congress, the lawmaking process itself is a major tool for affecting the behavior of bureaucrats. Huber and Shipan (2002) and Huber, Shipan, and Pfahler (2001) outline how legislators craft legislation in specific ways to dictate agency action. Through passing either intentionally vague or detailed legislation, Congress can afford the bureaucracy greater (or lesser) discretion to implement policy in a certain way. When Congress seeks to curtail bureaucratic discretion and limit its ability to implement policy in a manner inconsistent with the intent of the law, Congress will write detailed legislation. These studies show that legislative constraint is an effective means for influencing the behavior of agents in the implementation process.

Congress also can curtail agency behavior and affect bureaucratic outcomes through the oversight process. Oversight policy allows Congress to determine whether executive branch agencies are implementing policy in a manner consistent with the legislation passed. Although monitoring the bureaucracy can be an effective means of leverage it can be very costly for Congress with large opportunity costs, as any time and resources devoted to this practice are resources *not* being used elsewhere. Given the vast size of the executive branch and its countless departments and agencies, widespread oversight is difficult to conduct.

Given that traditional bureaucratic oversight is extremely difficult and costly, Congress developed other ways of monitoring agency behavior. As McCubbins and Schwartz (1984) note, one such means is implementing "fire alarms." This form of oversight consists of Congress establishing a set of detailed rules and procedures that allow Congress to deflect the job of monitoring agency behavior to those actors (individuals, interest groups, and so forth) who stand to benefit or suffer from the way specific policies are implemented. These actors, who have a vested interest in a particular policy area, will watch closely to ensure that relevant policy is implemented in a manner consistent with their interests. If they are dissatisfied with the way the policy is being implemented, they seek redress from Congress, agencies, or the courts. McCubbins and Schwartz argue that only sporadic or fire alarm oversight provides an effective stimulus for monitoring agency behavior. Alternatively, Aberbach (1990) argues that oversight deployed systematically is an effective tool. Wood and Waterman (1993), in this regard, found evidence of lagged House and Senate committee influence.

While the various tools afforded only to the president or only to Congress are often effective in influencing bureaucratic outcomes, the literature suggests that the most effective means of controlling agency behavior are those that are shared by both the president and Congress (most importantly, the appointment and budget powers). We have identified tools that give the president and Congress leverage over bureaucratic outcomes. How then can we apply these tools to policy outcomes?

Outcomes

Many studies demonstrate that presidents are successful in controlling the bureaucracy, though there is variation in terms of the
level of success. For example, Wood and Waterman (1991) examine
the response of seven different agencies to various political stimuli
initiated by both the president and Congress. They found that in six
of the agencies bureaucratic outputs shifted dramatically in response
to a Reagan appointee. Wood and Anderson (1993) and Moe (1982,
1985) also provide evidence that bureaucratic outputs respond to
cues from presidential appointees. Other research examining the *perceptions* of bureaucrats indicates that they considered presidential
appointees to be the most powerful political actors (even more powerful than the president, Congress, the Courts, the public, or interest
groups (Waterman, Rouse, and Wright 2004). Yet the evidence on
presidential appointments provides some important caveats as well.

Ronald Reagan appointed a loyalist, Anne Gorsuch (later Anne
Burford) as the EPA Administrator, along with a number of other
antiregulatory officials, to key agency positions. Many of these officials were vehemently opposed to the goal of environmental regulation and demonstrated limited political skill once on the job. While
the president used considerable leverage to accomplish his objectives
(e.g., the appointment power, budget cuts, reorganization, executive
orders) the political result was less than satisfactory (Waterman
1989). While there was a short-term reduction in enforcement and
compliance outputs (which was consistent with Reagan's goals), in
the long term agency officials rebelled and members of Congress
eventually put considerable pressure on the EPA to change its enforcement policy (Wood 1988). Thus the influence of bureaucrats
themselves (see Krause 1999) and of Congress prevailed. By 1983, the
Reagan administration essentially surrendered control of the EPA.
While Reagan used loyalists to send a clear message of his regulatory
intent, he did not adequately consider his appointees' qualifications
or the level of political opposition to his policy—evidence of limited
political skill. Though he used all of the leverage at his disposal, the
political outcome was unsuccessful. Reagan experienced a similar result with the Equal Employment Opportunity Commission (Wood
1990). Both cases then represent what we call the Incompetent President Model. The president did not use his leverage skillfully and he
did not achieve the outcome he preferred, even though he had considerable leverage at his disposal.

As noted, the Reagan approach was more successful at other federal regulatory agencies. At the Federal Trade Commission and the
Food and Drug Administration, the appointment of more qualified
personnel who shared the president's political philosophy resulted in
outcomes more consistent with Reagan's political preferences (Wood

and Waterman 1991, 1994). In these agencies, there was less public and congressional opposition to the president's policies (that is, there was less *countervailing leverage*). Agency personnel therefore were more amenable to following Reagan's policy direction. Combining loyalty with competence, and considering the nature of the external political environment, is therefore evidence of Reagan's greater presidential skill.

The Carter presidency also provides two interesting examples related to the appointment power. With regard to the Interstate Commerce Commission (ICC), Carter had a policy objective (deregulation of the motor carrier industry) which he clearly expressed. He also appointed highly qualified individuals who shared his policy perspective. These officials then put pressure on Congress to deregulate the industry, essentially stating that they would do so if Congress did not. The end result was what the president wanted: a deregulation bill was enacted (Waterman and Wood 1992). As with the Reagan cases (FTC and Food and Drug Administration) this is an example of a president displaying skill, using existing leverage, and securing a successful political outcome.

Carter was often not as fortunate in his dealings with the bureaucracy, however. In the case of the National Highway Traffic Safety Administration (NHTSA), an inadvertent appointment promoted exactly the opposite outcome to the one Carter desired (Wood and Waterman 1991). While Carter preferred the NHTSA to be more aggressive in promoting enforcement activity, his lack of political skill was evident when he appointed an individual who opposed his own policy. The president therefore did not display skill, though he had leverage, and the political outcome from his perspective was unsuccessful (that is, he did not get the policy outcome he preferred).

These examples illustrate that there is indeed variation across the three constructs or variables in our model. It also is evidence that the quality of presidential leadership varies, as well. It is more than a binary variable: presidential success or failure.

Conclusions

We argue that there is more to presidential leadership than the political outcome. Merely stating a president was a good or poor leader is not insufficient. Yet, too often scholars focus only on the outcome or anecdotal accounts of presidential skill, without considering how each of the three variables we delineate is related to the political outcome. We argue that in order to understand the nature of presidential leadership it is important to consider all three elements of leadership: presidential skill, the leverage the president possesses, and the policy or political outcome.

To further emphasize this point let's look at some examples from bureaucratic politics and show how they relate to our presidential leadership model. We use the example of Ronald Reagan's leadership approach. Regarding skill-related factors, the literature suggests the following:

- Reagan expressed a clear vision of smaller government and less regulation.

- His administration identified individuals who shared this vision and placed them in key positions within the bureaucracy.

- The administration's primary qualification for appointment was loyalty to the president and his program.

- The president tended to listen then to individuals with whom he agreed, rather than a wide group of individuals with divergent political opinions (as Bill Clinton did).

The literature also provides some insight with regard to the leverage that Reagan possessed.

- The president used the constitutional appointment power as leverage to force agencies to comply with his desired agenda.

- Using the large national budget deficit as a justification, he instituted a series of budget cuts designed to reduce a variety of federal agencies' budgets and hence their ability to enforce the law.

- Reagan issued executive orders on cost-benefit analysis and administrative procedures designed to limit bureaucratic enforcement.

- Reagan administration officials reorganized some agencies, such as the EPA, eliminating their enforcement divisions.

With regard to outcomes, the literature also suggests the following:

- There was a consistent reduction in bureaucratic outputs (compliance and enforcement) across a wide range of federal regulatory agencies.

- But in some agencies, particularly the EPA and EEOC, there was a political backlash as members of Congress responded to heavy-handed attempts by Reagan appointees to reduce environmental enforcement.

- These bureaucratic backlashes (and later the Iran-Contra scandal) raised questions about the effectiveness of using loyalty as a primary criterion at the appointment stage, and even raised serious questions about Reagan's competence. They suggest that presidents need to consider both loyalty and competence in their appointments in order to increase the chances that they will achieve their policy goals (i.e., a successful outcome).

We have presented eight distinct cases of presidential leadership and illustrated how our model works by referring to empirical studies from the literature on political control of the bureaucracy. These eight models provide a new way of thinking about presidential leadership. The next step is to provide more detailed cases for each leadership type and to determine a classification scheme for each president. In our typology we also treat each of our variables as dichotomous (e.g., success or no success, leverage or no leverage). We need to next develop more continuous measures for each of our three main constructs.

Notes

1. Neustadt (1960) discusses each of these three concepts in his path-breaking work. The power of persuasion requires personal political skill. He also discusses various tools presidents can use to achieve an outcome (e.g., they can gain leverage by using their personal reputation). He also discusses the results of various attempts at presidential leadership (e.g., Truman and the Steel Seizure case).

2. While we generally think of a successful political outcome in terms of a proactive presidency—that is, presidents have to do something to accomplish a successful outcome—sometimes presidents succeed by not acting. For example, Eisenhower's decision not to intervene in Vietnam in 1954 is generally viewed as a wise political choice and therefore can be characterized as a tangible presidential success, yet it required the wisdom not to act. Presidential outcomes therefore can be derived in a variety of ways.

3. One can also make the argument that no matter what the outcome Bush has shown leadership by securing the outcome that he desired: military intervention in Iraq and the overthrow of Saddam Hussein's government. Hence, whether the long-term situation is civil war or peace, Bush did achieve one of his primary short-term objectives.

References

Aberbach, Joel D. 1990. *Keeping a Watchful Eye: The Politics of Congressional Oversight.* Washington, DC: Brookings Institution.

Arnold, Peri E. 1986. *Making the Managerial Presidency: Comprehensive Reorganization Planning 1905–1980.* Princeton: Princeton University Press.

Bond, Jon, and Richard Fleisher. 1990. *The President in the Legislative Arena.* Chicago: University of Chicago Press.

Cameron, Charles M. 2000. *Veto Bargaining: Presidents and the Politics of Negative Power.* New York: Cambridge University Press.

Deering, Christopher. 1987. "Damned if You Do and Damned if You Don't: The Senate's Role in the Appointment Process." In G. Calvin Mackenzie (ed.), *The In-and-Outers:*

Presidential Appointees and Transient Government in Washington, 100–119. Baltimore: John Hopkins Press.

Dodd, Lawrence C., and Richard L. Schott. 1979. *Congress and the Administrative State*. New York: Wiley and Sons.

Edwards, George C. III. 2003. *On Deaf Ears: The Limits of the Bully Pulpit*. New Haven, CT: Yale University Press.

Fine, Jeffrey A., and Richard W. Waterman. 2004. "Divided Government: A Theoretical and Methodological Critique." Presented at the Annual Meeting of the Southern Political Science Association. New Orleans, LA.

Fisher, Louis. 1975. *Presidential Spending Power*. Princeton, NJ: Princeton University Press.

———. 1981. *The Politics of Shared Power*. Washington, DC: Congressional Quarterly Press.

Hargrove, Erwin C., and Michael Nelson. 1984. *Presidents, Politics, and Policy*. New York: Knopf.

Hess, Stephen. 1988. *Organizing the Presidency*. Washington, DC: The Brookings Institute.

Howell, William G. 2003. *Power Without Persuasion: The Politics of Direct Presidential Action*. Princeton, NJ: Princeton University Press.

Huber, John D., and Charles R. Shipan. 2002. *Deliberate Discretion? The Institutional Foundations of Bureaucratic Autonomy*. New York: Cambridge University Press.

Huber, John D., Charles R. Shipan, and Madelaine Pfahler. 2001. "Legislatures and Statutory Control of Bureaucracy." *American Journal of Political Science* 45 (April):330–345.

Kernell, Samuel. 1986/1997. *Going Public: New Strategies of Presidential Leadership*. Washington, DC: Congressional Quarterly Press.

King, James D., and James W. Riddlesperger, Jr. 1987. "Senate Confirmation of Appointments to the Cabinet and Executive Office of the President." Presented at the annual meeting of the American Political Science Association. Chicago, IL.

Krause, George A. 1999. *A Two-Way Street: The Institutional Dynamics of the Modern Administrative State*. Pittsburgh: University of Pittsburgh Press.

Mackenzie, G. Calvin. 1981. *The Politics of Presidential Appointments*. New York: Free Press.

Mayer, Kenneth R. 1999. "Executive Orders and Presidential Power." *The Journal of Politics* 61(2):445–466.

———. 2001. *With the Stroke of a Pen: Executive Orders and Presidential Power*. Princeton, NJ: Princeton University Press.

McCubbins, Matthew D., and Thomas Schwartz. 1984. "Congressional Oversight Overlooked: Police Patrols Versus Fire Alarms." *American Journal of Political Science* 28:165–179.

Moe, Terry M. 1982. "Regulatory Performance and Presidential Administration." *American Journal of Political Science* 26:197–225.

———. 1985. "Control and Feedback in Economic Regulations: The Case of the NLRB." *American Political Science Review* 79:1094–1116.

Nathan, Richard P. 1983. *The Administrative Presidency*. New York: John Wiley and Sons.

Neustadt, Richard E. 1960/1980. *Presidential Power: The Politics of Leadership from FDR to Carter*. New York: John Wiley and Sons.

———. 2002. "Presidential Power and the Research Agenda." *Presidential Studies Quarterly* 32:720–723.

Noll, Roger G. 1971. *Reforming Regulation*. Washington, DC: Brookings Institution.

Pfiffner, James P. 1988. *The Strategic Presidency: Hitting the Ground Running*. Chicago: The Dorsey Press.

Rudalevige, Andrew. 2002. *Managing the President's Program: Presidential Leadership and Legislative Policy Formulation*. Princeton, NJ: Princeton University Press.

Waterman, Richard W. 1989. *Presidential Influence and the Administrative State*. Knoxville: University of Tennessee Press.

Waterman, Richard W., Amelia Rouse, and Robert L. Wright. 2004. *Bureaucrats, Politics, and the Environment*. Pittsburgh: University of Pittsburgh Press.

Waterman, Richard W., and B. Dan Wood. 1992. "What Do We Do With Applied Research?" *PS: Political Science & Politics* (September):559–564.

Weingast, Barry R., and Mark J. Moran. 1983. "Bureaucratic Discretion or Congressio-
    nal Control: Regulatory Policymaking by the Federal Trade Commission." *Journal of
    Political Economy* 91:756–800.
Weko, Thomas J. 1995. *The Politicizing Presidency: The White House Personnel Office,
    1948–1994.* Lawrence: University of Kansas Press.
Wilson, Woodrow. 1885/1981. *Congressional Government: A Study in American Politics.*
    Baltimore, MD: John Hopkins Press.
Wood, B. Dan. 1988. "Bureaucrats, Principals, and Responsiveness in Clean Air En-
    forcements." *American Political Science Review* 82:215–234.
———. 1990. "Does Politics Make a Difference at the EEOC?" *American Journal of Polit-
    ical Science* 34:503–530.
Wood, B. Dan, and James E. Anderson. 1993. "The Politics of U.S. Antitrust Regula-
    tion." *American Journal of Political Science* 37:1–39.
Wood, B. Dan, and Richard W. Waterman. 1991. "The Dynamics of Political Control of
    the Bureaucracy." *American Political Science Review* 85 (September):801–828.
———. 1993. "The Dynamics of Political-Bureaucratic Adaptation." *American Journal of
    Political Science* 37 (May):497–528.
———. 1994. *Bureaucratic Dynamics: The Role of Bureaucracy in a Democracy.* Boulder,
    CO: Westview Press. ✦

Chapter 3

A Primer on the President's Legislative Program

Charles M. Cameron and Jee-Kwang Park

Presidential leadership often involves getting other policy actors to support or do what the president wants. Among these policy actors, the Congress is the most prominent. An important component of presidential leadership is therefore the ability to secure congressional approval for the president's legislative program, which Cameron and Park define as a "comprehensive set of requests for new or modified laws. . . ." In relation to the leadership model presented by Fine and Waterman in Chapter 2, success in passing the president's program provides a quantifiable measure of presidential outcomes.

Yet a president faces considerable obstacles when he or she tries to secure congressional passage of a program, including a greater propensity for divided government (where at least one house of Congress is not controlled by the party of the president). This often results in high levels of gridlock (and a larger gridlock region or interval in Congress that can block presidential initiatives). Presidential success in dealing with Congress, then, is *contingent* on these and other political factors, which in turn define whether opportunities exist for policy action. To use a metaphor, if *policy windows* are open (representing greater political opportunity), then a president has a greater chance of gaining congressional approval for his or her legislative program. When the policy window is closed, however, a president has much less chance of success with Congress. Whether policy windows are open or closed is contingent on many factors.

For example, presidential success with Congress is related to which actor takes the lead in writing legislation. On this point, Cameron and Park ask, "why should Congress pay any attention to a bill drafted by the president's minions?" Certainly, Congress and its individual members have their own policy preferences, some of which differ from the president's interests. How much influence

We thank Andrew Rudalevige for his exceptional generosity and he, Dave Lewis, Brandice Canes-Wrone, Jeff Cohen, Bert Rockman, and Rick Waterman for helpful conversations and suggestions. We also thank Princeton's Center of the Study of Democratic Politics for providing a stimulating and supportive home for the research.

the president has is therefore contingent on congressional policy preferences, as well as the salience that members have toward an issue. It also depends on how much political cost legislators are willing to invest in writing new legislation. If they can pass a bill written by the president that they agree with, or at least one that is close to their preferred policy position or preferences without having to invest valuable time writing the legislation, they will have more time for constituency service, campaigning, and raising campaign funds. However, the more a president's policy position differs from the median or middle member of Congress, or when the level of congressional salience increases and members care more about existing differences between the president's position and their own, a president will find it more difficult to secure the passage of legislation he or she prefers. Again, presidential success is contingent on a variety of political factors.

This chapter helps us to understand the contingent nature of presidential leadership. Following Richard Neustadt's idea of presidential *burden sharing*, Cameron and Park examine when Congress is likely to allow the president to write legislation, as well as when Congress is most likely to offer an alternative of its own. They also provide a series of innovative models that demonstrate the propensity of presidential leadership under different contingencies. In other words, "under the right circumstances the president can act as a bill-drafting service for Congress." As a result, "the president can use proffered bills not simply to stimulate congressional action, but to shape" its content. Presidents can be more active in this role when "policy windows" are open and when social movements exist to favor policy change.

The chapter therefore addresses in new and innovative ways an important relationship between the president and Congress. Sections 1–3A and 5 are easily accessible for all undergraduate students, while sections 3B and 4 are more methodologically sophisticated and may be more accessible for upper-division undergraduates and graduate students.

◆ ◆ ◆

1. Introduction

One of the most important tools of modern presidents is the "legislative program," a comprehensive set of requests for new or modified laws, typically in the form of draft bills, submitted to Congress for its consideration. Indeed, a leading authority calls the legislative program a "cornerstone of presidential-congressional relations, part of the definition of the 'modern' presidency" (Rudalevige 2002).

The president's legislative program has no constitutional or statutory basis. Rather, presidents began drafting bills and offering them to Congress on a piecemeal basis in the nineteenth century. Joseph

Cannon, Speaker of the House from 1903 to 1911, once explained the practice to a constituent:

> The President of the United States frequently suggests legislation that is desirable, and sometimes transmits drafts of proposed bills. Frequently, also, the heads of the executive departments, who are members of the President's cabinet, by communication, suggest to one or the other Houses of Congress legislation that is desired, and even communicates the forms or drafts of bills, the enactment of which they recommend. During the most strenuous years of the Civil War much of the financial legislation was drafted by Mr. Fessenden, Secretary of the Treasury, who had long experience in the Senate and was familiar with its methods. In later years the Senate has shown some sensitiveness at the activity of cabinet officers in drafting bills for its consideration, but in the House these drafts have always been, and still are, received as suggestions for legislation. (Cannon, n.d.)

As Cannon indicates, the practice of submitting draft bills could be controversial in a period when presidents and cliques of senators competed for political primacy. But presidents persisted in the practice. It was not until President Truman, however, that the chief executive fully institutionalized the legislative program, directing members of his administration to draft a comprehensive set of bills and present them to Congress. As Neustadt has related, President Eisenhower resisted the practice in his first year in office, but adopted it thereafter at Congress's insistence (Neustadt 1955). All subsequent presidents followed him in this regard.

By the late 1950s, administrative agencies submitted approximately 1,000 items to Congress annually, with the president himself providing messages and bills for about 100. Using *Congressional Quarterly,* the *Public Papers of the Presidency,* and records in the presidential libraries, political scientist Andrew Rudalevige identified more than 6,900 presidential proposals from 1949–1996 (inclusive), about 144 per year (2002, 166).

Scholars of the presidency have investigated the legislative program and uncovered some intriguing regularities, which we review below. Nonetheless, the conceptual foundations of the president's legislative program remain murky. Several questions stand out. On the one hand, why should Congress pay any attention to a bill drafted by the president's minions—why shouldn't Congress simply continue on its merry way, regardless of legislative musings from the other end of Pennsylvania Avenue? On the other hand, if congressmen swoon into submission when presidents proffer a bill (or do so regularly some percentage of the time), why doesn't the president inundate the legislature with a flood of bills, over and over and over again, until he achieves all his legislative objectives?

These questions alert us to the likely *contingent effectiveness* of the legislative program: under some circumstances, a proffered bill may dramatically alter what Congress would have done, absent the bill; but under other circumstances, the impact of a proffered bill may be negligible. If so, what factors make a proffered bill influential, and what factors limit its impact?

The goal of this chapter is to shed some light on these questions. We proceed as follows. In the following section, we survey known empirical regularities in the president's legislative program. We review what political scientists have learned about the volume of the president's proposals (presidential legislative activism), the content of proposals, Congress's response to proposals, and the policy impact of proposals.

In Section 3 we turn to theory. We review three theoretical ideas that have been advanced for understanding the president's program. Then, we develop one of these into a full-blown model, which we call the *burden-sharing model*. To the best of our knowledge, this is the first formal model of the president's legislative program. The burden-sharing model is based on an idea advanced by Richard Neustadt. He suggested that under the right circumstances the president can act as a bill-drafting service for Congress. The model shows how, by doing so, the president can use proffered bills not simply to stimulate congressional action, but to shape the content of legislation. The burden-sharing model helps explain some of the empirical regularities observed by political scientists.

In Section 4, we use the burden-sharing model to undertake a new analysis of presidential legislative activism. The burden-sharing model suggests that presidents should become legislative activists when policy windows open in Congress and simultaneously the public clamors for major new legislation. Using new data on social movement activism collected for this chapter, standard measures of congressional gridlock, and Rudalevige's counts of annual proposals from 1963 to 1996, we test the model's predictions. The data clearly display the predicted patterns. Section 5 concludes. An appendix provides additional technical details.

2. What Do We Know? The Empirical Regularities

Political scientists and historians have described how different presidents constructed their legislative program. Richard Neustadt, for example, described the process in the first Eisenhower administration (Neustadt 1955). According to Neustadt, the president first canvassed his administration for ideas. Then his top aides reviewed the suggestions, and in consultation with the president himself, selected a smaller number as "the program." These items were then worked up by the departments, the Bureau of the Budget, and top aides. Subsequently, the program was vetted by Republican leaders on the Hill. Most of the actual bill drafting was handled in the departments.

Historical accounts suggest that other presidents have done something similar. However, as Andrew Rudalevige convincingly documents, presidents have often preferred to craft innovative, high-priority programs "in house," using their own staff rather than that of the departments.

Beyond the bare facts about process, what do we know about empirical regularities in the legislative program? Several excellent studies use systematic data to uncover reliable patterns. Three studies stand out as particularly notable: Peterson (1990), Edwards and Barrett (2000), and Rudalevige (2002). A variety of other studies are also helpful.[1] In this section, we review what these studies uncover.

First, a brief word about research approach. Several scholars (e.g., Peterson and Rudalevige) attempted to identify all presidential proposals and then drew random samples (or subsets) of items to track. Consequently, their studies provide detailed evidence about what happens when a president proffers a bill—but they cannot tell us anything about what happens when he does not. In other words, they cannot say anything about what *difference* proffering makes (nor do they claim to). In contrast, Edwards and his coauthor explicitly compare presidential initiatives with purely congressional ones—but they limit their attention to the most "legislatively significant" proposals, those proposals sophisticated observers typically rank as the most important of a congressional session. So their study provides a highly selective view of proposals. Nonetheless, Edwards and Barrett can make statements about the apparent difference proffering makes, at least for very important bills. We say "apparent," however, because *presidents themselves select the bills they proffer, and presumably do so strategically.* Even if we perceive a big impact from the bills presidents chose to proffer, we cannot assume they would have gotten the same bang from bills they explicitly chose *not* to proffer. What social scientists call "selection bias" precludes this inference, however natural it seems.[2] (We return to this point shortly.) Edwards and Barrett do not try to correct for selection bias statistically. In fact, doing so would require either data of near-experimental quality or a well-developed theory of proffering decisions. By the same token, however, Edwards and Barrett are careful not to claim too much for their findings.

Volume: When Are Presidents Legislative Activists?

The data painstakingly collected by Rudalevige and by Edwards and his coworkers provides a solid base for charting periods of legislative activism by presidents. Figure 3.1 displays these data by Congress, from the 81st Congress (1947–48) to the 104th (1995–96).[3]

Figure 3.1. Legislative Activism by Presidents, 1949–1995

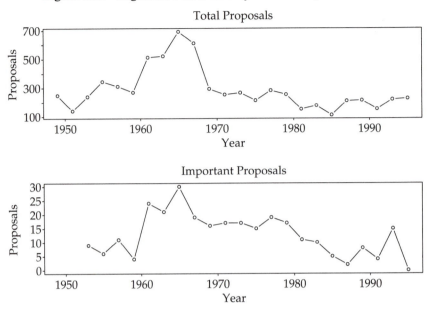

Figure 3.1 tells an interesting story. In the modern era, presidential legislative activism rose dramatically from a low period in the early 1950s to a historic high in the mid-1960s. The high water mark was the 89th Congress, LBJ's Great Society Congress. Presidential legislative activism then declined steadily for the next two decades, through the mid- to late 1980s. It then rebounded slightly, at least until the end of the first Clinton administration (the series end in 1996). Of course, even in the period of declining activism, presidents continued to present many important proposals, especially during the 1970s. Over the whole period, the number of important proposals tracked the total number of proposals, at least roughly. More specifically, in an average Congress in the post-War period "important" proposals (as scored by Edwards and Barrett) constituted about 4.5 percent of all proposals, with the percentage for most Congresses falling between 3 percent and 6 percent.

What explains the tides of presidential legislative activism? Very little attention has been directed at this question. We return to it in Section 5, where we present one of the first statistical studies of this data.

Content: What Do Presidents Proffer to Congress?

What do presidents choose for their legislative programs? For example, does the general tenor of items—liberal versus conservative—reflect the mood of the public, or is it more responsive to presidential ideology? Do presidents predictably respond to economic conditions, widely perceived social ills, and so on, or do they show little concern with those matters?

Unfortunately, the proposal data have not been analyzed from this perspective. However, it is possible to make some educated guesses, because scholars have examined a closely related question: which items do presidents emphasize in their public rhetoric? (Presidential rhetoric is part of a comprehensive legislative strategy, so presumably the program itself may show similar patterns.)

Particularly useful is the work of Jeffrey Cohen (especially 1997, Chapters 4–6). Cohen studied the statements presidents made in their State of the Union messages, focusing on economic policy, civil rights, foreign policy, and domestic policy. He examined the number of mentions of those areas, the specificity of the mentions, and their general liberalism.

Broadly speaking, Cohen found that presidents were somewhat responsive to objective conditions, but much less responsive to public opinion. (Interestingly, public opinion appears to respond to presidential rhetoric). Consistently, however, more liberal presidents and more conservative ones tend to emphasize more liberal and more conservative items, respectively. This finding—that presidents are driven more by their ideological agendas than responsiveness to the public—is quite consistent with micro-oriented case studies of presidential action, for example, Jacobs and Shapiro's recent study of the Clinton healthcare plan (2000). Those scholars show how President Clinton attempted to manipulate public opinion in favor of his preferred legislative outcomes, rather than shape his proposals to reflect public desires (such that they were).

It would be quite surprising if similar patterns did not hold for the legislative program as a whole. But, this remains an open question.

Response: What Happens to the President's Proposals in Congress?

Are the president's proposals seriously considered by Congress? Are they considered by both chambers? Do they pass both chambers? Do enacted proposals give the president most of what he wants? How do these patterns vary between unified and divided party government? In addressing these questions we are on firmer ground, as they are central to the work of Peterson, Edwards and Barrett, and Rudalevige.

First consider whether Congress takes the president's proposals seriously. In their study, Edwards and Barrett adopted an expansive definition, scoring a proposal as "on the agenda" if a committee or subcommittee held hearings on the president's bill. Among the 4–5 percent of presidential proposals between 1953 and 1996 that

Edwards and Barrett considered highly significant, congressional committees or subcommittees held hearings on an astonishing 98 percent. Peterson employed a more restrictive definition, requiring Congress either to pass or definitively defeat a proposal; otherwise, he classified it as terminated via inaction. Using this definition, he found Congress took serious action on 75 percent of the 299 bills he tracked in his random sample of presidential proposals from 1953–1984.[4] However, this number varied considerably depending on the importance of the proposal. He scored 22 percent of the proposals in his random sample as "most important," implying a far less restrictive definition than that of Edwards and Barrett. But in this large group of relatively important proposals, Congress took serious action on 84 percent. However, Congress did so for only 62 percent of the proposals Peterson scored as less important.[5]

At the top end of the importance scale these numbers are so large, apparently for both unified and divided party government, that they raise an interesting question: who is leading whom? Can presidents achieve a 98 percent consideration rate simply by tossing a major proposal into the legislative hopper? Or does a consideration rate like this indicate that presidents preemptively submit bills in areas that are likely to see major congressional action anyway? Then, at the lower end of the importance scale, presidents may submit bills in an effort to stimulate action, with considerable but far from universal success. We return to these points subsequently.

Now consider the success of presidential initiatives. Does Congress enact legislation that incorporates some or all of the position advanced by the president in his proposal? Peterson (1990); Edwards and Barrett (2000); Edwards, Barrett, and Peake (1997); and Rudalevige (2002) all address this question.

Table 3.1 summarizes Peterson's findings, calculated from data presented in Peterson (1990).[6] As discussed above, Congress was more likely to give a definitive resolution to more important proposals than less important ones (84 percent versus 62 percent, a 35 percent increase). But, if Congress acted on a less important proposal, it was much more likely to provide some success to the president (76 percent versus 58 percent, a 31 percent increase).

Table 3.1. Success of Presidential Bills in Congress (Peterson Data)

Proposals	N	Serious Action Taken	Proposal Rejected (if serious action taken)	Some Presidential Success (if serious action taken)
Most important	67	84%	41%	58%
Less important	232	62%	23%	76%

Calculated from Table 5.3 in Peterson (1990, 183).

Edwards and Barrett, who tracked 256 of the most significant proposals made by presidents between 1953 and 1996, found that 42 percent of those that made it onto the congressional agenda become law. Because the proposals they studied were apparently much more significant on average than those Peterson scored as "most important," this rate appears quite compatible with those reported in Table 3.1.

Importantly, Edwards and Barrett contrast the success rate for major proposals under unified government versus divided party government—and find a large difference. In particular, Congress enacted 53 percent of the president's major proposals under unified party government, but only 28 percent under divided party government, a decrease of 47 percent. Thus, Congresses controlled by the opposition party were far less likely to enact the president's proposals.[7]

Rudalevige tracked 384 presidential proposals initiated between 1949 and 1996. He scored these proposals similarly to the Peterson data, but did not distinguish between more important and less important proposals. Overall, he found some presidential success in 61 percent of proposals (2002, Table 7.1). This figure is intermediate between Peterson's 76 percent for less important proposals and 58 percent for more important proposals, and appears quite compatible with these estimates. It is considerably higher than Edwards and Barrett's 48 percent, but this is probably due to their focus on the most important proposals.

Although Rudalevige does not report data for unified versus divided party government per se, it is possible to calculate a measure using the data in his tables. In particular, he scored defeat or inaction as "0," some or marginal presidential success as "1," substantial presidential success as "2," and complete presidential success as "3." Using these measures, the mean or average overall presidential success score in his sample of proposals was 1.4—almost midway between marginal and substantial presidential success (2002, Table 7.1). In his sample, 42 percent of the proposals were unified government proposals while 58 percent were divided party proposals. For the unified party government proposals, the average success score was 1.7, somewhat shy of substantial presidential success. However, for the divided party government proposals, the average presidential success rate was only 1.2, slightly better than marginal success.[8] This 30 percent decline in average success score shows quite clearly the differential success rates discovered by Edwards and Barrett.

Aside from the significance of proposals and unified versus divided party control of the government, are there other reliable predictors of the success or failure of presidential proposals? Rudalevige's analysis is most helpful in this respect.[9] First, he found the percentage of seats held by the president's copartisans in Congress was an important predictor of success. This result is broadly similar to the unified/divided party government finding, and is also compatible with earlier studies of presidential success in roll call voting in Congress (see, e.g., Bond and Fleisher 1990).

Second, Rudalevige found evidence that success fell with increasing ideological distance between the president and the House Rules Committee. This finding may attest to the importance of that committee, but it is also helpful to remember that Rules is a "leadership" committee. In other words, this ideological distance may be a proxy for distance from the leadership of the majority party in the House— or, put differently, a measure of the ideological polarization between the president and the House majority party. Third, Rudalevige found that increased presidential popularity boosted the prospects of success. Fourth, he found that specific characteristics of proposals correlated with success. In particular, foreign policy proposals did better than domestic ones; simpler proposals tended to do better than more complex ones; reorganization plans did particularly well; and proposals developed in the White House seemed to do somewhat worse.

We now know that presidential rhetoric can have powerful effects on the public, and through them, Congress (Canes-Wrone 2005). Hence, the president's use of rhetoric may be an important contributor to the success or failure of programmatic initiatives. However, students of the legislative program have not yet integrated presidential rhetoric into their studies of program success. This is an obvious path for future research.

Impact: What Difference Does Proffering Make?

What difference does the president's legislative program make? That is, what would have happened to public policy if the president had not proffered a bill when he did? What would have happened if he had, when he did not?

These are hard questions to answer. As discussed earlier, presidents strategically choose which bills to proffer and what to include in them. Presumably, they intervene where they have a chance to affect outcomes in ways important to them. Consequently, inferences about counter-factuals are difficult. For example, Congress might well have passed a civil rights bill in 1964 or 1965. So President Johnson's intervention may not have affected the probability of passage of *some* civil rights bill at all. But the *form* the actual Civil Rights Bill took probably owed something to LBJ's intervention. More generally, if presidents focus on "hot" areas (i.e., those most likely to be passed by Congress anyway) and ignore "cold" ones, a simple comparison of passage rates between items in and out of the program will spuriously overstate the president's impact. And (conversely) if one fails to compare the content of enacted program items relative to enacted *non-program* items, one will miss a real impact from presidential intervention. On the other hand, presidents may proffer bills in areas

Table 3.2   Enactment Rates for Highly Important Proposals (Edwards and Barrett Data)

	Presidential Initiatives	Congressional Initiatives
Overall	42%	25%
Unified Party Gov't	53%	20%
Divided Party Gov't	28%	26%

From Table 6-6 in Edwards and Barrett (2000).

where congressional action is potentially malleable, and pass over those areas where it is not. So it may be quite false to suggest that a proffered bill could have made a difference in some area the president chose to avoid.

No analysis deals satisfactorily with these problems—nor would doing so be easy, absent near-experimental quality data or a well-developed theory of the presidential program. Nonetheless, Edwards and Barrett supply useful information by contrasting the enactment rates of significant presidential initiatives with those of comparably significant congressional ones. (No study contrasts the *content* of enacted presidential bills with the content of enacted nonpresidential bills.) These rates are shown in Table 3.2.

As shown, presidential initiatives are much more likely to pass than purely congressional ones—*but only under unified party government.* During divided party government, the respective passage rates are virtually identical. Moreover, the passage rate of nonpresidential (that is, purely congressional) proposals during unified government is lower than during divided party government. This may well indicate that presidents preemptively proffer bills during unified government in many areas in which enactments are likely.

Summary

Thanks to the hard work of some excellent scholars, political scientists have charted presidential legislative activism. In addition, data on the content of presidential programs now exists. At present, relatively little is known about why presidential legislative activism rises and falls or what determines the broad content of presidential programs. In contrast, much has been learned about the correlates of success in Congress. First, the most important presidential initiatives almost invariably receive scrutiny in Congress. On the other hand, Congress frequently ignores less important initiatives. Second, success is related to large majorities of copartisans in Congress, with an absence of ideological polarization between presidents and congressional leaders, with presidential popularity, and with simpler, less important initiatives, especially in the area of foreign policy.

More broadly, it is unclear whether presidents proffer bills pre-emptively in an effort to shape enactments that probably would have occurred anyway, or whether they proffer bills to stimulate action where it was unlikely. The almost invariable consideration by Congress of the most significant presidential proposals under both unified and divided party government suggests the "preemption" strategy—either that or an almost fantastic degree of presidential power. On the other hand, the variable success of presidents in gaining consideration of less important items seems to suggest the "stimulus" strategy.

These effects underscore the contingent nature of presidential influence. Nonetheless, even a modest degree of success in altering the content of the most significant enactments represents a huge impact on public policy by presidents. Small wonder, then, that the president's legislative program has become such an important part of the modern presidency.

3A. Theories of the President's Program

What explains the potency of bills proffered by the president? In this section, we review political scientists' theories about the presidential program. Then, we develop one of these ideas in detail.

Burden Sharing, Coordination, and Information Superiority

Political scientists have suggested three causal mechanisms by which a bill written in the administration and proffered to Congress could actually affect what Congress does: burden sharing, coordination, and information superiority.

The first causal mechanism, burden sharing, was originally suggested by Richard Neustadt. Neustadt observed that the presidential program is a "downtown" drafting service (1955). As he noted, "From a congressional point of view, 'service,' not domination, is the reality behind these presidential undertakings."

Neustadt, somewhat characteristically, did not elaborate his insight in much detail. However, the basic idea seems straightforward. As many case studies attest, legislative policy entrepreneurs (i.e., leaders in a policy area) need plausible vehicles to advance their ideas. Poorly drafted bills make poor vehicles, because everyone knows that sloppily drafted bills miss their policy targets, engender horrific implementation problems, provoke litigation or tests in court, and lead to a sea of red ink. Thus, legislative entrepreneurs must research a bill extensively, draft it carefully, and keep redrafting it as they continually negotiate with others. The process is extremely laborious. However, the president can dramatically reduce the burden facing a legislative entrepreneur by using the vast resources of the executive branch to craft a well-formulated bill and then assist its sponsor. In turn, the lower cost of legislating makes the president's ready-made product more attractive to legislative entrepreneurs, provided the content appears reasonable.

Subsequent analysts have not done much with Neustadt's idea. Yet it affords a simple way to model the president's program. Moreover, the resulting model makes strong empirical predictions. We will return to the burden-sharing model shortly.

The second theoretical lens for understanding the presidential program is the coordination approach. The basic idea is that, even in the same objective situation, multiple outcomes might hold together equally well as stable social situations (that is, there is the possibility of multiple equilibria in political situations). This can occur because people's expectations about one another's behavior create a self-reinforcing dynamic. For instance, everyone driving on the left-hand side of the road and everyone driving on the right-hand side are both stable outcomes for motorists in a country: given your expectations about other people's behavior, you have no incentive to alter your driving behavior.

In the driving example, either equilibrium seems equally good. In many other examples, however, a self-enforcing equilibrium may be very unattractive for the participants but no one can change it unilaterally. Suppose, for example, a small town refuses to hire teenagers from a particular neighborhood, because they believe these teens are poorly educated. Because employers will not hire them, the neighborhood's teenagers have little incentive to remain in school and work hard. This situation is an equilibrium, because no employer has an incentive to change his behavior (since if he does, he will hire a poorly educated teenager), and no teenager has an incentive to work hard in school (since no one will hire him if he does). But this is a bad equilibrium for both employers and the teenagers, since the employers would prefer a larger pool of educated teens as potential employees, and the teens would be very happy to stay in school if doing so would result in employment.

Using this logic, suppose most congressmen wish to legislate on a pressing national problem. But if most congressmen spend most of their time on constituency service, the prospects of successful legislation are low. And if the prospects of successful legislation are low, each congressperson should indeed spend most of his or her effort on constituency service—even though he or she, like the majority, would prefer to legislate.

As this example illustrates, unless the participants in a bad equilibrium like this find some way to coordinate their actions and expectations about each other's behavior, so everyone switches simultaneously, they will remain stuck in a bad equilibrium.

In the spirit of this insight, Gary Miller (1993), among others, suggested that presidents could exercise legislative leadership by creating "focal points." That is, a president can make particular legislative targets highly salient to congressmen, interest groups, and the public. Then, the interested parties can coordinate their efforts to pass a few bills, rather than fruitlessly scatter their efforts over a disjointed multitude of bills or other activities.

A closely related idea involves coordination failures, which occur when one chamber passes legislation but the other fails to follow, or the two chambers pass irreconcilable bills (nonidentical bills passed by the House of Representatives and the Senate). Such coordination failures could occur because the president did not supply a viable focal point. Edwards and Barrett report that during unified government some 11 percent of the president's major initiatives died from this kind of legislative coordination failure, but during divided party government 22 percent of major congressional initiatives did (2000, Table 6-9). The 11 percentage-point difference can be seen as (arguably) the benefit of presidential coordination across the chambers.

Although the basic idea of presidential coordination has a degree of appeal, it also presents problems. First, why can't the congressional leadership play the coordinative role? And if they can, why do members of Congress need the president's focal points? Second, if the purpose of the legislative program is simply to coordinate efforts in Congress, why must the president actually draft bills? Why can't he simply announce the focal points and save himself and his aides a great deal of work? Finally, what empirical predictions does the coordination theory actually make, aside from "presidential leadership can work"? Perhaps not surprisingly, the coordination approach has never been developed in much detail.

The third theoretical lens, the information superiority approach, is perhaps the most intriguing of all. This approach tries to ground the power of the president's program in the information advantages of the executive branch. And surely these are substantial, for the executive branch can call on the specialized expertise and programmatic knowledge of thousands of civil servants as well as top experts. Arguably, then, the executive can draft better bills than any congressional committee. These informational advantages may create a degree of deference to the president's proposals, particularly if the president and Congress are close to one another ideologically.

As promising as the information superiority approach is, however, it must resolve a number of difficult theoretical issues. For example, what can Congress learn from a bill proffered by the executive branch? Suppose Congress can "back out" the special information of the executive from the content of the president's bill.[10] Then the committee effectively expropriates the executive's expertise. It may then reject the president's bill in favor of one it drafts itself, since its own bill may bring it a more preferred outcome ideologically. Of course, if the committee can do this, the supposed information superiority of the executive vanishes—along with much of the president's incentive to proffer bills.

Despite these and other problems, the information superiority approach probably represents the best avenue for constructing a rich and convincing theory of the presidential program. But until the theoretical issues are resolved in a rigorous way, it remains only an intriguing notion.

3B. A Closer Look at Burden Sharing

Let us return to the simplest of the three theoretical lenses, burden sharing. The basic idea of the burden-sharing model is very simple. Suppose Congress must assume an "entry cost" or opportunity cost, k, when it writes a bill and tries to pass it (for example, k could represent a cost in time that could be dedicated to constituency service instead of writing legislation). This cost will be higher when policy is abstruse and technically complex or when Congress faces many demands on its time, for example, during crises or during the run-up to an election. If Congress bears k, the legislature can craft a bill to suit itself. Or, *the president can assume* k *for Congress, supplying it with a ready-made bill* (that is, the president assumes the cost of writing legislation, not the members of Congress). In this case, however, Congress must take the president's product without modification, since researching the subject matter and rewriting the bill would essentially require expending k (that is, Congress must accept the president's bill as is, otherwise it will cost them additional time to rewrite it).[11]

This simple idea seems to capture Neustadt's idea of a "downtown drafting service." And, it is easily explored in depth using the standard spatial model of legislating.[12] Within this framework, we can investigate what Congress would do in the absence of a presidential bill, when the president should offer bills, how he should position their policy content, and how the president can combine proffered bills and the veto power as two pillars of an integrated legislative strategy.[13]

Building Blocks

The key elements of the model are *players, policies, preferences,* and *sequence.* The *players* are the president, Congress (focusing on the median or ideologically middle voter in Congress and abstracting from bicameralism), and the veto-override player or legislator at the 60th percentile in Congress (as it were).

As shown in Figure 3.2, *policies* are indicated in a policy space, *X*, a line (e.g., a tax rate, tariff rate, extent of restrictions on abortion, extent of privatization of social security, or more generally liberalism versus conservativism). Specific policies are points on the line. A particularly important policy is *q*, the status quo, the policy in effect at the beginning of the players' (members of Congress and the president) interactions.

The players' *preferences* are indicated by utility functions or how much policy benefit or gain players receive from a particular presidential proposal, which show how a player regards policies—more preferred policies yield higher utility. Thus, in Figure 3.2, the median voter in Congress prefers a policy located at *c* (his or her "ideal point") to one located at *q* (the status quo policy). Thus, if we think of *X* as representing a policy and *c*, or Congress's ideal point, as being a more conservative alternative to the existing status quo or *q*, the median or middle member of Congress would prefer the more conservative position to the status quo. We assume the president and veto-override player have similar utility functions, but with ideal points $p,v > c = 0$. (Obviously, there are "mirror" cases when those players' ideal points lie to the left of Congress's.)[14]

An important aspect of the utility functions involves issue saliency. We assume greater or lesser saliency does not affect the location of the players' ideal points but does affect the intensity with which they feel losses from non-ideal policies. In terms of Figure 3.2, greater saliency increases the steepness of the utility functions; that is, the greater the saliency of an issue, the greater the potential intensity of legislative feelings on a particular issue, the greater their perceived gain/benefit or loss will be. Let the parameter α denote the saliency of

**Figure 3.2 Policies and Congressional Utility
in the Burden-Sharing Model**

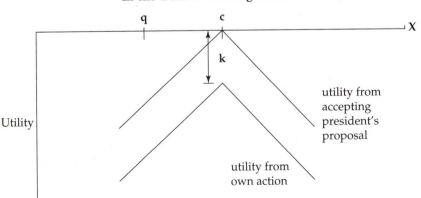

Summary

The burden-sharing model provides a simple rationale for a contingently effective presidential program. The model's empirical predictions are summarized in Table 3.3.

The model makes predictions both about the probability the president proffers a bill and about the content of proffered bills (based on the assumption that the president wishes the bills to be passed). First, the president has little incentive to proffer a bill if the policy lies in the gridlock region. Otherwise, however, the president has a powerful incentive to proffer bills, especially if the issue's public salience is great and the cost of legislating is low. In general, the president will proffer bills preemptively, in order to shape the content of enactments that Congress would likely undertake anyway. Typically, these preemptive bills will be "compromise" bills, but ones quite favorable to presidential interests. However, under special circumstances—for example, when the president's preferences are close to those of Congress (as in unified party government) or when policy is technical and abstruse or when Congress is distracted or overwhelmed or the issue salience is very low—the president can achieve his ideal policy. Greater issue saliency forces the president to make greater compromises to Congress, while greater legislation costs allow the president to offer fewer compromises in bills he chooses to proffer.

Does the model go any distance in explaining the empirical regularities discussed in the previous section? At least in some cases, the answer seems to be yes. For example, if the model is correct, the president proffers in policy areas that *Congress would have considered anyway* or in areas where *Congress will welcome the administration's bills*. If this is correct, it is hardly surprising that Congress considers 98 percent of the most important presidential bills.

The model also helps explain why presidents have so much success during unified party government. When the president's ideal point is close to that of Congress (see Figure 3.2), the president has wider latitude in placing bills that Congress will accept. In contrast, consider

Table 3.3   Empirical Predictions of the Burden-Sharing Model

	Probability President Proffers a Bill	Content of Proffered Bill
Policy in gridlock region	Zero	—
Policy outside gridlock region		
—Increased salience of issue	Up	Increased accommodation of Congress
—Increased cost of legislating	Down	Decreased accommodation of Congress

the situation when the president's ideal point is far from Congress (see Figure 3.4). In this case, small errors in placement (due to "incomplete information" about k or congressional preferences) can easily lead to rejection of the president's proposals.

The model also suggests that scholars may not have measured "presidential success" in quite the right fashion. Mostly, (the model suggests) the president is trying to shape congressional action by making it easier for Congress to "do the right thing" as the president might understand it. Thus, when the president is conservative, successfully proffered bills should "bend" policy in a more conservative direction *than would have occurred absent presidential intervention,* and similarly, the bills a liberal president successfully proffers should "bend" policy in that direction. Presidential success lies in these "bends" in policy, not in the percentage of what the president got relative to his initial request (which was strategically chosen anyway).

The burden-sharing model is just a starting place for thinking theoretically about the president's legislative program. Like all such frameworks, its success lies in explaining observed regularities, predicting new ones, and stimulating better theory. With the model in hand, let us turn to a closer look at presidential legislative activism.

4. Explaining Presidential Legislative Activism

The burden-sharing model suggests some simple ideas for structuring an investigation of an underresearched topic, presidential legislative activism. When does a rational president proffer many bills to Congress, and when does he proffer few?

First, as discussed in Section 3, the burden-sharing model emphasizes *preemptive action* by the president. So, straightforwardly, the model directs us to look at periods when large-scale congressional action is eminent. In such moments, presidents will want to be legislative activists in order to mold the content of the legislation Congress would likely enact anyway. So the critical question is: when will large-scale congressional action be eminent? The spatial model at the center of the burden-sharing approach points to periods when president and Congress can find legislative common ground for many status quos. In other words, it points to periods when the "gridlock interval" in Figure 3.4 is small, so that policy windows (or the opportunity to enact new policies) are open.

Critically, however, open policy windows are only a necessary condition for legislative activism, not a sufficient one. In addition, Congress must face intense *demands* to produce legislation, for even if Congress can legislate, it will not do so if organized groups and public opinion do not create the necessary incentives.

From the perspective of the burden-sharing model, then, it is the *combination* of open windows and intense demands on Congress that leads to presidential legislative activism. In these periods, the model suggests, presidents will want to proffer many bills, in order to shape the content of subsequent legislation.

Second, the burden-sharing model emphasizes the costly nature of legislating to Congress. For Congress, expending time and effort on legislation is always costly, if only in terms of forgone opportunities. The most obvious case when the opportunity cost of legislation increases is in the run up to congressional elections. Thus, the model leads us to expect fewer presidential proposals in those periods, as Congress is less likely to act on them.

A Closer Look at Presidential Legislative Activism

Figure 3.6 displays Rudalevige's data by year of term within administration. The mean annual number of proposals per administration is shown with a dotted line. Table 3.4 displays complementary data. Four patterns stand out.

First, *average legislative activism varied widely across administrations.* Three presidents, Truman, Reagan, and Bush (41), displayed relatively low levels of legislative activism, averaging less than 100 proposals annually. Eisenhower, Nixon, Ford, and Carter were "moderate" legislative activists, averaging between 120–150 proposals annually. Finally, Kennedy and Johnson were "intense" legislative activists, averaging more than 250 proposals annually. Notably, average activism rose and declined more or less symmetrically around the Johnson administration. President Clinton can be scored as either a nonactivist or a moderate activist, depending on the exact cutoff one chooses. If one scores Clinton as a moderate, then the moderate activists averaged about 50 percent more bills per year than the nonactivists, and the intense activists more than three times as many. (The annual averages across the three groups are 88, 132, and 293).

Second, *variation in activism over the years of a term within an administration was much smaller.* The nonactivists tended to be nonactivists or moderates every year; the activists were activists in almost every year of the administration. The presidents we labeled moderates often surged into activism or slumped in nonactivism, but nonetheless tended to stay fairly close to a moderate average. Variance (or changes from year to year) in proposing increased with average activism, a statistical pattern known as "heteroskedasticity." As is often the case, taking logarithms stabilizes the variance and eliminates heteroskedasticity. We can then see (in the fourth column of Table 3.4) that proposals in the first Eisenhower administration were particularly variable. The Ford presidency stands out for low variance.

Figure 3.6   Presidential Legislative Activism From Truman to Clinton (Rudalevige Data)

Annual Presidential Proposals, 1949–1995

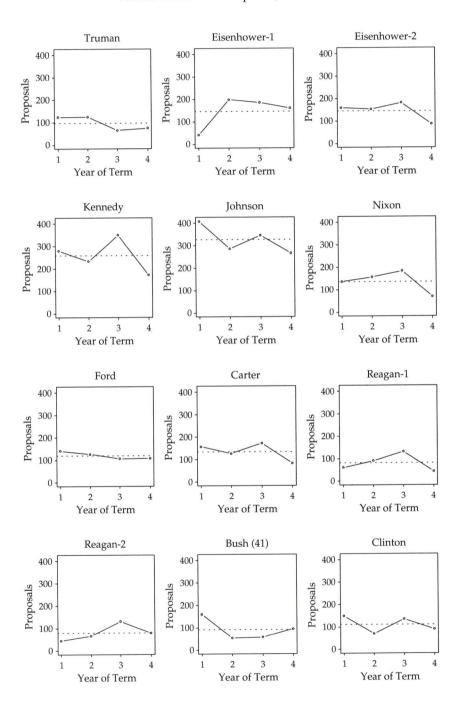

Table 3.4   Legislative Activism by Administration (Rudalevige Data)

Administration	Average Annual Proposals	SD of Annual Proposals	Average Annual Proposals (log)	SD of Annual Proposals (log)
Truman	97	32	4.5	.4
Eisenhower—1	146	71	4.8	.7
Eisenhower—2	145	40	4.9	.3
Kennedy	259	75	5.5	.3
Johnson	326	64	5.8	.2
Nixon	137	49	4.9	.4
Ford	120	17	4.8	.1
Carter	134	39	4.9	.3
Reagan—1	82	38	4.3	.5
Reagan—2	80	37	4.3	.4
Bush (41)	92	49	4.4	.5
Clinton—1	112	37	4.7	.3

Note: Logarithms are natural logarithms.

Third, *variation within terms was broadly predictable*. In particular, the first and third years of a term often displayed about the same number of proposals. The fourth year usually displayed a considerable decline, averaging about 25 percent relative to the third year. The second year was quite variable, but averaged about a 15 percent drop relative to the first year. From this perspective, the Carter administration displays the "most typical" pattern. The unusually high variance of the first Eisenhower administration was due to the low number of proposals in the first year (as noted by Neustadt), with many items that more typically would have appeared in the first year seemingly appearing in the second. The low variance of the Ford administration was due to an unusually elevated number of bills in the fourth year. The anomalous appearance of the Bush administration seems to reflect proposals deferred from the third year to the fourth, probably due to the Gulf War of 1991.

In sum, most presidents seem at least somewhat susceptible to a broad rhythm within the four years of an administration. But the underlying strategic situation determining the "baseline" of activism—low, moderate, or intense—varies widely across administrations. Explaining this "baseline" is a major challenge for any theory of presidential legislative activism. We now turn to the "baseline" conditions suggested by the burden-sharing model.

Policy Windows and Legislative Demands

In Section 3B, we discussed the gridlock configuration and the gridlock region (recall Figure 3.4). It is possible to measure this distance, using estimates of ideal points developed by political scientists.

Then, when the gridlock region is small, one can say the policy window is wide; when the gridlock region is large, the policy window is narrow; that is, the larger the potential for gridlock in Congress the less opportunity there is for presidents to successfully propose legislation. (We supply details in the Appendix.)

The left-hand panel in Figure 3.7 displays this measure of the policy window. In the period under study, the policy window was widest in the early Eisenhower administration and during the Johnson administration. It was narrowest in last two years of the second Reagan administration. Statistically, the right-hand panel shows the bivariate relationship between the policy window and the number of presidential legislative proposals. As shown, a wider window correlates with greater activism (the glaring outlier in the lower right-hand corner of the panel is 1953, year one of the first Eisenhower administration).

Political scientists do not have a standard measure of social demands for legislation. However, a plausible measure might look to the activity of social movements. As African Americans, environmentalists, and women mobilized in pursuit of social objectives, their conceptions of a better world led to demands for much new legislation. Thus, we create a simple measure of social movement activity: the number of front page stories in the *New York Times* mentioning "civil rights," "women," and "environment" and "movement." (We exclude clearly inappropriate stories and stories covering congressional action or legislation.)

The left-hand panel in Figure 3.8 presents this measure of social movement activity. After 1963, the measure has a degree of face plau-

**Figure 3.7 The Width of the Policy Window
and Presidential Legislative Activism**

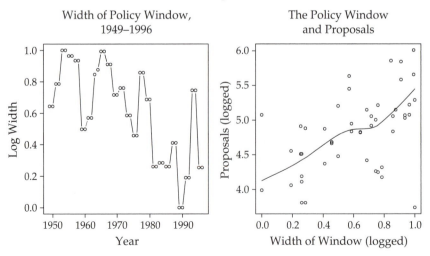

sibility—it appears to track common conceptions of social movement activity. Prior to 1963, however, the measure fails to capture the growing civil rights activity that actually existed. So the measure is hardly perfect. Nonetheless, the right-hand panel in Figure 3.8 suggests that the measure does correlate with presidential legislative activism. (The negative relationship at the lowest levels of activity may reflect the poor quality of the pre-1963 data.)

The burden-sharing model suggests presidents will become legislative activists when the policy window is wide *and* Congress faces intense demands for legislation. One can capture this idea by interacting (multiplying) the two separate measures. The interaction assumes large values only when both of the separate measures have large values. The left-hand panel displays this measure. As shown in the right-hand panel, the interaction correlates with presidential activism, perhaps even better than either of the two separate measures.

Figure 3.10 confirms the implications of Figure 3.9. The number of proposals and the extent of the interaction effect closely move together for the period examined, especially after 1962.

Multivariate Analysis

A sound analysis of presidential legislative activism demands a multivariate approach.[18] However, time-series data always require special care. Because the issues involved are rather technical (involving the stationarity of the series), we address them in an appendix. The results reported there indicate that straightforward ordinary least squares regression is appropriate for analyzing the data, but only after 1962. The earlier figures also suggested that measurement

**Figure 3.8 Social Movement Activity
and Presidential Legislative Activism**

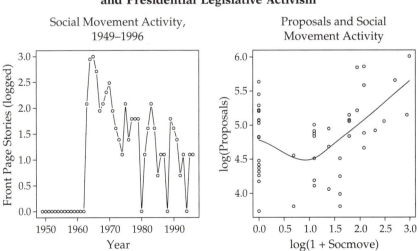

Social Movement Activity,
1949–1996

Proposals and Social
Movement Activity

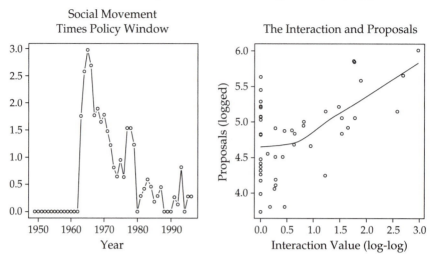

Figure 3.9 The Combination of Open Windows and Intense Demands, and Presidential Legislative Activism

error in the social movements variable precluded an earlier analysis in any event. Consequently, we focus on the post-1962 data in the statistical analyses that follow.

Table 3.5 presents six simple regression models for the post-1962 data using the variables discussed above. Model 1 is the simplest pos-

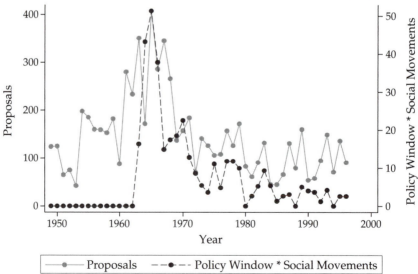

Figure 3.10 Time Series: Presidential Legislation Activism and the Interaction of Policy Windows and Social Movements

sible model. It contains only the key variable, the interaction of the policy window variable, and the social movement variable. Model 2 adds two variables indicating the second and fourth years of a term. Model 3 combines these into one variable indicating congressional election years. Models 4 and 5 add the policy window and social movement variables, each separately, to the interaction term and the election year variable. Model 6 adds both these variables simultaneously (this is the "saturated" model that many statistical analysts would see as most natural).

Most striking is the way the key variable, the interaction, strongly affects presidential legislative activism. By itself, the interaction term explains almost half of the variance in the number of proposals proffered to Congress. Using Model 3, a change in its value from its high point in the post-1963 period (2.97 in 1965) to its low point (0 in 1980 and 1988–90) is estimated to decrease presidential proposals from 389 to 85 in noncongressional election years, and from 300 to 66 in election years.[19] As long as the interaction variable is included in the model, adding its component parts singly or jointly adds essentially nothing to the model. The Durbin-Watson statistic indicates no problems with serial correlation, a finding confirmed by Breusch-Godfrey tests (not shown).

As expected, proposals drop in congressional election years. Moreover, the effect appears to be the same in the midterm and presidential election years, justifying combining the second- and fourth-year variables into one election-year variable.

Across all the models, the values of the variables are quite stable. This is clear for the election year variable, but taking into account the different specifications, the estimated effects of the policy window and social movement variables are also quite stable over the models.

Figure 3.11 compares the fit of Model 2 with the actual data. As shown, the model tracks the actual data remarkably quite well, with the exception of a few isolated years.

The message of the statistical analysis is quite clear: *when the policy window opens after a social movement gains steam, presidents become legislative activists.* Absent those conditions, the size of the president's legislative program is much smaller. The macrolevel counts analyzed here cannot prove that activist presidents move preemptively in order to shape prospective congressional legislation. But if they were doing so, these are the statistical results one would expect.

5. Conclusion

Political scientists have long argued that the president's legislative program is important. But in the absence of systematic data, that im-

Table 3.5 Regression Analysis of Presidential Legislative Activism

	Model 1	Model 2	Model 3	Model 4	Model 5	Model 6
ln(Policy Window) * ln(Social Movement)	.53*** (.08)	.52*** (.08)	.51*** (.07)	.40*** (.13)	.60*** (.13)	.34 (.35)
Year 2	—	-.25* (.15)	—	—	—	—
Year 4	—	-.27* (.15)	—	—	—	—
Congressional Election Year	—	—	-.26** (.12)	-.28** (.12)	-.28** (.12)	-.28** (.13)
ln(Policy Window)	—	—	—	.40 (.37)	—	.48 (.69)
ln(Social Movements)	—	—	—	—	-.12 (.16)	.04 (.28)
Intercept	4.30*** (.10)	4.45*** (.11)	4.45*** (.11)	4.35*** (.15)	4.56*** (.19)	4.28*** (.44)
Degrees of freedom	32	30	31	30	30	29
Adjusted R^2	.48	.62	.63	.63	.62	.62
Durbin-Watson Stat.	2.08	1.84	1.84	1.89	1.90	1.88

Note: The dependent variable in all models is ln(Proposals). In each cell, the topmost number is the coefficient and lower number is the standard error.

***: significant at the .01 level.

**: significant at the .05 level.

*: significant at the .10 level.

No mark: not statistically significant.

**Figure 3.11   Actual Versus Predicted Levels
of Presidential Legislative Activism**

Actual Versus Predicted Values of Proposals, 1963–1996

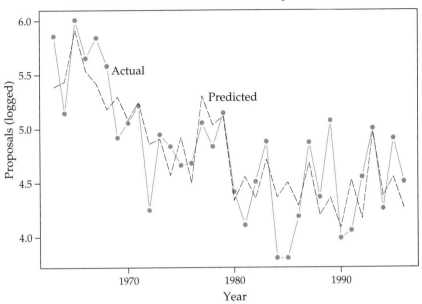

portance was hard to demonstrate. And in the absence of tightly argued theories, it was difficult to explain why proffering bills should matter.

Newly available data, painstakingly collected by presidential scholars, has dramatically expanded our knowledge of empirical regularities in the presidential program. At least for important bills, Congress is extraordinarily willing to consider presidential initiatives. And Congress is somewhat responsive to them, at least when the legislature contains a large band of copartisans ideologically proximate to the president. But this hardly exhausts the new data: much remains to be learned.

We have argued that the president's program is also theoretically tractable, in the same way that the presidential veto, presidential direct action, and presidential rhetoric are (Cameron 2000; Howell 2003; Canes-Wrone 2005). To that end, we constructed one of the first formal models of the presidential program, the burden-sharing model.

Although the burden-sharing model is just a first step toward a robust theory of the presidential program, it affords a simple way to understand some of the known empirical regularities. Moreover, it suggests new ways to think about the legislative program, including presidential legislative activism. Using the new data and some simple ideas from the model, we showed that presidents appear to respond in a sensible way to their legislative opportunities. In particular, presidents expand their legislative program when large-scale congressional action appears likely, as if they were trying to shape that legislation by preemptively proffering bills. They contract the legislative program when policy windows close, the public mutes its demands for legislation, and Congress is distracted by an impending election. Though much has been learned about presidential strategy in this area, much remains to be learned.

Appendix

The Policy Window Variable

We identified the gridlock region as the distance between the ideal point of the median voter in Congress and the nearer of the ideal points of the president and veto-override player. We measured this distance for the Senate, using Keith Poole's "optimal classification scores" (see http://voteview.com/). Call this measure "*grdlk*." Then we define

$$Window = 1 + 1.718 \frac{|\max(grdlk) - grdlk|}{\max(grdlk) - \min(grdlk)}$$

This creates a standardized measure ranging from 1 (when *grdlk* attains its maximum value in the series) to 2.718 (when *grdlk* attains its minimum value in the series). Log(Window) then has values between 0 and 1. This is the series used in the analysis.

Stationarity of Variables

A time-series variable is "stationary" if its mean, variance, and covariance are all time invariant. If the variables in a time-series analysis are not stationary and OLS is used, the regression will report a significant relationship between the explanatory and response variables that does not really exist, a so-called spurious regression (Granger and Newbold 1977). Accordingly, we examined the stationarity of the variables with a statistical test designed to uncover nonstationarity (a unit root test). We employed the DF-GLS test, which has shown particularly good properties in this regard. The results are summarized in Table 3.A.1.

When the DF-GLS unit root test is applied, all the variables except the policy-window variable are estimated as unit-root nonstationary. When the post-1962 data is used, however, all the variables are estimated as stationary, which allows us to use OLS for the post-1962 data.

Table 3.A.1 Unit-Root Test Results

	Whole Period	Post-1962
Ln(proposals)	Nonstationary	Stationary (Detrending)
Ln(window)	Stationary (Detrending)	Stationary (Detrending)
Ln(socmove)	Nonstationary	Stationary (Detrending)
Ln(window) * Ln(socmove)	Nonstationary	Stationary (Detrending)

DF-GLS (Dickey-Fuller Generalized Least Square) Test is used with SIC (Schwart Information Criteria) for lag length selection.

Notes

1. For example, Light (1999), Fett (1974), and related work on other parts of legislative strategy such as "going public," especially Cohen (1997) and Canes-Wrone (2005).

2. For a sophisticated treatment of the same problem in studying a president's decisions to "go public," see Canes-Wrone (2001).

3. The data on all proposals may be found in Table A1 in Rudalevige (2002) (Rudalevige splits 1974 into two periods, due to the change from Nixon to Ford—that year is combined here). The data on "important" proposals is from Table 6-1 in Edwards and Barrett (2000).

4. Peterson used data collected by *Congressional Quarterly* for 1953–1974 and then added similar data through 1984 using the *Public Papers of the President* and the *Weekly Compilation of Presidential Documents*. Peterson then drew a random sample from this universe, excluding foreign policy proposals.

5. Rudalevige scored his data similarly to Peterson's, but his tables combine the categories "no action" with "actively defeated." Thus, one cannot see how many proposals were actively considered by Congress.

6. If Congress took a presidential proposal seriously but it failed, Peterson scored it as "opposition dominance." If it passed in some form, he scored it as either "compromise," "presidential dominance," or "consensus." We aggregate the last three categories as "some presidential success."

7. Peterson does not report success rates by unified versus divided party government. He does so by administration (e.g., 1990, Table 7.1) but does not distinguish between more important and less important proposals, so that the meaning of different rates is not clear.

8. We calculate these using the data in Table A.7 in Rudalevige (2002, 184–185).

9. Edwards and Barrett did not undertake a multivariate analysis. Peterson did, for example, with respect to the innovativeness of proposals, but not with respect to success per se.

10. In other words, suppose there is a separating equilibrium in the implied signaling game between president and Congress. For a discussion

of related issues in the context of congressional committees and the floor, see Chapter 2 in Krehbiel (1991).

11. This is clearly an extreme assumption, which might comport better with an information-based model. Thus, one might see the burden-sharing model as a "reduced form" informational model.

12. We review the standard spatial theory of legislating below. Readers who wish to learn more may want to consult, for example, Krehbiel (1998).

13. The third pillar is presidential rhetoric, "going public." Using the approach created by Canes-Wrone and her coauthors (see Canes-Wrone 2005), one could integrate all three. But doing so is outside the scope of this chapter.

14. The function for Congress if it legislates on its own is: $-\alpha|x| - k$, where α is the saliency parameter discussed below and k is the cost of legislating.

15. The following subcase deserves quick mention: suppose q lies to the left of c but within k/α distance of it. In that case, a unilateral move of the status quo will not be worth the effort to Congress. Therefore, this policy will not be "on Congress's agenda." In this case, the president can proffer a bill located at $x^p = -q > 0$, successfully putting his bill on the congressional agenda, leading to an enactment. (If $-q \leq p$, the president would offer his ideal point.) In other words, the president's bill will stimulate Congress to enact legislation, when otherwise it would not.

16. Note that it does not matter whether $p < v$ or $v < p$, provided $q < \min\{p,v\}$.

17. The critical condition is $x^c + k/\alpha \geq p$. However, some simple algebra shows that $x^c = 2p - q$ when $c < p < q,v$ and $x^c = 2v - q$ when $c < v < q,p$. So the condition reduces to $k \geq \alpha(q - p)$ and $k \geq \alpha(q - v)$, respectively.

18. Because the dependent variable involves counts, some analysts would advocate Poisson or negative binomial regressions rather than the ordinary least squares estimates shown here. But given the magnitudes of the counts, these approaches are likely to gain little. And, of course, the OLS estimates are easier to interpret. Thus, we present the OLS estimates.

19. This is calculated as, for example, $e^{4.45+.51*2.97} = 389$.

References

Bond, Jon, and Richard Fleisher. 1990. *The President in the Legislative Arena*. Chicago: University of Chicago Press.

Cameron, Charles. 2000. *Veto Bargaining: Presidents and the Politics of Negative Power*. Cambridge: Cambridge University Press.

Canes-Wrone, Brandice. 2001. "The President's Legislative Influence from Public Appeals." *American Journal of Political Science* 45(2):313–329.

———. 2005. *Who Leads Whom? Presidents, Policy and Public*. Chicago: University of Chicago Press.

Cannon, Joseph G. No date. "How a Bill Becomes A Law," typescript transcribed from the original manuscript in the Illinois State Historical Library, Springfield Illinois.

Cohen, Jeffrey E. 1997. *Presidential Responsiveness and Public Policy-making.* Ann Arbor: University of Michigan Press.

Edwards, George C. III, and Andrew Barrett. 2000. "Presidential Agenda Setting in Congress." In Jon R. Bond and Richard Fleisher (eds.), *Polarized Politics: Congress and the President in a Partisan Era,* 109–133. Washington DC: CQ Press.

Edwards, George C. III, Andrew Barrett, and Jeffrey Peake. 1997. "The Legislative Impact of Divided Government," *American Journal of Political Science* 41(2):545–563.

Fett, Patrick. 1974. "Presidential Legislative Priorities and Legislators' Voting Decisions." *Journal of Politics* 56(2):502–512.

Granger, C.W.J., and Paul Newbold. 1977. *Forecasting Economic Time Series.* New York: Academic Press.

Howell, William. 2003. *Power Without Persuasion: The Politics of Direct Presidential Action.* Princeton, NJ: Princeton University Press.

Jacobs, Lawrence R., and Robert Y. Shapiro. 2000. *Politicians Don't Pander: Political Manipulation and the Loss of Democratic Responsiveness.* Chicago: University of Chicago Press.

Krehbiel, Keith. 1991. *Information and Legislative Organization.* Ann Arbor: University of Michigan Press.

———. 1998. *Pivotal Politics: A Theory of U.S. Lawmaking.* Chicago: University of Chicago Press.

Light, Paul. 1999. *The President's Agenda: Domestic Policy Choice From Kennedy to Clinton.* (3rd edition). Baltimore, MD: Johns Hopkins University Press.

Miller, Gary J. 1993. "Formal Theory and the Presidency." In George C. Edwards III, John H. Kessel, and Bert A. Rockman (eds.), *Researching the Presidency: Vital Questions, New Approaches,* 289–336. Pittsburgh: University of Pittsburgh Press.

Neustadt, Richard. 1955. "Presidency and Legislation: Planning the President's Program." *American Political Science Review* 49(4):980–1021.

Peterson, Mark. 1990. *Legislating Together.* Cambridge, MA: Harvard University Press.

Rudalevige, Andrew. 2002. *Managing the President's Program: Presidential Leadership and Legislative Policy Formulation.* Princeton, NJ: Princeton University Press. ✦

Chapter 4

Conditional Presidential Leadership
Pivotal Players, Gridlock, and Delegation

David Epstein, Ida Pagter Kristensen, and Sharyn O'Halloran

In Chapter 3, Cameron and Park argued that a president's influence on legislation is a function of how prevalent gridlock is and the incentives among members of Congress to allow the president to take the lead in proposing legislation. They emphasized that the greater the level of disagreement, the less likely Congress is to follow the president's lead and the more likely it is to try (but not often succeed) at writing legislation on its own. Because the costs of collective action in Congress are high and its members have political maintenance needs in addition to legislating, there are advantages to members of Congress in having the president propose legislation, meaning, in effect, that the president relieves Congress of some of the costs of coordination and gains some influence as a result.

In Chapter 4, Epstein, Kristensen, and O'Halloran discuss gridlock in relation to whether bills are enacted and how much discretion they grant the executive to determine the meaning of the enactments. Like Cameron and Park, they also find that presidential leadership is contingent—or in their words, conditional. They describe their chapter:

> In his book *Pivotal Politics*, Keith Krehbiel formulates a formal theory of the relationship between key legislative "pivot players," legislative gridlock, and policy production. Krehbiel claims that the size of the gridlock interval, as defined by the spatial distance between key legislative players, determines the ease with which Congress can pass legislation. The larger the gridlock interval, the more difficult it is to pass legislation, and we should therefore expect a negative relationship between the size of the gridlock interval and the amount of legislation passed by Congress. Large changes in the gridlock interval from one Congress to the next should correspondingly be associated with increased productivity. This chapter demonstrates that his theoretical model is slightly misspecified. Furthermore, although Krehbiel performs a variety of empirical tests in his book, he fails to test

his model directly. This chapter shows that when his key independent variable, the size of the gridlock region, is operationalized in accordance with his theory, Krehbiel's theoretical model performs poorly in empirical testing. Hence, neither the size of, nor changes in the gridlock interval are good predictors of gridlock, as measured by the amount of legislation passed. Furthermore, the paper proposes and tests three modifications of Krehbiel's original theory. None of these modifications makes the gridlock interval a significant predictor of legislative productivity.

✦ ✦ ✦

Introduction

The increase in the occurrence of divided partisan control of the branches of government in the United States ushered in a wave of new research assessing the impact of congressional-executive conflict on legislative behavior. The bulk of this literature addresses the question of whether divided government results in gridlock; that is, the inability of legislators to enact new policy initiatives. The central theme that has emerged from this literature is that divided government leads to policy stalemate and, consequently, legislative productivity should be highest when the same party controls both the legislative and executive branches.[1]

Mayhew (1991) challenged this notion, arguing that there is no significant difference between the number of "significant laws" passed under divided and unified party government. Following Mayhew, a vast amount of literature has either tried to show limitations to Mayhew's findings (Edwards, Barrett, and Peake 1997; Coleman 1999; Howell et al. 2000), or has developed further the idea of divided government not having an impact on gridlock. In the latter category, Krehbiel (1996, 1998) claims that it is not divided government per se but rather the size and location of "the gridlock interval," defined as the distance between pivotal legislative actors, which influence legislative production. In his empirical analysis, Krehbiel finds that the gridlock interval, as he operationalizes it, is a significant predictor of the amount of legislation being passed in Congress.

However, once the gridlock interval is operationalized in accordance with Krehbiel's theory, it fails to be a good predictor of the amount of legislation passed. Not only does it not predict the amount of "significant legislation" passed (as defined by Mayhew 1991), it also does not predict any of a variety of other definitions of the amount of legislation passed. This chapter also proposes three different modifications of Krehbiel's theory that can be expected to increase the predictive power of the model. Yet even after incorporating these modifications, the gridlock interval still does not predict legislative productivity.

The larger question of whether, or how, gridlock affects legislative productivity thus remains open. This chapter presents a competing theory of legislative production—conditional presidential leadership—that builds on both the presidential leadership and delegation literatures. It asserts that presidents can play a strong role in the policymaking process by convincing Congress to delegate more power to the executive branch. But this ability to influence Congress will be felt most strongly when delegation is attractive and congressional action is least efficient; that is, under unified government with high gridlock.

The paper proceeds as follows. After a literature review, we discuss Krehbiel's definition of the gridlock interval and suggest an alternative operationalization or way of measuring that corresponds more closely to his theoretical model. We then test the effect of changes in the absolute size and changes in the location of the gridlock interval on the amount of legislation passed, showing that in all cases gridlock is not a significant predictor of legislative outcomes. We next introduce our theory of conditional presidential leadership, and show that the size of the gridlock region does predict the amount of discretionary authority delegated to executive officials. The final section concludes by emphasizing the importance of institutional context for delegating authority to the executive.

Gridlock Theory

Pivotal Players

Krehbiel (1998) formulates a theory in which the size of and changes in the location of the "gridlock interval," rather than divided government per se, predict the ease with which Congress can pass legislation. The gridlock interval is identified as the distance between two key pivotal players among the following potential pivots: the veto-override pivot, the filibuster-override pivot, and the president. Which two players define the gridlock interval depends on the relative position of the ideal policy positions of these players in a one-dimensional policy space. In other words, it will vary by the existing political coalitions in Congress on each individual issue/policy/vote. Hence, if we think of ideology running along a scale from zero to one hundred, it would be (1) the ideological difference between the president's ideology and the ideology of the member of Congress who would provide the 33rd vote preventing the override of a presidential veto. Likewise, (2) the filibuster pivot would be the difference between the president's ideology and the 60th member of Congress who could prevent a successful cloture vote, thus ending a filibuster.

Figure 4.1a shows the ideal policy points of the pivotal legislators, the veto pivot, and the filibuster pivot respectively, when the president is liberal compared to Congress.[2] The veto pivot is the most extreme (in the direction of the president) of the legislators needed to override a presidential veto, while the filibuster pivot is the most extreme (in the direction opposite the president) of the legislators needed to override a filibuster.

Krehbiel's theory predicts that legislation cannot be passed when the status quo is located inside the gridlock interval—that is, anywhere between the veto pivot and the filibuster pivot in the example in Figure 4.1, while past research assumed that the median or middle voter was most important; that is, all the president needed to do was to get a simple majority vote in order to win. For instance, if the status quo is located between the veto pivot and the median legislator, a majority of the legislators prefers to move legislation in a more conservative direction. Any attempt to do so will be vetoed by the president, though, and a veto override is impossible, as the veto pivot opposes any shift in a conservative direction. Likewise, if the status quo is located between the median and the filibuster pivot, a majority prefers to move policy in a more liberal direction. This is impossible though, as a filibuster will be mounted, on which cloture cannot be invoked.

The larger the absolute size of the gridlock interval the more likely it is, *ceteris paribus,* that the status quo on a given issue will be lo-

Figure 4.1   Pivotal Players and Gridlock

Figure 4.1a. Pivotal legislators in Krehbiel's model

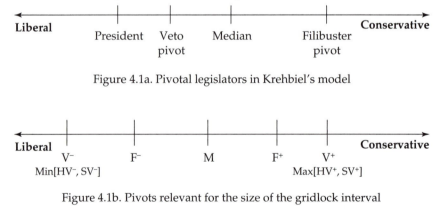

Figure 4.1b. Pivots relevant for the size of the gridlock interval

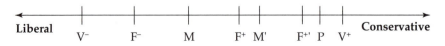

Figure 4.1c. Distribution of pivots with a moderately conservative president

cated inside the gridlock region and hence make legislating on the issue impossible. Therefore, Krehbiel predicts that the absolute size of the gridlock interval will be negatively correlated with Congress's ability to pass legislation. Furthermore, large changes in the location of the gridlock interval, which dramatically alter which part of the policy space is located inside this interval, are theorized to have a positive correlation with Congress's ability to pass legislation. Krehbiel argues that other scholars misclassify these changes as a "honeymoon effect" (Krehbiel 1998, 42).

Interestingly, whether the government is divided or unified does not play any role per se in Krehbiel's model, as many different preference distributions—and hence many different gridlock intervals—can exist under divided as well as under unified government. This implies that it is less important which party controls a simple majority in each chamber than whether any party controls 60 percent or two-thirds of the seats. The median legislator does have some impact in his model, though, as an extreme status quo will be changed to the median legislator's ideal point. On the other hand, a status quo located closer to the gridlock region will only to some extent be moved towards the median legislator, as the pivot player will block any bill that does not at least make her indifferent compared to the status quo.[3]

Extending the Original Model

As a definitional matter, a small theoretical inconsistency exists between Krehbiel's more general theoretical orientation and his precise definition of the gridlock interval. Krehbiel (1998, 39, footnote 24) defines the gridlock interval by:

$(F, \min[V, P])$ for $P > M$, or by

$(\max[V, P], F)$ for $P < M$,

where F is the filibuster pivot, V the veto pivot, P the president, and M the median legislator. This definition does not, however, take into account the possibility that the president's ideal point may lie between the two filibuster pivots. In those instances, the gridlock interval will be defined by (F^-, F^+); that is, the range of policies that lie between the ideal points of the two filibuster pivots. Here the veto pivots are irrelevant, as the president is moderate relative to Congress.

We also extend the original model to Congress's two-chamber setting. The filibuster pivots are necessarily defined for the Senate only; consequently, these remain the same. A veto override demands a two-thirds majority in both chambers, so it must be redefined as the more extreme of the Senate and House veto-override pivots.

Table 4.1   Gridlock Interval by President's Ideal Point

President's Ideal Point (P)	Augmented Gridlock Interval
$P \leq \min(V^-_H, V^-_S)$	$[\min(V^-_H, V^-_S), F^+]$
$V^- \leq P \leq F^-$	$[P, F^+]$
$F^- \leq P \leq F^+$	$[F^-, F^+]$
$F^+ \leq P \leq V^+$	$[F^-, P]$
$\max(V^+_H, V^+_S) \leq P$	$[F^-, \max(V^+_H, V^+_S)]$

Figure 4.1b maps the relevant ideal policy positions of the players in the legislative process into what we term the two-chamber, or the augmented, gridlock interval. In this figure, V^- (V^+) denotes the most liberal (conservative) member of Congress needed to overturn a liberal (conservative) president. F^- and F^+ denote the policy positions of the filibuster overrides while M denotes the policy position of the median legislator in the Senate. As long as the House median lies between F^- and F^+, the gridlock interval is defined as shown in Table 4.1 above based on the position of the president's ideal point.[4] As the table shows, the position of the median legislator in Congress does not influence the size or location of the gridlock interval. In each of the five examples it can easily be shown that any status quo inside the gridlock interval is invulnerable, while any status quo outside the interval will be altered in the direction of the gridlock interval.

Empirical Definition of Gridlock Interval

Krehbiel uses interelection swings as a proxy measure of changing preferences from one Congress to another. This measure, in turn, is used as an approximation of changes in his key independent variable, the gridlock interval (1998, 58). Krehbiel uses three steps to calculate this measure. First, he calculates the net percentage of seats that change party for each chamber after an election. He next calculates the average of these two values, weighing each chamber equally. Finally, he assigns a positive or negative sign to this net change in seats corresponding to whether the change denotes an expansion or a contraction of the gridlock interval from the president's perspective.

This approximation of the gridlock interval is, however, problematic, as interelection swings do not necessarily capture changes in the gridlock interval: large swings may take place without changing the gridlock interval, and the gridlock interval may change in the absence of an electoral swing; in other words, the focus should be on ideology, not partisan changes in seats. Consider the following hypothetical Senate faced with a Republican president P, and between 60 and 65 Democratic senators. This implies that V^-, F^-, M, and F^+ are all Democratic senators, while V^+ is a Republican senator, so the gridlock interval is defined by the region $[F^-, P]$. Figure 4.1c shows all the senators lined up by policy preferences from the most liberal to the most conservative.

Imagine next a Republican landslide at the midterm election where the Republican party seizes control over the Senate but where none of the 34 most liberal Democrats are replaced. This implies that F^- does not change and, since the President is still the same, the gridlock interval does not change either.[5] At the same time, the median legislator and the upper filibuster pivot move to the right, which in the figure are illustrated by M' and $F^{+'}$. In sum, we experience a significant interelection swing but this has no influence on the gridlock interval and hence should not influence the amount of legislation passed. Likewise, with the initial distribution of ideal points in Figure 4.1c, assume that five Democratic and five Republican senators are replaced, so that there is no net change in seat shares. Nonetheless, if a senator who is located on the liberal (conservative) side of F^- replaces a senator on the conservative (liberal) side of F^-, the gridlock interval will change.

Finally, while Krehbiel is concerned with the average of the interelection swings in the House and in the Senate, what happens in the House may be totally irrelevant for the size of the gridlock interval. This is in fact the case in the example provided above; another example would occur if the president is very liberal and the lower veto pivot is more extreme in the Senate than in the House, such that the gridlock interval is defined by $[V^-_S, F^+]$ (see Table 4.1). In this situation, a Republican landslide can take place in the House without affecting the gridlock interval since the House defines none of the relevant pivot points.[6] Again, interelection seat swings do not provide a reliable measurement of changes in the gridlock interval; indeed, the original idea of defining the gridlock interval was to measure the potential for policy production that did *not* rest entirely on swings in partisan control.

Alternative Operationalizations

Rather than seat shifts, we use Poole and Rosenthal's (1991, 1997) "Nominate" scores (a systematic measure of legislators' ideology compiled over time) to obtain estimates of the augmented gridlock interval for each Congress. In particular, we employ the common space coordinates, which allow for comparisons across different Congresses. For each Congress, we order all members of Congress by their Nominate scores and identify the filibuster and veto pivots in both the House and the Senate. We use the president's announced positions on congressional roll calls to assign him a Nominate score as well.

An issue arises with how to deal with a situation when an intraterm member replacement took place in the House or Senate, as this potentially changes the size of the gridlock interval in the middle of a congressional term. From the 84th to the 106th Congress, which is the period we use for our analyses,[7] there were 126 such changes in the House and 74 changes in the Senate. Upon closer examination, only 14 of the 126 changes in the House and 14 of the 74 changes in the Senate, representing 17 of the 23 Congresses in our sample, affect the size of the gridlock interval. Furthermore, the remaining potential changes in the gridlock interval are relatively minor, ranging from 0.001 to 0.022. These differences are small compared to the overall distribution of the gridlock variable and, not surprisingly, they never change the significance level of the results reported below. We therefore analyze only the estimated ideal policy position of the first member who held the seat in each Congress.

Once the policy positions of the key players are identified, we measure the distance between the two relevant pivotal players, and hence the absolute size of the gridlock interval, as defined in Table 4.1. Table 4.2 provides an example of such a calculation for the 106th Congress, showing that in 2000, Clinton was more liberal than any of the other pivotal players in Congress. Following Table 4.1, this implies that the gridlock interval is defined by $[V^-, F^+]$. As the veto-override pivot in the House was (slightly) more extreme then the veto-override pivot in the Senate (–0.273 compared to –0.223), the veto-override pivot in the House is the relevant V^-. Hence, the gridlock interval is [–0.273; 0.271] and the size of the gridlock interval is 0.271 – (–0.273) = 0.544.

Figure 4.2 shows the gridlock interval as well as the ideal point of the House, Senate, and president for the 83rd to the 106th Congress. As can be seen from the figure, there is significant variation in both the length and location of the gridlock interval. Only in the 84th and 85th Congresses is the president's ideal point moderate enough to fall within the gridlock interval; in all other cases the president is extreme relative to Congress. The size of the interval is noticeably small in the 95th and 96th Congresses (Carter's term in office), where it is also skewed in a liberal direction, while it is large in the 104th through 106th Congresses (Clinton's last three Congresses).

To revisit briefly the relationship between gridlock and partisan swings, we calculate a simple bivariate correlation between the absolute size of the gridlock interval and Krehbiel's interelection swing

Table 4.2   Example of Calculation of Gridlock Interval

Congress	Clinton	House V^-	Senate V^-	Senate F^-	House M	Senate M	Senate F^+	House V^+	Senate V^+	Gridlock
106th	–0.456	–0.273	–0.223	–0.203	0.146	0.178	0.271	0.35	0.314	0.544

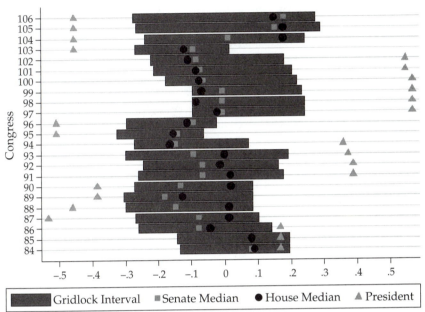

Figure 4.2   Pivotal Players and Size of the Gridlock Interval, 84th to 106th Congresses

variable.[8] The two measures correlate very weakly at 0.07, which implies that the difference between the two operationalizations is not trivial; the variables clearly measure two different things.

Testing Gridlock

In the following sections we examine whether the size as well as changes in the position of the gridlock interval have any impact on legislative productivity.

Data

To measure the amount of significant legislation passed, Mayhew (1991) employed a "two-sweep" method. The first sweep identified significant laws based on contemporary judgments made by political commentators in key newspapers, while the second sweep made use of retrospective judgments by policy specialists. The two sweeps identify 267 pieces of significant legislation between 1947 and 1990. Of these, an average of 12.8 pieces of legislation were passed by each Congress under unified government compared to an average of 11.7 under divided government—a difference that is not statistically significant. Mayhew has kept the data up to date on his web page since the publication of his book, and this update has not altered his initial conclusion that divided party government does not suppress the number of bills passed in a given Congress.[9]

Since Mayhew's original work, other researchers have offered a variety of alternative measures of legislative productivity. Binder (1999), for instance, suggests that gridlock should be measured by the proportion of bills on the legislative agenda that fail. To account for the success rate of bills, Binder argues that "intra-branch conflict—perhaps more than inter-branch rivalry—is critical in shaping dead-lock in American Politics" (1999, 519). Binder's key independent variables pertain to the ideological differences between members of Congress, and she finds that ideological polarization within each chamber of Congress is more detrimental to passing bills than divided government. Similarly, Edwards, Barrett, and Peake (1997) find that *potentially* important bills are more likely to fail during divided government.

Lately, Howell et al. (2000) argue that Mayhew's findings of no relationship between productivity and divided government are a result of an inaccurate statistical specification. The authors identify four different and mutually exclusive groups of legislation, denoted Groups A, B, C, and D. Group A identifies landmark enactments and is close but not identical to Mayhew's significant bills, Group B identifies major enactments, Group C identifies ordinary enactments, while Group D includes minor enactments. The authors show that once enactments identified by Mayhew's sweep one are separated from the sweep two enactments and the time-series structure of the dependent variable is taken into account, divided government does in fact depress the number of landmark enactments (their Group A) being passed in Congress; that is, fewer landmark bills are enacted during periods of divided government.

As dependent variables we use two specifications of Mayhew's number of significant laws as well as six specifications of the amount of legislation passed, taken from Howell et al. (2000). The first dependent variable is the total number of significant bills as defined by Mayhew (1991) and updated on Mayhew's web page. The issue with this is that the identified bills only include both sweep one and sweep two until 1986; after 1986, the bills are only identified by the first sweep.[10] To address the possibility of data source bias, we use the number of significant bills identified by sweep one as a second alternative measure of legislative production. Finally, we run all analyses with Howell et al.'s (2000) Group A, B, C, and D categories of bills, counting landmark enactments, major enactments, ordinary enactments, and minor enactments, respectively, as well as two alternative specifications of Group A and B measuring the space used in *Congressional Quarterly* (CQ) to describe the importance of the bills passed (see Howell et al. 2000 for details).

For our independent variables, we start with *divided* government, which is coded 0 whenever both chambers of Congress and the presidency are controlled by the same party, and 1 otherwise. The *seat share* measure is a more sensitive indicator of divided government, defined as the percentage of seats held by the party opposite the president less the percent held by the president's party, averaged across the House and the Senate. For example, when the president's party holds 45 percent of the seats in both chambers and the opposition 55 percent, seat share equals 10 percent.

From Mayhew's data we borrow a *start term* variable that takes on the value 1 for the first two years after a presidential election and 0 otherwise. Mayhew asserted that this variable captures the honeymoon effect that usually follows presidential elections. Therefore we should expect to see more policy production, or in our case more discretion, when the executive has just entered office. We also included an *activist* variable, which captures the public's demand for policy. Mayhew simply included a dummy variable for the years 1961 to 1976. We employ a more fine-grained version of this measure, which starts at 0, rises steadily one unit for each Congress between 1961 and 1968, and then declines steadily from 1969 to 1976.

Finally, Brady and Volden (1998) argue that during times of tighter fiscal constraints Congress is less able to arrive at a legislative compromise, and we should therefore see less policy movement. To account for this possibility we also controlled for the percent of the federal *budget surplus* as a share of total federal outlays, hypothesizing that Congress should grant the executive less discretion to set policy when the deficit is large. Table 4.3 provides descriptive statistics for all variables used.

Size of the Gridlock Interval

As hypothesized by Krehbiel's theory we expect the size of the gridlock interval to be negatively correlated with the amount of legislation passed. Figure 4.3 displays the bivariate relationship between the absolute size of the gridlock interval and number of Group A landmark enactments passed for the 83rd to the 103rd Congresses. The figure leaves no impression of the expected negative relationship between the two variables. In fact the simple bivariate relationship is in the opposite direction, as larger gridlock intervals seem to be mildly associated with higher productivity.

To examine the relationship while controlling for other variables, we ran ordinary least squares (OLS) regressions for all eight dependent variables listed in Table 4.3 to test the robustness of these findings. Table 4.4 shows the results of four models where the dependent variable is the amount of important legislation passed. While the first model includes Mayhew's variable measuring an activist mode, as the

Table 4.3   Descriptive Statistics for Included Variables

Group of variables	Variable	N	Minimum	Maximum	Mean	St. Dev.
Dependent variables	Mayhew's significant laws	23	5	22	12.04	5.06
	Mayhew's sweep one	23	1	12	5	2.59
	Group A	20	4	19	9.65	3.54
	Group B	20	2	22	12.9	5.63
	Group C	20	37	146	72.05	27.24
	Group D	20	403	978	591.8	141.37
	Group A-sum	20	55	271.5	125.9	53.94
	Group B-sum	20	13.5	261.2	157.24	69.82
Gridlock	Gridlock	23	0.26	0.55	0.38	0.08
	Unified government	23	0	1	0.30	0.47
	Seat Share	257	−0.17	0.15	−0.017	0.096
Economic variables	Real GDP	23	2100	9224	4956	2034
	Consumer Price Index	23	26.8	172.2	80.48	49.80
	Unemployment	23	3.5	9.7	5.85	1.48
Delegation variables	Discretion	257	0	1	0.183	0.161
	Deficit	257	−0.25	0.39	−0.072	0.095
	Divided	257	0	1	0.553	0.498
Other controls	Activist mood	18	0	1	0.44	0.50
	Start of presidential term	23	0	1	0.48	0.51

Note: The data from Howell et al. (2000) has not been updated since 1994 (103rd Congress). These dependent variables therefore have three fewer cases than Mayhew's dependent variables, which have been updated up to the 106th Congress. The delegation variables are used in the analysis below and are coded for each enactment in Mayhew (1991); hence their N is 257.

literature on divided government often does, the remaining models were run without this variable, to reflect the fact that the activist-mode variable seems to be arbitrarily defined by the empirical surge in legislation in the 1960s and in the first half of the 1970s. Since the variable lacks a theoretical foundation, it seems somewhat problematic to rely on model specifications that include it.

Table 4.4 shows that the absolute size of the gridlock interval never has the expected negative influence on the number (or size as in Model 4) of important bills passed. Using the length of the description of Group A enactments in the periodical *Congressional Quarterly* (CQ) as the dependent variable in the last column of Table 4.4, the positive coefficient is even significant. There is no obvious explana-

**Figure 4.3   Size of Gridlock Interval and Major Enactments,
by Administration**

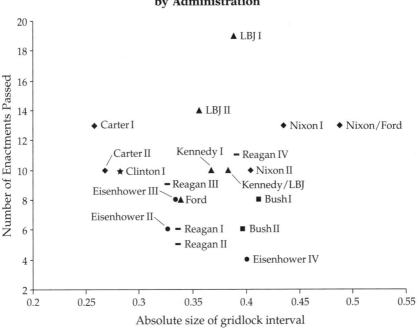

Absolute size of gridlock interval

tion for this. But as the absolute size of the gridlock interval has no significant impact on the number of Group A enactments passed (as shown in Column 3), the conclusion may just be that there is a qualitative (showing up as amount of space in CQ) but not a quantitative impact of the absolute size of the gridlock interval.[11] Similar to what Mayhew found, whether the government is unified or divided has no influence on the number of significant bills passed. In Howell et al.'s alternative operationalization, though, unified government does involve a higher average of enactments compared to divided government.

Table 4.5 shows OLS results for four different models, using the remaining of Howell et al.'s measurements of number of bills passed as well as the amount of space used in CQ to describe Group B enactments. As above, the absolute size of the gridlock interval never has a significant negative impact on either the number or length of bills passed in Congress. In Model 2, the gridlock interval even has a significant positive influence on the number of bills passed. Once again there is no obvious explanation for why we see a significant positive relationship between the absolute size of the gridlock interval and productivity for the C group of bills passed. To answer why this group and no other group is impacted, one would have to analyze Howell et al.'s (2000) criteria for dividing the bills into groups more carefully.[12]

Table 4.4 OLS Estimates of Important Legislation

	Model 1	Model 2	Model 3	Model 4
Dependent variable	Mayhew	Mayhew	Group A	Group A – sum
Absolute size of	6.16	19.51	3.97	457.7*
gridlock interval	(18.86)	(18.39)	(10.03)	(205.6)
Unified government	–0.09	2.13	2.75*	49.95*
	(1.74)	(2.36)	(1.11)	(22.84)
Activist mood	5.48*			
	(2.42)			
Start of pres. term	3.27*	2.78	1.90*	34.34
	(1.07)	(1.61)	(0.80)	(16.46)
Inflation (CPI)	–0.19	–0.27*	–0.18**	–1.40
	(0.09)	(0.09)	(0.05)	(0.94)
Real GDP	0.005*	0.005*	0.005**	0.04
	(0.002)	(0.002)	(0.001)	(0.02)
Unemployment	–0.50	0.35	–0.82	–6.98
	(0.58)	(0.84)	(0.40)	(8.11)
Constant	1.66	–4.34	3.39	–110.2
	(9.37)	(10.45)	(5.23)	(107.1)
N	18	23	20	20
R^2—adjusted	82.8%	43.9%	75.8%	56.2%

Note: standard errors in parentheses.
*Denotes significant on the 0.05 level (two-tailed).
**Denotes significant on the 0.01 level (two-tailed).

Table 4.5 OLS Estimates of Bills Passed

	Model 1	Model 2	Model 3	Model 4
Dependent variable	Group B	Group C	Group D	Group B – sum
Absolute size of	33.69	297.5*	–775.3	331.2
gridlock interval	(25.65)	(126.0)	(463.5)	(319.7)
Unified government	2.52	21.82	–101.86	3.25
	(2.85)	(14.00)	(51.49)	(35.51)
Start of pres. term	–0.10	12.04	6.36	7.61
	(2.05)	(10.09)	(37.11)	(25.59)
Inflation (CPI)	–0.34*	–0.61	6.54**	–4.38**
	(0.12)	(0.57)	(2.11)	(1.45)
Real GDP	0.009*	0.01	–0.20**	0.12**
	(0.003)	(0.01)	(0.05)	(0.04)
Unemployment	0.09	3.09	–53.79*	2.76
	(1.01)	(4.97)	(18.29)	(12.61)
Constant	–14.92	–70.35	1664.9**	–203.7
	(13.34)	(65.67)	(241.5)	(166.6)
N	20	20	20	20
R^2—adjusted	37.3%	35.4%	67.6%	36.7%

Note: standard errors in parentheses.
*Denotes significant on the 0.05 level (two-tailed).
**Denotes significant on the 0.01 level (two-tailed).

Changes in the Gridlock Interval

The above analysis focused on the absolute size of the gridlock interval, arguing that if Krehbiel's theory is correct we would expect larger gridlock intervals to be associated with less legislation being passed. It is important to test another aspect of Krehbiel's theory as well: the effect of changes in the gridlock interval on the number of bills passed. As the gridlock interval changes location we can expect issues that previously were gridlocked to move outside the gridlock interval, at which point new legislation may become possible.

For the following analyses, then, the "uncovered region" refers to the size of the nongridlocked policy space that was inside the gridlock interval in the previous Congress. To get a sense for the magnitude of this variable over time, Figure 4.4 shows the size and location of the gridlock interval as well as the number of Group A, B, C, and D bills passed in every Congress. The uncovered region has a lower bound at zero (see for example the 93rd Congress, where both the liberal and the conservative pivots are more extreme than in the 92nd Congress, so that no part of the gridlock interval is uncovered), while the largest value is 0.199, corresponding to the large conservative shift between the 96th and 97th Congresses. Note that the size of the uncovered region measures an entirely different phenomenon than does the size of the gridlock region itself. As an example, going from the 90th to the 91st Congress, the absolute size of the gridlock interval increases, as

Figure 4.4   Size of Gridlock Interval and All Levels of Enactments

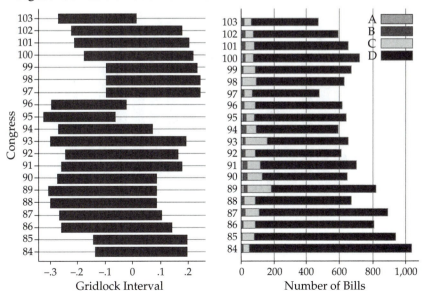

displayed in Figure 4.4, but since the liberal legislative pivot moved slightly to the right the uncovered region is only 0.012.

Following Krehbiel's logic, we would expect a smaller than average amount of legislation in, for example, the 85th and 89th Congresses, as Figure 4.4 displays that no amount of the gridlock interval was freed up from the 84th to the 85th or from the 88th to the 89th Congresses. Similarly, we would expect much more legislation in Congresses 97 and 103 where the uncovered region is relatively large. From the figure, no such trends are apparent.

Figure 4.5 shows the size and location of the gridlock interval by Congress, compared to the number of major enactments (Group A) passed. It also shows the absolute size of the gridlock interval as well as the size of the uncovered region. Casual inspection of Figures 4.4 and 4.5 suggests that the magnitude of the uncovered region from one Congress to the next is no more successful in predicting the over-

Figure 4.5   The Uncovered Region and Major Enactments

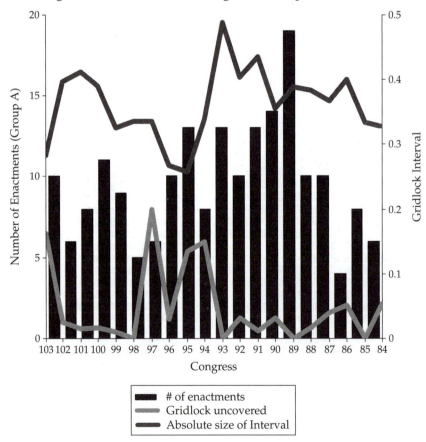

Table 4.6   OLS Estimates of Changes in the Gridlock Interval

	Model 1	Model 2
Dependent variable	Mayhew's # of sig. laws	Group A enactments
Gridlock uncovered	−11.65	−15.52*
	(14.45)	(7.17)
Unified government	0.89	3.12**
	(1.86)	(0.89)
Start of pres. term	2.97	2.28*
	(1.60)	(0.82)
Inflation (CPI)	−0.30**	−0.21**
	(0.09)	(0.04)
Real GDP	0.006**	0.005**
	(0.002)	(0.001)
Constant	3.62	0.33
	(3.81)	(2.05)
N	23	20
R^2—adjusted	45.2%	74.5%

Note: standard errors in parentheses.
*Denotes significant on the 0.05 level (two-tailed).
**Denotes significant on the 0.01 level (two-tailed).

all amount of legislation passed or the number of important bills than was the absolute size of the gridlock interval.

Table 4.6 summarizes a more thorough empirical investigation of the issue.[13] Model 1 uses Mayhew's number of significant laws as the dependent variable. It shows that the uncovered region, supposedly freeing up policy space and allowing for more legislation to take place, does not have a significant impact on the number of laws passed each Congress. The same pattern is seen in the second model where Howell et al.'s Group A enactments are used as the dependent variable.[14] In this specification, the size of the uncovered region is actually significant in the *opposite* direction than hypothesized, suggesting that large moves in the gridlock interval are associated with lower and not higher legislative productivity. Finally, we tested (regression results not shown) whether the midpoint of the gridlock interval has any independent effect on productivity; the result was again negative. In conclusion, looking at the uncovered region instead of at the absolute size of the interval does not enhance the model's predictive power.

Conditional Presidential Leadership

One might ask, then, whether the gridlock interval, theoretically attractive as it may be, actually predicts any relevant measure of legislative productivity. In answer to this question, we turn to the literature on congressional-executive delegation, which emphasizes the modern transfer of policymaking power to the executive branch and analyzes the conditions under which Congress will voluntarily choose to delegate discretionary authority to executive agencies.[15] Under this approach, the impact of legislative gridlock would not necessarily be manifested in the number of bills passed, but rather in the amount of discretionary authority ceded to executive branch actors.

Theory

To flesh out the theoretical implications of delegation as it relates to legislative gridlock, we introduce the concept of *conditional presidential leadership,* similar to the notion of conditional party government in Congress (Cooper and Brady 1981; Aldrich 1995). Under conditional party government, legislative majorities will delegate more policymaking power to party leaders when the majority party is homogeneous, and less willing to delegate when it represents diverse policy interests. Parties in Congress can have real power, the theory predicts, but only when the necessary conditions for delegation are present.[16]

Similarly, we hypothesize that Congress as a whole will delegate more authority to the executive under certain, specific conditions. As elaborated in Epstein and O'Halloran (1999), Congress will wish to delegate when legislative action is relatively inefficient, due to dispersed policy preferences within the chamber, and when its preferences are close to those of the executive; that is, under unified government. It will choose to make policy itself, through more explicit, detailed legislation, under the opposite circumstances.

Notice that the gridlock interval combines a measure of legislative heterogeneity with a measure of interbranch congruity of preferences. To disaggregate this relationship, and to deduce the relation between gridlock and delegation, Figure 4.6 presents predictions of both legislative productivity and delegation under high and low gridlock, and under unified and divided government.

Taking each possibility in turn, the upper left cell assumes low gridlock and unified government. This would describe conditions under which Congress is relatively coherent, and in which a legislative majority is of the same party as the president. Here we would expect high productivity, but ambiguous delegation or broad discretion, since both congressional action and delegation are relatively efficient from legislators' point of view. Similarly, in the lower right cell, high gridlock and divided government mean that both legislative and delegatory policymaking are *unattractive,* so productivity will be low, but given that a law is passed, the implications for delegation are ambiguous.

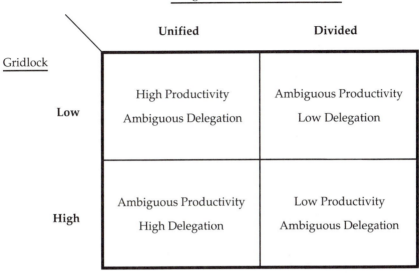

Figure 4.6 Conditional Presidential Leadership

The logic of policymaking in the off-diagonal cells should now be clear as well. The upper right, with low gridlock and divided government, describes a situation with a coherent Congress and a moderate president of the opposite party—were the president more extreme, gridlock could not be low. Here productivity is ambiguous; Congress can perform well, but it will be opposed by the president.[17] On the other hand, if policy is passed, it will tend to be explicit, with relatively little executive discretion. In the lower left, a disunited Congress and unified government mean that productivity will be variable, but if policy is passed, the majority party will be eager to delegate to the executive branch, rather than relying on the inefficiencies of congressional action.

Overall, then, the prediction regarding gridlock and delegation is that we should see more discretionary power ceded to the executive with high gridlock and unified government. In other words, the interactive term between these two variables should be significant in a regression, even if the signs on the coefficients for each of the terms individually may be affected by the ambiguous diagonal entries in the table. As a bonus, the figure also predicts a significant interactive relationship between gridlock and unified government when predicting policy production, but with the opposite sign.

Testing Conditional Presidential Leadership

To test the conditional presidential leadership hypothesis, we begin, as above, with the Mayhew (1991) data set of significant legis-

lation passed between 1947 and 1990. As opposed to the results by
Congress presented in the previous sections, though, our unit of analysis here is an individual enactment, of which there are 257 in
Mayhew's original study. Our dependent variable is the Epstein and
O'Halloran (1999) measure of executive discretion, defined as the delegation ratio (number of provisions that delegate over the total number of provisions) minus the constraint index (the number of
administrative procedures that constrain the executive's use of delegated authority).[18]

The theory of conditional presidential leadership predicts that delegation will be highest under unified government and high levels of
gridlock. As a first examination of the data, we divide the Congresses
according to whether their level of gridlock was above or below the
mean (39.7). Table 4.7 shows the average discretion afforded the executive when gridlock is high or low, and under unified and divided
government. As shown in the table, preliminary evidence seems to
support our hypothesis; executive discretion is highest under unified
government and high gridlock, and lowest in the opposite case.

Turning to the regression analysis, Table 4.8 shows the results from
performing robust regression using executive discretion as the dependent variable. The first two columns include only the variables
whose effects are predicted from our model, the second two include
all control variables, and the last two exclude the activist measure,
consistent with our previous analysis. We also tried including Bond
and Fleisher's (1990) rankings of presidential ability as independent
variables, and the uncovered region as a dependent variable. In no instance did these additions produce any significant effects.

As indicated, the interaction between partisan control of the legislature and gridlock is significant, whether one uses the simple divided government measure of partisan control or the more nuanced
seat share variable. The gridlock variable is never significant on its
own, however, reinforcing our previous findings that it does little to
directly predict legislative outcomes. The other independent variables
have the expected signs, even though they are not only significant.
Congress delegates more in times of fiscal downturns, and they also
delegated greater discretion in the "activist" period of the 1960s. Interestingly, the coefficient on delegation rates at the start of a presi-

**Table 4.7 Average Discretion,
by Gridlock and Divided Government**

	Unified Government	Divided Government
Low Gridlock	0.164	0.157
High Gridlock	0.230	0.172

Table 4.8 OLS Estimates of Executive Discretion

	Model 1	Model 2	Model 3	Model 4	Model 5	Model 6
Gridlock	-0.0006	.0002	-.0014	-.0007	-.0007	-.00004
	(0.0010)	(.0008)	(.0010)	(.0009)	(.0010)	(.0008)
Gridlock * Seat Share	-0.005*		-.005*		-.004*	
	(0.002)		(.002)		(.002)	
Gridlock * Divided		-.001*		-.0009*		-.0009*
		(.0004)		(.0004)		(.0004)
Deficit			.167*	.166*	.204*	.197*
			(.086)	(.086)	(.087)	(.086)
Start of pres. term			-.008	-.004	-.009	-.005
			(.016)	(.016)	(.017)	(.016)
Activist mood			.041*	.041*		
			(.017)	(.017)		
Constant	0.182**	.175**	.209**	.202**	.206**	.199**
	(0.039)	(.037)	(.039)	(.038)	(.040)	(.038)
N	257	257	257	257	257	257
F^k_{n-k-1}	2.59	2.83	3.33	3.44	2.72	2.77

Note: standard errors in parentheses.
*Denotes significant on the 0.05 level (two-tailed).
**Denotes significant on the 0.01 level (two-tailed).

dential term, the "honeymoon period," is always negative, though insignificant.

Conclusion

While Krehbiel (1998) offered a compelling theoretical model of the legislative process describing the relationship between the distribution of key players' ideal points and Congress's ability to pass legislation, his model nonetheless was a poor predictor of legislative productivity. This chapter showed that neither a consistent operationalization of Krehbiel's original gridlock theory, nor an alternative measure based on changes in the gridlock region, was significantly related to any of a series of productivity measures. These results cast significant doubt on the predictive power of Krehbiel's theory.

The ensuing analysis, however, presented an alternative view of policy production, one based on the amount of discretionary authority delegated from Congress to executive branch actors. Our theory, which we term conditional presidential leadership, predicts that delegation will be greatest under conditions of high gridlock and unified government. Indeed, our predictions were borne out in empirical analysis, even after controlling for the usual set of covariates that correlate with legislative productivity.

We conclude that presidential power must be understood within its institutional context. Gone are the days when presidents could act unilaterally on issues of great domestic import—witness George W. Bush's inability to make any headway on Social Security. And only occasionally can they induce spates of new legislative activism on the scale of the New Deal. Rather, executive power is now obtained through delegation from the legislative branch, and presidential leadership manifests itself in the president's ability to wring such concessions out of the hands of jealous legislative leaders. After all, major policy initiatives can be aimed at curtailing executive power as well as enhancing it (as in the 1973 War Powers Resolution and the Congressional Budget and Impoundment Control Act of 1974, both passed by Democratic congresses over Nixon's objections).

Further, presidential leadership seems to accrue on a schedule more attuned to the interbranch and intrabranch distribution of preferences, rather than the traditionally defined presidential bargaining ability. In particular, it is when Congress is most disunited, and when the president comes from the same party as the legislative majority, that authority is passed to executive hands. Presidents can lead, but just like the king who consulted with his royal astronomers before ordering the sun to rise at exactly 6:22 a.m., the time has to be right.

Notes

1. See for instance Sundquist (1988) and Cutler (1988).

2. See Figure 2.2 in Krehbiel (1998, 23).

3. See Figure 2.7 in Krehbiel (1998, 35).

4. Table 4.1 is an expanded version of figure 6.2 in Epstein and O'Halloran (1999, 127).

5. Assuming that neither the F^- senator nor the president has changed his policy stance.

6. As a Republican landslide probably moves V^- to a higher value, V^- will still be more extreme in the Senate and the gridlock interval stays the same.

7. Due to data constraints, the entire period is only used in the empirical tests using Mayhew's measure as the dependent variable. For the remaining tests, the period from the 84th to the 103rd Congress is used instead.

8. Taken from Table 3.3 in Krehbiel (1998, 59).

9. Mayhew's web page can be viewed at www.yale.edu/polisci/Faculty/DMayhew.htm.

10. This is because a significant amount of time has to pass by before retrospective evaluations can be made. Furthermore, after the release of his book, Mayhew has only updated sweep one and not sweep two.

11. We also estimated a model using Mayhew's sweep one as the dependent variable using robust Poisson regressions with a time variable and a squared time variable, when appropriate, following the approach used by Howell et al. (2000). The results were no different than the results presented in the text.

12. We also estimated these models using robust Poisson regressions as described above. None of these resulted in the gridlock variable having a significant negative influence on the amount of legislation passed.

13. For the OLS results displayed in Table 4.6, the parameter estimates for unemployment are not shown, as they were highly insignificant for both specifications.

14. The regressions were run for the remaining operationalizations of legislation passed as well, showing similar results.

15. For classic expositions of this theory, see McCubbins, Noll, and Weingast (1987) and Epstein and O'Halloran (1994, 1999).

16. For a related theory on parties as legislative cartels, see Cox and McCubbins (1993).

17. Contrast, for instance, the last Congress under Reagan, with its high productivity, and the tenure of the first President Bush, when relatively little was accomplished.

18. See Epstein and O'Halloran (1999), Chapter 5 for details on the construction of these variables.

References

Aldrich, John. 1995. *Why Parties? The Origin and Transformation of Political Parties in America.* Chicago: University of Chicago Press.

Binder, Sarah. 1999. "The Dynamics of Legislative Gridlock, 1947–96." *American Political Science Review* 93:519–533.

Bond, Jon and Richard Fleisher. 1990. *The President in the Legislative Arena.* Chicago: The University of Chicago Press.

Brady, David, and Craig Volden. 1998. *Revolving Gridlock.* Boulder, CO: Westview Press.

Coleman, John J. 1999. "Unified Government, Divided Government, and Party Responsiveness." *American Political Science Review* 93:821–835.

Cooper, Joseph, and David Brady. 1981. "Institutional Context and Leadership Style: The House from Cannon to Rayburn." *American Political Science Review* 75:411–425.

Cox, Gary, and Mathew McCubbins. 1993. *Legislative Leviathan: Party Government in the House.* Berkeley: University of California Press.

Cutler, Lloyd. 1988. "Some Reflections About Divided Government." *Presidential Studies Quarterly* 18:485–492.

Edwards, George C., Andrew Barrett, and Jeffrey Peake. 1997. "The Legislative Impact of Divided Government." *American Journal of Political Science* 41:545–563.

Epstein, David, and Sharyn O'Halloran. 1994. "Administrative Procedures, Information, and Agency Discretion." *American Journal of Political Science* 38:697–722.

———. 1999. *Delegating Powers.* Cambridge, UK: Cambridge University Press.

Howell, William, Scott Adler, Charles Cameron, and Charles Riemann. 2000. "Divided Government and the Legislative Productivity of Congress, 1945–94." *Legislative Studies Quarterly* 25:285–312.

Krehbiel, Keith. 1996. "Institutional and Partisan Sources of Gridlock: A Theory of Divided and Unified Government." *Journal of Theoretical Politics* 8:7–40.

———. 1998. *Pivotal Politics.* Chicago: University of Chicago Press.

Mayhew, David R. 1991. *Divided We Govern.* New Haven, CT: Yale University Press.

McCubbins, Mathew, Roger Noll, and Barry Weingast. 1987. "Administrative Procedures as Instruments of Political Control." *Journal of Law, Economics, & Organization* 3:243–277.

Poole, Keith, and Howard Rosenthal. 1991. "Patterns of Congressional Voting." *American Journal of Political Science* 35:228–278.

———. 1997. *Congress.* New York and Oxford: Oxford University Press.

Sundquist, James. 1988. "Needed: A Political Theory for the New Era of Coalition Government in the United States." *Political Science Quarterly* 103:613–635. ✦

Chapter 5

Power Without Persuasion
Identifying Executive Influence

William Howell and Douglas Kriner

In his classic work on the presidency, Richard Neustadt argues that presidents must bargain and compromise in order to achieve their goals. Yet, much has changed in the political environment since Neustadt wrote his seminal work in 1960. Washington politics, particularly involving the president and Congress, is now characterized by higher levels of polarization, with an increased propensity for divided government. Advocates of the polarization thesis note that gone are the days when legislators from both parties could work behind the scenes to craft compromise legislation. As a result, the leadership strategies that Neustadt recommends may be less amenable to the politics of the twenty-first century than they were almost a half century ago. If so, then new strategies of presidential leadership will be required.

In this chapter, William Howell and Douglas Kriner examine the idea of "power without persuasion" or the propensity of presidents of both political parties to use their *unilateral powers* to secure the policies they prefer. Presidents can employ executive orders, proclamations, and other tools of the unilateral presidency to advance their goals. Howell's (2003) own recent work demonstrates that presidents are more active in using executive orders to advance their policy goals, but the question remains, how successful are presidents in using this strategy? In this chapter, Howell and Kriner address this question by exploring four case studies from the presidency of George W. Bush. These case studies demonstrate both the potential and the limitations of the unilateral presidency approach. While there are limitations to the approach, importantly, these case studies reveal that in many situations presidents can employ their powers unilaterally to greatly increase their leverage over Congress, as well as to achieve their preferred policy outcomes. While presidents cannot ignore the need to bargain and work with Congress, it is no longer the only game in town for presidents.

✦ ✦ ✦

Modern presidents are put in a seemingly impossible position. On the one hand, they are saddled with enormous responsibilities, expected to respond at a moment's notice to everything from the latest terrorist attack to the "threat" that same-sex couples present to the institution of marriage. And on the other, the formal powers that the Constitution grants them are wholly insufficient to meet the task. Wielding only the powers to propose and veto legislation in order to stave off mounting public expectations is a bit like brandishing a wooden sword in the face of a rapidly approaching cavalry. Presidents, plainly, stand little chance at holding their line.

Fortunately for them, presidents have more options, and more opportunities, than all of this supposes. Drawing from a "tool chest" that they themselves have fabricated, presidents unilaterally can set public policy and thereby place upon others the onus of coordinating a response (Cooper 1997, 546). With executive orders, executive agreements, national security directives, proclamations, and other kinds of directives, presidents can exert power and initiate change to an extent not possible in a strictly legislative setting. And because of this, they stand a considerably better chance of beating back the public claims made on them, while also redirecting the doings of government in ways that better reflect their own priorities.

From the very beginning, presidents have exercised their unilateral powers, the Neutrality Proclamation, Louisiana Purchase, and Emancipation Proclamation being early highlights. In the modern era, however, the practice has really taken hold. Almost all of the trend lines point upwards. During the first 150 years of the nation's history, treaties (foreign agreements that must be ratified by Congress) regularly outnumbered executive agreements (foreign agreements that automatically take effect); but during the last 50 years, presidents have signed roughly 10 executive agreements for every treaty submitted to Congress (Moe and Howell 1999; Margolis 1986). With rising frequency, presidents are issuing national security directives (policies that are not even released for public review) to institute aspects of their policy agenda (Cooper 1997, 2002). Though the total number of executive orders has declined, the number of "significant" orders has increased by roughly an order of three (Howell 2003, 83).[1] Using executive orders, department orders, and reorganizations plans, presidents have unilaterally created a majority of the administrative agencies listed in the United States Government Manual (Howell and Lewis 2002; Lewis 2003). What is more, these policy mechanisms hardly exhaust the totality of options available to presidents, who regularly invent new ones or redefine old ones in order to suit their own strategic interests.

A variety of factors have contributed to the rising use of unilateral directives: Supreme Court rulings in the 1930s and '40s upholding the constitutionality of executive orders and executive agreements;[2] the rise of the administrative state (Weko 1995; Arnold 1998); and, perhaps most consequentially, the well-documented weakening of parties, devolution of committee powers, and polarization of Democrats and Republicans within Congress since the 1970s (Kernell 1997; Mann and Ornstein 1981; Heclo 1978; Oppenheimer 1980; Bond and Fleisher 2000), all of which have made the legislative process a less attractive venue for presidents to advance their policy agendas.[3] The real question, though, is whether this arsenal of unilateral powers has done presidents much good, enhancing his ability to cope with the rising expectations laid before them.

Conventional wisdom, for the most part, presents a rather dim view of these powers, arguing that presidents rely upon them only when efforts to persuade—the purported key to presidential power—have faltered. The mere issuance of commands, as it were, is less a sign of strength than of failure to achieve one's policy goals "by softer means" (Neustadt 1990, 24). This chapter takes a different view. Through a series of case studies, it demonstrates two facts about the politics of unilateral action. First, because presidents can issue executive orders in lieu of laws and executive agreements in lieu of treaties, they are able to institute policies that materially alter the doings of government. Rather than working at the fringes of the policymaking process, or instituting policies preferred by supermajorities within Congress, presidents use their unilateral powers to considerable and independent effect—sometimes creating policies that look very different from those that members of Congress might prefer, and other times issuing orders that would never survive the legislative process. Second, and critically, these powers have limits, for which any theory of unilateral action must account. Though they need not construct or sustain coalitions in support of their policy initiatives, presidents must carefully monitor, and even consult with, members of Congress and judges to ensure the sanctity of their orders. Acting in policy domains in which they lack adequate constitutional or statutory authority or issuing policies that anger too many legislators, presidents risk being overturned. The challenge, as such, is to recognize opportunities when they arise and to push policy as far as Congress and the courts will permit.

Straight out of the Gates

From the moment he took office, President George W. Bush began issuing executive orders, proclamations, and national security directives that would dramatically reshape the domestic and foreign policy landscapes.[4] In the spring of 2001, he issued an executive order that instituted a ban on all federal project labor contracts, temporarily setting in flux Boston's $14 billion dollar "Big Dig" and dealing a major

blow to labor unions. He later required federal contractors to post no-
tices advising employees that they have a right to withhold the portion of union dues that are used for political purposes. He created the
White House Office of Faith-Based and Community Initiatives, which
was charged with "identify[ing] and remov[ing] needless barriers that
thwart the heroic work of faith-based groups."[5] He has used the Office of Management and Budget to scrutinize the scientific basis for
regulating businesses and, in some instances, whole industries. He
set new guidelines on federal funding of fetal tissue research. In order
to block the release of presidential papers, he claimed the power for
presidents and their kin to invoke executive privilege years after leaving office. By including salmon raised in fish hatcheries in counts for
the Endangered Species Act, Bush managed to take salmon off the
list of endangered species and thereby lifted federal regulations that
applied to the rivers and streams where they spawn. Without securing
congressional authorization, Bush withdrew from the Kyoto Protocols, the International Criminal Court, and the Antiballistic Missile
Treaty. And just as Truman used a 1950 national security directive to
identify the doctrine of containment, which guided foreign policy
during the Cold War, Bush issued a national security strategy endors-
ing the principle of preemptive war, which may guide foreign policy
efforts to confront terrorism in the twenty-first century.

For Bush, scaling back environmental and industry regulations has
been a major priority. "Stymied in [their] efforts to pass major domestic initiatives in Congress," a recent *New York Times* feature story
revealed, "officials have turned to regulatory change." Under Bush's
watch,

> Health rules, environmental regulations, energy initiatives, worker-
> safety standards and product-safety disclosure policies have been mod-
> ified in ways that often please business and industry leaders while dis-
> maying interest groups representing consumers, workers, drivers,
> medical patients, the elderly and many others. And most of it was done
> through regulation, not law—lowering the profile of the actions. The
> administration can write or revise regulations largely on its own, while
> Congress must pass laws. For that reason, most modern-day presidents
> have pursued much of their agendas through regulation.[6]

The Bush administration has issued rules that alter the amount of allowable diesel-engine exhaust, that extend the number of hours that
truck drivers can remain on the road without resting, and that permit
Forest Service managers to approve logging in federal forests without
standard environmental reviews. These rule changes, moreover, represent but a fraction of the total.

Considerable activity has centered around the president's war on
terrorism. In the aftermath of September 11, Bush created a series of
agencies—the Office of Homeland Security, the Office of Global Com-

munications, and the Commission on the Intelligence Capabilities of the United States Regarding Weapons of Mass Destruction—to collect and disseminate new intelligence while coordinating the activities of existing bureaus. He issued a national security directive lifting a ban (which Ford originally instituted via executive order 11905) on the CIA's ability to "engage in, or conspire to engage in, political assassination"—in this instance, the target being Osama bin Laden and his lieutenants within Al Qaeda. He signed executive orders that froze all financial assets in U.S. banks that were linked to bin Laden and other terrorist networks. And perhaps most controversially, Bush signed an order allowing special military tribunals to try any noncitizen suspected of plotting terrorist acts, committing terrorism, or harboring known terrorists.

The most visible of Bush's unilateral actions consisted of military strikes in Afghanistan and Iraq. Having secured congressional authorizations to respond to the mounting crises as he saw fit,[7] in the fall of 2001 Bush directed the Air Force to begin a bombing campaign against Taliban strongholds, while Special Forces conducted stealth missions on the ground; and in the spring of 2003, he launched a massive air and ground war against Iraq, involving the United States in the most protracted military conflict since the Vietnam War. Though not packaged as traditional policy directives, these commands nonetheless instigated some of the most potent expressions of executive power. Within a year Bush's orders resulted in the collapse of the Taliban and Baathist regimes; the flight of tens of thousands of refugees into Pakistan, Iran, and Turkey; the destruction of Afghanistan's and Iraq's social and economic infrastructures; and the introduction of new governing regimes.

Bush hardly invented these powers, nor was he the first president to utilize them with such frequency and consequence. During his tenure, Clinton also "perfected the art of go-alone governing."[8] Though Republicans quashed his 1993 healthcare initiative, Clinton subsequently managed to issue directives that established a patient's bill of rights for federal employees, reformed healthcare programs' appeals processes, and set new penalties for companies that deny health coverage to the poor and people with preexisting medical conditions. During the summer of 1998, just days after the Senate abandoned major tobacco legislation, Clinton imposed smoking limits on buildings owned or leased by the executive branch and ordered agencies to monitor the smoking habits of teenagers, a move that helped generate data needed to prosecute the tobacco industry. While his efforts to enact gun-control legislation met mixed success, Clinton issued executive orders that banned numerous assault weapons and required trigger safety locks on new guns bought for federal law enforcement officials. Nor did this activity decline in the waning years of his administration. Instead, Clinton "engaged in a burst of activity at a point when other presidents might have coasted. . . . Executive orders have flown off Clinton's desk, mandating government action on issues from mental health to food safety."[9] Even as a lame duck president, Clinton drew upon his unilateral powers to turn literally millions of acres of land in Nevada, California, Utah, Hawaii, and Arizona into national monuments. Though Republicans in Congress condemned the president for "usurping the power of state legislatures and local officials" and vainly attempting to "salvage a presidential legacy," in the end they had little choice but to accept the executive orders as law.[10] Rather than wait on Congress, Clinton simply acted, daring his Republican opponents and the courts to try to overturn him. With a few notable exceptions, neither did.[11]

Nor are Clinton and Bush aberrations. Throughout the twentieth century, presidents have used their powers of unilateral action to intervene into a whole host of policy arenas. Examples abound: by creating the Fair Employment Practices Committee (and its subsequent incarnations) and desegregating the military in the 1940s and '50s, presidents defined the federal government's involvement in civil rights decades before the 1964 and 1965 Civil Rights Acts; from the Peace Corps to the Environmental Protection Agency to the Bureau of Alcohol, Tobacco, and Firearms to the National Security Agency to the Federal Emergency Management Agency, presidents unilaterally have created some of the most important administrative agencies in the modern era; with Reagan's executive order 12291 being the most striking example, presidents have issued a string of directives aimed at improving their oversight of the federal bureaucracy; without any prior congressional authorization of support, recent presidents have launched military strikes against Grenada, Libya, Panama, Bosnia, Sudan, and Kosovo. These, moreover, are just a small sampling of the policies issued and actions taken, via executive orders, proclamations, reorganization plans, and other kinds of directives.[12]

A defining feature of presidential power during the modern era, it seems fair to say, is a propensity, and a capacity, to go it alone. As Peter Shane and Harold Bruff (1988) argue in their casebook on the presidency, "presidents [now] use executive orders to implement many of their most important policy initiatives, basing them on any combination of constitutional and statutory powers that is thought to be available." Kenneth Mayer (2001, 4–5) echoes their assessment in his comprehensive survey of executive orders, which documents how presidents have used their unilateral powers to "make momentous policy choices, creating and abolishing executive branch agencies, reorganizing administrative and regulatory processes, determining how legislation is implemented, and taking whatever action is permitted within the boundaries of their constitutional or statutory authority." And according to Phillip Cooper (2002, 8–9), "Many presidents have felt the need to reach out with executive orders and proclamations, creating some of the most important debates over executive action and some of the most important policy moves in our history. . . . These tools of presidential direct action have been at the heart of the good, the bad, and the ugly of the presidency." Through executive orders, executive agreements, proclamations, and their ilk, presidents have managed to stem the rising tide of public demands and expectations placed upon them in the modern era, and to effect change in ways simply not possible in a strictly legislative setting.

The Demonstration of Influence

That presidents are using their unilateral powers with rising frequency does not necessarily indicate that they are getting more of what they want. Richard Neustadt fairly warns that one must distinguish the exercise of powers (plural) from the demonstration of power (singular) (1990, see note on p. 7), for one hardly guarantees the other. As *powers*, Neustadt would surely concede that unilateral directives are an integral part of the president's arsenal. His skepticism lies in whether these powers yield *power*; and he outright rejects the notion that commands enable presidents to meaningfully address the awesome tide of responsibilities laid before their feet (pp. 10–28). For Neustadt (p. 24), the exercise of these unilateral powers, as with virtually all formal powers, represents a "painful last resort, a forced response to the exhaustion of other remedies, suggestive less of mastery than of failure—the failure of attempts to gain an end by softer means." If anything, unilateral directives signal weakness, for when presidents issue them, they admit to having lost sway over other political actors, and, by extension, the political system more generally.

For a variety of reasons, Neustadt's claim that the mere issuance of orders demonstrates weakness greatly overstates matters (Howell 2005a). Still, his distinction between powers and power is a useful one. Obviously, presidents do not gain power simply by producing more executive orders, any more than they do so by issuing additional vetoes or proposing more legislation. The frequency with which formal powers are asserted says little, if anything, about the power that presidents wield (Cameron and McCarty 2004, 414), especially in a system of governance where numerous other political actors have their own independent authority and means to resist. If presidents and their staffs are merely acting on behalf of other political actors and issuing orders that otherwise would be printed as laws, or if the domain of delegated and constitutional authority in which presidents can act independently is highly restricted,[13] then unilateral powers hardly augment executive power.

To identify power, the president's actions must leave a unique imprint on the law and, ultimately, on the doings of government.[14]

Among social scientists, there is considerable confusion on this matter, and so it is worth drawing out at some length. To measure the influence that a president (or anyone else for that matter) has made, the proper comparison is not between the world that is and the world that he might prefer; nor is it between the worlds that exist before and after an action has been taken. Presidents can use their unilateral powers to considerable effect even though they do not achieve everything they might like, and even when the operations of government appear stable over time. *The right comparison, instead, is between the state of the world that exists in the aftermath of a presidential order and the one that would exist had the president not acted at all.* If the president is merely doing things that other political actors would have done themselves, then no difference between this observed and this imagined world will appear. Similarly, if members of Congress immediately undo every presidential order that does not perfectly reflect their own independent interests, then again these two worlds probably will look much alike. But if the president uses his unilateral powers to institute policies that otherwise would not survive the legislative process, or to issue policies that look substantially different from those that members of Congress might prefer, then genuine influence is revealed.

When will presidents exercise their unilateral powers, and how much influence do they gain from doing so? In two circumstances (derived formally in Howell 2003), presidents have strong incentives to issue unilateral policy directives; and in both, they create policies that differ markedly from those that other branches of government would produce, were they left to their own devices. First, when Congress is poised to enact sweeping policy changes that the president opposes, the president occasionally can preempt the legislative process with more moderate policy shifts. Recall, by way of example, the weakling Occupational Safety and Health Administration created under Nixon, the modest sanctions levied by Reagan against South Africa's Apartheid regime, and the narrow focus and minimal powers that Bush originally assigned to the independent commission investigating intelligence failures on Iraq and weapons proliferation. In each of these cases, Congress stood poised to create either a stronger agency or more robust public policy, and the president lacked the support required to kill these initiatives with a veto. And so in each, executive influence was measured by the president's ability to unilaterally impose portions of the proposed legislation, and thereby derail the support of moderates within Congress who were considering stronger and more sweeping policy change.

Presidents also use their unilateral powers to shift existing policies over which Congress remains gridlocked. Here, the signature of power is not an altered policy, but the creation of one that otherwise would not exist at all. As Congress failed to deal in any substantive way with civil rights issues during the 1940s and '50s, the classification of intelligence during much of the post-War era, or terrorism in the aftermath of September 11th, presidents stepped in and unilaterally defined the government's involvement in these policy arenas (Mayer 2001; Cooper 2002). As Justice Robert Jackson recognized in his famous concurring opinion to *Youngstown Sheet & Tube Co. v. Sawyer,* "Congressional inertia, indifference, or quiescence may sometimes, at least as a practical matter, enable, if not invite, measures on independent presidential responsibility."[15] Incapable of effecting policy change legislatively, presidents may step in, grab the reins of government, and issue policy changes that members of Congress, left to their own devices, would not enact. Doing so, they do not always get everything that they want, for should they push too far, their actions may galvanize a congressional or judicial response. And in some instances, presidents might well prefer to have their policy inscribed in law rather than in a unilateral directive, if only to guard them against the meddling of future presidents. But a window of opportunity nonetheless presents itself when members of Congress remain mired in gridlock—one that presidents can take without ever convincing a single member of Congress that they share the same interests or serve the same goals.

In both of these scenarios, the contours of executive influence are readily discernible. In the first, the counterfactual to a unilateral directive is a more radical policy shift by Congress—were it not for the president's actions, Congress would retain the votes of its more moderate members in support of sweeping legislative change. And in the second, the mark of presidential influence is not a public policy that is weaker (or stronger) than what Congress prefers—rather, it is the unilateral creation of a policy that otherwise would not exist at all. Absent the president's ability to change public policy unilaterally, the federal government would appear incapable of moving policy in either a liberal or conservative direction.

Unilateral Actions Taken: Four Recent Cases of Command

The rest of this chapter considers four case studies, each involving actions taken by Bush during the past several years. The studies are meant to serve two overarching objectives, the first of which concerns the identification of presidential power. For a variety of reasons, this can be a tricky business, and one ideally suited to case-study research. First, in our system of separated and federated powers, most every branch of government has its hands on policy—members of Congress, bureaucrats, judges, and White House staff all, and always, are leaning against the status quo, hoping to nudge it in their preferred ideological direction. Trying to gauge the contribution of each can be a bit like predicting what will happen to a bunch of pick-up sticks when one, and one alone, is removed from the pile. Second, clear winners are rarely declared. Though conflict is constant, and politicians remain engaged in a continual contest of will and strength, rarely do we witness two branches of government in a clear showdown, one rising up and exerting its powers and the other relenting. And finally, as previously established, power is properly assessed by reference to conditions that would exist had powers not been exercised; and because we do not observe realities that might have been, it can be extremely difficult to measure the magnitude, or even existence, of executive influence.[16]

The second objective served by these case studies is to highlight the institutional constraints on the president's unilateral powers. Plainly, presidents cannot institute every aspect of their policy agenda by decree. The checks and balances that define our system of governance are alive, though not always well, when presidents contemplate unilateral action. Should the president proceed without statutory or constitutional authority, the courts stand to overturn his actions, just as Congress can amend them, cut funding for their operations, or eliminate them outright.[17] When exercising unilateral powers, presidential power is defined in the negative—it is as big or small as Congress and the courts are weak or strong. Any account of a president's unilateral powers must take these institutional constraints seriously, identifying how they operate, when presidential power is checked, and what opportunities presidents have to strike out on their own.

Salmon and the Endangered Species Act

Since the enactment of the Endangered Species Act (ESA) in 1973, the federal government has devoted more resources to protecting the great salmon runs of the west coast than it has spent on any other species.[18] In the 1990s, President Clinton continued and strengthened this massive effort to preserve 26 species of salmon classified as endangered and to protect their expansive natural habitats ranging from southern California to Washington. Beginning in 2001, however, all of this would change, as the Bush administration made a clean break with precedent and began to systematically curtail protections for wild salmon.

For 30 years, in its counts for determining whether a species was endangered, the federal government only considered wild salmon and excluded populations raised in hatcheries. In September 2001, however, Oregon Federal Judge Michael Hogan demanded scientific justification for this policy. The District Court gave no explicit instructions for how stocks from hatcheries should factor into the determination of a species' endangered status. Instead, the court merely directed the National Marine Fisheries Service to "consider the best available scientific evidence" when constructing its standard rather than summarily excluding hatchery-bred fish from its determinations.[19]

To meet the court's mandate, the Fisheries Service hired a panel of outside experts to evaluate the nation's salmon stocks, while also commissioning its own internal review. Citing the genetic inferiority of man-raised stocks and the continued decline in the wild salmon population, the board of scientists rejected outright arguments that salmon from fisheries could stabilize natural populations. The Fisheries Service's internal review bolstered these conclusions, stating that production in hatcheries provided a poor gauge of the health of natural populations and that the determination of each species' status should be based only "on whether they are likely to be self-sustaining in their native ecosystem."[20]

The Bush administration, however, did not welcome these determinations. In search of a new regulatory policy that would ease restrictions on development, Bush turned to Mark Rutczik, who just three years prior as a timber lobbyist had proposed giving equal weight to hatchery-raised and wild salmon in federal endangered species determinations. As a newly appointed legal advisor to the Fisheries Service, Rutczik redrafted his earlier recommendations as an official proposed regulatory change, which promptly was published for public comment in the *Federal Register* on June 3, 2004. The proposed change pleased the Building Industry Association's Timothy Harris, who lauded the administration efforts: "It's about time. . . . I'm hoping this will finally result in de-listing some of these salmon populations."[21] A mere 11 days after the formal introduction of the proposed new counting procedures, the Fisheries Service proposed another new rule that would strip 23 of 27 species of their endangered status after reevaluating their populations in light of hatchery stocks.[22]

The response from the scientific and environmental community was swift and unambiguous. Upon learning that their conclusions about the viability of restoring natural salmon stocks with hatchery fish were "inappropriate for official government reports," the scientists who drafted the Fisheries' report made their findings public in *Science* and openly derided the proposed regulatory change in the press.[23] Dr. Ransom Myers of Dalhousie University charged, "this is a direct political decision, made by political people to go against the science." When asked to comment on the administration's arguments that the use of hatchery fish would be the swiftest solution to restoring natural stocks, Myers replied, "no credible scientist believes this."[24] Environmentalists were no less harsh in their criticism of the Bush administration's proposal. The National Wildlife Federation's Jan Hasselman summed up their views: "Rather than address the problems of habitat degraded by logging, dams and urban sprawl, this policy will purposefully mask the precarious condition of wild salmon behind fish raised by humans in concrete pools."[25]

Despite the outcry, the Bush administration hardly wavered in its support of the controversial proposals; and recently, it has only intensified its attacks on federal salmon protections. On November 30, 2004, the administration released a new draft proposal that would remove from federal protection 80 to 90 percent of the "critical habitat" for salmon currently protected by the Fisheries Service from logging and human development.[26] And in its latest movement against the old regime, the Bush administration seized on a 2003 District Court ruling to propose barring altogether the removal of four federal dams blocking salmon access to upstream spawning grounds.[27] Judge Redden, who issued the ruling that purportedly supported Bush's actions, announced his disapproval and warned that the Bush policy could be headed toward a veritable "train wreck."[28] Nevertheless, in stark contrast to the will of the District Court and 30 years of policy precedent, the Bush regulations remain unaltered and on course to becoming the law of the land.

As Bush has acted unilaterally to reverse long held tenets of federal environmental policy protecting wild salmon, Congress has been remarkably silent. A few members, particularly Western Democrats such as Maria Cantwell and Jim McDermott of Washington, have levied intense public criticism against the president and his regulatory attacks; however, no member has brought legislation challenging any of the proposed changes to the floor of either chamber.[29] What little action there has been on the Hill has attempted to write into law some of Bush's objectives pursued through regulatory change. In the fall of 2004, the House Committee on Resources reported to the floor HR 2933, which would amend the ESA to mirror the Bush policy of excluding from federal protection salmon habitats already governed by state or municipal environmental management policies. The legislative clock ran out on the bill, however, when Congress adjourned in December. Still, this amendment to the ESA did not go nearly as far as the Bush regulatory proposal of November 30, which would also exclude from federal protection vast tracts of land not deemed critically important to salmon survival by the new population survey and mapping techniques.

Rather than build the supermajorities required to enact new legislation in Congress, Bush has sought change through the regulatory process. Doing so, he has achieved reductions in federally protected salmon habitats much more drastic than those even contemplated by members of the House or Senate. Indeed, absent any legislative changes in the ESA that might justify the about face in policy, administratively Bush has orchestrated policy proposals that have revised one of the most important environmental policies enacted in the last half century. After a period for public comment, Bush's proposals took effect on June 28, 2005.[30]

Military Tribunals

Throughout our nation's history, presidential power has expanded most during times of war. In moments of crisis, Congress and the courts regularly defer to their Commander in Chief—and perhaps for good reason as, according to Alexander Hamilton in the 74th *Federalist*, national emergencies demand all the energy and dispatch that a unitary executive can muster: "Of all the cares or concerns of government, the direction of war most peculiarly demands those qualities which distinguish the exercise of power by a single hand. The direction of war implies the direction of the common strength; and the power of directing and employing the common strength forms a usual and essential part in the definition of executive authority." Examples of presidential wartime authority abutting and occasionally breaching constitutional limits include Abraham Lincoln's suspension of the writ of *habeas corpus,* Woodrow Wilson's assertion of unprecedented control over the national economy during World War I through measures such as the temporary suspensions of civil service hiring rules and eight-hour workday laws,[31] and Franklin Roosevelt's repeated efforts before and after the Lend Lease Act to supply arms and other war materiel to Great Britain, not to mention his now infamous internment of 110,000 Japanese Americans during World War II.

The contemporary "war on terror" and occupation of Iraq have proved no lesser catalysts for the aggrandizement of presidential power. Among the most visible assumptions of unilateral executive authority stemming from the current conflict is President George W. Bush's decision to deny Geneva Convention rights to militants captured in Iraq. From a purely constitutional perspective, however, President Bush's military order of November 13, 2001, creating military tribunals to try enemy combatants stands alone for the directness of its attack on the separation of powers and its unambiguous incursion into the domain of another branch of government, in this case the federal judiciary.

In the immediate aftermath of September 11, 2001, members of Congress reacted at lightning speed to grant the president new authority and tools to protect the nation's security. On September 14, both the House and Senate approved a joint resolution authorizing the president to use "all necessary and appropriate force against those nations, organizations, or persons he determines planned, authorized, committed or aided the terrorist strike, or harbored such organizations or persons, in order to prevent any future acts of international terrorism against the United States by such nations, organi-

zations or persons."[32] Similarly, to aid in the identification and
tracking of suspected terrorists already within the United States,
Congress bowed to administration pressure and passed the USA Patriot Act,[33] which granted federal law enforcement agencies unprecedented powers to spy on citizens and noncitizens alike, taking
advantage of roving wiretaps, secret "sneak and peak" warrants, and
access to information ranging from voicemail messages to library
records.

Not content with these specific delegations of power, and wagering
that he still had enough partisan and public support to ward off any
congressional challenge, the president unilaterally claimed even
greater authority over the conduct of the war on terror. A mere 18
days after signing the Patriot Act into law, President Bush issued a
military order granting himself and the Secretary of Defense sole authority over the detention, trial, and punishment of suspected terrorists.[34] Citing his constitutional powers as Commander in Chief and
those granted him by the recently enacted use of force resolution,
President Bush proclaimed his authority to detain any noncitizen he
had "reason to believe" was a member of Al Qaeda, had engaged,
aided or abetted, or conspired to commit acts of terrorism, or had
harbored such individuals. If ever charged and brought to trial, such
persons, regardless of whether they were captured on a foreign battlefield or in downtown Detroit, would face a military tribunal in
which only a two-thirds vote was needed for conviction. Possible sentences included death.

Bush left no doubt that any person charged under the military
order would be beyond the reach of the civilian judicial system: "The
individual shall not be privileged to seek any remedy or maintain any
proceeding, directly or indirectly, or to have any such remedy or proceeding sought on the individual's behalf, in (i) any court of the
United States, or any State thereof, (ii) any court of any foreign nation, or (iii) any international tribunal." The only authority oversee-
ing the process was the president himself, as the order required
"submission of the record of the trial, including any conviction or
sentence, for review and final decision by me or by the Secretary of
Defense if so designated by me for that purpose."[35] In a congressional
hearing on December 6, 2001, Senator John Edwards (D-NC) argued
that this clause was so vague that it even allowed the president to
overturn an acquittal. By this reading, the order essentially granted
Bush sole power over the fate of the accused, leaving Congress and
the judiciary with nothing but the administration's assurances that
individual rights would receive due consideration.[36] Such was heretofore only the power of kings and Caesars.

Not surprisingly, the order provoked fervent denunciations from
some of the more outspoken members of Congress. Bob Barr, a conservative Republican and civil libertarian from Georgia, lamented,

"the scope of this executive order takes your breath away."[37] At the opposite end of the ideological spectrum, Dennis Kucinich of Ohio warned, "the creation of military tribunals would permit secret arrests, secret charges using secret evidence, secret prosecutions, secret witnesses, secret convictions, secret sentencing, and even secret executions ... it is therefore a matter of protecting our constitutional rights that defendants in terrorism cases receive full due process under the law."[38]

Other members expressed unease that Bush, without Congress's consultation or approval, had effectively supplanted the traditional justice system. New York Democrat Jerrold Nadler quipped, "for the administration to do this without coming to Congress is a tremendous arrogation of power. If they had suggested military tribunals, they would have been laughed out of Congress. So instead they do it by executive order ... to avoid the Congress."[39] And Illinois Senator Richard Durbin expressed the frustration of many Democrats who had supported the president on the Patriot Act, but now felt blindsided by the administration:

> Because it seemed to us that this is a rather significant departure from what we considered to be the open statement here of our cooperation between the legislative and executive branch in dealing with terrorism. We felt we had been asked for and had given to the administration the tools they needed to fight terrorism. And then to the surprise of many of us came this new request for—perhaps not a request but an announcement about military tribunals and commissions.[40]

Wisconsin Democrat Russ Feingold went further, accusing the administration of not only doing unilaterally what it could not accomplish legislatively but even of timing the announcement of the order to the anthrax scare that gripped the capital in late fall 2001: "From a strategic point of view I guess it was pretty clever to throw the kitchen sink at us [then] ... every day you'd pick up the paper—first it was detainees. Then, gee, they're going to start listening in on attorney-client conversations."[41]

Though congressional Democrats challenged the order, none of their efforts materialized in legislation. In the House, Dennis Kucinich threatened to introduce an amendment to the Defense Appropriations bill (H.R. 3338) that would bar the use of federal funds to administer the tribunals. Although publicly supported by 38 other representatives, Kucinich yielded to pressure from others who wished to avoid a vote on the issue.[42] California Democrats Zoe Lofgren and Jane Harman then introduced a softer measure, H.R. 3468, that would sanction the tribunals, while still guaranteeing the accused *habeas corpus* rights. And in the Senate, Patrick Leahy of Vermont offered S. 1941 to provide for the judicial review of any convictions resulting from a military tribunal. Both bills, however, stalled in committee.

Lacking an effective legislative retort, Democrats and moderate Republicans turned to public hearings to air their grievances with the goal of influencing the final shape of the tribunals, whose *modus operandi* was still being determined by the Secretary of Defense. Republican Senator Arlen Specter of Pennsylvania hoped that such hearings would reestablish the central role of congressional oversight:

> Simply declaring that applying traditional principles of law or rules of evidence is not practicable is hardly sufficient. The usual test is whether our national security interests outweigh our due-process rights, and the administration has not yet made this case. . . . Even in war, Congress and the courts have critical roles in establishing the appropriate balance between national security and civil rights. . . . Vigorous Congressional oversight is the indispensable first step in determining what is "practicable" in finding that balance.[43]

Leahy brought a parade of civil rights groups and constitutional law scholars before the Senate Judiciary Committee who denounced both the military order's content and the president's gall in announcing it unilaterally. The ACLU decried the order as "unjustified and dangerous" and admonished, "while the order applies in terms only to noncitizens, the precedents on which the president relies makes no such distinction, thereby permitting the order to be extended to cover United States citizens at the stroke of a pen."[44] From the libertarian camp, Timothy Lynch, director of the criminal justice project at the Cato Institute, chided, "nobody is above the law, not even a president who enjoys very, very high approval ratings."[45] Harvard Law School's Phillip Heymann exhorted Congress to defend its institutional prerogatives and check the administration's seizure of power: "It should be a proud and patriotic responsibility of the Congress to protect the people of the United States against the unnecessarily dangerous path of recourse to military tribunals and detention without trial which the president has taken us in response to public fears."[46]

Renowned constitutional law scholar Laurence Tribe offered perhaps the most scathing critique of Bush's action: "The structure of the November 13 Order is so constitutionally flawed at its base that it cannot be saved by nimble TV spin [referring to Rumsfeld's 12/2/2001 *Meet the Press* interview] or by altering a detail here and a detail there." Tribe emphasized its potential for wanton abuse and the threat it posed to millions of legal aliens residing in the United States who paid taxes and steadfastly abided by the law. To illustrate his point, Tribe described how a hypothetical Irish national, who had lived in the United States for decades but contributed funds to the IRA before its disarmament, could be handed over to a military tribunal for trial and execution should the president, and the president alone, certify the action. Tribe concluded:

> Of course, as Secretary Rumsfeld must have recognized, any such threat, made in a manner that necessarily hangs like a sword of Damocles over millions of lawful residents of this nation, cannot possibly be defended under our Constitution. As Justice Marshall once wisely observed, such a sword does its work by the mere fact that it "hangs—not that it drops.". . . The Secretary's attempt to wish the sword away—to persuade us all that, until we feel the edge of the blade upon our necks, we need not worry—is no substitute for replacing the sword with a solid framework for the judicious use of executive force in bringing terrorists to justice.[47]

The administration, however, resisted this onslaught of objections.[48] While criticisms from Democrats and moderate Republicans would have killed any effort to create the tribunals legislatively, sufficient Republican support for the president remained to ensure that his opponents in Congress could not muster the two-thirds majority necessary to overturn his unilateral directive. Emboldened by Republican support and buoyed by high public approval ratings, President Bush defended the need for military tribunals to try suspected terrorists: "I need to have that extraordinary option at my fingertips. . . . It's our national interests [sic], it's our national security interest [sic] that we have a military tribunal available." Vice President Cheney dismissed concerns about the violation of suspects' rights, asserting that foreign terrorists "don't deserve the same guarantees and safeguards that would be used for an American citizen going through the normal judicial process."[49] At a December 6 hearing before the Senate Judiciary Committee, the Attorney General John Ashcroft signaled the administration's intransigence by branding those who questioned the president's authority agents of the terrorists:

> To those who pit Americans against immigrants, and citizens against non-citizens, to those who scare peace-loving people with phantoms of lost liberty, my message is this: Your tactics only aid terrorists, for they erode our national unity and diminish our resolve. They give ammunition to America's enemies and pause to America's friends. They encourage people of good will to remain silent in the face of evil.[50]

On March 21, 2002, the Defense Department finally announced its "refinement" of the military order, fleshing out details of how the tribunals would operate and what standards of proof would be required for convictions. In several respects, the administration gave ground: death sentences would require a unanimous vote; the proceedings, except portions relating to national security, would be public; defendants and their counsel would have the right to see the evidence against them; and the standard for conviction would be proof beyond a reasonable doubt. Yet, on other key elements, the administration remained adamant: hearsay evidence would be admissible; the process would remain insulated from any civilian review; and some defendants might be held even after an acquittal.[51]

Although the legislative branch initially failed to grapple with the president's effort to construct a new, parallel judicial system, challenges to the tribunals and the administration's tactics for dealing with suspected terrorists slowly percolated through the federal courts—and all of the previous outcries against the tribunals, not to mention the president's low approval ratings and a languishing occupation of Iraq, augmented the chances of a reversal. On June 28, 2004, the Supreme Court released three decisions regarding individuals deemed enemy combatants and held in military custody. The first two cases, *Rumsfeld v. Padilla* and *Hamdi v. Rumsfeld*, concerned the indefinite detention of American citizens, who by virtue of their citizenship were not subject to the military order of November 13.[52] However, the third case, *Rasul v. Bush*, bore directly on the right of the federal government to hold indefinitely noncitizens at Guantanamo Bay, Cuba. Writing for the majority, Justice John Paul Stevens struck down the military order's provision that detainees had no recourse to civilian courts, ruling that the U.S. District Court did have jurisdictional authority to hear petitions of *habeas corpus* because the United States "exercises plenary and exclusive jurisdiction" if not "ultimate sovereignty" over Guantanamo Bay.[53] Though it allowed detainees to challenge the legality of their detention, the decision remained silent on how such challenges should be decided and exclusively concerned those detainees incarcerated at Guantanamo Bay. Other detainees, including those sent to foreign countries for interrogation, remained beyond the purview of the Court ruling.

Although the *Rasul* case dealt a glancing blow to the administration's policies for dealing with Guantanamo detainees, its ambiguity over how civilian courts should handle detainees' petitions for redress raised altogether new questions. Less than two weeks after the *Rasul* decision, Bush directed Deputy Secretary of Defense Paul Wolfowitz to create a new military tribunal, the Combatant Status Review Tribunal (CSRT), which would grant all detainees a hearing and pass judgment on their status as enemy combatants. When the CSRTs upheld the continued detention of many at Guantanamo, new legal actions were filed in federal court. In one such case, *Hamdan v. Rumsfeld*, the U.S. District Court initially found in November of 2004 for the plaintiff, ruling that the CSRTs failed to comply with the Uniform Code of Military Justice and were therefore invalid.[54] The government appealed the decision, and on July 15, 2005, the Circuit Court of Appeals reversed. In a sweeping ruling, the D.C. Circuit refuted the petitioner's claim that the president lacked constitutional authority to create military tribunals; instead, the court ruled that Congress granted him that power *de facto* through its authorization to use all means necessary to prosecute the war on terror. The court then upheld CSRT's determination that Hamdan was an enemy combatant and denied him any legal grounds in U.S. or international law for a hearing in a civilian court.[55]

Given the dramatic conflict between the District and Circuit court rulings, the chances were high that *Hamdan* would soon reach the Supreme Court, and on November 7, 2005, the Court granted *Hamdan* certiorari. With Chief Justice Roberts recusing himself because he had previously participated (and found for the government) in the Appeals Court decision, the Court by a 5–3 ruling struck down the president's tribunal system as in breach of both the congressionally enacted Uniform Code of Military Justice (UCMJ) and the Geneva Conventions. In striking down the tribunals, the Court rejected the administration's arguments that the Authorization for Use of Military Force implicitly granted the president power to create a military tribunal system.[56] Absent explicit authorization for new tribunals, the Court ruled that § 836 and § 821 of UCMJ establishing guidelines for the creation of military tribunals were controlling, and that the president's military tribunals as constituted—specifically, the provisions refusing the accused the right to hear and contest all evidence presented against him and the admission of hearsay testimony—violated the requisite basic safeguards and protections. Moreover, because § 821 made all military tribunals subject to the laws of war, the majority insisted the Geneva Conventions, particularly Common Article 3, were also operable and violated by the Military Order procedures.[57]

Though the Court ruling struck down the Military Order *in toto*, the majority did not close the door on the use of military tribunals completely. In his concurring opinion, Justice Breyer responded to the dissenters' charge that the Court's ruling would "sorely hamper the President's ability to confront and defeat a new and deadly enemy" by emphasizing that the Court's ruling did not strike down the use of military tribunals in principle, but only the Bush administration's legal justification for not seeking congressional authorization for their creation. "The Court's conclusion ultimately rests upon a single ground: Congress has not issued the Executive a 'blank check' [Cf. *Hamdi v. Rumsfeld,* 542 U.S. 507, 536 (2004)]. Indeed, Congress has denied the President the legislative authority to create military commissions of the kind at issue here." Perhaps presciently, Breyer concluded, "nothing prevents the President from returning to Congress to seek the authority he believes necessary."

Indeed, in a press conference immediately after the decision's announcement, Bush proclaimed his willingness to work with Congress on drafting legislation to create a new system of military tribunals. Shortly thereafter, Senate Majority Leader Frist disclosed his intention to introduce new legislation authorizing tribunals after the 4th of July recess.[58] Judiciary Committee Members Lindsay Graham

(R-SC) and John Kyl (R-AZ) seconded Frist, announcing: "We intend to pursue legislation in the Senate granting the executive branch the authority to ensure that terrorists can be tried by competent military commissions. Working together, Congress and the administration can draft a fair, suitable, and constitutionally permissible tribunal statute."[59] Despite this newfound spirit of cooperation between the White House and the Republican congressional leadership, as of this writing we have yet to see how many concessions the administration will have to make to allay the considerable unease expressed within Congress over the president's original tribunal system and thereby garner the supermajorities required for legislative passage.

Liberia

Particularly since the Korean War, which Truman deemed a "police action" in order to circumvent the constitutional requirement that Congress declare all wars, presidents have seized a degree of control over the military that would have horrified the Framers. From Article II's Commander in Chief clause, modern presidents have assumed, and Congress and the courts have recognized, the unilateral power to deploy military forces abroad to pursue foreign policy goals ranging from bolstering allies in ongoing conflicts, to effecting regime change in a target state, to staging humanitarian interventions across the globe.[60] The exponential growth of presidents' war powers has led scholars to decry the advent of an "imperial presidency" and lament Congress's "abdication" of its constitutional prerogatives (Fisher 2000; Schlesinger 1973, 2004).

Presidents, however, do not heed every foreign crisis calling for military action—and domestic politics can be an important reason why (Howell and Pevehouse 2005; Auerswald and Cowhey 1997; Clark 2000; Howell and Pevehouse 2007). To see how domestic political institutions generally, and Congress in particular, can influence presidential decisionmaking in matters of war, consider Bush's dealings with Liberia during the third year of his first term. In this instance, the president achieved his policy goals by dispatching, without congressional authorization, a limited number of U.S. forces to stem the humanitarian crisis and project American power into Africa, and by simultaneously avoiding a commitment so large that it would detract from ongoing military operations in the Middle East. That Bush was the driving force behind the American response to the Liberian crisis is clear. Nonetheless, the timing of the intervention, its modest size, and the brevity of its duration all underscore the importance of domestic politics.

In June of 2003, the Liberian government announced its intention to seek a cease-fire in the 14-year civil war that had already claimed 200,000 lives in the small West African nation. Because of its historical ties to the United States, the contribution of freed American slaves to its foundation, and its alliance with America during both World Wars and the Cold War, Liberia, along with its neighbors and the United Nations, looked to American leadership to resolve the conflict. On June 28, United Nations Secretary General Kofi Annan called for an international peacekeeping force to end hostilities in Liberia, and on July 3 Liberian president Charles Taylor, who had already been indicted for war crimes perpetrated in Sierra Leone's civil war, agreed to step down and go into exile if international peacekeepers were dispatched to Liberia. Members of the Economic Community of West African States (ECOWAS), most notably Nigeria, also agreed to send troops. But all involved parties expressed their desire for American participation.

It is impossible to discern from the written record Bush's precise policy preferences for intervention in Liberia. A preponderance of evidence, however, suggests that he was genuinely disturbed by the situation in the small West African nation and favored a limited show of American military might to bolster African and UN peacekeeping efforts there. The president's words reveal a willingness and even desire to intervene in a limited capacity, but also indicate his sensitivity to calls across levels of government for any new American military intervention to be constrained in scope and duration. Meeting with Kofi Annan and reporters, Mr. Bush publicly stated: "I assured him that our government's position is a strong position. We want to enable ECOWAS to get in and help create the conditions necessary for the ceasefire to hold, that Mr. Taylor must leave, that we'll participate with the troops. We're in the process, still, of determining what is necessary, what ECOWAS can bring to the table, when they can bring it to the table, what is the timetable, and be able to match the necessary U.S. help to expediting the ECOWAS' participation."[61] If Bush had preferred inaction, he could have easily deferred to strong opposition among congressional Republicans, and he certainly could have compelled his Secretary of State to keep private his counsel urging intervention.

Instead, opening a five-day African tour in Senegal on July 8, President Bush demanded that Charles Taylor leave Liberia as a precursor to any American involvement, while assuring African leaders that the United States was "in the process of determining what is necessary to maintain the ceasefire and to allow for a peaceful transfer of power."[62] Although he refrained from promising to send American marines, the president did order 32 military experts to Monrovia to investigate the situation, and several thousand American marines moved into position off the Liberian coast. No immediate intervention, however, was forthcoming. On July 19, the ceasefire collapsed as violence erupted in the capital. The president's delay earned repeated condemnations in the press and a scathing critique from a former Assistant Secretary of State for African Affairs in the Clinton administration: "the dithering and delaying, particularly after raising expectations in Liberia and throughout Africa and in the international community, is bordering on the criminally responsible. I don't understand what they're waiting for."[63]

This hesitancy reflected both concerns about the stability of the situation on the ground in Liberia and, domestically, the deep divisions within the administration itself, in the military's ranks, and within the halls of Congress. Somewhat ironically, the chief advocate of military intervention within the administration was Secretary of State Colin Powell, the progenitor of the "Powell doctrine," which advocated using force only when clearly in the interests of national security and then only with overwhelming force to ensure expeditious victory. Powell acknowledged, "in Liberia, if you ask the question, 'What is our strategic, vital interest?' it would be hard to define in that way." Nonetheless, he insisted that "we do have an interest in making sure that West Africa doesn't simply come apart. We do have an interest in showing the people of Africa that we can support efforts to stabilize a tragic situation as we work with others to bring relief to people—people who are desperately in need."[64]

The Pentagon and Joint Chiefs, meanwhile, were more wary of committing American troops to a potentially perilous situation in Liberia, particularly with more than 150,000 American servicemen already deployed overseas in Iraq and Afghanistan.[65] General Richard Myers, the Chairman of the Joint Chiefs, warned, "It's not a pretty situation . . . whatever the fix is going to be is going to have to be a long-term fix." Testifying before Congress at his reconfirmation hearing, Marine General Peter Pace, who previously served in the operation to secure and then withdraw U.S. troops from Somalia in 1993–1994, alluded to the disaster in Mogadishu and warned that while the situation in Liberia was undeniably "very tragic," in his judgment, "it is a situation that poses great personal risk to forces, such as our forces, that could be injected into that very fast-moving and volatile situation there in Monrovia and in the greater Liberia."[66]

Congress, too, was strangely split on the question of military action.[67] Many Democrats who had staunchly opposed the administration's push to war in Iraq supported a humanitarian military intervention in Liberia, while erstwhile Republican hawks were wary of entangling American troops in a situation that did not clearly advance the nation's interests. The Congressional Black Caucus implored the president to act in late July. Acknowledging the contrast between her stance on Iraq and calls for action in Liberia, Representative Sheila Jackson-Lee (D-TX) argued that the two cases were not comparable and advocated forceful American intervention:

I too want to ensure that the young men and women who serve in the United States military are not put in harm's way. My position on the war in Iraq is well known, but this is a different set of circumstances. The people of Liberia are begging for our assistance, and our assistance is being asked for truly and only as peacekeepers and humanitarians.[68]

Similarly, while falling short of explicitly calling for armed intervention, the Iraq war's chief opponent Senator Robert Byrd (D-WV) chastised the president's inaction:

The questions are tough, but procrastination is not an acceptable response. Hundreds of innocent civilians are suffering and dying as a result of the conflict in Liberia. Monrovia is in shambles. . . . Indecisive, half-hearted gestures [the stationing of U.S. marines off the Liberian coast] serve no purpose. . . . The President needs to determine a course of action, he needs to consult with Congress and the United Nations on pursuing that course, and he needs to explain his reasoning and his strategy to the American people.[69]

As a symbol of support for military action, Tom Lantos (D-CA), Corrine Brown (D-FL), Donald Payne (D-NJ), and others introduced House Concurrent Resolution 240 calling on the administration and the Secretary of Defense to take a "leading role in creating and deploying an international stabilization force to Liberia."[70]

Still, most of the president's copartisans in Congress, even the stalwart supporter of the war in Iraq and Senate Armed Services Committee Chairman John Warner, had grave misgivings about any military action in West Africa. When the Pentagon abruptly canceled a scheduled briefing to the committee on Liberia (prompting ranking Democrat Carl Levin to lament: "the checks and balance in the Constitution must have been designed with this administration in mind"), John Warner took to the floor to express his dismay and his unease over military intervention in West Africa.[71] While Warner took great pains to assure the chamber that he did not question the Commander in Chief's authority to order unilaterally American troops into combat—"But for simplicity, clarity, and brevity today, I simply say the Constitution gives that right to the President and should not be ever in question"—he criticized the briefing cancellation and strongly questioned the merits of action in Liberia. With respect to the briefing, Warner admonished, "I will say in my 25 years in the Senate, it is most unusual to conduct our affairs in that way between the Senate and the Department of Defense." With respect to the merits of intervention, Warner called upon the Powell Doctrine and asked: "Is this situation following the doctrine in our national security interests? I have even seen the word 'vital' national security interests used. It has not been answered to my satisfaction."[72]

House Republicans expressed similar and even stronger sentiments against the use of force in Liberia. In stark contrast to the
proposed Democratic resolution, Ron Paul (R-TX) and several cosponsors introduced House Concurrent Resolution 255 expressing
the sense of Congress that the United States should not become involved. Noting the Army's existing heavy overseas deployments in
Iraq, Afghanistan, and South Korea, Paul warned of its overextension
and concluded: "Mr. Speaker, there is no U.S. interest in the conflict
and U.S. military involvement could well lead to resentment and
more violence against U.S. troops as we saw in Somalia. We must
ponder this possibility before yet again putting our men and women
in uniform in harm's way."[73]

However, the problems Congress posed to the White House diminished considerably when it adjourned for its summer recess shortly
after Warner's speech on August 1. The next day the United Nations
Security Council voted to authorize a multinational peacekeeping
force for Liberia and on August 4 the first Nigerian troops arrived as
part of the ECOWAS mission. Seven marines went ashore on August
6 to bolster the small U.S. contingent already in and around the
American Embassy, and 20 more followed two days later. Then, on
August 11, Liberian President Charles Taylor resigned and voluntarily
went into exile in Nigeria. With the last condition for U.S. involvement met, on August 14, five weeks after signaling in Senegal America's willingness to intervene and stop the killing, Bush finally
ordered 200 marines from the flotilla anchored offshore into Monrovia and informed Congress of the deployment "consistent with the
War Powers Resolution."[74] Though small, Jacques Klein, Kofi Annan's special envoy in Liberia, echoed the sentiments of many when
he said, "These few Americans on the ground—it makes all the difference." Unfortunately, thousands of Liberians already had died in the
interim between the dispatch of American military investigators during Bush's visit to Africa in mid-July and the larger deployment on
August 14.[75]

On September 2, the same day that the Senate reconvened following its August recess, American military officials speculated publicly
that the approximately 150 remaining American personnel in Monrovia could be withdrawn within a matter of weeks.[76] By the end of
the month, the Department of Defense announced that one battle
group including the USS Carter Hall and USS Nashville had already
left the region and that all U.S. peacekeepers, save a token force of 55
marines for embassy security, were pulling out of Liberia.[77] By limiting the scope of the military venture and carefully crafting the mission's timing and duration, Bush managed to accommodate
congressional Republicans and members of his own administration,
and thereby forestall potentially embarrassing congressional efforts
to speed the withdrawal of troops from the region.[78]

Ultimately, the decision on how to deal with Liberia fell upon Bush's shoulders, and Bush's shoulders alone. Under the president's orders, a small contingent of American marines entered Liberia, bolstered the ECOWAS forces already on the ground, and helped restore order and stability to the country. And well it was that way, at least from the president's perspective, for if Bush had had to first obtain a congressional authorization, the marines probably would never have left their ships. Still, in this instance, the institutional checks that constrain the president's unilateral powers are also on display. Vocal opposition from Congress, coupled with resistance from the Pentagon and among the Joint Chiefs, slowed the administration's response to the Liberian crisis. And the resulting delay had a serious human toll, as thousands perished in the intervening period between the United Nation's call for action and Bush's eventual reply.

The Arsenic Rule

Typically, newly elected presidents enjoy considerable discretion to revise or overturn their predecessor's executive orders, proclamations, and rules. And not surprisingly, the first actions of modern presidents typically consist of unilateral directives overturning past presidential policies.[79] Occasionally, though, past unilateral actions remake contemporary politics in ways that are effectively irreversible, tying a new administration to a status quo not of its own choosing. In such instances, unilateral powers grant presidents precious little influence over public policy. Bush's effort to undo a Clinton order on arsenic and drinking water represents a case in point.

By ordering the Environmental Protection Agency (EPA) to delay and review a Clinton rule lowering the existing standard for allowable levels of arsenic in drinking water, Bush hoped to unilaterally reverse a policy that otherwise could only have been changed either by enacting new legislation (an unlikely event given the 50–50 partisan split in the Senate) or by restarting the protracted rule-making process, which would require the presentation of scientific evidence justifying the change.[80] In this instance, though, Bush's unilateral powers faltered. A confluence of factors, from the transfer of Senate power to the Democrats in May 2001 to intense opposition from environmental and citizens groups, stacked the political deck against the president. The most formidable obstacle in Bush's path, however, turned out to be President Clinton's transformation of public debate in his favor, which Clinton achieved by virtue of having the advantage of acting first. According to one study, Clinton's midnight action created a "new reversion point [that] fundamentally altered the debate, which was no longer about whether it made sense to lower the permissible levels of arsenic. Instead, the question became why the Bush administration wanted to *raise* the permissible level" (Howell and Mayer

2005). Bush would quickly discover that by advocating on behalf of adding carcinogens to citizens' drinking water, he was inviting nothing less than a public drubbing from his political opponents.

For over a half century, a 1942 rule governed federal standards on arsenic in drinking water, setting the allowable limit at 50 parts per billion (ppb).[81] In amendments to the 1996 Safe Drinking Water Act,[82] however, Congress directed the Clinton administration to commence new scientific studies of the public health threat posed by arsenic.[83] A 1999 National Academy of Sciences study found that the existing requirement "could easily" cause a 1 in 100 chance of bladder or lung cancer and encouraged the administration to lower the levels immediately.[84] In response, the EPA initially proposed decreasing the tolerable limit ten fold to 5 ppb;[85] however, bowing to pressure from utility, mining, and lumber lobbies, as well as some of the affected communities that would bear the brunt of the costs of compliance, the administration settled on a 10 ppb rule, the same standard embraced by the World Health Organization.[86] Promulgated in the waning days of Clinton's administration, the rule was slated to be finalized in early 2001 and went into effect in 2006.

Almost immediately upon assuming office, Bush attempted to put a stop to all of this. New EPA Director Christie Whitman suspended the rule, awaiting further scientific research determining that the health benefits of the new standard justified the costs of implementation. "It is clear that arsenic, while naturally occurring, is something that needs to be regulated," said Whitman. "Certainly the standard should be less than 50, but the scientific indicators are unclear as to whether the standard needs to go as low as 10."[87]

The decision to halt the implementation of the arsenic standards was only one element of a larger campaign to roll back last minute Clinton orders. Invoking an infrequently used provision of the 1996 Congressional Review Act,[88] congressional Republicans passed S J Res 6, which the new president signed on March 20, 2001, to quash midnight Clinton rules on ergonomic safety in the workplace.[89] The president unilaterally suspended a Clinton rule to protect 58.5 million acres of national forests as "roadless" regions, a move that would have shut them off from logging. And on March 27, Bush announced plans to withdraw from the Kyoto Protocols on global warming.[90]

In Bush's environmental reversals, many Democrats saw an opportunity to score political points. James Jordan of the Democratic Senatorial Campaign Committee expressed his hope that while "Republicans did make some progress in the last cycle in talking like Democrats [specifically, on education]," the environmental issue would allow Democratic candidates "to get some clear, obvious, verifiable separation from the Republicans." While they objected to all of Bush's actions, Democrats harnessed their resources to publicize the image of an administration allowing more arsenic into drinking

water. New Jersey Representative Rush Holt explained: "Arsenic—
that hit a nerve because arsenic sounds like poison."[91] Holt and fellow Representative Frank Pallone Jr. capitalized on the issue, even
traveling to an arsenic-laced well in Hopewell Burrough, New Jersey
to dramatize their critique of administration policy. By late April, the
party launched an ad campaign featuring a young girl asking, "May I
please have some more arsenic in my water, Mommy?"[92]

Former executive branch members promptly entered the debate.
Clinton EPA official Chuck Fox, who had served as the agency's assistant administrator for water, told reporters the day of Whitman's announcement: "I'm stunned . . . this action will jeopardize the health of
millions of Americans, and it compromises literally a decade's worth
of work on behalf of developing a public health standard."[93] The following day, Fox chastised the Bush administration in a *New York
Times* op-ed. While emphasizing that the new standard "is widely supported by drinking water utilities, states, scientists, public health officials and environmentalists," Fox noted the continued opposition of
the mining industry and several Western states that were firmly in the
Bush column in 2000. The former EPA official concluded, "We answered those questions with a commitment to public health protection. I certainly hope that the new administration will approach this
issue in the same manner." Editorials from papers across the country added to the barrage of criticisms leveled against the Bush
administration.[94]

The reaction from Capitol Hill was equally swift. Representative
Henry Waxman (D-CA) minced no words when condemning Bush's
action as "another example of a special interest payback to industries
that gave millions of dollars in campaign contributions."[95] Referring
to the arsenic and ergonomic roll backs, among others, House Minority Leader Richard Gephardt (D-MO) derided the new president:
"what people are really beginning to see is that this administration is
of, by and for the special interest."[96] Several weeks later, when assessing the first 100 days of the Bush presidency, Gephardt returned to
the arsenic issue and charged that the president's reckless move endangered the health and safety of America's children and families.
"Ladies and Gentlemen," Gephardt concluded, "this is not compas-
sionate conservatism, this is not reforming with results; this is leaving no special interest behind, and it must not stand."[97] Yet, perhaps
the most trenchant critique was that of Senate Minority Leader Tom
Daschle (D-SD) immediately after the announcement:

> What is not helpful is what the administration decided to do yesterday
> on arsenic in water. . . . The level of arsenic that the administration
> now will tolerate is 10,000 times the amount that is tolerated in food.
> And the National Academy of Sciences has said that the likelihood of
> cancer at that level is 1 in 100. I can't imagine that any legitimate re-

view of the analysis of the facts, of the information available, would possibly provide a motivation to anybody in the administration to accept this rule. It is—it is baffling, just baffling. We're going to have to put warning labels on water bottles if this goes through. So you haven't heard the end of this. We're going to come back at it in some way in the not too distant future. But we will not allow this to stand. This is just not acceptable.[98]

The negative publicity and popular outrage prompted a series of public backtrackings by Christie Whitman and the administration. When announcing the decision on March 20, Whitman acknowledged that the current standard of 50 ppb was "certainly" too high, but expressed doubts as to "whether the standard needs to go as low as 10 ppb."[99] But with repeated polls showing a strong majority of Americans opposing the Bush administration policy, on April 18 Whitman raised the possibility that the administration might seek an even stricter standard than Clinton.[100] In an abrupt about-face, she directed the National Academy of Sciences to study standards ranging from 3 to 20 parts per billion a year.[101]

Early efforts by congressional Democrats to pressure the Bush administration legislatively were hampered by the ominous roadblock of the GOP-controlled Senate.[102] But the defection of James Jeffords (IN-VT) from the GOP and the resulting transfer of power in the Senate to the Democrats breathed new life into legislative efforts to force the administration's hand. Democrats considered attaching riders on arsenic to the Veterans Affairs, Housing and Urban Development, and Independent Agencies appropriations bill (H.R. 2620). During consideration of the bill, Senator Barbara Mikulski (D-MD) appeared before the committee and chastised the Bush administration for clinging to an antiquated 1942 standard despite recent scientific evidence of the danger posed by arsenic.[103] A month later, House Minority Whip David Bonior (D-MI) succeeded in amending the appropriations bill to prohibit the use of funds in the following year's EPA budget to implement an arsenic standard higher than 10 ppb (H. Amndt. 261 to H.R. 2620).[104]

Faced with the defection of 19 Republicans in the House and mounting opposition within the Senate, the White House eventually caved.[105] On October 31, 2001, a full three months before the EPA initially claimed that it would announce its final decision, Director Christie Whitman reported the agency's intention to implement the Clinton standard of 10 ppb.[106] As early as August, the Bush administration seemed to have known the game was lost. The president himself acknowledged in an *ABC News* interview, "I think we could have handled the environmental issue a little better. . . . [Whitman] pulled back a rushed piece of legislation [*sic*] to look at it, to make sure the science was sound, and therefore we got labeled for being for arsenic in water." Whitman concurred, telling the *USA Today*, "Politically, if

I'd been smart, I would have never changed it. . . . I would have let the courts decide. We were going to be sued anyway by the Western states and a bunch of water companies, and I should have just left it there."[107]

In June of 2003, the U.S. Circuit Court of Appeals upheld the Clinton standard of 10 ppb, dismissing a suit filed by the state of Nebraska.[108] The new standard went into effect in 2006, right on schedule with the original Clinton order.

Concluding Thoughts

Power is properly assessed by reference to conditions that would exist had power not been exercised. In at least two of the four prior case studies, the mark of Bush's influence is readily discernible. If regulations governing the counting of salmon populations and the protection of their habitats could only be modified by amending the Endangered Species Act, the endangered status of 23 species and federal protections for thousands of acres of streams and watersheds would almost certainly remain intact. Similarly, if the ultimate decision to send troops into Liberia had rested in Congress's 1,070 hands, rather than Bush's two, the United States probably would not have made even a modest contribution to diffusing the nation's civil unrest. Even in the military tribunals case, in which the Supreme Court's ability to check presidential power appeared on full display, the precedent created by Bush's 2001 Military Order may yet pave the way for legislative authorization of new tribunals closer in design to the president's true preferences than the administration could have achieved before through legislation alone. Moreover, all of the individuals who the administration intends to prosecute through military tribunals remain, as they have for the past four years, under the direct control of the president. Through executive orders, military orders, and rules, President Bush, along with all modern presidents, has managed to materially redirect public policy in ways not possible in a strictly legislative setting, using only those powers enumerated in the Constitution.

That the president's unilateral powers yield genuine influence over public policy, however, does not mean that the president necessarily gets everything he might want. Even in the cases of the Liberian interventions, limits to presidential power are readily apparent. Though Bush may have preferred to respond immediately and, perhaps, with greater force to the mounting African crisis, he instead bowed to congressional and Department of Defense pressures and ordered a relatively small and short-lived military Liberian intervention.

Less ambiguously, the military tribunal and arsenic cases dramatically underscore the limits of unilateral powers. As Yale Law School

Dean Harold Koh has noted, "[the *Hamdan*] opinion is a stunning re-
buke to the extreme theory of executive power that has been put forward for the last five years. It is a reminder that checks and balances
continue to be a necessary and vibrant principle, even in the war on
terror."[109] Similarly, if less dramatically, the arsenic case also illustrates the institutional constraints on presidential unilateral action.
Bush clearly wanted to raise the allowable levels of arsenic in drinking water, but facing widespread public and congressional opposition
to this move, he prudently abstained from altering Clinton's order.
And so it is with all presidents. Unilaterally, they do as much as they
think they can get away with. In those instances when a unilateral directive can be expected to spark some kind of congressional or judicial reprisal, presidents may hedge their bets; and knowing that their
orders will promptly be overturned, presidents may not act at all.
Hence, when trying to account for these constraints, it will not do to
simply inventory those instances when Congress or the courts actually overturn a presidential order. Scholars must stay attuned to the
ways in which presidents anticipate congressional and judicial reactions and adjust their actions accordingly.

Still, we would do well to keep the limitations to presidential
power in proper perspective. In the arsenic case, influence lost to
Bush redounded to the benefit of Clinton. For Clinton had previously
relied upon his own unilateral powers to strike first, lowering the allowable levels of arsenic in drinking water and thereby reshaping the
politics that surrounded the issue. Bush's failure to reverse the
Clinton rule demonstrates that while unilateral actions by one president are always in jeopardy of being reversed by another, under some
conditions they can continue to have lasting influence on public policy. When a president's order or regulatory action recasts the terms of
debate and mobilizes organized interests to defend it against subsequent incursions, even unilateral actions that can technically be reversed with the stroke of a pen prove remarkably resilient. In the
military tribunals case, meanwhile, the president's defeat at first
blush would appear absolute. Still, the administration may yet succeed in gaining congressional authorization for much of its agenda,
and it retains considerable discretion over the detention of the hundreds of individuals who continue to await trial.

The burden of checking presidential power ultimately lies with
Congress and the courts. And if recent political history is any indication of future trends, presidents will have continued reason to rely
upon unilateral directives to advance their policy agenda. As majority
parties retain control of the House and Senate by the slimmest of
margins, as multiple veto points and collective action problems litter
the legislative process with opportunities for failure, and as members
of Congress and judges remain reticent to take on the president during times of war, abundant opportunities and incentives for presi-

dents to exercise their unilateral powers remain. To be sure, presidents must proceed with caution, scaling back some initiatives and abandoning others altogether, especially when political opposition is strong and mobilized. Directives that immediately affect the electoral prospects of key members of Congress, or that deeply offend basic constitutional provisions, are likely to provoke some kind of legislative or judicial response, which may in turn redefine the boundaries of presidential power. But in an era where political gridlock is commonplace and judicial deference the norm, presidents can be expected to regularly strike out on their own. And if Bush's presidency teaches us anything at all, it reveals the extent to which unilateral powers can influence the production of foreign and domestic policy.

Notes

1. See also Mayer and Price (2002).

2. See *United States v. Curtiss-Wright*, 299 U.S. 304 (1936); *United States v. Belmont*, 301 U.S. 324 (1937); and *United States v. Pink*, 315 U.S. 203 (1942). Schubert (1973) contains a useful summary of these cases.

3. In addition to making administrative strategies more attractive, these forces also have changed the tactics presidents employ when they do attempt to guide policy proposals through Congress. See, for example, Kernell (1997) and Canes-Wrone (2005).

4. This section draws from Howell (2003, 2005a, 2005b).

5. For the full history on Bush's order to support faith-based organizations, see Farris, Nathan, and Wright (2004).

6. Brinkley, David. "Out of Spotlight, Bush Overhauls U.S. Regulations," *New York Times*, August 14, 2004, A1.

7. In many policy arenas, presidents find the authority they need to act unilaterally in some vague statute or broad delegation of power. And when doing so, it is difficult to make the case that the president is merely fulfilling the expressed wishes of Congress (more on this below). In this instance, it is worth noting that Congress refused to formally declare war against Afghanistan or Iraq. Rather, it passed authorizations in the falls of 2001 and 2002 that gave the president broad discretion to use the military as he deemed appropriate in the nation's campaign against terrorism.

8. Kiefer, Francine. "Clinton Perfects the Art of Go-Alone Governing," *Christian Science Monitor*, July 24, 1998, 3.

9. Ross, Sonya. "Searching for a Way to Make History Forget Impeachment," December 20, 1999, posted on CNN.com.

10. Quotes in *CQ Weekly*. "Clinton's Lands Designation Refuels Efforts to Narrow Monuments Law," January 15, 2000, 86. In 1999, the House

passed HR 1487 that would have restricted the president's authority to designate national parks, but the bill died in the Senate.

11. One of the more visible repudiations of an executive order issued by Clinton concerned the permanent replacement of striking workers. *Chamber of Commerce of the United States v. Reich* (D.C. Cir. 1996). For more discussion on the institutional constraints of presidential power, see below.

12. See Cooper (2002) for many more.

13. Much of the "congressional dominance" literature, which emphasizes the ways in which Congress controls the bureaucracy and president through delegation and carefully crafted statutes, also suggests as much (see, for example, Kiewiet and McCubbins 1991; Kernell and McDonald 1999). For critiques of this perspective, see Whittington and Carpenter (2004) and Moe (1987, 1999).

14. In one critique of this view, Matthew Dickinson insists that unilateral directives "must be evaluated in the context of their overall impact on [presidents'] bargaining power" (2004, 103). But this suggestion confuses power's means and ends. Presidents do not issue directives and commands in order to augment their bargaining stature. Rather, they do so in order to materially change the world around them; and to the extent that these unilateral powers accomplish as much, presidents are well advised to continue issuing them. In his contribution to this volume, Dickinson also points out that unilateral directives must be implemented, forcing presidents to "bargain" with members of the executive branch, just as Neustadt argued all along. While a useful reminder, this claim overstates the extent to which presidents must rely upon persuasion to have their way (Howell 2005a). When dealing with the bureaucracy, as opposed to a co-equal branch of government such as Congress, presidents have at their disposal all kinds of additional powers to ensure compliance, not least of which is the ability to hire and fire them (Waterman 1989; Moe 1999; Nathan 1983). Moreover, presidents regularly issue all kinds of unilateral directives that are designed to ensure that their policy orders are faithfully implemented. For one recent case study, see Farris, Nathan, and Wright (2004).

15. 343 U.S. 579 (1952), 637.

16. This, according to Paul Holland, is the "fundamental problem of causal inference" (1986).

17. Future presidents, too, can overturn the unilateral directives of their predecessors. Incoming presidents regularly relax, or altogether undo, the regulations and orders of past presidents, and in this respect, the influence sitting presidents wield is limited by the anticipated actions of their forebears. As Richard Waterman correctly notes, "subsequent presidents can and often do . . . reverse executive orders. . . . This is not a constraint if we think only within administrations, but for presidents who wish to leave a long-term political legacy, the fact that the next president may reverse their policies may force them, at least on occasion, to move to the legislative arena" (2004, 245). Because of these dynamics, should we downwardly adjust our assessments of

presidential power? Probably not, and two points help explain why. First, just as future presidents may subsequently overturn, or amend, his actions, a sitting president is not forced to abide by every standing order that he inherits from past presidents. And second, the transfer and exchange of unilateral directives across administrations is not always as seamless as all this supposes. Often, presidents cannot alter orders set by their predecessors without paying a considerable political price, undermining the nation's credibility, or confronting serious, often insurmountable, legal obstacles (Howell and Mayer 2005).

18. Jessica Kowal, "As Flow of Salmon Surges, U.S. Moves to Cut Protections; Critics Say Federal Plans Favor Dams," *Boston Globe,* September 19, 2004, A21.

19. *Alsea Valley Alliance v. Evans,* 143 F. Supp. 2d 1214 (2001).

20. Timothy Egan, "Shift on Salmon Re-ignites Fight on Species Law," *New York Times,* May 8, 2004, A1.

21. Craig Welch, "U.S. Shift on Salmon Could Cut Protection; Hatchery Fish Would Count as Part of State's Wild Runs," *Seattle Times,* April 30, 2004, A1.

22. "In proposed listing determinations described in this proposed rule, artificial propagation has been considered in (1) determining what constitutes an ESU, and (2) when evaluating the extinction risk of an entire ESU. . . . The consideration of artificial propagation in the subject proposed listing determinations is based on the proposed Hatchery Listing Policy (see second citation)." National Marine Fisheries Service, "Endangered and Threatened Species: Proposed Listing Determinations for 27 ESUs of West Coast Salmonids," June 14, 2004, 69, *Federal Register,* 33102. National Marine Fisheries Service, "Endangered and Threatened Species: Proposed Policy on the Consideration of Hatchery-Origin Fish in Endangered Species Act Listing Determinations for Pacific Salmon and Steelhead," June 3, 2004, 69, *Federal Register,* 31354. Note: 26 species were classified as endangered when the review began and an additional species was considered a candidate for the status, thus increasing the total to 27.

23. Ransom A. Myers, Simon A. Levin, Russell Lande, Frances C. James, William W. Murdoch, and Robert T. Paine, "Hatcheries and Endangered Salmon," *Science,* March 26, 2004, 303.

24. Egan, "Shift on Salmon."

25. Blaine Harden, "Hatchery Salmon to Count as Wildlife," *Washington Post,* May 10, 2004, A1.

26. Kenneth Weiss, "Salmon and Steelhead May Lose Protections," *Los Angeles Times,* December 1, 2004. National Marine Fisheries Service, "Endangered and Threatened Species; Designation of Critical Habitat for 13 ESUs of Pacific Salmon and Steelhead in Washington, Oregon and Idaho," December 14, 2004, 69, *Federal Register,* 74572.

27. The District Court struck down a Clinton policy that allowed for the removal of the federal dams, but only as a last resort. The Court deemed this language too vague and insufficient in its protections. *National*

Wildlife Federation v. National Marine Fisheries Service, 254 F. Supp. 2d 1196 (2003).

28. Felicity Barringer, "Government Rejects Removal of Dams to Protect Salmon," *New York Times*, November 30, 2004, A1.

29. Blaine Harden, "Pollsters Doubt Fish Rules Will Move Votes," *Washington Post*, May 6, 2004, A4. James McDermott, *Congressional Record*, June 16, 2004, H4268.

30. National Marine Fisheries Service, "Policy on the Consideration of Hatchery-Origin Fish in Endangered Species Act Listing Determinations for Pacific Salmon and Steelhead," June 28, 2005, 70, *Federal Register*, 37204–37216.

31. See, e.g., executive Orders 2570, 2572, 2605, 2617, 2705, and 2718.

32. SJ Res. 23 (PL 107-40), Section 2 (a).

33. PL 107-56.

34. Military Order of November 13, 2001, "Detention, Treatment, and Trial of Certain Non-Citizens in the War Against Terrorism," *Federal Register*, 66:57833. The military order is not an executive order per se and hence not found in executive order disposition tables. In choosing a military order, Bush followed the precedent of Franklin Roosevelt whose July 2, 1942, military order provided for the trial by military commission of eight suspected German saboteurs pursuant to his authority under the 38th Article of War (U.S.C. Title 10, Sec. 1509).

35. Military Order of November 13, 2001, "Detention, Treatment, and Trial of Certain Non-Citizens in the War Against Terrorism," *Federal Register*, 66:57833.

36. John Edwards and John Ashcroft, Senate Judiciary Committee, December 6, 2001.

37. Jennifer Dlouhy and Elizabeth Palmer, "New Assertions of Executive Power Anger, Frustrate Some on Hill," *Congressional Quarterly Weekly*, November 24, 2001, 2784.

38. Dennis Kucinich, *Congressional Record*, November 28, 2001, E2162.

39. Jennifer Dlouhy and Elizabeth Palmer, "New Assertions of Executive Power Anger, Frustrate Some on Hill," *Congressional Quarterly Weekly*, November 24, 2001, 2784.

40. Richard Durbin, Senate Judiciary Committee hearing, November 28, 2001.

41. Elizabeth Palmer and Adriel Bettelheim, "War and Civil Liberties: Congress Gropes for a Role," *Congressional Quarterly Weekly*, December 1, 2001, 2820. The attorney-client eavesdropping was the result of a Department of Justice rule, "National Security: Prevention of Acts of Violence and Terrorism," *Federal Register*, 66:55062.

42. Elizabeth Palmer and Adriel Bettelheim, "War and Civil Liberties: Congress Gropes for a Role," *Congressional Quarterly Weekly*, December 1, 2001, 2820.

43. Arlen Specter, "Questioning the President's Authority," *New York Times,* November 24, 2001, A25.

44. American Civil Liberties Union, Senate Judiciary Committee hearing, November 28, 2001.

45. Elisabeth Bumiller and Katharine Seelye, "Bush Defends Wartime Call for Tribunals," *New York Times,* December 5, 2001, A1.

46. Phillip Heymann, Senate Judiciary Committee hearing, November 28, 2001.

47. Laurence Tribe, Senate Judiciary Committee hearing, December 4, 2001.

48. For denunciations of the order in the press see: "Justice Deformed: War and the Constitution," *New York Times,* December 5, 2001, 4:14; William Safire, "Voices of Negativism," *New York Times,* December 6, 2001, A35; "A Tribunal Too Far," *Washington Times,* November 19, 2001, A16; "Ashcroft Overreaches," *St. Louis Post-Dispatch,* November 27, 2001, B6; "A Perilous Course on Civil Liberties," *Seattle Times,* November 19, 2001, B4; "Not Democratic Enough," *San Francisco Chronicle,* November 28, 2001, A20; "Rule of Law Needn't be Suspended in Wartime," *Houston Chronicle,* November 24, 2001, A40.

49. Jennifer Dlouhy and Elizabeth Palmer, "New Assertions of Executive Power Anger, Frustrate Some on Hill," *Congressional Quarterly Weekly,* November 24, 2001, 2784.

50. Adriel Bettelheim, "Hill Treads Carefully in Challenging Ashcroft Over Expansion of Anti-Terrorism Powers," *Congressional Quarterly Weekly,* December 8, 2001, 2903.

51. Katharine Seelye, "Government Sets Rules for Military on War Tribunals," *New York Times,* March 21, 2002, A1; William Safire, "Military Tribunals Modified," *New York Times,* March 21, 2002, A37; Katharine Seelye, "Rumsfeld Backs Plan to Hold Captives Even if Acquitted," *New York Times,* March 29, 2002, A18.

52. *Rumsfeld v. Padilla,* 124 S. Ct. 2711 (2004); *Hamdi v. Rumsfeld,* 124 S. Ct. 2633 (2004).

53. This assertion of American jurisdiction is one (of several) ways the Court claims it differs from the *Eisentrager* precedent, which ruled that "aliens detained outside the sovereign territory of the United States [may not] invoke a petition for a writ of habeas corpus." *Johnson v. Eisentrager,* 70 S. Ct. 936 (1950).

54. This judgment was echoed by D.C. District Court Judge Joyce Hens Green, *In Re: Guantanamo Detainees,* Civil Action No. 2002-0299, January 31, 2005.

55. *Hamdan v. Rumsfeld,* U.S. App. 14315 (2005).

56. *Hamdan v. Rumsfeld,* U.S. LEXIS 5185 (2006).

57. Common Article 3 requires all tribunals be conducted by a "regularly constituted court affording all the judicial guarantees which are recognized as indispensable by civilized peoples." A plurality of the Court (not joined by Justice Kennedy) also argued that the conspiracy charge

levied against Hamdan was not an "offense that by . . . the law of war may be tried by military commissions," 10 U.S.C. § 821, and therefore beyond the purview of the administration's tribunals, regardless of whether they were legally created.

58. CNN.com. 2006. "Bush Says He'll Work With Congress on Tribunal Plan." Available at http://www.cnn.com/2006/POLITICS/06/29/hamdan. reax/index.html.

59. Charlie Savage, "Justices Deal Bush Setback on Tribunals; High Court Says Guantanamo Action Illegal," *Boston Globe*, A1.

60. For trenchant critiques of this perspective, see Adler and George (1998) and Ely (1993).

61. Office of the Press Secretary, "President Reaffirms Strong Position on Liberia," July 14, 2003.

62. Office of the Press Secretary, "President Bush Discusses Liberia," July 8, 2003.

63. Richard Stevenson and Christopher Marquis, "Bush Team Faces Widespread Pressure to Act on Liberia," *New York Times*, July 23, 2003. See also, "America's Role in Liberia," *New York Times*, July 24, 2003; "Liberia Calls," *Washington Post*, July 1, 2003.

64. "Powell Backs U.S. Role to Aid Liberia," *New York Times*, July 24, 2003.

65. Bill Sammon, "Bush Won't 'Overextend' U.S. Troops; Downplays Liberia Mission," *Washington Times*, July 10, 2003; Rowan Scarborough, "U.S. Eyes Small Force for Liberia Duty; Unit Would Augment West Africans," *Washington Times*, July 24, 2003.

66. Christopher Marquis and Thom Shanker, "Pentagon Leaders Warn of Dangers For U.S. in Liberia," *New York Times*, July 24, 2003.

67. Typically, members of the president's party support a planned military venture, while members of the opposition party are the one to raise objections and roadblocks. For more on the partisan dynamics that fuel congressional reactions to the use of force, see Howell and Pevehouse (2005, 2007) and Kriner (2006).

68. Sheila Jackson-Lee, United States House of Representatives, *Congressional Record*, H7198, July 21, 2003.

69. Robert Byrd, United States Senate, *Congressional Record*, August 1, 2003.

70. H. Con. Res. 240, introduced in the House of Representatives, July 8, 2003.

71. Eric Schmitt, "G.O.P. Senator Criticizes Bush on Liberia Case," *New York Times*, August 2, 2003.

72. John Warner, *Congressional Record*, S10893, August 1, 2003.

73. Ron Paul, United States House of Representatives, *Congressional Record*, E1602, July 24, 2003.

74. Bradley Graham, "U.S. to Send 200 Troops To Liberia; Addition Follows Concerns About Pace of Peacekeeping," *Washington Post*, August 14, 2003. Office of the Press Secretary, "Presidential Letter to the

Speaker of the House of Representatives and the President Pro Tempore of the Senate," August 13, 2003.

75. Tim Weiner, "200 U.S. Marines Land in Liberia to Aid African Force," *New York Times*, August 15, 2003.

76. Eric Schmitt, "U.S. General Optimistic on Liberia Mission," *New York Times*, September 3, 2003.

77. Jim Garamone, "Liberia Mission Winds Down," *Armed Forces Press Service*, Release #1022-03-1041, September 30, 2003.

78. For example, not a single member of Congress was quoted objecting to the deployment in either the *Washington Post* or the *New York Times* in the two weeks following the action while both chambers were in recess.

79. Recall, for instance, the back and forth between Bush 41, Clinton, and Bush 43 over the so-called Mexico City policy, which granted federal aid to family planning clinics abroad that counseled clients on abortion.

80. For example, the Bush administration's proposed regulatory change that would lower standards for tuna to be labeled "dolphin safe" was recently struck down by the federal courts as based on unsatisfactory scientific evidence to justify the change. " 'Dolphin-Safe' Labeling Upheld," *Pittsburgh Post-Gazette*, August 12, 2004, A7.

81. U.S. Public Health Service. 1943. Public Health Service Drinking Water Standards. Approved Revisions to the 1925 Drinking Water Standards on December 3, 1942. *Public Health Reports*. 58(3):69–82. January 15, 1943.

82. Public Law 104-182.

83. Rebecca Adams, "Bush Attack on Regulations for Arsenic, Surface Mining Has Democrats Vowing Action," *Congressional Quarterly Weekly*, March 24, 2001, 670.

84. Subcommittee on Arsenic in Drinking Water, National Research Council of the National Academy of Sciences, *Arsenic in Drinking Water* 3 (1999).

85. National Primary Drinking Water Regulations; Arsenic and Clarifications to Compliance and New Source Contaminants Monitoring; Notice of Proposed Rulemaking," 65 *Federal Register*, 38888, (2000).

86. John Cushman, "E.P.A. Proposes New Rule to Lower Arsenic in Tap Water," *New York Times*, May 25, 2004. For the rule itself, see: E.P.A., "National Primary Drinking Water Regulations; Arsenic and Clarifications to Compliance and New Source Contaminants Monitoring; Final Rule," 66 *Federal Register*, January 22, 2001, 6976.

87. Christie Whitman quoted in Robert Schlesinger, "Drinking Water Rule Put on Hold; Effort Seen to Gut Arsenic Standard," *Boston Globe*, March 21, 2001.

88. Public law 104-121.

89. "Ergonomics Program; Final Rule," 65 *Federal Register* 68262, (2000).

90. "Special Areas; Roadless Areas Conservation; Final Rule," 66 *Federal Register* 3244, (2001).

91. Alison Mitchell, "Democrats See Gold in Environment," *New York Times,* April 21, 2001.

92. Rebecca Adams, "GOP, Business, Rewrite the Regulatory Playbook," *Congressional Quarterly Weekly,* May 5, 2001, 990.

93. Chuck Fox, "Arsenic and Old Laws," *New York Times,* March 22, 2001.

94. "A Sensible Arsenic Limit," *Boston Globe,* March 27, 2001; "Bush Going Backward With Ruthless Efficiency," *Atlanta Journal-Constitution,* March 26, 2001; "Poisonous Politics," St. Louis Post-Dispatch, March 22, 2004; "A Hostile Environment," *San Francisco Chronicle,* April 2, 2001.

95. See Douglas Jiehl, "E.P.A. To Abandon New Arsenic Limits for Water Supply," *New York Times,* March 21, 2001.

96. Richard Gephardt, Press Conference from Capitol H-206, March 22, 2001.

97. Richard Gephardt, Press Conference from the Capitol East-front, April 26, 2001.

98. Tom Daschle, Press Conference from S-224, March 21, 2001.

99. Helen Kennedy, "Christie is Laced on Arsenic Stand," *New York Daily News,* March 21, 2001.

100. A Princeton Survey Research Associates Poll, April 22, 2001, showed 57 percent of respondents disapproved of Bush's decision to halt Clinton rule. Similarly, *LA Times Poll,* April 21, 2001, showed 56 percent of Americans opposed Bush's decision to overturn the Clinton regulations.

101. Douglas Jehl, "E.P.A. Delays Its Decision on Arsenic," *New York Times,* April 19, 2001.

102. Immediately after the Bush decision of March 21, 2001, House Democrats introduced several measures to combat the action. On April 4, Henry Waxman introduced H.R. 1413, colloquially known as the "Get Arsenic Out of Our Drinking Water Act," which garnered 173 cosponsors before stalling in committee. An even more restrictive measure that would implement the Clinton standard by 2003 and then further reduce the tolerable level of arsenic in water to 3 ppb by 2006 drew 77 cosponsors before similarly dying in committee. Comparable measures calling for a restoration of the Clinton standard were also introduced in the Senate but garnered little support. See, for example, S. 632 and S. 635.

103. Barbara Mikulski, testimony before the Senate Appropriations Committee, June 13, 2001.

104. Adriel Bettelheim, "VA-HUD Spending Bill's Progress Slowed by Partisan Sparring in House," *Congressional Quarterly Weekly,* July 28, 2001, 1851. Douglas Jehl, "House Demanding Strict Guidelines on Arsenic Level," *New York Times,* July 28, 2001.

105. See U.S. National Resource Council, Subcommittee on Arsenic in Drinking Water. 2001. *Arsenic in Drinking Water: 2001 Update.* Washington: National Academy Press; see also the National Drinking Water Advisory Council's *Report of the Arsenic Cost Working Group to the National Drinking Water Advisory Council,* August 14, 2001; and the E.P.A. Science Advisory Board's own review, *Arsenic Rule Benefit Analysis: An SAB Review,* August 2001.

106. Katharine Seelye, "E.P.A. to Adopt Clinton Standard," *New York Times,* November 1, 2001.

107. Katharine Seelye, "Arsenic Standard for Water Is too Lax, Study Concludes," *New York Times,* September 11, 2001.

108. *State of Nebraska v. Environmental Protection Agency,* 356 U.S. App. D.C. 410.

109. Charlie Savage, "Justices Deal Bush Setback on Tribunals; High Court Says Guantanamo Action Illegal," *Boston Globe,* June 30, 2006, A1.

References

Adler, David, and Larry George. 1998. *The Constitution and the Conduct of American Foreign Policy.* Lawrence: University Press of Kansas.

Arnold, Peri E. 1998. *Making the Managerial Presidency: Comprehensive Reorganization Planning, 1905–1996.* Lawrence: University Press of Kansas.

Auerswald, David, and Peter Cowhey. 1997. "Ballotbox Diplomacy: The War Powers Resolution and the Use of Force." *International Studies Quarterly* 41(3):505–528.

Bond, Jon, and Richard Fleisher. 2000. *Polarized Politics: Congress and the President in a Partisan Era.* Washington, DC: Congressional Quarterly Press.

Cameron, Charles, and Nolan M. McCarty. 2004. "Models of Vetoes and Veto Bargaining." *Annual Review of Political Science* 7:409–435.

Canes-Wrone, Brandice. 2005. *Who's Leading Whom?* Chicago: University of Chicago Press.

Clark, David. 2000. "Agreeing to Disagree: Domestic Institutional Congruence and U.S. Dispute Behavior." *Political Research Quarterly* 53(2):375–400.

Cooper, Phillip. 1997. "Power Tools for an Effective and Responsible Presidency." *Administration & Society* 29(5):529–556.

———. 2002. *By Order of the President: The Use and Abuse of Executive Direct Action.* Lawrence: University Press of Kansas.

Dickinson, Matthew. 2004. "Agendas, Agencies and Unilateral Action: New Insights on Presidential Power?" *Congress & the Presidency* 31(1):99–109.

Ely, John Hart. 1993. *War and Responsibility: Constitutional Lessons of Vietnam and Its Aftermath.* Princeton, NJ: Princeton University Press.

Farris, Anne, Richard P. Nathan, and David J. Wright. 2004. *The Expanding Administrative Presidency: George W. Bush and the Faith-Based Initiative.* Washington, DC: The Roundtable on Religion and Social Policy.

Fisher, Louis. 2000. *Congressional Abdication on War and Spending.* College Station, TX: Texas A&M University Press.

Heclo, Hugh. 1978. Issue Networks and the Executive Establishment. In *The New American Political System,* edited by A. King. Washington, DC: American Enterprise Institute.

Holland, Paul. 1986. "Statistics and Causal Inference." *Journal of the American Statistical Association* 81:945–960.

Howell, William G. 2003. *Power Without Persuasion: The Politics of Direct Presidential Action.* Princeton, NJ: Princeton University Press.

———. 2005a. "Power Without Persuasion: Rethinking Foundations of Executive Influence." In *Presidential Politics,* edited by G. Edwards. Belmont, CA: Wadsworth.

———. 2005b. "Unilateral Powers: A Brief Overview." *Presidential Studies Quarterly* 35 (3):417–439.

Howell, William G., and David Lewis. 2002. "Agencies by Presidential Design." *Journal of Politics* 64 (4):1095–1114.

Howell, William G., and Kenneth Mayer. 2005. "The Last 100 Days." *Presidential Studies Quarterly* 35(3):533–553.

Howell, William G., and Jon Pevehouse. 2005. "Presidents, Congress, and the Use of Force." *International Organization* 59 (1):209–232.

———. 2007. *While Dangers Gather: Congressional Checks on Presidential War Powers.* Princeton: Princeton University Press.

Kernell, Samuel. 1997. *Going Public: New Strategies of Presidential Leadership.* Washington, DC: Congressional Quarterly Press.

Kernell, Samuel, and Michael McDonald. 1999. "Congress and America's Political Development: The Transformation of the Post Office from Patronage to Service." *American Journal of Political Science* 43 (3):792–811.

Kiewiet, Roderick, and Mathew McCubbins. 1991. *The Logic of Delegation.* Chicago: University of Chicago Press.

Kriner, Douglas. 2006. *Taming the Imperial Presidency: Congress, Presidents, and the Conduct of Military Action.* Cambridge, MA: Government Department, Harvard University.

Lewis, David E. 2003. *Presidents and the Politics of Agency Design.* Stanford, CA: Stanford University Press.

Mann, Thomas, and Norman Ornstein, eds. 1981. *The New Congress.* Washington, DC: American Enterprise Institute.

Margolis, Lawrence. 1986. *Executive Agreements and Presidential Power in Foreign Policy.* New York: Praeger.

Mayer, Kenneth. 2001. *With the Stroke of a Pen: Executive Orders and Presidential Power.* Princeton, NJ: Princeton University Press.

Mayer, Kenneth, and Kevin Price. 2002. "Unilateral Presidential Powers: Significant Executive Orders, 1949–99." *Presidential Studies Quarterly* 32(2):367–386.

Moe, Terry. 1987. "An Assessment of the Positive Theory of 'Congressional Dominance.'" *Legislative Studies Quarterly* 12(4):475–520.

———. 1999. "The Presidency and the Bureaucracy: The Presidential Advantage." In *The Presidency and the Political System,* edited by M. Nelson. Washington, DC: Congressional Quarterly Press.

Moe, Terry M., and William G. Howell. 1999. "The Presidential Power of Unilateral Action." *Journal of Law, Economics, and Organization* 15(1):132–179.

Nathan, Richard P. 1983. *The Administative Presidency.* New York: John Wiley.

Neustadt, Richard E. 1990. *Presidential Power and the Modern Presidents.* New York: Free Press.

Oppenheimer, Bruce. 1980. "Policy Effects of U.S. House Reform: Decentralization and the Capacity to Resolve Energy Issues." *Legislative Studies Quarterly* 5:5–30.

Schlesinger, Arthur. 1973. *The Imperial Presidency.* Boston: Houghton Mifflin.

———. 2004. *War and the American Presidency.* New York: W.W. Norton & Company.

Schubert, Glendon. 1973. *The Presidency in the Courts.* New York: Da Capo Press.

Shane, Peter, and Harold Bruff. 1988. *The Law of Presidential Power.* Durham, NC: Carolina Academic Press.

Waterman, Richard W. 1989. *Presidential Influence and the Administrative State.* Knoxville: University of Tennessee Press.

———. 2004. "Unilateral Politics." *Public Administration Review* 64(2):243–245.

Weko, Thomas. 1995. *The Politicizing Presidency: The White House Personnel Office.* Lawrence: University Press of Kansas.

Whittington, Keith, and Daniel Carpenter. 2004. "Executive Power in American Institutional Development." *Perspectives on Politics* 1(3):495–513. ✦

Chapter 6

Impediments to Presidential Leadership

The Limitations of the Permanent Campaign and Going Public Strategies

George C. Edwards III

The first four chapters demonstrate that presidential leadership is conditional: it depends on a variety of factors, often beyond the president's individual skill level, for a president to be successful. When presidents have little political leverage, such as when gridlock in Congress exists, presidential leadership ability is greatly constrained. While presidents have the ability to act unilaterally, even in these cases they sometimes find themselves constrained (and ultimately unsuccessful in their attempts to change policy). In short, there are significant boundaries to presidential leadership. While we may expect presidents to be strong and effective leaders, it is not realistic for us to expect them to do so at all times, in all political circumstances. We need to also understand what are the impediments to presidential leadership and what approaches presidents have employed to overcome them.

In this chapter, Edwards describes important impediments to presidential leadership, as well as how recent presidents have tried to overcome them. For example, the constitutional system of checks and balances and separation of powers makes it difficult for presidents to build coalitions with likeminded members of Congress. Presidents cannot depend on the opposition party in Congress for support, a factor that has more deleterious consequences for presidents in periods of divided government. In addition, over the past decades the two parties have become more ideologically polarized, which further complicates the process of building coalitions or securing compromise and cooperation from members of Congress. Presidents also are losing some advantages they once possessed. For instance, the number of members of Congress who are elected because they ride the president's coattails into office has declined precipitously in recent decades.

Because of these impediments, presidents have developed new strategies designed to promote their presidential leadership ability. In particular, they now employ a strategy of going public or a permanent campaign to go directly over the heads of members of Congress to the public at large. The idea is to get the public to put pressure on members of Congress. But as Edwards notes, "public support gives a president, at best, leverage, but not control." When presidents are not popular (overall or with regard to specific policies they support), which is often the case, "this strengthens the resolve of those inclined to oppose him. . . ." Edwards therefore finds, "Presidents not only fail to create new political capital by going public, but their efforts at persuading the public may also *decrease* their chances of success. . . ." He does so by presenting polling data on a variety of issues important to Presidents Reagan, Clinton, and George W. Bush. Edwards's chapter therefore represents a direct challenge to one of the most prominent models of presidential leadership.

◆ ◆ ◆

Leadership is the essence of the presidency. Previous chapters have explored the president's leadership in a variety of venues. We have seen that it is important to distinguish between attempts to lead and the success of that leadership. Presidents also often fail to influence the actions and attitudes of others and affect the output of government.

Building coalitions is at the core of governing in America. The necessity of forming coalitions is inevitable in a large, diverse nation in which political power is fragmented both vertically and horizontally. Because the president in most instances requires the approval of the legislature to make public policy, Congress is the proximate site of coalition building. Because advances in technology allow the president to reach the public directly and because the White House views public support as crucial to its success, presidents invest substantial time and effort in building support for themselves and their policies among the public.

In this chapter, I explore the president's ability to obtain support for himself and his policies within Congress and among the public. I show how presidents frequently fail to obtain the support they need to govern, but my particular focus is on explaining why presidents have so much difficulty leading others to support them.

Building Coalitions in Congress

Some presidents want to undo the work of their predecessors while others want to break new ground in public policy. All presidents, however, wish to produce a legacy of important legislation. Andrew Barrett and I identified 287 presidential initiatives of potentially significant legislation over the period from 1953 to 1996. These are the proposals that have the most potential to leave a mark on public policy. It is reasonable to infer that these are also the policies about which presidents care the most. Of these 287 presidential initiatives of potentially significant legislation, only 41 percent became law.[1] In other words, *in the majority of cases presidents lose on their major legislative initiatives.* In addition, many of the presidential initiatives that Congress does pass are delayed or diluted by legislative opposition. In sum, presidents are typically frustrated in their efforts to bring about major policy changes.

Constitutional Structure

The president faces many obstacles to obtaining congressional support. The first barrier to success is the structure of the constitutional system. The system of checks and balances is designed to produce sound, moderate legislation through a process of negotiation and compromise that accommodates minority viewpoints. The open and deliberative nature of the process is to confer legitimacy on the legislation that it generates. At the same time, checks and balances complicate coalition building. Indeed, the necessity of congressional support forces the president to build coalitions in the first place. The bicameral structure of Congress further complicates the process by requiring the president to build not one but two coalitions from among quite different sets of representatives.[2] In addition, the requirement that the Senate ratify treaties by a two-thirds vote is a structural provision that increases the burden of coalition building because it forces the president to gain a supermajority to achieve ratification.

Checks and balances alone do not explain the president's challenges in forming supportive coalitions in Congress. Theoretically, the two branches could be in agreement. However, checks and balances provide the context within which other potentially divisive factors may become obstacles to coalition building. For example, the Senate's rules, especially those regarding debate, protect minority interests and force advocates of change to build coalitions of at least 61 percent of the members.

Party Support

Members of the president's party almost always form the core of the president's support in Congress. As Table 6.1 shows, in the 1953–2000 period, presidents obtained support from the typical senator or representative of their party about two-thirds of the time. This is twice the rate of the support that they received from the opposition.

On one hand, the president can depend on the support of most members of his party most of the time. On the other hand, there is plenty of slippage in party support, and the opposition party opposes him most of the time. If the opposition party is in the majority, which

Table 6.1 Partisan Support for Presidents, 1953–2000*

	House		Senate	
	Democratic President	Republican President	Democratic President	Republican President
Democrats	71%	26%	70%	33%
Republicans	31	67	32	70
Difference†	40	41	38	37

*On roll-call votes on which the president has taken a stand and on which the winning side was supported by fewer than 80 percent of those voting.
†Differences expressed as percentage points.
Source: George C. Edwards III and Stephen J. Wayne, *Presidential Leadership*, 6th ed. (Boston: Wadsworth, 2002).

it frequently is, the odds are against the president building a winning coalition.

In recent years, congressional parties have become more ideologically homogeneous and, as a result, more cohesive.[3] This change has not advantaged presidents, however. Presidents have a more difficult time obtaining votes from the opposition party as the two parties become more polarized. When their parties are in the minority in Congress (as they were for most or all of the tenures of Ronald Reagan, George H. W. Bush, and Bill Clinton), polarization makes it more difficult for presidents to prevail on votes.

In addition, with the exception of Ronald Reagan, winning candidates in the past three decades have positioned themselves as more moderate than their congressional parties. At the same time that winning presidential candidates have moved to the center, their congressional cohorts have become more polarized. As the number of conservative Democrats and liberal Republicans has diminished, there has been less pressure to compromise within the party caucus. The inevitable tension between centrist presidents and polarized party caucuses has meant that party support for the president has not increased in conjunction with party homogeneity.[4]

Party Opposition

The most important resource the president can have in building coalitions is like-minded members of Congress.[5] Such members are most likely to be found among those in the president's party. We have seen that the president receives twice as much support on the average from members of his party as from members of the opposition party. Presidents have had little success in exercising legislative skills and systematically changing the minds of many senators and representatives as legislation comes to the floor.[6] As a result, the president is largely dependent on the cards voters have dealt him in previous elections.

There are a number of methods of electing chief executives and members of the legislature. The most common is a parliamentary system in which the chief executive is elected from a single legislative district during the general elections for parliament. Thus, the members of the legislature and the chief executive are elected at the same time. This simultaneous election encourages voters across the nation to support the leader's party by voting for candidates of the leader's party. Since the prime minister is selected by a majority of the legislature, the prime minister's party or party coalition must have the support of a majority in the legislature.

In the United States, voters cast their votes separately for executive and legislative officials, who have terms of different lengths. Thus they may split their votes between candidates of different parties. Not supporting the president's party is even easier during midterm elections, when the president is not on the ballot. In addition, one-third of the Senate is not elected in any election during a president's four-year term. The result is often divided control of the executive and legislative branches, which has occurred nearly two-thirds of the time in the past half-century and in all but two of the national elections since 1978.

Divided government has important consequences for the president's policies. Under unified government, the president succeeds in obtaining passage of 53 percent of his significant legislative proposals.[7] Under the less sanguine conditions of divided government, however, the success rate for presidential initiatives is cut nearly in half, falling to 27 percent because of the opposition of the majority party in Congress. Divided government matters.[8] Moreover, divided government exacerbates the tendency stemming from the Senate's filibuster rules to delay or dilute bills that eventually pass.

Intraparty Diversity

The president faces a second party-related obstacle to building coalitions: the diversity of policy preferences within his own party. In a large and diverse country with a two-party system, it is not surprising that representatives of each of the two parties reflect a range of constituents' policy positions. This diversity inevitably poses a challenge to intraparty cohesion.

The system of primaries for selecting congressional candidates undermines at a minimum the ability of party leaders to control who runs under their party's label, and thus weakens their ability to discipline errant members for not supporting the president. Most members of Congress gain their party's nomination by their own efforts, not the party's. Because virtually anyone can vote in party primaries, party leaders do not have control over those who run under their parties' labels. Moreover, even though national party organizations have been active in fundraising in recent years, candidates remain largely responsible for providing the money and organization for their own election, precluding party control over another aspect of electoral politics.

One way for the president to improve the chances of obtaining support in Congress is to increase the number of fellow party members in the legislature. The phenomenon of presidential coattails occurs when voters cast their ballots for congressional candidates of the president's party because those candidates support the president. The relative independence of presidential and congressional elections is illustrated by the modest number of coattail victories, in which presidential coattail votes provide the increment of the vote necessary for a representative of the president's party to win a seat. Such victories may provide the president an extra increment of support out of a sense of gratitude for the votes that winners of congressional races perceive were received because of presidential coattails or out of a sense of responsiveness to their constituents' support for the president. However, the outcomes of very few congressional races are determined by presidential coattails.[9] The change in party balance that usually emerges when the electoral dust has settled is strikingly small. In the 13 presidential elections between 1952 and 2000, the party of the winning presidential candidate gained an average of 7 seats (out of 435) per election in the House. Most House seats are too safe for a party, and especially for an incumbent, to have the election outcome affected by the presidential election.

Senate elections are more affected by the president's standing with the public.[10] Nevertheless, the opposition party actually gained Senate seats in seven of the presidential elections (1956, 1960, 1972, 1984, 1988, 1996, and 2000), and there was no change in 1976 and 1992. The net gain for the president's party in the Senate averaged less than one seat per election.

Presidents' frustration with their short coattails is nothing new: in 1792, George Washington easily won reelection, but the opposition Democrat-Republicans captured the House of Representatives.

Modern presidents have tried to increase the size of their party cohort in Congress and encourage party cohesion by taking an active role in midterm congressional elections. Typically, however, they are disappointed in the results of their efforts.[11] The results of George W. Bush's relentless campaigning in 2002 stand as an interesting exception as his party increased marginally its representation in each house. It was more a consequence of redistricting (in the House) and of the higher turnout among Republican loyalists than of any national shift in public sentiment toward the party or the president. It was also a consequence of the unique circumstances following the 9/11 terrorist attacks.[12]

Party leaders typically are not strongly positioned to enforce party discipline among those who are elected. What sanctions might be applied, such as poor committee assignments, are rarely used because legislators are very hesitant to set precedents that could be used against them. Nevertheless, party leadership, at least in the House, has been more effective in recent years. As the party contingents have become more homogeneous, there has been more policy agreement within the parties and thus more party unity in voting on the floor. Increased agreement has made it easier for the Speaker to exercise his prerogatives regarding the assignment of bills and members to committees, the rules by which legislation is brought to the floor, and the use of an expanded whip system—all developments that have enabled the parties to advance an agenda that reflects party preferences.[13] Following the Republican takeover of Congress in 1995, Speaker Newt Gingrich began centralizing power and exercising vigorous legislative leadership. By 1997, however, the leadership backed off. Weakened by his low ratings in the polls, Speaker Newt Gingrich gave committee chairs greater leeway to set their committee's agenda and promised to allow legislation to be first fashioned by committees. The fact remains, however, that committee chairs are not as powerful as they were before the reform era, and the party leadership in the House has much more control over legislation.

The independent tenures of the president and members of Congress also diminish cohesion in the president's party. In a parliamentary system, the government falls if the prime minister loses the support of the legislature. Typically, such a loss of support leads to new elections for the entire legislature. Since facing the electorate under circumstances of party disunity is usually not in the interests of the prime minister's party, its members have an incentive to support their leader.[14] No such incentive exists in the United States, however. Members of Congress retain their jobs (at least in the short run) independently of the president's legislative success.

Institutional Assets

The most important influences on congressional voting are party, ideology, and constituency.[15] These factors are largely beyond the president's control, especially in the short run. Aside from the veto power, the president has few institutionalized legislative powers. He may call Congress into special sessions and adjourn it in the case of disputes between the two chambers. Both of these powers have fallen into disuse and give the president little leverage in an age of year-round Congresses. The president also may give a State of the Union message and recommend legislation to Congress. The president's role in setting Congress's agenda is substantial, although it is difficult to see how the "right" to recommend legislation is at the core of it.

Given the First Amendment, the right to recommend legislation is a truism. How could anyone limit it? The White House has a modest-sized institutional staff devoted to congressional relations. Although presidents have employed this staff in a variety of ways and although some operations work more effectively than others,[16] the performance of the legislative liaison office is not at the core of presidential leadership in Congress.[17]

Summary

At the core of the president's challenges in building coalitions is the separation of powers and checks and balances. The electoral system of separate elections for separate terms and the independent tenures of the president and members of Congress follows from the premise of separate institutions. The greatest obstacles to presidential coalition building arise from this electoral system. It creates the potential for divided government; discourages intraparty unity; and invites the president and members of Congress to define their constituencies differently. Differences in the length of terms of presidents and members of Congress and limits on the president's tenure encourage the White House and Congress to adopt different time perspectives for considering legislation.

Presidents, then, face a range of obstacles to obtaining congressional support for their policies (see Table 6.2 for a summary), and the Constitution provides few assets for moving Congress. It is natural that they turn to an extraconstitutional source of political power: public opinion.

Table 6.2   Impediments to Presidential Coalition Building in Congress

- Checks and balances force the president to build multiple coalitions on any bill and supermajorities on treaties.
- The rules for separate elections for separate terms create the potential for divided government.
- The independence of the tenures of the president and Congress discourage intraparty unity. (The system for nominating and electing members of Congress also weakens party leadership.)
- The electoral system invites the president and members of Congress to define their constituencies differently.
- Limitations on the president's tenure encourage different time perspectives in the executive and legislature.
- The hierarchical nature of the executive, in contrast to the more decentralized legislature, highlights the president's accountability while obscuring Congress's.
- The hierarchical nature of the executive, in contrast to the more decentralized legislature, provides the president and Congress different bases for their decisions.

Leading the Public

Leading the public is at the core of the modern presidency. Even as they try to govern, presidents are involved in a permanent campaign. Both politics and policy revolve around presidents' attempts to garner public support, both for themselves and for their policies. Presidents clearly believe that they need to lead the public, and they "go public" more than ever, depending on a steadily expanding White House public relations infrastructure to take their messages to the American people.[18]

To understand whether public support can help the president overcome impediments to his leadership of Congress—or whether the inability of the president to influence public opinion is yet another impediment to leadership—we must examine the president's success in obtaining public support for himself and his policies and the utility of public support for governing.

Obtaining Presidential Approval

How well have presidents done in obtaining the public's approval? Table 6.3 shows the average approval levels for full terms of presidents over the past three decades. Presidents Nixon, Ford, and Carter did not receive approval from even 50 percent of the public on the average. Even Ronald Reagan, often considered the most popular of recent presidents, averaged only 52 percent approval—a bare majority. George Bush achieved the highest average approval, at 61 percent. Yet when he needed the public's support the most, during his campaign for reelection, the public abandoned him. He received only 38 percent of the popular vote in the 1992 presidential election.

The fact that Bill Clinton enjoyed strong public support during his impeachment trial should not mask the fact that he struggled to obtain even 50 percent approval during his first term and did not exceed such an average for a year until his fourth year in office. Clinton's failure was not from lack of trying. The president was an indefatigable

Table 6.3   Average Levels of Presidential Approval

President	Years in Office	Average Approval
Nixon	1969–1974	48%
Ford	1974–1977	47
Carter	1977–1981	47
Reagan	1981–1989	52
Bush	1989–1993	61
Clinton	1993–2001	55

Source: George C. Edwards III, with Alec M. Gallup, *Presidential Approval* (Baltimore, MD: Johns Hopkins University Press, 1990); updated by the author.

traveler on behalf of his efforts to move the public. Charles O. Jones reports that Clinton traveled to 194 places and made 268 appearances in the United States between his inauguration in January 1993 and the midterm election in November 1994, mostly to sell himself and his policy proposals. Yet, as Jones concludes, the president's efforts were "a colossal failure"—his approval ratings did not rise.[19]

George W. Bush reached great heights of approval following the terrorist attacks on September 11, 2001. This impressive support should not obscure the fact that on September 10, 2001, the president was at only 51 percent approval and by his fourth year in office—after the rally in public opinion had waned—he was below 50 percent approval.

Impact of Public Approval

It is easy to understand why the White House believes that members of Congress might respond to public opinion regarding the president. Members of Congress appear to anticipate the public's reaction to their decisions to support or oppose the president and his policies. Depending on the president's public standing, they may choose to be close to him or independent from him to increase their chances of re-election. Polls find that a significant percentage of voters see their votes for candidates for Congress as support for the president or opposition to him.[20]

Members of Congress spend more time in their constituencies when the president's approval ratings are low, explaining how they differ from him.[21] Similarly, members of the president's party try to distance themselves from him during election periods if he is low in the polls.

Congressional incumbents defeated in the election of 1974 had supported Richard Nixon more than their colleagues had who won reelection.[22] Regardless of party, the voters do not punish representatives who do not support the president's programs if the president's policies are perceived as unsuccessful, but strong supporters of the president are less fortunate.[23] In districts where Bill Clinton was weak in 1994, Democratic candidates were more likely to be defeated.[24]

Scholars have found that the president's popularity strongly influences the vote in individual Senate races.[25] It appears that voters in Senate elections express their support for or dissatisfaction with the president by respectively rewarding or punishing candidates of his party—a national referendum effect.

The White House encourages members of Congress to infer from the president's approval levels the public's support for his policies. Ultimately, the effectiveness of this strategy is tied to the potential for making the support of a senator or representative a campaign issue.

Presidents who are high in the polls are in a position to make such threats.

Members of Congress may also use the president's standing in the polls as an indicator of his ability to mobilize public opinion against his opponents. Senators and representatives are especially likely to be sensitive to this possibility after a successful demonstration of the president's ability to mobilize the public, as appears to have occurred in response to the efforts of Reagan's White House in 1981.[26] As Richard Neustadt put it, "Washingtonians . . . are vulnerable to any breeze from home that presidential words and sighs can stir. If he is deemed effective on the tube, they will anticipate."[27]

Looking at the matter from another perspective, low presidential approval ratings free members of Congress from supporting the president if they are otherwise inclined to oppose him. A senior political aide to President Carter noted: "When the President is low in public opinion polls, the Members of Congress see little hazard in bucking him. . . . After all, very few Congressmen examine an issue solely on its merits; they are politicians and they think politically. I'm not saying they make only politically expedient choices. But they read the polls and from that they feel secure in turning their back on the President with political impunity. Unquestionably, the success of the President's policies bears a tremendous relationship to his popularity in the polls."[28]

A president with strong public support provides a cover for members of Congress to cast votes to which their constituents might otherwise object. They can defend their votes as having been made in support of the president rather than on substantive policy grounds alone. Of course, a president without public support loses this advantage and may find himself avoided by members of Congress who will certainly not articulate their decisions as having been made in support of the president if the president is caught in the depths of the polls. Lyndon Johnson, for example, found fewer members of Congress eager to attend White House receptions or discuss matters of policy with him when his standing in the polls declined.[29]

In addition, low ratings in the polls may create incentives to attack the president, further eroding his already weakened position. For example, after the arms sales to Iran and the diversion of funds to the contras became a cause célèbre in late 1986, it became more acceptable in Congress and in the press to raise questions about Ronald Reagan's capacities as president. Disillusionment is a dangerous force for the White House.

Perceptions do not always match reality, however. How much do presidents actually benefit from public support? In 1998, Bill Clinton averaged well over 60 percent job approval, and about two-thirds of the public consistently opposed his impeachment. In addition, the Democrats gained seats in the midterm elections—the first time the president's party had gained seats in 64 years! Yet in the face of over-whelming public opposition, Republicans impeached and tried the president.

Many commentators were mystified at how congressional Republicans could act in defiance of public support for the president. They should not have been. Senators and representatives do not pay equal heed to all the voters they represent. Instead, they are most responsive to their reelection constituencies, those who compose their electoral coalitions. In addition, members of Congress are more likely to receive communications from their electoral supporters more frequently than from other constituents.[30] Not surprisingly, these communications are likely to support the views of the senator or representative.

In the 1998 congressional elections, the typical Republican House incumbent who faced a Democratic challenger *gained* 3 percent of the vote over his or her performance in the 1996 elections. Fifty-five other Republican incumbents faced no opposition at all. Thus, 74 percent of the Republicans voting on the question of impeaching the president had just won reelection unopposed or saw their share of the two-party vote increase. In addition, Republicans did *not* suffer losses in districts in which Bill Clinton had done well in 1996.[31]

So it was reasonable for Republican lawmakers to interpret the results in their districts as indicating that Clinton's national popularity did not affect their own elections and was not indicative of *their* constituents' views. In the end, the House impeached the president, who then was acquitted in the Senate. The votes in both houses were heavily partisan. Despite his widespread and sustained public support, the president was able to change the minds of hardly any members of Congress who were predisposed to oppose him.

In an entirely different context, George W. Bush learned of the limited effect of public support. Even as the country displayed great solidarity in the face of the terrorist attacks of September 11, 2001, and even when he enjoyed record levels of personal approval, Bush could not win on the issue of keeping airport security guards in the private sector. Nor could he pass his economic stimulus package, a bill to make the 2001 income tax cut permanent, or a host of other core initiatives.

Scholars have raised questions about the actual responsiveness of Congress to the president's public support.[32] At the most, we should expect this responsiveness to be modest. We know, for example, that no matter how low a president's standing with the public or how small the margin of his election, he still receives support from a substantial number of senators and representatives. Similarly, no matter how high his approval levels climb or how large his winning percentage of the vote, a significant portion of the Congress still opposes his policies.

The president's public support must compete for influence with other, more stable factors that affect voting in Congress, including ideology, party, personal views, commitments on specific policies, and constituency interests. Although constituency interests may seem to overlap with presidential approval, they should be viewed as distinct. It is quite possible for constituents to approve of the president but oppose him on particular policies, and it is opinions on these policies that will ring most loudly in congressional ears. Members of Congress are unlikely to vote against the clear interests of their constituents or the firm tenets of their ideology solely in deference to a widely supported chief executive. And, as we have seen, the electoral constituencies of senators and representatives may not reflect general opinion in the nation.

Both Neustadt and Edwards argue that presidential approval (or "prestige") should be viewed as a strategic influence, a factor that may affect the outcome in every case, but that will not necessarily determine the outcome in a specific case.[33] As Neustadt makes clear, public approval is a "factor operating mostly in the background as a conditioner, not the determinant, of what Washingtonians will do about a President's request." It "tends to set a tone and to define the limits of what Washingtonians do for him or do to him." However, "rarely is there any one-to-one relationship between appraisals of his popularity in general and responses to his wishes in particular."[34]

Widespread support should give the president leeway and weaken resistance to his policies. Thus, public support gives a president, at best, leverage, but not control. On the other hand, when the president lacks popular support, this strengthens the resolve of those inclined to oppose him and narrows the range in which he receives the benefit of the doubt. The president's options are reduced, his opportunities diminished, and his room for maneuver checked; he loses crucial "leeway."[35]

Moving the Public on Policy

Presidents typically are as interested in obtaining public support for their policies as they are for themselves. At the base of the strategy of governing by going public is the premise that through the permanent campaign the White House *can* successfully persuade or even mobilize the public. Commentators on the presidency in both the press and the academy often assume that the White House can move public opinion if the president has the skill and will to effectively exploit the "bully pulpit." In Sidney Blumenthal's words, in the permanent campaign "the citizenry is viewed as a mass of fluid voters who can be appeased by appearances, occasional drama, and clever rhetoric."[36] In reality, however, presidents typically fail to move the public.

Ronald Reagan. In contrast to his immediate predecessors, the public viewed Ronald Reagan as a strong leader, and his staff was unsurpassed in its skill at portraying the president and his views in the most positive light. This seeming love affair with the public generated commentary in both academia and the media about the persuasiveness of "The Great Communicator." Reagan's views were notable for their clarity, and there is little doubt that the public knew where the president stood on matters of public policy. The question for us is the degree to which the public moved in Reagan's direction.

In his memoirs, Reagan reflects on his efforts to ignite concern among the American people regarding one of his principal preoccupations: the threat of communism in Central America. At the core of his policy response to this threat was an effort to undermine the "Sandinista" government of Nicaragua through support of the opposition Contras. Reagan required congressional support to obtain aid for the Contras, and he made substantial efforts to mobilize the public behind his program of support for them. Yet he consistently failed—at no time did even a plurality of Americans support the president's policy of aiding the Contras.[37] As he lamented in his memoirs,

> Time and again, I would speak on television, to a joint session of Congress, or to other audiences about the problems in Central America, and I would hope that the outcome would be an outpouring of support from Americans who would apply the same kind of heat on Congress that helped pass the economic recovery package.
>
> But the polls usually found that large numbers of Americans cared little or not at all about what happened in Central America—in fact, a surprisingly large proportion didn't even know where Nicaragua and El Salvador were located—and, among those who did care, too few cared enough about a Communist penetration of the Americas to apply the kind of pressure I needed on Congress.[38]

One of Ronald Reagan's highest priorities was increasing defense spending. Support for increased defense spending was unusually high *before* Reagan took office. The Reagan defense buildup represented an acceleration of change initiated late in the Carter administration. A number of conditions led to broad partisan support of the defense buildup in both the Carter and Reagan administrations, including the massive Soviet increase in their strategic nuclear forces; a series of communist coups in Third World countries, followed by revolutions in Nicaragua and Iran; and the Soviet invasion of Afghanistan. American hostages held in Iran, Soviet troops controlling a small neighbor, and communists in power in the Western hemisphere created powerful scenes on television and implied that American military power had become too weak.

Nevertheless, public support for increased defense expenditures dissipated by 1982 (Table 6.4), only a year after Reagan took office.

Indeed, in his second term, a plurality of the public thought the United States was spending *too much* on defense. Public support for defense expenditures was decidedly *lower* at the end of his administration than when he took office.[39] As a result, Reagan suffered another disappointment, as Congress did not increase defense spending in real dollars during his entire second term.

Ronald Reagan was less a public relations phenomenon than the conventional wisdom indicates. He had the good fortune to take office on the crest of a compatible wave of public opinion, and he effectively exploited the opportunity the voters had handed him. Yet when it came time to change public opinion or mobilize it on his behalf, he typically met with failure. As press secretary Marlin Fitzwater put it, "Reagan would go out on the stump, draw huge throngs and convert no one at all."[40]

Bill Clinton. Bill Clinton's 1992 presidential election campaign kept a clear focus on the economy. On February 15, 1993, the new president addressed the nation on his economic program. Two days later he delivered a much more detailed address to the Congress on his policy plans. His economic proposals included spending for job creation, a tax increase on the wealthy, investment incentives, and aid to displaced workers. In the same month he introduced his first major legislative proposal, a plan to spend more than $16 billion to stimulate the economy. It immediately ran into strong Republican opposition. During the April 1993 congressional recess, Clinton stepped up his rhetoric on his bill, counting on a groundswell of public opinion to pressure moderate Republicans into ending the filibuster on the bill. (Republicans, meanwhile, kept up a steady flow of sound bites linking the president's package with wasteful spending and Clinton's proposed tax increase.) The groundswell never materialized, and the Republicans found little support for any new spending in their home states. Instead, they found their constituents railing

Table 6.4 Public Support for Defense Spending

Date	Decrease	About the Same	Increase
1980	11%	18%	71%
1982	34	33	33
1984	32	32	36
1986	39	29	32
1988	35	32	33

Source: National Election Study question: "Some people believe that we should be spending much less on money for defense. Others feel that spending should be greatly increased. Where would you place yourself on this scale?"
Note: Decrease = 1–3, About the Same = 4, Increase = 5–7 on NES's 7-point scale.

against new taxes and spending.[41] The bill never came to a vote in the Senate.

Public support for the president's economic plan peaked immediately following his speech on February 17 and then dropped dramatically a few days later. During the period when the president needed support the most and when he worked hardest to obtain it, it diminished to the point that by May a plurality of the public *opposed* his plan.[42]

Healthcare reform was to be the centerpiece of the Clinton administration. In September 1993, the president delivered a well-received national address on the need for reform. Yet the president was not able to sustain the support of the public for healthcare reform. The White House held out against compromise with the Republicans and conservative Democrats, hoping for a groundswell of public support for reform. But it never came.[43] In the meantime, opponents of the president's proposal launched an aggressive counterattack, including running negative television advertisements. As the figures in Table 6.5 show, by mid-July 1994, only 40 percent of the public favored the president's healthcare reform proposals, and 56 percent opposed them. The bill did not come to a vote in either chamber of Congress.

Bill Clinton based his strategy of governing on moving the public to support his policy initiatives. Despite his impressive political and communications skills, the evidence is clear that the president typically failed to obtain public support. He did succeed in defending the status quo against radical departures proposed by his Republican opponents, but he could not rally the public behind his own initiatives.

**Table 6.5   Public Support
for Clinton's Healthcare Reform**

Date	Favor	Oppose	Don't Know
09/24–26/1993	59%	33%	8%
10/28–30/1993	45	45	10
11/02–04/1993	52	40	8
11/19–21/1993	52	41	7
01/15–17/1994	56	39	6
01/28–30/1994	57	38	5
02/26–28/1994	46	48	5
03/28–30/1994	44	47	9
05/20–22/1994	46	49	5
06/11–12/1994	42	50	8
06/25–28/1994	44	49	8
07/15–17/1994	40	56	5

Source: Gallup Poll question, "From everything you heard or read about the plan so far . . . do you favor or oppose President Clinton's plan to reform health care?"

George W. Bush. Much to the surprise of many political observers, George W. Bush launched a massive public relations campaign on behalf of his priority initiatives soon after taking office in 2001. At the core of this effort was the most extensive domestic travel schedule of any new president in American history. Bush spoke in 29 states by the end of May, often more than once. The president also used his Saturday radio addresses to exhort members of the public to communicate to Congress their support for his tax cut and education plans.

As we have seen with Bill Clinton and Ronald Reagan, it is one thing to go public. It is something quite different to succeed in moving public opinion. Table 6.6 shows responses to Gallup Poll questions on the president's tax cut proposal, the central domestic and economic program of his administration. The results show that public opinion did not change in response to the president's efforts.

No issue was more important to George W. Bush's presidency than the war with Iraq. The context in which Bush sought this support was certainly favorable. In surveys conducted over the previous 10 years, stretching back to the end of the Gulf War, majorities had generally supported U.S. military action in Iraq to remove Saddam Hussein from power. The American public had long held strongly negative perceptions of Iraq and its leader. In September 2002, Gallup reported that most Americans believed that Iraq had developed or was developing weapons of mass destruction. Many Americans felt that if left alone, Iraq would use those weapons against the United States within five years. Most Americans felt that Saddam Hussein sponsored terrorism that affected the United States. A little more than half of Americans took the additional inferential leap and concluded that Saddam Hussein was personally and directly involved in the September 11, 2001, terrorist attacks.[44]

The war itself was over in a matter of weeks, but the pacification, reconstruction, and democratization of Iraq was to take much longer. The president needed to sustain support for his policy, especially as he sought reelection. Table 6.7 shows public support for the war with Iraq. Public opinion did not change in response to the administration's public relations blitzkrieg. Unfortunately for the president, the

Table 6.6   Public Support for Bush Tax Cut

Date	Favor	Oppose	No Opinion
2/09–11/2001	56%	34%	10%
2/19–21/2001	53	30	17
3/05–07/2001	56	34	10
4/20–22/2001	56	35	9

Source: Gallup Poll, "Based on what you have read or heard, do you favor or oppose the federal income tax cuts George W. Bush has proposed?"

public was less supportive of the war after a year, with a majority concluding the war was not worth fighting.

Going Public in Perspective. Although sometimes they are able to maintain public support for their policies, presidents typically do not succeed in their efforts to change public opinion. Even "great communicators" usually fail to obtain the public's support for their high-priority initiatives. Moreover, the bully pulpit has proven ineffective not only for achieving majority support but also for increasing support from a smaller base.

Presidents not only fail to create new political capital by going public, but their efforts at persuading the public may also *decrease* their chances of success in bringing about changes in public policy. The way presidents attempt to govern has important consequences for public policy. When political leaders take their cases directly to the public, they have to accommodate the limited attention spans of the public and the availability of space on television. As a result, the president and his opponents often reduce choices to stark black-and-white terms. When leaders frame issues in such terms, they typically

Table 6.7 Support for War With Iraq

Date	Worth Going to War	Not Worth Going to War	No Opinion
06/27–29/2003*	56%	42%	2%
07/18–20/2003*	63	35	2
07/25–27/2003*	63	34	3
08/25–26/2003*	63	35	2
09/08–10/2003*	58	40	2
09/19–21/2003*	50	48	2
10/06–08/2003*	55	44	1
10/24–26/2003*	54	44	2
11/03–05/2003*	54	44	2
11/14–16/2003*	56	42	2
12/05–07/2003*	59	39	2
01/09–11/2004	59	38	3
01/29–02/01/2004	49	49	2
03/05–07/2004	55	43	2
03/26–28/2004	56	41	3
04/05–08/2004	50	47	3
05/21–23/2004	45	52	3
06/03–06/2004	46	52	2
06/21–23/2004	46	51	3
07/08–11/2004	47	50	3

Source: Gallup Poll question: "All in all, do you think it was worth going to war in Iraq, or not?"
*"All in all, do you think the situation in Iraq was worth going to war over, or not?"

frustrate rather than facilitate building coalitions. Such positions are difficult to compromise, which hardens negotiating positions as both sides posture as much to mobilize an intense minority of supporters as to persuade the other side. *The permanent campaign is antithetical to governing.*

Traditionally, presidents attempted to build coalitions in Congress through bargaining. The core strategy was to providing benefits for both sides, allowing many to share in a coalition's success and to declare victory. Going public is fundamentally different. The core strategy is to *defeat the opposition,* creating winners and losers in a zero-sum game. In going public, the president tries to intimidate opponents by increasing the political costs of opposition rather than attracting them with benefits. If going public is not a successful strategy and actually makes coalition building more difficult, polarization, gridlock, and public cynicism, which characterize American politics today, are the likely results.

Obstacles to Leading the Public

The president's efforts to lead the public do not occur in a vacuum. Instead, the White House faces a number of obstacles to obtaining public support, including focusing the public's attention, framing issues to its advantage, obtaining an audience for the president's messages, and overcoming the public's predispositions.[45]

Focusing the Public's Attention. The first step in the president's efforts to lead the public is focusing its attention. People who are not attentive to the issues on which the president wishes to lead are unlikely to be influenced in their views on those issues. If the president's messages are to meet his coalition-building needs, the public must sort through the profusion of communications in its environment, overcome its limited interest in government and politics, and concentrate on the president's priority concerns. It is no exaggeration to conclude that focusing the public's attention is usually a substantial challenge.

There is little the White House can do to limit the overall volume of messages that citizens encounter or to make the public more attentive to politics. What it can do—in theory—is to repeat its own messages to the public so that they will break through the public's lack of interest in politics and the countless distractions from it. In addition, the White House could sustain its flow of messages for the many months of the legislative cycle and concentrate its communications on the president's priorities.

What actually occurs is quite different. Despite an enormous total volume of presidential public remarks, these statements are dispersed over a broad range of policies and wide audiences hear only a small portion of the president's remarks. The president rarely focuses a televised address on an issue before Congress and actually makes few statements on even significant legislation. In addition, the president faces strong competition for the public's attention from previous commitments of government, congressional initiatives, opposing elites, and the mass media. Even more importantly, the president often provides competition for himself as he addresses other issues, some on his own agenda and others that are forced upon him.

Framing the Message. Presidents make a substantial effort to frame issues in ways that will favor their preferred policy options and to place their own performance in a favorable light. If they succeed in setting the terms of debate on policies and on themselves, they will prime the public to view them as consistent with its core values.

There are substantial obstacles to structuring choices for the American people, however. The White House faces a great deal of competition from the opposition in its efforts to frame issues. In addition, many people are either unaware of the president's messages or too committed to a different view for the president to persuade them to support his views. Some people will listen but misperceive the president's point. The wide range of issues on which the president attempts to lead, the transience of opinion change, and the potential for overuse and heavy-handedness further complicate the president's efforts.

Perhaps no obstacle to setting the terms of debate is greater than the president's dependence on the mass media to transmit his messages. The media is unlikely to adopt consistently the White House's framing of issues. Instead, it makes independent judgments about which issues to highlight and how to frame them for its viewers and readers. Brief, superficial, negative, and interpretive press coverage of the president often leaves the public ill-informed about matters with which the president must deal. In addition, the press often primes criteria for evaluating the president and his policies that do not reflect positively on the White House.

The president, then, cannot depend on structuring the choices about himself or his policies for the public. Persuading the public to think about his policies and his performance in his terms is difficult to do. One can sympathize with Bill Clinton when he declared that "Americans don't want me to help them understand. They just want me to do something about it."[46]

Receiving the Message. If the president is going to lead the public successfully, it must *receive* his message. The nationally televised address offers the president the best opportunity to reach the largest audience of his fellow citizens in an unmediated fashion and in the context of the dignified surroundings of the Oval Office or a joint session of Congress.

However, the White House finds it increasingly difficult to obtain an audience for its views. Audiences for the president have been steadily declining. The options offered by cable television seem to be diverting public attention. No matter what the subject of his speech or press conference, the president can no longer depend on reaching even a bare majority of the public. The fact that those he needs to reach the most, people predisposed to oppose him, are not especially likely to tune him out is small solace for the loss of the bulk of the television audience.

For the president to influence public opinion, members of the public must not only receive his message but understand it as well. Those who are unaware of a message are unlikely to know the president's positions. Even those who pay attention may miss the president's points, and substantial percentages of the public do just that. In addition, individuals' predispositions affect how they process the president's arguments. Thus, only a small portion of the public is generally open to changing its opinions in response to the president.

Compounding the White House's problem, the networks are increasingly likely to refuse airtime to the president. Whereas once the networks automatically broadcast live primetime presidential policy speeches and press conferences, such events have become relatively rare. Aside from the State of the Union messages and statements regarding scandals or military actions, the president is not likely to speak directly to the American people. More than ever, the White House is dependent on the press to deliver its message.

Accepting the Message. The final link in the chain of communications from the president to the public is a weak one. The president must overcome the predispositions of his audience if he is to change their minds about his policies or his performance. This is very difficult to do. Most people ignore or reject arguments contrary to their predispositions. Nor can the president depend on those predisposed toward him to be especially responsive or to resist national trends opposed to his positions.

Conclusion

Building coalitions for governing among the public and within Congress poses a considerable challenge for the president. The very nature of public opinion and the institutional structure of the presidency (and Congress) pose an imposing set of impediments to presidential leadership. The reality of the president's predicament is that no matter how skilled the White House may be, the president is unlikely to be consistently successful in leading either the public or Congress. Only the presence of contextual conditions that encourage deference to the president, such as occurred in Franklin D. Roosevelt's first term, are likely to provide the president the opportunity to dominate the policymaking process.

I have approached the issue of impediments to presidential leadership from the perspective of the president. Thus, I have focused on how well the president can make the system work in response to his demands rather than the contribution the president makes to the functioning of the system. Some, following David Mayhew,[47] may conclude that the system works well enough and produces significant legislative change, even under divided government. (Such a conclusion, of course, begs the question of whether such changes meet our needs.) Charles O. Jones prefers "balanced participation" and does not feel that we will be better off with simplifying the system to encourage presidency-centered leadership.[48] Indeed, he warns against an excess of presidential power, such as he finds in the early Johnson and Reagan administrations when dominant presidents obtained sweeping changes that, he feels, were not necessarily wise. Moreover, the separated system may help avoid stalemate by giving the other branch the option of taking the lead on policy change.

On the other hand, those who believe that there is a pressing need for significant legislation at the national level are likely to be more concerned. Advocates of change might point out that both conservatives and liberals seek major changes in policy, and they typically want the president to take the lead in bringing about this change. If the president is pivotal to achieving the goals of those on both ends of the political spectrum, the ability of the White House to build coalitions is a prime concern as we evaluate our political system.

Notes

1. George C. Edwards III and Andrew Barrett, "Presidential Agenda Setting in Congress," in Jon R. Bond and Richard Fleisher (Eds.), *Polarized Politics* (Washington, DC: CQ Press, 2000), p. 128.

2. See Sarah A. Binder, "The Dynamics of Legislative Gridlock, 1947–96," *American Political Science Review* 93 (September 1999):519–533.

3. David W. Rohde, *Parties and Reform in the Postreform House* (Chicago: University of Chicago Press, 1991); John H. Aldrich and David W. Rohde, "The Consequences of Party Organization in the House: The Role of the Majority and Minority Parties in Conditional Party Government," in *Polarized Politics*.

4. Richard Fleisher and Jon R. Bond, "Partisanship and the President's Quest for Votes on the Floor of Congress," in *Polarized Politics*. See also Sarah A. Binder, *Stalemate* (Washington, DC: Brookings, 2003); and Gary C. Jacobson, "Partisan Polarization in Presidential Support: The Electoral Connection," *Congress and the Presidency* 30 (Spring 2003):1–36.

5. George C. Edwards III, *At the Margins: Presidential Leadership of Congress* (New Haven, CT: Yale University Press, 1989); Jon R. Bond and

Richard Fleisher, *The President in the Legislative Arena* (Chicago: University of Chicago Press, 1990).

6. Edwards, *At the Margins,* chapter 9; Bond and Fleisher, *President in the Legislative Arena,* chapter 8.

7. George C. Edwards III and Andrew Barrett, "Presidential Agenda Setting in Congress," in *Polarized Politics.*

8. George C. Edwards III, Andrew Barrett, and Jeffrey Peake, "The Legislative Impact of Divided Government," *American Journal of Political Science* 41 (April 1997):545–563; Binder, "The Dynamics of Legislative Gridlock, 1947–96."

9. George C. Edwards III, *The Public Presidency* (New York: St. Martin's, 1983), 83–93; Gregory N. Flemming, "Presidential Coattails in Open-Seat Elections," *Legislative Studies Quarterly* 20 (May 1995):197–212.

10. Alan I. Abramowitz and Jeffrey A. Segal, *Senate Elections* (Ann Arbor: University of Michigan Press, 1992), pp. 121, 233, 238; Lonna Rae Atkeson and Randall W. Partin, "Economic and Referendum Voting: A Comparison of Gubernatorial and Senatorial Elections," *American Political Science Review* 89 (March 1995):99–107; James E. Campbell and Joe A. Sumners, "Presidential Coattails in Senate Elections," *American Political Science Review* 84 (June 1990):513–524.

11. See Jeffrey E. Cohen, Michael A. Krassa, and John A. Hamman, "The Impact of Presidential Campaigning on Midterm U.S. Senate Elections," *American Political Science Review* 85 (March 1991):165–180.

12. Gary C. Jacobson, "Terror, Terrain, and Turnout: Explaining the 2002 Midterm Elections," *Political Science Quarterly* 118 (Spring 2003):1–22.

13. On the increasing importance of party leadership in the House, see Rohde, *Parties and Leaders in the Postreform House;* Barbara Sinclair, "The Emergence of Strong Leadership in the 1980s House of Representatives," *Journal of Politics* 54 (August 1992):657–684; and Gary W. Cox and Matthew D. McCubbins, *Legislative Leviathan* (Berkley: University of California Press, 1993).

14. Leon D. Epstein, *Political Parties in Western Democracies* (New York: Praeger, 1967).

15. Edwards, *At the Margins;* Bond and Fleisher, *President in the Legislative Arena.*

16. Kenneth E. Collier, *Between the Branches* (Pittsburgh, PA: University of Pittsburgh Press, 1997); Abraham Holtzman, *Legislative Liaison* (Chicago: Rand-McNally, 1970); Charles O. Jones, *The Trusteeship Presidency* (Baton Rouge: Louisiana State University Press, 1988); Stephen J. Wayne, *The Legislative Presidency* (New York: Harper & Row, 1978).

17. Edwards, *At the Margins;* Bond and Fleisher, *President in the Legislative Arena.*

18. See, for example, Kernell, *Going Public.*

19. Charles O. Jones, *Clinton and Congress, 1993–1996* (Norman: University of Oklahoma Press, 1999), pp. 90–91.

20. News release, CBS News/*New York Times* poll, October 30, 1986, tables 21, 27.

21. Glenn R. Parker, "Cycles in Congressional District Attention," *Journal of Politics* 42 (May 1980):547.

22. Walter D. Burnham, "Insulation and Responsiveness in Congressional Elections," *Political Science Quarterly* 90 (Fall 1975):418; "1974 Support in Congress: Ford Low, Nixon Up," *Congressional Quarterly Weekly Report,* January 18, 1975, p. 148.

23. John R. Alford and John R. Hibbing, "The Conditions Required for Economic Issue Voting: Actions Speak More Loudly Than Partisan Affiliation," paper presented at the annual meeting of the Midwest Political Science Association, Chicago, April 1984.

24. Gary C. Jacobson, "The 1994 Midterm: Why the Models Missed It," *Extension of Remarks,* APSA Legislative Studies Section, 1994; David W. Brady, John F. Cogan, and Douglas Rivers, *How Republicans Captured the House: An Assessment of the 1994 Midterm Elections* (Stanford, CA: Hoover Institution, 1995).

25. Abramowitz and Segal, *Senate Elections,* pp. 121, 233, 238; Atkeson and Partin, "Economic and Referendum Voting."

26. Kernell, *Going Public,* pp. 144–154.

27. Richard Neustadt, *Presidential Power and the Modern Presidents* (New York: Free Press, 1990), p. 264.

28. Quoted in Dom Bonafede, "The Strained Relationship," *National Journal,* May 19, 1979, p. 830.

29. Nigel Bowles, *The White House and Capitol Hill* (New York: Oxford University Press, 1987), pp. 99, 102, 104.

30. See George C. Edwards III, "Aligning Tests with Theory: Presidential Approval as a Source of Influence in Congress," *Congress and the Presidency* 24 (Fall 1997), pp. 123–124 and sources cited therein.

31. Martin P. Wattenberg, "The Democrats' Decline in the House During the Clinton Presidency: An Analysis of Partisan Swings," *Presidential Studies Quarterly* 29 (September 1999):685–689.

32. See, for example, Edwards, *At the Margins,* chapter 6; Bond and Fleisher, *President in the Legislative Arena,* chapter 7.

33. Neustadt, *Presidential Power,* p. 78; Edwards, *At the Margins,* pp. 109–114.

34. Neustadt, *Presidential Power,* p. 74.

35. Neustadt, *Presidential Power,* pp. 75, 77.

36. Sidney Blumenthal, *The Permanent Campaign,* rev. ed. (New York: Simon & Schuster, 1982), p. 24. See also pp. 297–298.

37. See George C. Edwards III, *On Deaf Ears: The Limits of the Bully Pulpit* (New Haven, CT: Yale University Press, 2003), pp. 51–54.

38. Reagan, *An American Life,* p. 479.

39. This may have been the result of the military buildup that did occur, but the point remains that while Reagan wanted to continue to increase defense spending, the public was unresponsive to his wishes.

40. Quoted in R. W. Apple, "Bush Sure-Footed on Trail of Money," *New York Times,* September 29, 1990, p. 8.

41. "Democrats Look to Salvage Part of Stimulus Plan," *Congressional Quarterly Weekly Report,* April 24, 1993, pp. 1002–1003.

42. Edwards, *On Deaf Ears,* pp. 35–36.

43. "Health Care Reform: The Lost Chance," *Newsweek,* September 19, 1994, p. 32.

44. Frank Newport, "Public Wants Congressional and U.N. Approval before Iraq Action," Gallup Poll News Release, September 6, 2002.

45. For a more thorough discussion of the obstacles to leading the public, see Edwards, *On Deaf Ears,* chapters 6–9.

46. Quoted in Bob Woodward, *The Choice* (New York: Simon and Schuster, 1996), p. 315.

47. David R. Mayhew, *Divided We Govern* (New Haven: Yale University Press, 1991).

48. Charles O. Jones, *The Presidency in a Separated System* (Washington, DC: Brookings Institution, 1994), chapter 8. ✦

Chapter 7

Presidential Leadership in an Age of New Media

Jeffrey E. Cohen

In the last chapter, George Edwards argued that "going public" and the permanent campaign have not proven to be effective strategies for influencing the U.S. Congress. Edwards's main focus was on the relationship between the president and the public. An important intermediary between these two actors is the media. It is the media that translates the president's message, reports on the president's activities, and informs (or in some cases misinforms) the public. In this chapter, Jeffrey Cohen examines how the media's relationship with the public has been utterly transformed over the past half century and the implications of this transformation for how the public perceives and evaluates presidents. In so doing, Cohen raises questions about the utility of the strategy of "going public."

In describing this chapter, Cohen writes,

> Despite a barrage of bad news in 1998, Bill Clinton still enjoyed strong and rising popularity with the public. Many have sought to explain this paradox. My intention is to describe the new news environment that began to emerge in the late 1970s and early 1980s. Four trends describe the news environment of the new media age. One, the news media have become increasingly competitive and decentralized. Two, reporting styles have changed. News is now softer and increasingly negative. Three, the public now consumes less news from traditional outlets than it once did. Four, public regard toward the news media has declined. To a degree, this news environment insulates the president from news, which helps explain Clinton's popularity rise in 1998 despite bad news. But this news environment also impedes the president's ability to lead the mass public. As a result, the president's governing style has changed. Instead of focusing their efforts on leading the nation, presidents spend more time targeting select constituencies. This narrow "going public" style reinforces the polarization in the political system, while also alienating the broad middle from American politics.

✦ ✦ ✦

I want to thank Tom Patterson and Lyn Ragsdale for allowing me to use data that they have collected. This paper would not be possible without access to that data.

Political leadership is a complex and often elusive topic and concept. Its complexity derives in part from the several and varied
meanings or definitions of leadership. Sometimes leadership is defined in positional terms. Thus, a person is considered a leader if that
person occupies a position of leadership. A leadership position often
entails sitting in a relatively high position of authority within an organization, where the leader can command or direct subordinates.
From a second perspective, leadership is defined as a personality attribute, that a person possesses the personal character and quality of
a leader. Hence, the colloquial saying that someone is "a born leader."
But leadership is also sometimes defined more actively, that is, one
engages in acts of leadership. Active leadership, as commonly used,
usually implies that a leader influences others, using Dahl's (1957)
definition of influence—influence occurs when a person gets another
person to do something that he or she would otherwise not do.

To a degree, common usage of the term *presidential leadership* en-
velops all three definitions. In this essay, I will use presidential leadership from the third perspective, that of actively trying to influence
others. The "others" that I will focus on are the mass public. Leadership as *active influence* is appropriate and useful when trying to understand the nature of presidential leadership of the mass public. The
president's ability to lead the public has evolved over the years, that
is, his degree of influence over the way that the mass public thinks
about politics and public policies has changed. The conventional
story about presidential leadership and influence over the mass public tends to emphasize an increasing ability to influence the mass
public. This account emphasizes the resources and organizational
skills that the presidency has acquired and developed over the past
century or so.

However, as I will argue in this chapter, the story of presidential
leadership of the mass public is not so simple. The ability of the president to influence the mass public depends only in part on the resources and skills that the president commands. It also depends on
the nature of the major institution through which the president tries
to influence the mass public, the news media. As the news media
changes, so does the ability of the president to influence the mass
public. Over the past quarter century or so, the news media has
evolved into what we now call the "new media age" (Davis and Owen
1998; Baum 2003; Hamilton 2003). This new media age ironically
both reduces the ability of the president to lead or influence the mass
public, but at the same time renders the news media less capable to
harm the presidency.

This understanding of presidential leadership has important theoretical implications. It leads us away from the positional understanding of presidential leadership. Surely presidents are leaders because
of the position that they hold. But in comparing presidential leader-

ship of the mass public over time, position is held constant.[1] Similarly, this understanding of leadership moves away from the personal definition of leadership, although it allows some room for variance in the individual ability of presidents to lead. And as to leadership as actively trying to influence, the perspective used here emphasizes the importance of structures in affecting the president's ability to lead.

Here I am most interested in the structure of relationships among the president, the news media, and the mass public, what I will call the *presidential news system*. As I will hope to show, changes in the presidential news system over the past quarter century or so affect presidential leadership and influence. Changes in structures often affect the president's ability to lead.

In the next section, I present a puzzle—presidential news has grown increasingly negative and critical, yet presidential polls do not seem to suffer much. Why? To answer this puzzle requires understanding how the presidential news system has changed in recent decades. These changes have lessened the president's ability to lead the public. As an actor bent on policy leadership, presidents have adapted with a new style of "going public" (Kernell 1993) leadership that increases the attention that presidents pay to friends and select publics, while deemphasizing the amount of attention that the president pays to a singular, national mass public.

A Puzzle: If the News Is So Bad, Why Are Presidential Polls So High?

By almost any standard, 1998 was a horrible year for any president. Bill Clinton's affair with Monica Lewinsky became public, leading to his impeachment. The Republican-controlled Congress heartily attacked him, and the news media, never easy on the administration (Kurtz 1998), escalated the degree to which it challenged and criticized the president.

Figure 7.1 traces the percentage of news stories about the president and the administration from 1981 that were coded as clearly negative or more negative than positive.[2] As the figure demonstrates, 1998 stood out in the degree of negative news reports. Only 1987, the year of the Iran-Contra scandal, produced a higher percentage of negative news stories on the president. But we should not overly interpret the 1987 figure because of the modest number of stories coded that year (25). Even 1994, the year of Clinton's ill-fated health care initiative, itself a bad press year for Clinton at 58 percent, is still less negative than 1998 by nearly 10 percent. Not surprisingly, nearly 22 percent of all news stories in 1998 about the president and administration focused on the scandal, and nearly all of those stories were negative. Without the scandal stories, only 47 percent of the news sto-

Figure 7.1   Percentage of Negative News About the President

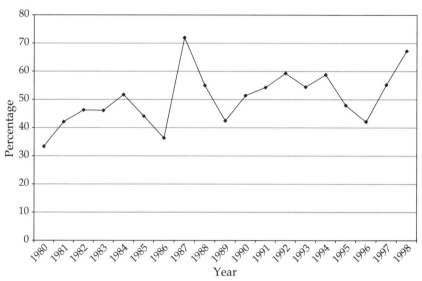

Source: Patterson (2000) Lexis-Nexis sample of news stories.

ries about Clinton would have been negative, which is similar to the amount of negative news that he received in any given year.

What is so remarkable about these figures is not that Clinton received so much bad press given the scandal and impeachment, but that his job approval polls rose that year.[3] Clinton received a 56 percent approval rating in the last Gallup poll of 1997. By the end of July 1998, his job approval rating had risen to 65 percent, the vicinity at which it remained throughout the remainder of the year. It spiked upward in very late 1998 and early 1999, reaching a peak of 73 percent in Gallup's poll of December 19–20, 1998.

That Clinton's polls did not plummet in the face of such bad press challenges many widely held assumptions about the role of news in shaping opinions. Brody's (1991) seminal book argues that the balance of positive and negative news about the president will affect public attitudes towards the president. When the news leans in a negative direction, presidential approval should drop. Erikson, MacKuen, and Stimson (EMS) (2002) follow up on Brody's approach in a time series analysis that covers the period 1975–1994. The Brody-EMS approach suggests that Clinton's approval should have declined in 1998, yet it rose! Our existing theories and understandings of the relationship among the news, the presidency, and public opinion cannot explain why Bill Clinton's approval rose in 1998.

Nor can they explain the general decoupling of news from presidential approval. Figure 7.2 plots data on the annual tone of presidential news and Gallup approval from 1949 through 1992 (Ragsdale 1997). Visual inspection of the two series reveal that they tended to diverge for the first half of the series, but some time in the mid- to late 1970s, negative news and approval began to track together.

The presidential news system, the interrelationships among the president, the news media, and the public, had undergone a major transformation over the past 20–25 years. Studies of the new media age are increasingly common (Davis and Owen 1998; Baum 2003) and often focus on the impact of changes in communications technologies, but these studies rarely relate such changes to the political system, instead focusing more narrowly on the impact of changes in communication technology on public opinion.

Here I identify four interrelated changes that have implications for the role of news in politics, opportunities for presidential leadership, and public opinion. These four changes are (1) the structure of the news industry, (2) the style of news reporting, (3) the audience for news, and (4) public regard towards the news media.

In the next section, I briefly describe the presidential news system during television's golden age (Baum and Kernell 1999; Cook and Ragsdale 1998) of the 1960s and early 1970s. Then I trace the four trends. The news environment that the president now faces is very different from what it was 20–25 years ago. A smaller news audience

**Figure 7.2 Trends in Presidential Approval
and News Tone, 1949–1992**

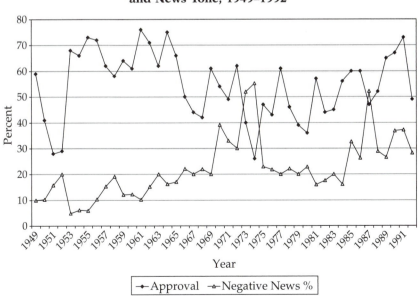

Source: Lyn Ragsdale data supplied to author. News tone data from the *New York Times*, approval data from Gallup.

that views the news media more cynically helps blunt the impact of the news on the president. Thus, negative news may do less harm to presidents than it did 25 years ago. But a smaller audience also lessens the president's ability to mobilize the mass public. As a consequence, presidents now build support not so much by rallying the mass public, but by selectively mobilizing segments of the public, usually special and often attentive publics. This reinforces the tendency toward polarization politics and public disenchantment in recent American politics. In the conclusion I return to the case of Clinton, the press, and public approval in 1998, illustrating how this new understanding helps us make a sense of what otherwise looks like a puzzle.

The Presidential News System in the Golden Age of Television

Baum and Kernell (1999) colorfully call the period of the late 1950s through 1970s the "golden age of presidential television." In that era, the president enjoyed a number of major advantages, but that system also posed grave threats to presidential leadership. During this period, the public received the bulk of its news from the three nightly news broadcasts. The news audience, for several reasons, was also relatively large (Baum and Kernell 1999). Through television, presidents had easy access to the mass public, a major advantage for presidents bent on leading the public.

News content during this era also advantaged the president. The president was perhaps the dominant news story, crowding rivals and other political leaders off of the news hole (Gilbert 1981, 1989). Additionally, news was reported objectively, which advantaged the president in that most news about the president portrayed him in a positive light (Grossman and Kumar 1981). While the seeds of interpretive and cynical news reporting were sown during this era, such a style was not yet the norm.

Still, this news system could pose a danger to a president if it turned against him, as it occasionally did. Two administrations, Johnson's and Nixon's, were cut short in part because the press turned against the presidents.

The Public and Television News

In the 1950s, television emerged as the most popular entertainment and news medium for American citizens. For instance, using American National Election Study (ANES) data, in 1952, 79 percent of respondents claimed to have read something about the presidential campaign in newspapers, whereas only 51 percent said that they watched a television program about the campaign.[4] By 1956 the pattern had shifted. Newspaper reading declined to 68 percent, while TV watching rose to 73 percent.

Moreover, the percentage of people who only relied on TV for news increased from about 8 percent in 1952 to 18 percent in 1956, ranging between 14 and 19 percent through 1968. From one-sixth to one-fifth of the public claimed that television was its sole source of news. At the same time, the percentage of the public that only used newspapers dwindled precipitously from over 35 percent in 1952 to 12 percent four years later. Thereafter it never rose above 10 percent. The public basically had bifurcated into two segments by the late 1950s, those who only watched TV for news about the campaign and those who used both TV and newspapers.

Presidents and Reporters in the Golden Age

It was not until John F. Kennedy became president in 1961, however, that the presidency understood and attempted to harness the power and reach of television. Truman and Eisenhower focused the bulk of their attention on print journalists and broadcast journalists were decidedly second-class citizens among reporters. The status differences between print and broadcast reporters narrowed, in part due to the behavior of President Kennedy. Kennedy viewed the new television medium as one to exploit rather than as one to fear. It offered him access to the mass public unlike any previous communications medium. He innovated in its use, appealing to the public directly, over the heads of the news media.

Unlike his predecessors, Kennedy offered live press conferences in primetime. Kennedy's televised press conferences altered the press-public connection. If people could watch a press conference, they no longer needed the newspaper story to fill them in on what transpired. From this experience, the Kennedy and subsequent White Houses began to favor the electronic over the print media, figuring that it could transmit its message directly to the public (Maltese 1992). They also figured that the television would be satisfied with film showing the president and in this way would become relatively passive transmitters of presidentially manufactured news to the public.

News Reporting Styles in the Golden Age

During this golden age, the president became perhaps the dominant focus of news attention. News tended to be reported objectively, although early signs of a new interpretive news style were emerging. The news also tended to portray the president in a positive light. The combination of these news reporting attributes conferred advantages on the president, enhancing his ability to lead.

Baumgartner and Jones (1993) randomly sampled news stories from the index of the *New York Times* from 1946 into the mid-1990s.

They identify from the index description whether the president was an actor in the story, as well as other actors (Congress, the Supreme Court, etc.). Figure 7.3 traces two trends lines using these data: presidential mentions as a percentage of all news stories and presidential mentions as a percentage of news stories about government.

Both trend lines display an unmistakable and similar pattern, a growth of presidential news from the 1940s into the 1970s. The two are highly correlated in spite of their differing bases (Pearson's r = .87, p = .000). From 1946 to 1959, presidents received on average about 5 percent of all news and 12 percent of government/policy news. These figures jumped to 8 and 17 percent, growth rates of 60 and 42 percent. The growth in presidential news continued in the 1970s, with the president receiving 11 percent of all news and 23 percent of governmental/policy news during that decade.

News reports on the president also tended to be objective and positive rather than negative. The best data on this attribute of presidential news comes from Grossman and Kumar (1981). They ambitiously content-analyzed news stories about the president from three news sources: *Time* magazine, the *New York Times,* and CBS News. For *Time* and the *Times,* the data spanned from 1953 through August 1978. The CBS data begin with August 1968, when the Vanderbilt Television Archives began collecting tapes of the broadcasts (254).

They find that all three news organizations reported on the president more favorably than unfavorably. Approximately 60 percent of

Figure 7.3 Presidential News Volume, *New York Times*, 1946–1994

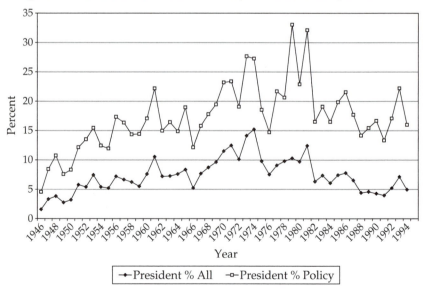

Source: Baumgartner and Jones (1993).

Time's stories were favorable, with about 11.8 percent neutral and 28.2 percent negative. The *New York Times's* breakdown resembles *Time's*. CBS, which spans a shorter time frame, displays a balance between positive (38.5 percent) and negative (38.6 percent) news, with 22.9 percent neutral.

The greater representation of the Watergate years in CBS's totals accounts for the difference between CBS and the other media. From 1953 to 1965, both *Time* and the *Times* gave the president a ratio of favorable to unfavorable news of approximately 5 to 1. From 1966–1974, news from both was more negative than positive, as was the case for CBS. In the post-Watergate years, 1975–1978, news for all three news organizations shifted, such that positive news again outweighed negative news, often by hefty margins. Thus, other than when extraordinary events led the press to view the president in a negative light, presidents during the golden age could count on favorable news.

All this would begin changing in the late 1970s. The news media decentralized. Competition and other forces led to a new style of news reporting that was more interpretive and negative than the style of the golden age. The audience for news also shrank, and people, perhaps because of the new style of news, became less positive in its own attitudes towards the news media (Patterson 2000). Together, these trends blunted the impact of the news on public attitudes toward the president. They also lessened the ability of the president to lead the public.

The Presidential News System in the New Media Age

The presidential news system in the new media age is characterized by competition among the news media, the rise of soft news, negativity in hard news, a shrinking news audience, and declining public regard for the news media. Such a news system ironically limits the damage that the news media can do to a president. It also limits the president's ability to lead the public, which forces changes in presidential "going public" behavior.

The Decline of Network Monopoly and the Rise of Competition

In the golden age, three national networks and a handful of other national news organizations dominated the production, definition, and dissemination of the news. All news outlets offered essentially the same basic portrait of the president, except that television could not portray the president in as much depth as the print media. Technological and economic forces came together in the late 1970s and 1980s to crack the control that these elite news organizations had over the news (Hamilton 2003). By the 1990s, the news production system had decentralized and splintered. Many news organizations competed for a shrinking news audience: to create a market niche, news programs and producers tried to differentiate themselves from their competitors by presenting distinctive voices and perspectives to the news.[5]

Cable television, the Internet, new printing technologies, hand-held cameras, and satellite systems all worked together to break the monopoly of the elite press of the golden age. Yet cable television had the greatest impact. It spawned dedicated news networks, like CNN, Fox News, and MSNBC, offering news around the clock. No longer did news-hungry viewers have to wait until the nightly broadcast to learn of events. Each cable network also tried to differentiate itself. CNN prided itself on international coverage. Fox News offers viewers news with a conservative tilt. Cable had another, perhaps more profound effect. Cable programming offered viewers a choice beside what the three major networks offered. By and large, the news-consuming public of the golden age had little programming choice. In the early evening, all three networks broadcast their national nightly news programs, sandwiched between local news broadcasts. If one was to watch television during these hours, one had to tune into a news program. The structure of television during the golden age effectively captured the public. People without an interest in news had little choice but to watch such programs, unless they decided to turn off the television.

With cable, people's tastes were better served. Reluctant news viewers had a myriad of entertainment offerings to watch in lieu of the network nightly news (and network entertainment fare). Across the board, the ratings of network programs, news and entertainment alike, eroded.

Less traditional news providers are also springing up on the Internet, challenging the dominance of the traditional media, in the process redefining news and affecting public regard for news organizations. The prime example of this phenomenon is Matt Drudge, who came to national prominence in late 1997, when he published on his web page the allegations that President Clinton was having an affair with Monica Lewinsky. *Newsweek* also had the story, but refused to publish because it could not be confirmed by a second source. Drudge turned the hand of the traditional news media, much as print tabloids had been doing for the past 10–15 years, forcing the news media en masse to cover the scandal.

The Rise of Negative News and the Decline of Political News

The decentralization of the news media and the ability of almost anyone to become a "journalist" and publish a web page (e.g., Matt

Drudge) threatened the traditional norms of news publishing, such as source protection and confirmation of information, norms that had evolved over the course of the twentieth century. Whereas news in the golden age was primarily objective and positive toward the president, news in the new media age became softer and more sensational (Patterson 2000; Sabato 1991). The boundary between entertainment and news blurred and journalist voices began to appear in the news in greater quantity than the voices of politicians.

Many commentators have noted the decline of traditional hard news, such as reporting on government and public policy, and the rise of crime stories, entertainment, and celebrity profiles (Patterson 2000; Hess 2000). The Project for Excellence in Journalism conducted a study that content-analyzed the news of seven major media outlets (the three networks, *Time*, *Newsweek*, the *New York Times*, and the *Los Angeles Times*) from 1977 to 1997. The Project's data give us a snapshot of change across the two decades, as they only code three time periods (1977, 1987, 1997). Still, their data reveal a dramatic decline in traditional news across almost all media.

In citing the Project's data, I categorized, as the Project did, traditional hard news as concerning government, military, domestic, and foreign policy. Their other subject categories include entertainment/celebrities, lifestyle, celebrity crime, personal health, other crime, business and commerce, science, technology, arts, religion, sports, weather and disasters, science fiction, and the supernatural. The Project coded entire network broadcasts, the front pages of the newspapers, and cover stories of the news weeklies.[6]

Only the major newspapers resisted the trend of replacing government- and policy-related news with other types of content. The decline among the three networks is striking, from about two-thirds or more of broadcast new stories dealing with government and policy in 1977 to about 40 percent in 1997. Similarly, the weekly newsmagazines, *Time* and *Newsweek*, which in the 1970s ran government- and policy-related figures and stories on about half of their covers, ran such stories on their covers about 20–25 percent of the time in 1997, a reduction rate of approximately 50 percent. The *Los Angeles Times* also displayed a minor drop in government and policy news, yet the bulk of the *Los Angeles Times*'s front page in the 1990s was still given to hard news. Only the *New York Times* clearly resisted the trend of declining news coverage on its front page.

Perhaps the most important point from these data is that from several different vantage points, coverage of traditional government and policy news has declined across a variety of news media. Moreover, there exists a severe decline in government and policy news in American's most relied upon news source, the network nightly news.

At the same time that the volume of governmental news, much of it about the presidency, has been ebbing, the lion's share of presidential news is no longer positive (Groeling and Kernell 1998). Again, the Project for Excellence provides some useful data. They compared nightly network news coverage of Presidents Bill Clinton and George W. Bush during their first 100 days.[7] In his first 100 days, Bill Clinton received positive coverage 22 percent of the time, negative news 28 percent, and neutral coverage 49 percent. George W. Bush received positive news 27 percent of the time, negative news 28 percent, and neutral news 44 percent. While not extraordinarily negative, that the figures are not lopsidedly positive is notable given that this is the traditional honeymoon period. If the honeymoon represents a period when presidents can expect their best overall news coverage, these figures do not bode well for the rest of the administrations' time in office.

These numbers differ markedly from those reported above that Grossman and Kumar collected for the 1953 to 1977 period, and they differ dramatically from the high degree of positive news that presidents received on average in the 1950s and early 1960s. Lyn Ragsdale has taken Grossman and Kumar's *New York Times* data and extended the series forward to 1949 and through 1992. Again, negative news on the president clearly trends upwards over this period.[8]

The Declining Audience for News

At the same time that the amount of political and presidential news declined and negative news rose, the news audience was shrinking. Commentators offer several explanations for the declining size of the news audience. Patterson (2000) attributes the decline to changing reporting styles. The rise of sensationalistic and soft news, according to Patterson, alienated some of the news audience. Baum and Kernell (1999) point to the effects of changes in the structure of the mass media. The arrival of cable television offered viewing choices besides the network nightly news. Indications are that large numbers of viewers left the networks for cable offerings, as well as other media, such as VCRs and the Internet.

All news media show declines in average usage from the 1980s to the 1990s. In the late 1980s and early 1990s, people on average watched the nightly network news broadcast from 4.6 to 5 days a week. Their news viewing dropped to less than 4 days a week from 1996 through 2000. On average, people now claim to watch the nightly network news about one day a week less than they did a decade ago. Coupling this decline with the decline in hard news content may lead to the conclusion that the public overall, which relies mainly on these broadcasts for news, is much less informed than it was two decades or more ago.

Newspaper consumption has also declined, although not as steeply. On average, people read a daily newspaper nearly 4 days a week from

1984 through 1994. From 1996 through 2000, they decreased their newspaper reading about one-half a day per week, to about 3.5 days per week, or about every other day, although we can not say whether the mix of stories that they read during the time frame changed or not.

The number of people who are heavy media users, that is, those whose combined use of television news and newspapers totals at least 11 days, declined as a percentage of the population from about 35–40 percent in the 1980s and early 1990s to 20–25 percent in the late 1990s (1996–2000). At the same time, light media users, those whose combined consumption totals no more than 4 days a week, increased as a percentage of the population from 15–20 percent across the 1980s and early 1990s to 30–35 percent in the second half of the 1990s.

Overall, these data indicate a shrinking audience for news for both major media. Moreover, not only is there a long-term deterioration in news consumption that began for newspapers in the 1960s and television in the 1970s, but a steeper decline that began sometime in the mid-1990s. The 1990s decline appears not to be just a short-term trough, but a step-like drop that is continuing.

When the decline in news content is combined with the shrinking news audience, one can make a strong case that the public is less well-informed than was the case in the 1950s and 1960s. Considering the limited consumption of news, whether the increased amount of negative news can easily affect public opinion is another question. Whether negative news about public figures and government can have much impact on public opinion when public confidence in that institution has also declined raises still another question.

Declining Trust in News Media

A fourth trend of significance is the declining public confidence in the news media. Considerable debate exists over whether declining confidence in the news media is just a function of overall confidence declines in all major institutions (Bennett, Rhine, and Flickinger 1998) or whether some aspect of the decline is particular to the news media itself (Cook and Gronke 2001).

The General Social Survey has been asking people about their confidence in the people running television and the press off and on since 1972. Although the press question clearly points to the news media, the television question is more ambiguous. Many people may think of television entertainment executives as well as news executives. But as the data on Figure 7.4 indicate, both series display a downward trend of similar magnitude from the 1970s through the 1990s. Linear trend lines have been added to the figure to highlight the downward trend and make the series, which are often broken due to missing data, more easily interpretable.

Patterson (2000) argues that the content and style of modern journalism has alienated many viewers and readers (also see Capella and Jamieson 1997). One path linking news styles, confidence, and consumption is that the modern news style erodes confidence and trust in the news, which in turn leads people to abandon the news.

What are the implications of these changes for the press, the presidency, and public opinion?

Implications for Presidents, the News Media, and the Public

Based on existing understandings of the impact of news on public opinion (e.g., Brody 1991), one would expect the increase in negative news to have a dampening effect on public support for the president. Not only does the case of Bill Clinton during 1998 belie this expectation, but a positive correlation between negative news and presidential approval since the late 1970s also confounds traditional

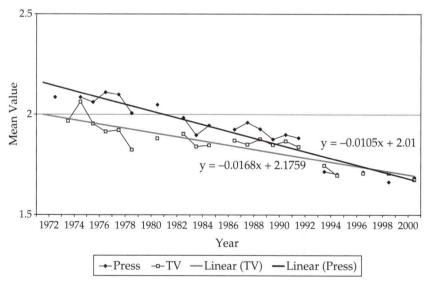

Figure 7.4   Mean Confidence in the Press and TV, 1972–2000

Source: GSS, 1972–2000. Question: "I am going to name some institutions in this country. As far as the people running these institutions are concerned, would you say you have a great deal of confidence, only some confidence, or hardly any confidence at all in them? Press. TV." The figure is constructed by coding "great deal" = 3, "only some" = 2, and "hardly any" = 1, and then taking the average for each year.

understandings of the connections between news and public support for the president.

Several factors about the news media may blunt its impact on public opinion. First, it is harder for the news media to reach and consequently affect public thinking because the news audience has shrunk. Fewer people are attentive to the news than was once the case. Furthermore, there is less news content for them to be attentive to. While it is true that people may encounter the news indirectly through conversations with friends and family, such indirect or two-stage flows of information may weaken the impact of the news, as content is filtered in the course of communication.

The rise of public discontent with the news media may blunt the impact of news reporting on the public even more than the shrinking news audience. Source credibility is an important ingredient in opening a person to communication effects. As source credibility declines, communication effects should also diminish. If we take the increasing levels of distrust and lack of confidence in the media as related to the source credibility of the press, then we can conjecture that the news has less impact on the public because the source that the information came from has lost some of its credibility.

Closely related, the fact that the news now is regularly negative may also undermine the ability of news content to affect public support for the president. In the golden age of broadcast television, negative news about the president was potent because it was rare. Its rarity signaled to the public that something was truly amiss in the White House. When all news about the president is negative, the signaling value of news to the public declines. The public can no longer tell if there are problems with the president and the administration that it needs to consider, or if the negative news is just the same old story that the news media always seem to be reporting. When the signal from the news media is so noisy, the public discounts it heavily.

The combination of a smaller news audience, the loss of credibility of the news media, and the noisiness of the news signal to the public all have undermined the ability of the media to affect the public as strongly as they seemed to do in the 1960s and 1970s. Hence, in a mass-mediated age, the public relies heavily on the news media to act as its eyes and ears about government. The information that the public receives from the news media is indispensable in the public's ability to hold its leaders accountable. As such, the news media play a vital role in democratic processes. When the public pays little attention to the news, when it views the news as incredible and its information as noise, then this linkage that binds the governed and the governors together is weakened.

This new system also has important consequences for the president and his ability to lead the public. One may read from the above comments that the president may be somewhat immunized from bad news. This is one way to read the Clinton example. But this new system is a double-edged sword for the president, too. It also limits his ability to lead the public (DiClerico 1993). Rather than trying to build widespread support across a national mass public, in this new environment the president must build support in a different way.

A smaller news audience means that the president can reach fewer people through the news media than he once could. Moreover, his ability to go public directly is undermined, as the audience for presidential addresses has declined (Baum and Kernell 1999; Welch 2000). As Edwards (2003) argues, one of the barriers to presidential leadership is gaining public attention. This barrier has always been in place, given the relatively low levels of public awareness and interest that polls have noted across the last 50 years. But the news system described here has raised the height of that barrier. First, presidents have increasing difficulty even getting the news media to pay attention to them, as the declines in news content indicate. And even when presidents make the front page and nightly news broadcasts, stories are more likely to be about scandals and less likely to be about policymaking than was the case several decades ago. Moreover, when the president wants to address the nation on primetime, the networks have been increasingly likely to deny his request, and sometimes when access is granted, only one of the networks will broadcast the presidential address (Foote 1990). The lack of news attention by average citizens adds to the barrier between the president and the public.

In place of building public support through appealing to the public writ large, the president engages in a more selective approach, targeting specific groups. We see this in the increase of presidential speaking, but not to the nation as a whole. Usually presidents target friends, ginning up their enthusiasm for the president. Presidential opponents counter with appeals to opposition groups.

In fact, from Gerald Ford's presidency onward, presidents delivered a larger number of minor speeches, mostly before smaller, specialized audiences. Over one-third of all presidential speeches occurred at ceremonies honoring some group or individual, while another 15 percent occurred at political rallies, with over half of all speeches occurring in these two types of settings. These findings suggest that presidents now speak more often before local audiences, special interest groups, and invited guests (Hart 1987, 157).

Neither presidents nor their opponents have much incentive to moderate their rhetoric or policy proposals in such a system. The moderate middle of the public is effectively left out of the picture. Instead, presidents and political elites in general try to mobilize already committed and loyal constituencies composed of people whose political beliefs tend to veer far from the middle. This system of leadership and opposition further polarizes an already polarized politics.

Thus, while the new system may immunize presidents to some degree from negativity in the news, this new system also limits opportunities for presidential leadership. Great events, like 9/11, that galvanize the public, must exist for presidents to lead the nation. Rather than being the nation's leader, with one *national constituency*, presidents in this new system act more as the leader of *many constituencies.*

A Coda: How Did Clinton Survive 1998, and the Presidency Into the Twenty-First Century

I opened this paper with the puzzle of how Bill Clinton's popularity could have risen while being pummeled with as bad and hostile a press as any president. This is only puzzling if we look at politics in the late 1990s as structurally similar to politics 25 years ago. It is not the same.

Bill Clinton survived 1998, a scandal with a young White House intern and a congressional impeachment, as well as uniformly bad press, because (1) much of the public was not paying much attention to what was going on, and (2) much of the public discounted what the press had to say about the president because the public had gotten use to the press knocking presidents. Bill Clinton's polls rose in part because of a good economy and in part because of a counterreaction of the public to the press's extreme negativity (Popkin 1998).

But it is also likely that Bill Clinton's public-relations strategy, built on a system fully expressed by Ronald Reagan, had a role to play in explaining Clinton's rising polls. If the public refused to pay much attention to what the press said about the president, the public may have paid some attention to what the president had to say about himself. Clinton's public-relations strategy was to emphasize his leadership and the effectiveness of his policies.

Unwittingly, the press may have enabled Clinton's strategy to reach the public by showing film of the president acting presidential and touting his accomplishments. In news stories, journalists would routinely comment on the "presidential strategy" in cynical terms. But the public discounted what the journalists had to say, instead absorbing some of the president's message. We do not see a groundswell of support behind the president; the audience is too small for that and many people's political attitudes are too hardened to change. But we do see a modest, perhaps somewhat more than merely incremental, increase in presidential support across 1998. The president reached a modest number of people through his public relations campaign, driving up his polls. He might not have been able to do this in the golden age of broadcast television.

Finally, the system described above seems well entrenched into the twenty-first century. Despite 9/11 and wars in Afghanistan and Iraq, public attention to politics and government has not risen beyond the levels of the late 1990s. Polls from the Pew Research Center for the People and the Press find continued high levels of public cynicism toward the news media. Heavy doses of soft news still fill news broadcasts. And the tone of news coverage of the Bush presidency does not seem to affect public approval of the president, as reported in a study of trends in Bush's approval across the first five years of his term in office by political scientists Brian Gaines and Brian Roberts (2005).

The case of George W. Bush's attempt to reform Social Security is instructive of the little that has changed in the news system described above. After his reelection in November 2004, Bush placed reform of Social Security as his top domestic policy priority. In March and April 2005, he embarked on a campaign to sell his reform by traveling to 60 cities in 60 days. That campaign was unable to generate the amount of publicity he desired. Moreover, the more he talked about Social Security reform, the lower the level of public support for his proposal. Upon the conclusion of his tour around the nation, Bush held a primetime address to the nation, a last ditch effort to overcome the barriers of the news system described above. Likewise, the president's attempts to build support for his immigration reform package and for declining support for the war in Iraq proved unsuccessful.

Trying to use the "bully pulpit" and other forms of the public presidency become increasingly difficult when the news media fail to produce the volume of news that presidents desire, when the public is uninterested in politics and government, and when the public is cynical about the news media. This is as true in the early twenty-first century as it was in the late twentieth century.

Notes

1. The only modification here is that the office may evolve over time.

2. These data come from Thomas Patterson's (2000) random sample of 5,000 stories from the Lexis-Nexis service from 1981 through 1998. His data cast a wide net beyond stories on the presidency; I only present presidential news stories here, about 20 percent of the entire sample. The number of presidential stories per year is often modest, which precludes making definitive statements about news coverage of the presidency. Yet because of the long span of time and the random selection of stories, we can gather a sense of the comparative tone of news reporting on the presidency across these nearly two decades.

3. In a perceptive analysis, Newman (2002) finds that the scandal actually hurt Clinton's ratings. Had the scandal not existed, Clinton's polls would have been about 2–3 points higher. Still, this is a meager effect

of scandal on presidential polls in light of Ostrom and Simon's (1989) analysis of the impact of Watergate and Iran-Contra.

4. We need to take these numbers with caution. People seem to inflate their news exposure, as they overreport voting turnout. Given that surveys indicate that some people consider programs like *Entertainment Tonight* and reality crime shows like *COPS* to be news, people may overstate their news consumption when all that they have done is watch an entertainment program. Similarly, newspaper-reading attention to the campaign may be inflated, as sports readers may glance at the news headlines about the campaign. Still, despite these sources of measurement error, assuming that such problems are relatively constant across years, we can track some trends. But it is quite likely that these numbers understate those who are inattentive to either medium. Other data suggests that the percentage of the population that is inattentive to all forms of hard news has increased (Patterson 2000).

5. Centralization was occurring in the newspaper sector, as many papers failed, leaving only a handful of cities with more than one daily paper, and as corporate chains took over many other newspapers. Yet, as Hamilton (2003) argues, the newspaper sector was not immune to competitive pressures. Corporate offices were often highly sensitive to the economic implications of their news product and altered daily papers to reflect these new economic considerations.

6. For more details of their study see http://www.journalism.org/node/442.

7. "The First 100 Days: How Bush Versus Clinton Fared in the Press." http://www.journalism.org/node/312.

8. A regression of negative news on a time counter (1949 = 1) is strongly statistically significant, and suggests that each year that the series progresses the president will receive about half a percentage point more negative news. The regression equation (standard errors in parentheses) is $y = 10.10 (2.93)$ Constant $+ .54 (.11)$ Counter; $R^2 = .35$. A similar regression for positive news finds a near mirror result. Each additional year subtracts about .4 percentage points of positive news. The resulting equation is $y = 50.41 (2.83)$ Constant $- .39 (.11)$ Counter; $R^2 = .23$.

References

Baum, Matthew A. 2003. *Soft News Goes to War: Public Opinion and American Foreign Policy in the New Media Age.* Princeton, NJ: Princeton University Press.

Baum, Matthew A., and Samuel Kernell. 1999. "Has Cable Ended the Golden Age of Television?" *American Political Science Review* 93 (March):99–114.

Baumgartner, Frank R., and Bryan D. Jones. 1993. *Agendas and Instability in American Politics.* Chicago: University of Chicago Press.

Bennett, Stephen Earl, Staci L. Rhine, and Richard S. Flickinger. 1998 "Assessing Americans' Opinions About the News Media's Fairness in 1996 and 1998." *Political Communication* 18 (April):163–183.

Brody, Richard. 1991. *Assessing the President: The Media, Elite Opinion, and Public Support.* Stanford: Stanford University Press.

Capella, Joseph N., and Kathleen Hall Jamieson. 1997. *Spiral of Cynicism: The Press and the Public Good.* Oxford, England: Oxford University Press.

Cook, Timothy E., and Paul Gronke. 2001. "Dimensions of Institutional Trust: Is Public Confidence in the Media Distinct from Other Institutions?" Paper presented at the Annual Meeting of the Midwest Political Science Association, Chicago IL.

Cook, Timothy E., and Lyn Ragsdale. 1998. "The President and the Press: Negotiating Newsworthiness in the White House." In Michael Nelson (Ed.), *The Presidency and the Political System*, 5th ed., 323–357. Washington, DC: CQ Press.

Dahl, Robert A. 1957. "The Concept of Power." *Behavioral Science* 11 (July):201–215.

Davis, Richard, and Diana Owen. 1998. *New Media and American Politics*. New York: Oxford University Press.

DiClerico, Robert E. 1993. "The Role of Media in Heightened Expectations and Diminished Leadership Capacity." In R. W. Waterman (Ed.), *The Presidency Reconsidered* 115–143. Itasca, IL: F.E. Peacock.

Edwards, George C. III. 2003. *On Deaf Ears: The Limits of the Bully Pulpit*. New Haven, CT: Yale University Press.

Erikson, Robert S., Michael B. MacKuen, and James A. Stimson. 2002. *The Macro Polity*. New York: Cambridge University Press.

Foote, Joe S. 1990. *Television Access and Presidential Power: The Networks, the Presidency, and the "Loyal Opposition."* New York: Praeger.

Gaines, Brian J., and Brian D. Roberts. 2005. "Hawks, Bears, and Pundits: Explaining Presidential Approval Rally Effects." Paper presented at the Midwest Political Science Association, Chicago, IL, April 7–10, 2005.

Gilbert, Robert E. 1981. "Television and Presidential Power." *Journal of Social, Political, and Economic Studies* 6(1):75–93.

———. 1989. "President Versus Congress: The Struggle for Public Attention." *Congress and the President* 16(1):91–102.

Groeling, Tim, and Samuel Kernell. 1998. "Is Network News Coverage of the President Biased?" *The Journal of Politics* 60(4):1063–1087.

Grossman, Michael Baruch, and Martha Joynt Kumar. 1981. *Portraying the President: The White House and the News Media*. Baltimore: Johns Hopkins University Press.

Hamilton, James T. 2003. *All the News That's Fit to Sell: How the Market Transforms Information Into News*. Princeton, NJ: Princeton University Press.

Hart, Roderick P. 1987. *The Sound of Presidential Leadership: Presidential Communications in the Modern Age*. Chicago: University of Chicago Press.

Hess, Stephen. 2000. "Federalism and News: Media to Government: Drop Dead." *Brookings Review* 18 (Winter):28–31.

Kernell, Samuel C. 1993. *Going Public: New Strategies of Presidential Leadership*, 2nd ed. Washington, DC: CQ Press.

Kurtz, Howard. 1998. *Spin Cycle: Inside the Clinton Propaganda Machine*. New York: Free Press.

Maltese, John Anthony. 1992. *Spin Control: The White House Office of Communications and the Management of Presidential News*. Chapel Hill: University of North Carolina Press.

Newman, Brian. 2002. "Bill Clinton's Approval Ratings: The More Things Change, the More They Stay the Same." *Political Research Quarterly* 55 (December):781–804.

Ostrom, Charles W. Jr., and Dennis M. Simon. 1989. "The Man in the Teflon Suit? The Environmental Connection, Political Drama, and Popular Support in the Reagan Presidency." *Public Opinion Quarterly* 53 (Autumn):353–387.

Patterson, Thomas E. 2000. "Doing Well and Doing Good: How Soft News and Critical Journalism are Shrinking the News Audience and Weakening Democracy—And What News Outlets Can Do About It." Joan Shorenstein Center for Press, Politics, and Public Policy, John F. Kennedy School of Government, Harvard University.

Popkin, Samuel. 1998. "When the People Decline to be Spun." *New York Times*, November 10, A29.

Ragsdale, Lyn. 1997. "Disconnected Politics: Public Opinion and Presidents." In Barbara Norrander and Clyde Wilcox (Eds.), *Understanding Public Opinion*, 229–251. Washington, DC: CQ Press.

Sabato, Larry J. 1991. *Feeding Frenzy: How Attack Journalism Has Transformed Politics*. New York: Free Press.

Welch, Reed L. 2000. "Is Anybody Watching? The Audience for Televised Presidential Addresses." *Congress and the Presidency* 27 (Spring):41–58. ✦

Chapter 8

Which Presidents Are Uncommonly Successful in Congress?

Richard Fleisher, Jon R. Bond, and B. Dan Wood

In Chapter 2, Fine and Waterman argued that there are three components to presidential leadership: personal skill, the resources available to a president (or leverage), and a political outcome. The idea was that skillful presidents can use political leverage to achieve a successful outcome. But what if the impediments to presidential leadership that Edwards described in Chapter 6 are so powerful that skill no longer matters? In that case, presidential success would depend only on whether presidents have sufficient leverage to offset the various impediments to leadership.

Fleisher, Bond, and Wood, as do Cameron and Park (in Chapter 3) and Epstein, Kristensen, and O'Halloran (in Chapter 4), find that opportunities for presidential success with Congress are "contingent" or "conditional." They also conclude that leverage, not skill, matters most. Describing this chapter, Fleisher, Bond, and Wood write,

> Scholarship on the presidency suggests that what the president does or fails to do is a crucial determinant of success in Congress. If presidential activity exerts a general and systematic influence, then when compared to a common baseline that accounts for political conditions that affect success rates, we should observe some presidents who are "uncommonly" successful and unsuccessful. We test this expectation with an empirical analysis of presidential success on roll call votes from 1953–2001. We construct a baseline model of presidential success grounded in theory and recent research, and evaluate which presidents appear "uncommonly" successful or unsuccessful relative to the baseline. We find that presidential success in Congress is largely determined by whether political condi-

We are grateful to the departments of Political Science at Fordham University and Texas A&M University for supporting this research, and to Christina Suthammanont for help with data coding. An earlier draft of this paper was presented at the 2002 Annual Meeting of the Southern Political Science Association, and we appreciate helpful comments from Richard Conley.

tions are favorable or unfavorable. Few residuals from this model could be considered "uncommon," and those that are unusual occur only slightly more frequently than random chance. Thus, we find no evidence that any of the 10 presidents analyzed here were "uncommonly" successful or unsuccessful.

◆ ◆ ◆

Which Presidents Are Uncommonly Successful in Congress?

Over four decades ago, Richard Neustadt (1960, i) focused the study of the presidency on presidential behavior, "what a President . . . can do, as one man among many, to carry his own choices through that maze of personalities and institutions called the government of the United States." Although students of presidential congressional relations have produced numerous innovative and high quality studies testing Neustadt's insight, a great deal of theoretical ambiguity remains. Empirical research provides clear and convincing evidence that political conditions existing in that "maze of . . . institutions called the government" affect presidential success in achieving his policy goals. Neustadt (1960) argues, however, that skilled presidents are able to capitalize on the advantages and overcome the disadvantages of whatever political conditions they face. Or as Roger Davidson (1984, 374) put it, some presidents are not just successful; they are "uncommonly successful." The evidence that the president's activities and performance systematically alter legislative success is less convincing.

Much of the difficulty in demonstrating the effect of skills results from theoretical ambiguity in how to define and measure this key concept. Rather than offering one more study testing one more measure of presidential performance, we approach the problem indirectly. In particular, we seek to leverage what we know with some confidence about the determinants of presidential success in Congress to test an empirical generalization about presidential performance: if presidential activity exerts a general and systematic influence on success in Congress, then when compared to a common baseline that accounts for political conditions, we should observe some presidents who are "uncommonly" successful and unsuccessful.

We test this expectation with an empirical analysis of presidential success on roll call votes in the House and Senate from 1953–2001. We construct a baseline model of presidential success grounded in theory and recent research, and then evaluate which presidents appear "uncommonly" successful and unsuccessful relative to the baseline. This analysis indicates that presidential success in Congress is determined largely by whether political conditions are favorable or unfavorable. None of the 10 presidents analyzed here were "uncommonly" successful or unsuccessful. Few residuals from this model could be considered "uncommon," and those that are unusual occur only slightly more often than would be expected from random chance. The few "uncommon" residuals are also inconsistent with common perceptions of which presidents had strong or weak skill. Although our analysis does not test the effects of presidential skill, these results do suggest that presidential activities are a marginal determinant of success in Congress.

Literature and Theory

The initial impulse of scholars who seek to understand political leadership is to focus on characteristics and activities of the leader. Yet leadership implies a relationship with followers, and the behavior of followers in this relationship is as important as the behavior of the leader. A fruitful strategy to understand the effects of leadership, therefore, is to focus on followers. The study of presidential-congressional relations can be viewed in a similar way.

The literature on presidential-congressional relations offers guidance on two key issues in the evaluation of whether a president is uncommonly successful with Congress. First, a number of scholars have attempted to analyze the effects of presidential activities on legislative success. The evidence is mixed at best. Although these studies have been unable to provide convincing evidence about the effects of presidential performance, they do offer clues for another research strategy. That strategy is to focus on Congress—that is, to analyze the behavior of followers. Second, the literature provides guidance about the specification of models of congressional behavior that predict and explain presidential success on roll calls.

Evidence of the Effects of Presidential Performance

Early efforts to analyze presidential leadership skill relied on in-depth case studies. Although conclusions from case studies may be based on sound scholarship, generalizing findings from a single case is problematic. Even a multiple-cases approach that applies common standards of assessment to analyze several presidents' performances on several important issues (Kellerman 1984) suffers from questions about selection bias and interpretation of findings (see Bond and Fleisher 1990, 34–40).

Several studies attempted to go beyond case studies and analyze the effects of presidential performance on legislative success quantitatively. These studies use two research strategies. One set of studies develops measures of one or two presidents' activities, and assesses the impact of these activities on success (Covington 1987a, 1987b, 1988a, 1988b; Covington, Wrighton, and Kinney 1995; Fett 1994; Lockerbie and Borelli 1989; Sullivan 1988, 1990, 1991). Recognizing the inherent difficulty of directly measuring presidential performance, other studies use an indirect approach. These studies assess the success of presidents relative to some baseline to determine if presidents reputed as skilled are more successful than those reputed as unskilled (Bond and Fleisher 1990; Edwards 1980, 1989; Fleisher and Bond 1983, 1992). Evidence from both types of studies provides only tenuous support for the hypothesis that presidential skill leads to uncommon success. And what supportive evidence there is cannot be generalized.

Lockerbie and Borrelli (1989) relied on journalists' assessments to measure the performance of presidents Carter and Reagan. They constructed a monthly measure of presidential performance from a content analysis of columns by George Will and Meg Greenfield. This measure may come closer than any other to testing Neustadt's (1960, chap. 4) notion that Washingtonians' perceptions of presidential skill are a more relevant "reality" than any actual activity. Although they found no overall effect of this variable on House roll calls in each month, further analysis focusing on "high skills" indicated that presidents were more successful in months when journalists reported most favorably on their skills.

Interpreting this evidence as support for the skills hypothesis is dubious for several reasons. First, the measure may be influenced by the outcome. Journalists are more likely to see and report about presidential competence when there is a visible success or failure. In other words, there is an endogeneity problem that must be addressed when using such a measure. To claim that skilled performance causes success, we must be sure that the outcome did not produce the assessment of skill. Second, this measure assumes that presidential reputation undergoes meaningful month-to-month change. While this study found month-to-month variability, much of this variation may be measurement error. Relying on assessments of only two journalists increases the chance of measurement error. Finally, even if we accept the measure's validity, we have assessments of only two presidents in one chamber. Although quantitative evidence is an improvement over qualitative assessments in traditional case studies, generalizing from two presidents in one chamber is risky.

Another attempt to assess presidential performance relies on data from administration headcounts (a series of prevote polls of members' positions). This research finds that some members change their position between the first poll and the vote (Sullivan 1991), and some copartisans abstain rather than vote against the administration (Covington 1988a). But attributing switches and strategic abstentions to presidential influence is debatable. Some "conversions" to a pro-administration position reflected insincere, strategic position taking on the initial count (Sullivan 1990). In addition, some members reverted to an antiadministration position (Sullivan 1988), indicating that even if such activity does influence members' votes, the influence is not always positive.

Other research suggests that presidents focus on influencing core supporters. Fett (1994) found that the more often a president mentioned an issue, the more likely core supporters were to vote with him. Covington (1987a) found that presidents mobilize core supporters more on issues important to them. While presidential activity might increase support among core supporters, it might also indicate that presidents place a higher priority on issues on which they and their core supporters already agree. If so, then these findings might indicate that the president is responding to key allies in Congress rather than skillfully influencing them. In addition, Fett's (1994) measure is just the number of times the president mentioned an issue rather than an assessment of how skilled the president's performance was or how Washingtonians perceived it, as with Lockerbie and Borrelli's (1989) measure. And each of these studies was limited to two presidents, raising questions about generalizability.

Finally, Covington, Wrighton, and Kinney (1995) focus on presidents' positions and their influence over the agenda. Their analysis demonstrates that both majority and minority presidents have about the same probability of winning votes on which the president supports passage, and votes that are on the president's agenda regardless of whether he supports or opposes passage. Although this innovative study offers important insights about the effect of presidential performance, it also shows why party control is such an important political condition affecting success in Congress. Compared to majority presidents, minority presidents are much less likely to support passage of bills that get to the floor, and they are much less likely to get their on-agenda items to the floor for a vote. And since this analysis is based on the experience of only three presidents who served between 1953 and 1975, questions of generalizability remain.

Thus, attempts to directly measure presidential performance have not produced convincing, generalizable evidence. Although we admire the innovative tests in these studies, the lack of progress in demonstrating general empirical effects suggests the need for another approach. Other studies have used an indirect approach to compare presidents since Eisenhower. These studies rely on general assessments of presidents' reputations, and then compare presidents' success against various baselines based on characteristics and conditions in Congress.

The case study literature does give an indication of which presidents have reputations as skilled politicians and which ones do not. Recall that Neustadt (1960, chap. 4) views perceptions of the president's professional reputation as most relevant even if these differ from more objective indicators. A review of this literature (Bond and Fleisher 1990, 198–204) indicates that Lyndon Johnson, Ronald Reagan, and Gerald Ford are reputed to be highly skilled, while Richard Nixon and Jimmy Carter are reputed to be unskilled. Historical assessments of Eisenhower and Kennedy are mixed, and reputations of more recent presidents are still being formed.

Edwards (1980, 1989) found that presidents reputed to be skilled did not receive more support from certain groups of members (i.e., northern Democrats, southern Democrats, Republicans) than other presidents of the same party. This finding was similar for measures of presidential support based on nonunanimous votes as well as on key votes in both the House and Senate. The analysis of key votes is noteworthy because it limits the analysis to a few issues likely to be viewed as highly important to presidents and members of Congress. Comparing presidents of the same party controls for a major factor known to influence individual presidential support scores, and the analysis of several presidents' success in both chambers of Congress contributes to generalizability of the findings.

Fleisher and Bond (1983, 1992) expanded on Edwards's approach with a statistical model that estimates the effects of party, ideology, and presidential popularity on individual House members' support for the president. They compared forecasts from this model to members' actual levels of support for Carter and Reagan during their first years in office. Consistent with perceptions of Carter as unskilled, this analysis revealed that on average members of Congress supported Carter less often than predicted. But contrary to perceptions that Reagan was unusually influential, Reagan also received less support from House members than predicted (Fleisher and Bond 1983). A similar analysis of the senior Bush's first year suggested that support for Bush was also below predicted levels, even among individuals identified as his close friends and political allies (Fleisher and Bond 1992). These studies, however, were limited to analysis of success in the House during these presidents' first years in office.

Bond and Fleisher (1990, chap. 8) used a similar statistical baseline to analyze annual success rates of presidents from Eisenhower to Reagan in the House and Senate. This analysis found that presidents reputed as highly skilled did not win more roll call votes given the political conditions they faced than did presidents reputed as less skilled.

Edwards's and Bond and Fleisher's studies may be criticized because their crude, global assessments treat leadership skill as static. Perceptions of skill are probably not as fluid as popularity, but they are likely to vary over the course of a term.

The choice of a baseline also has come under scrutiny. Joslyn (1995) criticized Fleisher and Bond (1992) for using a model based on data from 1953–1974 to forecast presidential support in 1989. Using a baseline so far removed in time from the behavior being predicted assumes that relationships estimated in the forecast model do not change over time. Joslyn (1995) found different results using a model that included observations closer to the period being forecast. This critique raises the more general point that assessments of presidential performance depend heavily on model specification. An improperly specified model will dump more unexplained variance into the error term, increasing the number of factors included in the residuals.

Thus, studies that compare presidential success to some baseline fail to find evidence that perceptions of skill have systematic effects. This approach, of course, is not a direct test of skills. Yet constructing a better-specified model than those used in previous research for both chambers would at least allow us to see which presidents were uncommonly successful and unsuccessful relative to the conditions they faced. This research strategy is likely to produce findings that can be generalized at least to presidents since Eisenhower for whom we have indicators of legislative success. The task we face is to estimate a properly specified model. We turn now to the literature on presidential success in Congress to identify the variables that belong in the baseline.

The Determinants of Presidential Success in Congress

To estimate a well-specified baseline model of presidential success in Congress requires a theory of congressional behavior. Fortunately, students of Congress and presidential-congressional relations have identified the basic determinants of congressional behavior and how presidential preferences and activities fit into members' decision-making calculus.

Our theory assumes that members of Congress are rational actors motivated by two goals: policy and reelection (Aldrich 1995; Aldrich and Rohde 2000; Arnold 1990; Fenno 1973; Mayhew 1974; Rohde 1991). Because members must make decisions with imperfect information under severe time constraints, they rely on cues, or shortcuts, to help them cast votes that advance their goals. Previous research establishes that the most important determinants of roll call votes in Congress are cues from party, ideology, and constituency, and only rarely does a member need to search more broadly for guidance (Jackson 1974; Kingdon 1981; Matthews and Stimson 1975). These cues tend to dominate decisionmaking in large part because of substantial overlap among them. Elections tend to select representatives with partisan and policy preferences that are compatible with their constituency, so members seldom experience conflict between constituent preferences and their party and personal ideology (Fenno

1978). For most members, following their party and ideology contributes to reelection—or at least does not threaten it.

If these primary cues are not in conflict, then members vote with the consensus. Only when there is conflict do members expand their search to other cues both in and out of government (Kingdon 1981). This expanded search may include inputs from staff, interest groups, bureaucrats, experts, the news media, and mass public opinion, as well as the president. But note that the president is only one of many competing outside influences, and seldom is he dominant in members' calculus. Cues from the president must always compete with the stronger influences of party, ideology, and constituency. Because the primary cues are strong and rarely in conflict, presidential influence on members' voting behavior is marginal, and most likely to occur when the primary cues are in conflict.

Developing a Baseline Model of Presidential Success

The literature suggests a number of variables that should be included in a fully specified model of presidential success. The first and most important determinant is party. Previous research shows that presidential support is higher among members of the president's party than among the opposition, and the president's position is more likely to win when his party controls Congress than when the opposition party is in power (Bond and Fleisher 1990; Edwards 1989).

We have solid theoretical reasons to explain why party exerts a strong influence on congressional behavior (Bond and Fleisher 1990). First, because members of the same political party must satisfy similar electoral coalitions, they share a wide range of policy preferences. Support is higher among members of the president's party because they and their constituents are more likely to agree with his policy preferences than are members of the other party. Second, members of a political party share a psychological attachment to a common political symbol; in a sense, they are part of the same political "family." Although diverse, decentralized parties and different institutional perspectives inevitably lead to disagreements between the president and his copartisans in Congress, "bargaining 'within the family' has a rather different quality than bargaining with members of the rival clan" (Neustadt 1960, 187). Third, members of the president's party must run on his record as well as their own, so they have an incentive to help him succeed.

This partisan support translates into higher success if the president's party has a majority in Congress. Part of the explanation of why majority presidents win more votes in Congress than minority presidents is simple arithmetic—majority presidents have more members on the floor with incentives to support their policy preferences. But more important than numbers is control of the levers of

power in Congress. The majority party in Congress controls committees as well as access to the floor. Consequently, the issues on the congressional agenda and how choices are presented to members on the
floor are more likely to reflect the president's preferences when his
partisans control the chamber (Covington, Wrighton, and Kinney
1995). Bond, Fleisher, and Wood (2003, Table 1) show that the percentage of the president's party in Congress has no effect on presidential success independent of majority control. The simple dichotomy
of unified or divided party control of the chamber, therefore, provides
a sound beginning for explaining presidential success.

A second explanation to add to the model is timing during the president's term. The notion of a "honeymoon" is a frequently noted aspect of presidential-congressional relations. The honeymoon refers to
the early part of a president's term when the public, the Washington
press corps, and members of Congress are predisposed to give him
the benefit of the doubt. An American government textbook hints at
the origin of the analogy: the "honeymoon" is the period "during
which, presumably, the president's love affair with the people and the
Congress can be consummated" (Wilson 1992, 344). This period is
widely viewed as the most propitious time for presidential initiatives.
But paradoxically, the first year is also a period of learning and ad-
justment for the president, so there is no guarantee that he will be
able to exploit the potential benefits of the honeymoon. Bond and
Fleisher (1990, 211–213) present evidence that Presidents Johnson
and Reagan had successful honeymoon years, while Nixon and Carter
had less impressive beginnings. They suggest that having unusually
successful first years may have contributed to Johnson and Reagan's
reputations as skilled, while Nixon and Carter's less than impressive
first years contributed to their reputations as unskilled.

The honeymoon concept is closely tied to presidential elections,
but there is a question of how to code cases if the president assumes
office without an election, and if a president wins reelection. President Johnson assumed office following the Kennedy assassination
when there was a strong rally of public support for American institutions. As a result, Johnson received an early honeymoon prior to his
election. In contrast, President Ford, who was appointed Vice President and ascended to the presidency after Nixon's resignation,
seemed to have no honeymoon. As he assumed the presidency, Ford
said to Congress, "I do not want a honeymoon with you. I want a
good marriage." Yet despite vows of "communication, conciliation,
compromise, and cooperation," Cronin (1980, 226) observes that
Ford's "hoped-for holy wedlock soured and unholy deadlock set
in. . . ." And renewal of vows for a second term also appears not to
merit a second honeymoon (Light 1982, 39).[1]

A third explanation of presidential success in Congress is popularity with the public. Neustadt (1960) proposes electoral self-interest as

a theoretical rationale for why public approval should affect success in Congress. The president's popularity affects calculations of electoral self-interest because members fear electoral retribution if they oppose a popular president or support an unpopular one. As Neustadt (1960, 86) explains, members of Congress "must take account of popular reactions to their actions. What their publics think of them becomes a factor, therefore, in deciding how to deal with the desires of a President. His prestige enters into that decision; their publics are part of his."

Presidential approval, however, has only a marginal effect on success. Presidential approval is not likely to cause members of Congress to systematically alter their behavior, because the public's evaluation of the president plays only a small role in deciding the outcome of most congressional races. Few voters have sufficient knowledge of their representative's level of presidential support to make a connection between their evaluation of the president and their decision of which congressional candidate to support. If presidential popularity influences congressional elections, it most likely works indirectly through the candidate recruitment process, helping or hurting members of the president's party without regard to their specific levels of presidential support (Jacobson 1990; Jacobson and Kernell 1983). Furthermore, because presidential popularity is fluid, using it as a guide in casting roll call votes is risky. The president's popularity on election day is more important than his popularity months or even years earlier when members must cast votes supporting or opposing the president. Members cannot predict with any certainty presidential popularity on election day. For these reasons, the effect of public approval on members' electoral self-interest is limited and uncertain. Since public approval has only a limited effect on members' electoral self-interest, its effect on their roll call voting decisions will also be marginal (Bond, Fleisher, and Wood 2003).

A final factor that affects presidential success in Congress is party polarization. But we do not expect polarization to directly raise or lower success. Instead, our theory predicts that polarization affects success by conditioning the effects of presidential popularity and party control. Bond, Fleisher, and Wood (2003) develop a theoretical rationale explaining why party polarization conditions the relationship between presidential approval and success in Congress. The level of partisanship in Congress systematically alters the relationship, because members search more or less broadly as primary cues change. Partisan behavior is a function of the consistency among cues from party, ideology, and constituency. During times of low partisanship, Congress has more cross-pressured members who experience conflicts among these primary cues (Fleisher and Bond 2000). When many members experience such conflict, public approval becomes more important as members expand their search. During periods of high partisanship with fewer cross-pressured members, primary cues are reinforcing. When few members experience conflict among the primary cues, the effect of public approval declines.

This theory may be extended to explain how party polarization should also condition the relationship between party control and presidential success. Presidents typically reflect preferences of their party mainstream (Aldrich and Rohde 2000, 69; Bond and Fleisher 1990). When parties are polarized, presidential cues reinforce primary cues of more members of his party resulting in fewer defections, leading to higher success if his party controls the chamber.

The effects of the interactions, however, are likely to differ in the House and Senate. Two features of the Senate tend to insulate senators from popular influences and might mute the effects of both public opinion and party. First, senators serve six-year terms and only one-third must face the voters in any given election. The president's popularity is less likely to affect the reelection chances of the two-thirds of senators whose next election is two or four years away. Second, Senate rules allow individuals and the minority party to block legislation they oppose, whereas House rules empower even a slim partisan majority to win if it is cohesive. Polarized parties, therefore, should increase the success of majority presidents in the House because they can win without votes from the minority. But majority control is less of an advantage in the Senate, and the interaction with polarized parties should be weaker than in the House.

Measures for the Baseline Model

Thus, the literature identifies the major determinants of presidential success in Congress. We turn now to a description of the measures used in our model.

Presidential Success in Congress

The dependent variable is presidential success on the floor of the House and Senate, measured as the annual percentage of conflictual roll calls from 1953 through 2001 on which the president's position won (presidential roll calls were identified by Congressional Quarterly, Inc. 1953–2001). A conflictual presidential roll call is one on which less than 80 precent vote in agreement with the president (Bond and Fleisher 1990; Fleisher and Bond 2000). We exclude consensual presidential victories to limit the analysis to relatively important issues. A check of issues passed by near unanimous margins with the president's support reveals that, with rare exceptions, these are minor and routine issues. Votes that the president lost with more than 80 percent voting against him remain in the analysis. These relatively unusual cases when the president stands alone against a united

Congress represent instances of important institutional conflict. Such cases are neither trivial nor routine, and belong in the analysis. Presidential success ranged from 17.6 percent to 89.0 percent with a mean of 55.36 and standard deviation of 20.54 in the House, and from 23.5 percent to 90.0 percent with a mean of 62.12 and a standard deviation of 17.07 in the Senate.

Party Control

We model the effect of party with a binary variable coded one when the president's party controls the chamber and zero otherwise. Consistent with findings in Bond, Fleisher, and Wood (2003), the size of president's party had no significant effect beyond the effects of majority status in any of our specifications, so we omit this variable. Substantively, this finding suggests that having the president's partisans control committees and the floor agenda is more important than incremental changes in the number of copartisans in the chamber.

Honeymoon

The honeymoon is indicated by a binary variable coded one for the first year after the president's first election and zero otherwise. Consistent with the discussion above, we coded Johnson with an early honeymoon in 1964, but Ford with no honeymoon. Second term presidents did not receive a second honeymoon.

Presidential Approval

We measure presidential popularity with the Gallup job approval question (Edwards with Gallup 1990; updates from Gallup), "Do you approve or disapprove of the way [the incumbent] is doing his job as president?" Our measure is the average annual percentage approving of the president's job performance. Approval ranged from 37 percent to 75 percent, with a mean of 56.48 and standard deviation of 10.67.

Partisanship in Congress

Partisanship in Congress is the frequency of party voting in each chamber during each year. Our measure is the annual percentage of all recorded votes on which a majority of Democrats opposed a majority of Republicans (Ornstein, Mann, and Malbin 1998; Willis 2002). The greater the percentage of party votes, the more often members are following partisan cues in deciding their votes. In the House, party voting ranged from 27 percent to 73 percent, with a mean of 47.02 and standard deviation of 10.73. In the Senate, party voting ranged from 30 percent to 69 percent, with a mean of 46.14 and a standard deviation of 8.97. We do not expect party unity to directly affect presidential success. Instead, we expect party unity to condition the effects of public approval and party control.[2]

Interactions

We analyze the House and Senate separately and expect similar, but not identical, relationships in both chambers. As discussed above, we expect the effects of presidential approval and party control to be weaker in the Senate than in the House, and the interactions should also be weaker in the Senate.

Results From the Baseline Model

Table 8.1 reports results as we sequentially add variables in constructing the baseline model for the House and Senate. To be conservative and to take account of potential autocorrelation and heteroscedasticity, we report t-statistics calculated using Newey and West (1987) autocorrelation and heteroscedasticity consistent standard errors. The full model for each chamber is in the last column of each part of the table. To assess the veracity of the full model, however, it is instructive to observe how the model changes as we sequentially add each theoretical component.

The first column of models for the House and Senate shows results of what we might term a naïve model that predicts presidential success from party control alone. This simple model suggests that majority party control yields a substantial bonus for the president in both chambers, but as expected, the benefit is somewhat stronger in the House than in the Senate. Although the ultimate result of majority party control is a predicted success rate of about 76 percent in both the House (i.e., 44.41 + 31.54 = 75.95) and the Senate (i.e., 50.59 + 25.68 = 76.27), the increase associated with majority status is larger in the House. Compared to minority presidents, the models predict that success rates of a majority president should be 31.54 percentage points higher in the House, and 25.68 points higher in the Senate. This naïve model is also fairly powerful, in that it explains about 55 percent of the variance in annual presidential success for the House, and about 57 percent in the Senate.

Adding the honeymoon effect (shown in the second column) improves the model substantially. The honeymoon effect is similar in the House (11.5 percent) and Senate (10.5 percent), suggesting that the president receives about the same amount of good will at the start of his term in each chamber.

Adding presidential approval to the model yields little additional explanation in the House, but a statistically significant increase in the Senate. Our theory suggests that approval should affect members' behavior only at the margins after party, ideology, and constituency are taken into account. The weak effect in the House, therefore, is consistent with this theory, but the significant effect in the Senate is not. Our theory suggests that six-year staggered terms should insulate

Table 8.1 Regression Analysis of Determinants of Presidential Success in the U.S. House of Representatives and Senate, 1953–2001

Variable	House				Senate			
	Party Control	Add Honeymoon	Add Approval	Add Polarization	Party Control	Add Honeymoon	Add Approval	Add Polarization
Party Control	31.54 (7.35)	27.88 (7.02)	27.96 (7.05)	−37.38 (−3.58)	25.68 (7.55)	23.51 (7.50)	24.61 (8.52)	5.91 (0.45)
Honeymoon		11.50 (3.48)	11.16 (2.88)	4.64 (1.41)		10.48 (3.29)	7.20 (2.17)	6.29 (1.70)
Approval			0.03 (0.23)	0.91 (5.46)			0.29 (2.36)	0.66 (4.24)
Approval* Polarization				−0.02 (−5.71)				−0.01 (−2.54)
Party Control* Polarization				1.44 (6.94)				0.41 (1.44)
Constant	44.41 (13.05)	43.33 (12.72)	41.68 (5.48)	38.72 (6.94)	50.59 (19.78)	49.43 (19.44)	33.23 (4.94)	32.87 (4.97)
N	49	49	49	49	49	49	49	49
R^2	0.55	0.59	0.59	0.77	0.57	0.63	0.66	0.70
σ	13.99	13.43	13.57	10.42	11.29	10.61	10.33	9.95

Note: The dependent variable is the president's annual percentage success on conflictual roll call votes from 1953 through 2001. The numbers in parentheses are t-statistics calculated using Newey and West (1987) autocorrelation and heteroscedasticity consistent standard errors.

senators from outside influences such as presidential approval, so we expected a weaker relationship in the Senate than in the House.

Our theory also suggests that the effect of approval on presidential success should be conditioned by the degree of polarization in Congress, and there is empirical support for this theory (Bond, Fleisher, and Wood 2003). In addition, we offered a theoretical rationale to expect a conditioning effect for majority control. Therefore, to evaluate the effects of public approval and majority control on presidential success, we need to test for interactions with party polarization.

The last column of models for each chamber reports results of adding the interactive effect of party polarization on presidential approval and majority party status. Consistent with the models reported in Bond, Fleisher, and Wood (2003), the interaction of presidential approval and party polarization is significant in both the House and Senate. The negative interaction indicates that the relationship between public approval and legislative success declines as partisanship rises. Consistent with our theory, the negative interaction effect is two times larger in the House than in the Senate. Each 1 percent increase in partisanship reduces the effect of public approval on presidential success about –0.02 (–0.017 rounded up) in the House, and –0.01 (–0.008 rounded up) in the Senate.

The coefficient for approval in this model indicates the effect at zero partisanship. In the absence of partisanship, the model suggests that the effect of public approval would be positive with a larger effect in the House than in the Senate—a 1 percent rise in approval is associated with nearly a 1 percent (.91) increase in success in the House and about a .66 percent increase in the Senate. But zero partisanship is not a realistic value. Consider now how polarization affects the relationship between presidential approval and success at average levels of party voting. The average percentage of party votes from 1953–2001 was about 47.02 in the House and about 46.14 in the Senate. Over the entire time period, the average effect of public approval on presidential success in the House was about 0.11 (i.e., 0.91 + [47.02*–0.017] = 0.11), and about 0.29 (i.e., 0.66 + [46.14*–.008] = 0.29) in the Senate. Thus, at average partisanship, a 10 percent increase in public approval produces about a 1.1 percent increase in success in the House and a 2.9 percent increase in the Senate. This result means that a relatively large 10 percent rise in presidential approval translates into about one additional House victory and two additional Senate victories (i.e., 65*.011 = 0.72 in the House; 72*.029 = 2.09 in the Senate).[3] These effects are small, especially compared to the effect of the president's party controlling the chamber. And if partisnship increases one standard deviation above the mean (to 57.75 in the House and 55.11 in the Senate), the effect of presidential approval is negative in the House (i.e., 0.91 + [57.75*–0.017] =

–0.07) and remains small in the Senate (i.e., 0.66 + [55.11*–.008] = 0.22).

Finally, consider how polarization conditions the relationship between party control and success. The interaction of party control and polarization is positive in both chambers, implying that unified parties produce higher success if the president's party controls a chamber.[4] With same party control in the House, each 1 percent increase in polarization produces a 1.44 percent increase in success. The coefficient is smaller and not significant in the Senate. It implies that under same party control each 1 percent increase in polarization would increase success about 0.41 percent.

Since the coefficient for party control indicates the effect of majority status at zero partisanship (no party votes), we need to evaluate the effects at more realistic levels. At average partisanship in the House, the majority party bonus is about 30 points (–37.38 + [1.44*47.02] = 30.33), and at one standard deviation above mean partisanship, the majority bonus increases to about 46 points (–37.38 + [1.44*57.75] = 45.78). At average partisanship in the Senate, majority presidents receive about a 25-point bonus (5.91 + [.41*46.14] = 24.83), and at one standard deviation above mean partisanship, the majority bonus is about 29 points (5.91 + [.41*55.11] = 28.51).[5]

These results indicate that polarization increases the success rates of majority presidents. And as predicted by our theory, the effects are muted in the Senate: the direct effect of majority control is smaller in the Senate than in the House, and the boost in success that majority presidents receive if the parties are polarized is also smaller in the Senate.

Which Presidents Do Better or Worse Than Expected?

The purpose of this analysis was to produce a well-specified model of annual presidential success in Congress in order to establish a common baseline. The residuals indicate whether any of the 10 presidents in the sample appear "uncommonly" successful or unsuccessful after accounting for political conditions that theoretically affect success in Congress.

Is the baseline model well specified? The final models with the interactions explain 77 percent and 70 percent of the residual variance in the House and Senate respectively. The standard errors of estimates show that the average residual error is about 10.42 percent and 9.95 percent respectively. In other words, if we used these models to predict presidential success, we could be wrong on average by about 10 percent in each chamber. We tried adding some other potentially interesting variables, including magnitude of the president's election victory, turnover in congressional seats in the prior election, and individual year dummies. None of these variables produced statistically significant change.[6] We also ran a fourth order Ramsey's (1969) RESET test for model misspecification; the test was not statistically significant. Based on these results and tests, we are confident that the model is well specified.

To determine if any of these 10 presidents were unusual, we calculated *studentized residuals*. These are standardized residuals made independent by calculating the model fit while sequentially omitting each of the i observations. This approach to constructing an index of the relative "unusualness" of observations takes into account both the leverage that an observation exerts on the regression, as well as the absolute size of each residual. *Studentized residuals* follow a t-distribution with T-k-1 degrees of freedom (43 degrees of freedom with our models). Using a 95 percent confidence interval, absolute values of *studentized residuals* greater than about 2.017 would be considered unusual. By random chance, we would expect one in 20 to appear unusual. For our sample of size 49, we would expect about 2.45 unusual observations by random chance in each chamber.

Figure 8.1 plots the *studentized residuals* for the House and Senate. We find only three "unusual" observations in each chamber. In the House, the "unusual" observations occur in 1960, 1971, and 1988; in the Senate, they occur in 1958, 1977, and 1999. These outliers occur for different presidents in different years in each chamber, and there is no systematic relation between chambers that would suggest simultaneous uncommon success of any particular president. Since we expect 2.45 "unusual" observations in each chamber by random chance, this analysis suggests there is little systematic in the residuals that would point toward "uncommon" presidential success or failure.

Of course, one might argue that the "unusualness" standard implied by *studentized residuals* is arbitrary and that there are patterns in the residuals that imply other factors. We do, of course, observe periods within presidencies when a president was more or less successful than predicted by the model. For example, Eisenhower appears more successful than predicted through most of the second term. Nixon was more successful in the House than predicted by the base model from 1971 through 1973. And Clinton was less successful than predicted during the second term.

Attributing such patterns to presidential performance and skill, however, is not appropriate. Although we are confident that our statistical baseline is well-specified, as with any statistical model it contains error resulting from unknown sources. Some presidency scholars emphasize the importance of leadership skill, and we know our model omits this potentially important variable. But we have no scientific way to determine how much of the error variance (if any) is attributable to this (or any other) omitted variable.

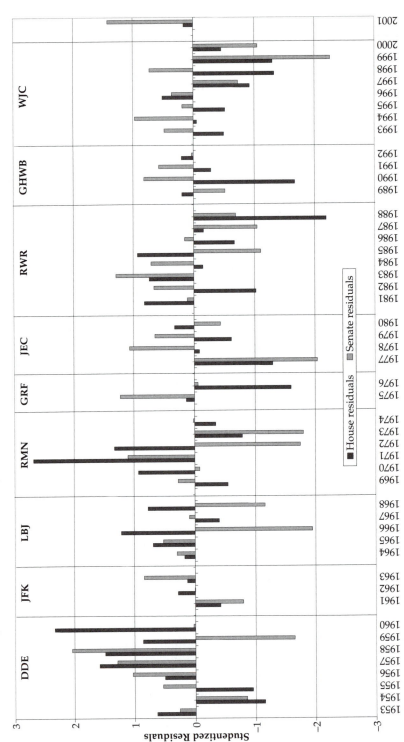

Figure 8.1   Which Presidents Were More or Less Successful Than Expected in Congress

Nonetheless, this analysis ought to raise serious questions about leadership skill as a systematic explanation of presidential success on roll call votes in Congress. Just as the clue of the dog that didn't bark pointed Sherlock Holmes to the true culprit in Sir Arthur Conan Doyle's mystery *Silver Blaze*, let's consider what this analysis does not find.

First, the failure to find more than a random number of cases of "uncommon" success suggests that the baseline model has identified the most important determinants of success. If leadership skills were an important and systematic variable omitted from the model, then we should see more presidents who did much better or worse than expected relative to the conditions they faced.

Second, theoretical discussions do not suggest that different skills are required to succeed in the House and Senate, or that skills operate differently in the two chambers. If political skills or the lack of them lead to uncommonly high or low success, then we would expect to see some uncommon cases for the same president in both chambers simultaneously. The few observations of uncommon success appear randomly distributed across president and chambers. No single president had uncommon success in both chambers in the same year. Eisenhower is the only president with more than one outlier and they are in different years (the Senate in 1958 and House in 1960).

Finally, the few "uncommon" cases do not match up to presidents identified by qualitative research as highly skilled or unskilled. Neither Johnson nor Reagan, who according to the journalistic and scholarly consensus were highly skilled, appear as uncommonly successful relative to the political conditions they faced. To the contrary, Reagan's success in the House in 1988 was one of the unusually low cases. And the presidents viewed as least skilled, Nixon and Carter, also fail to conform to expectations of the skills explanation. Although Carter's success in the Senate in 1977 was unusually low, Nixon's success in the House in 1971 was uncommonly high.

Conclusions

Presidency scholars claim that presidential success is a function of both skill and political conditions. Although students of presidential-congressional relations have been unable to demonstrate convincingly that presidential activities systematically affect success, the literature provides substantial theory and evidence regarding the political conditions that determine presidential success in Congress. Our analysis contributes additional evidence that presidential success on the floor of Congress is determined primarily by whether political conditions are favorable or unfavorable. Although our model leaves some variance unexplained, few of the residuals would be considered outliers. That is, none of the 10 presidents analyzed here were un-commonly successful or unsuccessful relative to the conditions they faced. The few instances of uncommon success could occur by ran-dom chance.

Presidential skill, nonetheless, continues to occupy a central, if not dominant, position in the literature. This analysis cannot refute skill as an explanation. Previous research has found a number of interest-ing and important cases on which a skilled performance (or lack of it) made the difference between success and failure. But the debate over the relative importance of skills cannot be resolved simply by agree-ing that skills matter some of the time on some issues. If presidential skill is to provide a theoretical understanding of presidential success on par with that provided by political conditions, then we should be able to observe more than idiosyncratic effects on a small number of issues. The burden of providing systematic evidence rests on pro-ponents of the skill part of the explanation. The persistent failure to find systematic evidence should raise doubts about skill as scientific theory.

We should also continue to work to improve our understanding of the conditions that affect presidential success, and how they operate. Our finding of significant interactions of party polarization with pub-lic approval and majority control is noteworthy. Party control sets the basic condition for presidential success, and presidents do somewhat better in their honeymoon year. The marginal effect of public opinion on success is conditioned by the level of partisanship in Congress. At low levels of partisanship, the president's standing with the public has a modest positive effect on success. But at high levels of partisan-ship, which have characterized Congress in recent decades, the mar-ginal effect of public approval diminishes (and even turns negative in the House). Party polarization also interacts with party control, en-hancing the benefit of majority status.

Thus, polarized parties further reduce the ability of presidential activities to affect success even at the margins. In polarized periods, electoral processes reduce the number of moderate and crosspres-sured members, the very members who are most inclined to search beyond the primary cues of party and ideology for guidance in mak-ing decisions. Fewer members who look beyond party and ideology means fewer members subject to presidential persuasion. This condi-tion places a high premium on having majorities in the House and Senate. Unless the level of partisanship in Congress declines, a ratio-nal strategy for a president who seeks to improve his legislative suc-cess is to focus on maintaining or winning partisan majorities in the House and Senate. President Bush seemed to have successfully fol-lowed this strategy in the 2002 midterm elections. Ironically, electoral activities aimed at electing sympathetic majorities in Congress are likely to contribute to more party polarization.

Notes

1. Other timing effects include a "cycle of increasing effectiveness" as the president's knowledge and expertise grow, and a "cycle of decreasing influence" as the president's political capital and energy are depleted (Light 1982). Since these are offsetting influences without precise measures, it is difficult to include both in a statistical model. The effects of midterm elections are captured by partisan influences in the model.

2. In a separate set of analyses, we measured party polarization using Poole and Rosenthal's DW-NOMINATE scores (Poole and Rosenthal 1997). The results were similar to those reported below, but somewhat weaker. We suspect the difference results because DW-NOMINATE scores vary only biennially.

3. The average number of party votes over the period of this study was 65 in the House and 72 in the Senate.

4. When interacting a binary and a continuous variable, one typically includes both in the model. But including polarization as well as the interactions produces severe multicollinearity, so we omit polarization. This omission imposes the theoretical restriction that polarization has no effect generally, but only in interaction with other variables. This restriction is consistent with our theory that polarization does not directly cause success to rise or fall.

5. Since the coefficient for majority party control is not significant in the Senate model, one might prefer to treat it as zero. If we do, the estimates are reduced to 18.92 at the mean and 22.60 at plus one standard deviation.

6. One study included the number of positions taken, as a measure of risk taking by the president (Brace and Hinckley 1992). This measure is nonstationary in time series terms and often produces spurious relationships (Granger and Newbold 1974). In addition, our dependent variable contains the total number of votes on which the president took a position, so the number of presidential positions would be endogenous in our analysis.

References

Aldrich, John H. 1995. *Why Parties: The Origin and Transformation of Political Parties in America*. Chicago: University of Chicago Press.

Aldrich, John H., and David W. Rohde. 2000. "The Consequences of Party Organization in the House: The Role of the Majority and Minority Parties in Conditional Party Government." In Jon R. Bond and Richard Fleisher (Eds.), *Polarized Politics: Congress and the President in a Partisan Era*. Washington, DC: CQ Press.

Arnold, R. Douglas. 1990. *The Logic of Congressional Action*. New Haven: Yale University Press.

Bond, Jon R., and Richard Fleisher. 1990. *The President in the Legislative Arena*. Chicago: University of Chicago Press.

Bond, Jon R., Richard Fleisher, and B. Dan Wood. 2003. "The Marginal and Time Varying Effect of Public Approval on Presidential Success in Congress." *Journal of Politics* 65 (February):92–110.

Brace, Paul, and Barbara Hinckley. 1992. *Follow the Leader: Opinion Polls and the Modern Presidents.* New York: Basic Books.

Congressional Quarterly, Inc. Annually 1953–2001. "Presidential Support." *Congressional Quarterly Almanac.* (Washington, DC: Congressional Quarterly, Inc.).

Covington, Cary R. 1987a. "Mobilizing Congressional Support for the President: Insights from the 1960s." *Legislative Studies Quarterly* 12 (February):77–96.

———. 1987b. "Staying Private: Gaining Congressional Support for Unpublicized Presidential Preferences on Roll Call Votes." *Journal of Politics* 49 (August):737–755.

———. 1988a. "Building Presidential Coalitions Among Cross-pressured Members of Congress." *Western Political Quarterly* 41 (March):47–62.

———. 1988b. "Guess Who's Coming to Dinner: The Distribution of White House Social Invitations and Their Effects on Congressional Support." *American Politics Quarterly* 16 (July):243–265.

Covington, Cary R., J. Mark Wrighton, and Rhonda Kinney. 1995. "A Presidency-Augmented Model of Presidential Success on House Roll Call Votes." *American Journal of Political Science* 39 (November):1001–1024.

Cronin, Thomas E. 1980. "A Resurgent Congress and the Imperial Presidency." *Political Science Quarterly* 95 (Summer):209–237.

Davidson, Roger H. 1984. "The Presidency and Congress." In *The Presidency and the Political System,* ed. Michael Nelson. Washington, DC: CQ Press.

Edwards, George C. III. 1980. *Presidential Influence in Congress.* San Francisco: W. H. Freeman.

———. 1989. *At the Margins: Presidential Leadership of Congress.* New Haven: Yale University Press.

Edwards, George C. III, with Alec M. Gallup. 1990. *Presidential Approval: A Sourcebook.* Baltimore: Johns Hopkins University Press.

Fenno, Richard F. 1973. *Congressmen in Committees.* Boston: Little, Brown.

———. 1978. *Home Style: House Members in Their Districts.* Boston: Little, Brown.

Fett, Patrick J. 1994. "Presidential Legislative Priorities and Legislators' Voting Decisions: An Exploratory Analysis." *Journal of Politics* 56 (May):502–512.

Fleisher, Richard, and Jon R. Bond. 1983. "Assessing Presidential Support in the House: Lessons from Reagan and Carter." *Journal of Politics* 45 (August):745 58.

———. 1992. "Assessing Presidential Support in the House II: Lessons from George Bush." *American Journal of Political Science* 37 (May):525–541.

———. 2000. "Partisanship and the President's Quest for Votes on the Floor of Congress." In Jon R. Bond and Richard Fleisher (Eds.), *Polarized Politics: Congress and the President in a Partisan Era.* Washington, DC: CQ Press.

Granger, C. W. J., and Paul Newbold. 1974. "Spurious Regressions in Econometrics." *Journal of Econometrics* 2 (July):111–120.

Jackson, John E. 1974. *Constituencies and Leaders in Congress.* Cambridge: Harvard University Press.

Jacobson, Gary C. 1990. *The Electoral Origins of Divided Government.* Boulder, CO: Westview.

Jacobson, Gary C., and Samuel Kernell. 1983. *Strategy and Choice in Congressional Elections,* 2nd ed. New Haven: Yale University Press.

Joslyn, Mark R. 1995. "Institutional Change and House Support: Assessing George Bush in the Postreform Era." *American Politics Quarterly* 23 (January):62–80.

Kellerman, Barbara. 1984. *The Political Presidency: Practice of Leadership From Kennedy Through Reagan.* New York: Oxford University Press.

Kingdon, John W. 1981. *Congressmen's Voting Decisions,* 2nd ed. New York: Harper and Row.

Light, Paul Charles. 1982. *The President's Agenda: Domestic Policy Choice From Kennedy to Carter (With Notes on Ronald Reagan).* Baltimore: The Johns Hopkins University Press.

Lockerbie, Brad, and Stephen A. Borrelli. 1989. "Getting Inside the Beltway: Perceptions of Presidential Skill and Success in Congress." *British Journal of Political Science* 19 (January):97–106.

Matthews, Donald R., and James A. Stimson. 1975. *Yeas and Nays: Normal Decision Making in the U.S. House of Representatives.* New York: Wiley.

Mayhew, David R. 1974. *Congress: The Electoral Connection.* New Haven: Yale University Press.

Neustadt, Richard E. 1960. *Presidential Power.* New York: Wiley.

Newey, W., and K. West. 1987. "A Simple, Positive Semi-definite, Heteroskedasticity and Autocorrelation Consistent Covariance Matrix." *Econometrica* 55 (May):703–708.

Ornstein, Norman, Thomas E. Mann, and Michael J. Malbin. 1998. *Vital Statistics on Congress, 1997–98.* Washington, DC: CQ Press.

Poole, Keith T., and Howard Rosenthal. 1997. *Congress: A Political-Economic History of Roll Call Voting.* Washington, DC: Congressional Quarterly Press.

Ramsey, J. B. 1969. "Tests for Specification Error in Classical Linear Least Squares Regression Analysis." *Journal of the Royal Statistical Society* B31:250–271.

Rohde, David. 1991. *Parties and Leaders in the Post Reform House.* Chicago: University of Chicago Press.

Sullivan, Terry. 1988. "Headcounts, Expectations, and Presidential Coalitions in Congress." *American Journal of Political Science* 32 (August):567–589.

———. 1990. "Explaining Why Presidents Count: Signaling and Information." *Journal of Politics* 52 (August):939–962.

———. 1991. "The Bank Account Presidency: A New Measure of Evidence on the Temporal Path of Presidential Influence." *American Journal of Political Science* 35 (August):686–723.

Willis, Derek. 2002 "Party Unity Background." *CQ Weekly,* January 12:142.

Wilson, James Q. 1992. *American Government.* Lexington, MA: D.C. Heath. ✦

Chapter 9

The Politicized Judiciary
A Threat to Executive Power

Forrest Maltzman

Congress is not the only other constitutional actor that presidents interact with at the federal level. The federal courts also play an important role in the outcome of political and policy decisions that are important to presidents. Yet, as Maltzman notes in this chapter, most of the literature on the presidency and the courts presents a "textbook" view in which the courts generally accede to the demands of the presidency. But is this view of judicial acquiescence accurate? That is the question Maltzman addresses. If the courts do not merely acquiesce, then they too could represent yet another impediment to presidential leadership.

Maltzman examines several primary methods used by presidents to influence the courts. Presidents use the solicitor general (S.G.) to present their legal arguments before the nation's highest court. When the U.S. government is a direct party to an ongoing legal challenge, the administration's success rate has been fairly consistent over time—on average they prevail in 63 percent of cases. In cases where the S.G. files an *amicus curiae* or "friend of the court" brief, however, the success rate has declined significantly over time. Many of these negative decisions are in substantively important, high-profile cases (such as affirmative action).

Given this propensity for the courts to decide against the president, what leverage do presidents have with the courts? One potential source is the solicitor general. Yet, when the S.G. files a brief advocating a conservative position, "justices who disagree ideologically with the administration are less likely to vote in a conservative direction." The same dynamic occurs when liberal S.G.s file *amicus curiae* briefs. Consequently, presidents do not have leverage to influence the justices' decisions. In fact, this evidence suggests precisely the opposite conclusion. Furthermore, while presidents do have leverage over the courts through their appointment power, the Senate also has the power to confirm justices. In recent decades, Maltzman finds that the time it takes for the Senate to confirm judges has increased, a sign of increased disagreement between the two branches of government. There also has been a substantial decline in the confirmation rates for judicial nominees. This can be explained in great part by the increased ideological polarization between presidents and members of their congressional opposition. This process is further exacerbated by the ideologically charged issues (e.g., abortion, gay marriage) that are coming before the courts. Thus, the courts represent yet another arena in which leverage has declined.

✦ ✦ ✦

On June 23, 2003, the United States Supreme Court affirmed a decision of the Sixth Circuit Court of Appeals that upheld the University of Michigan law school's affirmative action program (*Barbara Grutter v. Lee Bollinger et al.*). The decision was a stunning defeat for George W. Bush's administration. After debating the legal and political merits of filing a "friend of the Court" (*amicus curiae*) brief, the Bush administration had taken a clear position against the Michigan programs. Indeed, in a nationally televised press conference, the President himself had described the University's system as "divisive, unfair and impossible to square with the Constitution" (CNN, January 16th, 2004).[1] A year later, the Bush administration's conduct in the war on terrorism was directly challenged by the Court. In an 8–1 decision, the Court declared that citizens detained as "enemy combatants" were entitled to due process and access to an attorney (*Hamdi v. Rumsfeld*). In another 6–3 decision, the Court ruled that foreign "enemy combatants" held at Guantanamo Bay, Cuba should be given access to U.S. Courts (*Rasul et al. v. Bush*).

These three decisions illustrate the challenge presidents face in using the courts to further their policy and political goals. Indeed, the Court dealt the Bush administration major setbacks in two of the policy areas (civil rights and the war on terrorism) that were at the top of the President's agenda. The assertiveness of the judicial branch in these three cases is in many respects characteristic of the relationship that currently exists between the courts and the executive branch.

It is also a characteristic that violates our "textbook" understanding of the relationship between the judicial and executive branches. Scholars typically portray the judiciary as an institution that acquiesces to the demands of the executive branch. For example, Edwards and Wayne argue that "most presidents operate under few constraints from the courts" (2003, 400). That portrait of deference is consistent with almost 50 years of scholarly portraits of the relationship between the president and the federal courts (see Rossiter 1960, 52).

The textbook portrait of the Court has historically rested on several pillars. First, when the executive branch states a legal position as either a party in a case or by filing an *amicus* brief, the executive disproportionately wins. For example, Scigiliano discovered that when the United States was a direct party in a case, 64 percent of the Supreme Court's decisions reflected the position preferred by the executive. Scigliano noted that the executive branch's success ratio was "even better" when it participated as *amicus curiae* (1971, 179). For the period 1952 to 2000, Deen, Ignagni, and Meernik showed that the executive branch prevailed almost 75 percent of the time when it participated as *amicus curiae* (2001; see also McGuire 1998; Segal and Reedy 1988; O'Connor 1983).

Second, when the Court is directly asked to decide issues that involve the prerogatives of the executive, the Court has historically ruled in favor of the executive. Between 1792 and 1997, Ragsdale (1988) reports that only 76 decisions of the Supreme Court directly curtailed executive branch power. The pattern of executive success is even more remarkable if one excludes the 25 instances when the Court ruled against President Nixon. However, even here the Court has recently been willing to rule against the executive. For example, in 1998 the U.S. Supreme Court decided in *Clinton et al. v. New York City et al.* that the line-item veto (a bill that enabled the president to effectively remove particular line items from appropriation bills) was unconstitutional. The Court's willingness to deny President Clinton the line-item veto was not the only threat to executive power experienced by the 42nd president. The Court denied the president's petition to keep Paula Jones's civil suit out of the judicial branch (*Clinton v. Jones*) and executive privilege claims that would have prevented a special prosecutor from being able to compel testimony from Secret Service agents (*Rubin v. United States*).[2]

The Court's rejection of several pivotal arguments made by Presidents Bush and Clinton suggest that the textbook portrait of executive-judicial branch relations is dated. The judicial branch today is an assertive force in the American political system. Its decisions frequently run counter to the goals and preferences of the executive. Although the "textbook" portrait may have been an accurate description during an earlier period in time, it is not an accurate portrait of the past 50 years. Instead, the court is an independent force that on occasion accommodates the president, but also frequently challenges him. In this chapter, I explore those forces that have reshaped the relationship between the president and the judiciary. I argue that theses forces have undermined the president's ability to use the Courts to pursue his policy and political goals.

Executive-Judicial Relations

President Bush's experiences with the Supreme Court reflect an emerging pattern: the Court regularly challenges the decision of the executive branch. This point is illustrated in Figure 9.1. In this figure, I present the success rate of the executive branch before the Supreme

Court in two types of cases. In one set of cases, I report for the period 1954–2000 the success of the federal government before the Supreme Court when the United States is a party in a case. These cases are demarked with a solid line. In the 46-year period covered, the federal government prevailed when it was a party in 63 percent of the cases. Although this figure has varied from a high of 83.3 percent (1983) to a low of 44.1 percent (1956), the trend is essentially flat.[3] The federal government's record over this period is relatively consistent, prevailing in just under two-thirds the cases in which it participates.

The dashed line in Figure 9.1 explores the success rate when the federal government filed an *amicus curiae* ("friend of the court") brief. Whereas the first series involves cases where the United States is a party (e.g., someone commits a federal crime), the second set is cases that do not directly involve the federal government. The briefs in these cases (such as the Michigan affirmative action case discussed earlier) are usually filed at the discretion of the executive branch. As a result, they largely reflect the administration's attempt to use the Court to further the president's agenda (Pacelle 2003; Bailey, Kamoie, and Maltzman 2005). A different pattern emerges in these cases. Whereas at one time the solicitor general's participation may have been useful for a president seeking to further their policy goals, the Court increasingly rejects the arguments made by the solicitor general on behalf of the president.[4] Whereas the federal government's success rate when the United States is a party is essentially stable, its success rate when it participates as an *amicus curiae* has significantly

Figure 9.1   Executive Success Before the Supreme Court: 1946–2001

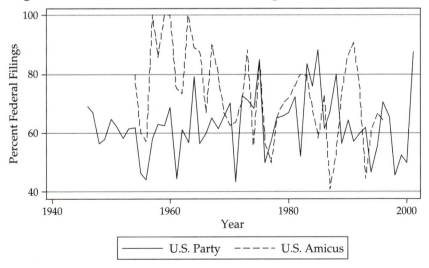

Source: Data compiled from Epstein et al. (2003), tables 7–12 and 7–15.

declined over time. Indeed, the fate the Bush administration encountered in *Grutter v. Bollinger* was encountered by the Clinton administration in almost one-third of all cases.

The ability of the executive branch to count on the Supreme Court to further its policy goals is not unique to the highest court in the land. Federal district and appellate court judges regularly reject claims made by the administration. Although precise data are difficult to come by, available evidence suggests that legislation that is designed to overrule a judicial decision frequently stems from a decision that was initially made by either a district or appellate court.[5]

Judicial Decisionmaking Criteria

According to the textbook model of judicial-executive relations, federal judges look to the executive branch to provide guidance as to the direction of the law. According to this model, the Court looks to the executive for several reasons. First, the executive provides the Court with information that is necessary to ensure the effective implementation of the law. It is also this argument that has led some to label the executive branch's lawyer before the Supreme Court (the solicitor general) "the tenth justice" (Caplan 1987; but see McGuire 1998). Second, the Court responds to the executive because of fear that its credibility will be undermined by the executive's refusal to comply or willingness to support a legislative override (Knight and Epstein 1996). As evidence for this view, scholars point to particular instances in time when the Court was reluctant to act in a manner hostile to the preferences of an administration (e.g., Knight and Epstein 1996; Caldeira 1987; Gely and Spiller 1990).

In contrast to these portraits of a constrained and responsive judicial branch, the dominant conclusion one draws from those who study the votes cast by justices is that their actions reflect their policy preferences and ideological values (Schubert 1965; Segal and Spaeth 2002). In other words, when justices review the positions embraced by the executive branch, they are guided first and foremost by their views of the law and their preferred policy outcomes.

Patterns of Judicial Responsiveness

To determine whether Supreme Court justices are responsive to the wishes of the executive, we can look at the voting behavior of individual justices when the executive participates as an *amicus*.[6] If the executive branch serves as a source of legal expertise to the bench or if justices are reluctant to see the executive ignore or overrule the Court, we should expect all justices to support the administration's preferred position. On the other hand, if justices vote in accordance with their policy preferences, we would expect justices who are ideological allies of the solicitor general to be more likely to support the position of an ideologically sympathetic administration. In other words, if the S.G.'s participation is viewed by individual justices as a signal regarding an administration's policy preferences, conservative justices (such as Clarence Thomas, Antonin Scalia, and William Rehnquist) should be more responsive to the arguments made by a conservative president's administration (such as George W. Bush or Ronald Reagan) than liberal justices (such as Ruth Bader Ginsburg, Thurgood Marshall, or William Brennan). Likewise, liberal justices should be more responsive to the arguments made by liberal administrations.

Table 9.1 reports the proportion of the time that each justice voted with the S.G. when he or she embraced liberal and conservative outcomes and the significance of this difference. The data are based upon all civil liberties and rights cases during the 1953–2002 period.[7] For example, Justice Marshall voted with the S.G. in 16 percent of the cases when the S.G. embraced a conservative position and 96 percent of the cases in which he or she embraced a liberal position. This difference is significant. Indeed, 15 of the 17 justices over this period gave markedly different levels of support to conservative and liberal positions embraced by the solicitor general.

Although this pattern is highly suggestive that justices do not defer to the executive simply because of their constitutional roles, it is not proof. First, the table does not tell us whether the liberals support a liberal administration because they share the same views or because presidents influence justices' votes. Second, sometimes liberal administrations embrace conservative positions, and vice versa. In these instances, we would expect a justice who is sympathetic with the predisposition of an administration to be particularly likely to vote contrary to their usual policy positions (see Calvert 1985, 552).[8]

To get a better understanding of the influence administration position taking has on justices' votes, we can examine the conditions under which justices are likely to support the positions of an administration. In Table 9.2, I look at whether a justice supports the position recommended by the solicitor general when the S.G. has filed an *amicus* brief. For explanatory variables, I look at each justice's ideological closeness to the sitting president. In the model, the dependent variable is whether the S.G. took a position that runs contrary to his administration's normal policy views.[9]

As shown in Table 9.2, the variable that taps a justice's ideological closeness to the administration (DISTANCE FROM S.G.) is negative and significant. This means that when the S.G. files a brief advocating a conservative position, justices who disagree ideologically with the administration are less likely to vote in the conservative direction. Likewise, when the S.G. advocates a liberal outcome, ideological foes of the president are less likely to embrace the administration's posi-

Table 9.1 **Support for the Solicitor General *Amicus* Positions**
(1953–2002 Terms)

Justice	Overall	Percent Support for S.G		Chi-Sq*	Number of S.G. Amicus *Briefs* Filed	
		S.G. Liberal	S.G. Conservative		S.G. Conservative	S.G. Liberal
Black	0.74	0.78	0.43	—	7	54
Reed	1.00	1.00	1.00	—	1	2
Frankfurter	0.73	0.80	0.00	—	1	10
Douglas	0.8	0.97	0.13	51.31*	15	59
Jackson	1.00	1.00	—	—		2
Burton	1.00	1.00	1.00	—	1	4
Clark	0.79	0.82	0.50	—	4	44
Minton	1.00	1.00	1.00	—	1	2
Warren	0.92	0.96	0.50	—	6	53
Harlan	0.47	0.49	0.25	—	4	51
Brennan	0.55	0.95	0.25	128.71*	157	115
Whittaker	0.75	0.75	—	—		8
Stewart	0.67	0.65	0.71	0.29	34	84
BWhite	0.79	0.74	0.82	2.78	192	117
Goldberg	1.00	1.00	—	—		25
Fortas	0.73	0.82	0.40	—	5	17
Marshall	0.42	0.96	0.16	138.23*	163	77
Burger	0.79	0.59	0.92	23.99*	96	58
Blackmun	0.61	0.85	0.51	28.94*	192	85
Powell	0.73	0.58	0.82	11.82*	107	59
Rehnquist	0.77	0.42	0.95	136.22*	246	130
Stevens	0.48	0.76	0.34	58.54*	236	123
OConnor	0.77	0.65	0.82	9.80*	217	95
Scalia	0.71	0.35	0.88	67.21*	151	72
AKennedy	0.73	0.48	0.86	32.01*	127	67
Souter	0.69	0.82	0.60	8.40*	92	65
Thomas	0.64	0.28	0.90	56.30*	80	60
Ginsburg	0.66	0.8	0.52	10.55*	60	56
Breyer	0.75	0.87	0.65	6.21*	54	45

*Significance of difference between support for S.G. when he urges a liberal and a conservative outcome. Critical value for $\alpha < 0.05$ is 3.84. If a justice participated in fewer than 10 cases where the S.G. participated as a liberal *amici* and 10 cases where the S.G. participated as a conservative *amici*, χ^2 is not calculated. A version of this table originally appeared in Bailey, Kamoie, and Maltzman (2005).

tions. This relationship holds even after controlling for the ideology of the justice (IDEOLOGICAL PROPENSITY), whose coefficient is also statistically significant. The statistically significant OUTLIER variable indicates that when the S.G. advocates a position that runs contrary to his usual ideological position, the cue is taken more seriously by justices who typically disagree with him. A justice is more

**Table 9.2 Probability of a Justice Voting
in a Manner Consistent with S.G. *Amicus* Brief**

Variable (expected sign) Signaling Variables	Distance from S.G. (–)	–0.26*** (5.82)	–0.23*** (5.49)
	Outlier signal (+)	0.20*** (3.52)	0.15** (2.67)
Justice-Specific Controls	Ideological propensity (+)	0.68*** (10.78)	0.71*** (11.05)
	Freshman (+)	— —	0.14* (1.39)
Case-Specific Controls	Legal salience (–)	— —	–0.30*** (3.96)
	Political salience (–)	— —	–0.31*** (4.98)
	Invitation (+)	— —	–0.13 (1.08)
	Complexity (+)	— —	–0.08 (1.22)
Constant		0.55 (9.31)	0.63 (3.66)
–2 Log Likelihood		–1915.3	–1852.9
Pseudo R^2		0.23	0.24
Correctly Predicted %		77.21%	77.23%
Reduction in Error %		30.1%	30.1%
Number of Observations		3888	3888

Note: Entries are unstandardized coefficients from probit estimation (t-statistics are in parentheses and based on robust standard errors). Fixed effects for each S.G. are included in the model, but not reported. A version of this table originally appeared in Bailey, Kamoie, and Maltzman (2005).
*p < 0.10; **p < 0.01; ***p < 0.001 (one-tailed)

likely to support a conservative S.G. when the S.G. advocates a liberal rather than a conservative outcome.

These patterns clearly demonstrate that different justices treat the information from the administration in a selective manner. Rather than merely deferring to the executive or viewing the executive as a valuable source of unbiased information about the law and the direction it should develop, justices view information from the administration as a signal about the policy implications of particular decisions. Thus, liberal justices value information from liberal administrations, and conservative justices prefer the positions of conservative administrations. This pattern is consistent with arguments that justices' decisions reflect their policy views.

This pattern also highlights one of the reasons why the executive branch has a hard time controlling the judiciary. Justices do not unquestionably defer to the executive when they hold different views about policy. Although this analysis is limited to the relationship between Supreme Court justices and the executive branch, there is little reason to suspect that lower-court justices are particularly prone to defer to the executive branch. Instead, the actions of lower-court judges appear to reflect the combination of three factors: the judge's ideology, the legal facts of the case, and the goal of avoiding reversal by acting in compliance with the decisions of the Supreme Court (Songer, Segal, and Cameron 1994; but see Klein 2002; Cross 2004). Indeed, scholars have found that federal district and appellate court judges appointed by Presidents Lyndon Johnson, Ronald Reagan, and George W. Bush quite often supported outcomes contrary to the views one would expect from the administration that appointed them.[10] Even though these three presidents actively sought to appoint judges who shared their ideological views, presidents were essentially powerless to control them once they were confirmed onto the federal bench.

Appointing Federal Judges

The fact that judges and justices frequently vote in a manner inconsistent with the preferences of the executives who appointed them stems in part from how judges make decisions once they are on the bench. However, judicial independence also grows from the politics of the appointment process. Although the president has the constitutional responsibility to nominate federal judges, the capacity of any single president to alter the nature of the judiciary is limited in several ways.[11] First, the opportunities for a single president to shape the judiciary are limited. On the federal trial and appellate benches, the turnover rate is approximately 4 percent each year (Carp, Manning, and Stidham 2004). On the Supreme Court, the turnover rate throughout our nation's history has been approximately one justice every two-year period.

Second, the vast majority of the vacancies presidents can fill have a small impact on the bench's ideological composition. Because judges have lifetime appointments, the ability of a president to change a bench's ideological tenor depends on both who retires and the ideological bent of that court. If the bench is overwhelmingly dominated by either liberal or conservative judges, no single appointment is likely to make a big difference in the partisan or ideological balance of the bench.[12] Likewise, if a judge or justice retires who holds views sympathetic to those of the president, the president will be unable to use the appointment to alter the composition of the Court. For example, if a conservative Supreme Court Justice (such as Antonin Scalia) retires, a conservative president can appoint another conservative, but that doesn't remove any liberals from the Court or change the status quo.

Third, the appointment power is a limited one, because predicting future judicial behavior is complicated. Once confirmed, a judge has his or her position for life. They therefore have virtually no incentive to defer to the views of the president by complying with his policy positions and legal arguments. Even if the administration uses a litmus test or screening process to identify judges who would be most likely to be "true" believers in an administration's positions, the administration is likely to encounter what economists often term an "adverse selection problem." That is, a president lacks the capacity to fully understand a nominee's policy preferences and such nominees have an incentive to present themselves in a manner that is favorable to the president's positions.

Fourth, the Senate can be a powerful constraint on the president's use of the appointment power as a tool for crafting the bench. Article 2, Section 2, of the Constitution stipulates that presidential appointments must be made with the "Advice and Consent" of the Senate. As a result, the president and the Senate share the appointment power. The constitutionally prescribed role of the Senate provides senators with the opportunity to influence the fate of presidential appointees and thus the chance to shape the makeup of the federal bench.

When it comes to district and circuit appointments, individual senators often have the incentive and power to restrict the president's choices. Senators' influence arises from several corners. First, the geographic design of the federal courts strongly shapes the nature of Senate involvement in selecting federal judges. Because federal trial and appellate level courts are territorially defined, each federal judgeship is associated with a home state, and new judges are typically drawn from that state. As a result, senators attempt to influence the president's choice of appointees to federal courts in their states.

Second, Senate procedures that empower individual senators curtail a president's power. Although the Constitution prescribes Senate "advice" as well as "consent," nothing in the Constitution requires the president to respect the views of interested senators from the state. In practice, however, judicial nominees must pass muster with the entire chamber. Senate procedures that enable a minority of senators to block a nominee with a filibuster make Senate leaders reluctant to consider nominees who do not have broad support.[13]

Therefore, presidents have an incentive to anticipate objections from home-state and other pivotal senators in making appointments. In the past, federal judgeships rarely elicited the interest of senators outside the nominees' home states, so the views of the home-state senators from the president's party were typically sufficient to determine whether or not nominees would be confirmed. Other senators would typically defer to the views of the home-state senator from the president's party, thus establishing the norm of *senatorial courtesy*. Moreover, the Senate Judiciary Committee in the early twentieth century established the "blue slip," a process in which the views of home-state senators—regardless of whether they hailed from the president's party—were solicited before the committee passed judgment on the nominees (Binder 2004). By granting home-state senators a role in the confirmation process, individual senators could threaten to block a nominee during confirmation and thus encourage the president to consider senators' views before making appointments. In other words, the blue slip and senatorial courtesy provided individual senators with some leverage over the president.

Third, the Senate rarely considers nominations that lack the support of the Senate Judiciary Committee. For example, Orrin Hatch (R-Utah) used his leverage as chair of the Judiciary panel to force President Bill Clinton to nominate Hatch's friend Ted Stewart to a Utah district court seat. Although Clinton was reluctant to nominate Stewart because of his perceived antienvironmental record as the head of Utah's Department of Natural Resources during the 1980s, Hatch held as hostage 42 other judicial nominations until Clinton made the nomination (Ring 2004).

Fourth, divided party control of the Senate and White House also limits the president's ability to stack the courts as he sees fit. In such periods, the opposition party controlling the Senate is unwilling to give the president much leeway to reshape the federal bench. Instead, the opposition will allow home-state senators and the judiciary committee chair to block nominees they oppose (Binder and Maltzman 2002, 2004).

Likewise, the fact that the Senate calendar is determined by the majority empowers the opposing president during periods of divided government (Binder and Maltzman 2002, 2004). During periods when the Senate is controlled by the president's party, the Senate is more likely to ignore the will of home-state senators and judiciary committee chairs are more likely to envision their role as one of shepherding through presidential nominations.

Because judicial selection has rarely in the past elicited national attention and because Senate nominations have only occasionally triggered open conflict, conventional wisdom emphasizes the tranquil relationship between presidents and senators in shaping the federal bench. Senate observers have portrayed the president as deferring to the views of the home-state senators from his party when selecting judges for the nation's district courts. Presidents are said to be less likely to defer to senators over the selection of appellate judges for the circuit courts of appeal. Nevertheless, even here the process is usually portrayed as reflecting cooperation between home-state senators and the White House.

Patterns of Confirmation Politics

Despite the conventional wisdom, trends in the nomination and confirmation process suggest otherwise. Figure 9.2 shows the increasing length of the confirmation process over the last half of the twentieth century, a measure that likely reflects the level of disagreement over nominees in that Congress. The data include all nominees for the federal district and circuit courts of appeal eventually confirmed by the Senate. If the amount of time it takes to move an appointee from nomination to confirmation reflects the level of disagreement over the nominee, charges that the confirmation process is newly politicized certainly hold some weight. The Senate took on average just one month to confirm the average judicial nominee during President Ronald Reagan's first term. By the end of President Bill Clinton's second term, the wait had increased on average five-fold for district court nominees and seven-fold for appellate court nominees. At least a fourth of Clinton's judicial nominees in the 106th Congress (1999–2000) waited more than six months to be confirmed, including U.S. District Court Judge Richard Paez, who waited nearly four years to be confirmed to the Ninth Circuit Court of Appeals. Confirmation delay continued to increase under President George W. Bush, reaching a record for appellate court nominees in the 107th Congress (2001–2002).

Figure 9.2   Average Confirmation Delay (in Days, Each Congress)

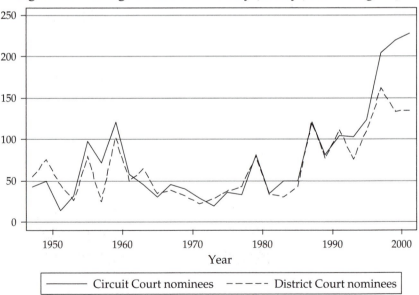

Source: Data compiled from *Final Legislative and Executive Calendars,* Senate Judiciary Committee, 80th–105th Congresses.

Still, delays weathered by recent presidents in securing confirmation of their nominees reflect more than Clinton's polarized relations with a Republican Senate or Bush's polarized relations with a Democratic Senate. Delays in the confirmation process were considerable in the mid-1980s, when Reagan saw Democratic Senates take on average nearly four months to confirm his judicial nominees. Even during a rare episode of unified Democratic control during 1993 and 1994, the Senate took on average three months to confirm the majority party's nominees.

The roots of today's impasse over federal judges are also visible in confirmation rates for judicial nominees. In Figure 9.3, a sharp decline in the rate of confirmation for district and appellate court appointees is quite striking. Whereas 100 percent of circuit court nominees were confirmed in the 1950s, less than 40 percent were confirmed in the 107th Congress (2001–2002). Overall, the data support the notion that the Senate confirmation process has markedly changed over the past 10 years, and suggest that presidents have an increasingly hard time stacking the bench to their advantage.

Of course, presidents also have a difficult time cherry picking the Supreme Court. Indeed, because of the visibility and importance of these positions, we would expect even more legislative review and re-

Figure 9.3   Confirmation Rates for Judicial Nominees, 1947–2002

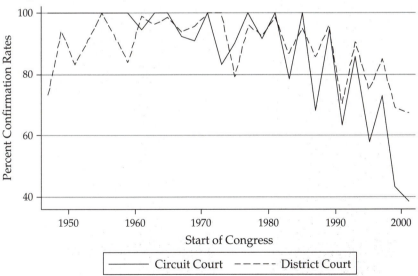

Source: Data compiled from *Final Legislative and Executive Calendars,* Senate Judiciary Committee, 80th–105th Congresses. Data for 106th and 107th Congresses compiled from United States Senate Committee on the Judiciary website, http://judiciary.senate.gov.

sistance. Over the past 40 years, less than 75 percent of presidential nominations to the Supreme Court have been confirmed.[14]

Although these figures and facts are indicative of the changing shape and tone of the nominating process, even these may exaggerate the president's influence on the bench. Strategic presidents frequently attempt to avoid protracted nomination battles by taking into account the preferences of the Senate. This dynamic was suggested by a Ninth Circuit judge, Stephen Reinhardt: "Clinton was not willing to have any fights over [the courts]," Reinhardt once observed, "so he just bowed to the Republicans, and he was careful not to nominate anyone who might be considered liberal" (cited in Ring 2004). Likewise, some prominent conservative commentators (such as Ann Coulter) felt that George W. Bush's choice of John Roberts was too big of a concession to the moderate wing of the Republican party.[15]

To more systematically explore the difficulty presidents face in shaping the bench, in Table 9.3 I model the probability that the Senate will act, during the 1947–1998 period, on a given appellate court nominee at a particular time.[16] Technically, the coefficients help us to understand whether a particular independent variable increases or decreases what is known as the "hazard" or "risk" of Senate action. The hazard of Senate action is thus roughly the probability of swift Senate action by the Senate to confirm a president's nominee.

The estimates generated by the analysis essentially indicate whether each independent variable increases or decreases how long it takes for the Senate to act. An independent variable whose coefficient has a positive sign means that increases in the value of the variable will speed up the probability of Senate action; negatively-signed coefficients show that as the value of the independent variable increases, the likelihood of swift Senate confirmation goes down. As independent variables, I use variables to tap the ideological distance between the median senator and the president and between that senator and the nominee. To determine whether the Senate is more reluctant to confirm a nominee when the vacancy is on a bench where the partisan balance of the sitting judges is evenly divided, we include a dummy variable to demark these "critical" nominations. To assess the impact of the Judiciary chair and home-state senator, I include variables to tap the ideological distance between the president and the furthest home-state senator and the chair of the Judiciary Committee. To assess whether partisan forces shape the confirmation process, I include variables to denote whether the Senate is controlled by the president's party; the ideological distance between the president and the opposing party's median, and whether a critical seat is being filled during a period of divided government. To determine whether the effect of the "institutional forces" variables are exaggerated during periods of divided government, these variables are interacted with a measure demarking the presence of divided government. Finally, I

Table 9.3 Cox Regression of the Timing of Senate Confirmation Decisions, 1947–1998 (Nominations to U.S. Circuit Courts of Appeal)

Variable (expected direction)	Coefficient (robust s.e.)
Ideological Forces	
Ideological distance between Senate and president (–)	1.00 (.79)
Ideological distance between Senate and nominee (–)	.16 (.40)
Nomination to a closely balanced court (–)	.36 (.15)
Senate Institutional Forces	
Ideological distance between Judiciary chair and president (–)	.16 (.36)
Home state senator is ideologically distant from president (–)	.49 (.19)
Partisan Forces	
Divided government (–)	–.10 (.30)
Ideological distance between president and opposing party (–)	–3.14 (1.06)**
Nomination to a closely balanced court during divided government (–)	–.82 (.25)***
Senate Institutional Forces During Divided Government	
Ideological distance between Judiciary chair and president during divided government (–)	–1.05 (.61)*
Home-state senator is ideologically distant from president during divided government (–)	–2.32 (1.20)*
Presidential Forces	
Well-qualified nominee (+)	.01 (.13)
Qualified nominee (+)	.49 (.65)
Temporal Forces	
Number of nominations pending (–)	–.02 (.00)***
Time left in session (+)	–.00 (.00)
Congress counter (–)	–.04 (.02)**
Log Likelihood	–1814.13
Chi^2	304.76***
N	413

Notes: The table reports results of a Cox regression model, based on Stata 8.0 *stcox* routine. Significance of coefficients is indicated as follows: * p < .05, ** p < .01, *** p < .001 (all one-tailed t-tests).

include variables to tap the quality of the president's nominees (as judged by the American Bar Association), the number of nominations pending, the time left in the session, and a countervariable to control for the trend seen in Figures 9.2 and 9.3.[17]

The results in Table 9.3 strongly suggest the Senate's institutional features and the rise of partisanship in recent years severely limits the president in shaping the bench. For example, when judgeships open up on closely divided benches during divided government, senators drag their heels and radically slow down the confirmation process. When home-state senators and the Judiciary Committee chair ideologically disagree strongly with the president, they exploit the Senate rules and practices to drag out the confirmation process.

These findings help explain why presidents often find themselves unable to fill vacancies on some federal appellate circuits. Take, for example, the Sixth Circuit Court of Appeals. In 1997 and 1998, the circuit was nearly evenly balanced between Democrats and Republicans, as Democrats made up roughly 45 percent of the bench. That tight ideological balance led the parties to stalemate over additional appointments to that bench, despite the fact that nearly a quarter of the bench was vacant. Michigan's lone Republican senator blocked the president's nominees by exploiting the blue slip in the late 1990s, and the Republican chair of the Judiciary panel recognized his objections. Michigan's two Democratic senators after the 2000 elections then objected to President Bush's appointments to the circuit. General disagreement over the policy views of the nominees certainly fueled these senators, but their opposition was particularly intense given the stakes of filling the judgeships for the ideological balance of the regional bench.

Most importantly, neither president was able to ensure confirmation for his preferred nominees for the federal bench. Hamstrung by opposition party control of the Senate and the Judiciary Committee and buffeted Senate rules and practices that enhance senators' ability to block confirmation, neither Bush nor Clinton could persuade the Senate to confirm their nominees to this closely balanced Court. The Senate, in short, can place a severe constraint on presidents seeking to mold a federal bench that strongly supports their policy agendas.

Judicial Politicization

The contentiousness of the confirmation process and the reluctance of judges to indiscrimately defer to the administration's legal opinions grows in large part from the politicization of the law (Kagan 2001; Lovell 2003; Burke 2004; Barnes 2004). The growth in litigation is apparent in a number of different ways. For example, in 1961 approximately 13,500 statutory claims were filed in federal district courts. In 1970, close to 40,000 statutory claims were filed; in 1980, more than 75,000 claims; in 1990, over 125,000; and by 1998, close to 160,000 claims (Barnes 2004; United States 2000). The pattern is obvious. The courts are increasingly being used to resolve questions that arise from the political arena.

Perhaps even more telling are changes in who uses the federal courts. Between 1958–1961, an average of 4.75 *amicus* briefs were filed each year by public interest groups or law firms. Between 1978 and 1981, interests groups filed an average of 45.5 briefs each term. Between 1986 and 1990, an average of 103 briefs were filed each year (Epstein, Segal, Spaeth, and Walker 2003, 689). Once again, the pattern is clear. Organized interests are increasingly using the courts as a vehicle for pursuing and protecting their policy agendas.

It is not surprising that gun-control groups, property-rights groups, antismoking groups, prochoice groups, organized labor, and environmentalists utilize the legal process to pursue agendas that might not be implemented by elected officials. When legislators seem unable and unwilling to definitively resolve controversial policy questions, adversaries not surprisingly turn to the courts to pursue their agendas (Lovell 2003). It is this phenomenon that recently led Justice Antonin Scalia to question "the propriety, indeed the sanity, of having value-laden decisions such as these [capital punishment, abortion, and physician-assisted suicide] made for the entire society . . . by judges" (Belkin 2004). As the courts have become increasingly controversial and accessible policymakers, rather than merely interpreters of legal facts and cases, the president's influence over the judiciary has been challenged. Given the stakes of Court decisions, few are willing to allow the president unfettered influence over the judiciary and its pivotal legal choices.

Likewise, the inability of presidents to control the judiciary is increasingly a threat to executive branch control of policy outcomes. With the courts having been transformed into a viable outlet for routinely determining important policy questions, the lack of presidential control has become an important threat to executive power and influence. The growth in policy by litigation has encouraged members of Congress and interest groups to challenge presidential influence over judicial nominations and executive branch success. Even without these challenges, the constantly growing and changing docket would make it virtually impossible for a president to use nominations to shape future outcomes. As Justice Sandra Day O'Connor recently explained:

> I frankly do not know how anyone going on the Court would be able to predict the thousands of issues that come before the Court. I myself couldn't have told President Reagan what I would do on all these issues, because I hadn't faced them. (Gibson 2005)

Conclusion

In *Federalist #78*, Alexander Hamilton argued "that the judiciary is beyond comparison the weakest of the three departments of power;

that it can never attack with success either of the other two." Hamilton's view is consistent with the textbook understanding of judicial-executive relations. This understanding suggests that the judiciary is neither a threat nor a hindrance to executive power.

The two pillars of the conventional wisdom—the president's appointment power and his superior legal guidance—have begun to crumble. No longer can we view judges and justices as simple followers of the executive's positions and opinions. As the judicial branch has been called on to resolve contentious policy political issues, executive influence has waned—challenged both by senators seeking to influence the makeup of the bench, by other litigants, and by the justices themselves as critical issues and issues are addressed by the Court. It is time to abandon the conventional wisdom.

Notes

1. http://www.cnn.com/2003/ALLPOLITICS/01/15/bush.affirmativeaction/.

2. The Court also refused to hear cases that would have overturned lower-court decisions that denied executive privilege claims that would have prevented the special prosecutor from having access to the notes taken by the White House counsel's office and that would have shielded the working papers of the first lady's healthcare reform task force.

3. There is no significant change over time in the federal government's success rate when the federal government is a party.

4. The Office of the Solicitor General (S.G.) is the Justice Department office that has the primary responsibility for representing the administration in all cases that have reached the Supreme Court.

5. Barnes (2004) randomly identified 100 cases that were overridden by Congress and the executive branch. Seventy-three of these overrides were designed to reverse a decision made by a federal district or circuit court.

6. Bailey, Kamoie, and Maltzman (2005) provide such an analysis for all civil liberties/rights cases that arose during the 1953–2002 period. The discussion that follows is based upon this analysis and data.

7. For details on how this was calculated, see Bailey, Kamoie, and Maltzman (2005).

8. Such an outcome would be consistent with theoretical work that has explored the dynamics behind "signaling" models.

9. The precise measurement strategy and a more extensive analysis is detailed in Bailey, Kamoie, and Maltzman (2005). The ideological measures are based upon Bailey (2005), which provides an ideological measure that is comparable across different branches of government.

10. Carp, Manning, and Stidham (2004) report that 36.1 percent of the votes cast by G. W. Bush's appointees and 35.8 percent of the votes cast by Reagan judges were in support of liberal outcomes. Likewise, 48.1

percent of Johnson appointee votes were in support of conservative outcomes.

11. For a comprehensive overview of the nomination and confirmation process, see Goldman (1997).

12. One of the reasons Sandra Day O'Connor's retirement from the bench was so important was because the natural Court she was retiring from was divided between conservatives and liberals and she was a swing voter. William Kristol, the editor of the conservative *Weekly Standard* explained, "The Court is the pivot point on social policy, and O'Connor's seat is the pivot point on the Court" (Balz 2005). For a discussion about the importance of pivotal seats, see Moraksi and Shipan (1999).

13. Senate Majority Leader Bill Frist (R-Tennessee) attempted in 2005 to eliminate filibusters of judicial nominees through a more radical approach that became known as the "the nuclear option." Under this approach, a simple majority of the Senate would seek through parliamentary appeals to establish the precedent that filibusters against nominations were unconstitutional. The approach was dubbed the nuclear option because of the anticipated consequences if the attempt were to succeed: Democrats would exploit their remaining procedural advantages and shut down most Senate business. Frist was forced to abandon adoption of this tactic when a bipartisan coalition refused to support such a procedure. Because the existence of the filibuster empowers every member individually, filibuster reform efforts usually fail (Binder and Smith 1997). Frist's 2005 failure will inevitably force Bush to take into account the views of a wider spectrum of senators prior to making a judicial nomination.

14. Between 1965 and 2006, the justices Abe Fortas, Thurgood Marshall, Warren Burger, Harry Blackmun, Lewis Powell, William Rehnquist, John Paul Stevens, Sandra Day O'Connor, Antonin Scalia, Anthony Kennedy, David Souter, Clarence Thomas, Ruth Bader Ginsburg, Stephen Breyer, John Roberts, and Samuel Alito were confirmed. Nominations for Homer Thornberry, Clement Haynsworth, Harrold Carswell, Robert Bork, Douglas Ginsburg, and Harriet Miers were not confirmed. Although President Reagan announced Ginsburg's nomination, it was never formally submitted to the Senate for consideration.

15. http://www.townhall.com/columnists/anncoulter/ac20050721.shtml.

16. In particular, Table 9.3 shows the results for a duration model. Because duration models include information about when a nominee is confirmed and whether the observation is censored (never confirmed), the model simultaneously helps one understand both whether, when, and how the Senate acts on any given nominee. Details on measurement of the independent variables, the construction of the dependent variable, and the estimation strategy appear in Binder and Maltzman (2002, 2005). The model reported here differs slightly from Binder and Maltzman (2002, 2005). Whereas Binder and Maltzman (2002) used fixed effects to capture the impact of specific presidents on judicial selection, this model includes a time counter ("Congress") that allows one to gauge whether the process of advice and consent has changed signifi-

cantly over time. To simplify presentation, the model presented here is more abbreviated than those that appear in Binder and Maltzman (2002, 2005).

17. The specific measures used and a more extensive theoretical justification for these variables is contained in Maltzman (2005).

References

Bailey, Michael E. 2005. "Bridging Institutions and Time: Creating Bayesian Common Space Preference Estimates for Presidents, Senators, and Justices, 1950–2002." Manuscript, Georgetown University.

Bailey, Michael E., Brian Kamoie, and Forrest Maltzman. 2005. "Signals From the Tenth Justice: The Political Role of the Solicitor General in Supreme Court Decision-Making." *American Journal of Political Science* 49 (January):72–85.

Balz, Dan. 2005. "Nomination Could Be Defining Moment for Bush." *Washington Post*, July 2.

Barnes, Jeb. 2004. *Overruled? Legislative Overrides, Pluralism, and Contemporary Court-Congress Relations.* Stanford, CA: Stanford University Press.

Belkin, Douglas. 2004. "Scalia Decries Judicial Activism in Harvard Talk." *Boston Globe*, September 29.

Binder, Sarah A. 2004. "Origins of the Senate 'Blue Slip': The Creation of Senate Norms." Paper presented at the annual meeting of the Midwest Political Science Association.

Binder, Sarah A., and Forrest Maltzman. 2002. "Senatorial Delay in Confirming Federal Judges, 1947–1998." *American Journal of Political Science* 46:190–199.

———. 2004. "The Limits of Senatorial Courtesy." *Legislative Studies Quarterly* 24:5–22.

———. 2005. "Congress and the Politics of Judicial Appointments." In Lawrence C. Dodd and Bruce I. Oppenheimer (Eds.), *Congress Reconsidered*, 8th ed. Washington, DC: CQ Press.

Binder, Sarah A., and Steven S. Smith, 1997. *Politics or Principle? Filibustering in the United States Senate.* Washington, DC: Brookings Institution Press.

Burke, Thomas F. 2004. *Lawyers, Lawsuits, and Legal Rights: The Battle over Litigation in American Society.* Berkeley: University of California Press.

Caldeira, Gregory A. 1987. "Public Opinion and The U.S. Supreme Court: FDR's Court-Packing Plan." *American Political Science Review* 81:1139–1153.

Calvert, Randall. 1985. "The Value of Biased Information: A Rational Choice Model of Political Advice." *Journal of Politics* 47 (June):530–555.

Caplan, Lincoln. 1987. *The Tenth Justice: The Solicitor General and the Rule of Law.* New York: Vintage Books.

Carp, Robert A., Kenneth L. Manning, and Ronald Stidham. 2004. "The Decision-Making Behavior of George W. Bush's Judicial Appointees." *Judicature* 88:20–28.

Cross, Frank B. 2004. "Explaining U.S. Circuit Court Decision Making." *Judicature* 88:31–35.

Deen, Rebecca E., Joseph Ignagni, and James Meernik. 2001. "Trends in the Solicitor General as *Amicus*, 1963–2000: When Is He a Friend? When Is He Influential?" Paper presented at the annual meeting of the American Political Science Association. San Francisco, CA: August 20–September 2.

Edwards, George C. III, and Stephen J. Wayne. 2003. *Presidential Leadership*, 6th ed. Belmont, CA: Wadsworth/Thomson Learning.

Epstein, Lee, Jeffrey A. Segal, Howard Spaeth, and Thomas Walker. 2003. *The Supreme Court Compendium*, 3rd ed. Washington, DC: Congressional Quarterly Press.

Gely, Rafael and Pablo T. Spiller. 1990. "A Rational Choice Model of Supreme Court Statutory Interpretation Decisions With Applications to the State Farm and Grove City Cases." *Journal of Law, Economics and Organization* 6:263–300.

Gibson, Gail. 2005. "Justice O'Connor Warns Against Harsh Political Rhetoric." *Baltimore Sun*, April 8.

Goldman, Sheldon. 1997. *Picking Federal Judges: Lower Court Selection from Roosevelt Through Reagan.* New Haven, CT: Yale University Press.

Kagan, Robert. 2001. *Adversarial Legalism*. Cambridge, MA: Harvard University Press.

Klein, David E. 2002. *Making Law in the United States Courts of Appeals*. New York: Cambridge University Press.

Knight, Jack, and Lee Epstein. 1996. "On the Struggle for Judicial Supremacy." *Law and Society Review* 30:87–130.

Lovell, George I. 2003. *Legislative Deferrals: Statutory Ambiguity, Judicial Power, and American Democracy*. New York: Cambridge University Press.

Maltzman, Forrest. 2005. "Advice and Consent: Cooperation and Conflict in the Appointment of Federal Judges." In Paul Quirk and Sarah A. Binder (Eds.), *The Legislative Branch*. New York: Oxford University Press.

McGuire, Kevin. 1998. "Explaining Executive Success in the U.S. Supreme Court." *Political Research Quarterly* 51 (June):505–526.

Moraski, Bryon, and Charles R. Shipan. 1999. "The Politics of Supreme Court Nominations: A Theory of Institutional Constraints and Choices." *American Journal of Political Science* 43 (4):1069–1095.

O'Connor, Karen. 1983. "The Amicus Curiae Role of the U.S. Solicitor General in Supreme Court Litigation." *Judicature* 66 (December–January):256–264.

Pacelle, Richard L. Jr. 2003. *Between Law and Politics: The Solicitor General and the Structuring of Race, Gender, and Reproductive Rights Litigation*. College Station: Texas A&M University Press.

Ragsdale, Lynn. 1988. *Vital Statistics on the Presidency*, rev. ed. Washington, DC: Congressional Quarterly.

Ring, Ray. 2004. "Tipping the Scales." *High Country News*, February 16.

Rossiter, Clinton. 1960. *The American Presidency*. New York: A Mentor Book.

Schubert, Glendon. 1965. *The Judicial Mind*. New York: Free Press.

Scigliano, Robert A. 1971. *The Supreme Court and the Presidency*. New York: Free Press.

Segal, Jeffrey A., and Cheryl D. Reedy. 1988. "The Supreme Court and Sex Discrimination: The Role of the Solicitor General." *Western Political Quarterly* 41:553–568.

Segal, Jeffrey A., and Harold J. Spaeth. 2002. *The Supreme Court and the Attitudinal Model Revisited*. New York: Cambridge University Press.

Songer, Donald, Jeffrey Segal, and Charles Cameron. 1994. "The Hierarchy of Justice: Testing a Principal-Agent Model of Supreme Court-Circuit Court Interactions." *American Journal of Political Science* 38:673–96.

United States, Department of Commerce. 2000. *Statistical Abstract of the United States*. Washington, DC: Government Printing Office. ✦

Chapter 10

The Evolution of the Institutional Presidency
Presidential Choices, Institutional Change, and Staff Performance

David E. Lewis

In the last few chapters we have examined various impediments to presidential leadership. Edwards identified several related to Congress. Both Edwards and Cohen then argued that a much touted strategy for promoting presidential leadership, the idea that presidents should go public (or follow a permanent campaign strategy), does not work. Fleisher, Bond, and Wood then demonstrated that presidents have to depend essentially on the cards they are dealt (that is, their existing leverage) when they deal with Congress. Finally, Maltzman argued that greater ideological polarization between the president and Congress also has contributed to a lesser presidential ability to appoint judges they prefer to the federal courts. In short, combined, the last four chapters portray a presidency that depends heavily on leverage to succeed, but which more often than not appears to be lacking that necessary leverage. Given this political dynamic, what then can presidents do?

One answer in the scholarly literature is that presidents can use the resources of their own executive branch to get things done. As Howell argued, presidents are moving toward a greater reliance on unilateral political techniques. Another mechanism at their disposal is the Executive Office of the President (EOP), its various units, and especially the White House staff. A major debate in the presidential literature revolves around the question of whether presidents should rely on greater centralization of these executive branch resources or whether this strategy actually further undercuts presidential leadership capacity. Lewis contributes to this debate in an innovative manner. He argues that presidents have employed a variety of different strategies to secure

I gratefully acknowledge the helpful comments of Stuart Jordan, George Krause, Nolan McCarty, Bert Rockman, Andrew Rudalevige, Michael Strine, and Richard Waterman. The errors that remain are my own.

greater control over the EOP. In so doing, however, they have increased the size of the EOP, accentuated the process of "thickening government," and perhaps ironically, in the long run reduced their capacity to control the very units and individuals they seek to hierarchically master. Thus, one potential source of leverage may come with considerable political costs.

✦ ✦ ✦

By virtue of their unique position, presidents have always felt pressure to manage the executive branch and their administrative tasks. The problem for presidents historically has been that their administrative tasks exceed their abilities. John Hart (1987, 13), for example, writes of George Washington:

> Washington and his immediate successors saw themselves as chief executive officers and took a close interest in the day-to-day business of the departments of the executive branch . . . and the presidential desire to be undisputed master of the whole executive branch generated an ever growing work load that took its toll on the incumbent.

In order to perform their administrative responsibilities, presidents from Washington forward have relied on personal staff.[1] Presidential staff traditionally provided clerical assistance, political advice, and managerial oversight of relations with administrative agencies, Congress, and other political actors. In some cases this presidential staffing arrangement worked well. In other cases, presidents were disappointed with their staff support. Andrew Johnson's son Robert, who filled the post, was according to one author an "incurable alcoholic and womanizer" whose incompetence not only led to poor administration, but also brought a sex for pardon scandal down on the White House.[2] In contrast, Daniel Lamont, Cleveland's "Assistant President," and George Cortelyou, McKinley's secretary, are widely regarded as having made a substantial positive impact on the administration of each man, serving as clerks, speechwriters, gatekeepers, and political liaisons.[3]

One of the primary motivations for Franklin Delano Roosevelt's appointment of the President's Committee on Administrative Management (Brownlow Committee) was a frank recognition on his part that the sprawling federal bureaucracy, which he had helped create, was beyond his control.[4] The result of the Brownlow Committee's recommendations is what we now refer to as the institutional presidency. The Executive Office of the President (EOP), created in 1939, is the structural basis of the institutional presidency.[5] The institutional presidency was originally comprised of a handful of presidential agencies (e.g., White House Office, Bureau of the Budget) and a limited number of personal aides whose occupation was to help the president perform congressionally delegated or constitutional responsibilities.

Over time, the institutional presidency has expanded dramatically, both enabling and constraining presidential action in a way inconceivable to earlier presidents. The number of agencies, employees, and dollars necessary for the EOP's activities has increased substantially. The institutional presidency has assumed more responsibilities and increased in organizational complexity. Whereas the original EOP had 5 fledgling agencies, 630 employees, and a budget of $17 million in real dollars in 1939, it now has 11 agencies, 1,750 employees, and a budget of $260 million.[6] These simple statistics mask substantial changes in the size and organization of the EOP over time, however.

Understanding the process of institutional change and development over time is necessary in order to understand the success or failure of modern presidential leadership. For example, without sufficient independence and professionalism parts of the institutional presidency, such as the National Security Council, can fall victim to dangerous groupthink and lead presidents into cataclysmic foreign policy and national security disasters. Without sufficient political influence and oversight, parts of the institutional presidency can send conflicting messages about the president's priorities on any number of important issues ranging from trade to science policy and budget projections. These conflicting messages hamper the president's ability to negotiate successfully and in good faith with Congress and direct the administrative machinery of government.

Scholars focused on the presidency have produced a number of competing explanations for the evolution of the institutional presidency over time, including (1) a steady Weberian march toward the division of labor, expertise, and stability in response to increased demands on the national government and the president; (2) a process of growth and decline dictated by interbranch competition; or (3) a connected series of developments driven by unique historical circumstances or the president's decisionmaking environment. In this chapter I argue that existing explanations are incomplete, that the institutionalization of the institutional presidency is driven by a natural internal logic of growth, expansion, thickening, and reorganization. The intensity of this expansion, thickening, and reorganization in a given period is determined by the extent to which the existing institution meets the needs of the new president in terms of loyalty and capacity to do what the president needs done. Changes in the EOP are evidence of presidential weakness relative to the responsibilities and expectations accompanying the job. Presidents seek to manage, change, and reorganize the institutional presidency in order to meet immense public expectations for presidential behavior that include virtually all aspects of governing.

The argument proceeds in four parts. In the first section I review some of the common explanations for the institutionalization of the EOP. In the second section I explain how presidents evaluate the existing institutional presidency when they assume office. I argue that presidents are more likely to add personal aides, politicize EOP agencies, or reorganize when presidents encounter agencies that have different policy views than the president, are hard to monitor effectively, or are not good at what they do (low capacity). In the third section I describe these organizational strategies for dealing with problems in the existing institutional presidency in more detail, providing examples from modern presidential administrations. In the final section I conclude, explaining how these presidential strategies influence the performance of the presidency as a whole and suggest that the internal dynamics that result naturally from turnover in the presidency hinder the performance of the institutional presidency.

I. Explaining the Evolution of the EOP

In a fundamental respect the office of the president, though always filled by one person with more or less institutionalized staff support, has always been an institution. In other words, the office described in the Constitution has always had the characteristics of an "institution." That is, it is an office that is stable, differentiable, coherent, and adaptable.[7] The president's actions have been enabled, defined, and constrained by the constitutional separation of powers system. What is commonly referred to as the institutional presidency, however, is the staff support system that has grown up around the office of the president. Most scholarly attention has focused on describing and explaining the growth, organization, complexity, and operations of this system. Existing research has mainly focused on the expansion of the national government, the strategic interaction of the two branches, and presidential choices to explain the institutionalization of the presidency.[8]

Several works describe the transformation of the presidency from a person to an organization as an irresistible Weberian march toward differentiation, complexity, stability, and coherence that occurs simultaneously with an increase in staff size and resources.[9] In other words, the growth of government and increased demands on the president lead naturally to the growth of a bureaucratic staff system.[10] In this view institutionalization follows an irresistible logic where staff units naturally develop and differentiate to divide labor efficiently and develop expertise. Over time these units in the institutional presidency develop procedures, norms, and processes to handle repeated tasks and interaction. Ultimately, they develop organizational identities shaped by their unique perspective in the division of labor. Once in existence, these units become adaptable and adopt strategies to ensure their own longevity.

Other works suggest that, in addition to the institutionalization caused by the growth of government, the strategic interaction between the executive and legislative branches helps predict institutional growth in the two branches.[11] In this view presidents are opportunistic actors who can exploit Congress's collective action problems to create and design units of the institutional presidency to their advantage.[12] Whether or not presidents can exploit Congress in the long term remains an open question.[13]

The final set of works suggest that unique historical circumstances or recurring political choices made by the president and Congress in response to policy priorities or bargaining needs shape the institutionalization process. A number of fine works mention the importance of specific historical events like World War II or one of the Hoover Commissions, the increasing role of presidents in international affairs, or the specific histories of the units themselves as important in explaining the institutionalization of the presidency.[14] Others generalize across presidential choices to theorize about how presidents interact with the institutional presidency in response to changes in policy priorities, managerial imperatives, or the bargaining environment.[15]

Each perspective adds to our understanding of the development of the institutional presidency. Agencies in the EOP are created and transformed in response to demands on government and the president specifically. Their evolution follows the path most agencies follow toward division of labor, greater specialization, and instincts for survival. The EOP is also influenced by the strategic interaction of the two branches and the unique needs of presidents as decisionmakers. What is overlooked, however, is how much the evolution of the institutional presidency is driven by systematic forces within the EOP itself and the president's relationship with each agency.

Presidents consistently need both competence and loyalty and these dual, often competing, needs systematically drive presidential staffing choices. Heclo (1975) famously argues that presidents should look for neutral competence in their staff agencies, particularly the Office of Management and Budget (OMB). By neutrality, Heclo means "giving one's cooperation and best independent judgment of the issues to partisan bosses—and of being sufficiently uncommitted to be able to do so for a succession of partisan leaders." The primary means of ensuring neutrality in executive office agencies is to have them staffed by career employees with an ethos of "speak up, shut up, carry up, carry out."

Moe (1985), on the other hand, suggests that presidents seek a more politically responsive staffing system. He is dubious of the responsiveness of career employees to presidential direction. He claims that the president is primarily a politician and is less concerned with efficiency or effectiveness than a staff structure that is responsive to his political needs. He cites the White House Office (with all political appointees) as an example of a structure that better meets the needs of the president than the Bureau of the Budget (later OMB). He also claims that while presidents largely inherit the basic institutional framework of the presidency, they try to make it more responsive by "manipulating civil service rules, proposing minor reorganizations, and pressing for modifying legislation . . . to increase the number and location of administrative positions that can be occupied by appointees" (p. 245).

How presidents negotiate these dual needs for competence and political responsiveness largely determines how the institutional presidency evolves.

II. Institutional Incentives, Presidential Staff, and the EOP

Upon assuming office, presidents confront a preexisting institutional support system. Some of the parts of the EOP will suit their needs effectively and other parts will be cause for concern. Each new president in the modern period makes a keep, reorganize, or discard decision with the units of institutional presidency that fundamentally depends upon presidential choice. While it is true that some parts of the institutional presidency are harder to change than others because of statutory authority, unusually high clientele support, or expertise, the fact remains that presidents have a significant amount of discretion over the personnel and structures that serve them directly.

The dynamics of the president's relationship with personal staff described in the introduction have an analogue in the institutional presidency. Some parts of the institutional presidency will be loyal and helpful and others can potentially be an embarrassment. Getting good staff help in the institutional presidency is complicated by the fact that a large portion of the personnel and structures of the institutional presidency carry over from administration to administration, meaning that presidents have little control over the selection and organization of a significant portion of their own staff. Not only is the institutional presidency substantially larger and more complex than the old staffing system, it is also populated with persons that the president did not select (and are hard to remove) and cannot monitor easily, and who vary in competence.

Of course, the characteristics of the institutional presidency that make managing it difficult are also a source of strength. Long service, job security, and stability generate expertise; they facilitate institutional memory, engender a long-term perspective, and systematize valuable informal information flows that facilitate governance. This perspective reflects the institutional interest of the presidency disconnected from sectoral and partisan claims on the office. Some agencies in the EOP like the Office of Management and Budget have a long history, established routines, professional expert staff, and substantial institutional memory that carries over from one administration to the next. Others like the White House Office turn over all of their personnel, remove all of their files, and by so doing eliminate continuing institutional knowledge.

Some parts of the institutional presidency will be well enough suited to a new president, but others present substantial challenges. Presidents will be concerned about some units in the EOP because presidents will question their loyalty to the president and his policy priorities. For example, both the Eisenhower and Kennedy administrations were concerned about the loyalty of the Budget Bureau because of long tenures under the opposition party's leadership.[16] Each was successful in substantially changing and reorienting the BOB to reflect his individual concerns. Presidents will be concerned about other EOP agencies because, frankly, they do not have a reputation for being good at what they are supposed to do. Upon assuming office in 1993, President Clinton targeted the Office of National Drug Control Policy for personnel cuts as a way of fulfilling his pledge to cut "White House" staff. The drug office was a natural target both because Clinton was not enthusiastic about the drug war started by his Republican predecessors but also because the drug office had a reputation for being ineffective. It was the home for a number of political appointees chosen for their political connections rather than their expertise.

When Do Presidents Make Institutional Changes?

What are the factors that explain when presidents are likely to change an EOP agency that will significantly alter the speed or character of its institutionalization? Problems that exist between units of the institutional presidency and the president are the same as those that characterized presidents' relationship with their personal staffs in earlier periods—agencies in the institutional presidency do not always have the president's interests in mind when they act, they are hard to monitor, and they vary in quality. In some cases presidents can have problems with parts of the institutional presidency because the preferences of a particular unit or staff differ from those of the president. This can be the case for a number of reasons including differing policy perspectives, self-seeking, or simply miscommunication between the president and his staffs. Of course, if presidents could monitor their subordinates effectively, these problems would be diminished. Finally, in the same way that some presidential aides are prone to error or incompetence, some parts of the institutional presidency are less expert or useful than other parts. Presidents respond to such problems by increasing White House attention, altering the number of political appointees in part of the EOP, or reorganizing in order to solve these problems.

Divergent Preferences

The loyalty of particular units in the EOP can vary as a function of their purpose embedded in law and personnel. Some units in the EOP are designed with a specific policy goal in mind. For example, the Office of Economic Opportunity was the hallmark of Lyndon Johnson's Great Society. It was anathema to Richard Nixon and he set about dismantling it in the early 1970s. Of course, some units of the EOP are entirely pliable in terms of what they do because of the dramatic turnover in personnel. The National Security Council (NSC), for example, has no career service protections on employment, making it supremely pliable and responsive relative to other offices. Of course, one wonders whether it is correct to call the NSC institutionalized given the dramatic turnover from administration to administration. The Office of Management and Budget and the Council on Environmental Quality, on the other hand, are substantially filled with employees from the competitive service. Presidents can work diligently to ensure that the preferences of his staff coincide with his own through the selection process but civil service protections limit the extent to which they can choose their personnel.[17]

Monitoring

We should expect that outcomes contrary to the president's wishes frequently occur in cases where presidents have a difficult time monitoring. Presidents who are willing to put forth the effort can vigorously monitor individual agencies or activities but they cannot monitor all parts of the EOP at the same time, particularly as the institutional presidency grows. Presidents can remedy some of the problems with monitoring their staff by organizational design and personal initiative. Franklin Delano Roosevelt, for example, tried to assign multiple aides to the same task, leaving lines of jurisdiction unclear, and inducing competition.[18] He hoped that competition would produce both more information and additional incentives for staff to demonstrate loyalty. A number of scholars have noted the different ways of organizing the White House staff and its impact on presidential performance.[19] Despite their best efforts to organize staff effectively for oversight or politicize selection processes, however, a growing EOP means greater monitoring difficulties.

Competence

Outcomes contrary to the president's interests can also arise because of incompetence or failure. Presidents can get bad advice, be misrepresented, or have their staff fail in implementation. Historically, presidents have ensured the competence and ability of their subordinates either through the personnel selection process or by keeping existing personnel on the job. Some staff competence attaches to the persons brought in by the president; other competence is achieved through experience in the job. Existing staff support and personnel from past administrations are attractive to the president precisely because of their experience or competence developed through work.

In the EOP, units develop informational and relational assets over time that help presidential decisionmaking and increase efficiency in action. Politicizing or reorganizing EOP units is a costly action precisely because the act of replacing the unit and its expertise is a difficult one. In most cases, the longer an agency has been in existence, the longer its institutional memory, the more developed its routines and processes, and the more informed its advice and activities.

III. Presidential Strategies for the EOP

The hallmark of early presidential aides, as described in the Brownlow Report, was to be anonymous and loyal. Over time, both the president and Congress recognized the need for expert help in addition to loyal help. In fact, it was partly congressional concern over Roosevelt's and Truman's decisionmaking that led Congress to create the Council of Economic Advisers and the National Security Council (Hart 1987; Seidman 1998). Congress wanted to institutionalize in the presidency a means of getting good advice on issues of critical importance to the country. Unfortunately, the first presidential transition after their creation revealed the difficulties with this arrangement.[20] Presidents still needed the type of loyal help and advice they got from their personal aides, and existing institutional arrangements, while situated to provide expertise, did not always have the president's best interests in mind.

The president's response in each case was to substantially reorganize the units to enhance his control. President Eisenhower submitted Reorganization Plan 9 to Congress on June 1, 1953. The plan strengthened the power of the chairman of the CEA by giving all authority heretofore delegated to the CEA as a whole to the chair instead. It also abolished the position of vice-chair.[21] For the NSC he created two new units, the Planning Board and the Operations Coordinating Board, to do policy planning and ensure implementation, respectively.[22] Congress also provided the president with an Economic

Adviser to the President outside the CEA and a National Security Adviser to serve partly as a buffer between the president and these agencies.

When presidents decide that certain parts of the institutional presidency do not meet their needs they have a number of different techniques for remedying these problems. Presidents will buffer a new agency by increasing White House staff, politicize agencies, or reorganize the EOP in order to make it more responsive. The regular use of these techniques shapes the evolution of the EOP over time. The techniques can be used as substitute or complementary strategies depending upon the circumstances which differ in the extent of political costs and the difficulty of implementation.

Buffering

One technique presidents use upon encountering the preexisting institutional presidency is buffering. If the president feels that one part of the EOP is not loyal or performing poorly, one low-cost way of dealing with the problem is to assign a personal aide, a special assistant, or a counselor to the president to deal with the agency. The White House aide can filter information coming from the agency, monitor the activities of the agency, and direct the unit's operation for the president. This is illustrated in a specific way in the addition to the White House Office of an Economic Adviser and National Security Adviser. It is illustrated in a generic way in Figure 10.1 where a new special assistant is added to the institutional presidency and given a portfolio that includes EOP Agency 1.

Sometimes the new special assistant and his staff will not only monitor the subordinate staff but also take over their responsibilities. This is what is commonly referred to as *centralization*.[23] Centralization is the transfer of functions from the executive branch or broader EOP into the White House.

One institutional consequence for such actions is that they are sticky. Once a position has been created, a precedent has been established, expectations developed, and processes altered to accommodate organizational change. This makes eliminating the position costly. Positions once added often remain even when the original motivation for the position has been removed. New positions and the persons filling them develop routines and relationships, get office space and staff support, rearrange organizational charts, and adopt new responsibilities. This normal Weberian bureaucratic behavior makes it increasingly unlikely that a position will be removed in the normal course of organizational activity. As the number of special assistants proliferates, the White House bureaucracy is often organized with increasing hierarchy and the White House itself becomes hard to manage. This is one explanation for the systematic expansion in

Figure 10.1   White House Buffering

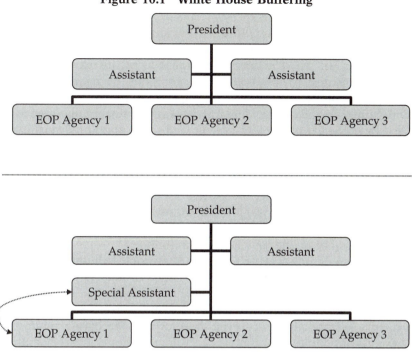

White House staff during the modern period until the unusual events of Watergate stemmed the tide.

Of course, as the CEA and NSC cases illustrate, there are other means of getting control of parts of the institutional presidency, including politicization and reorganization. Presidents can exercise special care in selecting personnel at the top of EOP units and they can work to politicize an EOP agency by adding more personnel selected by the president. This latter strategy can have dramatic consequences for institutionalization.

Politicization

Presidents politicize parts of the institutional presidency in five ways: replacement, layering, increasing ministerial staff, internal reorganization, and reductions in force. For example, in Figure 10.2 a generic EOP agency has a director and three divisions, each headed by a career manager carried over from the last administration. If one of these career managers is underperforming in the eyes of the director or the White House, the status of the manager's position can be changed from a career position to an appointed position. In most cases this is performed simply with a request to the Office of Personnel Management (or earlier, the Civil Service Commission) for a change in position classification. Most experienced personnel officers know how to use the appropriate terms of art to ensure their applications are approved.[24] The Office of Personnel Management director and many of his or her subordinates serve at the pleasure of the president, easing the way for the White House to get its way. The official forms requesting reclassification of positions by agencies include space for White House opinion and input as a way of signaling White House opinion and intent. The drawback of requesting that a position filled by career appointment be changed to an appointed position is that the career employee serving in this position at the time of its change may have tenure rights either in this job or a comparable job, or has connections with interest groups or Congress that make removal difficult. Of course, there are a number of techniques that are well known in bureaucratic lore about how to get unwanted employees to leave their current jobs, including the frontal assault, the unwanted transfer, or the new activity technique.[25]

Presidents can also layer appointees on top of the existing structure to get control. Layering is the practice of adding politically appointed managers on top of career managers as a means of enhancing political control. For example, in Figure 10.3 two associate directors are added between the director and the career managers. These new appointees can more carefully monitor the career managers and assume some of their policy-determining responsibilities through their influence in budget preparation, personnel decisions, and other administrative responsibilities.

Figure 10.2   Replacement

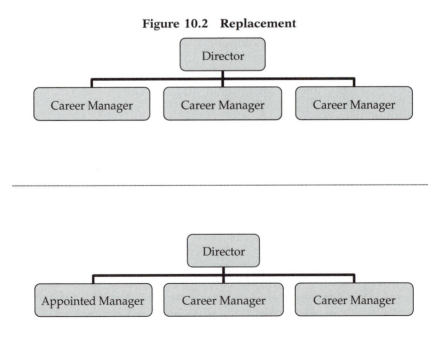

A good example of the way layering can be used to enhance control is the reorganization of the Bureau of the Budget into the Office of Management and Budget in 1970. In 1960 the Budget Bureau had fewer than 10 political appointees, the director, the deputy director, three assistant directors, and a handful of personal staff.[26] The 1970 reorganization was supposed to focus increased attention in the budget agency on federal management and the reorganization included a new appointee to head the management effort. The reorganization also included four new program associate directors, however.[27] These new appointees, the program associate directors (PADs), were put in below the existing appointed officials but above the permanent examining divisions. The examining divisions have always held a lot of power in federal budgeting. They review and control agency budget requests in the executive branch and are an important source of power and policy influence in government. Whereas before the examining divisions were headed by career employees with access to the top of the agency, now they were subordinate to politically appointed directors. In total, the number of appointees in the budget agency increased from 10 in 1960 to 20 in 1973. The increase was comprised equally of positions with formal authority and ministerial staff for these positions. The Carter administration subsequently added more layers to the OMB.[28] In 1977, the Carter administration added two

Figure 10.3   Layering

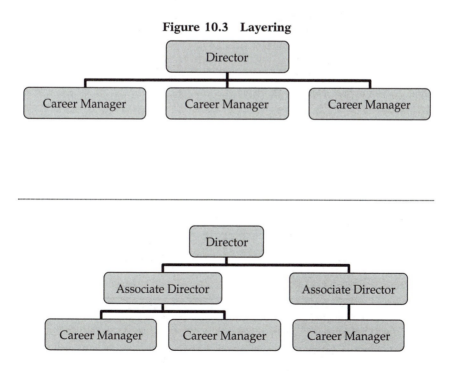

executive associate directors above the PADs added by Nixon. OMB also added six noncareer deputy associate directors below the PADs.

A similar strategy is to add appointed ministerial staff. In Figure 10.4 the director adds a special assistant. Titled positions like directors often acquire title-riding appointees like chiefs of staff, special assistants, counsels, and public affairs personnel to help them perform their jobs.[29] The strategy of adding ministerial staff is different from layering in that the added appointees have little formal authority. The function of ministerial staff is to help the director perform his or her existing duties, particularly to help manage the existing divisions by monitoring subordinate behavior, coordinating agency activity, and communicating the director's preferences to subordinates. While ministerial staffs have little formal authority, such appointees can acquire substantial informal authority as experts, gatekeepers, and public spokespeople.

Figure 10.5 illustrates a fourth common politicization technique, internal reorganization. Internal reorganization has been used strategically by managers to diminish the influence of problematic career managers and enhance political control. In the illustration, the agency is reorganized so that the career manager is put in charge of a

Figure 10.4   Increase Ministerial Staff

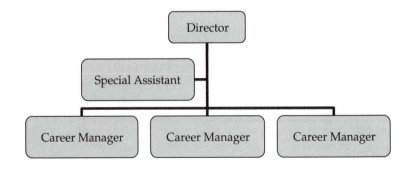

new division or project. This division can be entirely new, a nascent initiative, or it can simply be comprised of preexisting personnel, responsibilities, and budgets put together in a new way. The nominal purpose of the reorganization can be to align organizational structure to better meet the bureaus stated goals or to increase efficiency but have the real or dual purpose of getting better control of the bureau. In large modern agencies with complicated organizational structures, reorganizations can be subtle and effective means of getting political appointees in charge of important administrative responsibilities. In reorganizations, positions are created and disbanded, upgraded and downgraded and these decisions are informed by the political needs of administration officials.

Another prominent technique for politicizing is reductions-in-force (RIF).[30] Through RIFs federal officials cut employment as a way of getting control of the bureau. According to a general rule of "save grade, save pay," those career employees with the least experience lose their jobs first during RIFs but those who stay with more

Figure 10.5 Intra-Agency Reorganizations

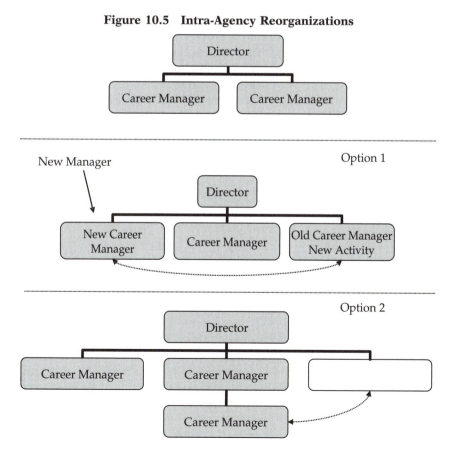

seniority are bumped down in position and often assume new or different tasks. They often have to do more work for the same amount of pay and the new tasks they assume are frequently jobs not performed by people in their pay scale. These ripple effects increase attrition beyond that caused by the initial RIF. Career managers in charge of these divisions and their subordinates will have to do more work with fewer employees and manage through declining morale for an administration with whom they likely disagree ideologically. The Reagan administration's treatment of the Council on Environmental Quality (CEQ) is a good example. In 1982 the CEQ's staff had been reduced from 49 under President Carter to 15.[31] The administration fired all of the immediate council staff, some of whom had served since the Nixon and Ford administrations.[32] Appointees from the campaign staff replaced those removed.

In practice, politicization can jeopardize expertise. Expertise or competence is attached to agencies with continuing professional personnel. When career professionals are removed or frozen out of policy decisions in order to implement the president's new agenda, performance often suffers because of increased turnover, lower morale, and difficulties in recruitment and retention. Presidents also lose the benefits of institutional memory and professional expertise. In his critique of President Nixon's reorganization of the Bureau of the Budget into the Office of Management and Budget (OMB), Hugh Heclo (1975) detailed how Nixon's changes decreased impartiality, hampered communication, threatened OMB's brokerage function, and endangered cooperation among OMB units. The reorganization also threatened continuity and institutional memory to the detriment of both the agency and the presidency.[33]

EOP Reorganization and Agency Termination. The final presidential strategy when faced with problems of preference divergence, monitoring difficulties, or a lack of bureaucratic capacity in the institutional presidency is to reorganize more dramatically. Reorganization can take many different forms (see Figure 10.6). On some occasions presidents eliminate parts of the institutional presidency that do not suit their needs and fold their responsibilities into one of the existing departments or agencies in the executive branch. On other occasions presidents reorganize by combining EOP units with other parts of the EOP or agencies and personnel from outside the institutional presidency. In 2001, President Bush attempted to quietly close two small White House offices, the Office of National Aids Policy and the Office on the President's Initiative for One America. His decision angered AIDS and race activists who questioned Bush's commitment to those issues.[34] Bush also closed the Office of Women's Initiatives and Outreach.[35] He is not the only president to have closed offices in the institutional presidency. President Clinton tried to eliminate the Council on Environmental Quality and succeeded in closing

Figure 10.6 Reorganization

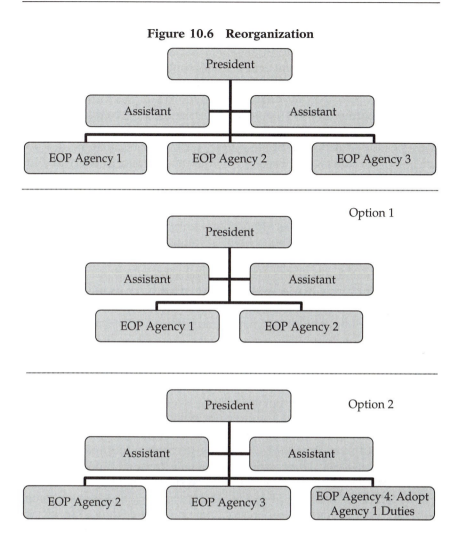

the Council on Competitiveness, the Critical Materials Council, and the National Space Council. Among others, President Reagan shut down the Council on Wage and Price Stability, Carter the President's Economic Policy Board, and Nixon the Office of Economic Opportunity.[36] Short of termination, presidents have also substantially reorganized units of the institutional presidency upon assuming office. President Eisenhower substantially reorganized the Council of Economic Advisers, Kennedy the National Security Council, and Nixon the Bureau of the Budget.[37]

Of course, the extent to which presidents are forced to rely on parts of the institutional presidency varies. If presidents do not have to rely on the staff agencies they inherit they are less motivated to shape them to fit their political needs. Monitoring, politicizing, and reorganizing require time, attention, and political resources that presidents have in limited supply and they focus their attention on the most important areas. Presidents are most likely to neglect agencies in the institutional presidency that perform tasks that are neither salient nor presidential priorities. For example, Richard Clarke, former Clinton and Bush administration counterterrorism official, complained that President George W. Bush neglected and downgraded counterterrorism operations in his National Security Council because he did not recognize the severity of terrorist threats prior to the 9/11 terrorist attacks.[38] Presidents also frequently neglect parts of the institutional presidency when agencies in the wider executive branch or partisans in Congress can perform the same role. For example, during Nixon administration discussions about plans for a second term, the administration talked openly about how "retaking" the State Department would allow them to downgrade the importance of the National Security Council.[39] When presidents have successfully politicized an executive agency or when presidents govern with partisans from their own party in Congress, there is less of a need for them to tinker with the institutional presidency.

Choosing Among Strategies

The strategies presidents use to deal with the problems in the presidency they inherit differ in important ways. First, some strategies are easier to implement than others. In particular, it is often easier to add positions than to either replace career employees or initiate reductions in force. Reorganizations are disruptive, complicated, and politically involved. The costlier strategies in time and political capital are reserved for cases where there are substantial problems in the relationship between the president and the agency or cases where an issue area is particularly salient to a particular president. Nixon's actions to dismantle the Office of Economic Opportunity and Eisenhower's reorganization of the National Security Council come to mind. The first is a case where differences of opinion were strong enough that the president had to fundamentally restructure the agency. The second is a case where foreign policy and national security were enough of a policy priority that the president was willing to pay the cost in time, political capital, and loss of immediate expertise to reorganize the NSC structure.

Of course if positions proliferate and persist, this can create organizational problems that require significant reorganization to remedy. As the number of positions proliferates, the increase generates management problems in its own right. Information flows slow, accountability is diffused, and management becomes more complicated. As the number of people speaking for the president increases, the clarity of the president's message and priorities can decrease.

Fiscal constraints also limit the number of positions that can be added and shape the content of reorganization plans. Fiscal constraints make reductions in force and certain types of reorganizations more attractive relative to creating new positions. The choice of strategies can also be influenced by the political ideology of the president. Conservative presidents may be more willing to cut government since they are more willing to take on the difficulties associated with upsetting federal employee unions representing government employees.[40] Rather than add positions, conservatives should be more likely to cut positions, reorganize, and implement reductions-in-force in response to preference divergence, monitoring difficulties, and competence problems.

IV. Consequences for the Evolution of the Institutional Presidency

The repeated interactions of transient presidents with a continuing institution affect the development of the institution in systematic ways. All presidents want their staffs, both continuing institutional staff and transient president-specific staff, to be loyal to the president and expert. The institutional structure the president inherits, however, does not always provide the president with loyal and expert staff. When parts of the institutional presidency do not have the president's interests in mind because staffs are self-serving, view the world differently than the president, or misunderstand the president's interests, presidential efforts to lead can be jeopardized. When staff are hard to manage and monitor, the chances the staff will stray from the president's preferences and hamper rather than help presidential leadership increases. Similarly, when staff are ill-equipped for the job they have been given it is harder for presidents to lead. Once these staff problems cross a threshold defined partly by the cost of action, presidents act to alter the institutional presidency. They add White House personnel, politicize the institutional presidency, or reorganize.

The net effect of presidential changes every four to eight years is a thickening of hierarchy in both the White House and the agencies of the institutional presidency. The repeated interactions of presidents and the continuing institution also produce a relatively deep penetration of political appointments in the institutional presidency relative to the departments and bureaus of the executive branch. Gradual thickening and increasing politicization are followed by regular episodes of reorganization to rationalize bureaucratic structure, cut hierarchy, and reconstruct low-capacity institutions.

The performance of the different parts of the institutional presidency is influenced by where an EOP unit falls in this cycle and where it falls in the history of the institution. Bureaucracies characterized by persistent reorganization, politicization, and growing hierarchy are unlikely to be the most effective.[41] Presidents have a short time horizon determined by elections and a two-term limit on service. All presidents confront an existing institution but few think holistically about the performance of the institution or how the institution will suit future presidents. They are more concerned about their immediate political needs. As a consequence, the evolution of the institutional presidency is not the product of self-conscious forward-looking design. On the contrary, it is produced in response to regular short-term political pressures that produce predictable variation in structure and design but a variation that mitigates against performance advantages stemming from stable, professional staffing characterized by a long-term perspective. The institutional presidency may grow in size, expense, and complexity, but not in competence, and variation in the performance of the institutional presidency can determine the success or failure of presidential leadership in a given policy arena.

Notes

1. I draw most of this discussion from Hart (1987). Early presidents funded their staff support from salary provided them by Congress. It appears that Congress appropriated money for presidential salary and support with both the president's salary and clerical expenses in mind. Later Congress would explicitly appropriate funds for presidential staff.

2. See Hart (1987, 20).

3. Hart (1987).

4. Dickinson (1997); Hart (1987). Dickinson (1997, 46) argues that Roosevelt feared his administrative shortcomings would hurt his reelection chances in 1936.

5. For detailed accounts of the EOP and its development see Burke (1992) and Hart (1995).

6. Sources: Relyea (1997); Stanley and Niemi (1999) supplemented with data from the *Budget of the United States Government* (Washington, DC: Government Printing Office), various years; Krause (2002) supplemented with data from the *Budget of the United States*.

7. Ragsdale and Theis (1997).

8. See, e.g., Berman (1979), Tomkin (1998), and Zegart (1999).

9. Ragsdale and Theis (1997) examine four characteristics of institutionalization to determine when the presidency became institutionalized. They conclude that the presidency became institutionalized in the 1970s and that national government activity had the greatest impact on the institutionalization of the presidency. Walcott and Hult (1995)

similarly suggest that increasing task demands lead to institutionalization but they also suggest that organizational dynamics shaped by
growing informational assets lead to the stability and persistence of organizational forms.

10. See, for example, Rossiter (1949) and Seligman (1956).

11. Howell and Lewis (2002); Krause (2002); Moe and Wilson (1994).

12. Moe and Wilson (1994); Howell and Lewis (2002).

13. George Krause (2002) examines the growth in the presidential and legislative branches and argues that the institutional dynamics in our
separation of powers system allow presidents short run advantages in
increasing their institutional resources vis-à-vis Congress. He also
finds, however, that presidents cannot permanently exploit Congress.

14. See, for example, Berman (1979), Tomkin (1998), and Zegart (1999).

15. Walcott and Hult (1995) mention the influence of presidential policy
priorities and presidential management needs. Dickinson (1997) argues that the bargaining needs of modern presidents drive presidential
staffing decisions.

16. Heclo (1975).

17. Weko (1995) argues that the increase in size and importance of the
White House Personnel Office is attributable to presidential attempts
to screen staff, partly for loyalty.

18. Dickinson (1997).

19. See, for example, George (1980) and Hess (1976).

20. In fact, Truman himself was cool to the new structures. See Falk (1964)
for an account of how little Truman used the National Security Council
structure.

21. For a full history see Hood (1954).

22. See Relyea (1997, 185–188).

23. For a full discussion see Moe (1985) and Rudalevige (2002).

24. See the "Federal Political Personnel Manual" (or "Malek Manual") reprinted in *Presidential Campaign Activities of 1972*, vol. 19: *Watergate
and Related Activities, Use of Incumbency-Responsiveness Program*. Executive Session Hearings before the Select Committee on Presidential
Campaign Activities 93 Cong. 2 sess. (Washington, DC: Government
Printing Office), 8903–9050.

25. For a full description see the "Federal Political Personnel Manual,"
8903–9050.

26. See Heclo (1975); Heclo (1977, 78–81); U.S. Congress. Senate. Committee on Post Office and Civil Service. Policy and Supporting Positions. 86th Congress, 2d Sess.

27. See Heclo (1975) and U.S. Congress. Senate. Committee on Post Office
and Civil Service. *Policy and Supporting Positions*. 93rd Congress, 1st
Sess.

28. See Causey (1977).

29. See Light (1995).
30. See Durant (1992, 37) for a discussion of RIFs as one part of the Reagan administration's strategy for gaining control of the bureaucracy.
31. See Mosher (1982).
32. See Davies (1984).
33. For an analysis of whether the pre-Nixon Budget Bureau really was as depicted in the critiques of Nixon's politicization see Dickinson and Rudalevige (2004).
34. See Hall and Keen (2001).
35. See Kornblut (2001).
36. See Relyea (1997).
37. See Hood (1954), Falk (1964), and Berman (1979), respectively.
38. See Clarke (2004).
39. "The Second Administration Team: A Concept." 1972. Frederick Malek papers. Stanford, CA: Hoover Institution, 6. As quoted in Rudalevige and Lewis (2005).
40. See, however, Light (1995), who argues that the number of layers in the bureaucracy increased significantly under Republican presidents.
41. See Boylan (2004) and Gilmour and Lewis (2006).

References

Berman, Larry. 1979. *The Office of Management and Budget and the Presidency, 1921–1979*. Princeton, NJ: Princeton University Press.
Boylan, Richard T. 2004. "Salaries, Turnover, and Performance in the Federal Criminal Justice System." *Journal of Law and Economics* XLVII:75–92.
Burke, John P. 1992. *The Institutional Presidency*. Baltimore, MD: John Hopkins University Press.
Causey, Mike. 1977. "Political Aides See Shift." *Washington Post*, May 25, 1977, C2.
Clarke, Richard. 2004. *Against All Enemies*. New York: Free Press.
Davies, J. Clarence. 1984. "Environmental Institutions and the Reagan Administration." In N. Vig and M. Kraft (Eds.), *Environmental Policy in the 1980s*. Washington, DC: CQ Press.
Dickinson, Matthew J. 1997. *Bitter Harvest: FDR, Presidential Power and the Growth of the Presidential Branch*. New York: Cambridge University Press.
Dickinson, Matthew J., and Andrew Rudalevige. 2004. "Presidents, Responsiveness, and Competence: Revisiting the 'Golden Age' at the Bureau of the Budget." *Political Science Quarterly* 119 (Winter):633–54.
Durant, Robert F. 1992. *The Administrative Presidency Revisited: Public Lands, the BLM, and the Reagan Revolution*. Albany: State University of New York Press.
Falk, Stanley L. 1964. "The National Security Council Under Truman, Eisenhower, and Kennedy." *Political Science Quarterly* 79(3):403–34.
George, Alexander L. 1980. *Presidential Decisionmaking in Foreign Policy: The Effective Use of Information and Advice*. Boulder, CO: Westview Press.
Gilmour, John, and David E. Lewis. 2006. "Political Appointees and the Competence of Federal Program Management." *American Politics Research* 34(1):22–50.
Hall, Mimi, and Judy Keen. 2001. "Bush to close offices on AIDS, race." *USA Today*, February 7, A1 (on-line edition).
Hart, John. 1987. *The Presidential Branch*, 1st ed. New York: Pergamon Press.
———. 1995. *The Presidential Branch*, 2nd ed. New York: Chatham House.
Heclo, Hugh. 1975. "OMB and the Presidency—The problem of 'neutral competence.'" *The Public Interest* 38 (Winter):80–98.

———. 1977. *A Government of Strangers: Executive Politics in Washington.* Washington, DC: Brookings Institution.

Hess, Stephen. 1976. *Organizing the Presidency.* Washington: Brookings Institution.

Hood, Ronald C. 1954. "Reorganizing the Council of Economic Advisers." *Political Science Quarterly* 69(3):413–37.

Howell, William G., and David E. Lewis. 2002. "Agencies by Presidential Design." *Journal of Politics* 64(4):1095–1114.

Kornblut, Anne E. 2001. "Shut office signals shift on women." *Boston Globe,* March 28, A1 (on-line edition).

Krause, George A. 2002. "Separated Powers and Institutional Growth in the Presidential and Congressional Branches: Distinguishing Between Short-Run Versus Long-Run Dynamics." *Political Research Quarterly* 55(1):27–57.

Light, Paul. 1995. *Thickening Government: Federal Hierarchy and the Diffusion of Accountability.* Washington, DC: Brookings.

Moe, Terry M. 1985. "The Politicized Presidency." In John Chubb and Paul E. Peterson (Eds.), *New Directions in American Politics.* Washington, DC: Brookings.

Moe, Terry M., and Scott A. Wilson. 1994. "Presidents and the Politics of Structure." *Law and Contemporary Problems* 57(2):1–44.

Mosher, Lawrence. 1982. "Environmental Quality Council Trims Its Sails in Stormy Budget Weather." *National Journal,* July 24, 1982.

Ragsdale, Lyn, and John J. Theis III. 1997. "The Institutionalization of the American Presidency, 1924–92." *American Journal of Political Science* 41(4):1280–1318.

Relyea, Harold, ed. 1997. *The Executive Office of the President: A Historical, Biographical, and Bibliographical Guide.* Westport, CT: Greenwood Press.

Rossiter, Clinton L. 1949. "The Constitutional Significance of the Executive Office of the President." *American Political Science Review* 43(6):1206–17.

Rudalevige, Andrew. 2002. *Managing the President's Program.* Princeton, NJ: Princeton University Press.

Rudalevige, Andrew, and David E. Lewis. 2005. "Parsing the Politicized Presidency: Centralization and Politicization as Presidential Strategies for Bureaucratic Control." Paper presented at the 2005 annual meeting of the American Political Science Association, Washington, DC.

Seidman, Harold. 1998. *Politics, Position, and Power: The Dynamics of Federal Organization.* 5th ed. New York: Oxford University Press.

Seligman, Lester G. 1956. "Presidential Leadership: The Inner Circle and Institutionalization." *Journal of Politics* 18(3):410–426.

Stanley, Harold W., and Richard G. Niemi. 1999. *Vital Statistics on American Politics 1999–2000.* Washington, DC: Congressional Quarterly.

Tomkin, Shelley Lynne. 1998. *Inside OMB: Politics and Process in the President's Budget Office.* Armonk, NY: M.E. Sharpe.

Walcott, Charles E., and Karen M. Hult. 1995. *Governing the White House: From Hoover Through LBJ.* Lawrence: University Press of Kansas.

Weko, Thomas J. 1995. *The Politicizing Presidency: The White House Personnel Office.* Lawrence: University Press of Kansas.

Zegart, Amy B. 1999. *Flawed by Design.* Stanford, CA: Stanford University Press. ✦

Chapter 11

Understanding Presidential Personality

Fred I. Greenstein

Fine and Waterman identify three dimensions of presidential leadership: personal presidential skill, the tools or resources presidents require to lead—that is, leverage—and the nature of the policy or political outcomes that are produced. Thus far the emphasis in this book has been on leverage, both in terms of what leverage presidents possess (and under which circumstances) and the impediments that constrain presidential leverage. On the other hand, skill has been less prominent in the discussion. When it has been discussed, such as in the Fleisher, Bond, and Wood chapter, the emphasis has been that leverage matters, while skill does not.

Is personal presidential skill really irrelevant? This is a difficult question to answer because while, as Fine and Waterman note, it is easy to find multiple measures of political leverage and political outcomes, it is more difficult to develop quantitative measures for skill. As a result, the literature on skill has tended to be qualitative, with frameworks presented to describe what it takes to be an effective leader. Two of the most prominent such frameworks were presented by Richard Neustadt and James David Barber. In this chapter Fred Greenstein provides a critique of each. Then, Waterman presents a discussion of how skill can be quantified.

✦ ✦ ✦

Plumbing the Presidential Psyche: Building on Neustadt and Barber

The political institutions of the United States make it a virtual certainty that the occupant of the Oval Office will have a significant impact on political outcomes. The president heads one of three branches of government that are granted coequal status by the Constitution. Barring impeachment by the House of Representatives and conviction by the Senate, the president is entitled to remain in office until the end of his term. During that period, he has at his disposal an imposing array of political resources, including the power to veto legislation and a wide range of possibilities for taking unilateral action in his capacities as his nation's leader in the international arena, the commander-in-chief of its military establishment, and the administrator of its laws.

One could imagine a political system in which the highest executive had great formal powers but did not leave a distinctly personal imprint on political outcomes, because he or she was the agent of a powerful political party, military junta, or other political entity. But that is far from the case in the United States, where the political parties are decentralized, the military is subordinated to civilian authority, and there are many centers of power. One could also imagine that the norms governing the behavior of a nation's highest leader would be highly specific, leaving little room for personal discretion, but throughout the course of American history presidents have varied widely in the conduct of their responsibilities.

For much of American history the political influence of the president was limited by the modest role of the federal government in the life of the country, the nation's isolation from world affairs, and the tendency of Congress to take the lead in the initiation of policy. That changed dramatically during the presidency of Franklin Delano Roosevelt, when the United States became a world power and a nascent welfare state, and the program of the chief executive became a crucial determinant of the nation's political agenda. The capacity of presidents to make a difference was also magnified during the Roosevelt years by the creation of the Executive Office of the President, which provides chief executives with the support system they need to carry out their expanded responsibilities.

There is no more compelling illustration of the importance of presidential political psychology than the Cuban Missile Crisis of October 1962. President John F. Kennedy was faced with starkly opposed options by his advisors, some of whom called for launching a surprise air strike on Soviet missiles that had secretly been installed in Cuba and others of whom recommended less severe courses of action. The buck stopped at the presidential psyche. Kennedy, who in his personal life was a self-indulgent risk taker, proves to have been the epitome of caution in his public capacity. In the missile crisis, he went beyond the most moderate members of his advisory group, secretly acceding to the Soviet demand that the United States remove its missiles from Greece and Turkey. The importance of Kennedy's caution is highlighted by the evidence available from the post–Cold War historical record, which strongly suggests that an attack on Cuba would have escalated into nuclear war between the United States and the Soviet Union.

This and countless less apocalyptic episodes highlight the importance of understanding the personal qualities of presidents. In what follows, I ask how these qualities can be productively studied. I begin by reviewing the answers provided in two canonical analyses of presidential leadership, Richard E. Neustadt's 1960 *Presidential Power* and James David Barber's 1972 *The Presidential Character* at greater length.[1] After discussing Neustadt's work in brief and Barber's at length, I review my own approach to the study of presidential political psychology, showing how it relates to their analyses and where it modifies or expands on them.[2] I conclude with an observation about an objection sometimes voiced to a preoccupation with the personal qualities of White House incumbents—the claim that to be so closely attentive to a single actor within a large and complex political system with a multitude of participants is inappropriate.

Neustadt's Highly Political Focus

Neustadt's *Presidential Power* is not commonly thought of as an exercise in political psychology, but it is just that, albeit with the emphasis on the adjective "political." Neustadt brought to his analysis the experience that derived from his service in the Bureau of the Budget and the White House under President Truman. Having worked for a president who was severely constrained by the political forces of the time, Neustadt set out to examine the qualities that make it possible for the occupant of the Oval Office to make a difference in the often intractable American political order.

Neustadt argues that a president has three broad means of advancing his purposes. He can employ the formal and informal powers of his office as resources for achieving his goals by striking bargains with other political actors. He can seek to win the cooperation of other members of the political community by making it evident that he has the skill and will to get his way. And he can further win the support of his fellow policymakers by demonstrating that he has a high level of public support. From this Neustadt concludes that an effective president should have a number of attributes: He should be well grounded in the ways of American politics. He should have a high level of sensitivity to power relations. He should be self-confident about his own suitability for the presidency, and he should be resolute in his desire to place his stamp on political outcomes.[3]

Neustadt's classic has been repeatedly reprinted, each time with added chapters on post-1960 developments. But all of the book's editions retain the 1960 text in which he spells out his thesis. As Peter Sperlich has pointed out, that formulation falls short of being comprehensive.[4] Neustadt overemphasizes the importance of bargaining in presidential leadership, Sperlich argues. His analysis needs to be amplified to take account of nonbargaining sources of presidential power, such as shared ideology and personal commitment to the chief executive. Sperlich also holds that Neustadt overemphasizes the personal actions of the president, ignoring the role a president's aides play in his leadership. To these points I would add another on which I will expand below—Neustadt's formulation needs to be amended to take account of the importance of harnessing a president's political skills to a realistic vision of public policy.

Barber's More Psychological Focus

In the political psychology of Barber's *The Presidential Character* the accent is on the noun. Barber's well-known classification of presidential character had its origins in a less well-known study in applied politics reported in his 1965 book *The Lawmakers.*[5] In that work Barber's concern was with the problem posed for the quality of leadership in the American states by the high rate of turnover of state legislators. To gain insight into this issue Barber surveyed first-term members of the Connecticut legislature, exploring their willingness to seek additional terms in office, the extent of their legislative activity, and their satisfactions and dissatisfactions with legislative life.

Positing that the level of activity of a legislator would be associated with his or her motivation to remain in the legislature for a number of terms, Barber arrayed his data in a four-fold table. He was taken aback to discover that the legislative activists—those who made speeches and introduced bills—were evenly divided about whether they were prepared to seek future terms. So also were the legislators who tended not to engage in such activities.

Each of the four types of legislator that emerged from Barber's cross-tabulation proved to have a distinctive profile. Those activists who hoped to remain in the legislature (what Barber called the *lawmakers*) tended to be policy-oriented problem solvers. The activists who did not propose to remain in the legislature (what Barber called the *advertisers*) had typically sought office in the hope of advancing their private careers by increasing their visibility. The inactive legislators who did not want to run again (the *reluctants*) tended to be respected local citizens who had been prevailed on to run out of a sense of obligation. The inactive legislators who did want to remain in office (the *spectators*) tended to be motivated by the social recognition resulting from legislative service.

When Barber adapted his classification to the presidency, he made significant modifications in the indicators of his four categories. Instead of assessing activity with such precise indicators as giving speeches and introducing legislation, he made a global distinction between whether a president was active or passive in the conduct of his duties. Rather than measuring political motivation by the willingness to remain in office for a number of terms (an irrelevance in the era of the two-term limitation on presidents), he made another broad distinction, classifying presidents in terms of whether the feelings they invested in politics were predominantly positive or negative. He also introduced a significant change in the psychological claim he makes for his typology, arguing that his four-fold classification reflects the deeper levels of a president's psychological make up (his character) and not merely his adaptation to his political role.

In their transformed status Barber's types closely resemble the influential earlier categorizations of a pair of pioneering social scientists—the sociologist David Riesman and the political scientist Harold D. Lasswell. Barber's *passive-positive* and *passive-negative* presidential categories parallel what Riesman referred to as other-directed and inner-directed characters. The actions of the former are dependent on cues from their social environment and those of the latter are driven by their consciences. Barber's *active-positive* and *active-negative* presidents resemble what Lasswell referred to as democratic and power-centered character structures.[6] The former are emotionally robust individuals who approach their leadership out of a desire to get constructive results; the latter are emotionally unsettled individuals, whose political actions serve to vent their insecurities.

Barber embeds his revised classification in a commendably comprehensive framework, positing that a president's actions result not only from his underlying character structure, but also from his belief system and political style, as well as two broad aspects of his political environment: the distribution of political forces during his time in office and the state of public opinion. In practice, however, Barber focuses almost exclusively on character in his case studies of individual presidents.[7]

The Presidential Character has exercised a continuing intellectual influence. Summary accounts of Barber's formulation routinely appear in American government and presidency textbooks, and the book has gone into four editions, each of them adding new presidents to its analysis. There appear to be a number of reasons for the book's appeal. It contains vividly written case studies of the bulk of the twentieth-century presidents. It powerfully illustrates a thesis that most Americans find self-evident: that the personal qualities of the president are of fundamental importance. Neustadt's categories resonate with the insights of others, notably those of Lasswell and Riesman. Moreover, they provide an easily grasped basis for identifying meaningful patterns in the personal qualities of the bewilderingly diverse occupants of the presidency.

Yet *The Presidential Character* is also a work that has not stood up well to rigorous scholarly scrutiny. As Alexander L. George points out in an influential review article, many of the presidential actions Barber attributes to character (for example, Hoover's reluctance to make vigorous use of the government to combat the Depression) appear to be a function of ideology. Moreover, George continues, there is no empirical evidence for Barber's claim that the complex and varied manifestations of the psyche can be compressed into four categories.[8] (The diagnostic manual of the American Psychiatric Association consumes a full eight pages, with an enumeration of dozens of personality types.[9]) Indeed, the very dichotomies on which Barber builds his classification have analytic shortcomings. Presidents cannot be neatly partitioned into those who are active and those who are passive. They may be active in some spheres and passive in others. (Ronald Reagan was passive when it came to mastering the details of his administration's policies but indefatigable when it came to communicating with the public.) Nor are presidents either positive or negative in the emotions they invest in politics—some of them (for example, Theodore Roosevelt and Lyndon Johnson) may have bipolar tendencies, alternating with their moods.

There is still another problem with Barber's approach, one that provides a transition to my own trait-based approach to presidential political psychology. Barber's types are defined by externals, but people who differ in the surface may be similar under the skin, and those with similar appearances may have different underpinnings. Consider the case of a president who served after the appearance of the final edition of *The Presidential Character*—William Jefferson Clinton. On the face of it, the hyperactive, ever-ebullient Clinton would seem to be a quintessential example of Barber's emotionally robust active-positive character type. But in fact, Clinton's presidency was marked by the kinds of self-inflicted wounds Barber predicts for active-negative presidents. While he was not marked by the simmering anger and dark suspicions of a Richard Nixon, he was conspicuously lacking in self-discipline, most strikingly (but far from only) in entering into the sexual liaison that led to his impeachment.

Building on Neusdadt and Barber

Although my own approach to analyzing the presidential psyche builds on Neustadt and Barber, it contrasts with the former by considering the personal as well as the political qualities of the president and with the latter by not seeking to compress presidential political psychology into a master typology. My approach is in part inductive and interpretive in that I steep myself in the available evidence of particular presidents and characterize them in their own terms. But I also apply a set of common criteria for analyzing and comparing presidents, criteria that relate to the role demands of the presidency.

The first of these is the president's proficiency as a public communicator. The second is his organizational capacity, which includes his ability to select able colleagues and structure their activities to good effect. The third is the president's political skill. The fourth is the extent and nature of his vision of public policy. The fifth is the cognitive style with which he processes the tidal wave of advice and information that comes the way of a president. The last is what has in recent years come to be called "emotional intelligence" and what Max Weber referred to as "the firm taming of the soul"—the president's ability to control his emotions and turn them to constructive purposes, rather than being dominated by them and allowing them to diminish his leadership.[10]

This analysis yields a number of observations, some of which are consistent with the positions taken by Neustadt and Barber and others of which are not:

1. *Public Communication.* For an office that places so great a premium on public rhetoric, the modern presidency has been surprisingly lacking in effective public communicators. Most presidents have not addressed the public with anything approximating the professionalism of countless educators, members of the clergy, and radio and television broadcasters. Roosevelt, Kennedy, and Reagan—and Clinton at his best—are the shining exceptions. The critical importance of the bully pulpit to the modern presidency was underscored by the actions of President George W. Bush, who had minimized the role of public rhetoric in the initial months of his presidency, but responded to the terrorist acts of September 11, 2001, by addressing the public frequently and forcefully, winning a dramatically high level of public support for his leadership.

2. *Organizational Capacity.* A president's capacity as an organizer includes his ability to forge a team and get the most out of it, minimizing the tendency of subordinates to defer to him, rather than present him their unvarnished views. It also includes a quite different matter: a president's proficiency at creating effective institutional arrangements. The modern president who had the most demanding organizational experience, especially in his capacity as the commander of the allied theater of operations in World War II was Dwight D. Eisenhower, who had a highly developed view of the matter. "I know of only one way in which you can be sure you have done your best to make a wise decision," he declared in a 1967 interview:

> That is to get all of the [responsible policymakers] with their different viewpoints in front of you, and listen to them debate. I do not believe in bringing them in one at a time, and therefore

being more impressed by the most recent one you hear than the
earlier ones. You must get courageous men of strong views, and
let them debate with each other.[11]

Not all of the modern presidents have been open to vigorous
give and take. Nixon and Reagan were uncomfortable in the
presence of face-to-face disagreement. Johnson's Texas-sized
personality had a chilling effect on some of his subordinates.
His National Security Council staff member Chester Cooper recalled recurrent fantasies of facing down LBJ at NSC meetings
when Johnson sought his concurrence on a matter relating to
Vietnam by replying, "I most definitely do not agree." But
when LBJ turned to him and asked, "Mr. Cooper, do you
agree?" Cooper found himself replying, "Yes, Mr. President, I
agree."[12]

3. *Political Skill.* If there ever was reason to doubt Neustadt's em-
    phasis on the importance of the president's political skill, it
    was eliminated by the experience of Jimmy Carter. Lyndon
    Johnson, who seemed almost to have taken his methods from
    Neustadt, was the virtual antithesis of Carter when it came to
    skill. Within hours after Kennedy's assassination, Johnson had
    begun to muster support for major domestic policy departures.
    He cultivated his political reputation by keeping Congress in
    session until Christmas 1963 in order to prevail in one of his
    administration's first legislative contests. Moreover, his actions
    won him strong public support, making it apparent to his op-
    posite numbers on Capitol Hill that it would be politically
    costly to ignore his demands. Johnson, however, also illustrates
    the incompleteness of Neustadt's formulation, in that his politi-
    cal virtuosity was not complemented with a viable policy vi-
    sion, especially in the international arena.

4. *Policy Vision.* Despite his political virtuosity, Johnson led the
    United States into an open-ended military intervention in Viet-
    nam, not pausing to ask how long the commitment would last
    and what its economic and human costs would be.[13] Of the
    presidents since FDR, three had particularly explicit visions of
    where they sought to lead the nation—Eisenhower, Nixon, and
    Reagan. Presidents are better able to set the terms of political
    discourse if they have a clear sense of direction. In effect they
    serve as anchors for the rest of the political community. Presi-
    dents who are vision-free, on the other hand, tend not to set
    priorities for the nation and their administrations. They are
    prone to advance internally contradictory programs, as well as
    a course of action such as that Johnson pursued in Southeast
    Asia that have unintended and undesired consequences.

5. *Cognitive Style.* Here I mean to identify the variety of ways in which presidents' cerebral qualities may affect their role performance, including their capacity to master information and comprehend arguments, the extent to which their thinking is concrete or abstract, their capacity to get to the nub of problems and arrive at analytic or strategic conclusions. Presidents, like everyone else, vary in their cognitive styles. Jimmy Carter had an engineer's proclivity to reduce issues to what he perceived to be their component parts. That style served him well in his highly successful 1978 Camp David negotiations with the leaders of Egypt and Israel, but it was ill-suited for providing his administration with a sense of direction. Carter's narrow cognitive qualities contrast with the broader, more analytic intelligence revealed by Eisenhower in 1954 in his response to the communist encirclement of US-supported French military forces at the Indochinese fortress of Dien Bien Phu. His immediate response was to reach a strategic judgment, declaring that the jungles of Indochina would "absorb our divisions by the dozens."[14] Sheer brain power has not been a guarantee of effective presidential performance. Lyndon Johnson, Richard Nixon, Jimmy Carter, and Bill Clinton had impressive minds, but their presidencies suffered from their characterological shortcomings. Harry Truman and Ronald Reagan rose above their intellectual limitations in their conduct of their responsibilities.

6. *Emotional Intelligence.* The term "emotional intelligence" and its opposite, which might be dubbed "emotional obtuseness," provide convenient rubrics for addressing Barber's concern with the emotional underpinnings of presidential leadership. The first of these notions provides a useful way of referring to presidents who are able to channel their emotions into productive leadership—the ability Barber associates with the active-positive type. The second serves to identify presidents who lack emotional self-control and whose emotions sabotage their leadership. This is the vulnerability Barber ties to the active-negative type, but as noted above, it can encompass a Bill Clinton, whose appearance was emphatically active-positive.

A Concluding Remark

The historian Thomas Cochran once warned of the shortcomings of the "presidential synthesis" as an organizing principle in historical analysis.[15] More recently, the political scientist Charles O. Jones stressed that the president "is not the presidency" and "the presidency is not the government,"[16] arguing against a presidency-centered approach to the study of American politics. Is a preoccupation with the personal qualities of presidents a distraction from attention to the larger political system? An answer is suggested by the following analogy. Compare the structures and processes of the American political system to the complex machinery of a ballistic missile and the president to a small, but vital, component of the missile—its trigger mechanism. A defective trigger mechanism could be a prescription for disaster. Would paying close attention to that mechanism preclude closely examining the entity in which it is contained? Obviously not! By the same token, there is no conflict between intensive analysis of the American political system and comparably close analysis of the pivotally placed occupant of 1600 Pennsylvania Avenue. Both are mandatory and neither excludes the other.

Presidential Skill and Greatness: An Addendum

Richard W. Waterman

As Fine and Waterman note in Chapter 2, presidents do possess identifiable skill sets. Greenstein categorizes six areas of presidential skill: (1) public communication, (2) organizational capacity, (3) political skill, (4) policy vision, (5) cognitive style, and (6) emotional intelligence. Most people can agree that these skills are important attributes for presidents serving today. But as Waterman and Rockman noted in Chapter 1, expectations of the presidency have changed over time. As a result, the skill sets that are appropriate for presidential leadership also have changed. Presidential communication and organizational capacity are more important skills for presidents today than they were during the eighteenth or nineteenth centuries. The same is true of policy vision. Thus, while political skill always has been important, particular types of political skills were likely more beneficial at different periods in American history.

For instance, Lincoln's extraordinary skill at uniting the often dissonant voices within his own cabinet was accomplished with quiet skill and diplomacy, tactics that may be less effective in an age of 24/7 media coverage and increased political polarization. While Lincoln's tactics might be less successful today, or for that matter Franklin Roosevelt's leadership style (he actively encouraged administrative overlap, which today would be seen as evidence of duplication and gross inefficiency), there is no question that *these skills served these presidents very well during their time as president.* In other words, we know presidential skill exists and we know that it is important. We can identify it repeatedly when we qualitatively examine individual presidencies. We can even create frameworks that identify qualities that presidents should possess. Yet, when it comes to systematically measuring skill, we generally are at a loss. What does political communication mean over time? In the nineteenth century, Lincoln was continually involved in political communication, but whereas today communication is generally verbal, for Lincoln as president it tended to be written and directed at a specific audience. He communicated through letters, some provided to influential policymakers, while others meant to be disseminated more broadly were leaked to the press. This leadership and communication style befitted the technologies and expectations (e.g., the idea that presidents should not speak publicly) of his time. Therefore, one can rate Lincoln high on communication skills. But we cannot compare these skills directly with Ronald Reagan or Bill Clinton; both had extraordinary skill in front of an audience, particularly on television, but substantively had much less to say about policy than did Lincoln in his political correspondence.

Skill is not the only attribute of presidential leadership to change over time. The same can be said of the nature of political leverage, but we have more of an identifiable pattern in this case. Presidents today have more leverage politically than did their nineteenth-century cohorts. The movement of the United States onto the world stage provided presidents with considerably greater leverage in international affairs, as has the presence of a constant threat as exemplified by nuclear weaponry, the Cold War, and now terrorism. The centralization of the U.S. economy focused greater attention on the president as economic policymaker. It also tended to make the White House the center of attention in policymaking on other issues, thus accentuating the importance of the president's policy vision as a leadership characteristic. While it is true that there are palpable impediments to presidential leadership, as noted throughout this volume, we can identify the development of specific leverage mechanisms with a greater sense of continuity over time (that is, a clearer pattern of development) than we can with personal leadership skills. Skill is much more responsive and susceptible to the existing public expectations of a particular time and often varies with the particular abilities of each president.

How then can we evaluate presidential skill? One admittedly imperfect way is to examine the historical rankings of the "great" presidents. The data presented in Table 1.1 of Chapter 1 presents the historical rankings from a 2000 ranking of the presidents. While historical rankings are far from precise measures of presidential skill, they do at least tell us who historians believe excelled at the presidential job. They also tell us which presidents historians perceive as unsuccessful. We can then examine these individuals to see if there are identifiable traits shared by the subset of successful or failed presidents.

Lincoln ranks as the greatest president, followed by Franklin Roosevelt, George Washington, Theodore Roosevelt, Harry Truman, Woodrow Wilson, Thomas Jefferson, John Kennedy, Dwight Eisenhower, and Lyndon Johnson. Of these 10 presidents, seven served during the twentieth century, two during the nineteenth century, and one during the eighteenth century. Consequently, there is a bias toward twentieth-century presidents, though two of these (T. Roosevelt and Woodrow Wilson) governed before the era generally identified as the "modern presidency" (which many scholars demarcate as beginning in 1933). Again, while there is a bias, many of these twentieth-century presidents served prior to the invention of television (and two even prior to radio) and before the personalization of the presidency (and the decline of the political parties) that occurred with the development of the presidential primary process. Consequently, there is more variation in the types of presidents selected than one might at first suspect.

What qualities then do these 10 presidents exhibit? We know that Lincoln was a master of politics behind the scenes, Franklin Roosevelt exhibited the same capability, as well as great communication skills, Washington was a bedrock whose personal principles were beyond reproach, Theodore Roosevelt was both charismatic and energetic, Truman was determined, honest, and unyielding once he had made up his mind, Wilson was equally inflexible (often with disastrous policy results) but also was skilled at uniting his congressional party, and Jefferson was also skilled at leading Congress, but through an entirely different mechanism (dinners at the White House, with copious amounts of wine). Kennedy was noted for his political vision and communication skills and Eisenhower for his steadiness. Eisenhower, once criticized for his passivity, is now more fully appreciated by historians, especially given the abuses of power of some of his successors. For example, Lyndon Johnson led the nation into a war in Vietnam, often using deception to do so, but he also demonstrated incredible political skill in maneuvering momentous civil rights legislation through an often hostile Congress.

This synopsis, which is far from a detailed analysis of these presidents, suggests that each had admirable qualities associated with presidential leadership but that these qualities varied considerably from president to president. Not all were great communicators. Not all had a clear policy vision. But each president seems to have excelled at least in one of the categories Greenstein identifies. This may be one reason why it is so difficult to identify systematic effects related to presidential skill. There is no one way to be a successful president. If so, identifying great presidents a priori would be an easy task for pundits and the electorate. But among contemporaries, who would have guessed that Abraham Lincoln or Franklin Roosevelt would be a great president, though Neustadt assumes we could? They seemed to lack the experience and basic qualities of leadership. On the other hand, when they entered the White House Herbert Hoover and Richard Nixon seemed to have extraordinary levels of experience. Yet they obviously lacked other skills that could have made them great presidents. Skill, then, operates in a much less predictable and less systematic fashion than political leverage. The same qualities that promote leverage (the more seats held in Congress by members of the president's party) should help all presidents. We cannot say the same thing about skill.

What then explains who is a great president? According to Simonton, four-fifths of the variation in historical polls is explained by six variables: the number of years a president serves in office, whether they serve during war years or during a scandal, whether they were assassinated, whether they exhibited war heroism, and their intellectual brilliance.[17] Thus, situational factors predominate; that is, presidents must find themselves in the proper circumstances in order to be successful. For example, Lincoln, Franklin Roosevelt, Harry Truman, Woodrow Wilson, Dwight Eisenhower, and Lyndon Johnson all governed during time of war (though Korea certainly did not add to Truman's prestige nor Vietnam to Johnson's). Franklin Roosevelt also dealt with the crisis of the Great Depression, Kennedy with the Cuban Missile Crisis, Eisenhower the Suez Canal Crisis, and Jefferson the potential for war with England (though the Embargo of 1807 proved to be one the biggest failures of his presidency). Conflict and crisis can provide a stage for presidential greatness. They also can provide an extraordinary opportunity for presidents to demonstrate their personal leadership skill. Without crises, it is difficult for presidents to demonstrate anything but perfunctory skills.

Of course not all presidents who serve during times of crisis are considered to be great leaders. The flip side of the leadership equation is those presidents who failed during crisis situations; that is, those who did not demonstrate capable skill or leadership qualities. If we next examine the 10 lowest-ranked presidents we see that most of them failed to live up to historical or contemporary expectations in a time of crisis, or governed during periods of corruption (e.g., Grant and Harding). It is noteworthy that only two of these presidents served in the twentieth century (Hoover and Harding). Most governed in the period just before or just after the Civil War (Buchanan, Johnson, Pierce, Fillmore, Grant). Tyler was a lame duck president from the moment he assumed office. He was a Democrat elected on a ticket with a Whig, while William Henry Harrison lived just 30 days after his inauguration. None of these presidents were activists nor did they exhibit extraordinary political skill, though a few did prior to their presidencies. Grant showed skill on the battlefield, while Hoover demonstrated extraordinary skill in every position he held prior to the presidency, as well as after it. Buchanan also had been a well-regarded Secretary of State.

These presidents were not merely pawns of the times in which they governed, overwhelmed by events that no president could handle. Hoover failed in his attempts to deal with the Great Depression, and while Franklin Roosevelt's policies most often were not successful, he led the nation through a most difficult time in its history, providing the public with a much needed sense of hope. Likewise, while Pierce and Buchanan proved inept in dealing with the onslaught of Civil War, often making decisions that expedited it rather than averting it (e.g., Pierce supported the Kansas-Nebraska Act while Buchanan favored the Lecompton Constitution and the Dred Scott decision), Lincoln demonstrated extraordinary political skill in restoring the union. The conclusion we can draw from these cases, then, is that presidential skill matters.

Yet, we are still left with the nebulous conclusion that while skill matters, we are unable to systematically show how it matters in similar ways across presidents and across time. We know that activism is usually a sign of leadership, but not always. Some activist presidents do not fare particularly well in the poll. Prior political experience also is not always at a premium; otherwise presidents like Martin Van Buren, Richard Nixon, Herbert Hoover, and George Herbert Walker Bush would be ranked more highly. Even intelligence is not necessarily a requirement, despite Simonton's conclusion. If Franklin Roosevelt did indeed possess a "first class temperament and a second class mind," as Oliver Wendell Holmes famously declared, it did not limit his ability as president. Reagan lacked curiosity and even fell asleep at Cabinet meetings (and once did so in a meeting with the Pope), yet he ranks 11th in the poll, ahead of James Madison (ranked 18th), who is widely considered to be a political genius. Clinton and Carter are among our most intelligent modern presidents, yet they rank only 21st and 22nd, respectively. And again, Hoover is generally described as one of our smartest presidents, yet ranks only 34th.

Measuring skill, therefore, is a less precise task than is measuring political leverage or political or policy outcomes. While we know that skill matters, it is more difficult for us to measure it systematically than it is other attributes of presidential leadership. As a result, it is easy to conclude that skill does not matter. One goal for future research, then, will be to develop more systematic and reliable measures of presidential skill over time.

Notes

1. Richard E. Neustadt, *Presidential Power: The Politics of Leadership* (New York: Wiley, 1960). Reprinted repeatedly with added text, the last time with the title *Presidential Power and the Modern Presidency: The Politics of Leadership From Roosevelt to Reagan* (New York: Free Press, 1990). James David Barber, *The Presidential Character: Predicting Performance in the White House* (Englewood Cliff, NJ: Prentice-Hall, 1972), with three later editions, the last published in 1992.

2. Fred I. Greenstein, *The Presidential Difference: Leadership Style From FDR to Clinton* (New York: The Free Press, 2000). Paperback with an afterword on George W. Bush, Princeton University Press, 2001.

3. Neustadt, *Presidential Power,* 179–180.

4. Peter W. Sperlich, "Bargaining and Overload: An Essay on Presidential Power." In Aaron Wildavsky (ed.), *The Presidency* (Boston: Little Brown, 1969). Reprinted in Wildavsky's *Perspectives on the Presidency* (Boston: Little, Brown, 1975).

5. James David Barber, *The Lawmakers: Recruitment and Adaptation to Legislative Life* (New Haven, CT: Yale University Press, 1965).

6. Harold D. Lasswell, "Democratic Character," in *The Political Writings of Harold D. Lasswell* (Glencoe, IL: Free Press, 1950). Lasswell, *Psychopathology and Politics* (Chicago: University of Chicago Press, 1930).

7. In the third and fourth editions of *The Presidential Character,* Barber does raise the possibility that a president's belief system may affect his actions, classifying Gerald Ford, Jimmy Carter, and George H. W. Bush as active-positive presidents whose presidencies were diminished because they lacked the mental sets required for effective leadership.

8. Alexander L. George, "Assessing Presidential Character," *World Politics* 26 (1974), 234–282, reprinted in Alexander L. George and Julliette L. George, *Presidential Personality and Performance* (New York: Westview Press, 1998), 145–197.

9. *Diagnostic and Statistical Manual of Mental Disorders: DSM-IV* (Washington, DC: American Psychiatric Association, 1994), 793–802.

10. Daniel Goleman, *Emotional Intelligence* (New York: Bantam Books, 1995). This appears to be what Max Weber refers to as "the firm taming of the soul" in his classic essay on the political vocation. Max Weber, "Politics as a Vocation" in *From Max Weber: Essays in Sociology,* ed. H. H. Gerth and C. Wright Mills (New York: Oxford University Press, 1956), 19.

11. Dwight D. Eisenhower, Columbia University Oral History interview, 20 July, 1967, 103. See also Fred I. Greenstein and Richard Immerman, "Effective National Security Advising: Recovering the Eisenhower Legacy," *Political Science Quarterly* 115 (Fall 2000), 335–345.

12. Chester I. Cooper, *The Lost Crusade: America in Vietnam* (Greenwich, CT: Dodd, Mead, 1970), 223.

13. John P. Burke, Fred I. Greenstein, Larry Berman, and Richard Immerman, *How Presidents Test Reality: Decisions on Vietnam, 1954 and 1965* (New York: Russell Sage Foundation, 1988).

14. Ibid., 32.

15. Thomas C. Cochran, "The 'Presidential Synthesis' in American History," *The American Historical Review* 53 (1948), 748–759.

16. Charles O. Jones, *The Presidency in a Separated System* (Washington, DC: The Brookings Institution, 1994).

17. Dean Keith Simonton, *Why Presidents Succeed: A Political Psychology of Leadership* (New Haven: Yale University Press, 1987), Chapter 5. ✦

Chapter 12

The Politics of Persuasion
A Bargaining Model of Presidential Power

Matthew J. Dickinson

Does presidential skill matter? In Chapter 2 Fine and Waterman identified skill as one characteristic of presidential leadership. In Chapter 8, however, once they established a baseline model of presidential success rates with Congress, Fleisher, Bond, and Wood found no support that presidential skill matters. As Dickinson notes in this chapter, they are far from the only scholars who have come to this conclusion. In fact, there seems to be a growing tendency to minimize the impact of presidential skill on political outcomes, at least in domestic policy formulation. This may be because of the intrinsic difficulties involved in measuring skill, as Waterman notes in his addendum to Chapter 11. But it also reflects a wide-ranging research agenda which has challenged one of the most prominent models of presidential leadership: Richard Neustadt's model of presidential power.

In this chapter Dickinson offers a persuasive argument that skill matters. As do Fleisher, Bond, and Wood, Dickinson recognizes that presidents' behavior is conditioned by their institutional setting, and that it is increasingly constrained by organizational rules and processes. But this does not alter a president's analytic purpose. A president remains focused on what he or she, as an individual, can do to wield influence within this more institutionalized setting.

Presidency scholarship is often maligned, not least by presidency scholars (Edwards, 1981; Edwards, Kessel, and Rockman 1993; Heclo 1977a; A. King 1975; G. King 1993; Moe 1993; Peterson 1990; Wayne 1983). Critics bemoan the subfield's focus on individual presi-

I wish to thank Erwin Hargrove, Chuck Jones, and Andy Rudalevige for helpful comments on an earlier version of this article.

dents (the infamous n = 1 problem), its reliance on detailed case studies and ad hoc or nonexistent theorizing, the use of thick description
instead of systematic data analysis, and the failure to generate testable hypotheses. The result, they argue, is a body of work that lacks
cumulative findings; compared to scholarship on Congress or election studies, presidency research remains something of an intellectual backwater. As evidence, they point out that the subfield's
best-known work, Richard Neustadt's *Presidential Power* (hereafter
PP) is more than 40 years old. Neustadt's core argument—that a president's power is weak, that it depends primarily on persuasion, and
that persuasion is tantamount to bargaining—has remained essentially unchanged through five editions (1960, 1968, 1976, 1980, 1990).
To critics, it is indicative of the subfield's intellectual stasis that a single book has been dominant for so long, particularly given *PP*'s emphasis on the "man in office." Neustadt's "personal" approach to
studying the presidency, they suggest, in which presidential power
appears contingent on the attributes of individual presidents, is
hardly conducive to the theory building and testing necessary to build
cumulative and generalizable findings.

To be sure, one can overstate *PP*'s intellectual ascendancy within
presidency research; the bargaining model of presidential leadership
is not now and never was the only game in town (Edwards 2000, 11;
Hargrove 1998, 1–48; Hart 1998; Tatalovich and Engeman 2003).
Neustadt's argument has received extensive criticism,[1] and scholars
have periodically sought to supplement, if not replace, the bargaining
paradigm with alternative models of presidential leadership.[2] But if
these efforts helped extend and refine scholars' understanding of
presidential power, they did not relegate *PP* to the bookshelf of "classic period pieces" as some critics recommended (Skowronek 1987,
430). In the words of those editing a recent compilation of presidency
research, "Political scientists still consider [*PP*] as the seminal book
on the American Presidency—the one that still influences not only
their thinking and research about presidential power, but also that of
presidents and their advisers who have come to learn directly or indirectly about Neustadt's advice . . ." (Shapiro, Kumar, and Jacobs
2000, ix).

This chapter explains why Neustadt's bargaining paradigm remains at the heart of presidency research more than four decades
after *PP* was first published. The answer, I argue, has less to do with
the weaknesses of the presidency subfield than with the dictates of
the constitutional system that prompted Neustadt to write it in the
first place. Simply put, in a system of separated institutions sharing
powers (Neustadt 1990, 29) presidents have no reasonable alternative
to bargaining as a means of exercising influence on an ongoing basis.
Although Neustadt's work is perhaps the most famous articulation of
this thesis, it is by no means the only one. Several scholars have pre-

sented theories of presidential leadership that are entirely compatible with Neustadt's bargaining-based model (Jones 1994; Kellerman 1984; Seligman and Covington 1989). And, as described below, there is a strong case to be made that Neustadt's substantive claims have been largely validated. In fact, the most trenchant criticism of *PP* is directed not at Neustadt's empirical argument, but at his mode of analysis (Ragsdale 2000). If Neustadt's prescriptive, participant-observer analytical method has fallen out of fashion, however, his bargaining paradigm continues to guide most presidency research.

Because bargaining is woven into the constitutional fabric of the American political system, then, it should surprise no one that Neustadt's book has served as the intellectual foil for successive generations of presidency scholars. Nonetheless, *PP* is best understood as a prototheory to be tested and refined, not as the last word on presidential leadership. It presents an initial framework for a bargaining model of presidential power, but that framework continues to be modified and more fully fleshed out from subsequent research by scholars of different methodological persuasions. As a result, after four decades of studies, much of it inspired by Neustadt's insights, scholars have a more complete understanding as to why bargaining remains the essence of presidential leadership.

The chapter begins with an overview of Neustadt's basic thesis, as first presented in 1960 and elaborated by him in subsequent editions of *PP*. It then describes scholars' efforts to test the bargaining model—how well is it supported by the empirical evidence? How, if at all, should it be changed in light of additional research? The review is not meant to be exhaustive. Instead, I pay particular attention to Neustadt's critics—what can we learn about the basis of presidential power from them? Finally, I conclude by highlighting areas of additional research that may be helpful in clarifying scholars' understanding regarding the sources of presidential leadership. At the risk of overlooking important parts of the presidency literature, I focus my presentation on a specific subset of research in order to isolate and highlight areas in which substantial progress has occurred, and to point out potentially fruitful avenues for future scholarship. Neustadt's bargaining paradigm provides a wealth of testable hypotheses, some yet to be addressed. To do so, however, scholars need to move beyond the methodological parochialism that has often hindered progress in the field.

1. Bargaining, Power, and the *PP* Paradigm

PP's origins are rooted in Neustadt's return to academia in 1953, after several years as a high-level bureaucrat in the Truman administration. As Neustadt immersed himself in the political science literature in preparation to teach a course on American politics, he discovered, ". . . [T]he descriptions, particularly about the Presidency, seemed to be very remote from what I had experienced. The effort to get that straight is what underlies *Presidential Power*" (Jones 2003, 1).

In writing *PP*, however, Neustadt sought to do more than simply correct academic accounts of presidential leadership that stressed the importance of the president's formal powers (Corwin 1957), or the many leadership "hats" presidents wore (Rossiter 1960). Neustadt had a more ambitious, prescriptive, goal: explaining how a president could exercise authority in fact, and not just in theory. "My interest is in what a President can do to make his own will felt within his own administration," he says at the outset of *PP* (Neustadt 1990, xx—unless otherwise noted, all references to *PP* are from this edition). The book is essentially a primer on this topic, oriented as much, or more so, to political practitioners—including presidents—as to scholars. This prescriptive bent influenced Neustadt's writing style and use of evidence; he sought clarity in exposition and illustration above all else, even if it meant straying from strict adherence to social science's methodological canons.[3]

How does a president gain and retain power? The answer, Neustadt advises, is to think prospectively. A president must continually ask how his (someday her) choices today influence his sources of power down the road. By power, Neustadt means nothing more than a president's effective influence on government's processes and outcomes. That influence, Neustadt writes, is largely predicated on three related factors:

> [F]irst are the bargaining advantages inherent in his job with which to persuade other men that what he wants of them is what their own responsibilities require them to do. Second are the expectations of those other men regarding his ability and will to use the various advantages they think he has. Third are those men's estimates of how his public views him and of how their publics may view them if they do what he wants. In short, his power is the product of his vantage points in government, together with his reputation in the Washington community and his prestige outside. (1990, 150)

In making this argument, Neustadt draws a critical, and often overlooked, distinction between a president's formal "powers" and his power (1990, 29, endnote 1). Powers refer to the constitutional, statutory, and traditional authority designated to the president. These are the primary source of a president's "vantage points" from which to bargain; in a system of shared powers, other institutions and actors must cultivate presidential support in order to fulfill their own responsibilities.[4] Formal powers, however, do not translate fully into power—effective influence—because the president's bargaining audiences view their exercise from dissimilar vantage points; they are separated institutions, responding to different constituencies, and with different time frames and operating incentives.[5]

If formal powers are no guarantee of bargaining success, they do ensure that presidents will be locked into mutually dependent relations with other "Washingtonians" (defined by interest in the president's action, not geography)—that they will be clerks, if not leaders. Of course, this dependence yields advantages to the president. But to capitalize on these advantages, presidents must cultivate two additional sources of influence: their professional reputation and their public prestige.

By professional reputation, Neustadt means a president's "skill and will . . . to use his advantages" (1990, 50). Simply put, presidents develop a reputation through time for the effectiveness (or lack thereof) with which they employ the powers of their office to achieve desired ends. Presidents largely determine this reputation through their own presidential actions, with first impressions weighted more heavily than subsequent ones. Indeed, a president's reputation is not infinitely pliable; once fixed in the minds of Washingtonians, it thereafter becomes difficult to change. Because Washingtonians use a president's reputation to calculate his likely behavior in the bargaining process, it is a potential source of leverage: "What other men expect of him becomes a cardinal factor in the president's own power to persuade" (1990, 52). In particular, Neustadt argues, Washingtonians want to know what price, if any, they might pay for *opposing* the president. By creating uncertainty among Washingtonians in this regard, presidents can increase their bargaining influence (1990, 55).

A president's public prestige—his standing with Washingtonians' various publics—provides a third source of influence. But prestige does not refer to a president's overall public support as measured, for example, by monthly Gallup polls. Rather, it signifies the president's standing in the "aggregate of the publics as diverse and overlapping as the claims Americans . . . press on Washington" (1990, 73). As such, prestige takes a subtler and more variable form, one not easily captured by opinion polling. It often changes depending on the bargaining audience and topic, and the "quality" of that prestige is as important, if not more so, than its quantity. Moreover, Neustadt suggests that prestige operates mostly in the political background, providing "leeway" regarding what a president might accomplish, rather than directly determining bargaining outcomes.

As with reputation, presidents can influence their prestige, but in a much more limited manner. This is because prestige varies according to the publics' changing conceptions of what they want from the presidency, as an office. And those conceptions are based predominantly on events happening to them, in their lives. Presidents are rarely positioned to control these events; at best, they might interpret them in ways that redound to their bargaining advantage. This "teaching" is often more effectively accomplished by action, rather than talk. But even here a president's influence is limited by the public's willingness to listen, and by the president's previous actions in this area, particularly if those actions contradict the lesson he is trying to teach.

Neustadt's analysis is institutionally based, but his perspective is decidedly personal (Moe 1993); he writes from the president's vantage point—what must he do to maximize his chances of influence?[6] But if *PP* is a primer on personal influence, it is decidedly not a study of individual presidents; his generic advice applies to all presidents, regardless of personality "type." Neustadt is often accused of personalizing the study of the presidency, at the expense of understanding how the presidency as an institution shapes the exercise of presidential power (Jacobs and Shapiro 2000, 492; Mayer 2001, 11; Ragsdale 2000, 39).[7] But this ignores Neustadt's clearly articulated purpose in writing *PP*.[8] He recognizes that presidents' behavior is conditioned by their institutional setting, and that it is increasingly constrained by organizational rules and processes (1990, 218–220). But this does not alter his analytic purpose; he remains focused on what the president, as an individual, can do to wield influence within this more institutionalized setting.[9]

Neustadt fine-tuned his analysis in subsequent editions of *PP* to take account of new political developments.[10] But his central argument does not change from the first edition to last: "Presidential weakness was the underlying theme of *Presidential Power*. This remains my theme. It runs through the eight original chapters . . . and through five later ones that are meant to supplement, bring up to date, revise and reconsider, as befits a new edition. The doing has not brought a change of theme" (1990, ix). Why is presidential weakness Neustadt's constant refrain? Because of the constitutionally mandated system of many separated institutions sharing powers. "To share is to limit; that is the heart of the matter, and everything this book explores stems from it" (1990, x).

For many scholars, however, Neustadt's consistency in argument and method across four decades is not a virtue. Instead, it dates *PP*'s intellectual origins to a time and research tradition increasingly less relevant to presidency studies. "[T]he study of the presidency is unmistakably, though not exclusively, moving away from the direction charged by Richard Neustadt's *Presidential Power*" write Jacobs and Shapiro. ". . . Neustadt's work . . . no longer offers a reliable roadmap embodying the consensus among contemporary scholars. The current study of the presidency is motivated by different concerns and is pursuing new theoretical and substantive research questions" (Jacobs and Shapiro 2000, 489).

This claim that *PP*'s model of presidential leadership is outmoded and perhaps inaccurate is frequently voiced in the presidency literature, and as such deserves careful consideration (Moe 1993, 342;

Howell 2003, 10; Ragsdale 2000, 41; Mayer 2001, 22). The next section takes up this task. I argue that Neustadt's critics make several significant errors in their interpretation of *PP*. In particular, they often confuse his analytic perspective "looking over the president's shoulder" for a presidency-dominated "personal" model of political power. And they frequently caricature Neustadt's argument in order to more effectively contrast it with their own methodological and substantive claims. In so doing, however, they diminish the degree to which Neustadt's bargaining framework is consistently supported by subsequent research. In fact, not only do Neustadt's insights fuel many of the subfield's most significant research programs to date—they show every indication of continuing to do so for some time to come.

2. Assessing the Bargaining Paradigm

Since its initial publication in 1960, *Presidential Power* has had a profound and enduring impact on presidency research. Now in its fifth edition, the book has sold over 1 million copies and continues to be assigned in presidency courses at both the undergraduate and graduate levels. It is likely the most heavily scrutinized book on the presidency yet published. Certainly no serious presidency scholar can ignore its argument. As Jones puts it, "It defies standard political science classification, yet compels political scientists' notice. No one had written a book like it then. No one has since" (Jones 2003, 8).

What explains the books' popularity and continuing relevance, 40 years after Neustadt first presented its core argument? In part, it reflects Neustadt's deft writing touch, his finely honed examples, and the air of authenticity he brings to his analysis. He writes for an audience broader than presidency scholars, often based on his personal experiences, and using language that is accessible to non–social scientists. But style alone cannot explain its lasting success. A more fundamental reason is that Neustadt's empirical claims ring true, particularly to political practitioners—but also to scholars who have put them to the test. Although social scientists often lament Neustadt's failure to couch his argument in terms of testable hypotheses (Ragsdale 2000, 41–43), this criticism overlooks the fact that much of what he writes has in fact been subjected to conceptual and empirical assessment. The findings are generally consistent with Neustadt's original bargaining model of presidential leadership, even as they have broadened and refined it in important respects.[11]

It would be a mistake, however, to assess *PP* as if it were written in the style of modern social science (although this has not stopped critics from doing so!). As one of *PP*'s first reviewers pointed out, Neustadt's argument was "not completely systematic, and not very scientific" (Price 1960, 736). The book's historical examples—Truman seizing the steel mills and firing MacArthur, Eisenhower integrating a Little Rock high school and his 1957 budget proposal—at best illustrate the themes Neustadt advanced; they were not meant to, nor could they, constitute "proof."[12] But Neustadt wrote with a broader audience than social scientists in mind; as he noted in the preface to the 1990 edition, "I have always tried to turn participant observership to the account of scholarship that might assist participants. I leave to others, or at least to another time, all wider tasks" (1990, xxvii).

If Neustadt did not present his argument in the form of testable hypotheses, it is nonetheless written with a clarity that makes many of its basic postulates amenable to empirical testing. And, as the book attained classic status, scholars took on this task with increasingly sophisticated tools and approaches. Before examining this literature, however, several caveats are in order.

To begin, for the most part only empirical and conceptual critiques of *PP* are addressed here. Although Neustadt is sometimes criticized for advising presidents how to gain power, but without providing guidelines for its exercise (in this regard, Neustadt himself tells a sobering story about Nixon's White House aides [1990, xvi])—I eschew any review of normative critiques. The focus is on the logic of Neustadt's claims, and their empirical validity, not their normative content.

A second caveat: presidency research as a subdiscipline has always been characterized by a heavy reliance on qualitative case studies. Not surprisingly, efforts to test *PP* often use this methodology (Greenstein 1982; Kellerman 1984). However, it is difficult to assess this literature because the case-study methodology often does not meet modern social science criteria; although useful for descriptive purposes and hypothesis generation, the cases are rarely based on common analytic frameworks, and it is difficult to ascertain the reliability of conclusions derived from what might be idiosyncratic events (Bond and Fleisher 1990, 36–38; G. King 1993). As a result, for the most part the findings of specific case studies are not addressed. Finally, there is no pretense that my literature survey is exhaustive. Rather, the review is limited to the major research programs that are specifically linked to Neustadt's argument, and on results from those programs that have undergone peer review, broadly defined.

Keeping these caveats in mind, how well has *PP* withstood empirical and conceptual scrutiny? First-generation efforts to systematically test Neustadt's bargaining model frequently centered on studies of legislative outcomes in Congress (Bond and Fleisher 1990; Edwards 1980, 1989; Mouw and MacKuen 1992a; Peterson 1990), and utilized multivariable statistical techniques associated with the behavioral revolution that emerged in the 1960s and '70s. Typically this literature measured a president's power in terms of his influence on various legislative processes. How thoroughly, if at all, were the president's legis-lative priorities enacted? How frequently did members of Congress (MCs) support the president in different types of roll-call votes? Be-cause scholars found it difficult to find direct measures of presiden-tial influence or "skill," however, they often tried to estimate it indirectly, after first establishing a baseline model that explained these outcomes on other factors, including party strength in Con-gress, MCs' ideology, the president's electoral support and/or popular approval, and various control variables related to time in office and political context. With the baseline established, one could then pre-sumably see whether individual presidents did better or worse than the model predicted. Despite differences in modeling assumptions and measurements, however, these studies came to remarkably simi-lar conclusions: individual presidents did not seem to matter very much in explaining legislators' behavior (but see Lockerbie and Bor-relli 1989, 97–106). Bond, Fleisher, and Krutz summarize the find-ings: "Recent quantitative studies . . . provide little support for the skills hypothesis" (1996, 127; see also Edwards 1989, 212.)

To be sure, one can raise serious objections to efforts to define presidential power vis-à-vis Congress solely in terms of "wins" or "losses," whether these are determined by roll-call votes, individual legislator's support, or the quantity or quality of legislation passed. Nonetheless, several scholars interpret the null findings of much of this research as evidence that Neustadt's argument is wrong (Bond and Fleisher 1990, 221–223). However, the aggregate results are in fact consistent with Neustadt's assessment that presidents are not very powerful: ". . . Weakness is still what I see: weakness in the sense of a great gap between what is expected of a man (or someday woman) and assured capacity to carry through" (1990, ix). The confu-sion stems in part from scholars' difficulty in defining and operation-alizing presidential influence (Cameron 2000a; Dietz 2002, 105–106; Edwards 2000, 12; Shull and Shaw 1999). The authors of several policymaking studies seem to misinterpret *PP* as proposing a "president-centered" model of power in which presidents are the pri-mary determinant of political outcomes. In fact, Neustadt's desire to understand what presidents must do to influence policymaking should not be misconstrued to mean that he believes presidents are the dominant influence on that process. He writes from the presi-dent's perspective, but without adopting a president-centered view of power.

Neustadt, then, recognizes that a president exercises influence "at the margins" (Edwards 1989). "The essence of a President's persua-sive task . . . is to induce [Washingtonians] to believe that what he wants . . . is what their own appraisal of their own responsibilities re-quires them to do in their interest, not his" (1990, 40). But how, in practice, do presidents exercise persuasion? His answer: "[A] president's own prospects for effective influence are regulated (insofar as he controls them) by his choices of objectives, and of timing, and of instruments . . ." (1990, 90). As applied to the legislative process, this suggests that presidential influence is predominantly exerted "upstream" (Covington, Wrighton, and Kinney 1995, 1023), through a president's choices regarding what initiatives to present to Congress, and when. Although there is extensive evidence documenting the president's ability to get his initiatives considered by Congress (Bond and Fleisher 1990, 230; Edwards 1989, 146; Edwards and Barrett 2000, 109–133; Light 1999; Peterson 1990, 218–231; Rudalevige 2002a), there are surprisingly few studies measuring whether this agenda-setting prowess increases legislative success. In one of the few tests of this proposition, Covington, Wrighton, and Kinney demonstrate that Congress is more likely to pass the president's legislative initiatives compared to other proposals. This is because, they theorize, the president can shape a bill's content in ways designed to increase the likelihood of passage. And by selectively backing bills that have already survived the legislative process to arrive at a floor vote, presidents enhance their legislative "success" rate (Covington, Wrighton, and Kinney 1995, 1001–1024.)[13] Edwards and Barrett also find a higher success rate for the president's initiatives in Congress. But because this success is limited to periods of unified government, they suggest that the president's advantage reflects his status as party leader, rather than any additional bargaining skill. In their words, "[T]he president demonstrates no unusual persuasiveness with Congress" (Edwards and Barrett 2000, 133).

A president's success in Congress, then, appears partly predicated on his ability to obtain a hearing on his priority items. Outside of agenda setting, however, is there evidence that a president can influence legislative outcomes? Case studies provide some support in this regard (Kellerman 1984), but they are subject to the methodological caveats cited above. Spatial models of legislative voting that focus on vote switching by median, veto, and filibuster "pivots" within Congress (Krehbiel 1998, 147–164; Brady and Volden 1998, 125–136) provide more systematic empirical support that presidents possess limited persuasive powers, but again that influence must be inferred.[14]

More convincing proof that presidents matter required scholars to develop better measures of presidential bargaining, both conceptually and empirically. Second-generation models took on this task, often by building on Neustadt's insight that presidents can increase their bargaining leverage by utilizing informational advantages to exploit legislators' uncertainty regarding the worth of their vote to the president (1990, 55).[15]

In a series of articles, Terry Sullivan provides an early effort to more formally model and test Neustadt's information-based hypothesis (Sullivan 1988, 1990, 1991). Using internal administration headcounts gleaned from presidential archives, Sullivan gauges presidential influence in terms of the number of MCs who switched positions during legislative debate, from initially opposing the president to supporting him in the final roll call. Sullivan shows that in a bargaining game with incomplete information regarding presidential and MCs' preferences, there are a number of different possible bargaining outcomes for a given distribution of legislative and presidential policy preferences. These outcomes depend in part on legislators' success in bartering their potential support of the president's policy for additional concessions from the president. In threatening to withhold support, however, MCs run the risk that the president will call their bluff and turn elsewhere for the necessary votes. By capitalizing on MCs' uncertainty regarding whether their support is necessary to form a winning coalition, Sullivan theorizes that presidents can reduce MCs' penchant for strategic bluffing and increase the likelihood of a legislative outcome closer to the president's preference. "Hence, the skill to bargain successfully becomes a foundation for presidential power even within the context of electorally determined opportunities," Sullivan concludes (Sullivan 1991, 1188).

Although critics (Bond, Fleisher, and Krutz 1996, 128–129; see also Edwards 1991) point out that Sullivan infers presidential influence, rather than directly measuring it, his research is among the first to model at the individual level how presidents use informational advantages based on uncertainty to bargain with Congress, and to provide empirical evidence that is consistent with the bargaining model. Further progress in delineating how presidents bargain, and with what effectiveness, however, required scholars to begin to differentiate bargaining strategies according to the institutional setting in which they took place. For example, do bargaining strategies vary depending on whether the president moves first, as when submitting a nominee to the Senate, as opposed to responding to Congress by, for example, vetoing an enrolled bill (Cameron 2000a, 65–68)?

To illustrate, consider Charles Cameron's perceptive study of presidential vetoes (Cameron 2000b). Cameron models the veto bargaining process between president and Congress as a sequential game with imperfect information. Under these circumstances, he demonstrates that it may benefit a president to threaten to veto a bill—even if he prefers that bill to the status quo—in the hope that Congress will pass a revised bill closer to the president's preference. The effectiveness of the president's veto strategy, however, depends on his professional reputation, which influences legislators' judgment regarding the president's "take it or leave it point"—"the point beyond which he will not go because he would rather veto and retain the status quo" (Cameron 2000b, 110). By using veto threats to manipulate legislators' uncertainty over exactly where this point lies, presidents can achieve a more favorable legislative outcome. A president's professional reputation, Cameron concludes, is an important part of a president's veto-related bargaining effectiveness, much as Neustadt surmised.

First-generation efforts to assess presidential power in Congress using aggregate data, then, are consistent with Neustadt's thesis that presidents only marginally influence the legislative process. But by unpacking the black box of presidential bargaining, second-generation models reveal a more finely grained rendering of the details of bargaining. In particular, these studies provide initial conceptual support for Neustadt's claims regarding the importance of a president's professional reputation and the strategic use of uncertainty. But even as they confirm Neustadt's basic insights, they also suggest the importance of explicating the logic underlying his bargaining model in different institutional settings, rather than seeking generalizations that hold across all forms of presidential bargaining.[16] This is consistent with Neustadt's observation that bargaining "is a game played catch-as-catch-can, case by case" (1990, 32).

Presidents and Public Prestige

Even as scholars found evidence that a president's political reputation mattered in bargaining, others examined Neustadt's claims regarding the role of public prestige. Two related issues drove research in this area: what explains presidential approval levels, and how useful are those levels to a president's overall influence? Although the earliest approval studies coincide with the apex of the behavioral revolution in the 1970s (Kernell 1978; Mueller 1970), their number and methodological sophistication increased, not coincidentally, in the aftermath of the Reagan presidency. Recall that several books during the 1980s argued that Reagan's presidency heralded a fundamental shift in the basis of presidential power away from presidential bargaining within a system of "institutionalized" pluralism composed of relatively durable coalitions of political elites, and toward a strategy of "going public" within a system of "individualized pluralism" constructed from more ephemeral and ideological-based coalitions of political activists (Kernell 1997; Lowi 1985). In this new political context, presidents who adopt strategies designed to enlarge their public support can then use this resource as leverage against Washingtonians, much as Reagan appeared to have done to convince Congress to pass his first-year package of tax and spending reductions. As Samuel Kernell argued, "The sensitivity of self-reliant politicians to public opinion is their vulnerability and the key to his influence" (1997, 28).

Although the evidence that presidents were increasingly "going public" is clear (but see Hinckley 1990), its effect on presidential power is less so. Kernell's original thesis regarding the efficacy of going public rests in part on case studies of Reagan's first year legislative successes, and the President's subsequent failure to pass his legislative priorities when his popular approval declined. But others who look at the empirical record argue that Reagan's legislative effectiveness in this period owe much more to his use of the traditional bargaining tactics cited by Neustadt (Bodnick 1990; Pfiffner 1988, 104–108).

More systematic efforts to test the utility of going public produce mixed empirical results. Again, much of the research employs quantitative analysis and focuses on legislative outcomes as a measure of presidential influence. Some studies claim a positive correlation between increases in aggregate levels of presidential approval and presidential influence in Congress (Brace and Hinckley 1992; Rivers and Rose 1985). But others find a more variable effect, with the impact of presidential approval depending on the legislators' partisan affiliation (Edwards 1989; Bond and Fleisher 1990), and some see no relationship at all (Mouw and MacKuen 1992b; see also Collier and Sullivan 1995).

It is not clear, however, whether studies utilizing aggregate levels of presidential popularity are appropriate tests of Neustadt's more nuanced claim regarding the power of a president's public prestige. Neustadt warns that, "[O]ne rarely finds a one-to-one relationship between appraisals of his general popularity and responses from some public in particular" (1990, 77). Instead, he argues that the relationship between a president's public prestige and bargaining effectiveness varies based on several factors, including the parties involved, the issue saliency and complexity, the affected publics' level of interest and knowledge, and prior presidential statements (Neustadt 1990, 78–85). The latest scholarly studies support Neustadt's more textured assessment; they find that rather than a direct correspondence between presidential popularity and legislative outcomes, a president's prestige influences congressional behavior in a more variable, less direct fashion. Simple generalizations regarding prestige and power, then, are difficult to make.

Thus, looking at the first year of the Carter and Reagan presidencies, Fett uncovers evidence that presidents who publicly identify their legislative priorities increase the likelihood of support from their "core partisan" supporters in Congress (1994, 507–511). In their analyses of congressional policymaking during the Eisenhower and Reagan eras, Mouw and MacKuen show that, when presidents "go public," they force legislative agenda-setters to make strategic concessions in the content of legislative proposals in order to increase the likelihood of legislative passage (1992a, 87–105). Canes-Wrone examines presidents' budget requests for 43 agencies across four decades, and finds that presidents' televised appeals increases the likelihood that Congress funds their requests. However, this strategy works only for agencies with programs for which the president's position was already popular with the public, and for which Congress would otherwise not likely have supported the presidents' budget request (2001, 313–329). Similarly, Canes-Wrone and de Marchi examine House roll-call votes during the first Bush and Clinton presidencies and find that higher levels of presidential approval do increase the probability of legislative success, but only for "complex" legislation—that is, legislation about which citizens have little "technical" knowledge and no fixed opinions, but which is highly salient to voters (2002, 491–509; see also Canes-Wrone and Shotts 2004, 690–706). More generally, Canes-Wrone argues that it is the popularity of the issue, rather than the president's approval level, that largely determines the effectiveness of "going public" (2004, 477–492).

If higher approval ratings can augment a president's persuasive power in select cases, Neustadt remains skeptical that presidents can substitute "going public" for bargaining as a general means of influence. "Public appeals," he argues instead, "are part of bargaining, albeit a changing part since prestige bulks far larger than before in reputation" (1990, xv). A key reason why presidents cannot expect to rely on prestige to augment their power is that approval levels are largely governed by factors outside their control. "[L]arge and relatively lasting changes [in Gallup Polls measuring popular approval] come at the same time as great events with widespread consequences" (Neustadt 1990, 81).

Again, empirical studies confirm Neustadt's assertion; they find that the primary determinants of a president's popular approval are significant events and macrolevel factors such as the state of the economy and whether the nation is at war, as directly experienced by voters and as reported by the media (Brace and Hinckley 1992; Brody 1991; Hibbs 1987; Kernell 1978; Mueller 1970; Page and Shapiro 1992). These factors are mediated, however, through individuals' partisan attachments and their degree of attentiveness to public events (Ostrom and Simon 1988; see also Ostrom and Simon 1985). Thus, in their examination of the determinants of public opinion change during Carter's last year as president—a study based on panel data—Ostrom and Simon conclude: "[O]ur empirical evaluation provides reasonable support for a model of citizen evaluations of presidential performance that is . . . consistent with Neustadt's original characterization of the president's public" (1988, 1115).

If events and conditions, as mediated by the public's preexisting dispositions, largely determine a president's public prestige, Neustadt suggests nonetheless that a president can influence this potential bargaining resource at the margins, by interpreting events that are salient to the public in ways that cast a favorable light on the president. "If he wants to guard his popular approval he must give real-life experience a meaning that will foster tolerance for him. . . . He has to ride events to gain attention. Most members of the public grow attentive only as they grow concerned with what may happen in their lives. When they become attentive they will learn from what he does" (Neustadt 1990, 89).

Jeffrey Cohen has undertaken perhaps the most comprehensive study of presidents' efforts to shape opinion formation. He finds that presidents can use their State of the Union address to make certain issues more salient to the public (Cohen 1997, 56–58; see also Iyengar and Kinder 1987). Nonetheless, their impact on public opinion is relatively short-lived and must compete with objective events. Nor will the public necessarily support the president's issue stance. In fact, as George Edwards argues in his book-length overview of the literature on presidents and public opinion formation, "presidents are rarely able to move the public to support their policies." This is because they cannot control the terms of public debate, their message usually competes with alternative messages pushed by other political actors, and the public only rarely listens in any case (Edwards 2003, 79). Edwards concludes that rather than "going public," presidents are likely better served by "staying private"—conducting "quiet negotiations" behind the scenes with interested parties (Edwards 2003, 251–254; see also Covington, 1987). This strategy bears obvious similarities to Neustadt's prescription that presidential power depends on bargaining with those who share the president's power.

3. Current Critiques

Based on the account to this point, it may seem that presidential studies have come full circle, with recent research largely substantiating Neustadt's original insights. But not all scholars accept the accuracy of Neustadt's bargaining model of presidential leadership. Those working in two relatively recent research programs, using distinctly different methods, and focusing on different areas of presidential leadership, find fault with *PP*'s premises. Neither research program has as yet undergone the extensive evaluation characterizing studies of presidential-congressional relations, so assessments regarding their validity must remain somewhat more tenuous. Nonetheless, I argue that rather than undercutting the bargaining paradigm, both appear to support it in important respects.

Presidents, Bargaining, and Political Time

In an important work, Stephen Skowronek suggests that Neustadt's bargaining model is of limited historical applicability. This is partly because Neustadt restricts his study to "mid-century," thus creating an artificial distinction between modern and premodern presidents (Skowronek 1993, 5). In fact, Skowronek argues, the leadership dilemmas confronted by presidents that Neustadt classifies as modern are often quite similar to those for presidents serving in the premodern era. At the same time, Neustadt mistakenly assumes that the modern presidents face similar operational problems. In truth, Skowronek claims, they often preside during quite different periods of "political" (as opposed to "secular") time.

By political time, Skowronek means "the historical medium through which authority structures have recurred" (1993, 30). Specifically, two related dimensions largely determine the scope of a president's political authority: the existing political regime's resiliency, and whether the president is affiliated with that regime. From this Skowronek classifies most presidents as falling into one of four leadership authority structures—reconstructing, articulating, preempting or repudiating the existing regime—each of which presents its own leadership opportunities and constraints (1993, 36–45). This classification scheme enables Skowronek to highlight leadership similarities and differences even—especially—among presidents who served years or decades apart in secular time. In contrast, by focusing on the "modern" presidents, Neustadt both misses important commonalties across the premodern/modern presidential divide and too readily blurs important distinctions among the modern presidents.

Indeed, Skowronek argues that Neustadt's "operational" focus ignores an essential component of presidential leadership. Neustadt judges a president's effectiveness by his ability to make the political system work to his advantage. But Skowronek argues that "the assumption that a system is given and that presidents make it work more or less effectively" ignores an important leadership criterion. "[P]residents disrupt systems, reshape political landscapes, and pass to successors leadership challenges that are different from the ones just faced" (Skowronek 1993, 6). To Skowronek, then, a president's effectiveness cannot be judged only by how well he operates within a given political context—presidents must also be assessed by how well they reshape that context to their own advantage. Effective presidents, Skowronek argues, are those who understand the opportunities and constraints associated with their place in political time—the "warrants" of authority—and act accordingly.[17]

Moreover, Skowronek claims, Neustadt's bargaining model is of limited applicability; it is most relevant to presidents of the pluralist era (1900–1972), a period during which effective leadership demanded "bargaining with leaders of all institutions and organized interests as the steward of national policymaking" (1993, 53). By the mid-1970s, however, bargaining no longer dominates presidential politics. Instead, presidents enter the plebiscitary era, " a period distinguished by new tools of mass communications, by international interdependence, and by intensified international competition," as well as a new presidential selection process (Skowronek 1993, 54).

How accurate are Skowronek's criticisms? He is certainly correct that Neustadt situated his original analysis at midcentury, a time he characterized as "emergencies in policies with politics as usual" (Neustadt 1990, 5). But Neustadt's decision was driven less by a belief in the distinction between premodern and modern presidents than by evidentiary considerations. Because his empirical examples were drawn from a narrow band of presidents, he thought it prudent not to generalize beyond his data (Neustadt 1990, xi; see also Jones 2003, 19).[18]

Successive editions of *PP* clearly track contextual developments that potentially alter the foundation of presidential power (Neustadt 1990, 4).[19] Thus, in the 1980 edition of *PP* Neustadt recognizes that technological developments had likely permanently altered the relationship between prestige and reputation: "At the same time that prestige seems likelier than formerly to reflect reputation, it may come to matter more in reputation. A president's capacity to draw and stir a television audience seems every bit as interesting to current Washingtonians as his ability to wield his formal powers" (1990, 264).

But if Neustadt's presidents preside in different political contexts (1990, xiii), he believes their "power problem" remains much the same. In fact, Neustadt found the nature of presidential leadership remarkably stable in the 30 years between the first and last editions of *PP*: "I did not think it likely that three decades later all the changes in the setting would have taken such a shape as to leave the problem roughly what it was then, if not more so" (1990, xiv).

In part, the apparent disagreement between Skowronek and Neustadt regarding the substance of presidential leadership may be largely due to their adopting different levels of analysis (Lieberman 2000, 276). Skowronek, as a scholar surveying the sweep of presidential history, looks more broadly at presidents' efforts to place themselves in political time, and judges their effectiveness as presidents accordingly. Neustadt, standing behind the president looking over his shoulder, tries to understand how he might "make politics" on a strategic level, whether reconstructing, articulating, preempting, or repudiating the existing regime.

By adjusting for these differences in perspective and intent, one finds more overlap between the two leadership models than Skowronek acknowledges. Indeed, the transformational possibilities that Skowronek suggests inheres in the presidency seem to depend on the skillful harnessing of the power sources specified by Neustadt in *PP* (Riley 2000, 435–436). Skowronek claims that effective presidents must understand where they are in political time in order to exploit the available warrants of authority. But, as Hargrove recognizes, "Skowronek does not set up a repertoire of skills required for each kind of presidency, but broadens, without rejecting, the role of bargaining . . ." (2001, 251). From a president's perspective, then, Skowronek's wider focus on a president's place in history offers precious little in the way of concrete advice regarding how to turn an understanding of time and place into effective influence. For advice on these lines, presidents must turn to Neustadt. In Robert Lieberman's words, "[A] president must recognize his regime position . . . but he must also recognize that his leadership depends on his ability to manage precisely the political forces that Neustadt describes . . ." (2000, 301).

Skowronek's failure to address these operational issues is especially problematic in light of his view that political time is waning; he sees "a secular convergence toward opposition leadership in a resilient regime" (1993, 444). An increase in presidential responsibilities against the backdrop of a gradual institutional thickening appears increasingly to limit presidents' opportunities to reshape the political landscape. Skowronek's modern presidents thus seem stuck in a political landscape facing operating problems remarkably similar to those described by Neustadt in *PP*. By conceding the point that political time is becoming less important to understanding the presidency, Skowronek raises a potentially troubling question for his analysis: which is more important for presidential leadership—secular time, or political time? Are the problems and opportunities Jimmy Carter faced, for example, more like those his fellow "disjunctive" president John Quincy Adams (or Buchanan or Hoover) confronted? Or was his situation more similar to that of his "modern" counterparts, like Harry Truman? The question can only be answered empirically, but Neustadt would likely see a greater affinity among the leadership opportunities and constraints affecting the "moderns" Carter and Truman than among those affecting Carter and his fellow disjunctive presidents. In the end, then, Skowronek's work seems to reaffirm Neustadt's basic insights regarding the prerequisites for effective leadership in a system of diminished political time, where an increasing number of separated institutions now share—and compete for—power.

The Administrative Presidency: A Politics of Unilateral Action?

A second recent challenge to the bargaining paradigm is by scholars who claim that it underestimates the importance of the president's formal powers. Although this has been a longstanding critique of *PP*, it has received renewed attention in recent years from scholars who believe that presidents can wield power unilaterally, by issuing executive orders, proclamations, memoranda, and national security directives (Cooper 2002; Howell 2003; Mayer 2001; Moe and Howell

1999; Moe and Wilson 1994). By stacking the executive branch with loyalists who share their ideological and policy preferences, and by centralizing decisionmaking within a larger, more functionally specialized White House Office (Moe 1985), presidents can use these administrative directives to exercise power "without persuasion" (Howell 2003).

As with strategies of going public, scholars have been better at documenting the increase in presidents' use of these administrative strategies than in demonstrating their efficacy. Indeed, there are good reasons to doubt that these strategies provided unalloyed benefits. By politicizing the appointment process, presidents often gain loyalty at the expense of competence, and may stimulate greater congressional scrutiny and a more protracted confirmation process (Aberbach and Rockman 1988; Mackenzie 2001; Pfiffner 1987). More powerful White House staffs, history shows, sometimes undercut presidential authority as much as extend it (Dickinson 1997, 19–41; Hart 1995, 195–233). Detailed case studies of presidents' efforts to utilize administrative strategies indicate that they do not always achieve desired outcomes, and often embroil the president in controversy (Cooper 2002; Durant 1992; Waterman 1989). And White House centralization of the policymaking process has been shown to actually decrease presidential legislative success in Congress (Rudalevige 2002a, 134–151).

This evidence notwithstanding, several scholars assert that presidents can use unilateral means of power. Their claim rests in large part on presidents' efforts to achieve policy objectives by issuing executive orders (EOs) (Howell 2003; Mayer 2001). In a direct critique of the bargaining model, Howell argues that EOs provide a useful tool for moving policy otherwise stuck in legislative "gridlock" closer to a president's preference point.[20] A president's ability to act unilaterally in this fashion, he shows, is positively correlated with increasing ideological fragmentation within Congress. This is because an ideologically divided Congress cannot muster the supermajorities necessary to move policy out of the gridlock area. But neither can it prevent a president from using an EO to move policy within the gridlock area closer to his preference point.

Presidents, Howell asserts, can also act unilaterally to preempt and moderate more extreme policy measures that Congress is poised to pass. More generally, because presidents move first through executive action, and because Congress suffers all the debilitating effects of collective decisionmaking, presidents find the politics of unilateral action very appealing (Howell 2003).

The unilateral politics model has yet to receive extensive scrutiny from presidency scholars (but see Sullivan 2004). Nonetheless, there are grounds for believing that it will not radically alter scholars' belief in the centrality of bargaining to presidential leadership. To begin, advocates of unilateral action are principally concerned with "how policy is made, not how it is carried out" (Howell 2003, 22). But this ignores a fundamental dimension of presidential power, captured in Neustadt's oft-cited reference regarding Truman's warning to Eisenhower—". . . he'll say, 'Do this! Do that! And nothing will happen! Poor Ike. . . ."[21] As a former White House aide, Neustadt was well aware that a presidential directive is not tantamount to the exercise of power, even when that directive takes place in a policy arena, such as national security policy, where presidents presumably hold the most discretionary authority. Indeed, Neustadt saw first-hand how General Douglas MacArthur repeatedly ignored Truman's presidential directives regarding military strategy during the Korean War until Truman was finally forced to remove him, at great political cost. More generally, as Scott Sagan and Jeremi Suri demonstrate in their analysis of Richard Nixon's 1969 decision to put the country on nuclear alert, "presidential orders [are] actively fought against, sometimes manipulated or ignored, and often honored only in part" (2003, 153).

Indeed, the phrase "unilateral action" is somewhat misleading in the context in which scholars touting its effectiveness often employ it. The words imply that when utilizing administrative directives, the president enacts policy singlehandedly, in contrast to the legislative process in which policy is made collectively by working through Congress. However, there is extensive evidence demonstrating that policymaking via administrative action is no less subject to bargaining and compromise than is policymaking through the legislative process (Heclo 1977b, 235; Nathan 1983, 82–85). The difference in administrative and legislative policymaking is not that it signifies a shift between a "unilateral" and a "multilateral" process. Instead, it is a change in where, and with whom, bargaining takes place. As numerous case studies of "unilateral" action reveal, from Roosevelt's decision to intern Japanese Americans during World War II (Robinson 2001) to Ronald Reagan's efforts to curtail federal spending (Stockman 1986, 101–102) to Bill Clinton's failed 1993 effort to issue an executive order ending the ban on gays serving openly in the military, presidents typically bargain with members of their own executive branch during the drafting and implementation of executive orders and other presidential policy directives.

These and other studies show that the transaction costs of unilateral action—haggling over the details of presidential directives, estimating bureaucrats' preferences, attracting interest-group and public support, and ensuring bureaucratic compliance—often rival the costs of acting through Congress. Indeed, Neustadt explicitly warns scholars not to succumb to "the illusion that administrative agencies comprise a single structure, 'the' executive branch, where presidential word is law. . . . Like our governmental structure as a whole, the exec-

utive establishment consists of separated institutions sharing powers," and thus is not impervious to the bargaining that characterizes
politics elsewhere (1990, 33–34). For this reason, unilateral action is
likely less "unilateral" than its advocates suggest. At the very least,
substantiating its theoretical premises will require looking more systematically at the compromises and deal-making presidents must
make when drawing up such orders, and examining whether and to
what degree they are implemented.

At a more fundamental level, unilateral politics advocates tend to
view EOs from a tactical level, as a reliable indicator of presidential
influence. But this misconstrues the essence of Neustadt's argument:
executive commands—firing MacArthur, integrating the Little Rock
high school, seizing the steel mills—he asserts, must be evaluated in
their strategic context. What impact did these orders have on the
president's sources of bargaining influence? "There are two ways to
study 'presidential power,'" Neustadt writes. "Strategically, the question is not how he masters Congress in a peculiar instance, but what
he does to boost his chance for mastery in any instance, looking toward tomorrow from today" (1990, 4). To accurately gauge the effectiveness of unilateral action as an alternative to Neustadt's bargaining
paradigm, then, scholars must assess its strategic implications by discerning the impact of unilateral action on a president's sources of
bargaining influence. Consistent with Neustadt's claim, scholars have
documented numerous instances in which presidents' assertions of
unilateral "command" power produced a political backlash that led to
Congress restricting presidential power in other bargaining spheres
(Sundquist 1981, 203–209; Mayer and McManus 1988, 70–74; Waterman 1989, 188–189).

More generally, theories of unilateral power must be assessed by
reference to conditions that would exist had those powers not been
exercised. If by issuing an executive order or directive presidents
weaken their influence across a range of other issue areas, one would
be hard pressed to label the unilateral action an example of "power."
At the very least, scholars must make some effort to weigh the relative
tradeoffs between using administrative means to achieve an immediate objective and its impact on a president's effective influence in
other areas and at other times. Similarly, presidential directives that
are derived from compromise and consultation with other political
actors can hardly be said to illustrate "unilateral" action. Instead,
they seem more consistent with Neustadt's claim that bargaining
takes place within the executive branch as well as within Congress.

It is not unprecedented for scholars working in a relatively new research area to overstate the implications of their findings, in order to
more effectively contrast it with previous research. Recall that the initial assessments regarding the president's lack of bargaining skills, or
his power to "go public," were also overdrawn. After further concep-

tual clarification and empirical testing, however, scholars' understanding of both fell more closely in line with Neustadt's views as
described in *PP*. This is often how "normal" science proceeds: scholars stake out new and sometimes extreme positions relative to the
status quo, the claims are subject to further debate and analysis, and
initial assumptions are revised and reconciled with the standard
model. In this regard, the unilateral politics framework will serve a
valuable purpose if it forces scholars to more explicitly model how
presidents bargain within their "own" executive branch.

4. Further Research: Bargaining, Power, and the Institutional Presidency

Although perhaps not definitive, the cumulative evidence of four
decades of research is consistent with the bargaining model of presidential leadership as first laid out by Richard Neustadt in *PP*. Nonetheless, I believe that scholars have for the most part ignored a key
portion of Neustadt's fundamental purpose in writing *PP*. The book's
first five chapters are essentially a ground-clearing exercise, designed
to reveal why presidential power depends on bargaining. Neustadt's
subject in these pages is what might be called the demand-side of the
presidential power equation—how presidents can use others' demands for presidential services as leverage to obtain their own objectives without sacrificing their sources of influence. Scholars have
focused on this portion of *PP* in their research primarily because it is
the most conceptually detailed part of Neustadt's argument. But I
claim that these first five chapters are best read as a prelude to
Neustadt's central, supply-side concern addressed in chapters 6–7 of
PP: "What helps [the president] guard his power stakes in his own act
of choice?" Neustadt asks (1990, 90). The answer, he suggests, is information—"A president is helped by what he gets into his mind. *His
first essential need is information*" (1990, 128–129, italics added). It is
this supply-side informational perspective, I argue, that potentially
offers a way to integrate Neustadt with "new" institutionalist approaches (Hall and Taylor 1996; Jepperson 1991; March and Olsen
1984) to studying presidential organizations and decisionmaking.

Consider that bargaining takes place strategically, under conditions of bounded rationality; no participant is entirely sure of his or
her optimal bargaining strategy (Simon 1976; Williamson 1975). The
upshot is that bargaining terms are never fixed; they must be negotiated. To reduce bargaining uncertainty and clarify the likely outcome
of particularly negotiating choices, presidents seek information and
expertise. These resources are conceptually distinct from political
capital, but similar to what new institutionalists label transaction
costs—the resources that parties in a transaction must expend to de-

termine the actual worth of the goods being exchanged, and what must be spent to negotiate and enforce the details of that transaction (North 1990, 27–35; see also Alchian and Woodward 1987, 110; Coase 1937; Epstein and O'Halloran 1999, 34–47; Miller and Moe 1986, 169).

Drawing on Neustadt's insights regarding the importance of mitigating bargaining uncertainty, I argue that it is an increase in transaction costs that helps explain the growth of the institutionalized presidency during the last six decades. Presidency scholars have thoroughly documented the growth of a White House–centered system of advisers, functionally specialized and hierarchically arranged, in this period (Burke 1992; Hart 1995; Hess and Pfiffner 2002; Hult and Walcott 2004; Kernell 1989; Kumar and Sullivan 2003; Patterson 2000; Sander 1989; Walcott and Hult 1995). It is less clear, however, what drives this process. "Functional" explanations based on an increase in the size and complexity of the president's workload do not seem to be the primary cause (Dickinson and Lebo 2007).

Recall that transaction cost theory says that when the cost of determining product quality and negotiating the details of an exchange within the marketplace increase, partners to an exchange may find it more efficient to substitute hierarchical authority relations for market-based transactions. That is, the transaction is reconstituted within the organizational parameters of a business firm.[22] This, I suggest, is precisely what happened with the presidential staff during the post-FDR period. In a series of articles (Dickinson 1996, 2000, 2003), I show that a breakdown in the traditional "protocoalitions" (Kernell 1997, 16–17) of political elites, particularly during the 1960s and early 1970s, raised the transaction costs of bargaining; it became harder for presidents to negotiate and enforce the details of their transactions with Congress, the bureaucracy, party leaders, and other influential political actors. In response, successive presidents began institutionalizing their own in-house sources of bargaining expertise within the White House Office.

Hiring staff experts, however, is no guarantee presidents will gain access to the information they need. As Neustadt warns: "On the one hand [a president] can never assume that anyone or any system will supply the bits and pieces he needs most; on the other hand, he must assume that much of what he needs will not be volunteered by his official advisers" (1990, 129). The reasons why are clearly articulated in a second strand of new institutionalist thought, formally labeled principal-agent theory. The upshot of this literature is that, due to the problems of adverse selection, moral hazard, hidden information, and hidden action, presidents cannot expect advisers to provide the information they need to protect their sources of influence, when they need it (Miller 1992; Moe 1984; Pratt and Zeckhauser 1985).[23] Instead, they must create structural incentives within their advisory organizations so that presidential aides will be more likely to provide the requisite information. In short, how advisers are organized will prove crucial in determining what information reaches presidents.

Presidency scholars have long surmised that presidential staff structures can influence decisionmaking outcomes. However, although they have developed extensive typologies of White House staff structures (George 1980; Hess and Pfiffner 2002; Johnson 1974; Porter 1980), they have not demonstrated whether or how these structures might influence aides' behavior (but see Haney 1997). However, research by new institutionalist scholars, regarding the relationship between organizational structure, hierarchy, and information offer the potential to put this empirically rich presidential staffing literature on a more sound theoretical footing (Dickinson 1996, 1997, 2005; Rudalevige 2002b).

To illustrate how new institutionalist theories buttress Neustadt's insights regarding the link between presidential staff and power, consider his claim that Franklin D. Roosevelt's use of competitive staffing practices protected his sources of bargaining power (Neustadt 1963). Building on new institutionalist scholarship, I argue that FDR utilized staff structures that collectively created incentives for his advisers to transmit information to him that they might otherwise have preferred to use strategically to advance their own interests (1997; 2005, 274–278). This includes the use of redundant staff structures in which two or more groups of aides reported separately to FDR on the same advising task. Studies by Landau (1969) and Bendor (1985) demonstrate how parallel staff structures of the type FDR used can reduce the likelihood of decisionmaking errors. At the same time— and in contrast to the standard White House organizational model in which specialists control the flow of advice and information in their substantive areas to the president—FDR did not countenance the development of specialized policy staff structures. Instead, he relied on White House generalists whose jurisdictions mixed policy and political specialties. This is consistent with Hammond's claim (1986; 1994, 152) that chief executives may be advantaged by organizing their staffs to cut across the major elements by which they classify their environment because this practice exposes disagreements among those charged with advising in these critical areas. Moreover, there is evidence that the effectiveness of FDR's administrative practices was not simply a function of his personality attributes; other presidents with different temperaments, experiences, and operating styles have also found them useful. Thus, in a study of crisis decisionmaking in five presidencies, I find that presidents who employ redundant staffing structures composed of aides with different areas of expertise performed better on a variety of measures of decisionmaking effectiveness (Dickinson 2005, 259–288).

Space constraints prevent a more detailed explication of the relationship between Neustadt's supply-side concern with information and theories of advising, organizational structure, and presidential decisionmaking. The essential point, however, is that Neustadt's insights can be used to construct an *institution*-based model of presidential power. Differences in nomenclature and approach, then, should not obscure the common conceptual foundation underlying Neustadt's *PP* and new institutionalism. Both are constructed on assumptions about asymmetries in information and expertise among bargaining participants (see also Hammond and Miller 1985; Miller 1992). And each suggests that presidential bargaining effectiveness is partly predicated on a president's institutional choices, particularly the informational benefits and management costs associated with specific staff structures. By marrying the insights of new institutionalist theories of structure and hierarchy, then, with the rich empirical literature on presidential staffing, presidency scholars should be able to subject Neustadt's supply-side insights regarding information and bargaining to more rigorous conceptualization and testing, much as they have done with his notions of professional reputation and public prestige.

5. Some Final Thoughts

"Presidents and their staffs seek advice; they need it; they deserve the best the rest of us can offer," Neustadt reminds us (1990, 293). So do scholars, I might add. Methodological and conceptual disputes ought not prevent us from heeding his counsel. Indeed, despite differences in assumptions, nomenclature, and professional training, presidency scholars agree on much more than they have heretofore acknowledged. In this chapter I have tried to identify a core set of findings inspired by Neustadt's basic insights regarding the importance of bargaining to presidential leadership. This is not to claim that *PP* is the last word on the topic. Instead, Neustadt's work is best understood as presenting a series of hypotheses to be tested, elaborated, and, if necessary, refined. To date, efforts along these lines indicate that the bargaining paradigm presents the most comprehensive understanding of presidential leadership. At the same time, new conceptual insights and better empirical measures have broadened and deepened Neustadt's model in important respects. By continuing the process of building on and refining Neustadt's bargaining framework, presidency scholars are most likely, in my view, to achieve generalizable and cumulative findings regarding presidential power, and to elevate presidency research to the level of other subfields in American politics.

This does not mean limiting ourselves to his mode of analysis. Neustadt's particular methodology reflects a different time, and a different purpose. Still, there remains an important need for detailed, well-written historical studies of presidents exercising power, all the more so because, as Neustadt noted, "[S]o many of us fail to discipline ourselves to write in accessible language—a harder task . . . than writing in professional code, to say nothing of mathematics" (Neustadt 2000, 462). Clearly written and thoroughly researched presidential history provides useful data for scholars' broader theories, and sparks additional conceptual insights.

Neustadt's larger lesson, however, is that methodological parochialism ought not stop presidency researchers of different stripes from talking to one another. In truth, this is easier said than done; trends in professional training and recruitment make it both much more likely that presidency scholars will specialize within a narrow area of expertise, and that they will find it more difficult to appreciate the work of those who toil in other research areas. Nonetheless, breaking down these research barriers is well worth the effort. As evidence, one need only see how scholars of different research traditions, from case study analysts to behavioralists to "old" and new institutionalists, repeatedly utilize Neustadt's insights in their own work.

This intellectual homage partly reflects the clarity with which he stated his argument as well as the originality of his insights. But at a more fundamental level, Neustadt's bargaining model has served as the intellectual foil for successive generations of presidency scholars because it is derived from the constitutional framework established by the Framers more than two centuries ago. Presidents operate in a system of separated institutions sharing power, and therefore they must bargain to exercise influence. Regardless of changing intellectual fashions, then, presidency scholars continue to recognize the significance of Neustadt's bargaining paradigm to their own research agenda. Barring fundamental change to the Constitution and the authority structures that are derived from it, the bargaining model will likely remain the key to understanding presidential leadership for the foreseeable future.

Notes

1. Indeed, scholars took issue with Neustadt's argument from the start. Some saw it as too instrumentalist; Neustadt counseled presidents on how to husband their power, but provided few ethical guidelines for its exercise. Others argued that Neustadt underplayed both the president's formal and symbolic authority (Greenstein 1982; Pious 1979; Ragsdale 2000, 41). In some areas, such as foreign affairs, presidents' command authority seemed greater than Neustadt acknowledged. And, as an

elected official with a nationwide constituency, presidents did not always have to bargain to achieve objectives; they could appeal to others' sense of loyalty and duty to the highest office in the land (Sperlich 1969).

2. These efforts have been partly driven by political scientists' embrace of new modes of analysis, including the quantitatively oriented behavioralist revolution of the 1960s, and the various strands of "new institutionalism" that became fashionable during the late 1970s and 1980s. They also reflect scholars' belief that changes in the political system since 1960 render Neustadt's leadership model less accurate.

3. Thus, because Neustadt's examples are used to illustrate his theory, they cannot also serve to test it.

4. Chuck Jones takes Neustadt's insight a step further: in the American political system, Jones points out, separated institutions do not simply share powers. They actively *compete* for them (Jones 1994, 18).

5. As evidence regarding the weakness of formal powers, Neustadt presents three cases of command—Truman seizing the steel mills, Truman firing MacArthur, and Eisenhower integrating public schools in Little Rock, Arkansas. In each, a president is forced to utilize formal powers after persuasion fails. In so doing, however, they suffer significant damage to their sources of bargaining power.

6. In the chapter titled "Men in Office" Neustadt speculates as to why some presidents, like FDR, seem more adept at thinking prospectively than do others, such as Eisenhower. Differences in presidential temperament and prior experience, he suggests, must be part of the explanation: "The Presidency," he famously writes, "is no place for amateurs" (1990, 151). In subsequent editions of *PP*, however, he reacts to the failed presidencies of LBJ and Nixon, both of whom were experienced politicians, by exploring this issue in much greater detail; indeed, much of his later scholarship is devoted to helping public officials think more clearly about their power prospects. Thus, *Thinking in Time*, a book Neustadt coauthored with Ernest May, is essentially devoted in its entirety to this issue, although their intended audience goes beyond presidents to include other public officials (Neustadt and May 1986).

7. As this chapter documents, the evidence suggests that rather than personalizing presidency research, *PP*—particularly its first five chapters—steered the subfield toward more institutionally based analyses rooted in the bargaining model of presidential power.

8. Indeed, Neustadt characterized the notion that one could analyze personal power without reference to the institutional setting as "cuckoo" (Jones 2003, 18).

9. In this regard, Neustadt is less sanguine than others regarding whether the additional staff support helps presidents. Presidential advisers, he notes, are frequently "holier than the Pope;" they zealously serve the president without always fully comprehending his true bargaining interests. The combination of well-intentioned loyalty and the lack of a shared perspective can prove deadly to presidential interests, as

Neustadt illustrates through his discussion of the Reagan administration's Iran-Contra affair (1990, 269–294).

10. Chapter 10, "Reappraising Power," written for the 1980 edition, explores contextual developments in the president's environment since *PP*'s first edition. The 1990 edition, in addition to the Iran-Contra affair, included two case studies of presidential successes: Kennedy's handling of the Cuban Missile Crisis in 1962 and Eisenhower's 1954 decision not to intervene at Dien Bien Phu.

11. Interestingly, given Neustadt's intended audience, President John F. Kennedy was an early critic of *PP*. Kennedy reportedly confided that Neustadt "makes everything a President does seem too premeditated" (Schlesinger 1965, 678–679). There is a double irony here, for this is exactly the charge that is frequently leveled at rational choice scholars, who themselves have been quick to label *PP* as overly focused on the "personal" presidency. In truth, as JFK's critique suggests, Neustadt's implicit assumption that presidents act purposively to maximize power is perfectly compatible with—indeed, anticipates—rational choice approaches to presidential power.

12. See footnote 3 in this regard.

13. Because of data restrictions, they only look at the period 1953–1973.

14. Krehbiel analyzed successive votes by legislators in the context of a presidential veto and found "modest support for the sometimes doubted stylized fact of presidential power as persuasion" (Krehbiel 1998, 153–154). Similarly, Brady and Volden (1998) look at vote switching by MCs in successive congresses on nearly identical legislation and also conclude that presidents do influence the votes of at least some legislators.

15. Dietz (2002) provides a useful overview of recent formal models and quantitative studies of presidential-congressional relations.

16. In this vein, see Chuck Jones's proposal for measuring the importance of professional reputation (Jones 2001).

17. In assessing Skowronek's argument, it is often unclear how much freedom of action presidents possess to rework their institutional surroundings; that is, do presidents make politics, or do the politics make the president?

18. Neustadt recalled that his Columbia colleague David Truman said, "[O]therwise you are going to get killed by people who'll say you're being too presumptuous about generalizations and hypotheses on too narrow a band" (Jones 2003, 19).

19. For example, in the first edition of *PP*, Neustadt argued that prestige and reputation were usually separate sources of influence; one rarely affected the other. Thus, even as Truman's prestige plummeted during the Korean War, he retained a comparatively high professional reputation among Washingtonians. Conversely, although Eisenhower's prestige as a former war hero remained elevated throughout his presidency, his professional reputation grew comparatively weaker until late in his second term. But in the aftermath of the 1973–1974 Water-

gate scandal, Neustadt noted that Nixon's professional reputation seemed more directly tied to his public prestige; it was as if Washingtonians were using the one to gauge the other.

20. By gridlock, Howell means a situation in which the existing policy cannot be changed by any new policy proposal.

21. Mayer (2001, 17) argues that issues of implementation affect legislative directives as well. Neustadt would surely agree—but this is no reason to assume that bureaucrats are more likely to comply with unilateral directives. Indeed, because bureaucrats may find it easier to appeal to Congress against the president when asked to implement a presidential directive, one might expect bureaucratic compliance with administrative orders to be more problematic than with legislative directives.

22. Note that, beyond a general agreement that transaction costs matter, the field is far from unified on even basic concepts, including what constitutes a transaction cost.

23. Briefly, theories of adverse selection suggest why presidents might consistently hire assistants who are patently unqualified for the job. Moral hazard explains why presidents must devise methods to ensure that aides pursue the president's bargaining interests, rather than their own. Hidden action and hidden information are related problems having to do with the difficulties supervisors have in determining how much effort subordinates are putting into the job.

References

Aberbach, Joel, and Bert Rockman. 1988/1991. "Mandates or Mandarins? Control and Discretion in the Modern Administrative State." In James Pfiffner (Ed.), *The Managerial Presidency*. Pacific Grove: Brooks/Cole Publishing Co.

Alchian, Arman, and Susan Woodward. 1987. "Reflections on the Theory of the Firm." *Journal of Institutional and Theoretical Economics* 143:110–136.

Bendor, Jonathan. 1985. *Parallel Systems*. Berkeley, CA: University of California Press.

Bodnick, Mark. 1990. "Going Public Reconsidered: Reagan's 1981 Tax and Budget Cuts, and Revisionist Theories of Presidential Power." *Congress and the Presidency* 17 (Spring):13–28.

Bond, Jon R., and Richard Fleisher. 1990. *The President in the Legislative Arena*. Chicago: The University of Chicago Press.

Bond, Jon R., Richard Fleisher, and Glen Krutz. 1996. "An Overview of the Empirical Findings on Presidential-Congressional Relations." In James A. Thurber (Ed.), *Rivals for Power*. Washington, DC: Congressional Quarterly Press.

Brace, Paul, and Barbara Hinckley. 1992. *Follow the Leader: Opinion Polls and the Modern Presidents*. New York: Basic Books.

Brady, David, and Craig Volden. 1998. *Revolving Gridlock*. Boulder, CO: Westview Press.

Brody, Richard. 1991. *Assessing the President: The Media, Elite Opinion, and Public Support*. Stanford: Stanford University Press.

Burke, John P. 1992. *The Institutional Presidency*. Baltimore, MD: Johns Hopkins University Press.

Cameron, Charles. 2000a. *Veto Bargaining: Presidents and the Politics of Negative Power*. New York: Cambridge University Press.

———. 2000b. "Bargaining and Presidential Power." In Robert Shapiro, Martha Joynt Kumar, and Larry Jacobs (Eds.), *Presidential Power: Forging the Presidency for the 21st Century*, 47–77. New York: Columbia University.

Canes-Wrone, Brandice. 2001. "The President's Legislative Influence from Public Appeals." *American Journal of Political Science* 45, 2 (April):313–329.

———. 2004. "The Public Presidency, Approval Rating and Policy Making." *Presidential Studies Quarterly* 34, 3 (September):477–492.

Canes-Wrone, Brandice, and Scott de Marchi. 2002. "Presidential Approval and Legislative Success." *The Journal of Politics* 64, 2 (May):491–509.

Canes-Wrone, Brandice, and Kenneth W. Shotts. 2004. "The Conditional Nature of Presidential Responsiveness to Public Opinion." *American Journal of Political Science* 48, 4 (October):690–706.

Coase, Ronald. 1937. "The Nature of the Firm." *Economica* 4:386–405.

Cohen, Jeffrey. 1997. *Presidential Responsiveness and Public Policymaking: The Publics and the Policies That Presidents Choose.* Ann Arbor, MI: University of Michigan Press.

Collier, Kenneth, and Terry Sullivan. 1995. "New Evidence Undercutting the Linkage of Approval with Presidential Support and Influence." *The Journal of Politics* 57, 1 (February):197–209.

Cooper, Phillip J. 2002. *By Order of the President: The Use and Abuse of Executive Direct Action.* Lawrence: University Press of Kansas.

Covington, Cary R. 1987. " 'Staying Private': Gaining Congressional Support for Unpublicized Presidential Preferences on Roll Call Votes." *The Journal of Politics* 49, 3 (August):737–755.

Covington, Cary R., Mark Wrighton, and Rhonda Kinney. 1995. "A Presidency-Augmented Model of Presidential Success on House Roll Call Votes." *American Journal of Political Science* (November):1001–1024.

Corwin, Edward S. 1957. *The President: Office and Powers,* 4th ed. New York: New York University Press.

Dickinson, Matthew J. 1996. "Neustadt and New Institutionalists: New Insights on Presidential Power?" Occasional Paper, Center for American Politics Studies. Harvard University.

———. 1997. *Bitter Harvest: FDR, Presidential Power and the Growth of the Presidential Branch.* New York: Cambridge University Press.

———. 2000. "Staffing the White House, 1937–1996: The Institutional Implications of Neustadt's Bargaining Paradigm." In Robert Shapiro, Martha Joynt Kumar, and Larry Jacobs (Eds.), *Presidential Power, Forging the Presidency for the 21st Century,* 209–234. New York: Columbia University.

———. 2003. "Bargaining, Uncertainty, and the Growth of the White House Staff." In Barry C. Burden (Ed.), *Uncertainty in American Politics,* 27–47. New York: Cambridge University Press.

———. 2005. "Neustadt, New Institutionalism, and the Presidential Decision Making: A Theory and Test." *Presidential Studies Quarterly* 35, 2 (June):259–288.

Dickinson, Matthew J., and Matthew Lebo. 2007. "Reexamining the Growth of the Institutional Presidency, 1940–2000." *Journal of Politics* 69:206–219.

Dietz, Nathan. 2002. "Presidential Influence on Congress: New Solutions to Old Problems." In James A. Thurber (Ed.), *Rivals for Power.* Lanham, MD: Rowman & Littlefield.

Durant, Robert. 1992. *The Administrative Presidency Revisited.* Albany: State University of New York Press.

Edwards, George C. III. 1980. *Presidential Influence in Congress.* San Francisco: W.H. Freeman & Co.

———. 1981. "The Quantitative Study of the Presidency." *Presidential Studies Quarterly* 11 (Spring):146–150.

———. 1989. *At the Margins: Presidential Leadership of Congress.* New Haven, CT: Yale University Press.

———. 1991. "Presidential Influence in Congress: If We Ask the Wrong Questions, We Get the Wrong Answers." *American Journal of Political Science* 35 (August).

———. 2000. "Neustadt's Power Approach to the Presidency." In Robert Shapiro, Martha Joynt Kumar, and Larry Jacobs (Eds.), *Presidential Power: Forging the Presidency for the 21st Century.* New York: Columbia University.

———. 2003. *On Deaf Ears: The Limits of the Bully Pulpit.* New Haven, CT: Yale University Press.

Edwards, George C. III, and Andrew Barrett. 2000. "Presidential Agenda Setting in Congress." In Jon R. Bond and Richard Fleisherm (Eds.), *Polarized Politics: Congress and the President in a Partisan Era.* Washington, DC: Congressional Quarterly Press.

Edwards, George C. III, John H. Kessel, and Bert A. Rockman (Eds.) 1993. *Researching the Presidency: Vital Questions, New Approaches.* Pittsburgh: Pittsburgh University Press.

Epstein, David, and Sharyn O'Halloran. 1999. *Delegating Powers.* New York, Cambridge University Press.

Fett, Patrick. 1994. "Presidential Legislative Priorities and Legislators' Voting Decisions: An Exploratory Analysis." *The Journal of Politics* 56, 2 (May):502–512.

George, Alexander. 1980. *Presidential Decisionmaking in Foreign Policy.* Boulder, CO: Westview Press.

Greenstein, Fred. 1982. *The Hidden-Hand Presidency: Eisenhower as Leader.* New York: Basic Books.

Hall, Peter, and Rosemary Taylor. 1996. "Political Science and the Three New Institutionalisms." *Political Studies Quarterly* 44, 5:936–957.

Hammond, Thomas H. 1986. "Agenda Control, Organizational Structure, and Hierarchy in Bureaucratic Politics." *American Journal of Political Science* (May):379–420.

———. 1994. "Structure, Strategy, and the Agenda of the Firm." In Richard P. Rumelt, Dan E. Schendel, and David J. Teece (Eds.), *Fundamental Issues in Strategy: A Research Agenda.* Boston: Harvard Business School Press.

Hammond, Thomas H., and Gary J. Miller. 1985. "A Social Choice Perspective on Expertise and Authority in Bureaucracy." *American Journal of Political Science* 29, 1 (February):1–28.

Haney, Patrick Jude. 1997. *Organizing for Foreign Policy Crises: Presidents, Advisers, and the Management of Decision-Making.* Ann Arbor: University of Michigan Press.

Hargrove, Erwin. 1998. *The President as Leader.* Lawrence: University Press of Kansas.

———. 2001. "Presidential Power and Political Science." *Presidential Studies Quarterly* 31, 2 (June):245–261.

Hart, John. 1995. *The Presidential Branch, From Washington to Clinton,* 2nd ed. Chatham, NJ: Chatham House Publishers.

———. 1998. "Neglected Aspects of the Study of the Presidency." *Annual Review of Political Science* (1):379–399.

Heclo, Hugh. 1977a. *Studying the Presidency.* New York: Ford Foundation.

———. 1977b. *A Government of Strangers: Executive Politics in Washington.* Washington, DC: The Brookings Institution.

Hess, Stephen, and James P. Pfiffner. 2002. *Organizing the Presidency,* 3rd ed. Washington, DC: Brookings Institution.

Hibbs, Douglas A. 1987. *The American Political Economy: Macroeconomics and Electoral Politics.* Cambridge, MA: Harvard University Press.

Hinckley, Barbara. 1990. *The Symbolic Presidency: How Presidents Portray Themselves.* New York: Routledge Press.

Howell, William. 2003. *Power Without Persuasion.* Princeton, NJ: Princeton University Press.

Hult, Karen, and Charles E. Walcott. 2004. *Empowering the White House.* Lawrence: University Press of Kansas.

Iyengar, Shanto, and Donald Kinder. 1987. *News That Matters.* Chicago: University of Chicago Press.

Jacobs, Larry, and Robert Shapiro. 2000. "Conclusion: Presidential Power, Institutions, and Democracy." In Robert Shapiro, Martha Joynt Kumar, and Larry Jacobs (Eds.), *Presidential Power: Forging the Presidency for the 21st Century.* New York: Columbia University.

Jepperson, Ronald. 1991. "Institutions, Institutional Effects, and Institutionalism." In Walter W. Powell and Paul J. Dimaggio (Eds.), *The New Institutionalism in Organizational Analysis.* Chicago: University of Chicago Press.

Johnson, Richard Tanner. 1974. *Managing the White House: An Intimate Study of the Presidency.* New York: Harper & Row.

Jones, Charles O. 1994. *The Presidency in a Separated System.* Washington, DC: The Brookings Institution.

———. 2001. "Professional Reputation and the Neustadt Formulation." *Presidential Studies Quarterly* 31, 2 (June):281–295.

———. 2003. "Richard Neustadt: Public Servant as Scholar." *Annual Review of Political Science* 6:1–22.

Kellerman, Barbara. 1984. *The Political Presidency*. New York: Oxford University Press.

Kernell, Samuel. 1978. "Explaining Presidential Popularity." *American Political Science Review* 72:506–522.

———. 1989. "The Evolution of the White House Staff." In John E. Chubb and Paul E. Peterson (Eds.), *Can the Government Govern?* Washington, DC: The Brookings Institution.

———. 1997. *Going Public: New Strategies of Presidential Leadership*, 3rd ed. Washington, DC: Congressional Quarterly Press.

King, Anthony. 1975. "Executives." In Fred I. Greenstein and Nelson W. Polsby (Eds.), *Handbook of Political Science*, vol. 5. Reading, MA: Addison-Wesley.

King, Gary. 1993. "The Methodology of Presidency Research." In George C. Edwards III, John H. Kessel, and Bert A. Rockman (Eds.), *Researching the Presidency: Vital Questions, New Approaches*. Pittsburgh: Pittsburgh University Press.

Krehbiel, Keith. 1998. *Pivotal Politics: A Theory of U.S. Lawmaking*. Chicago: University of Chicago Press.

Kumar, Martha J., and Terry Sullivan (Eds.). 2003. *The White House World*. College Station, TX: Texas A&M University Press.

Landau, Martin. 1969. "Redundancy, Rationality, and the Problem of Duplication and Overlap." *Public Administration Review* 29, 4 (July–August):346–358.

Lieberman, Robert C. 2000. "Political Time and Policy Coalitions." In Robert Shapiro, Martha Joynt Kumar, and Larry Jacobs (Eds.), *Presidential Power: Forging the Presidency for the 21st Century*. New York: Columbia University.

Light, Paul C. 1999. *The President's Agenda: Domestic Policy Choice From Kennedy to Carter*, 3rd ed. Baltimore: Johns Hopkins University Press.

Lockerbie, Brad, and Stephen A. Borrelli. 1989. "Getting Inside the Beltway: Perceptions of Presidential Skill and Success in Congress." *British Journal of Political Science* 19 (January):97–106.

Lowi, Theodore. 1985. *The Personal President*. Ithaca, NY: Cornell University Press.

Mackenzie, G. Calvin. 2001. "The State of the Presidential Appointments Process." In G. Calvin Mackenzie (Ed.), *Innocent Until Nominated*. Washington, DC: The Brookings Institution.

March, James, and Johan Olsen. 1984. "The New Institutionalism: Organizational Factors in Political Life." *American Political Science Review* 78:734–739.

Mayer, Jane, and Doyle McManus. 1988. *Landslide: The Unmaking of the President, 1984–1988*. Boston: Houghton-Mifflin.

Mayer, Ken. 2001. *With the Stroke of a Pen*. Princeton, NJ: Princeton University Press.

Miller, Gary J. 1992. *Managerial Dilemmas: The Political Economy of Hierarchy*. New York: Cambridge University Press.

Miller, Gary J., and Terry Moe. 1986. "The Positive Theory of Hierarchies." In Herbert F. Weisberg (Ed.), *Political Science: The Science of Politics*, 167–198. New York: Agathon Press.

Moe, Terry M. 1984. "The New Economics of Organizations." *American Journal of Political Science* 28 (November):739–777.

———. 1985. "The Politicized Presidency." In John E. Chubb and Paul E. Peterson (Eds.), *The New Direction in American Politics*, 235–271. Washington, DC: The Brookings Institution.

———. 1993. "Presidents, Institutions and Theory." In George C. Edwards III, John H. Kessel, and Bert A. Rockman (Eds.), *Researching the Presidency: Vital Questions, New Approaches*. Pittsburgh: University of Pittsburgh Press.

Moe, Terry M., and William Howell. 1999. "The Presidential Power of Unilateral Action." *Journal of Law, Economics, and Organization* 29, 4:850–872.

Moe, Terry M., and Scott A. Wilson. 1994. "Presidents and the Politics of Structure." *Law and Contemporary Problems* 57, 2 (Spring):1–44.

Mouw, Calvin, and Michael MacKuen. 1992a. "The Strategic Agenda in Legislative Politics." *American Political Science Review* 86:87–105.

———. 1992b. "The Strategic Configuration, Personal Influence, and Presidential Power in Congress." *The Western Political Quarterly* 45, 3 (September):579–608.

Mueller, John. 1970. "Presidential Popularity from Truman to Johnson." *American Political Science Review* 64 (March):18–34.

Nathan, Richard. 1983. *The Administrative Presidency*. New York: John Wiley & Sons.

Neustadt, Richard E. 1963. "Approaches to Staffing the Presidency." *American Political Science Review* LVIX, 4 (December):855–863.

———. 1990. *Presidential Power and the Modern Presidents: The Politics of Leadership from Roosevelt to Reagan*. New York: The Free Press.

———. 2000. "A Preachment from Retirement." In Robert Shapiro, Martha Joynt Kumar, and Larry Jacobs (Eds.), *Presidential Power: Forging the Presidency for the 21st Century*. New York: Columbia University.

Neustadt, Richard E., and Ernest May. 1986. *Thinking in Time: The Uses of History for Decision-Makers*. New York: Macmillan.

North, Douglas. 1990. *Institutions, Institutional Change, and Economic Performance*. New York: Cambridge University Press.

Ostrom, Charles W., and Dennis M. Simon. 1985. "Promise and Performance: A Dynamic Model of Presidential Popularity." *American Political Science Review* 79:334–358.

———. 1988. "The President's Public." *American Journal of Political Science* 32, 4 (November):1096–1119.

Page, Ben, and Robert Shapiro. 1992. *The Rational Public*. Chicago: University of Chicago Press.

Patterson, Bradley. 2000. *The White House Staff: Inside the West Wing and Beyond*. Washington, DC: The Brookings Institution.

Peterson, Mark A. 1990. *Legislating Together: The White House and Capitol Hill From Eisenhower to Reagan*. Cambridge, MA: Harvard University Press.

Pfiffner, James. 1987/1991. "Political Appointees and Career Executives: The Democracy Bureaucracy Nexus." In James Pfiffner (Ed.), *The Managerial Presidency*. Pacific Grove: Brooks/Cole Publishing Co.

———. 1988. *The Strategic Presidency: Hitting the Ground Running*. Chicago: Dorsey Press.

Pious, Richard. 1979. *The American Presidency*. New York: Basic Books.

Porter, Roger B. 1980. *Presidential Decision Making: The Economic Policy Board*. Cambridge: New York.

Pratt, John W., and Richard Zeckhauser. 1985. "Principles and Agents: An Overview." In Pratt and Zeckhauser (Eds.), *Principles and Agents: The Structure of Business*. Boston, MA: Harvard Business School.

Price, Don K. 1960. "Presidential Power." *American Political Science Review* 54, 3 (September):735–736.

Ragsdale, Lyn. 2000. "Personal Power and Presidents." In Robert Shapiro, Martha Joynt Kumar, and Larry Jacobs (Eds), *Presidential Power, Forging the Presidency for the 21st Century*. New York: Columbia University.

Riley, Russell. 2000. "The Limits of the Transformational Presidency." In Robert Shapiro, Martha Joynt Kumar, and Larry Jacobs (Eds.), *Presidential Power: Forging the Presidency for the 21st Century*. New York: Columbia University.

Rivers, Douglas, and Nancy Rose. 1985. "Passing a President's Program: Public Opinion and Presidential Influence in Congress." *American Journal of Political Science* 29:183–196.

Robinson, Greg. 2001. *By Order of the President*. Cambridge, MA: Harvard University Press.

Rossiter, Clinton. 1960. *The American Presidency*. New York: Time Incorporated (paperback ed.).

Rudalevige, Andrew. 2002a. *Managing the President's Program*. Princeton, NJ: Princeton University Press.

———. 2002b. "The Structure of Leadership: Information, Organization, and Presidential Decisionmaking." Annual Meeting of the American Political Science Association.

Sagan, Scott, and Jeremi Suri. 2003. "The Madman Nuclear Alert: Secrecy, Signaling and Safety in October 1969." *International Security* 27, 4 (Spring):150–183.

Sander, Alfred Dick. 1989. *A Staff for the President: The Executive Office, 1921–52*. New York: Greenwood Press.

Schlesinger, Arthur Jr. 1965. *One Thousand Days*. Boston: Houghton-Mifflin.

Seligman, Lester G., and Cary R. Covington. 1989. *The Coalitional Presidency*. Chicago: The Dorsey Press.

Shapiro, Robert, Martha Joynt Kumar, and Larry Jacobs (Eds.). 2000. *Presidential Power: Forging the Presidency for the 21st Century*. New York: Columbia University.

Shull, Stephen, and Thomas A. Shaw. 1999. *Explaining Congressional-Presidential Relations*. Albany: State University of New York Press.

Simon, Herbert. 1976. *Administrative Behavior*. New York: The Free Press.

Skowronek, Stephen. 1987. "Review of Jeffrey Tulis' 'The Rhetorical Presidency.' " *The Review of Politics* 49, 3 (Summer):430.

———. 1993. *The Politics Presidents Make*. Cambridge, MA: Harvard University Press.

Sperlich, Peter. 1969. "Bargaining and Overload: An Essay on Presidential Power." In Aaron Wildavsky (Ed.), *The Presidency*, 168–192. Boston: Little, Brown.

Stockman, David. 1986. *The Triumph of Politics: How the Reagan Revolution Failed*. New York: Harper & Row.

Sullivan, Terry. 1988. "Headcounts, Expectations, and Presidential Coalitions in Congress." *American Journal of Political Science* 32 (July):567–589.

———. 1990. "Explaining Why Presidents Count: Signaling and Information." *Journal of Politics* 52 (August):939–962.

———. 1991. "Bargaining with the President: A Simple Game and New Evidence." *American Political Science Review* 84, 4 (December):1167–1195.

———. 2004. "Review of Power Without Persuasion: The Politics of Direct Presidential Action." *Presidential Studies Quarterly* 34, 2 (June):459–461.

Sundquist, James L. 1981. *The Decline and Resurgence of Congress*. Washington, DC: The Brookings Institution.

Tatalovich, Raymond, and Thomas S. Engeman. 2003. *The Presidency and Political Science Two Hundred Years of Constitutional Debate*. Baltimore: Johns Hopkins University Press.

Walcott, Charles, and Karen M. Hult. 1995. *Governing the White House: From Hoover Through LBJ*. Lawrence: University Press of Kansas.

Wayne, Stephen. 1983. "Approaches." In George C. Edwards III and Stephen J. Wayne (Eds.), *Studying the Presidency*, 17–49. Knoxville: University of Tennessee Press.

Waterman, Richard. 1989. *Presidential Influence and the Administrative State*. Knoxville: The University of Tennessee Press.

Williamson, Oliver. 1975. *Markets and Hierarchies: Analysis and Anti-Trust Implications*. New York: The Free Press. ✦

Chapter 13

When It Comes to Presidential Leadership, Accentuate the Positive, but Don't Forget the Normative

Bert A. Rockman

This book focuses on the conditions when, and the arenas in which, presidents can exercise leadership. Since the exact nature of leadership is not always clearly defined, as we observed in our introductory chapter, it often reflects personal opinion: presidents one agrees with exercise leadership, while presidents one disagrees with are capricious aggrandizers. In other words, the concept of leadership is thoroughly infused with ungrounded normative preconceptions (for example, Burns 1978). One president's leadership is another's aggrandizement of power (Andrews 1975). A scientific exploration of presidential leadership, however, requires some precision of definition. That, however, often turns out to be elusive. Most of the chapters in this book focus on the conditions that affect presidential discretionary behavior, asking explicitly or implicitly, in other words, how much leeway a president—any president—has under varying conditions. With some exceptions (notably the chapters of Greenstein and of Fine and Waterman, and ultimately, this one), more emphasis is placed on the conditions that influence presidents' discretionary capabilities—that is, the potential of presidents for exercising leadership—and much less on how particular presidents exercise leadership.

✦ ✦ ✦

Positive and Normative Conceptions of Leadership

As a subject, leadership endlessly wavers between its positive and normative aspects. How do we, and should we, evaluate

311

leaders? Should we evaluate them, as we discussed in the introduction, by their political success, by their policy impact, by the wisdom of their policies, or by their ways of making decisions? How do we assess outcomes for the polity or the society? These issues are befuddling and we have little to guide us in assessing them. The general characteristics, conditions, causes, and boundaries of presidential leadership are more amenable to inquiry. Description, explanation, prediction, and unraveling causality are the bases of any scientific understanding. Theories based on these characteristics are ordinarily described as positive, whereas theories based on "oughts" are ordinarily described as normative.

We do know that logically consistent and empirically plausible theories are necessary to provide a broad comprehension of the institution of the presidency and of the constraints and opportunities that presidents are likely to face. The empirical conditions facing any given president may help us to make predictions about the probability of certain aspects of that individual president's behavior. Unless generalizations derive from laws that cover all instances, like, say, the Second Law of Thermodynamics (whereby matter can neither be created nor destroyed, only converted from one form to another), the best we can do is to estimate likelihoods. What, in other words, are probable outcomes and plausible expectations? And how much are individual leaders a part of this equation?

Let me take an illustrative case. Upon George W. Bush's ascendancy to the presidency, he had very few resources with which to govern. There was a very tight division of political forces after the 2000 presidential election. The incoming president, having lost the popular vote in a highly disputed election, lacked broad support (although he came into office with more support than Reagan had at the same point in time). The party division within Congress was extremely close. There were bitter feelings on the part of partisans of the defeated candidate, Al Gore. Further, the new president's repeated statements proclaimed him to be a problem solver interested in uniting the country rather than dividing it (Rockman 2004). There are, of course, plausible scenarios based on partisan polarization that might have predicted Bush's subsequent behavior, governing virtually exclusively from his political base. The incentives to do that may have been powerful. But few predicted it. A more likely—or at least conventional—prediction was that Bush, having so little room to maneuver, would try to govern between the parties and build majorities from the center outward. It would have been reasonable to expect Bush, as had other closely contested winners such as Kennedy and Nixon during the early part of his first term, to proceed cautiously or to partially adopt, as Clinton also did, plays from the opposition's handbook.

Of course, we know that Bush did nothing of the sort. Instead, he embarked on a path designed to keep his party base content and to govern from it. There were conditions, to be sure, that were conducive to that. With the parties so polarized, it was difficult to find a middle ground. Bush didn't create polarization, but his track record in the White House reinforced it. Bush's strategy, though, was high risk, and would depend mainly upon getting his partisans out in 2004, while governing from a narrow base. This was not a probable scenario, but it worked pretty well until midway into the second Bush term. What we would have needed to know was how Bush thought strategically, the extent to which he was committed to what he said publicly about his conciliatory style of governing, and the extent to which his advisers were feeding him a common and compelling strategy that he digested. In other words, we clearly needed to know not only about Bush's strategic situation and what degree of freedom that afforded him, but we also needed to know something about Bush as a person—what made him tick and to what he was responsive. In other words, is a president merely a random error term in the study of the presidency or can we know something about the president that helps us to understand differences across administrations?

In this regard, one set of presidency scholars can plausibly argue that it is vital to understand and clarify the strategic circumstances under which any president would be likely to act, whereas another set can plausibly argue that people make a difference even when objective conditions appear to be similar. There is little doubt the first claim has greater theoretical purchase. But what it tends to purchase are necessary rather than sufficient conditions. The second claim lacks a consistently clear theoretical base, yet mainly focuses on sufficient conditions. Like the proverbial horses being led to water, not all presidents will drink from it. Why or why not is the question. Neither claim is invalid. Both are indeed essential. This chapter assumes the first claim of necessary conditions and therefore focuses on the latter: sufficient conditions.

Political science deals with generalizations likely to be found in variations of context. Political biography tends to deal with the idiosyncrasies of public figures as they confront critical decisions. If the leaders being scrutinized deal with these decisions in consistent ways, we may have some leverage as to how they will continue to deal with them. However, politicians adapt to changing circumstances and usually recognize when the path they are on is unlikely to yield success. And that, of course, raises a fundamental issue in understanding presidents who, after all, are politicians. To what extent are they free agents? To what extent are they bound by past commitments or by the constituencies and selectorates who will play a large role in their current and future political success? Studying conditions under the assumption that political leaders are adaptive and will respond to altered incentives seems a fairly safe bet. But political leaders also have to figure out how to balance past commitments with current opportu-

nities. In other words, can they discover how to loosen the constraints placed on them by those who helped them get where they are
now in order to take advantage of opportunities that will help them
further fulfill their ambitions? It is certainly plausible that political
leaders calculate differently the extent to which they can loosen the
constraints currently binding them so as to expand their options.

Inevitably, more idiosyncrasies remain in studying the exercise of
leadership than in the conditions allowing for its exercise. People are
different, and that likely makes a difference. The trouble is that, first,
we do not have good theories, data, or measures as to how people differ in the exercise of leadership, and, second, while the role of an individual leader may be extremely important, it is rarely primarily so,
at least in a statistical sense. Regarding the first point, as a vantage
point for analysis, it is best to start with how we think any person
would behave under the same circumstances. That is, what are the incentives for the person to act in a certain way? Or, how do individuals
cognize complexity or filter advice when time is short and demands
for action intense? While these are far from easy questions to answer,
they at least provide us with the analytic leverage that comes from
how we could expect anyone to behave under like circumstances or
conditions.

In the case of the second point, we know, for example, that chim-
panzees and human beings share 99 percent of their genetic endow-
ment. But obviously, the 1 percent that they do not share makes a
huge difference. We also know that we can explain from a statistical
point of view the outcome of an election by reference to party, but
party itself rarely decides elections unless party distribution is highly
lopsided. In other words, what is currently bereft of clearly and
uniquely identifiable influence on outcomes often turns out to make
the critical difference. Consequently, individual variability across
presidents is likely to be a crucial consideration, especially once we
account for similarities and differences in context, as Fine and Waterman point out in their chapter in this book. The problem is how we
can discern what these differences in individuals may be and how
they come to matter.

Positive theories of the presidency as an institution and of leadership as a general phenomenon are essential to making progress in describing, explaining, and predicting presidential leadership. Yet, as
noted, we know less about leadership than about the conditions affecting the capacity for its exercise. And we know even less about how
to deal in a meaningful way with the normative side of leadership—
are we able to distinguish between good leadership and bad? Normative theory emphasizes the justificatory grounding of "good policy"
based upon a theory of "the good." That theory could be based on religious or other ethical absolutes, or it could be based upon a form of
consequentialism. Only the latter can be analytically and potentially

empirically justified. Consequentialism implies a rule or set of rules for discerning the effects of policy choices. For example, will some be better off and none worse off by a given choice (Pareto optimality)? Will more people be better off even if some will be made worse off by a given decision (the greatest good for the greatest number)? Will a given process of decisionmaking (such as markets) ultimately lead to more productive choices that result in the overall benefit to society, even if some (rent seekers) are adversely affected in the short term? These are, of course, merely a few of the possible streams of consequentialist theory. And they present, in essence, the criteria brought to bear on policy by policy analysts. To ask whether a given choice will be productive or counterproductive requires a baseline for what would be a bettering or worsening of the status quo.

Neither presidents in particular, politicians in general, nor students of the presidency, however, are typically philosophers. Presidents are usually interested in what advances their political standing. Political scientists who study the presidency usually take that—and reasonably enough—as a first premise regarding presidential behavior. Nevertheless, it may well be that the most fundamentally important aspect of the presidency is the set of decisions that only presidents can make. Therefore, one might reasonably ask what is the type and level of preparation of each president to make those decisions, and what ways do different presidents have of engaging such decisions? What is the level of a president's involvement? What is the level of a president's curiosity? To what extent do presidents have sufficient knowledge or ability to be skeptical inquirers of others' priorities? To what extent, as Neustadt forewarned, can they see the stakes for themselves in the decisions they make (1990)?

The conditions for the exercise of leadership are necessary ones. They are essential and represent the foundation of our knowledge about the presidency. But, as in the case of human and chimpanzee genomes, the missing 1 percent, so to speak, is less about the presidency and more about the president. The president may be statistically marginal, but certainly not trivial regarding how leadership is executed.

While the positive foundations of presidential power that are derived from identifying strategic contexts are growing firmer from the progress of science, both theoretical and empirical, the normative foundations for the uses of presidential power have failed to similarly progress. Is that because everything is merely a matter of taste? I have my preferences and you have yours, and is there no meaningful way to distinguish between them from the standpoint of merit? In a society with heterogeneous preferences and a divided polity, who is to say that any set of preferences has standing over any other? That is, I would hazard to guess, the main reason that presidency scholars have shied away from dealing with the normative issues surrounding presidential leadership. But there also are others. Among them is the understandable view that those studying the presidency are rarely experts on issues or moral philosophy and, thus, can bring no special knowledge to bear on complicated policy issues. If we cannot bring special knowledge of this sort to bear, then we are in the realm of merely heterogeneous tastes and preferences. Another possible reason is that social scientists in general, and political scientists in particular, are very disproportionately to the political left of the public and disproportionately favorable to Democrats and unfavorable to Republicans (Rose 1993). Can a group of presidency scholars so skewed speak legitimately to normative issues of presidential behavior? Political scientists may believe that in the absence of justified grounded assessments, it is better to keep political judgments private since our expertise lies in specifying conditions in which presidential power has the capacity to be exercised or not. Whatever the precise constellation of reasons, political scientists who study the presidency are more comfortable examining what presidents do or might be able to do and what they are likely inhibited from doing than what it is they *ought* to do.

This chapter, then, assumes the importance of identifying the empirical conditions for the exercise of leadership and the scope of its exercise, on the one hand, while on the other it focuses on the role of the president as a decisionmaker. What can we know about presidents as decisionmakers that would suggest the likelihood of their being able to make informed choices? The president, of course, is preeminently a politician who needs to keep together a coalition of political constituencies, not a philosopher or policy analyst. A president who operates mainly as a policy analyst may well alienate those who are needed for his or her presidency to be successful. Alternatively, a president who operates solely to placate political constituencies will have lost his or her independence and, in essence, the claim to leadership.

Why Leadership?

Ultimately, without leadership there is drift, not merely the status quo. So, the subject has been an important element of political theory, especially in regard to the characteristics of effective leadership. Yet leadership may come from many sources, not merely one. Moreover, leaders may help (intentionally or otherwise) to set the stages for other leaders to build upon the accomplishments of past leadership. Alternatively, leaders may find themselves contesting with one another seeking different outcomes. This, of course, not only raises the question of what is leadership, it also raises the question of whom to regard as a leader. The diffusion of power designed in the U.S. Constitution, in fact, creates many potential leaders, not just one. Conventional wisdom equates leadership with the chief executive, but other actors are also in leadership roles and can exert extensive leadership from their vantage points. Within the last two decades, for example, Newt Gingrich, the voluble member of Congress from Georgia, was a successful agitator on behalf of his party's congressional wing. He rode that role to knocking off the Democratic Speaker of the House, Jim Wright, for alleged abuses of his role. He also rode his status as a powerful partisan figure all the way to the Speakership of the House himself from where substantial changes were made in how the House did its business. The Speaker's role was enlarged during Gingrich's brief but volatile tenure as House Speaker. Similarly, Tom DeLay, whose downfall was as swift as his rise, became the House Majority leader, but was, in effect, the de facto leader of the House Republicans even when he held only the third ranking leadership role of party whip. DeLay successfully positioned his party to be a disciplined, cohesive force in the House and to align producer and business interests, who cared more about outcomes favorable to themselves than to either party, to bestow large amounts of money on behalf of the Republican Party and to DeLay's foundation. Arguably, Gingrich and DeLay may have been the most important political figures in Washington—or at least, among them—during their periods of ascendancy.

Leadership, however, is rarely the product of a single person nor does it emanate from a single role, although entrepreneurship is often essential. Nor does leadership even necessarily emanate from within government, despite the existence of leadership roles. In fact, often social or political or policy activists exert significant influences over the shape of agendas and initiate important societal and political changes. Martin Luther King Jr., Rachel Carson, and Ralph Nader, for example, played powerful roles in bringing civil rights, environmental protection, and consumer safety to public attention. Others such as Jerry Falwell and Pat Robertson helped bring the tenets of religious fundamentalism into the political arena. In many ways, politicians only ratify issues that leaders in society, rather than officeholders, have brought to public attention. But leaders need to match up with opportunities for leadership, and as Bill Clinton often complained, he had few such opportunities, or at least believed he had few. Uninteresting times may do little to burnish politicians' reputations for leadership but they are usually more favorable to the citizens themselves and to the health and stability of democratic political processes.

Leadership roles facilitate but do not monopolize the exercise of leadership functions. Leadership can be provided from many sources, and the fewer the filters to becoming a leader, the more degrees of freedom exist. Some leaders have been self-anointed publicity hounds with few constraints on them: for example, Al Sharpton, who neither heads an organization nor holds office, but did run for president. But if leadership is everywhere, it also may be nowhere. Taken to an extreme, leadership everywhere is simply anarchy. Indeed, if leadership is strong everywhere, there may be only Hobbes's "war of all against all." Although leadership can occur in a wide variety of places and in multiple roles, which is ideally how new leaders are able to make claims for greater responsibilities, we tend to fix our attention on the executive leadership, particularly the principal executive leader in any organization, including government. If things go well below the top, we might be inclined to say that the leader knows how to put together a team, or inspire her or his subordinates. If things get messy, we may note deficiencies in these respects on the part of the chief.

Achievement is the product of luck, opportunity (threat is sometimes an opportunity, because it may provide a wider berth for leaders), and collaborative partners who have incentives to go along. But there are also indispensable elements of leadership that enable one to take advantage of the opportunities, lay the groundwork for change into the future, and create incentives for others to cooperate. We also know that some elements of leadership tend to be in contradiction to others. Rhetorical flourishes and bold moves may run counter to figuring out and assessing situations, and may induce potential blowback. Bargaining behind the scenes may allow for the syndication of success. Yet, a wily leader is unlikely to be seen as inspirational.

The one thing we can be sure of about leadership is that it is no single thing, nor is it vested in a single person. In fact, like other seemingly simple, yet very complex, concepts such as intelligence, personality, and so on, leadership has multiple and often contradictory aspects to it. This makes it a very difficult subject to study, because if we study individuals presumably exercising leadership, we may be led into considering counterfactuals—how else could the story have turned out? Was the intervention crucial to the outcome? Could a different style of involvement or even noninvolvement have produced a similar result? Did the exercise of leadership actually worsen the situation?

One might say that a subject as malleable and inconclusive as that of leadership is not worthy of much serious consideration, because the concept holds little interpersonal comparability and seems so remarkably confounded with other influences on outcomes. It is elusive and subjective. The scientific study of politics, thus, can focus on the conditions for potential influence but not its exercise or, above all, how it is used.

Obviously, the subject of leadership has been around much longer than the American presidency. Machiavelli had some notable things to say by way of advice based upon observational or intuitive generalities in *The Prince* (1999). But going back even farther to a figure from the biblical Old Testament, Aaron Wildavsky (2005) drew upon interpretations of Moses as a leader in bringing his people to the Promised Land. (His people are apparently one of several who seem to have been promised this land.) Other theorists, such as Max Weber (1964, 224 *passim*), focused on the bases of authority noting, in essence, that the rule of law diminished the role of leaders and their rule by institutionalizing transactions through legal and impersonal standards, thereby eliminating charisma as a basis of authority. But, of course, legal change, not to mention the institutionalization of legal systems, could not happen without leadership.

Both positive and normative elements of leadership are drawn from the parables of Moses leading his people's emancipation from ancient Egypt and their trek across the Sinai Desert. Millennia later, Machiavelli (1999) sought, like many modern political scientists, to render advice to his "Prince" on the basis of theoretically grounded observation involving both the attributes of the leader and the conditions for exercising leadership.

So, the study of leadership and leaders is hardly new. However, there tends to be an especially strong emphasis on the role of leadership in the United States as a process rather than on leaders as a class. There could be several reasons for this, although these are speculative, not definitive.

First, the individualistic nature of the American culture may place unusual emphasis on the role of skillful manipulation of resources and the application of wit and inspiration to managing enterprises, whether corporations, athletic teams, nonprofit organizations, or politics and government. A more traditionally conservative or systemic view might focus more on the realm of constraints.

Second, and derivatively, it is possible that because self-promotion plays such a significant role in the United States that we tend to focus more on the role of the outsider than the insider. The insider gets where she or he is going typically by playing within the rules and gaining support because of a reputation for reliability rather than inspiration. Organizations, such as parties, typically have been more important in parliamentary systems as focal points for the emergence of leaders than they have been in the United States. Perhaps this is because other affluent democratic polities traditionally have been less kind to the ambitions of those working outside of an established institutional/organizational framework. To some extent, this has a lot to do with the nature of parliamentary systems, where freelancing displays of political bravado are discouraged.

Third, the separation of powers system in the United States makes the reliability of support for the president something that can never be assumed. Despite parties having become much more important and, thus, constraining of leaders in American politics in the early twenty-first century than they had been at the midpoint of the twentieth century, the structural incentives for teamwork across party members, while growing stronger and perhaps close to their historical zenith in the United States, are still relatively weak by the standards of parliamentary systems. Predictability is still less powerful than in parliamentary systems across legislators and executives of the same party. When the going gets tough, the president's partisans in Congress do not have overpowering incentives to stay the course as the president defines it. One possible reason for that, however, is that unlike parliamentary systems where there usually is required consultation in the cabinet between prime ministers and other party leaders, American presidents are often first movers, and the circle of advice is often centered in the White House itself. Others may be informed but not necessarily consulted. Still, it is an unresolved and, unfortunately, largely hypothetical question as to whether even if there were such consultations before decisions were made, members of Congress would remain committed to those choices when it was no longer in their interest to do so.

From Institutions to Behavior Back to Institutions

In his landmark book *Presidential Power* (1990), Richard Neustadt focused attention precisely on the notion that presidents as often as not had to fend for themselves if they were to succeed. The focus on the leadership capabilities of the presidential officeholder in the United States, as suggested, stems from the variability in the conditionals under which presidents operate. When a president is elected (or occasionally selected), no government comes in with the new officeholder. Rather, as the Madisonian system of separation of powers would have it, a president may face widely varying conditions under which leadership might be exercised. How presidents exercise power and leadership under these varying conditions provide opportunities to assess the political agility of the individual incumbent. Does the incumbent, as Neustadt emphasized, have a feel for power—whatever that might mean? The "feel for power" that Neustadt emphasized was not merely the ability to issue edicts or strike poses but the ability to safeguard one's stakes in decisions—to avoid going out on limbs that could be cut off. What a president needed to know most was to know what he or she needed to know. The implication was that the presidency was not a job for the incurious or indolent, or for the unschooled—Neustadt famously warned that the White House is "no place for amateurs"—or for those given to heroic gestures (rash behavior) without comprehending the down side of such gestures.

Parliamentary systems can also provide numerous opportunities for leadership strategies, especially in multiparty systems. Examinations of individual leaders tend to be less frequent in such systems (however, see Olaf Ruin's political biography [1990] of the former leader of the Swedish Social Democratic Party [SAP] Tage Erlander) because more emphasis is placed on the strategies of parties facing critical options as to with whom they should align themselves or with related choices about the size of a governing coalition. In parliamentary systems, coalition building is a more formal process and commitments must be deemed to be credible because they involve the formation of a government, not just the outcome of a bill. Strategy, therefore, tends to be emphasized more at the organizational actor level in parliamentary systems than it has been in the case of the U.S. presidency, where individual leaders—their styles, psychologies, and political skills—more often have been the focus of analysis.

The history of presidential studies actually began with less emphasis on individuals and more on the institutional and constitutional moorings of the presidency. What were the president's powers? The study of the presidency was, to a considerable degree, the study of the president's formal powers or accumulated roles. Although scholars from time to time brought in different perspectives, it was largely Richard Neustadt's examination of presidential power, initially published in 1960 and read by the then President-elect John F. Kennedy, that shifted the emphasis from constitutional and institutional foci to personal behavioral ones.

Neustadt emphasized examining presidential power rather than the formal powers of the presidency, which he found to be limited. He assumed that any president would face a complex and fragmented political system that would be hard to lead or be given much central direction. In that sense, American political institutions constituted the parameters from which Neustadt's analysis took off. How could presidents gain traction in such a system? That was Neustadt's central question. His answer to that question was deceptively simple, yet extraordinarily vague. Effective presidents had to be individuals with an exquisite sense and comprehension of politics and power. They in turn would have to be drawn from among a pool of highly experienced professional politicians. Ambiguities are encountered at nearly every turn. What types of professional politicians, for example, would best compose this pool? Are they those with lengthy experience in Washington or outside of Washington? Are they to be drawn from legislative institutions or executive ones? And should they be drawn from elected or appointed positions? It remains unclear as to precisely what experiences count. And Neustadt's exemplar of presidential leadership, Franklin D. Roosevelt, had only a brief career in Washington as an appointed midlevel official in the Department of the Navy before later being elected governor of New York.

Nor is it much clearer what skill sets a president must have to be a successful leader. Adeptness at politics, to be sure, can't hurt but it—if it can be defined in a nontautological way—may not necessarily be crucial either for a president's success. By political skill, Neustadt seems to have meant the ability of the incumbent to manipulate organizations and people so as to create information asymmetries; that is, the president needs to know what others do not, but cannot let it be known that he does. Such a president, by definition, had to be hands on. Such a president surely was not, let us say, Ronald Reagan, though Reagan had great interpersonal skills as a kibbitzer-in-chief and did well in the office compared to his immediate predecessors from the standpoint of moving government in his preferred directions, as well as in generating a reasonably high level of sustained public approval (despite a low level of approval upon coming to office) in the context of presidencies that he succeeded as well as the one that immediately succeeded him. In policy direction and especially in governing style, however, Reagan was the anti-Roosevelt. Where Roosevelt was hands-on and guileful, Reagan was detached and dependent upon his associates. What then can we know or predict—if anything—about any given president? Since approval has been consistently measured, two of the most popular figures in the presidency are notably individuals of utterly divergent backgrounds and political and governing styles—Franklin D. Roosevelt and Dwight D. Eisenhower. Is the search for the ideal leader merely illusory? Are not the things we really need to know, therefore, in the context and situations of leadership and the fortunes over which no one has much control rather than the attributes of leaders themselves?

Furthermore, one could glean opposite conclusions from the tales that Neustadt spun regarding what he characterized as Eisenhower's political naiveté. For example, in *Presidential Power*, Neustadt (1990, 91–103) makes much of Eisenhower's difficulties in controlling his Treasury Secretary George Humphrey, who obviously took his dispute with the administration's 1958 FY budget plans public after the budget was released. Neustadt concluded from Eisenhower's reluctance to disavow his Treasury Secretary in public that Humphrey was allowed to diminish Eisenhower's leverage to sell his budget—a budget that was popular neither among his party's committed fiscal conservatives nor among the Democrats' liberals. Neustadt concludes that Eisenhower, by not reprimanding his Treasury Secretary, was placed in an indefensible situation publicly defending Humphrey while Humphrey publicly lambasted his boss's budget. But an alternative interpretation would suggest that the worst thing a leader can do is to express a lack of public confidence in his personnel choices. Humphrey was, after all, appointed by Eisenhower. One might equally conclude that a better way to go about it was to stammer around as Eisenhower did, making it unclear whether he supported his own budget without reservations or associated himself with Humphrey's remarks, which he partly did. It is plausible that Eisenhower concluded that the Humphrey dust-up was a here today, gone tomorrow story that would have been made worse by a public humiliation of his own appointee. Several months later, Humphrey left office. Perhaps Eisenhower used his authority in the most politic way possible, allowing both the issue and the principal (Humphrey) to fade away.

A similar episode could be derived (though not in Neustadt) from President George H. W. Bush's (Bush 41) protracted and difficult negotiations with the majority Democratic leadership on Capitol Hill in 1990–1991 over legislation to raise taxes and cut spending. Bush had made a famous but foolish pledge in his speech accepting the Republican Party's nomination for the presidency at his party's national convention in 1988. He promised not to raise taxes and, for emphasis, added "read my lips, no new taxes." He promised as well to veto any new tax bill. His pledge, delivered with partisan gusto before a flock of believers, gained him the enthusiasm of his party's core activists, which heretofore had been less than notable. However, the pledge obviously painted him into a corner once he took office. Nearing the halfway point of Bush 41's first term, and amidst a recession, cyclical and structural deficits combined to further deepen the federal government's deficit management problem.

A shadow mating dance subtly began in 1990 between the Bush 41 White House and leading Democrats on Capitol Hill who controlled the committee chairs. Dan Rostenkowski (D-IL) was the Chair of the House Ways and Means Committee responsible for writing tax legislation, which constitutionally has to originate in the House of Representatives. Rostenkowski signaled through the press that he was looking for a negotiation with the White House to stem the mounting federal fiscal deficit by raising taxes and limiting spending. As such signals are, these were muted—the very opposite in style of pledges made before partisan audiences.

Congressional Democrats were not so keen to limit spending and congressional Republicans, especially in the House, were uninterested in raising taxes. President Bush was thus placed in a very difficult bargaining situation. The Bush administration's Budget Director, Richard Darman, played hard to get as a negotiating partner with Rostenkowski, likely in order to bolster the administration's bona fides with its own constituencies.

As the negotiations continued and became more formal, a majority coalition was becoming harder to form. Republicans resisted raising taxes; Democrats resisted curtailing spending. Within his congressional party and among party activists, Bush was excoriated for failing to provide leadership, on the one hand, and for reneging on his tax promise, on the other. The Democrats and elements of the establishment press criticized Bush for also failing to provide leadership and for having made a campaign promise that he couldn't keep but also couldn't ignore. At an especially difficult point in the negotiations, Bush proclaimed (legitimately, from a constitutional standpoint) that it was Congress's job to come up with a package. From one perspective, this looked like a virtual dereliction of duty on the president's part, as though he had abdicated his leadership role in forging an accommodation. Yet, from a different perspective, Bush's ploy may have been more subtle and nuanced. Obviously, Bush was between a rock and a hard place. He was unable in either chamber to bring along a majority in his own party for any tax increases and, consequently, was left to work with a coalition of a minority of his own party and a majority of the Democrats. The fainter the White House's fingerprints were on an agreement, the better for Bush's prospects.

These ambiguities in the study of leadership and the presidency make the topic of leadership endlessly fascinating but often intractable. More traction could be had with greater emphasis on systematically identifying and modeling constraints in the president's environment and also opportunities for exploitation. That is, to gain analytic traction one might have to take the president out of the presidency and emphasize the conditionals influencing presidential possibilities for leadership. Two broad streams of work, both of which are represented in this volume, focus on the conditionals of presidency research. One is rich in data, the other rich in theory. The first of these emphasizes political behavior, communications, social psychology, and sociology, by examining the role of public approval, party cohesion and support for the president, the role of communications and persuasive efforts, and, accordingly, public susceptibility to persuasion efforts. Above all, such research often focuses on the ability to tie together the conditionals affecting the available space for presidential leadership.

The second stream of work, however, has rediscovered the role of institutions as definers of presidential imperatives, constraints, and opportunities. Broadly speaking, the return to institutions has come with a different twist. The formal legal bases of institutions could serve to define incentives for behavior and, in turn, as Terry Moe (for example, 1985 and 1995), one of the leading proponents of the institutional return to presidential studies emphasized, actors have incentives to cement their preferences into laws founding agencies and programs which then define the likely participants and set of problems on which agencies have discretion to work. Incentives as a basis of behavior derive from the assumptions of political economy, and a central such assumption is that actors will seek to advance their interests.

Institutional factors are important because they establish the parameters under which leadership occurs. Because of the growth and development of the White House staff and the larger Executive Office of the Presidency (EOP), presidents today have much greater capacity for leadership than did presidents of the premodern era. For example, presidents now can receive advice from a variety of organizations located under the president's direct control. Hence, there is a potential for presidents to receive more information and more detailed analysis, all of which can contribute to better decisionmaking in both foreign and domestic affairs.

Yet, the expansion of the institutional presidency has not been synonymous with improved presidential leadership. It is hard to identify better presidents, qualitatively speaking, after the establishment of the modern presidency than before it. In part, this is because institutions do not represent a panacea for effective leadership. While the National Security Council (NSC), through the staff of the President's National Security Advisor, can provide presidents with a valuable source of information and facilitate decisionmaking on key foreign policy issues, different presidents have used the NSC in decidedly different ways. Kennedy and Johnson often ignored it, while Nixon centralized U.S. foreign policy in the White House. Reagan, who set the broad parameters for foreign policy then let subordinates decide on the details, sat back passively while his various foreign policy and national security lieutenants bitterly fought with one another, raising serious questions about Reagan's leadership competence. Bush 41 then returned the NSC to its more traditional position as a neutral arbiter of information as had Gerald Ford earlier. Under George W. Bush (Bush 43), the policy nerve centers seem to have largely emanated from the Office of the Vice President and the Office of the Secretary of Defense. As these cases demonstrate, each president used the NSC in different ways. Some (e.g., Bush 41) proved more useful than others. However, under Johnson, Nixon, Reagan, and Bush 43, the NSC became subject to criticism, though for different reasons—in Nixon's case the NSC was thought to have too much power, in Reagan's too little oversight, and under Bush 43 too little influence.

Thus, while institutions can have an impact on leadership, their influence is variable. The decisive factor in the leadership equation is not the institutions themselves, but the leader. Each president decided how to use the NSC and the various departments and agencies differently with somewhat different consequences in their decisionmaking. Rather than a consistent pattern of NSC operation from president to president, the NSC appears to reflect the idiosyncratic variations of each president's leadership style. Thus, we can make no predictions about how future presidents will use the NSC based on its past usage. Instead, the best predictor will be the identity of the next president. In that sense, even when we consider the importance of institutions, it is important to keep in mind that individual leadership matters, and matters most when there are available degrees of freedom. Consequently, while it is true that the presidency today has become more organizationally elaborate and makes available more information for presidents, we cannot know how presidents will use this apparatus or whether they will succeed or fail as a result.

To succeed, presidents often need to know what they do not know. They need to ask hard questions and be skeptical of easy answers. Experience helps. So too, perhaps even more, does a mindset skeptical of certainties. Personal qualities and leadership, in sum, remain indispensable to an understanding of the presidency.

Presidents, being foremost politicians, however, rarely fare well unless they exude a sense of positive certainty and confidence about the future. They are, in part, selling a vision and an agenda and forging or sustaining a political coalition. But policy and decisionmaking require careful attention to facts. Visions need to be adjusted in accordance with troublesome facts. Policies and decisions need to be managed. Presidents are not likely to be evaluated, at least positively, by the mistakes they have wisely managed to avoid. The mistakes a president makes, however, especially when avoidable, bite back and ultimately diminish that president's political standing and weaken thereby the president's political and policy leverage. Listening, reading, assessing, and monitoring are essential for presidents to avoid self-destruction, but there is still no guarantee that they will not come to grief. Carter did all of these and even insisted on talking turkey, as he understood it, to the American public in what is now known as the infamous "malaise" speech. Carter, as we know, wound up less a turkey-talker than turkey hash.

Synthesizing the political and policy sides of the president's role is no simple task. Not surprisingly, few have done it well. Reagan had the political side down pat, but was more interested in watching *The Sound of Music* than attending to his briefing books. By contrast, Carter read voluminously and reacted to the details, but had few political instincts or clarity of vision. Reagan made it look easy once the economy began to perk up until events that Reagan apparently encouraged but knew little about, such as Iran-Contra, came down on the administration. Carter made a hard job look harder. The obvious conclusion is that fate and leadership style play important roles in how presidents fare. But, of course, leadership style is nested within other more powerful variables.

Thus, fortune or misfortune influence the fate of presidents regardless of their abilities. Good fortune smiled on some and misfortune on others. No president is fully the master of his or her fate. That is obvious. Indeed, this book demonstrates the possible spaces that presidents have to exploit leverage or escape blame. How successfully and, above all, how wisely presidents can exploit leverage depends upon their leadership abilities. Ultimately, leadership is indispensable. The person in the Oval Office is critical to presidential performance, especially when no one else can substitute his or her authority for the president's—in other words, when it truly matters, even if it doesn't always matter to political scientists.

Since leadership is indispensable we can therefore infer that it is a critical factor in what makes a good president. Yet this assertion on its own does not seem satisfactory, because leadership itself remains such a nebulous characteristic. What then is it specifically about leadership that makes one president a great president, another simply a good president, and others average or failed presidents? This is a question that scholars have attempted to answer without notable success.

We are therefore left to ask, what are the qualities of presidential greatness? Presidential popularity is treasured, and presidents are driven to seek high approval ratings. But popularity is not a proxy for leadership. Presidents who are forced to make tough and unpopular decisions, such as Lincoln during the Civil War, did not primarily quest popularity. George W. Bush's 2007 proposals to increase troop levels in Iraq flew in the face of public sentiment, and provide evidence of a president willing to set popularity aside for other objectives (see Jacobs and Shapiro 2000). While Lincoln's fortitude led to his coronation as one of the great presidents, there will likely be less consensus as to whether Bush 43's decision reflected great leadership skill and judgment, or merely a stubborn inability to face a tragic reality. Some of the latter was also said of Lincoln and Wilson during their terms in office. A presidential willingness to stand up to public opinion does not by itself, however, signify presidential leadership or greatness.

What about decisiveness? Bush 43 has made much of the fact that he is the "decider," the one who makes the tough decisions based on the information he receives. Yet there already is much reporting suggesting that the evidence Bush 43 received was either inadequate or even heavily biased in favor of the president's preferred course of action. Regarding the invasion and occupation of Iraq, there was little discussion or debate over key issues—including follow-through actions and the ramifications of an invasion. Indeed, there is clear evidence that professional skepticism was viewed as undesirable, as reflected in the unceremonious dumping of General Eric Shinseki, who warned of the need for far more troops necessary to establish order in Iraq. Thus, the mere willingness to be a "decider" is not necessarily evidence of presidential leadership. It may merely be evidence of obstinacy and stubbornness.

Still, one can hardly imagine the concept of leadership without a consideration of decisionmaking skill, for it goes to the very heart of what we generally think about when we consider the concept of leadership. Franklin Roosevelt developed and employed a chaotic decisionmaking structure, while Eisenhower was criticized for using one that was far too structured and deliberative. Carter gained a reputation for micromanagement, while Reagan liked to think that all he had to do was to make the big decisions, then let others fill in the details, as if the details did not matter. Nixon's decisionmaking style varied by policy area: he paid strict attention to issues of foreign policy, but cared little for domestic policy. Alternatively, Lyndon Johnson was more concerned with domestic policy, though foreign policy came to dominate his presidency. Clinton liked to discuss issues from various angles on into the night, but did not appear to actually like making decisions. Each president had a different approach to decisionmaking. Each was criticized in his time and since for the shortcomings of his decisionmaking approach. Yet, each approach apparently served the interests or personalities of that particular president. What is less obvious is what is the best decisionmaking style. When it comes to the knotty question of how do we know good leadership when we see it, the answer is likely to be normative. You will like the decisions if you like the decisions! But is that really leadership?

What we can say is that presidents are indeed very often the ultimate decisionmakers, and whatever approach they use, they will be judged in some, but probably insufficient, measure on the basis of the decisions they make. Some will have limited opportunities to make big decisions, as Teddy Roosevelt and Bill Clinton apparently regretted. Others, such as FDR and Bush 43, will be asked to make monumental decisions. The outcomes of these decisions, as well as how they were implemented and conceived, will have much to do with whether we consider these presidents to be effective leaders or not.

Since decisionmaking is critical to the presidency, all presidents should have certain characteristics in common. While qualities such as prior experience in elective office may not be correlated with presidential success (Rockman 1984, 210–211), an ability to seek information, to be both curious and skeptical (as Reagan said, "trust but verify"), should be at the center of the presidency. Presidents who come to 1600 Pennsylvania Avenue without a clear sense of where they want to lead the nation (e.g., Bush 41) will be at a distinct disadvantage. Having what Bush 41 called the "vision thing" is also important. It is not enough to lead. One must know where to lead. Too much vision, however, impairs one from seeing things as they really are. And it is vital for leaders to be attached to the Reality Principle. Presidents who lack inquisitiveness may find their options and their legacies held hostage to others in their administrations.

There is little doubt that the presidency can be a hard challenge, though conditions clearly vary for different presidents. The implications of Neustadt's argument are that wise presidents don't paint themselves into corners. Avoiding doing so requires shrewdness and judgment. Those qualities may save presidents. Perhaps more important, they may save us.

References

Andrews, William G. 1975. "The Presidency, Congress, and Constitutional Theory." In Norman C. Thomas (ed.), *The Presidency in Contemporary Context.* New York: Dodd, Mead.

Burns, James McGregor. 1978. *Leadership.* New York: Harper & Row.

Jacobs, Lawrence R., and Robert Y. Shapiro. 2000. *Politicians Don't Pander: Political Manipulation and the Loss of Democratic Responsiveness.* Chicago: University of Chicago Press.

Machiavelli, Nicolo (Tr. Luigi Ricci). 1999. *The Prince.* New York: Signet Classics.

Moe, Terry M. 1985. "The Politicized Presidency." In John E. Chubb and Paul E. Peterson (Eds.), *The New Direction in American Politics.* Washington: The Brookings Institution.

———. 1995. "The Politics of Structural Choice." In Oliver E. Williamson (Ed.), *Organization Theory: From Chester Barnard to the Present.* New York: Oxford University Press.

Neustadt, Richard E. 1990. *Presidential Power and the Modern Presidents: The Politics of Leadership from Roosevelt to Reagan.* New York: The Free Press.

Rockman, Bert A. 1984. *The Leadership Question: The Presidency and the American System.* New York: Praeger.

———. 2004. "Presidential Leadership in an Era of Party Polarization—The George W. Bush Presidency." In Colin Campbell and Bert A. Rockman (Eds.), *The George W. Bush Presidency: Appraisals and Prospects.* Washington: CQ Press.

Rose, Richard. 1993. "Evaluating Presidents." In George C. Edwards III, John H. Kessel, and Bert A. Rockman (Eds.), *Researching the Presidency: Vital Questions, New Approaches.* Pittsburgh: University of Pittsburgh Press.

Ruin, Olof (Tr. Michael Metcalf). 1990. *Tage Erlander: Serving the Welfare State, 1946–1969.* Pittsburgh: University of Pittsburgh Press.

Weber, Max (Ed. Talcott Parsons). 1964. *The Theory of Social and Economic Organization.* New York: The Free Press of Glencoe.

Wildavsky, Aaron. 2005. *Moses as Political Leader.* Jerusalem: Shalem Press. ✦

Chapter 14

Two Normative Models of Presidential Leadership

Bert A. Rockman and Richard W. Waterman

Scholars note that presidents face a series of excessive and unrealistic public expectations. Presidents face an uphill battle in providing effective leadership on a wide variety of issues. For example, they must deal with conflicting public attitudes in the fields of domestic and foreign affairs. As a result, many presidents face diminished public approval ratings, an increased threat to reelection success, and increased probability of failed presidencies. While this is a dominant theme in the presidential literature, concomitantly, presidential scholars also note that presidents have too much power, and that through a series of newly developed "unilateral" powers an "imperial presidency" has been established. This powerful presidency threatens our civil liberties and our democratic form of government. Both of these normative models are prevalent in the presidential literature, yet there are obvious inconsistencies between them. In particular, how can the presidency simultaneously be both too weak and too powerful? In this chapter we attempt to reconcile these two normative models using the various chapters from this book as the basis for our analysis. We argue that an essential finding from many of the chapters in this book is that presidents require political "leverage" in order to lead. When leverage is not available through traditional constitutional means, presidents have sought out new political resources that can extend their influence. In so doing, the limitations of the presidential office, as exemplified by the weak presidency model, provide an inducement for the development of new and more aggressive leadership techniques. As a result, the presidency is transitioning from its constitutional foundations and toward a stronger "imperial presidency."

✦ ✦ ✦

A synthesis of the literature on presidential power plausibly boils down to two starkly simple cases. They contain diametrically opposite conclusions about the state of the presidency. We refer to them as Case A and Case B.

CASE A: The presidential office is weak and individual presidents are doomed to failure. The office has limited constitutional authority, and while presidents may try to lead through persuasion or other techniques, they have few tangible resources at their disposal to promote effective presidential leadership. As a result, we face a "doomed presidency" characterized by a procession of failed presidents. Only rarely should we expect to see evidence of presidential greatness or presidential success.

CASE B: The presidential office is too powerful. An "imperial presidency" has been established whereby presidents can and regularly do defy the law when they believe it is in the nation's interest (or in some cases, when they believe it is in their own narrow personal political self-interest). This imperial presidency is unaccountable and threatens the very existence of our basic constitutional freedoms. In the long term, it also threatens the framework of American democracy.

Which of these cases best describes the state of the contemporary American presidency? If we are to believe what most close observers of the presidency currently think about the office (including journalists, Washington pundits, politicians, the public, and many presidential scholars) the answer appears to be both! Widely different published and televised accounts reveal that presidents both lack the necessary authority to satisfy basic public expectations of presidential leadership (CASE A)—that is, they cannot provide effective leadership on such important issues as the economy—and yet also possess dangerous, excessive, and even dictatorial power (CASE B).

To illustrate this point, let's take a look at how President George W. Bush was portrayed by the media in the summer of 2006. News accounts indicated that he lacked popular support (his poll ratings had fallen into the 30 percent range). While he continued to attempt to build bridges with his base, polls indicated that even support among his strongest partisans, including members of the Christian Coalition, had diminished. As a result of this declining popular support, he was unable to secure legislative support from his own Republican party on such key issues as Social Security, tax, and immigration reform. When he issued his first veto, of a bill that would have provided an expansion of stem cell research, he broke with the leadership of his own party. With the economy also showing signs of slowing down, he had little leverage on the economic front, other than calling for additional tax cuts, threatening to increase the deficit (which he had promised to reduce). His leverage in international affairs also was declining, as the war in Iraq turned into a stalemate and even showed signs of devolving into an open civil war. This view of the Bush presidency is consistent with CASE A. By these accounts, widely publicized in the media, George W. Bush was not able to satisfy public expectations in foreign or domestic affairs, and therefore paid the price in terms of diminished leadership capacity. Speculation therefore was rampant as to whether the nation could endure three years of a lame duck Bush presidency.

But there is a second installment to media coverage of the very same Bush presidency. The press also noted that George W. Bush used signing statements to essentially ignore the will of Congress by declaring that he would not implement or enforce certain legislative provisions. He also created military tribunals that provide him with near dictatorial powers. Numerous reports on domestic surveillance activities raised the specter of a tangible threat to the nation's civil liberties, and noted that these actions would set precedents for the further accretion of presidential power. In short, the Bush presidency was portrayed as out of control and contributing to the expansion of an unaccountable imperial presidency (see Rudalevige 2005).

As the Bush example indicates, the presidency and individual presidents often are portrayed in contradictory ways. For example, according to the "imperial" or omnipotent presidency theory, presidents can act unilaterally in a wide range of policy areas, but particularly in the realm of foreign affairs. They can issue a broad series of executive orders and use other unilateral techniques to affect the behavior of the bureaucracy or to set policy without consulting Congress. These actions are dangerous because they are not constrained by constitutional provision and often occur outside of the purview of congressional oversight or the media spotlight.

Contrarily, according to the excessive expectations or weak presidency theory, if presidents have influence at all it occurs only during limited periods of time, such as a crisis situation or early in a president's first term, during the so-called honeymoon period. Even in the latter case, however, presidents may not have the skill or knowledge to take full advantage of this political opportunity (Light 1983). For most of their terms in office, then, they must react to events, rather than lead them.

In short, listening to the pundits or reading the vast and growing presidential literature can easily give the impression that we have a bipolar presidency—one that is both too powerful and yet not powerful enough. Obviously, in order to better understand the contemporary American presidency we need to reconcile these divergent models. That will be the goal of this final chapter.

Presidential Leadership and Presidents

Generally speaking, the presidential literature has examined issues largely from a perspective that focuses on short time periods, with a particular emphasis on the period of the so-called modern presidency. It is not uncommon for scholars to focus attention on one or at most two successive presidencies at a time. Hence, during the 1970s, following the presidencies of Nixon and Johnson, many scholars noted that the presidency was out of control and cautioned against what Schlesinger (1973) famously called the "imperial presidency." The remedy was to constrain presidential power and to make it more accountable to other constitutional actors. By the late 1970s and following the perceived failures of the Ford and Carter presidencies, the focus changed again. Buchanan (1978) and other scholars noted that the job of president was too big for any one man. The idea soon evolved that the presidency was, as Lowi (1985) proclaimed, doomed to failure, because public expectations of presidential performance simply were out of step with the realities of presidential power. While the Reagan presidency temporarily raised hopes that a strong, rhetorically gifted president could provide necessary leadership, the Iran-Contra scandal dashed these hopes, again promoting a pessimistic view of the presidential office.

Thus two contradictory normative models came to dominate the presidential literature. While one normative framework searched for stronger presidents, the other sought a more accountable and constrained presidency. Obviously, it is difficult to reconcile these two models. How can both be simultaneously appropriate when they essentially represent polar opposites on a continuum of presidential power and leadership? Yet since both themes permeate the discussion of the current state of the American presidency some attempt to reconcile them is required.

In an attempt to do so we will apply the findings from the various chapters described in this book. Throughout this book the subject of presidential leadership has been examined from various perspectives using numerous analytical frameworks including rational choice, empirical, and normative approaches. The goal has been to develop a better understanding of what presidential leadership entails. To this purpose the book has addressed such questions as (1) what is meant by the term presidential leadership; (2) under which circumstances is presidential leadership most likely to succeed (that is, produce results consistent with the president's policy preferences); (3) what are the impediments to effective presidential leadership; (4) how does leadership depend on the individual attributes (style, skill) that presidents bring with them to the office; and (5) how do the office of president itself and its decisionmaking structures promote presidential leadership? In sum, we are interested in better understanding the multiple factors that both contribute to and impede presidential leadership. These factors should also help us to better understand the state of the contemporary American presidency.

In particular, a key finding spans several chapters of this book: the idea that presidents depend on leverage to succeed. In this final chapter we discuss how the concept of leverage may provide a basis for reconciling what at first appear to be two widely divergent normative models of presidential leadership.

Expectations: The Presidency Is Not Strong Enough

As noted, one dominant normative theme that runs throughout the presidential literature is the idea that the public expects too much from its presidents. As presidential scholar Richard Neustadt (1980, 7) presciently writes, the public believes that "the man inside the White House [can] do something about everything." In fact, a "major political trend of our time is the growth in public expectations of the presidency and the expanding scope of presidential action" (Seligman and Baer 1969, 18). Today, when the public demands governmental action it looks first to the president for leadership. In particular, as Louis Brownlow (1969, 35, 43) one of the main engineers of the Executive Office of the President wrote, the public expects the chief executive to be "a competent manager of the machinery of government; . . . a skilled engineer of the economy of the nation, . . . [and] a faithful representative of the opinion of the people." In addition, in time of war the public also expects the president as commander-in-chief "to lead us to victory."

Unfortunately for presidents, while our expectations may be admirable they also are excessive and unrealistic. For example, when the public simultaneously demands increases in defense spending and balanced budgets its expectations are unreasonable. Under such circumstances, as Brownlow (1969, 35) stated, "The nation expects more of the President than he can possibly do; more than we give him either the authority or the means to do. Thus, expecting from him the impossible, inevitably we shall be disappointed in his performance."

For example, presidents have limited ability to influence the economy. They are often spectators to events in other countries (reactive rather than proactive). Crime rates and many other issues actually depend on political activity at the state or local level. Other problems, such as cleaning up the environment, can only be dealt with incrementally and may also depend on the participation of a variety of other policy actors including private businesses and environmental groups, the level of public demand for services and goods, and the dictates of bureaucracies of state, local, special district, and county governments. Even other countries and international organizations are generally involved. The president, then, is but one player. On other issues, such as morality, presidents can set an example, but morality is often an issue that lies in the eye of the beholder. Hence, discussion of morality also can divide the electorate. In sum, excessive expectations can place such extensive demands on presidents that by any reasonable standard it is unlikely that they can satisfy them.

Given the challenge that an expectations gap presents, is there evidence that excessive public expectations actually exist? Empirical studies indicate that the public does have lofty expectations (see Stimson 1976, 1976/1977; Edwards 1983; Waterman, Jenkins-Smith, and Silva 1999; Jenkins-Smith, Silva, and Waterman 2005). Though these studies do not support the idea that excessive public expectations guarantee a failed presidency, they do show that expectations are related to lower poll ratings and an increased possibility that the incumbent will not be reelected (both of which are hypothesized by the expectations gap thesis).

One prescription for this dilemma is to lower public expectations, though how this can be done is not clear. When Jimmy Carter tried to convince the American public that it needed to sacrifice in order to meet the challenges of the energy crisis of the 1970s he was widely ridiculed and subsequently defeated in his reelection bid. Similarly, when George H. W. Bush tried to convince the public that little governmental action was required to deal with a relatively mild recession, his poll ratings collapsed in 1991 and 1992. He was subsequently defeated, as well. Pundits charged both presidents with being out of touch politically and few subsequent presidents sought to copy their model of presidential leadership.

If presidents cannot lower expectations, what then can they do? A second way of thinking about the expectations gap is the idea that presidents lack the necessary political resources to satisfy ever-increasing public demands for action. In other words, they lack what several contributors to this book have referred to as political *leverage*. As Terry Moe (1985) persuasively argues, because the public expects so much from its presidents, presidents themselves are constantly seeking to develop new institutional resources that will help them to promote their influence. This new institutionalized presidency is but one manifestation of a presidential attempt to increase leverage in the face of excessive expectations.

The President and Congress

To illustrate this point let us examine one key nexus of presidential leadership: presidential-congressional relations. One of, if not the, key works in this regard is Richard Neustadt's classic book *Presidential Power*, which in 1960 enunciated a bargaining model of presidential leadership. As Dickinson writes in Chapter 12 of this volume, and as Neustadt well understood,

> Presidents operate in a system of separated institutions sharing power, and therefore they must bargain to exercise influence. Regardless of

changing intellectual fashions, then, presidency scholars continue to recognize the significance of Neustadt's bargaining paradigm to their own research agenda. Barring fundamental change to the Constitution and the authority structures that are derived from it, the bargaining model will likely remain the key to understanding presidential leadership for the foreseeable future. (p. 302)

Still, as Dickinson notes, politically speaking much has changed since Neustadt first articulated his bargaining model in 1960. In this regard Dickinson notes, "Neustadt's work is best understood as presenting a series of hypotheses to be tested, elaborated, and, if necessary, refined" (301). Many of the works in this current volume do precisely that by at least implicitly beginning with Neustadt and then addressing presidential-congressional relations using various methodological approaches. Three chapters in particular are dedicated specifically to presidential-congressional relations and each comes to a similar conclusion regarding the future of this relationship: presidential success ultimately is dependent on political leverage, which is at the fulcrum of presidential leadership of the legislative branch.

Consequently, in Chapter 8 of this book Fleisher, Bond, and Wood note,

> Presidency scholars claim that presidential success is a function of both skill and political conditions. Although students of presidential-congressional relations have been unable to demonstrate convincingly that presidential activities systematically affect success, the literature provides substantial theory and evidence regarding the political conditions that determine presidential success in Congress.[1] (p. 209)

Their findings with regard to political conditions are most relevant here. They note,

> Our finding of significant interactions of party polarization with public approval and majority control is noteworthy. Party control sets the basic condition for presidential success, and presidents do somewhat better in their honeymoon year. The marginal effect of public opinion on success is conditioned by the level of partisanship in Congress. At low levels of partisanship, the president's standing with the public has a modest positive effect on success. But at high levels of partisanship, which have characterized Congress in recent decades, the marginal effect of public approval diminishes (and even turns negative in the House). Party polarization also interacts with party control, enhancing the benefit of majority status. (p. 210)

The authors then conclude,

> . . . polarized parties further reduce the ability of presidential activities to affect success even at the margins. In polarized periods, electoral processes reduce the number of moderate and crosspressured members, the very members who are most inclined to search beyond the primary cues of party and ideology for guidance in making decisions.

> Fewer members who look beyond party and ideology means fewer mem-
> bers subject to presidential persuasion. This condition places a high pre-
> mium on having majorities in the House and Senate. Unless the level of
> partisanship in Congress declines, a rational strategy for a president
> who seeks to improve his legislative success is to focus on maintaining
> or winning partisan majorities in the House and Senate. (p. 210)

To restate the matter, increased party polarization reduces the
number of members of Congress that presidents can reasonably expect to negotiate or bargain with—that is, polarization provides presidents with less leverage over Congress and its deliberations. How
can presidents increase their leverage? They can work to elect more
members from their party to Congress, but the evidence here is that
presidential coattails have diminished in recent decades (see Jacobson 1990). It also is unlikely that they can decrease the level of political polarization, since this phenomenon appears to be related to
systemic political factors that transcend the presidency. Consequently, one can argue that presidential success with Congress depends on how much leverage presidents possess. Unfortunately, the
amount of presidential leverage has been declining in recent decades.
This does not mean that presidents are inattentive to the opportunities for action.

Cameron and Park in Chapter 3 also examine the contingent nature of presidential leadership with Congress. Using data on the president's legislative program they show that:

> presidents appear to respond in a sensible way to their legislative op-
> portunities. In particular, presidents expand their legislative program
> when large-scale congressional action appears likely, as if they were
> trying to shape that legislation by preemptively proffering bills. They
> contract the legislative program when policy windows close, the public
> mutes its demands for legislation, and Congress is distracted by an im-
> pending election. (p. 76)

In other words, as Cameron (2000) did with his enunciation of a rational choice model of "veto bargaining," Cameron and Park demonstrate that presidents act strategically within the limitations of the
leverage that is available to them. When circumstances provide them
with greater leverage they are more likely to be proactive. Presidential leadership is therefore "contingent" on political circumstances.

In Chapter 4, Epstein, Kristensen, and O'Halloran make a somewhat similar argument. Their theory of "conditional presidential
leadership" again examines the circumstances under which presidents can be expected to be most successful. Their theory predicts
that authority delegated from the legislative to the executive branch
"will be greatest under conditions of high gridlock and unified government" (102). But their prognosis is consistent with a more limited
view of presidential power over time. They write,

Gone are the days when presidents could act unilaterally on issues of great domestic importance. . . . And only occasionally can they induce spates of new legislative activism on the scale of the New Deal. Rather, executive power is now obtained through delegation from the legislative branch, and presidential leadership manifests itself on the president's ability to wring such concessions out of the hands of jealous legislative leaders. (p. 102)

Again leverage is key to any positive action. They note,

presidential leadership seems to accrue on a schedule more attuned to the interbranch and intrabranch distribution of preferences, rather than the traditional defined presidential bargaining ability. In particular, it is when Congress is most disunited, and when the president comes from the same party as the legislative majority, that authority is passed to executive hands. Presidents can lead, but just like the king who consulted with his royal astonomers before ordering the sun to rise exactly at 6:22 a.m., the time has to be right. (p. 102)

While the authors of the three chapters do not agree on all points, a similar logic emerges—presidents can only be expected to lead Congress when certain characteristics are present. Otherwise, presidents are prisoners of the amount of leverage they possess. It is not surprising, then, that presidents would be interested in expanding the leverage that is available to them, often in creative ways.

For example, in Chapter 5, Howell and Kriner discuss the unilateral powers of the presidency. They note that presidents have developed a wide range of unilateral powers including executive orders, presidential proclamations, presidential signing statements, and national security directives. As Howell and Kriner demonstrate, while presidents can't ignore the need to bargain with Congress, it is no longer the only game in town. In particular, "Through executive orders, military orders, and rules, President [George W.] Bush, along with all modern presidents, has managed to materially redirect public policy in ways not possible in a strictly legislative setting, using only those powers enumerated in the Constitution" (133).

Howell's (2003) path-breaking book systematically examined the expanded use of presidential executive orders. It is therefore worth keeping in mind as Howell and Kriner do in Chapter 5 of this book that while "the president's unilateral powers yield genuine influence over public policy . . . [this] does not mean that the president necessarily gets everything he might want" (133). Still, the fact that the president and his advisors can craft executive orders without congressional participation or sanction is a significant agenda-setting tool. It is also important to note that the

    . . . burden of checking presidential power ultimately lies with Congress and the courts. And if recent political history is any indication of future trends, presidents will have continued reason to rely upon uni-

lateral directives to advance their policy agenda. As majority parties retain control of the House and Senate by the slimmest of margins, as
multiple veto points and collective action problems litter the legislative
process with opportunities for failure, and as members of Congress
and judges remain reticent to take on the president during times of
war, abundant opportunities and incentives for presidents to exercise
their unilateral powers remain. To be sure, presidents must proceed
with caution, scaling back some initiatives and abandoning others altogether, especially when political opposition is strong and mobilized. Directives that immediately affect the electoral prospects of key members
of Congress, or that deeply offend basic constitutional provisions, are
likely to provoke some kind of legislative or judicial response, which
may in turn redefine the boundaries of presidential power. But in an
era where political gridlock is commonplace and judicial deference the
norm, presidents can be expected to regularly strike out on their own.
And if [George W.] Bush's presidency teaches us anything at all, it reveals the extent to which unilateral powers can influence the production of foreign and domestic policy. (pp. 134–135)

Here we reframe Howell's argument in a slightly different way. We
hypothesize that as the leverage available to presidents in their relations with Congress decreases, presidents have greater incentives to
develop and employ various unilateral powers. Hence, if it is more
difficult for presidents to negotiate treaties with Congress, they can
turn to executive agreements that presidents can negotiate unilaterally with other nations, and that have the same legal effects as treaties. Likewise, if presidents cannot control the type of legislation that
Congress enacts they can either veto a larger number of bills (which
puts them on the defensive) or they can make greater use of presidential signing statements (PSS). A May 5, 2006 *New York Times* editorial
(A24) noted that George W. Bush had to that date issued over 750
presidential signing statements "declaring he wouldn't do what the
law required." The editorial noted, "Perhaps the most infamous was
the one in which he stated that he did not really feel bound by the
Congressional ban on the torture of prisoners." While noting that
other presidents had used this technique, devised during the Reagan
administration by Edwin Meese III, the editorial concluded "none
have used it so clearly to make the president the interpreter of a law's
intent, instead of Congress, and the arbiter of the constitutionality,
instead of the courts." The editorial then referred to it as one of
Bush's "imperial excesses."

While one can certainly question the legitimacy of the greater use
of executive orders (especially for policy purposes), executive agreements, national security directives, and presidential signing statements, they all have one key idea in common. Each represents a new
source of presidential leverage in its dealings with the legislative
branch (as does the less constitutionally suspect use of veto-bargaining).
In short, presidents are seeking out new leverage precisely as many

scholars note that their ability to lead congress is conditional, contingent, and constrained. If presidents cannot satisfy expectations for action (by playing the game as it is presently devised), then they will seek out new ways to gain advantage. Thus, for presidents who want to succeed in spite of often excessive public and elite expectations, these new sources of leverage must indeed be of considerable interest.

Alternatives to the Unilateral Presidency

Presidents could of course develop other alternatives to the controversial set of unilateral powers Howell describes. But here the presidential literature, including many of the chapters in this book, provides us with further insight about the difficulty of developing alternative sources of political leverage. Presidents could take the approach recommended by Kernell (1997), and attempt to go over the heads of elected officials directly to the public. Certainly, presidents such as Ronald Reagan and Bill Clinton have used this approach. But is it systematically viable? According to Edwards in Chapter 6 and Cohen in Chapter 7, the empirical evidence suggests it is not. As Edwards notes,

> Building coalitions for governing among the public and within Congress poses a considerable challenge for the president. The very nature of public opinion and the institutional structure of the presidency (and Congress) pose an imposing set of impediments to presidential leadership. The reality of the president's predicament is that no matter how skilled the White House may be, the president is unlikely to be consistently successful in leading either the public or Congress. Only the presence of contextual conditions that encourage deference to the president, such as occurred in Franklin D. Roosevelt's first term, are likely to provide the president the opportunity to dominate the policymaking process. (p. 165)

And such contextual conditions are not likely to occur with any regularity. Therefore, to succeed either Congress must be predisposed to the president's proposals, or the president must be successful at persuading the public to support his program. The former is unlikely for reasons discussed earlier in this section (e.g., a greater propensity toward polarization). The latter is unlikely because the

> final link in the chain of communications from the president to the public is a weak one. The president must overcome the predispositions of his audience if he is to change their minds about his policies or his performance. This is very difficult to do. Most people ignore or reject arguments contrary to their predispositions. Nor can the president depend on those predisposed toward him to be especially responsive or to resist national trends opposed to his positions. (p. 165)

Why is the public so inattentive? Cohen provides one explanation when he writes,

> presidents have increasing difficulty even getting the news media to pay attention to them, as the declines in news content indicate. And even when presidents make the front page and nightly news broadcasts, stories are more likely to be about scandals and less likely to be about policymaking than was the case several decades ago. Moreover, when the president wants to address the nation on primetime, the networks have been increasingly likely to deny his request, and sometimes when access is granted, only one of the networks will broadcast the presidential address. The lack of news attention by average citizens adds to the barrier between the president and the public. (p. 186)

Thus, while it is tempting to suggest that presidents can turn to the public, as Kernell recommends, the empirical evidence suggests that this may not be an effective alternative. If so, then presidents have even greater incentives to develop and utilize unilateral powers.

In this regard, beyond dealing with Congress, presidents also have developed new unilateral techniques at the bureaucratic level to facilitate the implementation of presidential preferences. For example, as Fine and Waterman discuss in Chapter 2, presidents have used a wide range of techniques derived from the "administrative presidency" strategy (see Nathan 1983) in an attempt to secure greater control of the bureaucracy. Presidents have developed a wide range of potential sources of leverage. Again, as Howell warns, not all of these attempts have been successful. Lewis writes in Chapter 10 that there are political risks to using the institutional presidency in lieu of the bureaucracy.

> All presidents want their staffs, both continuing institutional staff and transient president-specific staff, to be loyal to the president and expert. The institutional structure the president inherits, however, does not always provide the president with loyal and expert staff. When parts of the institutional presidency do not have the president's interests in mind because staffs are self-serving, view the world differently than the president, or misunderstand the president's interests, this can jeopardize presidential efforts to lead. When staff are hard to manage and monitor, the chances the staff will stray from the president's preferences and hamper rather than help presidential leadership increases. Similarly, when staff are ill-equipped for the job they have been given it is harder for presidents to lead. Once these staff problems cross a threshold defined partly by the cost of action, presidents act to alter the institutional presidency. They add White House personnel, politicize the institutional presidency, or reorganize. (p. 255)

The greater use of the institutionalized presidency also can have long-term deleterious effects. As Lewis continues,

The net effect of presidential changes every four to eight years is a thickening of hierarchy in both the White House and the agencies of the institutional presidency. The repeated interactions of presidents and the continuing institution also produce a relatively deep penetration of political appointments in the institutional presidency relative to the departments and bureaus of the executive branch. Gradual thickening and increasing politicization are followed by regular episodes of reorganization to rationalize bureaucratic structure, cut hierarchy, and reconstruct low-capacity institutions. (p. 255)

Since there are negative repercussions to the development of these new techniques, why then do presidents adopt them? Lewis provides an insightful answer.

Presidents have a short time horizon determined by elections and a two-term limit on service. All presidents confront an existing institution but few think holistically about the performance of the institution or how the institution will suit future presidents. They are more concerned about their immediate political needs. As a consequence, the evolution of the institutional presidency is not the product of self-conscious forward-looking design. On the contrary, it is produced in response to regular short-term political pressures that produce predictable variation in structure and design but a variation that mitigates against performance advantages stemming from stable, professional, staffing characterized by a long-term perspective. (p. 256)

Unanticipated Long-Term Consequences and the Imperial Presidency

Lewis suggests that presidents are motivated by short-term political considerations. They therefore are interested in developing leverage that can help them to prevail in the short term. While they may consider potential threats to their authority or alternatively the valuable accretions of presidential power they will leave to future presidents, their primary motivation is to increase their ability to succeed politically; that is, to achieve a preferred policy outcome. Hence, generally they are not persuaded by constitutional arguments, even when ideologically they would seem to have a common predisposition with those constitutional views.[2]

There is an irony in all of this. For instance, George W. Bush has long condemned judicial activism and called for a strict constructionist interpretation of the Constitution. Yet, constitutionally speaking, if we adopt a strict constructionist interpretation—and consider the Founders' "original intent"—the presidency is an office of limited power. It is clear that the Founders decided to invest greater power in the legislative branch than in the executive. Yet, it also can be argued that the constitutional relationship that existed in 1787 was more conducive to American political life (and world affairs) as it existed at that time. Specifically we can ask, does the presidency today require more power and active presidential leadership than the Founders intended? Most of us would answer yes, even emphatically so, though many would vehemently disagree with precisely how much power the presidency should possess. Consequently, when we move beyond the Founders' original vision it is not clear what the appropriate boundaries are for presidential power. What is clear is that an essentially new presidency has been created since 1787, one that the Founders would not recognize if they were alive today, and one that they might even fear.

Normatively speaking, no clear boundary can be drawn that provides the nation with the potential benefit that it requires from a strong presidency while also protecting the nation from the risks presented by presidential power. While accountability is desired, there is no mechanism other than the imperfect sanction of impeachment that can guarantee its implementation. Instead, in normative terms we are left to struggle between two political views, one of which often places security first and constitutional protections second. As Schlesinger (1973) notes in his classic book (see also Berger 1974; Rudalevige 2005), real dangers are posed by an imperial presidency. Yet there may be no obvious alternatives. The idea that we can put the genie of presidential power back in the bottle is unrealistic. We therefore are left with the potential that the presidential office can lead to abuses of power, such as those that occurred with the various Watergate-related scandals of the Nixon presidency and the Iran-Contra scandals of the Reagan administration. Abuses are inherent with strong executive leadership.

The alternative would be to develop a presidency that is not powerful enough, and is thus susceptible to an expectations gap. This is an alternative that most presidents confront on a daily basis. They must try to figure out how to get their programs enacted by Congress, how to satisfy public demands for action even when those demands are contradictory, how to mollify competing factions in the Middle East, and so on. As a result, developing new sources of leverage is of primary political importance. But with additional unilateral leverage can come a concomitant potential for abuses of power.

It is this intersection between the short-term development of new leverage mechanisms designed to satisfy public expectations and their possible long-term repercussions that provides the bridge between the two normative models that we introduced at the beginning of this chapter. Excessive expectations encourage presidents to develop new leverage mechanisms. In so doing they are motivated by short-term political gains. The end result, however, is often the construction of a new, powerful, and "imperial" presidency. By design or accident, then, power continues to accrue to the executive, and unless the legislative branch or the courts actively seek to redress this situation, the trend will continue.[3]

Does It All Come Back to Neustadt?

While unilateral power therefore does provide presidents with the potential for awesome power (at least in the short term), particularly in foreign affairs, there also is a very real potential for a political backlash should scandal or policy failure prevail. While Congress thus far has been passive in the face of the development of such powers, there have been some faint signs that the legislature's patience is beginning to wear thin, particularly in the wake of the 2006 midterm elections, with the return of Democratic control over both the House and the Senate. Even with Republican George W. Bush in the White House, many members of his party in the House and the Senate complained that they had not been given a vital role in policy development. (Such sentiments are hardly new. They also go back to the Nixon era, long before the days of Watergate, when Republican members of Congress felt themselves unheeded and disrespected by the Nixon White House.) A few mavericks opposed key issues on President Bush's political agenda, such as rewriting the Geneva Convention rules on torture. While there is no sign at present that Congress will eventually openly rebel against the development of the president's unilateral powers, there does appear to be at least the hint that there are limits to how far presidents can go in this direction, even in foreign affairs.

This is particularly the case when the use of unilateral power results in a policy failure. With the war in Iraq going poorly, by 2007 the Bush administration's strategy and leadership approach was called into question. Policymakers in both political parties asked if the administration had listened to all of the relevant evidence before making its decision to go to war. Had the president anticipated an insurgency or adequately planned for the postwar phase of the conflict? Negative answers to these questions encouraged critics to postulate that the president was living in a bubble controlled by a select few neoconservatives, and thus not receiving the full intelligence benefits offered by the traditional bureaucracy, including the Central Intelligence Agency, the State Department, and the many experts in the Defense Department who had disagreed with the initial war plan. This criticism in turn led to a renewed sense that presidents need to rely on what can be called *intelligent leadership* (as Rockman discusses in Chapter 13). Intelligent leadership requires a president to carefully sift through the evidence, skeptically analyzing it, and then use careful self-discipline when making policy choices. In so doing, presidents need to be open to all points of view, reaching out for information rather than excluding it. This is a point that Neustadt (1960/1980) stresses when he argues that presidents must be careful when they use their power. Presidential power is finite and presidents who act impulsively, whether through unilateral means or otherwise, will discover their power sources have diminished. Thus, as Neustadt wrote in 1960, the intelligent use of power is essential to the use and preservation of presidential power. Consequently, while presidents since Neustadt's time have made greater use of unilateral power, it can be argued that they are gaining benefits primarily in the short term, but not necessarily in the long term, as Lewis suggests in Chapter 10.

If so, there is another dynamic involved in the development of unilateral power; Neustadt's bargaining model and his prescriptions for presidential power remain relevant today, almost 50 years after his seminal book was written. There is a difference, however. Edward Corwin (1984) wrote that there is an "invitation to struggle" between the president and Congress. One can now argue that we have a new "invitation to struggle" between presidents' constitutional powers and their unilateral ones. If so, then while Moe (1985) may be correct that presidents secure influence by accentuating "responsive competence," developments over time also show that presidents risk their political influence, as well, when they rely only on loyal advisers. Likewise, unilateral powers may promise greater power and influence, but also entail inherent political risks. Thus, we postulate that for the foreseeable future, the new "invitation to struggle" will be a theme that will dominate the attention of both presidents and presidential scholars. It also will have important implications for the future of American democracy.

Notes

1. For a discussion in this book of the role of skill and its relationship to the presidency, see Fine and Waterman, Chapter 2; Greenstein, Chapter 11; Waterman's addendum to Chapter 11; and Rockman, Chapter 13.

2. Maltzman's argument in Chapter 9 of this book also raises this same issue. One can ask, is the nation better off with a politicized or nonpoliticized judiciary? The answer for most of us would be easy: the latter. Yet, as presidents attempt to deal with a series of controversial issues that have found their way to the judicial branch, such as abortion, gay rights, and physician-assisted suicide, the choice of judicial nominations has been increasingly drawn into the political process. Thus, as with other aspects of presidential decisionmaking, choices about the judiciary are being politicized.

3. As Rudalevige (2005) persuasively argues in his book on the new manifestations of the imperial presidency, if it had the political will power

Congress could more effectively counter presidential attempts to shift the balance of power toward the executive. But when it has done so in the past, the legislative branch eventually has backed down. Institutionally, then, the legislative branch seems ill-designed to limit presidential power in the long term.

References

Berger, Raoul. 1974. *Executive Privilege: A Constitutional Myth.* Cambridge, MA: Harvard University Press.

Brownlow, Louis. 1969. "What We Expect the President to Do." In Aaron Wildavsky (Ed.), *The Presidency.* Boston: Little, Brown and Co.

Buchanan, Bruce. 1978. *The Presidential Experience: What the Office Does to the Man.* Englewood Cliffs, NJ: Prentice-Hall.

Cameron, Charles M. 2000. *Veto Bargaining: Presidents and the Politics of Negative Power.* New York: Cambridge University Press.

Corwin, Edward S. 1984. *The President: Office and Powers, 1787–1984.* Randall W. Bland, Theodore T. Hindson, and Jack W. Peltason (Eds.). New York: New York University Press.

Edwards, George C. III. 1983. *The Public Presidency: The Pursuit of Popular Support.* New York: St. Martin's Press.

Howell, William G. 2003. *Power Without Persuasion: The Politics of Direct Presidential Action.* Princeton: Princeton University Press.

Jacobson, Gary C. 1990. *The Electoral Origins of Divided Government: Competition in U.S. House Elections, 1946–1988.* Boulder, CO: Westview Press.

Jenkins-Smith, Hank C., Carol L. Silva, and Richard W. Waterman. 2005. "Micro and Macro Models of the Presidential Expectations Gap." *Journal of Politics* 67 (August):690–715.

Kernell, Samuel. 1997. *Going Public: New Strategies of Presidential Leadership.* Washington, DC: Congressional Quarterly Press.

Light, Paul C. 1983. *The President's Agenda: Domestic Policy Choice From Kennedy to Carter.* Baltimore: John Hopkins University Press.

Lowi, Theodore J. 1985. *The Personal Presidency: Power Invested Promise Unfulfilled.* Ithaca, NY: Cornell University Press.

Moe, Terry M. 1985. "The Politicized Presidency." In John E. Chubb and Paul E. Peterson (Eds.), *New Directions in American Politics,* 235–71. Washington, DC: Brookings Institution.

Nathan, Richard P. 1983. *The Administrative Presidency.* New York: John Wiley and Sons.

Neustadt, Richard E. 1960/1980. *Presidential Power: The Politics of Leadership from FDR to Carter.* New York: John Wiley and Sons.

Rudalevige, Andrew. 2005. *The New Imperial Presidency: Renewing Presidential Power After Watergate.* Ann Arbor: University of Michigan Press.

Schlesinger, Arthur Jr. 1973. *The Imperial Presidency.* Boston: Houghton Mifflin.

Seligman, Lester G., and Michael A. Baer. 1969. "Expectations of Presidential Leadership and Decision-Making." In Aaron Wildavsky (Ed.), *The Presidency.* Boston: Little, Brown and Co.

Stimson, James A. 1976. "Public Support for American Presidents: A Cyclical Model." *Public Opinion Quarterly* 40 (Spring):1–21.

———. 1976/1977. "On Disillusionment With the Expectation/Disillusion Theory: A Rejoinder." *Public Opinion Quarterly* 40 (Winter):541–43.

Waterman, Richard W., Hank C. Jenkins-Smith, and Carol L. Silva. 1999. "The Expectations Gap Thesis: Public Attitudes Toward an Incumbent President." *Journal of Politics* 61 (November):944–66. ✦

What psychoanalysis presents as its knowledge is accompanied by a kind of intellectual and emotional terrorism that is suitable for breaking down resistances that are said to be unhealthy. It is already disturbing when this operation is carried out between psychoanalysts, or between psychoanalysts and patients, for a certified therapeutic goal. But it is much more disturbing when the same operation seeks to break down resistances of a completely different kind, in a teaching section that declares itself to have no intention of "looking after" or "training" psychoanalysts. A veritable unconscious blackmail is directed against opponents, under the prestige and in the presence of Dr. Lacan, in order to impose his decisions without any possibility of discussion. (Take it or leave it, and if you leave it, "the disappearance of the department would be imperative, from the point of view of analytic theory as well as from that of the university . . . " — *disappearance decided on by whom? in whose name?*). All terrorism is accompanied by purifications: unconscious washing does not seem any less terrible and authoritarian than brainwashing.

13

Endurance and the Profession

(1978)

It has become an enviable rarity these days to obtain a salary in exchange for the kind of discourse that is commonly called philosophy. As the twentieth century draws to a close, the statesmen and families who run the French secondary school system seem to want to have nothing to do with it. For according to the spirit of the times, which is theirs, to do is to produce— that is, to reproduce with a surplus value. Those who teach philosophy are thus condemned to decimation or worse, while those who have studied remain unemployed or give themselves up as hostages to other professions. Here, we will turn our attention to a minor but unexpected consequence: despite the adverse pressures in the socioprofessional context, and at a time when the philosophy department at Vincennes (University of Paris VII) has been stripped of its right to grant those degrees and research diplomas that it is a university department's duty to issue, the rate of attendance in philosophy courses has, little by little, been on the rise.

Why do they come? One day you asked this question solemnly during class. They told you it was their business, not yours.

A public institution of higher learning is by law an organ by which a nation ensures the education of its children. The state is the guardian of such institutions. When the state removes all credibility from the department of philosophy at Vincennes, one expects it to die out. But the nation's children—grown-up children at that, and even foreigners—persist in attending the courses in large numbers. Would you conclude that the mere existence of this department refutes the ideas of the state and of its educational guardians?

You enter; they are waiting for you. You have nothing in particular, nothing set to say, which is the general condition of philosophical discourse. But here, in addition, you have no long- or short-range aim set by an institutional function (to prepare degrees, monitor competitions, follow programs and syllabi, and keep track of things through examinations). There you are, given over to indeterminate requirements. (You are generally a few readings ahead of them, but in any case readings done with the frightful and shameful disorder of the philosopher).

Does this mean that each teacher in your department speaks of what he or she likes? — No, it means that no one is protected, and above all in his or her own eyes, by prescribed rules. And all must give their names to what they say, without pleading necessity; and all, like stutterers, must head toward what they want in order to say it. — You're exaggerating. — Don't forget they wait for you every week; and without telling you what they're expecting. — All the same, you know what you are driving at . . . — for the day's session, yes, very precisely; for example, demonstrating the machinery of an "antistrephon" put in the mouth of Protagoras by Diogenes Laertius. — So, you really did have an idea in the back of your mind!

Is it an idea, this strength of weakness that, from year to year, makes you believe that with the analysis of this or that fragment of Diels and Kranz, and with many others like it, some in the discernible framework of the week's thought, others at the horizon, for later on, two months, a semester from now, eventually you'll succeed?

— Succeed at what? at holding on for another year? — It's not to be laughed at. You're in free-fall in the atmosphere and it's a matter of not landing too hard. So you're crafty, you stall. So, this slowdown, due to an institutional void, which is the opposite of the feverishness experienced by a teacher anxious to cover course work in a limited time, creates or presupposes a soft and gentle "tempo." — That of research? — No, you've known researchers in the exact sciences. Their rhythm is one of athletic, economic, bureaucratic competition. More like the rhythm of study. But not of studies. Studies are something you work at, you pursue. In these classes, study goes along in its own way. You announce that you will study Thucydides, and three years later you still haven't begun.

— But yet, you, too, want something. — When one was younger, one might have wanted to please, or help, or lead by argument or revelation. Now, it's all over. You no longer know exactly what's wanted. How can you make others understand what you haven't really understood? But when the course works out well, you also know that since you made them understand what you didn't, it didn't really work out. The anguish, when you enter the classroom, especially at the beginning of the year, is not the stage fright of the actor or the orator (although it can be), the feeling of claustrophobia (all of us will burn in here), or the predicament of not knowing everything (rather reassuring). It is the sovereign pressure of an imbecilic "you must go there," which does not say where.

Just two years ago, this or that leftist commando was bursting in, denouncing the magisterial function, the star system, alienation, apathy; cutting the electricity; raising his clubs; locking up the teacher awhile; and abusing the students. In their eyes, our palaver, our readings, our affectations are gimmicks at best, and at worst treasons; for them, it's a state of war, an emergency. To ponder a metalepsis in the narration of book 9 of *The Laws* is not futile, it's criminal. They know where to go.

We used to fight a bit. Only once did it lead to something worthwhile. It was on the day of an active strike. What could we do? At the time we were working on the operators in persuasive discourse, making use of Plato's dialogues and Aristotle's *Rhetoric* and *Sophistic Refutation*. We subjected the statements relative to the strike to the same analysis. Once again we were speaking of Platonic pragmatics. Enter the commando unit armed with clubs, shouting that we were breaking the strike. A fight starts, quickly followed by palavers between the two groups, the besiegers and the besieged. The latter argue as follows: on the one hand, our "normal" activity is to study persuasive discourse, especially political discourse. On the other hand, to participate in an active strike is to occupy the workplace and to think together about the discourses that persuade or dissuade us from striking. The difference between these two activities is not distinguishable. You demand that it be, and you think it could be if we used certain words (*exploitation, alienation* . . .), a certain syntax ("it is not by chance that . . . "), certain names (Marx . . .). Question: In your eyes, how many Marxes per sentence would it take for our discourse to become one of active strikers? Most of the assailants backed off, admitting that we were as much "out of it" as they were.

The rhythm of work in progress seems tentative and peaceful. But on the occasion of each of these pointless classes, it becomes asceticism, impatience, and fear. You get up well before dawn and tell yourself that this particular part of the current work has to be done for tonight—for example, express the temporal logic of Protagoras's antistrephon before midnight—because the day after tomorrow you must explain it to those who are waiting for you. By looking straight at them, and not at your notes. And, as you aren't protected by an institution, make them furthermore understand that it's opportune or bearable to speak about such things.

So you sit down at your desk, and nothing has ever assured you that, by midnight, you will have understood. What if you didn't understand? Or what if it were to take longer than expected? What if you were extremely tired? Or what if you entertained the idea that, after all, who gives a damn about the antistrephon of Protagoras or another? Or else, what if you got your hands on a good Italian or American article supplying the interpretation you had imagined yourself giving?

In this last case, you're happy, you'll be able to do your course with this article. But at the same time, you're annoyed: there's something you have received and transmitted without transformation, without being transformed by it. This isn't work. You put it off till next week. What are you thus putting off? Confrontation, challenge, and the judgment of God. This is why you can wade through the antistrepha; I mean, dabble around them for six months. Audiences are surprising.

Sometimes you allow yourself to think that your working notes keep accumulating, you're making progress. But, with age, you know the opposite is true, that you hoard waste, scraps, that the thing to be thought slips away from you, as in interminable evasions and metastases.

As for making this mortification the substance of what you have to say, this seems henceforth a paltry resource. For such a solution proceeds only from your memory, allowing you to compare what you wanted to obtain with what you hold, and not from your imagination, which is indifferent to your grasp of anything. Moreover, here, amnesia rules. So much so that it is not even true that anything "slips away." Don't be satisfied with this shoddy pessimism. There's nothing to compare.

A few books are written this way out of the weekly rumination. There was a horizon sketched, uncertain. You have made headway here and there for two, three, four years. Sometimes bits of analyses are already published as articles. Nevertheless, you collect all of those attempts and you publish them as a book. Producing such a book means only one thing: that you're fed up with this approach, this horizon, this tone, these readings. Of course, the notes and even the parts already written don't exempt you from writing the book; that is, from rethinking almost everything. But you do it to get it over with. What makes you happy, gives you the sense of well-being you have with the book, is that you'll be done with the work. Whereas teaching is as endless as study itself.

But in order to finish and thus write the book, you must reach a certain satisfaction with what you thought, or believed you thought. And this is so to speak a grace momentarily granted, and you're truly unfortunate if you don't jump to exploit it. But also unfortunate if it stays with you.

The media have the truly unintelligible habit of making you speak about your latest book. How do you convince the *mediators* that, obviously, you wrote it to be done with it, and that once done, it really is finished? They believe it is false modesty. And they say they're doing you a favor. You become proud, you forget about this sort of publicity, you rely on another kind of distribution, osmosis or capillary action. After a little while, you no longer have a choice.

You aren't cut out for thinking; you're a philosopher. You believe it's not natural to think. You are envious of—but after all you disdain—your colleagues and friends who work in the human sciences, who seem to be in symbiosis with their work, who have a corpus, a method, a bibliography, a strategy, exchanges. That's what makes you different even from those close to you, like historians of philosophy, whom you admire nonetheless. You like what is unfinished. Nothing of what you write will be authoritative. You lend yourself willingly to this prescription: "to go there, without knowing there." You're certain that nobody can do it, least of all yourself. You know you're doing what you're not cut out to do. You're an imposter. You hate all this. Little by little you cease to draw any vanity from it. And this department at Vincennes, if it is pleasant, it is because its total lack of aims and imposed airs lends itself to suprisingly few bursts of vanity: imposters cannot be convicted here, the masks hold, and so does honor. You don't edit a journal, you're not a school.

The media and the worldly wise smile in vain at your humility, insinuating that many paths lead to importance, and that to vegetate in your prefab bungalow in "the sticks" is one way to acquire it — but you know this isn't true. In better established professorships you become tempted to say what should be thought. Here, in Vincennes, this infatuation is not protected.

This doesn't at all prevent this pitiful state of affairs from trading on its misery and catching the eye of a few cynics. You fight it, eliminating from your discourse most connotations, making yourself, if possible, even more temperate and meticulous. For example, you give up the metaphysical euphoria of energies and convert to logic, especially that of prescriptives, severe and fastidious. Now, this dissuades a few cynics from staying, but not the most cynical.

— They would have a certain function in your economy, as long as they also force you incessantly to take a new line. And after all, how do you know what their cynicism is all about?

Taking a new line: the metaphor is reassuring. What is behind you isn't more certain than what you are facing; in fact, it's more uncertain. To go beyond is an idea that makes you smile. What has been studied energetically for a year, two years, ten years you've let lie fallow. Study doesn't order it; it disorders. They tell you to keep your cool.

Which you wouldn't be doing if you believed that what you have to do is name the unnameable, say the unsayable, conceive the unconceivable, pronounce the unpronounceable, or decide the undecidable — and this is what it means to philosophize. You leave these poses to others.

Of course you speak of what you don't comprehend. But it doesn't necessarily follow that it's incomprehensible. You read and give your course to see if others, by chance, might have understood. The idea of a mission fades away.

They ask questions. So sometimes questions are posed, and sometimes people are only posing as they question. You're caught between your duty to listen and be patient and your right to impatience. Others write to you, point to references, share thoughts—and question. A few are or will be your mentors.

You try for two kinds of understanding: first, that which permits you to situate the antistrephon of Protagoras within the writing of temporal logic tomorrow. A strong understanding, and ultimately useless. The other is totally different: to learn obscurely, after months and years of study, why this bizarre verbal argument interested you. You first included it within a general examination of ruse, for example, and that had attracted you because you saw it as a weapon against the powerful. We're weak, you used to say as a justification. All this seemed directed toward some political end; you were inspecting the available arsenal. You easily refuted those who judged you as too picky, too slow in moving on toward action. You compared the funeral oration of Overney by Geismar with the one Socrates parodies in *De Sophistis Eleuchis*. You analyzed the jail letters and the declarations of the RÖTE ARMEE FRAKTION [Red Army Fraction], in the file constituted by Klaus Croissant, in the light of the alternative between the nonpedagogical struggle and the Platonic pragmatics of dialogue. The antistrephon found its place naturally in this general strategy and you studied it as such. Now, two and a half years later, you confess the vanity of your Manichaeism. The antistrephon may very well be a weapon at the disposal of the weak; it is also the strength of philosophical discourse, for this latter is made up of reflexive (or speculative) statements of which it is one type. Your general approach to paradoxes is mollified by it, as are your "politics." You say so. Your listeners, especially foreigners from poor countries, believe that with this move you have lost even more pugnacity, that you have become even more of a product of that cold thought and refined style that they call French and that exasperates them. On your side, little by little you stop justifying your interests, your tribulations, giving a good front to your disorder. It can even look like a challenge.

Who's going to follow you if you no longer even say where you want to go? But you take a certain pleasure in this silence. You feel its opacity as an interesting resource against Hegelianism or absolutism in general. You think you're making a contribution, however minute, to the destiny of what you believe philosophy to be: figuring, and not just conceiving. You find yourself in agreement with this department, which is a figure now more than an organ.

The concessions to what you feel is expected become rarer. You'd like to neglect even what your own mind desires, make it accessible to thoughts it doesn't expect. You don't read anymore to strip authors, but to steal away from yourself. You aim at this deculturation in every direction: science fiction, underground cinema, linguistics, and singular logics, monsters of plastic and sound, suprising banalities, oblique rereadings. You are unfaithful in your alliances like the barbarians of Clastres,[1] but for a different reason, opposite at least. You're at war with institutions of your own mind and your own identity. And you know that with all this, you're probably only perpetuating Western philosophy, its laborious libertinage, and its obliging equanimity. At least you also know that the only chance (or mischance) to do so lies in setting philosophy beside itself.

14

Ersiegerungen

(1989)

U. is guiding me.[1] We enter the lounge. S. is in the process of picking up the reins after his absence. You sit attentive, the semester gets going, you greet our arrival by banging on the table with your fist, S. picks up on it. This is not the climate of a much more ostensibly self-governing American seminar.

I come here with the assurance that we will speak freely about everything, like last year. But what everything? Everything that is attached to the name of Germany for a French philosopher of my age: a language, a way of being and thinking, acquired as well as can be expected as a child, through Schiller, Heine, Rilke, as an adolescent through Hofmannsthal and Storm; spat out, interrupted by the occupying forces; the moan of a young dying soldier, "*Mutter*," on a stretcher in the aid station at the Passage Saint André des Arts, July 1944, Paris; taken up again as a dead language from Husserl, Marx (1844 manuscripts, '44 once again, my twenties), from Hegel, Freud, Frege, Nietzsche, later Kant, Wittgenstein, Heidegger, Adorno. Throughout my life, Germans on my bedside table.

The anguish of your impossible identity come to nurture my melancholy and retard its resolution, behind the mask of the brave bicentennial citizen.

Is it always your anguish? Have you forgotten everything? Become excellent students? Honest Lutherans or Catholics? Accomplished postmoderns? Can you share this ridiculous pain that I believe comes to me from you?

It is, after all, your affair. Are you telling me to mind my own business? I feel myself burdened by a concern, burdening you with a presumption, both too European. My excuse for this sentimental Europe is that political masters, German or French, have both created and devastated it for centuries in order to carry out the program of an empire. The heritage of forced union must be worked out, and a horizon of thought drawn from it.

This intention substantiates, in my eyes, though you know nothing of it, my concern, my pain, and my presence. I come with my "jewish question." To make it understood that it is the question that must not be forgotten, after your Third Reich, which forced Europe to forget this question. And with this question, to forget one of the secrets, perhaps the most secluded secret, *abgeschieden*, of Europe's thought.

I come with my weakness or my lack of proper thought, with an endemic historicism, with the presumption to diagnose my time. My times, for the age puts time in the plural. Diagnostics puts it in the past. I always diagnose "postsomethings," stupidly: postwar, post-Marxism, and postrevolution, post-1968, postmodernism. Thus revealing the stubborn persistence of a single sickness, that of diagnosing.

My unconscious whispers to me that there ought to be an incommensurability between a young German student and an old philosopher "à la française." The misunderstanding ought to be as inevitable as that between an old man and a young girl. Will it nevertheless be possible to touch you? And for you to touch me? I look at you, impenetrable.

I announce the program of the seminar: to supplement *Le différend* in terms of space, time, and the body. A university gesture that I love, in which the sobriety of the enunciation of a problem placates the anxiety from which it is born.

An opportunity, I add a little more pathetically, to critique the rampant communicationalist ideology, aesthetics, the problematic of representation, the politics of forgetting. Four large sessions, then. We'll begin around two or three in the afternoon, we'll find ourselves ending at eleven at night. Without counting the interminable discussions at the Rimini.

It will have pleased you, it seems to me, to see that I did not know what I was talking about; that I "felt" my way along, firm on some points, as when a blind person assures himself of the identity of an object with his hands, uncertain about the others. We wander across questions and answers, in the three languages (S. adds a little Spanish). We pose reference points. I will have taught you only one thing, that there is no method in the first place. You are kindly told: that is called thinking.

The role of English between you and me. The neuter. The guarantee that no one is gaining the advantage by using his mother tongue. I speak it much worse than most of you. That wonderfully undermines a position of authority. You take charge of me as of a debutante.

We are making sand castles of thoughts together. I think it was Schiller who wrote that nothing is more serious than the game. But not every game is serious. If it were serious, one would find that out later on, perhaps. You keep an eye on each other, like children making sure that the others play by the rules. When one of you lets himself go too far in the direction of parody or pathos, the brows are knit, you give questioning looks, bothered.

S. untiring *Sprecher*. Picks up on my argument every time, displays, fixes, and transcribes it into points to be questioned. Your big brother, my younger brother.

Not a second of boredom during these sessions. Hours of boredom during the ecology conference. I dispel them to observe an unknown lovely face. During a pause, I go to apologize for my insistence on her. She bears the name of her eyes, Waltraud.

The tables are arranged in an irregular circle. The central space is empty. Sascha, D. B.'s dog, dwelt there peaceably during the interminable ecology discussion. Smiles, giggles, looks, heads tilted or raised circulate swiftly from one side to the other, weave the tense network of the things left unsaid.

Do you form a group other than by virtue of S.'s presence? Is your relation anything other than functional? I catch signs of particular affinity between some of you. But I can't be sure. Our lengthy association, in the course of which the most serious questions are engaged, will remain within the bounds of tact.

Sometimes you are loquacious, vehement: W., M. Cheerful and sad: R. As lively in questioning as an American student: K. Passing wicked notes, slid down tables, like an Italian: O. Reserved and direct: V. Somber and slow: B. Scatterbrained: F. After forty years of teaching, I feel a real pleasure at a time when I believed myself to be insensible to the ritual and the habits of school. And the smooth eyes of I., a wall of lapis lazuli.[2]

And in general, the fact that you are Germans surprises me.
   I find you to be the kind of Germans that frighten me at the time of the clumsy final ceremony. (For the reader: they had the idea of putting a crown of laurels on my head on the last day.) Of course, the Greek student was given the task of anointing. It was the act of a great naked affection (I'm trying to play upon your *Akt*). You laughed. I was touched by the awkwardness [*maladresse*] of the testimony: poorly addressed [*mal adressé*]. You knew it, I knew it. It was funny because it was sad. But it's difficult to say

what kind of sadness this was. We were going to leave one another, we were touched, had we understood each other? We refrained from being too serious and too funny.

You know, one thing comes back to me, evident today, essential — your absence of toadying. And its opposite, the absence of aggressiveness. Rarities in the teacher-student relation. At least I did not have any sense of either. Even in the car heading for the return (or departing) flight, R. and K. make me give yet another small talk, informally, on the question of sexual difference. You had the virtue of occasionally setting my thought in order, by questioning, objecting, resisting, documenting. Isaac's *Akeda* kept on giving us food for thought, thanks to R.

You called me "philosopher, the philosopher." It was ironic. Germany is filled with philosophers, as always. But most of you were not philosophers. And as for me, I am not one in the German sense, you know (Sch. in Apel's seminar in Bad Homburg: how do you expect us to believe that you are philosophers, you write!)

We must (we, French "philosophers") play a double game in Germany, in the United States, in Italy, everywhere where we run up against the disciplinary structure established by the constitution of the University of Berlin at the beginning of the last century, which has been adopted almost everywhere.

The *Kolleg* follows a completely different model, like the American humanities centers, where the "disciplines" cross, confront one another, make each other undisciplined. In the same way as, in a context different from that of Berlin, the Polytechnic Institute of Philosophy at the University of Paris VIII, and especially the International College of Philosophy.

To sum up, it is only in this frayed and rewoven tissue, wherever it may have been found, Penelope-like, that we have been able to "teach" — I mean: reflect publicly in common. In this dump where the thoughts of each are transplanted and placed side by side right on the table of thought. To institute, or quasi institute, this rather vague place is to give it a name that authority can tolerate, to offer credits, to become able to grant degrees, and to prove that it can train acceptable graduates, indeed more-than-acceptable ones.

It is a place that remains suspect, under surveillance, surrounded by prejudices, hostility. It has to be defended, and in order to defend it, it has to be constantly criticized. This critique forms part of the objects of discussion and debate in this place. Quite evident in the *Kolleg*. The institution of the *Kollege* contains the critique of its institution within itself. It is never safe from a summary administrative decision nor from accusations of superficiality, of a late-sixties mentality, of demagogy, of media small talk. Nonetheless, in this dump, rich or poor according to the country or the moment, the question is posed and has to be posed of what thought requires to find its place and an occasion today. How could it do without not only the philosophical tradition, of course, but also the question of its unconscious, of what mocks thought in literary, artistic, and scientific work, in political and religious institutions, in contemporary internationalism? We dream of a collegial network of European colleges.

"The philosopher" did not come to teach you philosophy (impossible, says Kant), he came to make what he believed he had thought bend under the requirements of other regimes of thought. *Exerciti*: we tested ourselves.

N. L., hardly loquacious, calculating his words with his Baudelairian elegance (which is much more than a systematic strategy), knows this kind of complexity. He wants to simplify a different kind of complexity. And he can only do it at the cost of a supplement of differentiation. It is this apparent "aporia," assumed with calm and tact, that I liked most in his thought, from which I am in a sense so distant. It was possible for us to form a small common front against the waves of ecologist eloquence. A two-sided front. There is no nature, no *Umwelt*, external to the system, he explained. And I added: of course, but there remains an *oikos*, the secret sharer [*hôte*] to which each singularity is hostage.

There remains a remainder. I called it *unbehandlich*(?), intractable. No, I said it more pathetically, *abgeschieden*.

It was a good thing to use guerrilla tactics against both ecologist phraseology and communicationalist ideology (with its often scatterbrained desire to restore the *Öffentlichkeit*),[3] it was a good thing to recall the *Unheimliche*.[4]

Siegen must represent more or less what happens to a *Heim* (the generic mode of being of Germans [in my prejudice]) when it is subjected to development. The church and its large village perched on a hillside, the highways crossing around it, businesses, industries, and offices flanking the valley road that has become the main street with its rush hours, traffic lights, and so forth. Double sadness, that of a culture of the land and that of a culture of communication [*messagerie*], the former asphyxiated by narrowness of spirit, the second by vacuity (the medium is the message).[5]

We, *Kollegiaten*, lodged on the opposite hill, are contented by nothing. It is what we call culture, this well-meaning nastiness. The result is that Siegen isn't sad.

One or two Sundays, we wander in the hills and the landscaped forests, we enter into the hostels full of humans come from secondary culture to re-immerse themselves in primary culture. We view all of this — the large sterile lands of Westphalia or the Westerwald, the *Holzwege*, and the soups, the beers — with the eye of the third culture. This frightens me a little. One might say that they dwell in the village as if it were part of the culture of communications, and, especially, the culture of communications as if it were a village. But this isn't true. They come on vacation to the *pagus*, and not to be *at home*,[6] on the margins of the *Heim*, in order to take in the air of the indeterminate. What difference, after all, from the visitors to Joshua Tree National Park in California? A single, terrible one. An American is always an immigrant, without *Heim*.

The Europe that we built at Siegen, briefly and to some extent, will only be made in Europe if its nationals emigrate right where they are. Become indeterminate. *Kollegiaten*, we were certainly not good villagers, and we did not want to be the talented messengers that the megalopolis claims for its own. We tried to work through our moments of rootlessness.

**Part III
Big Brothers**

15

Born in 1925

(1948)

No one knows whether this youth of ours is a youth. Any definition scatters it, revolts it, makes it laugh. We are on Radiguet's side, with nuances. We engage in a sustained refusal to be whatever isn't us—and to qualify this "we." However, let's be honest, we should not eliminate the part of this generation that gives itself over to parties, to dogmatisms. Questioning is not our common denominator. We have our indifferent elements, our submissive or our ambitious ones. Those whom maturity wins over. One would run out of breath trying to define what we are. Let's not suffocate.

Still a qualification is possible: we were fifteen in 1940. For a Czech, that meant clandestine action; for a German, *Gott mit uns*; for a French person, introversion. In any case, there is only a problem, at this moment, within the limits of Europe. Once again "European youth" is awake. The war and subsequent events have taught us that our own awareness must go hand in hand with historical consciousness: our only aesthetes are aggressive ones, and humanism has become a political attitude. Certain values have found themselves committed to battle, above all committed to the justification of that battle. Hence their swift degradation. We come out of the twentieth century's most concrete achievement, the war, in a state of monstrous poverty. We were twenty when the camps vomited into our laps those whom there had not been time or energy to digest. These hollow faces plague our reflections: in the camps Europe put its liberalism to death, killed three or four centuries of Greco-Latin tradition. The world is amazed. Secretly the shock spreads, and, when Gandhi's murder exposed the collapse of our raison d'être to a light made dazzling by our bitterness, we were twenty-three years old.

Thus we thought we were old. We are satisfied with a philosophy of the absurd: logically there is no beyond, and we love the easy cruelty of logic. This philosophy marks out our closed horizons, our ports without ships, our ships without moorings, a world where there are no more deserts to cross and no more virgin forests to ravish. We are chaste in our ventures. But this philosophy nevertheless teaches us that since nothing has been given to us, everything remains to be done. The absurd negates itself; a door is only closed to someone who claims to open it. This door was broken down by the war, the Resistance, and then the war again in such a way that the twenty-three-year-old activists, if they are clear-sighted, know that they are ineffective. Action is cut off from its purpose, an enterprise devoid of ambition; but engagement and action are worthwhile in themselves. In parallel fashion, art abandons figure, representation drowns the represented, and Raphael bores us. The object undergoes the same process of breakdown as had the field of concrete actions and undertakings. Surrealist expression has made us used to works whose very meaning is given over to chance as the summit of human freedom. *L'amour fou* is so optimistic.

Even so, this freedom overwhelms us. "Innocence beyond repair," says Camus. It is not young. It is as old as war or, more precisely, as old as postwar periods. But its crushing strength is surprising. The other postwar period had the Russian Revolution, Freud, surrealism. The bonds of traditional academism were broken by the institution of economic, moral, and artistic forms that not only questioned ways of living, interpreting, or acting, but also directly provoked innovative work. Now, for our part, we have not laid waste what our predecessors held dear; those attachments have simply died out. Nietzsche makes us ashamed: Europe is not overthrowing its values but suffering its fate. We became intelligent just in time to see communism decline into orthodoxy. And existential philosophy gives us, perhaps for the first time, a humanism that is resolutely pessimistic. (Black) humor is the last resort by which we can affirm ourselves against the world, and even it is complicitous. From *Conquérants* to *The Plague*, revolt becomes anemic, it internalizes itself. Despite appearances, this is not a Renaissance, for we have not broken out of slavery and rejected a faith, we have merely been present at the death throes of liberalism and freedom. We are entering into (a) middle age.

The so-called civilization of progress has just completed its own negation. First, the monuments of order collapse. The alienation that lies at the origin of our republic in the repression practiced from Versailles was first underscored by anarchist attacks. It had already given rise to surrealist scandals and been the target of the Communist International. In 1944–45, many called the (French) democratic regime into question. The minor reforms that were made served as poor camouflage for its failure, and the present crisis of this regime is a matter of public opinion. Europe no longer knows how it should behave, and therefore cannot understand itself. In 1918 Germany alone knew how to grasp the meaning of its chaos, and nazism, the hard line of capitalism, germinated from the horror of this chaos. The Germans, incapable of creating their own freedom, were susceptible to a destiny (to a

style). We failed to interpret this instinct of theirs: despair underlies all totalitarian systems. And it is in Germany that the industrial tradition comes
to fruition; the camps show us where the exploitation of humanity leads
when taken to the limit. The history of the nineteenth and early twentieth
centuries had combined a certain liberalism in trade and speculative thought
with a positivism that led to the disappearance of people into economics.
Our generation lived in the slow undermining or the catastrophic breakup
of both liberalism and positivism.

The second great movement, originating with Rimbaud, has also lost its
truth. The interwar period had its crisis of language, which was a crisis of
expression in the widest sense. Our generation has its own as well. There
might seem to be little difference here, were it not that we make nothing of
our crisis of language. *Lettrisme*[1] is mistaken, at any rate, in its claim to be
pursuing the objectives of surrealist explosivity. Firstly because (Breton is
right about this) there is no way to think of a beyond to surrealism. After
surrealism, you have to do *something else*. Secondly because: is this really
what we need? Today Jarry is stuck at *L'univers concentrationnaire*. Of
course, he is attempting to develop its meaning fully, but he is also emptying
it of meaning, if Jarry has created a scandal, and if that scandal is now no
longer an issue. After the recent conflict, revolt is now cut off from its occasion and its source, cut off from the possible. This is certainly the most
serious crisis in expression for some time: expression is no longer able to
surpass its material, no longer knows how to assign a "beyond" to the event.
The best novel of this period is a book devoid of dreams, *Les jours de notre
mort*. There is no longer any delirium that can live up to our tidy violence.
Chance and arbitrariness have entered our everyday life along with horror,
and often it is no longer desire that produces surreality, but remorse. One
might even say that Lautréamont's icy lyricism brought on the world of the
SS: the poets of the interwar period, who sought to kill the poet by revealing
the magic at the heart of the act or the object in themselves, seem to have
rediscovered the old soothsayer's privilege, perhaps too heavy, of foretelling
the future and of calling forth being through their speech. The most concrete
examples were Breton and Malraux, prophets. Speaking often takes on this
power at the dawn and the twilight of civilizations.

A sequence has begun. Expression has not found its proper measure,
since the century has already taken the measure of a new excess on the part
of humanity, an excessive cruelty. An Inquisition without any theological
pretext, this cruelty has been nakedly revealed, devoid of any justification,
with a disturbing beauty. Now it lies behind us, and we do not know what is
going to happen to us. What is new about this generation is its unconquer-
able appetite for the concrete. Poetry does not get much of an audience
among us, the adventure of the *Nourritures terrestres* makes us smile, Gide

will be the Bibliothèque Verte[2] of our sons, while we find T. E. Lawrence more persuasive than Mallarmé because we prefer the object of discourse (we are ripe for the detective novel). A radical breach with our elders: the world, which they told us was at human disposition, hardens in its hostile thickness. We have lost the fundamental complacency of all earlier undertakings whatsoever. On Bikini the earth split in two; the earth gave off a mushroom of dense smoke, like a belch. We were the only ones to laugh, while the adults said, keeping an eye on the health of the guinea pigs: "Reason will end up being right." Gradually, we betray (but do I still have the right to use this collective pronoun?), we desert the party of humanity for the party of things (for the *parti pris des choses*).[3] Rimbaud ("If I have any taste, it's only for earth and for stones"), Van Gogh, Braque, Ponge, T. E. Lawrence writing to Curtis, "If the world had belonged to me, I would have banished animal life from it," are so many permissions requested by "our common desire to exist in the manner of the in-itself."[4] The triumphant revolt that founded our humanist civilization on the dispersal of medieval consciousness is transfigured into desertion. We are reenacting a transition in the opposite direction, and just as Roman representation reduces the solitude of humanity in the interests of its complicity with matter, so we begin to no longer give ourselves priority over a universe in which our face and our indifference are sketched out.

Man's dream has been exiled from the city of man. How distant seems the claim to be master and possessor of nature! The forest eats our dwellings, thinking animal substance briefly grabs the machine man, adults cry freedom in order to give themselves courage. But who among those born in 1925 would not rather have been born a tree?

Of course, it's time to come clean; I am speaking of a certain kind of youth, so-called intellectual youth. It is nothing new if "young persons" of the bourgeoisie feel themselves situated out of joint with the movement of the world. What is somewhat new is that the consciousness of what we are, and especially the consciousness of what we are not, has come upon us more and more decisively. This is because, at the time when we were young people of fifteen or sixteen with our own enigmas to explain or escape, history forced us to pay attention to its problems. Now, at our present age, the age at which these same youths are primarily concerned to return to their class alignments, history once more evokes our distaste for compromises with oneself. Our isolation is the product of our malaise, our desire to look clearly at our belonging to the century. And, since all truth is reversible, our malaise is the product of isolation. This false situation occurs under a thousand different forms. The temptation or the attempt to make a break is among the more valid of these. Adventure, setting aside all passion, still passes as a means of giving oneself a reason to live. Many run to the political parties. And so on. In short, we are in a state of dispersal, with the decay of the speculative and a desire for the concrete as our common denominator, especially in the political sphere.

This dispersal occurs in all perspectives. In art, great painters are no longer those who possess skill, but those who have something to say, and who have skill to back them up. African art, Central Asian objects, and Roman frescoes prefer being and doing to technique. Picasso returns to his sources, and Klee, who could have been anything, chooses to be Klee. Heidegger, in philosophy, reconsiders all thought since Aristotle and observes that it has incessantly avoided the question of being: thus poetry presents itself as the means by which being reveals itself immediately. Hölderlin, or silence, crushes Valéry quite dead.

In thirty years we will have found a meaning for this empiricism, and reconstructed a civilization. But we will have lived in the interregnum.

We still have to make do with the provisional, to take threats of war into account, to think of ourselves without a future. For some this is easy, for many it is disturbing. Here individuals decide and consent only in their own good time. At least, among my class a young bourgeois is someone who, after a fairly general questioning of self and others, gives himself or herself answers in terms of "difference." We are tired of being obliged to represent a situation we did not create. We don't even have the hope anymore that what we stand for is a situation that remains to be created. They have killed our notion of humanity, it is said. Let's be consistent: we don't give a damn for tradition. And let's choose an extravagant personal adventure.

16

A Podium without a Podium: Television according to J.-F. Lyotard

(1978)

[The following is the text for a television program prepared by Lyotard as part of an access series entitled "Tribune Libre" on the French channel FR3 on March 27, 1978.[1] Responding to an invitation to appear as an intellectual, Lyotard employs a strict division between voice and appearance. Except for one moment, the sound track is not synchronized with the image of Lyotard's mouth. After an initial voice-over without an image of Lyotard, the sound track is out of sync with the speaking mouth that appears to produce it but doesn't. In the text, I have marked these instances as "voice-over," "sound track out of sync," and "synchronized sound track."—Trans.]

J. C. Courdy: Good evening. As usual on Mondays, here is our intellectual, Jean-François Lyotard.

Jean-François Lyotard is professor of philosophy at the University of Vincennes, but a rather unusual professor.

In effect, he begins by observing himself in order to observe others. From 1950, he has broken with the ideology of the French Communist party in undertaking a critique of bureaucracy. For twelve years he participated in a group of intellectuals and workers who aimed at developing the revolutionary critique of society. Author of numerous works, he identifies a fraying of discourse, the exhaustion of sociological discourses, in his most recent book, *Rudiments païens*. In *Rudiments païens*, he observes that societies seem able to function independently of all political, economic, and ideological discourses. Tonight, Jean-François Lyotard has been brought before you to critique his own discourse and to ask himself questions concerning his presence among us on television this evening.

Jean-François Lyotard (voice-over): You are going to see him; you are going to hear him. You do not know who he is . . . he's an intellectual, he has written several books that are attempts to philosophize. You have seen them, you see them now, you do not recognize them . . . You didn't ask him to speak this evening. You think that he must have friends at FR3; if he has any, they are unknown to him. The truth is even simpler than that. The producer of "Tribune Libre" thought he should give intellectuals some space on this program.

(*Lyotard, sound track out of sync*) The questions you should ask Lyotard and the others, the questions that he perhaps asks himself, are these: Why is he allowed to speak in these conditions? What is expected of him . . . ? If he were famous, his appearance would obviously be of benefit to the program. . . . But he isn't famous. Does someone want to do him a favor by giving him a chance to become well-known? Certainly, and he thanks the program's producer for it.

Yet, can he make something known by speaking for a quarter of an hour one evening in front of a camera . . . maybe his face, take a good look . . . maybe also his name, but that's less likely . . . and what is least likely is that he will make known what he believes he has to say, since that has already taken him one or two thousand written pages and several years (he is not young), so that it should be impossible for him to say all that in fifteen minutes.

I bet that he won't tell you anything about what he does. He doesn't just write books, he is professor of philosophy at the University of Vincennes; hence he does philosophy. No one has ever been quite sure what that consists of.

When one does medicine or politics, when one is a toolmaker, train driver, shopkeeper, one does something that performs a service for others . . . These are jobs; they have an obvious social utility; no one asks these professions to justify their existence—quite the contrary. People trust politicians, doctors, train drivers, because they know that these professionals know more . . . than the client or the user about what has to be done to make things work . . . in their own field.

Now, when one does philosophy, one asks oneself what it means to know that it works . . . and what it means to know what has to be done to make things work.

For example, what is a social, political, economic, or cultural body that works . . . and how do we know when it works? For example, does a body work when it doesn't make any noise, when there is no agitation, although this silence is perhaps that of oppression . . . ? Does it work when everyone feels safe? But how can one know that security is the ideal . . . for a social body, rather than adventure, resourcefulness, or abnegation? And besides, how can we know what must be done to reach a goal like silence or security . . . ?

What constitutes health does not seem any more obvious in medicine than in politics. Does health consist in not feeling one's body at all . . . ? And that is fainting or even death . . . A human being always feels its body. So, on the basis of what kind or intensity of bodily sensations should a human be called sick and be prescribed treatment in order to cure him or her . . . ?

Another example: When can you say that the work of a worker on an automatic lathe works? When it meets the productivity targets established by the technicians and controlled by chronometers?

But then, how do these technicians know what is good for the work and the worker?

They say that the finished product has to be sold, hence it must be competitive, it must be as cheap as possible, whence the productivity targets . . . But why? Can economic relations between people work well only if they produce and buy the greatest possible number of manufactured products . . . ? And a man and a woman together, what does it mean for them, for each of them and for the two of them together . . . what does it mean to say that things are going well between them?

These are the kinds of questions the philosophers ask themselves, philosophers like the one you are looking at . . .

These are utterly mundane questions. All people ask questions of this kind someday, questions about their work, about the area they live in, about their family, about their love life. . . . Has Lyotard been put on the air for a quarter of an hour just to ask these questions? You really don't need to be a philosopher to ask them . . . But maybe he is expected to answer them. Is he supposed to make a declaration about what constitutes true work, true health, the true society, and the true couple, or at least a declaration of the truth according to him? Maybe he is supposed to give his opinion on these subjects after all . . .

(*Lyotard, synchronized sound track*) We TV watchers have the habit of listening to and looking at masses of people who come onto our screens to give us their opinions, but we distinguish, or at least we believe we can distinguish, between a simple opinion and true expertise . . . When a great surgeon comes to speak to us about a heart transplant, for example, we know very well that he knows what he is talking about and that he is competent to perform it. Well, when I say that we know very well, that's just a phrase . . . Suppose that someone does know that the surgeon knows what he is talking about . . . Were that not the case, he would not be a great surgeon. We don't claim to be able to judge for ourselves in this matter.

(*Lyotard, sound track out of sync*) Really, though, if we are being presented with a philosopher this evening, it is because someone knows that this fellow is going to do more than simply give us an opinion on the question that interests us. If he has been allowed to speak, it is because, basically, someone does know that he knows what he is talking about.

And as in the case of the surgeon, we are not the ones who can tell whether he knows what he is talking about. We have not studied enough. We cannot judge it.

Except that he ought to know that he is learned. In any case, if he has been asked to appear, it's certainly for that reason. And if he is learned, it is precisely because he can answer those questions, that is, what is fair work, what is a good society, what is a perfect couple, and so forth. This is, in effect, what he is expected to do. He is expected to be an authority on these matters . . . because if he is authorized to speak freely for a quarter of an hour to hundreds of thousands of his fellow citizens, it is because he has the authority to do it.

Now, when I said that a philosopher is someone who thinks about the common questions, he reflects particularly and principally on questions of authority. For example, when he asks how the person who determines working practices knows that what he decides is good . . . what does the philosopher do? He ponders the authority of bosses over matters of production. The same thing for health, the same thing for the couple, for the rest: he ponders the authority of the physician, of the psychological counselor, and so on . . .

And, obviously, when he is put in the position of being an authority, as is the case for Lyotard at this moment, he wonders about the authority he is asked to have, and he tells himself that you are in the process of believing that there is indeed someone somewhere who knows that he is competent, because this someone has allowed him to speak . . .

Except that he, because he is a philosopher, knows that this is not the case at all. He knows that this someone cannot know if he, Lyotard, is competent . . . because that would be to say that this someone is himself competent to answer the questions that interest the philosopher—love, work, society, health, and so forth—and that he can thus knowingly judge Lyotard's competence, or that of someone else.

But how can one know that this someone, this second person, is himself competent? Of course, you are going to ask why there shouldn't be a knowledge and an authority on these everyday matters . . . There is indeed a knowledge and an authority, a recognized competence, in scientific and technical matters . . . they are the affair of specialists, very learned folks, and Lyotard himself, when he gives a course at Vincennes, when he writes books, does indeed know more than most of his students or his readers.

I believe he would grant us this last point, but he would have you note that it is one thing to know a question inside and out and another to answer it correctly, which is the essence of knowledge as such.

To admit that competence in scientific and technical matters is not illusory and that scientists, engineers, and technicians really are learned, although at times there is evidence to the contrary, does not prove that the same thing goes for all questions. One can, for example, provide a rigorous demonstration that the just is not an object of knowledge and that there is no science of justice.[2]

One can show the same thing for what is beautiful, or for what is agreeable. Hence there is no true and certain competence and authority in these domains, domains that, however, have a great significance in everyday life. In these domains there are only opinions. And all these opinions have to be discussed . . .

This philosopher thus refuses to appear before your eyes and ears as an authority, as he is asked to do . . . And for the rest, if he has chosen this little mechanism of transmission by which you don't see the one who is speaking and you don't hear the one you see, he has done so in order to destroy the image of authority that inevitably comes to frame itself in your screen, every time it makes you see anything other than fictions, films, or plays . . .

By refusing to offer you this image, he refuses to provide a service. This service is the only one that has always been required of philosophers. Since they do not provide any service to society by virtue of their profession itself, because they lack competence and authority in their field (which, besides, is not even a field because it is in reality made up of the most mundane questions), they can at least be asked to make themselves useful by agreeing to appear learned, to incarnate the authority of knowledge in the eyes of those who do not possess it.

One can ask these philosophers to at least appear learned. But if they accept that, to what do they provide a service, to whom and to what do they provide a service . . . ? Only to those who need to believe that there can be competence and authority in these matters where there isn't any.

For example, in matters of justice, in matters of beauty, of happiness, and perhaps even of truth . . . And does one have to believe in competence and authority in these matters if there isn't any?

Well, that's the big question . . . It's the need to believe in an authority, authority's need to be believed, its need to believe in itself . . . it's a very old affair, it's the affair of politicians or, rather, of political parties. Now this same question is raised by the slightest appearance on television. The presence on the screen of the least little philosopher, of the least little handyman, of the least little employee, of the least little variety show artist, devoid of authority as he may be, contributes and even suffices to give them an authority for a few moments . . .

And you believe that none of it will remain afterward? But the general idea will remain that there are always, in all domains, competent folks who are always those who decided to program what one sees or what one hears and who deserve to have authority.

If philosophers agree to help their fellow citizens to believe in authority in matters where there isn't any, to legitimate this authority, then they cease to ponder in the sense in which I spoke of thinking, and they thereby cease to be philosophers.

They become what one calls intellectuals, that is, persons who legitimate a claimed competence . . . their own, but persons who above all legitimate the very idea that there ought to be competence in everything. And then they all fill the same role, even if some are Catholic and others free thinkers or Marxists, even if some are on the left and others on the right. For a long time, in the West, philosophers have been exposed to the temptation of the role of the intellectual, they have been tempted to turn themselves into the representatives of an authority. And there are not many, since Plato, over the past twenty-five hundred years, who have not succumbed to this temptation. It seems to me that Lyotard would like to belong to this minority; that's what he told me to tell you.

17
Oikos
(1988)

The Dog

I want to begin here by saluting the mistress of us all in matters of ecology, Sascha, Dieter Beisel's dog.[1] She resides wherever Dieter Beisel is. She occupies a voice, an odor, a silhouette, a set of movements: such is the *oikos*. She takes no one to court to safeguard her property. She doesn't need a soil, a blood, or even an apartment; all she needs is to belong, *oikeion*.

The Humanism of War

The necessity of identifying an enemy is not, properly speaking, ecological; it has more to do with the political theology of a Carl Schmitt. It is curious that the need to identify an enemy makes itself felt at the very moment when there is no longer an enemy, in the absence of an alternative to the system. This enemy is identified as the death of *Menschheit* [mankind], and thus the war has to be begun all over again, which is to say we open a trial for war crimes.[2] Thus, a kind of prophetic or pathetic psychosis develops and—as Holger Strohm put it admirably yesterday—as always in psychosis you have to escape from *Verdrängung* [repression], for *Verdrängung* is only neurosis. Therefore you have to attack, organize, defend yourself, and it is on the basis of this mechanism that the very concept of *Grenze* [border] can appear. That said, this is not a diagnosis. *Das ist keine Diagnose*. Only a feeling. *Nur ein Gefühl*. Obviously, technoscientific development is accompanied by dangers. I remember texts written in France in 1840: prophetic, pathetic texts on the pollution caused by the railroads. It can be argued that these dangers proceed from the development of capitalism, and I think that what is generally called "capitalism" greatly exceeds "capitalism" proper. Capitalism is only a socioeconomic name for a process of development of which no one is master. This threat is not new, it is only stronger than it used to be because the system is more improbable, more complex, and more difficult to control. But I hear it said that people want to live in the humanism of war, to live one's life, as Strohm put it, to live without fear, to eliminate fear, that is, to obtain security. I think the enemy is not outside, but within, peculiar to and for each of us. And I would say that in the humanism of war there occurs a projection in the psychoanalytic sense, a projection of this enemy and this interior distress onto an external other, hence an exteriorization or an externalization.

When people say that the media lie, this is not news. The question is to know what it means to say this and how it is that the media lie. Their lies always work in the same direction, so as to produce a feeling of safety, sometimes by recourse to paradox. They work for safety. But the ecologism of war also wants safety, because it wants to eliminate fear. If you ask me, this is probably the reason for its success, particularly in the Federal Republic of Germany.

And yet the *oikos* in the Greek tradition (*domus* in the Latin tradition), is not, and I insist on this, the place of safety. The *oikos* is above all the place of tragedy. I recall that one of the conditions of the tragic enumerated by Aristotle is precisely the domestic condition: relationships are tragic because they occur in the family; it is within the family that incest, patricide, and matricide occur. Tragedy is not possible outside this ecologic or ecotragic framework.

The Grenzen *and the Question of the System*

It is obvious that recourse to the opposition between Man and nature (*Mensch/Natur*) and of course the simultaneous placing of this opposition in a dialectic, particularly in Marx (more precisely in the young Marx whose texts of 1843 and 1844 are quite clear on this point) are habits of speculative thought, notably Hegel's. This opposition of the inside to the outside belongs to a very specific philosophical tradition, namely, that of the metaphysics of the subject: a thinking, perceiving, or speaking subject can carry out its operations only by objectifying what it thinks, perceives, and speaks of in the form of a *Gegenstand* [an objectivity], which comes down to a process of exteriorization or even alienation in the Hegelian sense.

But there is another metaphysical tradition where this opposition is not relevant. It is a philosophy of substance that distinguishes between potential and action, a tradition that originates in the West with Aristotle's stress on energy, on the move to action, on putting into action *energeia*, which is also called "labor" and "technè." This philosophy of substance requires a kind of finality (I set this problem aside), but the opposition between outside and inside is not relevant to it; rather, the opposition between matter and form is what counts.

Now (and now I am going to get to *Systemtheorie*), the thought of Leibniz is an extreme condition of this philosophy, in which the question of outside and inside, that is, of the border between the outside and the inside, is not relevant. Leibniz's thought is thus the extreme state of the metaphysical tradition of the West, and his monadology pushes the suppression of the *Grenze* [border] a very long way because for him, precisely, there is no difference or border between matter or object and thought or subject. There are only different degrees of memory. Consciousness remains matter with a great deal of memory. And at that point, one has already broached the problem of cybernetics. Matter is consciousness with very little memory. That implies that every entity (*alles Seiende*, if you prefer), may be and ought to be thought in mechanical, dynamic, or economic terms, hence in terms of relationships of force and efficiency. A monad or a weak entity is one that does not have much memory and that reacts simply to information, namely, to shock, insofar as it can record it. On the other hand, a very rich monad has the wherewithal to process the information at length before reacting: it can take its time, which is what we are doing now. According to Leibniz, there is thus only a difference in complexity between monads, a difference in storage capacity and the capacity to make use of information.

What Niklas Luhmann calls the "reduction of complexity" is not the suppression of complexity at all, it is what might be called feasibility, the capacity to make use of a complex memory. The complexities of which he speaks are complexities of use and execution, since the memory of complex systems is a complex memory. With contemporary technoscientific systems, which have the capacity to address mental operations (even if only very simple ones), humanity (or at least the part of humanity that is called "developed") may be and should be thought of as a rich monad endowed with a more and more complex memory. This memory ought to make the information it stores useful. We should carefully analyze the effects of this situation on what we call "memory," on intelligence, on education, on the economy, and of course also on discourse and its nature. In any case, it is certain that the single principle of optimal performance predominates everywhere, optimal performance that consists in contributing to the development of this great monad in which humanity is caught.

This monadology was still a philosophical system that presupposed a finality, particularly that of a benevolent God ensuring the harmony of the whole. However, systems theory is not a philosophical system but a description of reality, "a so-called reality" ["die sogenannte Wirklichkeit"] that has become entirely describable in terms of general physics, which stretches from astrophysics to particle physics (electronics, information technology, and cybernetics are only aspects of this general physics) and of course also in economic terms. In this description, the alive or the human appear as particular cases, very interesting cases of complex material systems. This means that, from this perspective, conflict (and ultimately war) does not arise between human and nature; rather, the struggle is between more developed systems and something else that is necessarily less developed and that the physicists know as entropy, the second principle of thermodynamics. The section of humanity that is not developed can be considered as entropic in relation to the system (and this is already the way it is thought of, particularly by the central banks of the developed countries).

From the point of view of development (which is not mine, but which I can espouse for a moment), the Third World is nothing but a source of entropy for the *autopoesis* of the great monad. And either it will join the system or it will have to be excluded from it. I'm very pessimistic on this point, because I'm afraid that in the race for survival (after the explosion of the sun) the major part of the Third World is already lost.

Oikeion *and Entropy*

It is not the human and the inhuman that are at odds, for no clear-cut border exists between these two terms; the conflict or challenge is between negative entropy, negentropy, or development on the one hand and entropy on the other. On this basis the general hypothesis should be made that humans (I do not say "men," [*les hommes*], I say "humans" [*les humains*], to indicate complex systems capable of autoreferentiality) are only the bearers of and the witnesses to a process of negative entropy that can be located at the planetary level: a tiny little planet, a tiny little earth, in a tiny little system, around a little star, the sun, in a little galaxy. But this process takes no interest in humans; it is only interested in itself. Perhaps this negentropic self-development is related to Luhmann's *autopoesis*.

If one tries to reformulate *oikeion* in terms of *Systemtheorie*, is it the same thing as entropy? Probably it is possible to qualify what I mean by *oikeion* as an entropy, but this is only an external qualification, because it presupposes precisely the general assumption that the system functions according to the law of what I call general physics. If we preserve this metaphor derived from the vocabulary of physics (telling whether it is a metaphor or not is another problem), I have to make a neat distinction between ecology and economy. Probably this difference matches up exactly with the Kantian difference between determinant judgment and reflective judgment. Economy is the *nomos*, that is, the regulation of the circulation of forces and information or messages (I know that these are not the same, but let me put it that way for the moment), it is a question of regulation, that is to say, of the ability to preserve, conserve, store, and use the past, past events, the effects that past events have had on the system or the apparatus, and to use this information in order to adjust for efficiency, optimal performance.

What do we mean by "function"? It is a metaphor from biology or mathematics that designates a rule for operating, nothing more. The economy functions precisely insofar as people and instances observe rules that are something like what is called a "memory" in cybernetics, a sort of set of rules. Engineers distinguish between a living memory and a dead memory: the dead memory consists of stocks of ways of dealing with new information and the living memory is the memory useful for programming certain reactions. That is probably the difference between code and program. I am sure that it is possible to describe current society in terms of a program and I can understand this approach; probably it is also possible to understand the function of an individual in these terms (at least hypothetically) because if you consider that what we have to understand is the mode of functioning, you have already assumed the hypothesis of functions. The main point is that something is understood in terms of function.

What I mean by *oikeion* or my version of ecology precisely does not fall under the rule of that sort of memory. That is to say that it is impossible to describe it in terms of function. You can look at it as an entropy and certainly, functionally speaking, the unconscious (to use Freudian terminology) is the dysfunctional entity par excellence. It provokes only trouble, that is, paradoxes and even silences or noises, which are the same thing. It would be interesting to know where this sort of dysfunction or malfunction comes from. Is it possible to reduce it, to transform either an individual or collective apparatus into a totally transparent entity without any sources of dysfunction except the sources Luhmann assumed, that is to say, the sources coming from the function itself without any otherness? My *oikeion* is an otherness that is not an *Umwelt* at all, but this otherness in the core of the apparatus. We have to imagine an apparatus inhabited by a sort of guest, not a ghost, but an ignored guest who produces some trouble, and people look to the outside in order to find out the external cause of the trouble. But probably the cause is not outside, that is my idea. So we can call it entropy, but probably the more interesting thing is to try to touch it, not approach it, because it is not an object available for a cognitive touch. For example, psychoanalysis is not a science at all, not a knowledge, properly speaking; it is a different practice, a practice of something like writing. That is the reason why I connect, I have connected, and I will connect this topic of the *oikeion* with writing that is not a knowledge at all and that has, properly speaking, no function. Afterward, yes, when the work is written, you can put this work into an existing function, for example, a cultural function. Works are doomed to that, but while we are writing, we have no idea about the function, if we are serious.

As for the negentropic process, it is only a matter of a hypothesis; the scientists are very clear on this point if you ask them about it. Hence, one makes the hypothesis that in this corner of the universe, there is a negentropic process, because it is evident that something happens that contradicts the second principle of thermodynamics. Why, how? We know how, but no one knows why. Let's make a scientific hypothesis that allows us to understand many things. Philosophically, one can say that the general physics of this developing system is the realization of traditional metaphysics and more specifically of Leibniz's last great metaphysics of substance. And this is "reality." That means that for the philosopher, what we call reality is the realization of the monadology, which means that metaphysics has come to an end because physics has realized it. We are thus in a universe—*universe* is too big a word; it's time to say *Umwelt*—we are in an *Umwelt* that is the realization of metaphysics as a general physics under the name of cybernetics. This, I believe, is the heart of Jürgen Habermas's critique of Niklas Luhmann, when he calls Luhmann's system theory an ideology. But I would like to ask whether the philosophy of the subject that Habermas opposes to Luhmann, a philosophy that is explicitly counterfactual, but that nonetheless remains a philosophy of the subject, of a subject that has to constitute itself collectively as consensus, is not itself an ideology. My questions are, if you prefer, the following: In the framework of development, does not all philosophy transform itself into ideology? Is it not simply useless? There is a theme particularly dear to the French (at least to those who are called "the French"; I don't know who "the French" are), the theme of an ending, of a limit to philosophy. In the *Umwelt* I am describing, all politics is certainly nothing other than a program of decisions to encourage development. All politics is only (I say "only" because I have a revolutionary past and hence a certain nostalgia) a program of administrative decision making, of managing the system.

Ecology as Discourse of the Secluded

In conclusion, I would like to interrogate the word *ecology*, a word made up of *oikos* and *logos*. Do we speak of the *oikos*, or is it the *oikos* that speaks? Do we describe the *oikos* as an object, or is it rather that we listen to it, to what it wants? In Greek, there is a very clear opposition between *oikeion* and *politikon*. The *Oikeion* is the women, whose sex is *oikeion*; the children, whose generation is also *oikeion*; the servants, everything that can be called "domesticity" in the old Latin sense, that which is in the *domus*, like the dogs, for example. In the final analysis, *oikeion* is everything that is not *öffentlich* [public]. And the opposition between the *oikeion* and the *politikon* exactly matches up to that between the secluded (the *Zurückgezogene* or the *Abgeschiedene*)³ on one side and the *Öffentliche* on the other. The political is the public sphere, while the *oikeion* is the space we call "private," an awful word that I'm trying to avoid in saying "secluded." It is the shadowy space of all that escapes the light of public speech, and it is precisely in this darkness that tragedy occurs.

Answers to Questions

The Body as Destiny: Birth, Death, Sexual Difference

The assumption that the *oikos* is located inside us is based on a view according to which the body is not only an object but also an entity carrying the traces of a destiny that implies narratives and even tragedy, for it has a certain relationship with time that is definitively different from the computed, stored, differentiated time, time as money, that I sketched out in our first session. At that point I introduced the term *destiny*, and I will try to come back to that later on.

This destiny inscribed in the human body (which is its proper *oikos*) is connected to a double ontological fact: I was born and I have to die—a past and a future, and it is impossible to set the one off against the other. I have to be born, I am to die; that is a problem. And when we reflect on that for a moment we are conscious that this time is precisely not reversible. And the second aspect of this same ontological fact is my being sexed as a male or female, and I have no choice about it. It is impossible to have any thought about the human body that does not take into account this double fact of death and birth on the one hand and sexual difference on the other. My idea is that sexual difference is something like an ontological difference.

Being Dropped

In both schedules—I mean those of life and death and of female and male—we are dropped into a situation whose meaning is unknown to us, at least in the beginning. We have to learn something that has already happened. That is the sense I would like to give to the term "to be dropped." We have to learn something that is already here. We have to learn what it is to live, what it is to die, what it is to be a female or male. We have to answer these questions, and as we are growing up, we come up against a lot of answers from a lot of institutions. By "institutions" here I mean both little narratives, told around us and about us, by our family, relatives, friends, schoolmates, and colleagues, and I also mean norms and formal institutions, in principle operating in our society to provide answers to the questions of what it is like to be male or female, to be alive, to go to our deaths, and so on. We also have imaginary representations—literature, movies, and so on—in order to answer these questions.

Questions from Children and Philosophers

What is relevant here is the fact that we are questioned before we are able to answer, that is to say, that questions come too soon. We are unprepared for them. Childish questions like Where was I before I was born? That is a good question, a very good question, a philosophical question. Where will I be after death? Why don't females, and first of all my mother, have a penis? And why do males have one? How is it possible for females to give birth to children? What is giving birth? And what is the role or function of fathers with regard to mothers and children? I think that all these questions are properly philosophical questions and in general we have no proper answer to them, not only in childhood, but also now.

The Struggle with the Already-found Language

Such questions are uttered only when we are able to speak. At that moment we can formulate questions as questions requiring answers, and answers, too, if we can formulate them. But with respect to language we are late, too. We have to enter language as if it were a world already constituted. Language is already speaking before I am able to speak. Words (or phrases, if you prefer) do say something beforehand, and we are able to use them—so that we are in a kind of double bind relationship with words. We need them in order to express and formulate our questions. The questions we may formulate with words are only questions allowed by words so that we have to fight them, to fight words, to fight phrases to make them more appropriate to our questions. But what is the appropriateness, the property of a word? When can we say that this word, this phrase, is proper for expressing my question?

Supplementarity and the Secluded

We need something like a way to express that *oikeion*, which is not an *Umwelt* at all, but a relation with something that is inscribed at the origin in all minds, souls, or psychic apparatuses. We are not prepared (and that is our difference from computers, the fact that we are unarmed or undefended, in being born), not prepared to speak, not prepared to control the *Umwelt*, and so on. In this sense we are born too soon.

But at the same time we are born too late because a lot of meanings or stories have already been narrated about our birth. In this sense we are already the object of a lot of meanings, and we have to conquer these meanings afterward and probably we try all our lives to understand what was expected of us. It is too late, because these expectations are already part of our lives. That is to say that this belatedness [*Nachträglichkeit*] (this paradoxical relationship with time) probably characterizes what I called the *Abgeschiedene*. Any communication strives to resolve this paradoxical situation with regard to time. In this respect I do not agree at all with the parallel that Ferdinand Schmidt has drawn between our minds and computers precisely because no computer has ever been a child.

Coming Too Late and Supplementarity

Before we have access to language, questions about death, life, and sexual difference have already been asked in the child's psyche. And please conceive psyche as both body and mind. These questions are not asked as questions, but are present to the psyche as diseases. We are fearful or at least threatened and the psyche must overcome the distresses and diseases linked to those questions.

Repression

Thus, the psychic apparatus (the division between body and mind is introduced with language and there has been a phase that precedes language) is led to build defenses against feelings as tacit questions. Those defenses may be as much physical as mental, the difference between body and mind having not yet been made, that is to say, somatic conversions, dreams, phobias, aggressiveness, manias, and so on. All of them can be viewed as effects of defense against anxiety. Repression [*Verdrängung*].

The Character Filter as Effect of the Repressive Process

These effects of defense must be conceived as primary answers to the questions I mentioned. And with the ways according to which we *verdrängen*, we repress anxieties and diseases, the shape of our character, both physical and mental, is developing. This shape is like a filter that later on filters situations, issues, and answers we may need. And presumably this shape as a filter is the root or the source of the so-called ideologies and devotions, *Berufe*. Certainly, in this filter is rooted what I initially called "destiny."

Writing as Anamnesis and Working through

Insofar as we are concerned with the task of thinking or writing, we have to fight the heritage of meaning implicit in words and phrases in order to make words and phrases appropriate to what we need to say. We also have to de-construct, to dismember, to criticize the defenses that are already built into our psyche, impeding us from hearing original fundamental questions. I imagine the filter also as a sound filter, as a sort of noise that allows us not to hear the real questions. The task—I call it "anamnesis"—involves the *Durcharbeitung*, that is to say, a working through the filter or the screen preserving our quietness.

Childlike Fear of the Given

Thus, the task implies that one admits a large element of childish anxiety that is a result of the fact that something is given, has been given, and will have been given to us before we are able to receive it, before we are in the condition of agreeing to it, before becoming aware of it. And this something is merely that there is something, more than nothing. This "there is" is necessarily linked with questions of birth, death, and sexual difference.

I think that when Freud speaks of a "psychic economy," he would have done better to speak of a "psychic ecology," for the term "libidinal economy" (in the Freudian sense, not mine),[4] presupposes that something necessarily escapes publicity, *Öffentlichkeit*, that something resists openness and hence communication. Call it what you will, the "unconscious" or whatever. One can only describe this something as contradiction, tension (physical operation), *Verdrängung* [repression], *Verschiebung* [deferral] (physical operations), *Verstellung* [displacement] (physical operation), and in general *Entstellung* [distortion]. All these concepts are terms of transport, of the modification of forces, masses, and volumes. Precisely the order of passion or pathos, and this pathos is described in physical terms.

Today, economics belongs to *Öffentlichkeit*, what we call *Wirtschaft* [the economy] is precisely part of the public sphere. I would even say that the economy is the very substance of *Öffentlichkeit*, because it is simply the regulation, the *nomos*, of goods, values, and services. When *oikos* gives rise to *oikonomikos* or *oikonomikon*, a complex transformation of the word *oikos* occurs. If "economic" means *öffentlich*, it implies that the *oikos* itself has slipped away elsewhere. It would certainly be wrong to believe that it has disappeared. I mean simply that, for me, "ecology" means the discourse of the secluded, of the thing that has not become public, that has not become communicational, that has not become systemic, and that can never become any of these things. This presupposes that there is a relation of language with the logos, which is not centered on optimal performance and which is not obsessed by it, but which is preoccupied, in the full sense of "pre-occupied" with listening to and seeking for what is secluded, *oikeion*. This discourse is called "literature," "art," or "writing" in general.

Writing and Presence

I am describing a situation of distress, of suffering that is at the same time the mere condition of thinking and writing. And especially when we question the property of words, it is obvious that the answer to the question of what is proper in the realm of words lies in our ability to pay attention to a feeling, the feeling that the question we try to ask is of this or that kind. This feeling is what leads us in search of the proper word or the proper phrase, but feeling is not a phrase, it is only the sketch of possible phrases. It implies uncertainty about meaning, as if meaning were present before being present. That is to say, I am obliged to admit a sort of presence different from the explicit linguistic and communicable present.

Many Bodies

There are a lot of "bodies" that form the subject matter of various sciences or practices. The body can be dealt with under different rubrics: growing up and coming of age, *Gesundheit* [health], developing fitness (sports), cultivating intensity (eroticism, using drugs, etc.), exploring resistance and flexibility (life in space, underwater, underground, in freezing conditions), challenging artificial conditions (surgery, prosthesis).

Thus nobody can be said to be the owner of this body as a whole. Bodies are shared according to various rubrics among various claims and practices.

Preparation of Bodies for Emigration into Space

In my mind, the reason for the number of experiments challenging the human body lies in the necessity for the human body to be made either adaptable to or commutable with another body, another device, more adaptable to extraterrestrial conditions, and it seems to me that this horizon has to be thought in the general perspective of technoscientific development, insofar as this development is aimed at the emigration of humankind from the earth. That is the general perspective of development, negentropy, and the complexification at work in this part of the cosmos. And in order to achieve emigration from the earth, it is necessary to multiply the knowledge we have of the abilities of the human body. It is certainly not a question of making this body happier or more comfortable, but of making this body capable of survival in conditions to which it is not adapted.

Survival after the Explosion of the Sun — Creativity and Childhood

I agree with the idea that the atom bomb makes war impossible, and that the ideal of tension is a sort of trick of reason. Under the atomic umbrella, something else is possible, namely, war, which is interesting. I think that in

Schmidt's perspective, the only stake (in an evolutionary prognosis) is not the explosion of a bomb, but the explosion of the sun. The sun is due to explode quite soon, in four and a half billion years, which is not very long. And probably genetic manipulation and the development of electronics are ways of challenging this catastrophe; that is to say, ways to permit what will be called humankind at that time (probably just meaning computers, very intelligent computers) to be saved and to emigrate from this dead cosmological system. I have the idea that under these conditions so-called evolution or development will have erased the question of birth, the question of childhood, the question of a certain anxiety concerning the internal rather than the external situation. In this case we have to take into account that the relation that we can have with this internal *Fremde* [stranger], this *unheimliche Heimliche* [uncanny familiarity], is the source of every invention, creation, and writing—even in science, let me add, even in science. That is the big difference between an everyday scientist and somebody like Einstein. Unquestionably, Einstein has been a child and has remained a child, and we have to be children if we are to be capable of the most minimal creative activity. If we are sent to space after the explosion of the sun (I don't even know if it will be us), if something is sent to space without this extraordinary complexity that is precisely the paradox of childhood, I am afraid that this complexity is not complex enough. In this case, we could call this by the terrible name of mere survival, which is not very interesting. I am not interested in surviving, not interested at all.

I am interested in remaining a child.

18

The General Line

(for Gilles Deleuze)
(1990)

"Since my earliest youth, I have believed that every person in this world has his *no man's land*, where he is his own master. There is the existence that is apparent, and then there is the other existence, unknown to everyone else, that belongs to us without reserve. That is not to say that the one is moral and the other not, or that the one is permissible and the other forbidden. Simply that each person, from time to time, escapes all control, lives in freedom and mystery, alone or with someone else, for an hour a day, or one evening a week, or one day a month. And this secret and free existence continues from one evening or one day to another, and the hours continue to go on, one after another.

"Such hours add something to one's visible existence. Unless they have a significance of their own. They can be joy, necessity, or habit, in any case they serve to keep a *general line*. Anyone who has not made use of this right, or has been deprived of it by circumstances, will discover one day with surprise that he has never met himself. One cannot think about that without melancholy."

The right to this *no man's land* is the most important human right.

The narrator of *Roseau révolté*[1] knows this, and adds: "Let it be noted in passing that the Inquisition or the totalitarian State cannot admit of this second existence that escapes their control." Orwell in *1984* spoke of the resistance of a man to the annihilation of his second existence by the powers that be.

Humanity is only human when all individuals have this "country without man" for themselves, this *no man's land*. They are not necessarily solitary there. "Alone or with someone," all persons can "meet themselves" there. There is room for many people in this second life—me, you, the other.

On the other hand, "it must not be thought that it is a celebration, and that everything else is the everyday. The border does not lie there, it lies between life as such and the secret existence," specifies the same voice.

Nor is it exactly a matter of the right to secrecy. The right to secrecy allows you on occasion to keep quiet about something you know. But the "secret existence" is "free," because you don't have any idea what you should say, were you to speak of it. You give over your free time to this "secret existence" because you have a need to go on not knowing. This is how you get the chance to encounter what you are ignorant of. Meanwhile, you wait for it. And you can even try to make it come to you. You can read, drink, love, make music, give yourself over to the ritual of minor obsessions, write. But all these means of provoking the encounter are also part of the mysterious region. They keep the secret and there is no way to be sure that they will work.

The region is secret because it is set apart. The right to this second existence is the right to remain separate, not to be exposed, not to have to answer to others. They used to call this keeping oneself to oneself. (But we don't quite know what the self is. Keeping oneself to one's something else.) This right should be accorded to everyone and be respected.

This is not oneself, it is something one encounters. It is certainly *no man* because there is no need for such moments in order to encounter *man*. One's self is only there to protect *no man* and to keep guard around one's *land*.

It does not mean that one is irresponsible because one does not have to answer to others for what happens in this secret region. All that this means is that the secret life does not happen by means of questions and answers. It is not something to be argued for.

Nina Berberova has her narrator say that these moments "serve to guard the *general line*." The "general line" is not the line of general life, of life "as such." However, this second existence treats "apparent existence" gently. It suspends it a little, it lodges itself momentarily in apparent existence and divides it, but one is not aware of it. The secret life does not really harm apparent existence, it opens small parentheses in it.

It is when life in general seeks to grab hold of the secret life that things go awry. Then the human right to separateness, which governs all overtly declared rights, is violated. It doesn't take a totalitarian power, a defamatory rumor, expulsion, imprisonment, torture, starvation, enforced unemployment, or homelessness, censorship, occupation, deportation, segregation, or hostage taking in order for the right to separateness to be violated.

Of course, these are powerful methods by which to intimidate the forces that protect our second existence. They are direct, evident, and infallible ways of weakening it, making the second life impossible, invading it, annexing it to general life. There's no doubt that the masters of general life, whoever they may be, are haunted by the suspicion that something escapes them, that there is something that can conspire against them. They want the entire soul, and they want it to surrender unconditionally to them.

There is also a less obvious method, which works with less glaringly evident violence to insinuate itself into the white or gray area in which man
separates himself from men and feels his way according to his own general
line. This process of insinuation does not come across as at all terroristic.
The appeal to human rights, to publicly declared rights, can easily legitimate
and cover it. Express yourself freely. Have the courage of your convictions,
your opinions; communicate them, enrich the community, enrich yourself,
act, enter into dialogue. Only good can come from the use of your rights
provided you respect those of others. Mingle, everything is possible within
the limits fixed by law or convention. And what is more, this rule can itself
be revised.

I am speaking of liberal democracies, of "advanced" societies in which
human rights are granted, respected as much as possible, in any case always
appealed to and defended, and gradually extended to those who are called,
in North America, minorities. These commandments of liberal democracy
are good. They allow Amnesty International to exist, they even demand that
it should exist. They allow me, on occasion, to publish these minor reflections without difficulty. Anyone who does not agree with them can always
discuss them.

This does not, however, stop the repeated invitation to exercise rights and
to make sure that they are respected from becoming so pressing as to be oppressive. A small rise in pressure, and that will be it for our hours of secrecy.
Each person will be seized by others, by responsibilities, caught up in defending the proper enjoyment of his or her rights in general life, diverted
from his or her guard over the "general line" that belongs to him or her.

This is a kind of proof that exercising one's rights and making sure that
they are respected can come to be exacted as a duty, as infallible a proof as
any that a totalitarian order can supply. Infallible proof of the ruin of keeping oneself to oneself. Why did you not do this or say that? — you had the
right to!

Bergson said that no one is forced to write a book. The activity of writing
books belongs to the existence in which each person "escapes all control,"
including his own. Writing is one of the necessarily hazardous means at
one's disposal for bringing about an encounter. One writes because one does
not know what one has to say, to try to find out what it is. But today's slogan is *Publish or perish*! If you are not public, you disappear; if you are not
exposed as much as possible, you do not exist. Your *no man's land* is only
interesting when it is expressed and communicated. Silence is subjected to
extreme pressure to give birth to its expression.

Does this pressure only affect writers, "intellectuals"? Not at all. Everyone has the same duty to exercise the right to be informed and to be heard.
Everyone must be able to (exercise the right to) bear witness. The institu-

tions see to it that we are all positioned on the threshold of ourselves, turned outward, people of goodwill, ready to hear and to speak, to discuss, to protest, to explain ourselves. Thanks to surveys, interviews, opinion polls, roundtables, "series," "dossiers," we see ourselves in the media as humans occupied with fulfilling the duty of making rights prevail.

We are told again: no problem, everything is possible. There is legislation governing your case. If there isn't, then we will legislate for it, you will be authorized. We are even going to help you to have recourse to the law. All of which is good. Who would dare to complain about it? Certainly not those who are deprived of access to the law. This pressure makes general life more just and more attentive.

However, all of this does not take place without a certain "melancholy." It is true that we owe it to others to respect their rights and that they owe us the same. And that we all owe it to ourselves to be respected absolutely. But in this self there is an other, this or that thing whose company we keep or seek to keep during our secret hours. This other exercises an absolute right over the self, a right that has never been the object of any contract and that knows nothing of reciprocity. It is completely other to other people. It demands our time and our space in secret, without giving us anything in return, not even the knowledge of what it is or of what we are. We have no rights over it, no recourse against it, and no guarantees of safety.

Now, completely occupied with the legitimacy of exchanges with others in the community, we are inclined to neglect our duty to listen to this other; we are inclined to negate the second existence it requires of us. And thus we will become perfect ciphers, switching between public and private rights without remainder.

After that, in what terms would we still be respectable? We only deserve rights and respect for law because something in us exceeds all acknowledged law. The only ultimate significance of the law is to protect what lies beyond or beside it. What do we know of poverty, of sin, of the unconscious, of suffering, of shame, or indeed of inspiration, energy, passion, grace, and talent?

If we do not preserve the inhuman region where we can encounter this or that something, that which completely escapes the exercise of rights, we do not deserve the rights granted to us. What use is the right to freedom of expression if we have nothing to say but what has already been said? And how can we have any chance of finding a way to say what we don't know how to say if we don't pay attention to the silence of the other inside us? This silence stands as an exception to the reciprocity that characterizes rights, but it is its legitimation. We should indeed accord an absolute right to this "second existence" because it is what provides the right to have rights. Yet since it has nothing to do with rights, it will always have to make do with an amnesty.

19

The Wall, the Gulf, and the Sun: A Fable

(1990)

1

I intended to take advantage of the opportunity provided by this talk to take a bearing on the current historical conjuncture.[1] That's what I used to do in the fifties and sixties as a militant member of the critical theory and practice institute named Socialism or Barbarism whenever it was my turn to undertake the risky exercise we called situation analysis [*analyse de la situation*]. After having selected the events that we considered to have prominent significance in the contemporary historical context, we based our analysis on them with a view to formulating an accurate picture of the world.

While the purpose of this exercise was, of course, to gain as correct an understanding of "reality" as possible, it was also concerned with developing appropriate practical interventions within the complex and ever changing network of forces making up the historical situation. Thus, theoretical analysis was closely related to potential praxis. Indeed, besides the task of faithfully representing the world conjuncture, the question What could be done in such a situation? also had to be addressed. "What could be done" meant, more specifically, how could we help exploited and alienated peoples to emancipate themselves from exploitation and alienation, and what kind of practice would enable us to realize this goal, here and now?

To begin by recalling what "situation analysis" was for me in those days is not a matter of nostalgia. It helps me to realize just how different the circumstances for "situation analysis," and the expectations we can have of it, are today. Unlike a critical practice institute, we are of course not required to outline the direction of interventions. The only interventions we may envisage take form in the publication of papers and collections. This is not to say that it's a small matter to intervene in this manner. It is something else. And change doesn't come from the way a critical group is named. Rather, the difference emerges from a change that does effectively affect the historical situation and subsequently the state of criticism itself.

112

Briefly and generally speaking, let us say that militant praxis, in our countries at least, has become defensive praxis. We are constantly having to assert the rights of minorities, women, children, homosexuals, the environment, animals, citizens, culture and education, the South, the Third World, and the poor. We have to sign petitions, write papers, organize conferences, join committees, take part in polls, and publish books. In doing so, we assume the regular responsibilities attached to the position of intellectuals. I say "regular" because these practices are permitted and even encouraged by the law, or, at least, by the implicit or formal rules of our positions. Western society not only allows us to participate in these practices, in fact it requires us to take part in them; it needs the specific contributions that we are able to provide for the development of the system as a whole.

In these conditions, we may keep alive the feeling that we continue to fight for emancipation. And it is true. Nevertheless, there are signs that the nature of the struggle has changed. The price to pay for taking up the struggle — I mean the quantity of energy and time that must be spent in order to actualize critical practices — has been reduced. This reduction clearly indicates that our strategy has changed from an offensive one, as it formerly was, to a defensive one. According to Clausewitz, the amount of time and energy required for an offensive strategy to offset an adversary power is seven times greater than that needed for a defensive strategy. By moving from an offensive to a defensive strategy, we could save 86 percent of the energy previously devoted to the task of emancipation and still get the same effect!

We know in fact, however, that the effect can't be the same. Emancipation is no longer the task of gaining and imposing liberty from outside. It no longer represents an ideal alternative that can be opposed to reality. Rather, emancipation is taken as one goal among many pursued by the system, an ideal that the system itself endeavors to actualize in most of the areas it covers, such as work, taxes, marketplace, family, sex, race, school, culture, communication. Of course, emancipation is not always successful in each area; it is confronted with obstacles, both internal and external, that resist it. All the same, such efforts of resistance encourage the system to become more complex and open and promote spontaneous undertakings. That is tangible emancipation. Programs that improve what already exists are inscribed in its very mode of functioning, including venture programs that allow for greater complexity and more flexible institutions to be introduced into the system's network.

I know that the idyllic picture I am painting is as trivial as political discourses, commercial messages, and administrative policy documents may be and are. It is the critic's job to detect and denounce all of the cases in which the system fails to improve the process toward emancipation. I am merely suggesting that the critic's position now presupposes that the system itself is understood by criticism as being put in charge of promoting emancipation and that critiques, whatever forms they may take, are needed by the system for improving its efficiency in the direction of emancipation. I would say that criticism contributes to changing differends, if there are still any, into litigations.

2

Thereby, the situation might inspire observers and commentators with the feeling that the grand narrative issued from the Enlightenment has finally prevailed over the other representations that previously competed for the theoretical and practical lead in human affairs. Throughout the twentieth century, various different attempts—imperialism, fascism, nazism, and communism—have been made to govern human communities differently. Most of them have now been put out of the competition. The oldest and most all-encompassing Western grand narrative, Christianity, stopped shaping the social, political, economic, and cultural institutions of Western communities long ago. Marxism, the last shoot stemming from both the Enlightenment and Christianity, seems to have lost all of its critical power. When the Berlin Wall fell, it failed definitively. By invading the shops in West Berlin, the East German crowds gave evidence that the ideal of freedom, at least of the free market, had already invaded Eastern European minds.

Thus, the practical critique of communism has been carried out. But what about the practical and theoretical critical power of Marxism? Having been in East Berlin in June and December 1989, I was able to observe how anxious and concerned the East German intellectuals were (even if they had been more or less compromised with the communist bureaucracy) to save, maintain, or elaborate a view enabling all of us to criticize both Eastern totalitarianism and Western liberalism. For somebody coming from the tradition of radical Marxism, this request sounded like an appeal to go backward and start again with the double-edged criticism, directed against both "late capitalism" and so-called "communist" society, that we had undertaken in the fifties and sixties. Although it's attractive, the purpose is vain.

Of course, it still remains quite possible to analyze the current situation of Eastern and Western Europe in terms of the rise of capitalism and the fall of bureaucratic regimes and organizations. But something would necessarily be missing from the picture, something that has cast its tragic light over the historical stage for a couple of centuries: the proletariat. According to the rigorous Marxist notion, the proletariat was not to be confused with the laboring classes. The latter are social entities that are more or less recognizable (and falsifiable) by the means of sociology and cultural anthropology, and the former was supposedly the name of the authentic subject of modern human history. The proletariat was the subject whose unique property, its labor force, had, on the one hand, been exploited by capitalism, and that had, on the other hand, been taken by Marxism as the real motive force behind all human history. The proletariat was divested of its labor force in order to allow capital to appropriate the fruits of its peculiar and precarious capacity: to produce more value than this force consumes in the production process (an outstanding case of "good productivity" or, rather, "good productivity" itself).

What was ultimately at stake for Marxism was the transformation of the local working classes into the emancipated proletariat, that is, the conversion of the diverse communities of workers chained up in capitalist relationships into a unique self-conscious and autonomous collective subject, capable of emancipating all humanity from the disastrous effects of the injury it had suffered. Something sounded tragic in this vision: society was viewed as being possessed by the *mania*, haunted by a ghost, doomed to a tremendous *catharsis*. For the injury was a wrong that, unlike a mere damage, could not be redressed by litigations, since the court required (the court capable of equitably hearing the two parties, labor and capital) didn't exist. The rights of the workers were the rights of mankind to self-government, and they were to be fought for through class struggle. I mean class against class, with no reference to nation, sex, race, or religion.

The mere recall of these well-known guidelines of Marxist criticism has something obsolete, even tedious, about it. This is not entirely my fault. It is also because the ghost has now vanished, dragging the last critical grand narrative with it off the historical stage. The regimes that have pretended to represent the hero have fallen into appalling buffoonery. They collapse one after the other, allowing the stage to be opened up to reconstruction in accordance with Western models. This can take years and years and can cause tremendous convulsions. Nevertheless, the process of rebuilding in this way (an unexpected, practical form of critique) cannot be resisted. And in this process of practical critique, the working classes as such have played, are playing, and will play no role. The international labor movement has been dissipated into local institutions that claim only to defend the rights of specific groups of workers. Local class struggles work in the same way as the other efforts of resistance I have mentioned, that is, as impediments by which the system is confronted and that it needs in order to improve itself.

Thus, the discourse that Marxists called the bourgeois discourse of emancipation and the communal organization connected with it, that is, liberal "late" capitalism, now look like the only survivors and winners after two centuries of struggle that sought to impose another way of reading and leading human history. This system has good reasons to claim to be the true supporter of human rights and freedom, including the right and freedom to critique. How could the demands for radical criticism, as formulated by our East German colleagues, be satisfied if criticizing, questioning, and imagining, as Castoriadis and Lefort would say today, actually require the openness that only an open system provides?

3

In terms of the current situation, the fall of the Berlin Wall is a significant event that implies a lot of historical consequences. It also has a crucial influence on the scope of critical approaches. The Persian Gulf crisis, which, at the moment I am writing, still remains in a state of suspense, is no less significant, though in a different way. It is not the first time, and perhaps not the last, that the Western system as a whole has been severely challenged by the direct and indirect effects of its imperialist policy. Obviously, the aggressive Iraqi dictatorship is a consequence of the situation created by the presence of Western powers in the Middle East for two centuries. They divided up the area according to their respective interests, reciprocal power relations, and common attempts to "solve" the contradictions that affected them, especially on the occasion of the crisis that gave birth to the First and Second World Wars. Saddam Hussein has literally been produced by the Western chancelleries and business firms in a way that is even more cynically flagrant than the way Hitler, Mussolini, and Franco were produced by the "peace" policy adopted by the winners after the First World War. By "produced" or "a product of," I mean that they were the result of the imposition of the capitalist system's aporias upon less developed, defeated, or, in any case, less resistant countries.

Of course, there are a lot of differences between the situations I am comparing. Let us point out two that are of great relevance to our purpose. The first is that the challenge faced by the Western system comes at a moment when the extension of its power has reached the greatest lengths ever known (especially with the opening up of the communist regions). In this regard, it seems that Saddam Hussein has not taken a good look at this worldwide change symbolized by the fall of the Berlin Wall. In contrast, the crisis that struck Germany and Italy during the interwar years affected both American and all other European societies as well.

As to the second difference, I would like to linger over it for a while, since it merges with the general idea of this paper. That which forms the basis of and makes possible the dictatorships to which I have referred is obviously linked to social and economic distress. Such distress is accompanied by a feeling of resentment resulting from humiliation, a feeling of which most contemporary Western minds hardly can have an appropriate representation since they have no experience of it. A necessary condition for humiliation is that the community and culture to which one belongs is judged to be at least as eminent as the community and culture of the adversary. When it is only a matter of a recent and casual defeat, humiliation remains episodic and resentment can be overcome. This is what we expect in the case of a unified Germany.

Here is the difference that I want to underline. The Arab populations living in the Middle East belong to a long, brilliant, and worldwide civilization, Islam. They are aware of this thanks to the Muslim tradition. And they know that Islam and Arab culture have been subjected to humiliation by the West for centuries. Undoubtedly, the Desert Shield policy has awakened once more the resentment that is the permanent experience of the Islamic peoples. Moreover, as divided as the Arab states may be (an effect of the Western policy), the Arab populations do and undoubtedly will react as belonging to the ancestral community that they recognize as their own, the Islamic *Umma*. And they are undoubtedly ready to invest in any Arab figure they see as being capable of making the names of Islam and the *Umma* recognized and honored all over the world.

It is here that the force of Saddam Hussein lies, not in his military weapons. It is not by chance that this leader of the secularized Arab movement, the Baas, appeals to the *Umma* to resist the violation of Muslim holy places. And it is also here that the very challenge posed by the Gulf crisis lies. In the short term, the Baghdad dictator will undoubtedly be defeated in one way or another. In the mid-term, the Middle East map, including Lebanon, Jordan, Israel, and Palestine, will undoubtedly be revised. The point, however, is whether in the long run Islam can continue to resist the wholly secularized way of life that prevails in contemporary Western and Western-identified societies, whether it will still be able to oppose the secularized West with the spiritualization or, let us say, the symbolization that completely encompasses the details of everyday life and makes Islam a total civilization rather than a specific religious belief. It represents a way for human beings to be together, one that is completely extraneous to the Western way. Like God's voice, a voice heard by Abraham and Mohammed long ago, the muezzin's voice sounds over cities and deserts recalling that the Law itself is the unique source of authority in human affairs.

Let us take the position of authority as a touchstone in order to separate the two parties facing each other in the Middle East conflict and to consider what is actually at stake there, beyond the noise of declarations and weapons. In the modern or, rather, the postmodern system, authority is a matter of arguing. It is only attributed or lent, as it were, to an individual or group that comes to occupy a place for a period of time. In principle, this place of authority remains vacant. Thus, although it is the ultimate voice of the Law, authority is designated by contract. This is the paradox of democracy in that the supreme agency or foundation for making decisions concerning the whole community is based on the decision of the community. In this sense, the transcendence or Otherness attached to the notion of the Law that is considered as the ultimate court of appeal remains immanent to the community's sameness. The vacancy of the space of authority that I have just mentioned is a perfect example of the blankness or looseness that the open system preserves within itself, in order to allow it to criticize, correct, and adjust its own performances. To the extent that authority may be analogically represented by the figure of the father, it could be said that the father is elected by the sons and daughters among themselves.

In the Islamic tradition (like the Jewish one), however, the "father" elects his people, designates his representatives and prophets and dictates the Law to them. Posited as unfathomable, the transcendent Law is accessible only by reading the letters (the voice itself is unheard except by the prophets) that have been inscribed in the Book by the first witnesses and passed on to successive generations. Authority is a matter of interpretation rather than of argumentation—an interpretation of a special kind, which adds nothing to the letters, but only attempts to "fill up" the blank spaces between them, let us say something like a Talmudic reading.

In fact, the notion of authority as pure Otherness is common to Muslims and Jews. The difference lies in the way the moral content formulated by the reading of the Book is to be actualized. And this difference in actualization stems from the fact that the Hebrew tradition had already been crossed over by the Christian message when the Koranic law was laid down by Mohammed. The "good news" brought by Christianity is that thanks to the mystery of the incarnation, that is, the sacrifice of God's son (and thanks to the reading of it that Paul of Tarsus elaborated and imposed), the law of obedience is turned into the law of love, and the spiritual community linked by the reading of the Book may itself embody a concrete—first political (the empire), then economic (Protestant capitalism)—community. Although a theology of incarnation is missing from it, Islam retains the message that the political actualization of its Law is required as evidence. Thus, it is concerned with the task of manifesting the authority of the Book by fixing the significance of the Koranic verses and inscribing it into the worldly reality (as does Christianity, with analogous dogmatic and political consequences). As such, authority becomes a matter to be testified by secular achievements, and when such achievements are lacking, humiliation ensues. And this has not failed to be the case. When confronted with the modern and classical West, Islam was defeated because the Koranic law didn't allow the Muslim political states to develop economic power, whereas the West was authorized to do so by the dogma of the incarnation, a dogma that could legitimate success in all secular areas. In the final analysis, this was the reason for the failure of the powerful medieval caliphates. In the modern, postmodern, and even classical Western age, the holy war seems inappropriate while wars are only economic conflicts carried on by other means. (As for the Jews, they themselves, or perhaps their circumstances, have prevented the attempt to form political communities, at least for a very long time. Humiliation is impossible when the Law requires only subtlety in reading, humbleness in realizing, and humor in judging. But the price is having to suffer at the hands of other political, social, and economic communities.)

The previous description, which is too brief and too ambitious in its scope, can be concluded in the following way: neither the liberal nor the Marxist reading can account for the current historical situation marked by both the fall of the Berlin Wall and the Gulf crisis. As to the latter, the good conscience of the West appears impoverished in the assertions that Saddam Hussein is a tyrant, that Arab people are hysterical and fanatical, that international rights are being violated, and so on, as if the West was exempt from the same sins, even recently. On the other hand, if the Marxist reading could legitimate its own discourse, it wouldn't have to confuse the Third World, the South, or the masses of the Middle East who have been and are made wretched by imperialism with the figure of the proletariat — a confusion that is absurd in theoretical and practical terms and shameful with regard to the responsibility for thinking. With regard to the fall of the Berlin Wall, things are clearer and can help us gain a better understanding of the current situation. For the fall of the wall, on the one hand, provides evidence that the more open the system, the more efficient it is; while on the other hand it shows that closed and isolated systems are doomed to disappear, either by competition or merely by entropy (Brezhnev should have studied thermodynamics a bit). In the context of the Gulf crisis, the issues are predictable, though for different reasons. However respectable Islam is as a sample of spirituality, it cannot match the concrete performances achieved by the Western system and is therefore obliged either to change its positioning (for example, by turning into merely one religious faith and practice among others) or to disappear.

Therefore, the important aspect seems to be the openness (or looseness) of systems competing with each other. With this point, two questions arise. First of all, does this mean that the whole situation should be thought of in terms of utilizable forces, that is, in terms of the notions drawn from dynamics? Secondly, why is it necessary for systems to compete? In Leibnizian metaphysics, which was also a systems theory, there wasn't anything like a struggle for victory between monads. What then is the prime mover of the competitive process?

4

To these metaphysical questions, is it necessary to give metaphysical answers? Perhaps. But the metaphysical avenue is closed. Or, at least, it has become the object of critique. This critique has developed in the empty interior space that the open system maintains and protects within itself. The system no longer needs to be legitimated on a metaphysical basis. Rather, it only needs a free space. Critique is and will always be possible and desirable. But, it has to be remarked, its conclusion is deferred; some "blanks" always remain in the "text," whatever text it is. This blank is the resource of critique. It is also the trademark that the open system affixes to the works (*oeuvres*) of the mind.

And yet, this blank allows something besides critique: imagination. For example, it allows for a story to be told freely. I would like to describe the present historical situation in a way that is hardly critical. In fact, I would like to describe it in a manner that, quite frankly, is "representational," in the sense of referential, imaginative rather than reflexive—in a word, naive, if not childish. It could be taken for a Voltairean tale, if I had some talent. My excuse is that this "story" is reasonably well accredited in the very serious milieus that the communities of physicists, biologists, and economists represent. It is accredited in an informal, somewhat timorous, way, as if it were the unavowed dream that the postmodern world dreams about itself. It could be said that this tale represents the grand narrative that this world stubbornly tries to tell about itself, even though the grand narratives have obviously failed. This much could be said about this fable, if it weren't for the fact that the hero is no longer Man.

The system said:

In the incommensurable vastness of the cosmos, it happened that energy dispersed in random particles was gathered together here and there into bodies. These bodies constituted closed, isolated systems as galaxies and stars. They used the finite amount of energy with which they were provided to maintain themselves in aggregate systems resulting in the transformation of particles, a transformation that is called work. As a result of this work, energy was partially released into unusable forms, such as heat and light. Since additional energy could not be imported, however, the isolated systems were doomed to collapse after a certain period of time, as they lost their internal differentiation. Energy that had previously been gathered together into bodies was subsequently dispersed all over space. Entropy is the process whereby isolated systems are led toward the most probable distribution of their elements, that is, toward random distribution.

In a very small part of the incommensurable cosmos, there was a small galactic system called the Milky Way. Amid billions of stars, there was a very small star named the Sun. Working like any other closed system, the Sun emitted heat, light, and diverse radioactive waves toward the bodies or planets that it had attracted around itself. Furthermore, like all closed systems, the Sun also had a fixed life expectancy. At the moment when this story was being told, it was in its middle age. The Sun still had four and a half billion years before it would collapse.

Among the planets, there was Earth. And it happened that something unexpected occurred on its surface. Thanks to the contingent constellation of various energy forms (molecules constituting terrestrial bodies, water, the atmosphere selecting solar radiations, and temperature) it happened that molecular systems were gathered together into more complex and improbable systems called cells. Here lies the first enigmatic incident whose occurrence was the condition for the continuation of this story as well as its narration. With the advent of the cell, the evidence was given that systems with some differentiation were capable of producing systems with increased differentiation according to a process that was the complete opposite of that of entropy.

What was especially amazing was the ability of unicellular bodies to reproduce themselves by spontaneously dividing into two parts, both of which were identical to the originary body. Technically referred to as scissiparity, this process of cell division seemed to ensure the perpetuation of this kind of cellular organism.

Thus, birth was born and death with it. Unlike molecules, these "living" systems were required to regularly consume external energies for survival. On the one hand, this dependence made them very fragile because they were threatened by a lack of energy. But, on the other, it "spared" them the misfortune of being doomed to collapse like isolated systems; as a result, their life expectancy wasn't mechanically predictable.

Then another event occurred among the "living" systems: sexed reproduction. In addition to being immensely more improbable than scissiparity, this way of reproducing also allowed the offspring to be distinguished from their progenitors (thanks to the association of two different genetic codes). Hence, the "space" for unexpected events to interfere in the process of reproduction became wider, and the chance of mutations ("misreadings") also increased.

Thereafter, the story has already been told by Darwin. What is remarkable, however, is the fact that "evolution" did not imply purposiveness. New systems appeared fortuitously. They were mechanically confronted with the existing context, that is, the existing set of systems. The challenge that thus arose was how to provide oneself with energy. Given that the available amount of energy was finite, competition was unavoidable. War was born.

As a result, the most efficient or productive systems were statistically selected.

After some time (quite short in relation to astronomical time), the system called Man was selected. This was extremely improbable for the same reason that it is improbable for a superior monkey to remain upright on its hind legs. The vertical position freed the hands and allowed for the extension of the brain pan. Both manual techniques and those that operate by symbols called languages began to develop. Such techniques constituted additional prostheses enabling the human system to overcome the extreme weakness that was concomitant with its improbability.

As with unicellular systems, something equally unexpected had to happen with Man. Like the capacity of single cells to reproduce themselves in the unicellular system, Man's symbolic language had the peculiar characteristic of being recursive, that is, of being able to bring together diverse linguistic elements indefinitely (while still making sense). In addition, symbolic language had the particularity of being self-referential, that is, of taking itself as an object. Since they enjoyed similar benefits, thanks to these peculiarities of language, material techniques likewise underwent a mutation. Because of language, they could be referred to, improved upon, complexified, and accumulated.

Language also allowed individual human beings to inflect the rigid modes in which they had been living together in "primitive" communities. Various improbable forms of human aggregation arose, and they were selected according to their ability to discover, capture, and save sources of energy. In regard to this ability, there were two noteworthy "revolutions:" the Neolithic and the Industrial.

For a long time ("long," that is, when calculated in terms of human time) techniques and communities appeared at random. The probability of survival for improvable and fragile systems remained out of control. Sophisticated techniques could possibly be neglected as curiosities and fall into oblivion. Politically and economically differentiated communities could be defeated by simpler but more vigorous systems.

Nevertheless, because of the previously mentioned particularities characteristic of language, the ability to reproduce and anticipate unexpected events, including failures, an ability that had been introduced by language itself, was developing autonomously. Thus, the task of controlling unexpected occurrences, be they external or internal, became the primary task for systems to fulfill if they wanted to survive. In addition, a number of authorities began to appear in the social, economic, political, cognitive, and representational (cultural) fields.

After some time, it happened that systems called liberal democracies came to be recognized as the most appropriate for the task of controlling events in whatever field they might occur. By leaving the programs of control open to debate and by providing free access to the decision-making roles, they maximized the amount of human energy available to the system. The effectiveness of this realistic flexibility has shown itself to be superior to the exclusively ideological (linguistic) mobilization of forces that rigidly regulated the closed totalitarian systems. In liberal democratic systems, everybody could believe what they liked, that is, could organize language according to whatever system they liked, provided that they contributed to the system as energetically as they could.

Given the increased self-control of the open system, it was likely that it would be the winner in the competition among the systems all over Earth. Nothing seemed able to stop it, or even to direct it in ways other than contributing to its development. Incidents like the collapse of the communist societies and the Gulf crisis were, on the one hand, the opportunity for the system to increase its influence while preventing it from reducing its "blank" internal space as bureaucratic regimes had already done, and, on the other hand, the occasion for the system to improve its control over other sources of energy. Moreover, the system had also started to moderate its victory over other terrestrial systems by extending its ability to regulate the ecosystem so as to ensure its survival.

Nothing seemed able to stop the development of this system except the Sun and the unavoidable collapse of the whole star system. In order to meet this predictable challenge, the system was already in the process of developing the prosthesis that would enable it to survive after the solar sources of energy, which had contributed to the genesis and maintenance of the living systems, were wiped out.

All the research that was in progress at the time this story was told—that is, taken at random, research in logic, econometrics, and monetary theory, data processing, physics of conductors, astronomy and astronautics, biology and medicine, genetics, dietetics, catastrophe theory, chaos theory, strategy and ballistics, sports, systems theory—all this research was devoted to the problem of adjusting or replacing human bodies so that human brains would still be able to work with the only forms of energy left available in the cosmos—and thus preparing for the first exodus of the negentropic system far from Earth with no return.

What Man and "its" brain or, better, the Brain and its man would look like in the days of this final terrestrial challenge, the story did not say.

**Part IV
More "jews"**

20

German Guilt

(1948)

Right from the start of *Schuldfrage*,[1] Karl Jaspers takes a hard look at something that has not yet been *thought*, in the strict sense of the word: German guilt. This clear-sightedness has an ethical aim, that of purging the complexes attendant upon the German reaction to the accusation or the feeling of guilt. Hence, from the beginning, Jaspers implicitly makes the assumption that the effective, lived will to clear-sightedness leads to a catharsis and thence to a reconstruction (*Wiedergutmachung*) of the self and of things. Consequently, he locates the answer to the *Schuldfrage* in the individual rather than the political sphere. A number of designs converge, in excess of the problem proper, so as to appear to sketch an entire moral (or religious) system, founded on the twin assumptions of a sin against oneself and against God and of the absolute efficacy of the understanding. An initial hesitation between Kierkegaard and Socrates ends up as a strong desire for the concrete. It indeed seems, despite various contradictory formulas, that for Jaspers the concrete is the individual: the individual as self-consciousness.

1. The introduction explains that the book is neither a justification in the eyes of the world nor an apology for Germany. On the contrary, Jaspers seeks to enter into a struggle not against world opinion, but against the opinion that the Germans have of themselves, and especially against the opinion that they acquire as a result of an excessive confidence in the immediacy of feeling. In extreme circumstances, affectivity might be able to organize and govern an existence, to support its morality; yet it would not know either how to constitute this morality or how to explain this life. The confused awareness of a sin must become a clear knowledge.

2. There is responsibility. Legal responsibility (*Kriminelle Schuld*): obedience to or breach of the law, which falls under the jurisdiction of the national or international tribunal; political responsibility (*Politische Schuld*): insofar as

a people is responsible for the state that it gives itself or to which it gives itself and has to answer to the conqueror for it; moral responsibility (*Moralische Schuld*): if every consciousness is free to act according to its judgment and to judge itself in terms of its action; lastly, metaphysical responsibility (*Metaphysische Schuld*) because all individual intervention or nonintervention engages human solidarity, in its widest and most precise sense: God alone is the judge of this.

3. Of course, the distinction between these four responsibilities is an abstraction: in actuality, they are interpenetrating. Metaphysical sin, whether individual or collective, always requires the judgment of the self by the self, often that of the tribunal; and the other sins thus fall into this category: every human fault has a metaphysical meaning. Likewise, the moral engages with the political, whether it integrates itself in the political by virtue of the free participation of the members of the collectivity or whether it separates itself from the political, either in calm acceptance of the imposed order or in the blindness of a mass ideology: the deliberate refusal of politics by the moral is still a form of control. Jaspers, following Herodotus, thus opposes the freedom of the Greek system to Persian despotism, West to East. On the other hand, there remain, in law, categorical distinctions: it is not possible to judge a collectivity like an individuality, that is, to bring an accusation of a moral order against a political grouping. "Typological" thought (*the* Germans, *the* Jews), presupposes a degradation of the individual as such: this was the basis of the profoundly abstract Nazi systematization. In short, there is no collective *soul*. On the other hand, if metaphysical error entails actionable legislative moves, this error would not, as such, be conscious of any particular legal condemnation. "What matters in the eyes of God does not, nevertheless, matter in the eyes of men" (p. 20). Metaphysical responsibility concerns humanity not as individuals but as a group: individuals are not the judges of human nature. Finally, political guilt is not a criminal guilt because it pertains only to the one who was engaged in the struggle in which this guilt arose: the conquerors alone, who have risked their lives, can decide on the life of the conquered, who *must* carry out the sentence. The conquerors must do so by virtue of the Hegelian dialectic of master and slave, that is, by virtue of a necessity of historical evolution, which seems to me here a little superfluous, stuck on. The fact remains, however, and rightly so this time, that a neutral country is not in any position to judge the political guilt of belligerent parties.

4. After a brief examination of the possible systems of defense, Jaspers goes to the heart of his subject: the German problem that will be explained by the preceding analyses.

Of course there was a crime. It makes no difference to invoke the fact that the international legal statutes of Nuremberg were established after the fact, that the judges were sometimes criminal themselves, or that their justice serves only to mask brute force: Oradour and Auschwitz belong to history. You can't even excuse the Wehrmacht by setting it apart as an honorable machine for producing heroism. Nor can you wish the Germans as a whole to be also judged in the trial. There is no outrage at the German nation in the institution of the Nuremberg tribunal; the only matter at issue there is to draw out the consequences of the Germans' inability to free themselves from their regime: their national shame was to *let themselves* be liberated. Jaspers next insists on the significance of this international tribunal: a promise of peace, he says, if not an institution of peace. (Two years later, we don't think about it anymore; the judge comes after the crime.)

5. Furthermore, German political responsibility is obvious. The only problem to be posed, according to Jaspers, is whether this responsibility must be borne by individuals. In reality there was, generally, no lived or thought participation in the regime and what it entailed, namely, violence; on the contrary, there was a secret and profound resistance at the level of conscience. There is thus no collective moral culpability of the people (as there is of institutional organizations such as the Gestapo, the SS, or the Reichskabinett), but a collective guilt insofar as the collectivity allowed a minority to act. The notion of an apolitical individual no longer makes sense in this century: "there is nothing external to the modern State" (p. 40). Malraux said, after Napoleon: "Tragedy, now, is politics." Abstention is a policy; Germany's lassitude in the passionate movements after 1918 and under Weimar was, whether one likes it or not, a political attitude, as is now clear.

6. Moral guilt is an absolute; though it takes diverse forms, each is equally keen: moral secrecy ("Das Leben in der Maske"),[2] bad conscience (it was the duty of the military itself to contest certain orders, a scandalous notion among the heirs of Frederick the Great), half measures ("the regime did away with unemployment"), present acceptance of the worst with an eye to a better future (this was how German intellectuals let themselves be sucked in), omission, inaction, fence sitting—or sheer opportunism. The denazification tribunals must judge adherence to the party in terms of these various modalities: here action draws its meaning from intention.

7. Metaphysical sin: to prefer life and a bad conscience to a clear conscience and death. Morally this is not sinning because, morally speaking, consciousness must first be preserved in order to be improved: here the alternative is decisive, it is only thinkable in terms of a human bloc, abstracted from his-

tory, and at the same time polarizing it—which one may follow Jaspers in naming as God, if one pleases. In 1938, with the burning of the synagogues and the first massive deportations of Jews, Germany killed itself, and let itself get stuck in fear. At that time, the only good consciences were in the camps, political deportees organizing themselves in the face of the direct terrorist regime of the SS or the indirect regime of common law—an active negation of the master by the slaves, an acceptance of servitude insofar as it affirms a dogged freedom.

8. What Jaspers then calls "excuse" (Entschuldigung) is rather a bundle of possible explanations, all valid, in my opinion, and more of which might have been found than the author does: but this would be the work of a historian. "Germany under the Nazi regime was a house of correction": ergo the detainees are not responsible for the actions of the administration. It may be answered that this is an easy excuse; they chose the regime. But we should not criticize before understanding: we know that it is not easy to disorganize a terrorist police system. Historically, a collective psychosis that leads to silence develops. Secondly, frontiers without defenses and a country without unity give rise on the one hand to the establishment of a powerful militarized whole, and on the other hand to an economic and political instability that authorizes violent force. In the same way, the rupture with the spiritual traditions and the still-uncertain institution of new forms of labor—common phenomena in all the postwar nations—reach their breaking point in Germany. In the third place, the errors of Allied policy at Versailles, its weakness in the face of the indecisiveness of fascist Italy and the de facto situations created by the Hitler regime gave very little prompting to the German democrats or communists to harden themselves into an eventual resistance. Jaspers ends this quite valid analysis with a somewhat sentimental exhortation to the Western democracies not to give themselves over to despotism.

9. There is only individual salvation. Purification (Reinigung) will be an action of self on the self, without which Germany will once more plunge into the mechanism of violence. Neither reciprocal accusations, the contempt and the abandonment of the self, wicked pride, stubborn self-justification (often valid) at the individual level, taking refuge in a notion of historical evolution with a more or less moral end (what goes around comes around), nor the mystical invocation of an expiation will open the path of purification. "Purification is the route of man as man" (p. 93). Renewal (Wiedergutmachung) can only be the effect of a purification. The latter gives its meaning to the former; interiority takes precedence over the act. And this new interiority can be acquired only through an assiduous, honest, abstract

reflection on the complexes with which Germany has lived and thought since 1933 (and perhaps earlier), a reflection taken up with an eye to a future that will belong to it: "Clarifying our responsibility is at the same time clarifying our new life" (p. 93). Jaspers has a philosopher's confidence in the ethical consequences of any serious achievement of self-awareness. He has performed a psychoanalytic task: revealing to the invalid the sources, the modes, and the consequences of its sickness. It is up to the invalid to cure itself. That will take "humanity and moderation."

In short, one has to be sick in the first place (and, effectively, the Germans do not know that they are sick), the better to recover later on. A roundabout route. Of course, the ethical path is not the most direct one. Nor is it evident whether or not it leads to a true end: for what proof can there be of a German sickness, that the thought of sickness is not merely the product of the thought of healing? It can be argued that, for Jaspers, ignorance is itself a sickness. But ignorance of what, one may ask.

The passage from isolated consciousnesses to a collective consciousness is not a matter of addition: democratic freedom is not the achieved sum of individual liberations. By dint of interiorizing freedom one betrays it, and the exasperation of individual rights brings back despotism. Most importantly, it is not clear in the name of what the collective transfiguration of the individual as such that Jaspers calls for could take place. The people's desire for a clear conscience does not extend so far as to produce a catharsis on its own account. A catharsis can only be imagined, strictly speaking, in a social form in which the individual participates as an individual, that is, in a religious movement. And the very word *purification* already betrays a theology (or a mythology) in which ethics comes to an end, opens out into contemplation. But where could such a religious movement find a place in the reality of present-day Germany? The most clear-sighted Christians agree with Kogon (in his *SS Staat*) that what overcame the SS system proper in the concentration camps so as to establish a *society* in the camps was not their religious belief, their purity, but the organization of political blocks and compromises. In short, they accept that private belief is in fact subordinate to the conditions of history. Good politics do not go hand in hand with pious sentiments, especially in tight situations: we belong to the age of the assassinated Gandhi. And indeed Camus, in his "Letters to a German Friend" reminds us that effective combat requires the use of the enemy's own weapons, however odious they may be. Likewise, you cannot escape from a suffocating collective situation by means of individual salvation.

Therefore, no reflection upon the past as past (instead of as sin) can be effective. One cannot seriously expect the Germans to understand their present clear-sightedly, that is, in the light of their past. If they have to, they will understand their present in the shadow of this past; in any case, they have better things to think about and do. At the level of the history of peoples, the past as such is either dead or only of concern insofar as it conditions the current situation. For a people, the consciousness of its past, even if it is without illusions, can only be bad conscience. (Good) conscience requires that they examine what remains to be done. A nation does not need a spotless past to conquer itself, but a past pure and simple, that is, the opportunity to think itself concretely and to turn experience and trial into *knowledge*. The Germans must first shed their collective mythology if they want to integrate themselves into Western political civilization, which is liberal, realistic, and bloodless. They must define themselves in terms of conditioning rather than identify themselves in terms of destiny. Jaspers's all-too-brief attempt to bring to light the diverse factors in terms of which the recent history of his country has been written has more to offer than the ethical solution he proposes. But why give this reflection the shameful name of *Entschuldigung* [excuse]? This name nips its fecundity in the bud. Above all, it admits that this reflection is perhaps in effect nothing but a way of easing remorse, of imposing too heavy a burden of guilt on history and the nations that make it. A study of the responsibility of other nations would indeed be worthwhile as part of an ensemble of objective reflections; from the perspective immediately adopted by Jaspers, such a study seems equally pointless or disastrous, seems to be an avoidance of the issue.

This sharing, this dispersal of responsibilities, remains the paradoxical defining characteristic of the book. The desire to be concrete, affirmed at the beginning, eventually loses its way in a conclusion that pays more attention to its logic than to its efficacy. Drawing distinctions between various levels of responsibility is legitimate, in itself. But if criminal guilt ends up applying only to a few accused, if political error becomes blurred when one admits that individuals did not in general have a hand in it, and if the only result is a generally diffused bad conscience, there remains an ethical and metaphysical responsibility, honestly admitted, of course, but of which it is also said (and rightly so) that it does not fall under human jurisdiction, since moral consciousness and religious consciousness elude our tribunals; the human condition alone is in question. It is no longer only a matter of constructing a system of philosophy: that was already the case, as is well known. In beginning his work, Jaspers took care not to detach the political from the individual, who is at the root of the political. However, the individual was the one who was torn away from the political: nazism, a specific event localizable in history and in the world, cannot be brought to trial by any moral or metaphysical law, except in terms of its consequences. This political phenomenon is not allowed its autonomy anywhere in the world.

And this is doubtless the case because Jaspers has agreed to pose the problem in the terms in which the foreigner poses it to Germany on a daily basis, the terms of accusation and defense. Jaspers pleads guilty. *Confiteor*, he says, since he is inward-looking and since penitence is moral. Now, he should have asked the preliminary question of whether the polemic of guilt was capable of producing conclusions that might have a concrete validity. No one nowadays is unaware of the importance of the Nazi phenomenon: it introduces, as Jaspers feels, a new conception and a new formation of humanity (perhaps the most ancient); it installs a radical breach between the nineteenth century and the present one, emphasizes the probable failure of our Western civilization and of "Italianism," crushes liberal thought under forces of destiny. Jaspers wants to save this civilization, this thought, from the mortal sickness in which national socialism left them languishing. But Germany's guilt is one fact, and Germany's future is another. Is it not illusory, and hence illegitimate, to tie the two together, to rely on the former to prepare for the latter?

To which Dufrenne and Ricoeur respond that Jaspers "is not in the least concerned to open a political debate."[3] The excellent analysis they present of *Die Schuldfrage* justifies Jaspers's position because it understands and clarifies it from the inside. The only freedom that remains for each German is to assume responsibility for his fault, a solitary freedom par excellence. This assumption of guilt requires a lucidity that points out and condemns any blockage. Here, rationality comes to their aid and directs the guilty conscience toward the consciousness of its guilt. Individuals, having been freed in this way, not from their fault, but from their ignorance, are animated with a rigorous desire to "make amends" and open themselves to happy willingness and to goodwill. They can then say, "It is enough that God exists." Dufrenne and Ricoeur close by emphasizing the moral generosity of this thought, and above all its coherence with previously developed philosophical themes, which *Die Schuldfrage* applies to the ("tragically") concrete test of history. One cannot refuse to pay this compliment: Jaspers's book shows a great deal of honesty, and noblesse.

Once the book has been read, however, one question remains: *why* was this book written? Not to what purpose, but for what motives? On the one hand, it is clear that Jaspers's aim is not political, and that the "concrete" of which he speaks is not that of history; on the other hand, his final conclusion is given as the promise of a regeneration *for Germany* (or at least of the Germans). On the one hand, the *Reinigung* [purification] is a conversion that can be thought independently of any collectivity. On the other hand, this purification is offered to the German collectivity. And so on. In short, he is trying to pose a political problem nonpolitically. A solution is even claimed: the book does not present itself as a set of remarks but is dogmatic;

it condemns errors, it indicates a path to salvation. Whence proceed my criticisms: politically, "accepting guilt" means nothing. Jaspers cannot prevent this prescription from being understood politically: a solution to the German problem can only be political. The recent strikes by unions in the Ruhr, whether or not they have been infiltrated by the Kominform, have a significance completely different from that of a retrospective analysis. After the ordeal of the camps, German politicians correctly gauge the measure of a hope that torture has only spared. Such is the material of which the future history of a people is made.

21

Heidegger and "the jews": A Conference in Vienna and Freiburg

(1989)

I

Introduction to the Vienna Conference

I come to Vienna with fear. When I was twelve, I studied German as a "living language." My lycée had found me a German-speaking correspondent who studied French. He was, at that time (1937) he could only be, Austrian. He was Viennese. A year later, our correspondence was interrupted: 99.73 percent of the vote in favor of the Anschluss. German became a dead language for me, spoken only by the men of death, the army and the police of the Third Reich.

I continued to read and study the language. It became and has remained the language of culture, of literature, of philosophy—in particular when it comes to us through the constellation of great names that marked the beginning of the twentieth century here. But the pleasure of the intellect and of sensibility that the language gives me is and will always be a wounded pleasure. For half a century, this wound has borne the symbolic name of Auschwitz, which is also called Theresienstadt. I know that the *Shoah* is something other than this wound, which is, when all is said and done, a personal one. All the same, I would like to dedicate the pages that follow to my lost correspondent.

I fear Vienna more than Berlin or Frankfurt for one simple reason, which is perhaps imaginary. Austria is Catholic. As a child, I was raised in Catholicism. It was of course "à la française," and I know Italy well enough to know that there are differences between Catholicisms.

But I also know the power for healing and forgetting, of seduction that can be exercised over individual and collective consciousness by *one* Catholicism that is present in all the national Catholicisms, and that is Roman. What I fear here is the conjunction of catholicity and the tradition of the Reich. For historic, geographical, and political reasons, Austria has been able to heal the *Shoah* without working it out: that is my fear, and my prejudice.

If I come to Vienna nonetheless, it is first of all because of the courageous stubbornness of my editor, Peter Engelmann; and thanks to the invitation of the direction of this prestigious museum *für angewandte Kunst* [for applied art], and also because in suggesting that I speak of *Heidegger und "die Juden,"* they offer me the occasion to make a modest contribution to recalling something that never stops making itself be forgotten.

But I have a third reason. His name is Aurelius Freytag. In the name of the Österreichische Hochschülerschaft [Austrian university association], Monsieur Freytag has invited me to take part in a colloquium organized by that association concerning the condition and the destiny of the university institution today, in particular in the framework of European integration.

I did not reply to his invitation, and if he is here, I apologize publicly. It was only for lack of time and because I knew that I was not free at the planned date. For Aurelius Freytag attached a dossier to his letter. This dossier is the description and program for a series of workshops and lectures organized by the Austrian university association last November on the fiftieth anniversary of the *Kristallnacht*.

I have only one thing to say about this dossier: it *authorized* me to come to Vienna. My imagination was no longer preoccupied by "Austria" but by real Austrians, committing themselves to the task of working through the poorly healed trauma completely.

I also want to add one more preliminary remark: I have not forgotten that my country, alone among those of "democratic" Europe, managed to produce a "state" capable of active collaboration with Hitler. Thus I do not come before you to speak as a Frenchman to Austrians. We speak together, if you like, as Europeans who are trying not to forget.

Introduction to the Freiburg Conference

Forty years ago I took part in the first postwar international training course organized in Freiburg im Breisgau, at which young German and French students met for a month. Freiburg was a city in ruins, and Baden-Wurtemberg was still under French occupation. Both groups were still traumatized. Although their encounter no longer took place in terms of domination, it was not yet on an equal footing. They sought a common understanding of their encounter in their trauma.

On this occasion Jean Beaufret, who sponsored the French group, took some of us to visit Heidegger at Todtnauberg. Beaufret had been one of the very first to introduce Heidegger's thought to France, by translating and commenting on his works.

I remember a sly peasant in his *Hütte*, dressed in traditional costume, of sententious speech and shifty eye, apparently lacking in shame and anxiety, protected by his knowledge and flattered by his disciple. This picture was enough to prevent me from becoming a "Heideggerian." I take no pride in this. These were fugitive impressions, due no doubt to the prejudices of a young Parisian. I continued to read his work.

This was 1947. It seems to me that we have to begin our encounter again. For another "war" has kept us apart for some forty years. I come here with the intention of putting an end to it, no doubt unconsciously animated by the spirit of the time, which is interested in commerce rather than war; but also with an eye to understanding something and making it understood here, something that is not understood on either side of the Rhine. And I cannot believe that it is by chance that the occasion is provided by the name of the former rector of Freiburg im Breisgau.

II

My book *Heidegger and "the jews"* belongs to the group of French publications that followed the release of Victor Farías's book *Heidegger and Nazism*: articles in the major press, in magazines, in specialized journals, books, "dossiers," radio and television programs.

In this lively and sometimes violent debate, I wanted to intervene to try to understand Heidegger's silence on the subject of the *Shoah*, to which Adorno had given the generic name of "Auschwitz."

In doing this, I was working with a distinction that Philippe Lacoue-Labarthe had made in *Heidegger, Art and Politics*, and even more clearly in *La poésie comme expérience* (where he reflects on Paul Celan's interview with Heidegger at Todtnauberg). Heidegger's political engagement within the National Socialist party in 1933 and 1934 is one thing; his absolute silence (except for one phrase) concerning the *Shoah* right up to his death is another.

Both these facts are extremely serious. By serious, I mean that they demand to be thought rigorously. But they cannot both be thought in the same terms or under the same rubric. It is possible to think of the Nazi engagement in terms of philosophical politics (certainly not in terms of political philosophy, in the usual sense). But I do not think that the silence about the extermination of the Jews arises in the least from a political critique. First, because the extermination itself *is not* a political fact and second, and most importantly, because the prohibition on speaking of the genocide, or at least his inability to say one word about it, is by no means the product of a political attitude. Rather, this silence affects what is most essential to

Heidegger's thought, as is attested by the fact that it continued for forty years.

III

I will briefly restate the rules that I set myself when dealing with this double problem in my book:

1. One must admit the importance and the greatness of Heidegger's thought.
2. One must admit the seriousness of the compromise with what Heidegger calls "the movement" (whose "internal truth and greatness" he affirmed even in 1953), and one must admit that his persistent silence on the genocide is not the product of a *lapsus* or a minor failure of memory.
3. One must maintain both assertions—that of the greatness of the thought and that of the objectionable nature of the "politics"—without concluding that if one is true then the other is false, according to the implication that if Heidegger is a great thinker, then he cannot have been a Nazi or, if he was a Nazi, then he cannot be a great thinker.
4. Dealing with this double assertion must not mean just noting the conflict, but finding its internal logic.

IV

The German intellectual class has often been surprised that Heidegger's nazism and his silence should give rise to a whole "affair" in France. They tend to point out that the facts had already been known for a long time. And for this reason, they add, Heidegger's thought has been removed from the German philosophical heritage. How can it be that the same thing did not happen in France?

It is now over a year since Farías's dossier was published in France, and it has just been published in Germany. I am not claiming that this disparity is the *cause* of the difference in reaction in the two countries. Rather, it is an effect, the effect of an intellectual situation that has been marked by the isolation of our two countries for at least thirty or forty years. I can summarize (and therefore caricature) this situation in the following way (a French way).

Since the end of the eighteenth century, after the French Revolution and during the difficult formative period of the nation-states of Europe, there has been no important French philosophy. By this I mean no philosophy adequate to the world in its development. Philosophy was German. The French articulated the facts of this new world, the bourgeois world, in terms of history, sociology, and politics, and also (perhaps above all) in terms of literature and painting. The French philosophers were politicians and writers at the same time, as they had been since the Enlightenment. To put this another way, they were dedicated to exploring social and linguistic relations along with the relation to thought.

On this side of the Rhine, the great tradition of speculative thought developed, the heir of theology (herein lay a profound difference with French thought), which attempted to overcome the Kantian crisis. This thought was at the origin of the institution of the German university. Thus the philosophy of the professor-doctors arose, the summit of intellectual activity and a model of knowledge and wisdom offered to the nation. In France, it was understood that it was the people who possessed this wisdom, and that the function of education was to turn the individuals who compose that people into enlightened and free citizens, capable of deciding their lot in "full knowledge of the facts." If there is philosophy, it consists above all in a reflection on being-together, on its ideals and the means to achieve it, beginning with language.

The "crisis of the people" is as it were permanent in French history since the Revolution, not only in the social and political reality of the people, but in the way it is understood, and in the way in which one writes one's history and one's mind. I summarize.

Starting with the great (international) crisis at the end of the 1920s, French thinkers took over those elements of the most radical critical tradition (and hence of German language) that could help them to continue a reflection on the profound transformations affecting the nature of community and on the hidden aspects of the so-called "subject" of that community revealed by those transformations. Thus they invoked Marx, Freud, Nietzsche, Husserl and Heidegger, a version of Hegel reread by Kojève, the later Wittgenstein, and then Benjamin and Adorno. They subjected the philosophy of the subject (the legacy of Descartes and the "philosophes" of the eighteenth century) to a strong critique, along with the ideas of transparency or self-evidence, of free will, of communication, of the adequacy of reason. Even in an heir of Husserl like Merleau-Ponty, the late writings bear witness to an inclination to look for a nonphenomenological ontology drawn from Heidegger and from Freud as reread by Lacan. Little by little, by widely divergent routes, they developed the ideas of writing, of figure, of textuality, of difference (the differend), which characterize what foreigners call French thought (completely wrongly, since it is almost unknown in France and it is not homogeneous). And all this took place in close collaboration between philosophers, writers, and artists.

After 1945, the German intellectual class, essentially made up of professor-doctors, takes fright at the use that the French have been able to make of the thinkers that I mentioned. Mainly concerned to establish the conditions of democratic debate in a country where the people seem to have been doomed, for two centuries, to be first of all subject to a *Reich*, German thinkers direct their attention to the problems of the rationality of language, of dialogue, of shared certainty, and of consensus. They find the resources for this inquiry in the tradition of the *Aufklärung* [Enlightenment] and in contemporary philosophies of language, especially Anglo-American philosophy.

For them, the Heidegger affair does not exist, it is already done with. It is the last episode of a century of irrationalism. For the French, Heidegger's "politics" constitute an affair because they mean that the task of rewriting and deconstruction that they have undertaken along with Heidegger is not innocent of the worst kind of erring. And thus the question is asked as follows: what do "worst," "erring," or "fault" mean, if you have to run the risk of "analytic" thought in Freud's sense or of "genealogical" thought in Nietzsche's sense, or of "existential-ontological" thought in Heidegger's sense? Here we encounter a deficiency in our capacity to think Heideggerian "politics" (the engagement and the silence): the lack of a faculty of judgment or a feeling for the Law, to put it in Kant's terms, or the lack of a dependence on the Other and a responsibility that is other than ontological, if we phrase it in Emmanuel Lévinas's terms.

V

It is precisely on this issue that my idea of "the jews" comes in. I quote a summary of it from *Heidegger and "the jews"*:

> I write "the jews" this way neither out of prudence nor for lack of
> something better. I use lower case to indicate that I am not thinking of a
> nation. I make it plural to signify that it is neither a figure nor a political
> (Zionism), religious (Judaism), or philosophical (Jewish philosophy) subject
> that I put forward under this name. I use quotation marks to avoid
> confusing these "jews" with real Jews. What is most real about real Jews is
> that Europe, in any case, does not know what to do with them: Christians
> demand their conversion; monarchs expel them; republics assimilate them;
> Nazis exterminate them. "The jews" are the object of a dismissal with
> which Jews, in particular, are afflicted in reality. They are that population
> of souls to which Kafka's writings, for example, have given shelter only to
> better expose them to their condition as hostages. Forgetting souls, like all
> souls, but to whom the Forgotten never ceases to return to claim its due.
> The Forgotten is not to be remembered for what it has been and what it is,

something that never ceases to be forgotten. And this *something* is not a concept or a representation, but a "fact," a *Factum* (Kant II, A56): namely, that one is obligated before the Law, in debt. It is the "affection" of this "fact" that the dismissal persecutes.

To put it another way, the expression "the jews" refers to all those who, wherever they are, seek to remember and to bear witness to something that is constitutively *forgotten*, not only in each individual mind, but in the very thought of the West. And it refers to all those who assume this anamnesis and this witnessing as an obligation, a responsibility, or a debt, not only toward thought, but toward justice.

VI

Here I ought to give a detailed account of the figure, or rather the nonfigure, of this forgotten thing. I will content myself with providing an example, by way of the Freudian concept of *Urverdrängung* [primary repression], in the following series of quotations from *Heidegger and "the jews"*:

> The hypothesis of an unconscious without "representational formations" (which Freud proposes when he seeks to understand unconscious affect and *Urverdrängung*) necessitates a break from the philosophy of consciousness, even if the term "unconscious" still refers to it. It can only be deployed in what Freud calls metapsychology, that is, a topics, a dynamics, and an economy that deal respectively with the instances, the forces, and the conflicts of force (attraction and repulsion), and the results (effects) assessed quantitatively (Freud, *Métapsychologie*, 1915-17).
>
> Are the above terms metaphors? They are the elements of a metaphysics that is inherent in all modern physics, and which, under the name of metapsychology, Freud directs toward the determination of the state of the soul itself, which has, ever since, been considered a system of forces. (11-12)[1]

Once the physical hypothesis of the mind is accepted, it suffices to imagine that an "excitation"—that is, a disturbance of the system of forces constituted by the psychic apparatus (with its internal tensions and countertensions, its filtering of information onto the respective paths, the fixing in word and thing representations, and the evacuation of the nonfixed through the respective paths of the system[—]affects the system when it cannot deal with it: either at the point of entry, inside, or at the point of exit. Not even the protective shield of banal temporality can deal with it. It is an excitation that is not "introduced": it affects, but does not enter; it has not been *introduced* [in English in the original] and remains unpresented (Freud, "Repression," *Standard Edition* vol. 14). It is thus a shock, since it "affects" a system, but a shock of which the shocked is unaware, and which the apparatus (the mind) cannot register in accordance with and in its internal physics; a shock by which it is not affected. This excitation need not be "forgotten," repressed according to representational procedures, nor through *acting out* [in English in the original]. Its "excess" (of quantity, of intensity) exceeds the excess that gives rise (presence, place and time) to the unconscious and the preconscious. It is "in excess" like air and earth are in excess for the life of a fish.

Even so, its "effect" is there nevertheless. Freud calls it "unconscious affect." Freud was the very first to say to himself: pure nonsense, an affect that does not affect consciousness. How can one say it affects? What is a feeling that is not felt *by anyone*? What is this "anyone"? How can I, he asks (Freud, "The Unconscious," *Standard Edition* vol. 14), even be led on the path of this insane hypothesis if there exists no witness? Is not the affected the only witness to the affect? In a sense, this problem is even more insoluble than Wittgenstein's idiolect. For the silence surrounding the "unconscious affect" does not affect the pragmatic realm (the transfer of a meaning to the listener); it affects the physics of the speaker. It is not that the latter cannot make himself understood; he himself does not hear anything. We are confronted with a silence that does not make itself heard as silence.

Something, however, *will make* itself understood, "later." That which will not have been introduced will have been "acted," "acted out," "*enacted*" [in English in the original], played out, in the end—and thus represented. But without the subject recognizing it. It will be represented as something that has never been presented. Renewed absurdity. For instance, as a symptom, a phobia (Emma in the store). This will be understood as feeling, fear, anxiety, feeling of a threatening excess whose motive is obviously not in the present context. A feeling, it seems, born of nothing that can be verified in the "present" situation in a perceptible, verifiable, or falsifiable way, and which therefore necessarily points to an elsewhere that will have to be located outside this situation, outside the present contextual situation, imputed to a different site than this one. And how can this site be localized without passing through a "memory," without alleging the existence of a reserve where this site has been retained, in nonlocalized and nonlocalizable fashion, and without consciousness having been informed about it? This sudden feeling is as good as a testimony, through its unsettling strangeness, which "from the exterior" lies in reserve in the interior, hidden away and from where it can on occasion depart to return from the outside to assail the mind as if it were issued not from it but from the incidental situation. (12-13)

A few further observations:

1. Since this unconscious affect is, as Freud puts it elsewhere, a representative without a representation, it eludes the general critique of representa-

tion. The discussion of philosophical representations in the West, which have been the object of the Heideggerian anamnesis since 1934, is dedicated to leaving this affect forgotten.

2. As long as this unconscious affect remains forgotten, it will give rise to inexplicable formulations (expressions, symptoms). It will repeat itself without letting itself be recognized. Its "expressions" form a tissue of "screen memories" that block the anamnesis. The *Durcharbeitung* [working through] is a work that passes through these screens. Anamnesis is not an act of historical memorization.

3. In a sense, anamnesis is interminable. In effect, the original shock is not *representable*, having never been presented. Or at least its representation is always a trap.

4. In Western history, the Jewish condition, and it alone, is the impossible witness, always improper (there are only bad jews), to this unconscious affect. It alone admits that an event has "affected" (does not cease to affect) a people without that people being able or permitted to represent it, that is, to discover and restore its meaning. This event is called the Covenant that the (unnameable) Lord has imposed on a people (the Hebrews) who are not ready to submit to and respect it. The anguished (exultant and painful) violence of this seizure is accompanied by a Promise of forgiveness. While waiting for the Messiah, the Covenant and the Promise are once more violently recalled to (unworthy) memory by the prophets. Anyone who represents himself as the Messiah (Jesus) is suspect. He is suspected of being only a "screen memory" that betrays the immemorial event of the Law. This suspicion is practiced in the name of fidelity to the affect that stems from this event, an event that is always on the point of being forgotten.

Thus it is that the Jews cannot manage to find their place in the systems by which thought is represented in the politics and social practices of the European West. They cannot form a "nation" in the medieval sense, nor a people in the modern sense. The Law forbids them to acquire the communitarian status of an ethnic group. Their relation to the event of the Covenant and the Promise is a relation of dependence, not a relation to a land and a history but a relation to the letters of a book and to a paradoxical temporality. The book is not the object of a hermeneutic reading that might expose and accumulate its meaning, but of a talmudic reading that tries to get at that meaning through the screens of previous interpretations.

They are not missionaries, having no representation to spread, no formula suitable for remedying evil. The Final Solution was the project of exterminating the (involuntary) witnesses to this forgotten event and of having done with the unpresentable affect once and for all, having done with the anguish that it is their task to represent.

VII

Let me come back to the Heidegger affair. What matters to me in it is both to determine the relation between his thought and nazism and to make his silence on the *Shoah* intelligible.

Things are clear on the first point:

1. Heidegger's nazism, or rather his engagement with the movement, is not a *necessary* consequence of his thought at the time. To put it another way, it is not true that *Sein und Zeit* is, in itself, a Nazi or proto-Nazi book. On the other hand, it is true that this book *allows* or *leaves open* the possibility of such an engagement. The political texts of 1933 and 1934 are riddled with terms that are central to the existential-ontological thought of 1927. The very same tone is present. This proximity between the political and philosophical texts prevents us from conceiving of his engagement in the movement as a circumstantial "joining up," as a simple taking out of a party card. The realization of a thought is at stake.

2. The activity of the rector of Freiburg im Breisgau within the National Socialist party can only be divergent from, and in excess over, the party line. I would sketch this divergence and this excess in the following way.

The Nazi party expressed the immense anguish into which the country had plunged once it had been defeated in 1918, crushed by the Treaty of Versailles and pulverized by the crises of 1921 and 1928, and the Nazis exploited this anguish in order to seize power. The party claimed to have a cure for this anguish. Heidegger meditated on and articulated this anguish. He recognized that it had an existential-ontological status and authenticity. Under the cover of the swastika, he addressed the student generation, offering them the knowledge of their distress. He thought that by this narrow and perilous route he could protect the future of German thought (which would be embodied in this generation) from the double threat that he saw hanging over its institution, the university. The double peril consisted of (1) the threat of academic neutrality, of deafness to reality and (2) the threat that the means and the ends of thought would be subordinated to the interests of a contemptible political clique.

3. The rectorate is thus a key position in this strategy. It is like a hinge between the militant of the "movement" and the philosopher of *Sein und Zeit*. For the rectorate, if one thinks about it, can be analyzed according to two ideas or two themes. A rector is a scholar and a guide. The terms *Wissen* [to know] and *Führung* [to guide] correspond to these two themes, in *Sein und Zeit* as well as in the political speeches of 1933.

I do not have the time to analyze these terms fully here. I supply a sketch, itself too brief, in sections 19 and 20 of my book.

That sketch at least shows how authentic *Wissen*, elaborated in paragraphs 38, 54, 67, 68, and 69 of *Sein und Zeit*, finds its faithful echo in the Tübingen Conference on November 30, 1933, and, of course, in the rector's address of May 1933. The same demonstration can be performed as regards the authentic content (established in 1927) and the political use (in November 1933) of the term *Führung*. It would also be possible to extend this investigation to words like *Entscheidung* [decision], *Geschick* [destiny], and *Volk* [people].

In all these cases, the filiation between the political and the existential-ontological is indisputable. It is what allows one to understand Heidegger's engagement in the movement. Under cover of nazism, the rector "enacts" the thought of *Sein und Zeit*.

4. The engagement is thus not simply "Nazi," it has a completely different import, which might be called "differentially subversive." The introduction of the key terms of *Sein und Zeit* into the political address cannot fail to arouse suspicion of the Rosenberg Amt[2] and the whole Nazi apparatus responsible for culture.

However, Heidegger also plays on the ambiguity of these terms, which he knows are acceptable to party discourse. The shift from *Führung* to *Führer* is easy. Even the *Entscheidung* can find some protection in Carl Schmitt's decisionism. Not that Schmitt is exactly a Nazi; he is a political theologian, and in this respect very different from the Nazis and from Heidegger. But he nevertheless belongs to a family of thought that can on occasion support Hitler and that is a branch of European fascist thought. A vast "compromise," to employ Heidegger's own term, establishes itself among readings of the crisis, readings that are simultaneously divergent from and related to one another. Heidegger can stretch this compromise to the point of introducing a word that is (as far as I know) absent from *Sein und Zeit*, a word such as *Arbeit* [work] into his political text. The advantage of this word is that it refers to the *Arbeiter* published by Jünger in 1930, which had found an echo in the National Socialist party ideology of the *workers*. Jacques Derrida, in *Of Spirit*, has meticulously demonstrated how the term *Geist* [spirit], a term present in *Sein und Zeit* as well as in the political texts, was taken from a certain theological and poetic source that was shielded from deconstruction. When the rector takes his place on the podium, deconstruction seems to have to supplement itself, to take on some additional ballast, be it by employing doublespeak or by borrowing from Schmitt and Jünger or by the "forgetting" of deconstruction.

Thus, in Heidegger's "Nazi" engagement there is at the same time an intrinsic consistency with the existential-ontological thought of *Sein und Zeit*, and an inconsistency. This inconsistency consists in missing the deconstructive task of thought in various ways. This failing is not a minor one: it affects a major thought and allows it to accommodate itself to a totalitarian politics that was already known, at the time, to be criminal. It is, however, not the most serious charge that has to be made in the dossier of the Heidegger affair.

VIII

In this dossier, the most serious charge is written on blank pages: Heidegger's stubborn silence on the extermination. It is much more embarrassing, for those who consider his thought to be radical, than any failures of deconstruction, than what remains unthought, than the "supplements" required by political *Agieren* [enacting]. For unlike those lapses, this silence will not let itself be deconstructed; it calls into question the import of Heideggerian deconstruction itself.

This blank, which extends over some forty years (from *Kristallnacht* to the philosopher's death), is in my opinion the consequence of the exclusionary fashion in which thought "installs itself" in philosophy, that is, in the Greek heritage.

I am taking the word *installation* from Lacoue-Labarthe, who attempts to use it as a translation of *Stellung*. Heidegger identifies a Platonic *Stellung* that, after the pre-Socratics, circumscribes the space of European thought within metaphysical closure: henceforth it will only be a matter of thinking being.[3] The forgetting of Being becomes constitutive of Western philosophy.

I think that Heidegger's silence is due to another *Stellung* [enframing], another *closure*, and another forgetting: the exclusion of what I have called the event of the Covenant, the forgetting of a silent Law that takes the soul hostage and forces it to bear witness to the violent obligation it has undergone. One can attempt to rid oneself of this thematic of the Just (as one might seek to rid oneself of a vestige of theology) and of the ethics that accompanies it. Heidegger's reading of the *Critique of Practical Reason* in 1930 is an example of this elimination or exclusion: from the Kantian text of the law and obligation, the author of *Sein und Zeit* extracts only a commentary on freedom. Where Kant emphasizes the suffering and the violence that any finite will endures by virtue of being seized by an inexplicable and empty but inevitable prescription, Heidegger in *On the Essence of Truth* (also 1930) produces freedom "as in-sistant ek-sistence of *Dasein* . . . of the originary essence of truth, of the sign of the mystery of erring." Texts like these set the seal on Heidegger's deafness to a problematic of justice. This deafness governs his silence on great injustice, on Auschwitz. As far as the truth of Being is concerned, the *Shoah* is only a being.

And this ignorance will perpetuate itself, perhaps even more blinded, after the *Kehre*. From 1934 and 1935 onward, by way of a rereading of Hölderlin and Nietzsche, the *Kehre* will divert Heideggerian thought from the themes of *Geschick* [destiny] and *Entscheidung* [decision] toward those of shelter and of listening to Being in the work of art. Living as a poet on one's native soil is certainly not waiting, in the desert of the diaspora, for the last of the Just to come. If one is wholly Greek, and only Greek, above all pre-Socratic and hence also prepolitical, one has no motive to pay attention, *Achtung*, to the extermination.

If Heidegger is at *fault*, as Lacoue-Labarthe says, and if this fault is not simply a flaw in the rigor of thought, it cannot be assessed on the basis of an existential-ontological or poetic-deconstructive "installation." This installation forgets that the Forgotten is not (only) Being, but the Law. The difference that is incessantly forgotten is not only ontico-ontological, there is also the difference between good and evil, between justice and tort, no less elusive than ontico-ontological difference and, like it, always demanding reinscription. One can never settle accounts with this difference even if one is the most pious of believers. This difference cannot in the least be determined within theological or metaphysical doctrine. It requires the recognition of an immemorial liability. It is this liability, so contrary to its (simultaneously archaic and modernist) ideals of virility, control, and empire, that nazism wanted to exterminate.

IX

I will stop here. The problem I am trying to pass on to you is this: the techno-economico-scientific megalopolis in which we live (or survive) employs these same ideals of control and saturation of memory, directed toward goals of efficiency.

Unlike nazism, it has no need to have recourse to an aesthetic, ideological, and political mobilization of energies.

Heidegger gave this "new" ontological formation the name *Gestell* [enframing]. There is no question of escaping it. But how to resist it is in question. With what can we resist, if it is not the *Durcharbeitung* [working through]? This *Durcharbeitung* is the absolute opposite of a recollection. We certainly do have to bear witness to the Forgotten in thought, writing, art, and public practice. But the negative lesson that the "forgetting" of the *Shoah* by the great thinker of Being teaches us is that this Forgotten is not primarily Being, but the obligation of justice.

22

The Grip (*Mainmise*)

(1990)

I will only make a few observations. I will have, and I would have, difficulty in identifying the place from which they will have been made. This is not, I presume, the place of knowledge of presumed knowledge. For I *know* nothing about what I have to say. Nor do I know anything of this love of knowledge and wisdom with which the Greeks have infected us under the name of philosophy. For it seems to me that I have only ever loved what will not let itself be known or what will not create wisdom in the common way. Perhaps these remarks will not even have been made from a place. In any case, not a named locality. And not a utopia either. I would prefer to grant it the privilege of the real. Let us leave its name, its label, in suspense.

Manceps

Manceps is the person who takes hold, in the sense of possession or appropriation. And *manicipium* refers to this gesture of taking hold. But it also refers to *that* (it's a neuter word) which is taken hold of by the *manceps*. The slave, that is, designated in terms of the regime of belonging rather than of service. The slave does not belong to itself. Hence it does not have the capacity to appropriate anything at all, either. It is in the hands of another. Dependence is an inadequate term to designate this condition of being seized and held by the hand of the other. It has been the case that adults or self-styled adults have believed that the child could be defined in this way: the one that one holds by the hand. What I have in mind, however, is the following reversal and another tradition: we are held by the grasp of others since childhood, yet our childhood does not cease to exercise its *mancipium* even when we imagine ourselves to be emancipated.

This theme of childhood recurs in the idea or the ideology of emancipation. Born children, our task would be to enter into full possession of ourselves. Master and *possessor*, as Descartes put it, thus insisting on the act of seizure, an act to be carried out on the set of existing things (called nature).

But master and possessor of what *in us*, if we are fully emancipated? Would some childhood remain, after childhood? Something unappropriated after appropriation has carried out its act of seizure so that we have become owners in our own right? Kant defines the Enlightenment as the emergence of mankind from its self-imposed immaturity ("Answering the Question: 'What is Enlightenment?' "). If childhood persists after childhood, it is "laziness and cowardice," he writes, "it is so easy to be immature." The task of emancipation thus belongs to courage (in the double sense of resistance to fatigue and resistance to fear). To the courage of the very thing that is taken in hand by the *manceps*, and that consequently lacks courage. This banal theme is familiar; it is inherent to the West. It governs the aporias of freedom (one must be free in order to free oneself) and salvation (one must be good in order to redeem oneself from evil and become good).

Roman law had the merit of a cruel clarity: emancipation was in the hands of the *manceps*, in principle. Only the proprietor holds the power to relinquish his property, to transfer it. He who has set his hand upon the other may withdraw it. It is doubtful whether this relinquishing of the grip [*mainmise*] can be *deserved*. Who can tell what price the slave must pay in order to free himself? Is there even a common standard of measurement for those who are held and those who are free, a common standard of measurement shared by both the property owner and the expropriated, that would allow the price passing from one condition to the other to be calculated? Can there be emancipation by ransom? Is not the relinquishing of his grip always an act of *grace* on the part of the *manceps*? Grace, in principle, has no price. Can it even be obtained? Isn't the slave's prayer to the master to pardon him from his childhood inherently presumptuous? Does it not already contain the arrogance of a demand? Is it appropriate for someone who does not own himself to formulate a demand as if he were his own property? The exodus of the Hebrews is not the result of the clemency of the king of Egypt, but only of the pain that followed their prosperity. And they only escaped from the pharaoh's *mancipium* by placing themselves under Yahweh's.

By childhood, I do not only mean, as the rationalists have it, an age deprived of reason. I mean this condition of being *affected* at a time when we do not have the means—linguistic and representational—to name, identify, reproduce, and recognize what it is that is affecting us. By childhood, I mean the fact that we are born before we are born to ourselves. And thus we are born of others, but also born to others, delivered into the hands of others without any defenses. We are subjected to their *mancipium*, which they themselves do not comprehend. For they are themselves children in their turn, whether fathers or mothers. They do not attain emancipation from their childhood, either from their childhood wound or from the call that has issued from it. Thus they do not know, and they will never know, how they affect us. Not even if they were to try their hardest. Their very love for their son or their daughter may well turn out to have been a calamity. That is, their love may turn out to have exerted such a grip on the child's soul that it will always remain unknown to the child, even as an adult. It may be the case that the child will be so affected by this grip that it will not occur to the child to rebel, or that the child will not even be granted the grace to beg for release from this grip. I am not only thinking of deep neuroses or of psychoses. For the child, everything is trauma, the wound of a pleasure that is going to be forbidden and withdrawn. The resulting suffering and search for an object, more or less analogous to emancipation, stem from this plague. The flight from Egypt is also called vocation. We have been called by our name to *be* this name, we know not who or what calls us, and we do not know to what we are called. We know only that it is impossible to ignore this call and that fidelity to this requirement cannot be avoided, whatever we do and even if we try to ignore it.

Humanism, whether Christian or secular, can be summed up by this maxim: humanity is something that ought to be freed. There are several different versions of that freedom, the essence of modern philosophy from Augustine to Marx. And the distinction in the West between Christians and secularists is no doubt not absolutely relevant with regard to this freedom, since there is a social and political Christianity that aims to release the creature from the *mancipium* of the temporal powers and there is a spiritual secularism that searches for its internal truth and wisdom, as in late pagan stoicism. But what would constitute liberty itself, the state of emancipation? Innocence, autonomy, or the absence of prejudices? Adamic innocence is not autonomy—quite the contrary. Jacobin autonomy is not innocent. A state of the will is not a state of affection. And the condition of emancipated intelligence, of free thinking, is yet another thing. What matters here is to keep separate the three orders distinguished by Pascalian thought, or the three kinds of judgment isolated by Kant (these are not the same as Pascal's three orders: it is of course the case that along with knowledge and practice there is a third order, that of the heart, in both thinkers; but the heart is dedicated by Pascal to the love of Jesus, by Kant to the feeling of the beautiful and the sublime).

Even so, the modern Western ideal of emancipation mixes all three orders together. Emancipation consists of establishing oneself in the full possession of knowledge, will, and feeling, in *providing oneself* with the rule of knowledge, the law of willing, and the control of the emotions. The emancipated ones are the persons or things that owe nothing to anyone but themselves: Freed from all debts to the other. Denatured, if nature signifies an initial expropriation, a native state of *mancipium*, such as innate ideas, an already spoken destiny, or the "nation."

For two millennia, in political, epistemic, economic, ethical, technical, and perhaps even poetic thought and practices, modernity has traced its path by criticizing supposed "givens." The West does not accept gifts. It takes up, elaborates, and gives back to itself whatever is assumed to be given, but it treats the given as only a possible case of the situation (whether political, epistemological, poetic, etc.). Other cases are thus possible. They are conceived and carried out. That is called development or complexification. What was held to be the essence of the situation (political, economic, mathematic, etc.) ceases to be essential. Situational *axiomatics* are installed. This is true not only of geometries, of mechanics, of political constitutions, of jurisdictions, of aesthetics, but also of erotics (Sade's *120 Days of Sodom*) and of techniques, even of material (so that we speak of the "materiological").

This "emancipation" is the story of a Faust who didn't need to sell his soul because one had not been entrusted to him, so he was under no obligation to return it to the donor, nor did he have the power to steal it from its donor. On the other hand, Thomas Mann's *Doktor Faustus* remains an apparent and intentional product of ancient belief: the independent and autonomous constitution of music by Leverkühn or of politics in the Third Reich will have to be paid for with devastation. It incurs the wrath of God, the only *manceps*. Thenceforth, emancipation asserts that it is itself emancipated from the anxiety of conscience that can be the effect of the sin of ontological pride. General opinion holds that mankind has no obligation but to free itself, and that it owes this duty to itself alone. Only thus can we respect ourselves and be worthy of respect. We acknowledge instances of being grasped or seized only in order to deny them. They are thus conceived as cases, represented and treated according to scenarios. One frees oneself from the other by locating it as an exteriority and then taking a grip on it.

The Fable

I am not attempting to draw a distasteful portrait of this long movement that has agitated the West for two millennia (and the human world along with it). I confess that in my darker moments, I imagine what we still call emancipation, what the decision makers call development, as the effect of a process of complexification (called negative entropy in dynamics) that has affected and still affects the small region of the cosmos formed by our sun and its minuscule planet, Earth. Humanity, far from being the author of development, would only be its provisional vehicle and temporarily its most completed form. This process, once it has been started and set to expand, would develop far beyond the capacities of the human brain. The brain, considered as the most complex known aggregate of matter, possesses within its structure and mode of operation capacities for complexification that have yet to be exploited in the minute of cosmic time one calls human history. And so on, and so on. I will spare you this fable, popular with so many people, and not just the scientists.

This fable has the very emancipated virtue of enforcing no prescription upon the one who hears it, and therefore not requiring to be believed. It does away with the horizon of a call. In order for it to be verified it is enough for humanity to keep alive the will to emancipate itself. The fable "only" says that this will does not belong to humans, is not even a will, nor the obedience to any call, but the mental echo of a necessity resulting from cosmological chance. The fable nevertheless anticipates a contradiction, which we are just beginning to identify: the process of development ends up in contradiction with the human plan of emancipation. We have signs of it in the disastrous effects of the most developed civilizations, effects that motivate the ecology movement, incessant curricular reforms, ethics commissions, the crackdown on drug trafficking. Leaving aside the measures that humanity may employ in an attempt to make development bearable, without, however, bringing it to a halt, one question remains, the only question: Which man, or human, or which element in the human is it that thinks of resisting the grip of development? Is there some instance within us that demands to be emancipated from the necessity of this supposed emancipation? Is this instance, this resistance, necessarily reactive, reactionary, or backward looking? Or is it perhaps the product of a *remainder*, the element that all the memory data banks forget: the uncertain and slow resource, heavy with promise, that immemorial infancy lends to the (art)work, to the (art)work as expression of the desire for the *act* of bearing witness? Is there an ever-present zone of captivity that does not require the remembering and fixing in place of the infantile past, but demands indeterminate and infinite anamnesis?

Mancus

Anyone in the grip of a *manceps* is *mancus*, *manchot*, missing a hand. The one who lacks a hand. Emancipating oneself in these terms means escaping from this state of lack. In freeing himself from the other's tutelage, the *manchot* takes things in hand once more.[1] He believes that his castration has been healed. This dream that we may put an end to lack is what gives rise to the emancipation of today. The dream of having done with my lack, with what I lack, with what made me lack, what made me have lack. I would make the claim, without defending it here, that the preeminent mode in which lack appears is time, and that time is also, inversely, what requires emancipation in order to put an end to the lack that is time.

Contemporary life attests, by evidence of which the modern tradition is still ignorant, that time is the name of lack and therefore the adversary that must be defeated in order to emancipate oneself. Accelerated transmission, the rush of projects, the saturation of data banks, fascination with what the computer engineer calls "real time," that is, the near-perfect coincidence (almost at the speed of light) between the event and its reformulation as information (as a document), all bear witness to a convulsive struggle against the *mancipium* of time. Another example, one among many: credit financing performs an analogous function. It lends borrowers the time they don't have. And they will have to hurry to pay back this time in time. But insurance guarantees that the lender will get this time back, no matter when the borrowers may die. Enough . . . Does all of "developed" life bring to light this temporal aspect of emancipation *a contrario* (despite itself)? I say *a contrario* because emancipation does not only attempt to loosen the grip of the castrating force of temporal duration, nor that of death as the end of this duration. Emancipation seeks to undo the grip of history itself, the grip of the postponed time of the promise, since there is no history without the promise.

Among the moderns, since Paul and Augustine, the promised emancipation is what orders time as the course of a history or, at least, according to a historicity. For the promise required the undertaking of an educational journey — an emergence from an initially alienated condition toward the horizon of the enjoyment of selfhood or freedom. Thus, duration takes on the directed significance of waiting and working toward this horizon. Duration gave a rhythm to the adventure of trial and announced its end. Pagan Europe had endowed itself with this time in the structure of the Ulyssean cycle. Christian Europe postponed the *denouement*, the moment of homecoming. The holiness of *being released* (the state of freedom) was put off to a last day, in the future. Release (the act of freeing) became the daily bread of the healthy will, the effort of a sacrifice, which will have its reward. Modern philosophy in its phenomenological, speculative, and hermeneutic forms takes this ethical tension and grafts onto it the eschatology of a knowledge that is also the desire for the emancipation of meaning, permanently at work.

As it shortens the postponements or delays of this emancipation, the contemporary world liberates itself from this horizon of history or historicity in which emancipation was a promise. What do today's machines lack with their lightning speed? They are built to lack nothing, except lack. They certainly do not know that they are going to die, but I do not believe that this is the essential point of their stupidity or their wickedness. Rather, their essential weakness is that they have not been born. They had no childhood, in the sense I have given it. There is no lack, and thus no history in the sense of the narrative of a promise to be kept, unless we bear the enigma and the wound of a birth that we missed, our birth. Only when the machines are handicapped [*manchot*] in this way will they be able to think, that is, able to try to free themselves from what has already been thought, before them.

Mancipium

A major uncertainty about childhood, about binding and releasing, governs my thinking. An uncertainty, that is, about the very core of what governs emancipation. Hence this uncertainty concerns the nature of the call and of what calls: the father. Jesus' answer to the question Who is the greatest in the kingdom of heaven? vibrates like an arrow that has hit the target: the little one, the child (Matthew 18:1-5)—*parvulus*, in the Latin of the Vulgate. That is why the child ought not be "offended" [*scandalisé*] (Matthew 18:6). Under the name of *wound*, I have said that this scandal (which Freud called seduction) is inherent to infancy, insofar as childhood is subjected to the *mancipium* of adults (*mancipium* in the double sense: the *mancipium* they exercise over the child and the *manicipium* that their childhood exercises over them, even when they exercise it over the child). Jesus adds, "Woe to the world because of offenses [*scandales*]. For it must need be that offenses [*scandales*] come; but woe to that man by whom the offense [*scandale*] cometh!" (Matthew 18:7).

There are thus two meanings of the word *infancy*: the infancy that is not bound in time and that is the heavenly model of those who do not need to be emancipated, having never been subjected to a grip other than that of the father; and an infancy inevitably subjected to scandal or offense, and thus subject to the abjection of not belonging to the truth of this call. Everything that leads this call astray is scandal or offense: violence, exclusion, humiliation, the seduction (in the original sense)[2] of the innocent child. He who causes scandal exercises a *mancipium* over the child, which distracts and separates it from the only true *manceps*, the father. This scandal and this distraction are necessary. It is necessary to be *bound*, expropriated, appropriated by humanity, instead of by the father.

There is a principle of seduction, a prince of seduction. The fable of Eden clearly states that this principle is that of sexual difference and that this prince[3] is the evil that speaks in woman. To be freed would be to emancipate oneself from the seduction of this woman whom every child has "known" before knowing that it was a woman, his mother. The fable also makes it known that the woman desires the man to forget that he cannot have knowledge. The woman's desire is for man to set himself up as a rival to the All-Powerful and, at the same time, for man to cease to obey the call of the All-Powerful, that is, to cease to be bound to his *mancipium*. This is the wicked emancipation, the one that the hysteric whispers to her man: you are not castrated. This emancipation is paid for in suffering, toil, and death. And fratricide.

Things are not that easy, however, neither on the mother's side nor on the father's. On the mother's side, I would draw a parallel (but I am not the first: the comparison is already suggested in Luke 1:7 onward, by the figure of Elizabeth) between Sarah's sterility, the trait that characterizes the mother in the Hebrew tradition, and Mary's virginity in the Christian tradition. These traits are far from being identical, assuredly. Fecundation by the word of Yahweh—Sarah greets it with laughter. That is why the child will be called "He laughed," Isaac. And Sarah will drive Hagar from her house, Hagar her servant whom she had nevertheless given to Abraham when she was barren so that he might have his only son, Ishmael, by her. Laughter of disbelief, and laughter of revenge. Compare this with the simple faith of the Virgin in Luke 1:37 and 1:46, with her smile perhaps. But these two traits lend each a kind of assurance of exemption. I am tempted to say Jewish be-latedness and Christian prematurity. The fact of being too late or too early to bear children assures these women, Sarah and Mary, of a kind of exemp-tion from the seductive destiny of mothers. As a result, their sons, Isaac and Jesus, will have little or no experience of the distractions of the maternal *mancipium*. Their mothers will have hardly been women at all.

The trial of binding and release comes to the son from the father himself. It will hardly come as news to you[4] when I say that each of these elements, binding and release, takes a completely different turn in the Torah and in the New Testament. And by the same token, emancipation, good emancipation, is thought completely differently in each of the two.

In each case, good emancipation for the child consists in meeting the call of the father, in being able to listen to him. It is not a question of freeing oneself from this path one iota. Freeing is opposed to listening. Paul is very clear on this subject, in Romans 6:19 on, when he expresses himself "after the manner of men, because of the infirmity of your flesh," and when he writes: "As ye have yielded your members servants to uncleanness and to iniquity unto iniquity; even so now yield your members servants to righ-teousness unto holiness" (Romans 6:19). He also says that the only freedom from death lies in welcoming "the servitude of God," which has "holiness" as its "fruit" and "everlasting life" as its end (Romans 6:22).

As for the Jewish side, it is unnecessary to supply a further gloss on lis-tening, which I would like to call absolute (in the sense that a musician may be said to have an absolute ear), or indeed to expatiate upon the ear that Abraham and Moses lend when they are called by name.

Christians and Jews are in agreement on this point, that emancipation is listening to the true *manceps*, and that modernity breaks this agreement.

Modernity tries to imagine and carry out an emancipation in the absence of any other. This can only appear, in terms of the Scriptures, as weakness and impurity, a recurrence of the Edenic scenario. However, modern emancipation did bring forth a horizon. A horizon of liberty, let us say. Of the liberation of liberty. Yet to the extent that liberty "conquers" itself, as it extends its *mancipium*, its hold, and we get to what I have tried, rather poorly, to identify by the name of postmodernity, this horizon (historicity) disappears in its turn, and it is as if a paganism without Olympus and without pantheon, without *prudentia*, without fear, without grace, without debt and *hopeless* is reconstituting itself. This return of paganism takes place under the aegis of the cosmological rule of development, which is not a testament at all, neither a law nor a faith.

Although Jews and Christians agree on the impossibility, inanity, and abjection of an emancipation without *manceps*, without voice, they are nevertheless profoundly at odds. I would characterize their disagreement as concerning the value that each gives to sacrifice. For present purposes, I took another look at the Epistle to the Romans 2:17 on and the Epistle to the Hebrews. But I also reread Genesis 22, which tells the story of what is called the sacrifice or the holocaust of Isaac. I was struck that Paul, demonstrating the superiority of the new covenant over the old, does not make any allusion to the trial of Abraham (except in Hebrews 11:17, and then only to exalt the faith of the patriarch, which Paul considers as a forerunner of Christ-like faith). Paul attacks the Jewish ritual faith of the annual sacrifice, the arrangement of the temple into two tabernacles, with the second accessible only to the high priest, the sacrificial sovereignty of the Levites, and the Mosaic gesture of spilling the blood "of calves and goats" on the book, on the people, on oneself, and on the tabernacle (Hebrews 9:19-21). But he does not say the thing that seems to me essential to our subject, precisely that Yahweh demands that Abraham sacrifice his son, but prohibits him from carrying it out.

When I say "demand," I am transcribing poorly. Reinhard Brand, a young theologian and philosopher who learned the square letters of the Hebrew alphabet in the faculty of Hebrew theology at Heidelberg (and homage should be paid to this old city for this fact), and with whom I did some work at Siegen University, has explained to me that the letters in the Torah that name this demand of God have their closest equivalent in German in the verb *versuchen*. This means to make an attempt, to try out, with a suggestion of temptation. Yahweh *tests* Abraham in demanding his son from him, this son that he gave him in a most unusual, even insolent, way, this son who will always provide the Jews with a way to laugh at their own improbability, and perhaps even at Yahweh, the unpronounceable. Yahweh tests, and he renounces, he sends the ram. There will have been no sacrifice of the child.

Only a perpetual threat. The threat that Yahweh might forget to send the ram.

As Georges Steiner ably expresses it in the small volume entitled *Comment taire?*, every Jewish son knows that his father might be called to lead him to the hill henceforth named Adonai-Yerae, which means "God will provide" (rabbinic translation), for him to be sacrificed to Yahweh. And he knows that he cannot be sure that God will provide.

Even so, Yahweh did not take back the son he had given. That is why it is absurd that what the Jews simply call the *Shoah*, the disaster, should be called the holocaust. There is nothing sacrificial in this disaster. The principle that a sacrifice, the sacrifice of the child (which of course Christian anti-Semitism blamed on the Jews), can obtain grace (i.e., the emancipation of souls otherwise destined to internal death) is radically absent from Judaism. All that one can say is that God will provide for emancipation. But God is not foreseeable. He has promised. How the promise will be kept, no one knows. We must scrutinize the letters of the book. Scrutinizing the letter of the book does not just mean observing the rites to the letter, as Paul meanly suggests. Jewish emancipation consists in the pursuit of writing, writing about writing, and writing on the occasion of the event.

These letters are those of a history, of a host of stories. These stories are what we call Jewish jokes [*histoires juives*]. I mean by this that, in the case of the names that are called, the pure signifier (the tetragram, which should make these names into saints by calling out to them) can always end up lacking, end up by signifying something other than what the one who has been called thought that it said. It is this breakdown that makes one laugh. But it can also go so far as to let these names plunge into the horror of what Elie Wiesel has called *the night*. The night of the ear, and the night of meaning. No call can be heard except the call of the kapos, heard when standing for hours in the night.[5] No sacrifice to the signifier can or ought to hope to obtain a guarantee of redemption from him. One must ceaselessly read and re-read the letter that promises redemption. I will borrow a joke from Daniel Sibony, in *La juive* (1983): "A beggar comes into a community in eastern Europe, asking for money to rebuild the synagogue of his village (his *shtetl*) where *everything has been burned*. Moved by this disaster in which the letter and the place were finally *consumed* (although the letter ought to burn without being consumed), the leader of the community gets ready to make a *gift* to him, a rather rare and difficult gesture, when he suddenly thinks of a precautionary measure: 'Where's the report of the fire?' The other's answer: 'It got burned along with everything else.' Of course, the absurdity makes one laugh, but it here goes further, to the limits of laughter: in the very *telling* of this joke there *is a burning*, if the letter that tells it has burnt" (p. 25).

The bond passes around Isaac's body; its "bonding" [*liance*],[6] following Sibony's translation of the Hebrew *akedat*, can be undone by Yahweh, thus marking the precariousness of the "bonding," almost encouraging the people of Israel to forget it, encouraging renewed sinning and trial, encouraging rereading and rewriting without end. The letters of the book are both the letters of the stories it tells and the letters that tell the stories of the reading of these stories. The letter burns the letter; there can be no dogma of emancipation in this relation to the evanescent signifier. Dogma means that a matter of opinion, *doxa*, is fixed and established once and for all.

You know more than I do about the new covenant. As Paul explains, it puts faith in the place of the letter. This faith is possible only because the bond with the signifier has been guaranteed "once and for all," a recurring expression in the apostle's Epistles. The father has not asked for the son and has not bound him so as to then release him, he has given his own son as a sacrifice, and he has actually sacrificed him. The letter has been consumed, but the report of the fire (the Passion) did not burn along with it. For the child is reborn and leaves his tomb to come into the *mancipium* of the father. Emancipation through belonging to the father's voice and liberation from the *mancipium* of secular history *did occur*. This emancipation transfigures suffering, humiliation, and death into passion. This transfiguration is *already* emancipation. Here the signifier plays no tricks. He has made himself into bread and wine. Even aesthetics is sanctified, when the flesh receives pardon.

Of course, this confidence in forgiveness can give rise to bad emancipation, to appropriation, to privilege and temporal power. You have been aware of this and you have protested. But it didn't take a "new" New Covenant for Christianity to be emancipated from the grip of the vanities. All that was needed was to unleash the dialectic of works and faith that had been inaugurated by the son's sacrifice and redemption. This dialectic of transfiguration has suffused the thought and politics of secular Europe since the Enlightenment. I do not think that this is the case any longer.

It would be possible to go further in exploring the differend that sets the Christian testament against the Torah by clearing up the question of pardon. This question governs the problems of emancipation directly. It also has a decisive effect on the relation to time, above all to the past. Hannah Arendt wrote in *The Human Condition* that pardon is forgiveness for past actions. Not a forgetting, but a new deal. It would be necessary to examine the relation between pardon and emancipation, to ask who has such an authority over the *res gesta*, over what is finished. And what does this mean for the unfinished past, the past of an infancy that will have been affected without having known it?

23

Europe, the Jews, and the Book

(1990)

Unification for Europe also means the unification of its hatreds. Among them, it is essential not to confuse racism or xenophobia with anti-Semitism. These are two different kinds of hatreds. Both can go as far as cold-blooded murder, lynching, arson, the looting of homes, the destruction of community buildings. In setting anti-Semitism apart, there is no question of neglecting, of "swallowing" or letting the almost regular assassination of Maghrebi children, adolescents, or adults in France be forgotten.

The profanation of the tombs and the displaying of a corpse torn out of its coffin on a stake in the Jewish cemetery of Carpentras say something specific: after the *Shoah* the Jews have no right to their dead or to the memory of their dead. There is a long tradition of the profanation of Jewish cemeteries in Europe. The "final solution" martyred and killed millions of Jews for no political reason, but it also made them disappear, and it tried to erase all trace of the annihilation.

My claim is that the Jews represent *something that Europe does not want to or cannot know anything about.* Even when they are dead, it abolishes their memory and refuses them burial in its land. All of this takes place in the unconscious and has no right to speak. When the deed is done in full daylight, Europe is seized for an instant by the horror and the terror of *confronting its own desire.*

Europeans behave like rich relatives toward their poor cousins when dealing with foreign immigrants, especially if they are Europeans. The violence of their passions, their blindness, the many criminal acts are all family matters. All tragedy is a family matter.

But the Jews are not part of the family, although they have been "installed," as they say, at Carpentras for more than a millennium, and in Prague, Budapest, and Rhenanie for centuries. The Jews are not a nation. They do not speak a language of their own. They have no roots in a *nature*, like the European nations. They claim to have their roots in a book.

Do people have something against books, against their book, against the readers of this book that would lead them to the point of violating Jewish tombs to kill their dead? In principle, not at all. Europe is enlightened; they respect letters and scholars there. In fact, yes. Nothing is as slow, difficult, and unprofitable as learning to read, which is an endless activity. In a society avid for performance, profit, and speed, it is an exercise that has lost its value, along with the institution that trains people for it. Hence the general crisis of education, contempt for teachers, and generalized anti-intellectual-ism that extends to even the "cultural tasks" of the media. But the fact that the Jews are the "People of the Book" does not for all that explain the pro-fanation of their cemetery.

What does begin to explain it is *what* their book *says*. For what it says is something that Europe, initially Christian, then republican, now rich and permissive, does not want to know or cannot know. This book, which is at the base of Europe's whole culture, remains within that culture as excluded from it.

It is an old story. It begins with the Epistles addressed to the Romans and the Hebrews by the Apostle Paul. Forgive my brevity and consequent mis-representation. The book of the Jews says God is a voice; no one ever gains access to his visible presence. The veil that separates the two parts of the temple, isolating the Holy of Holies, cannot be crossed (except once a year by the priest, chosen by God). Anyone who passes himself off as divine is an impostor: idol, charismatic leader, supreme guide, false prophet, Son of God. The law of justice and peace does not become incarnate. It gives us no example to follow. It gave you a book to read, full of history to be inter-preted. Do not try to come to terms with it. You belong to it; it does not belong to you.

However, Paul says that this is not so, that the veil of the temple was torn "once and for all" at the moment when Jesus died on the cross. His sacrifice redeemed your sins "once and for all," repeats the apostle. The law gave you grace, God gave you his son and the death of his son as a visible example. Through him the voice was made manifest. It said clearly: love each other like brothers.

This was a revolution. It is the beginning of modernity. Christianity is es-tablished and spreads by (almost) effortlessly supplanting moribund ancient paganism. But what is to be done with Judaism, with those who cannot manage to believe in the Christ myth, those who nevertheless provided the first book, the ancient law — the fathers, in Europe, of written religion? And what is to be done with a religion that reveals that the veil does not rise?

The whole social, political, religious, and speculative history of Christian Europe bears witness to a permanent undertaking, using various means (in-quisition, conversion, expulsion, censorship) to neutralize the Jewish message and banish the community of unbelievers. Not until the twentieth century will the church revise its position on this matter. Which does not mean that the villages and towns of Europe will follow its teaching . . .

I am accusing no one. A differend as to the relation to the symbolic—that is, to the law and to death—is at stake. The Christians announce to us that, finally, we are all reconciled brothers. The Jews remind us that we are always sons, blessed but insubmissive. The message of redemption is more pleasant to hear, easier to "exploit" and propagate than the memory of indignity.

But today, after the *Shoah*? Is it not over? It will never end. The Christian churches had introduced the motif of fraternity. The French Revolution extended it, by turning it on its head. We are brothers, not as sons of God but as free and equal citizens. It is not an Other who gives us the law. It is our civic community that does, that obliges, prohibits, permits. That is called emancipation from the Other, and autonomy. Our law opens citizenship to every individual, conditional on respect for republican principles. The Jews are allowed in like anyone else. That is called assimilation.

But how could someone who professes *heteronomy* be transformed into one who exercises *autonomy*? A Christian can manage to reconcile things: the debt to the Other has been paid symbolically, once and for all; autonomy is permitted, within certain limits (these vary from one church to another). But for a Jew, the debt has not been symbolically wiped away, its extinction has only been promised. Redemption does not depend on works or even on intentions. God alone will emancipate.

What then can a "French or German citizen of Israelite profession" be—above all if he is an officer like Dreyfus or a head of government like Blum?[1] In the European unconscious, it is recognized that his debt to the Other will prevail over his duties to the others, to the national community. And that he is bound to be a potential traitor. Unless he forgets himself as Jew. This is the great temptation for the "assimilated" themselves. The "final solution" will come as a monstrous reminder to them that they are always, even *despite themselves*, witnesses to something about which Europe wants to know nothing.

People are surprised that anti-Semitism persists after the "final solution." But look at contemporary society. It no longer speaks of fraternity at all, whether Christian or republican. It only speaks of the sharing of the wealth and benefits of "development." Anything is permissible, within the limits of *what is defined* as distributive justice. We owe nothing other than services, and only among ourselves. We are socioeconomic partners in a very large business, that of development. The past has importance only insofar as it is capitalized into powers of all kinds that allow us to hold sway over "the future." Now that politics is also a discredited profession, it serves only to encourage development by taking care of the redistribution of its effects.

Politics has lost its monopoly on tragedy. So much the worse and so much the better. This will be the case for all of this brave new Europe.

As it rushes forward, what interest can Europe have in the words of the unknown voice in the book of the Jews? What can it make of these obscure stories of law and debt among bands of shepherds, already several millennia old? What can it do with these commandments from another age? The stubborn readers of this book, the witnesses to the Other are no longer even bothersome, but picturesque. A postmodern form of repression: they are made obsolete, they become kitsch. The Jews are just fine, when all is said and done.

Thus the annihilation of what the book of the Jews says continues in the unconscious of a permissive Europe. Thus continues the annihilation of the message that the law does not belong to us and that our reconciliation with it remains pending. This is the constitutive anti-Semitism of a Europe that has, in one way or another, always thought the opposite of this message, has always thought its self-constitution. What is shameful in the profanation of the Carpentras cemetery is, I fear, that it was truly an action from another age. Abject with respect to contemporary "values." But how do these contemporary "values" relate to the book that the dead of Carpentras used to read?

Part V
Algerians

24

The Name of Algeria

(June 1989)

The journal *Socialism or Barbarism*, in which these articles [chapters 25-34] appeared, was the theoretical mouthpiece of a few militants, workers, employees, and intellectuals who had banded together with the aim of carrying on the Marxist critique of reality, both theoretical and practical, even to its extreme consequences.[1]

An act was being repeated. In 1937, Trotsky had founded the Fourth International to fight the Stalinist bureaucracy and the criminal policy that it was imposing on political leaderships and workers' groups throughout the world, from China to Spain. Ten years later, a group of militants from several countries "left" the Fourth International with a negative attitude.

Blinkered by "classist" orthodoxy, Trotsky had not been able to define the class nature of "communist" societies, refusing to see in their bureaucratization the formation of a new exploitative ruling class. Enslaved by an "economism" that is perhaps justified in societies where "youthful" capitalism exploited the work force without restraint, Trotskyism does not profoundly rethink the desire for autonomy (or dis-alienation) that animates workers' struggles in developed capitalist societies. Attached to the principle of "democratic centralism," it learns no lessons from "workers' democracy," from the modes and forms of organization that workers spontaneously invent in their struggles, be they major conflicts or day-to-day resistances. And lastly, Trotskyism does not perform an analysis of the changes that capitalism itself undergoes (by virtue of its own development), even after capitalism has reached the "highest stage" identified by Lenin half a century ago.[2]

As one can see, there was plenty to be done. The group inherited the entire revolutionary tradition, both theoretical and practical, then in existence, including ideas that came to it from sources other than Trotskyism: Pannekoek's "Workers' Council" movement, the POUM,[3] revolutionary Trade Unionism, "Bordigaism,"[4] workers' opposition, the shop steward movement, the "News and Letters" movement . . . One thing was clear from this tradition: the workers' movement had been incessantly defeated over the past century. Some defeats had been heroic, some obscure (that is, insidious). But it was no longer enough to blame these defeats on weakness, on betrayal, on the leadership of the movement, whether reformist or Stalinist. The leitmotif of the traitor or the fool only served to put off the work that had to be done. It kept alive the malaise afflicting emancipation, the malaise that it claimed to denounce. It was necessary to rebuild the framework of ideas governing the emancipation of workers throughout the world from the ground up, while remaining as faithful as possible to what arose from their struggles—in order to give it back to them. (For the inventive quality of the immediate practice of workers' struggles is so common that its value tends to go unnoticed.) That value lies in the fact that this inventiveness is *already* emancipation. And the role of the revolutionary organization is not to direct workers' struggles, but to provide them with the means to deploy the creativity that is at work in them and the means to become aware of that creativity so as to direct themselves.

Today, anyone who describes the group Socialism or Barbarism as having been the hybrid offspring of Parisian intellectuals, whose sole worth lay in not having been too much in error about the nature of either the socialist and communist "left" or the liberal and conservative right during the time of the cold war and decolonization, only perpetuates the very thing against which the group fought. Such a description perpetuates the forgetting of what was actually at stake (this is a common idiocy in historical and sociological studies).

Such an analysis perpetuates the forgetting of what is and remains absolutely true about what was at stake. True even today, when the principle of a radical alternative to capitalist domination (workers' power) *must* be abandoned (something that allows many people, innocent or guilty, to relinquish all resistance and surrender unconditionally to the state of things). This stake, which motivates the carrying on of resistance by other means, on other terrains, and perhaps without goals that can be clearly defined, has always been, and remains, the *intractable* [*intraitable*].

A system can be as exhaustively provided as possible with information, with memory, with anticipatory and defensive mechanisms, even with openness toward events—the idea that guided Socialism or Barbarism was ultimately, even if it was expressed in other terms, the idea that there is something within that system that it cannot, in principle, *deal with* [*traiter*]. Something that a system must, by virtue of its nature, overlook. And if history, especially modern history, is not simply a tale of development, the result of an automatic process of selection by trial and error, this is because "something intractable" is hidden and remains lodged at the secret heart of everything that fits into the system, something that cannot fail to make things happen in it [*d'y faire événement*].

Under the names of "inventiveness," "creativity," self-government," along with a principle of autonomy already present in the actuality of the class struggle (names and a principle that could at times give rise, and that have given rise, to spontaneist or anarchist political organization), Socialism or Barbarism identified, I believe, the secret from which all resistance draws its energy. It identified that secret in the hope that by showing the motive of their resistance (actually inexpressible) to those who resist, the group would help them to remain faithful to this motive, help them to not let themselves be robbed of it under the pretext that it is necessary to organize oneself in order to resist.

If the group's existence, over some twenty years, was itself extremely turbulent, this was certainly not because of conflicts over status or personal interests—as is the rule, or so it seems, in the Parisian intelligentsia. Just as there is an ethics of psychoanalysis to be respected, so the group respected the ethics of political anamnesis. Controversies, resignations, and splits all took place over how to understand the struggle that was taking place and how to take part in it. This was the turbulence of an interminable cure, where the past of the revolutionary tradition was at work, but in the daily laceration of modern life. Nothing less academic. It was indispensable to re-read texts and actions, in sum, to prepare the Acts of the Workers' Movement, but this work was worthless unless it was directed by an open attention, a free-floating attention,[5] to living contemporary struggle, in which the intractable continued to show itself.

There was plenty of "work," as there is for the patient in analysis. As much as possible the group entered into these struggles. It was not "like a fish in water"[6] (because, after all, water only serves the fish for its survival, as the masses serve the party apparatus). Rather, it was like mind and memory bending in the face of free associations, bending before them the better to *reflect* them. For a long time, the group respected the ascesis of self-effacement in order to give the workers the opportunity to speak. The group only appeared on what is called the political stage in 1968, when the student government foregrounded some of the motives that had been animated by Socialism or Barbarism.

I have recalled this situation (in my fashion and under my sole responsibility) only in order to underline how much these writings about Algeria are indebted to Socialism or Barbarism. The signatory would have been completely incapable of writing them had it not been for the education that he received from the group (in both the tradition and in an attention to what I have already mentioned) and had not everything that he wrote on the issue been submitted to the merciless and sincere criticism of comrades.

In recognizing this obvious debt, I hope also to make today's reader understand why my picture of the Algerians' war is so unlike the one that appears in the memoirs, log books, and chronicles (good or bad) in which people bear witness to their experience of the "Algerian War." My picture is only sketched with difficulty, only corrects itself from moment to moment over seven years, on the basis of the thought and practice of the group. And these texts are certainly those of a combatant, but one who is neither French nor Algerian, but internationalist. Had I been a conscript or a *fellagha*, that would not have changed any aspect, I am sure, of what this picture, in all revolutionary probity, should have been.

It was my lot, as it was of many others (which was something that was discussed in the group), to lend practical "support" to the militants of the FLN [National Liberation Front] in France at the very same time that I was making theoretical criticisms of the organization in the journal. I did not find it necessary to adjust my diagnosis to fit in with my practice, nor did I desire to give up the latter because of the former. It was just, we told ourselves, for the Algerians to enforce the proclamation of their name upon the world; it was indispensable to criticize the class nature of the independent society that their struggle was preparing to bring about. This intimate differend *should* remain unresolved, unless we wish to lend credence to the false and dangerous idea that history marches at the same pace everywhere, in the Aurès[7] and at Billancourt,[8] or unless we wish, even more stupidly, to count on the peasants of the Third World to revolutionize the industrialized societies.

But I have also remembered my debt to the group for another reason. By placing our struggle under the sign of a fidelity to the intractable, I mean that the "work" we did can and must be continued, even when everything indicates that Marxism is finished with as a revolutionary perspective (and doubtless every truly revolutionary perspective is finished with), when the intractable voice or the voice of the intractable is no longer heard in Western societies on the social and political wavelengths. The radicality of Socialism or Barbarism, if one were to be faithful to its form, would remain a dead letter under present conditions.

Fidelity does not consist in maintaining the revolutionary tradition at any cost when the intractable has fallen silent in the realm in which it has spoken for over a century, that is, in the realm of social and political struggles. I am not claiming that one should cease to take an interest in that realm. Rather, those struggles no longer demand "work," this work of spirit, of body and soul, that was required in order to hear them and take part in them only thirty years ago. It seems to me that they do not demand anything more than intellectual, ethical, and civic probity.

This does not mean that the system has digested the intractable. It has assimilated everything that could be the legacy of the social and political struggles of the oppressed for over a century. In our own backyard, one has only to consider how the great impulses of 1968, which made young people build barricades and spread strikes to the point where the system broke down, in order for them to make these impulses felt, are now "well understood," almost obvious, and, by virtue of that very fact, unrecognizable.

Even in the article of 1960 included here, the suspicion of a significant part of the group appears, the suspicion that the political was ceasing or would cease to be the privileged site in which the intractable appeared. We spoke of a "depoliticization." It was on account of this that the group split up.

From this political crisis, which subsequently became even more evident, I preserve only one belief: that it is inaccurate and intellectually dishonest to impose the hope that, as Marxists, we should only invest in the revolutionary activity of the industrial proletariat, upon the freely spontaneous activities of such as young people, immigrants, women, homosexuals, prisoners, or the people of the Third World. This is not to say that these activities are negligible. But thought must yield to the evidence that the grand narratives of emancipation, beginning (or ending) with "ours," that of radical Marxism, have lost their intelligibility and their substance.

The presumption of the moderns, of Christianity, Enlightenment, Marxism, has always been that another voice is stifled in the discourse of "reality" and that it is a question of putting a true hero (the creature of God, the reasonable citizen, or the enfranchised proletarian) back in his position as subject, wrongfully usurped by the imposter. What we called "depoliticization" twenty-five years ago was in fact the announcement of the erasure of this great figure of the alternative, and at the same time, that of the great founding legitimacies. This is more or less what I have tried to designate, clumsily, by the term "postmodern."

The task that remains is to work out a conception and a practice completely different from the ones that inspired "classical" modernity. To readjust the latter, even subtly, to the present state of things would only be to mint and distribute counterfeit coin. Certainly, something of the intractable persists in the present system, but it is not possible to locate and support its expressions or signs in the same areas of the community and with the same means as those of half a century ago.

I would like to be able to honor the name of Algeria in a manner suitable to the sentiment that links me to it. It would be quite a singular anamnesis.

Who could be interested in my little story? A free ascent toward smells and sights, the sound of a poor and ancient wisdom in the city, a sharp light on the slopes, on the unquestionable ridges, the eruptions here and there of an endemic violence, of anguish, and a few names. I am thinking of Constantine[9] between 1950 and 1952.

I owe Constantine a picture of what it was for me then, when I arrived from the Sorbonne to teach in its high school. But with what colors should I paint what astonished me, that is, the immensity of the injustice? An entire people, from a great civilization, wronged, humiliated, denied their identity.

My few names, Bouziane, Champeaux, Souyri, Harbi, come to me from the institution where this aporia reached boiling point: the school.

The French Republic contrived to burden a few young Algerians with a borrowed culture while their own culture, that of their people—its language, its space, its time—had been and continued to be devastated by a century of French occupation.

Constantine suddenly caught me in this intense complication, and it kept me at a distance. What inner weight did this severe city have that made me quickly put myself at the service of its people?

The War of the Algerians[10] is written to this city, perhaps without my knowledge. It is the correspondence of a lover. From a distance, the lover confesses his jealousy of everything that deceives or will deceive the loved one. He admires the loved one, he encourages the loved one. He complains, knowing the loved one will not meet the fate that courage and beauty deserve.

When the group Socialism or Barbarism gave me responsibility for the Algerian section in 1955, Algeria did not name a "question" of revolutionary politics for me, it was also the name of a debt. I owed and I owe my awakening, *tout court*, to Constantine. The differend showed itself with such a sharpness that the consolations then common among my peers (vague reformism, pious Stalinism, futile leftism) were denied to me. This humiliated people, once risen up, would not compromise. But at the same time, they did not have the means of achieving what is called liberty.

Almost all the companions of that time are dead today, and dead because of this differend. Mohammed Ramdani, still an Algerian student, comes to tell me that I must publicly offer to them what is rightfully theirs.[11] The debt will not be paid off for all that. At least testimony will have been made to this intractability that, at one time, bore the name of Algeria, and that endures.

25

The Situation in North Africa

(1956)

Tunisia: in January 1952, riots at Bizerta and Ferryville are bloodily put down and a general strike is called.

Morocco: in December 1952, riots in Casablanca; in August, throughout the country. Proclamation of the internal autonomy of Tunisia in July 1954, independence of Morocco in March 1956.

Indochina: Battle of Dien Bien Phu from February to May 1954; French forces evacuate Hanoi on October 9, 1954, and the whole of North Vietnam in mid-May 1955.

In Algeria the National Liberation Front (FLN) and the Army of National Liberation (ALN) unleash on November 1, 1954, the "uprising" that is their declaration of war. On April 2, 1955, the French Chamber of Deputies passes the law declaring a state of emergency in Algeria. The elections of January 1956 are postponed in Algerian provinces. In the metropole, they are won by the Republican Front of Mendès-France. Mollet is made president of the Council of Ministers. He is welcomed in Algeria, where Lacoste is the resident minister, on February 6, 1955, by tomato-throwing crowds. On March 12, the council accords special powers for the government of Algeria.

The most obvious significance of the events in North Africa since 1952 is that of a new phase in the decay of French imperialism. To clarify this particular meaning, it would be necessary to show how and why the French bourgeoisie has shown itself generally incapable of preserving its colonial "empire" since the Second World War. Here I only want to note the essential elements of the recent history of the Maghreb: on the one hand, why the national-democratic objective of *independence* has constituted, and still constitutes in part, a platform capable of bringing together all the "popular" forces from the middle bourgeoisie to the agricultural subproletariat. On the other hand, I want to examine what perspectives of struggle are opened up once states and their apparatuses of repression have or will have been handed over by the colonists to their "valid interlocutors."

171

The conspicuous fact is, in effect, that the imperialist political apparatus has *broken down* in the three countries of the Maghreb since 1954, and has *given way* in Tunisia and Morocco. From the perspective of the global struggle of the proletariat, this fact is apparently of limited significance: a mere shift in the regime of exploitation. However, it is of crucial significance in relation to the conditions of overexploitation of the North African proletariat and must be immediately taken into account. I will then go on to consider which class will seize or has already seized control of the administrative organs that ensure exploitation, in order to ask what line the revolutionary movement ought to take, after we have defined the structure of power.

The Colonists Take a Step Backward

Why is there, why has there been, fighting "with bombs and revolvers" since 1952[1] in North Africa? For independence at most, at the least for internal autonomy. The right to self-determination is the common denominator of the MTLD, the Néo-Destour, and the Istiqlal.[2] Leaving aside Jacobin phraseology, a concrete objective remains: to end the colonists' control of the administrative and repressive apparatus, at least in its internal functioning. Thus, the discussions of the Franco-Tunisian conventions only ran into "serious difficulties" when tackling the essential elements of this apparatus: the municipal and central administrations, the police, the army. Indeed, the agreements concerning these points have already been called into question: Bourguiba [leader of independent Tunisia] wants a little bit of an army. The problem will soon be as pressing in Morocco.

Why did the struggle of the Maghrebi peoples occur in this domain and with such unanimity? Because the organization of the administrative and repressive mechanisms assumes considerably greater importance in North Africa than in technologically advanced countries. In short, in the Maghreb the police perform an essential *economic and social* role. The nature of their role must be understood in light of the brutally reactionary character of French colonialism in these countries.

Is North Africa an outlet for French manufactured goods? Yes, of course.[3] Manufactured goods in general constitute 54 percent of its imports.[4] But the absolute volume of these imports remains very low in relation to the population: manufactured goods find an outlet only in the privileged stratum of the colonists and the top administrators and in the semiprivileged stratum of the salaried "aristocracy," and this stratum is very thin. It is clear that an effective imperialist policy, whether it is "neocolonialist" or "progressive," must aim at developing an outlet for manufactured goods through large-scale investments, industrialization, and the creation of a middle class and a "modern" proletariat with increased buying power. In short, an effective imperialist policy necessitates the constitution of a market.

Yet capital investment is very weak: the Commission of Investments calculated the value of the annual investment per inhabitant in 1954 at 9,400 francs[5] for Algeria, at 8,700 for Morocco, at 5,500 for Tunisia (versus 54,900 francs for France).[6] Public investment is notoriously lacking: for example, North Africa is insufficiently provided with energy. As for private investment, it is directed toward the commercial, financial, or insurance sectors rather than toward industry.[7] In this sphere, the interest of the French cartels coincides with that of the colonists: both seek to maintain the North African economy in a preindustrial state. If agriculture were industrialized, writes the director of agriculture to the government of Algeria, the fellahs would become agricultural wage earners: "Is it really in our interest to proletarianize future elements of the population, *when social stability presumes an inverse development?*"[8] The direct occupation and direct rule of the Maghreb by France, whether as fact or as tendency, allows France to seal off these territories against all "foreign interference," that is, against any capitalist investment that might weaken "social stability."

But does this situation only call for economic agreements? Far from it. Among the traditional functions of the colony in the imperialist system, the only one that North Africa fulfills effectively is that of agricultural and mining production.[9] This function requires the appropriation of the means of agricultural and mining production to the greatest extent possible. "Social stability" rests, then, on the radical expropriation of 18 million Muslims by 1.5 million Europeans. In Algeria, of the 4.5 million hectares actually cultivated, 2 million belong to the Europeans, and precisely 1.5 million to 7,000 colonists.[10] The ratio of European to Muslim property ownership seems less discriminatory in Tunisia and in Morocco, but this apparent lack of discrimination arises only because imperialism consolidated the power of Muslim feudal lords in those countries. The result is the same for the fellah. Since the worst lands are left to the "natives," the poor soil combined with small landholdings make 70 percent of Muslim farms economically unviable.[11] The formidable mass of peasant smallholders[12] and expropriated peasants[13] cannot find employment either in industry[14] or on the large farms[15] because of mechanization. The fate of the North African peasantry is henceforth clear: it dies of hunger. And this is not just an image.[16] Permanent scarcity, permanent unemployment, permanent emigration, even without taking periodic famines into account. India has nothing on the Maghreb.

This ragged subproletariat exerts a formidable pressure on the pay scale. The average *annual* income of an Algerian peasant is 20,000 francs, and that of an industrial worker 100,000. The average Algerian industrial wage is a third of the minimum industrial wage in France: neither the agricultural wage earner nor the independent worker is entitled to Algerian family benefits, and in 1953 only 143,000 workers were registered on welfare![17] In 1951, the daily wage of the seasonal workers in the vineyards of the Constantinois ranged between 200 and 250 francs in return for eight, ten, and sometimes twelve hours of work. And there were still Tunisian peasants crossing the border who would accept 180 francs.

Such a level of exploitation of labor ultimately provides companies with unbeatable profit margins,[18] and this is the real meaning of "social stability." I cite these figures only so as to gain agreement, without further demonstration of the essential economic and social role played by the administrative apparatus: you do not create 70 percent profit margins innocently; you extract those profits from millions of dispossessed workers in the shape of sweat and death.

You have to take precautions; you interpose bribed or bribable bosses, administrators who are careful not to administer, cops, even occasional legionnaires, who employ the double-bottomed jars of Berber myths as their ballot boxes, the bloody bric-a-brac of a society where exploitation can no longer be discreet. You do not only seize the means of production; you also crudely sabotage the means of understanding—paying off the Muslim clerics, propagating illiteracy, outlawing the mother tongue, humiliating.

The entire daily life of almost all Muslims is thus taken over and ground down by the handful of colonists: Maghrebi society is a totalitarian society, where exploitation presupposes terror. And since class frontiers are almost exactly homologous with "ethnic" frontiers, class consciousness is impossible: a person is crushed for being an Algerian or a Tunisian as much as for being a worker or a peasant. The cop who clubs or who tortures is European, the boss or the foreman is European, the officer is European, the professor is European: scorn is European and misery is "Arab." Therefore, the struggle situates itself immediately at the national level; it spontaneously seeks to suppress the apparatus of state terror where oppression takes on its most obvious shape and independence. That is to say, the suppression of the apparatus of state terror appears to be a counter to exploitation.

In reality, there is no other alternative to exploitation than socialism; in reality, the national-democratic struggle of the North African people contains within it the seeds of a new mode of exploitation. But for all that the subjective and objective content of the goal of independence must not be underestimated. Its aim subjectively expresses the maximum possible consciousness for a proletariat ground down by material and moral terror; it crystallizes the meaning of a rediscovered dignity. Objectively, the conquest of national "independence" forces the colonists to take a step backward, to abandon the terrorist apparatus that was the precondition for overexploitation; in this way it creates a revolutionary situation characterized by power sharing: economic power to the colonists, political power to the "national-ists"; within this situation the problem of property ownership has to be faced.

We in France can therefore do nothing other than support this struggle in its extreme consequences. Contrary to the totality of the "left," our concern is in no way the preservation of the "French presence in the Maghreb." We are unconditionally opposed to all imperialism, French included. We are un-conditionally hostile to the pursuits of terror.

The "Valid Interlocutors" Take a Step Forward

There remains the question of which line to take in the dominated country. In order to establish this line, it is necessary to specify whether the "valid interlocutors" are actually valid, whether the "qualified representatives" of the Maghreb peoples are qualified by anyone other than themselves or the French bourgeoisie.

First it is necessary to point out that this question cannot be answered in the same way for the three North African countries. Each is characterized by differences in economic and social structure. In Algeria, expropriation was so pervasive and colonial administration so direct that there was practically no place left for the development of a Muslim bourgeoisie: shopkeepers and intellectuals, the only representatives of a well-to-do Arab class, are com-pletely marginalized by the administrative apparatus, and their economic role is limited to mercantile capitalism. In Tunisia and above all in Morocco, on the contrary, there exists a Muslim bourgeoisie that occupies a more prominent position in economic life: the old preimperialist mercantile bour-geoisie and some elements of the agrarian feudal system were enriched in the interests of the protectorate, and the capital accumulated by them in agri-culture or foreign trade was partially reinvested in industry. Consequently, in the protectorates, the conditions exist for domination by the local bour-geoisie. These particularities of development are explained by the respective dates of French expansion: Algeria was invaded by a dying aristocracy and occupied for a long time merely for the benefit of commercial companies who contented themselves with controlling the ports. Tunisia and Morocco were, on the contrary, the indispensable "cures" for a capitalism that was undergoing its first great imperialist crisis.

Yet these structural differences show through in the present nationalist movements: Tunisia and Morocco have produced parties with a specifically bourgeois leadership and program. In contrast, their Algerian equivalent, the UDMA, is a very weak party, while the Etoile nord-africaine, the first nucleus of the present MTLD, originated among the Algerian workers who had emigrated to France.[19] Of course, the social content of these parties is not as simple as it may seem: we have demonstrated that their ideology brings together an entire "people," which means that they contain social contradictions. But the nationalist platform, specific to a bourgeoisie seeking to constitute and monopolize a domestic market, proved sufficient in Morocco and Tunisia to group together all the social forces, and the best proof of this is the expansion of the left-wing nationalist parties since the last world war: the creation of the Destourian UGTT after 1945 and the infiltration of the Moroccan Trade Union Congress by the militants of the Istiqlal in 1948. The division of forces between Muslim bourgeoisie and proletariat favors the UGTT, largely owing to the support given by the colonists to the bourgeoisie in its struggle against Stalinist unionism. From this it is clear that even if the European oligarchy agrees to relinquish a part of the state apparatus to the Tunisian and Moroccan nationalists, it is because the Europeans know that this bourgeoisie is sufficiently differentiated as a propertied class to preserve the conditions for an "honest" exploitation. The rate of profit will perhaps fall from 70 percent to 40 percent, but that fall is tolerable, even prudent, and the oligarchy will end up convincing itself that it has succeeded. For its part, the "enlightened" French bourgeoisie seeks to bring about such a turn of events in Morocco, just as it has in Tunisia.

There can be no negotiations in Algeria, however, because "it is France." In reality, it is well known that there are no valid interlocutors in Algeria — that is, a local bourgeoisie already capable of having arms distributed to the underground forces (as in Tunisia) and of diverting the attention of the peasantry and proletariat away from land sharing, by one means or another. The peculiarity of the Algerian independence movement is evident in the splitting of the MTLD in the summer of 1954 into a "collaborationist" faction and an "intransigent" faction. The disarray of the party's base after the rupture favored a regrouping under the auspices of the activists of the CRUA, and the absence of a central workers' organization directly controlled by a bourgeois party, along with the cooperation of the nationalists with the Stalinists at the heart of the Algerian and French CGT, lent further specificity to the Algerian situation. The Chamber of Deputies' successive and apparently contradictory votes on Moroccan and Algerian policy are explained by the awareness of the French bourgeoisie of the fact that it cannot depend on any local bourgeoisie in Algeria. As a result, the Algerian problem is the problem of a power vacuum.

The French Communist party solves this problem in familiar terms: "Some will not fail to claim that there are no valid interlocutors in Algeria in order to try to disguise their hostility to all negotiation. If one truly wanted discussions with the Algerian people, it would be easy to find interlocutors who are capable of speaking in its name" (*L'Humanité*, July 30, 1955). And Duclos develops the thesis that the "shrewd" Gilles Martinet had already elaborated in *L'Observateur*: "loyal elections." More cautious than our progressives, Duclos requires some preliminary guarantees: basically an end to the repression, the release of detainees, and the suppression of mixed local councils. These are the very same conditions set by the leaders of the National Liberation Front and the National Liberation Army, through the mouth of Barrat's interlocutor (*L'Observateur*, September 15, 1955). But what point of view do these condition represent? Insofar as the elected representatives are to negotiate with the French government they represent "the new ties that will unite Algeria and France." As for the Stalinists, they address the reformists (through the authorized voice of Maurice Thorez) in the following terms: "Have we not already shown that we support a policy of negotiation with the peoples of North Africa for *the creation of a true 'Union française'*?" (*L'Humanité*, November 5, 1955).

Stalinists thus objectively take the position of a "very enlightened" bourgeoisie on the Algerian question. Why? First, because they have little support in Algeria: "about twenty officials, appointed by the French Communist party, who have no real influence over the Algerian masses" (a fellah leader, *L'Observateur*, September 15, 1955). This is the case in all of North Africa, so that their only hope for expansion in the Maghreb lies in France. Second, because the chances of American imperialism in an "independent" North Africa are currently much greater than those of the Russian bureaucracy. By keeping the French bourgeoisie there in one way or another, the French Communist party protects the future possibility of a Stalinist imperialism, already prefigured in the Near East. Its support of the FLN is thus a formality, and for the rest, the Algerian Communist party has always been uncertain about the underground resistance forces. In this matter, the colonists did the Communist party a service in lumping them together with the MTLD.

The question that remains to be asked is that of the social content of the National Liberation Army. Recruitment is easy among the unemployed. But who are the leaders? The recent study undertaken by Delmas in *Combat*, a study that is a monument to dishonesty, concludes that they are "nihilist" bandits sent from Cairo by religious fanatics. This is a well-known refrain. There is only one conclusion to be drawn from the material Delmas cites: that the fellah cadres are in effect hostile to the two older factions of the MTLD and to all "Bourguibist" attempts to make a "valid interlocutor" out of Messali.[20] Why such hostility? Apparently, the underground resistance hopes to assume the role of valid interlocutor, which Barrat's interlocutor confirms elsewhere, but the French bourgeoisie, for whom Delmas faithfully interprets, does not intend to negotiate with the leaders of the underground forces and would prefer negotiation with a broad-minded politician. The bourgeoisie looks for such a politician in the person of Messali or anyone else. Yet there is no bourgeoisie in Algeria strong enough to support a Bourguiba. One can conclude that negotiation has no future, even with all the "popular fronts" one might wish for in France. The development of the situation will essentially be determined by the underground resistance forces and one may expect, in the absence of all proletarian consciousness, the evolution of an embryonic military and political bureaucracy, which the scattered elements of the Muslim commercial and intellectual stratum will likely join.

Elsewhere, the situation has not stabilized in either Morocco or Tunisia. In the case of Morocco, the incapacity of the Destourian bourgeoisie to resolve social problems leads the former fellahs to support Salah ben Youssef; in Tunisia, the underground fighters of the Rif, supported by El Fassi, have not disarmed since the return of the sultan. In effect, it is evident, on the one hand, that bourgeois nationalism alone is fundamentally incapable of redistributing land in accordance with the hopes of the peasantry and that the concept of independence runs up or is going to run up against the immediate necessity of resorting to the kind offices of America or the Soviet Union for investment; and on the other hand, it is clear that the workers' movement in the North African countries, even if it did away with its bourgeois leadership, would not be in a position to set socialist objectives in the short term. Under such conditions, the growth of conflicts seems inevitable, conflicts between privileged factions who will make themselves into the mirror image of imperialist greed and conflicts between the new masters and the exploited, on whose side all those dissatisfied with the dominant policy will stand.

In North Africa, like anywhere else except even more intensely, the task of rigorous ideological clarification presents itself. We must recognize the possible revolutionary impact of a struggle for independence. It is also necessary, however, to know how to denounce the aims of nationalist leaders who, under cover of this struggle, seek to impose an indigenous ruling class as new exploiters. To this end, the nationalist leaders will have to integrate themselves into one of the imperialist blocks, be it American or Russian. Lastly, it is important to understand and to make it understood that the only solutions (the solutions that none in the struggle can provide) are class solutions, the first of these being the direct appropriation of the land by the peasantry.

26

The North African Bourgeoisie

(1957)

> *Mollet's policy is carried out. Franco-British offensive*
> *launched against the Suez canal (nationalized by Nasser) in*
> *autumn 1956 (while Khrushchev is "pacifying" Budapest).*
> *In October 1956, interception of the Moroccan airplane*
> *carrying five "historical leaders" of the FLN, among whom*
> *is Ben Bella. They are interned in France. In January 1957,*
> *Massu is given full powers to maintain order in Algiers. The*
> *"Battle of Algiers" begins.*
> *General embarrassment of Maghreb neighbor states*

The hour of truth has come in Morocco.[1] Is not the Moroccan bourgeoisie publicly accusing its proletariat of being "the cause of the morass in which it flounders?": "Remember, dear compatriots, that we needed all our courage and all our faith in our future, as well as all our love for our venerable sovereign, in order to accept cheerfully the month-long strikes that had such profound repercussions on commerce and industry." And President Bekkai, author of these pious words, added with a realist despair, "Billions of unpaid drafts block our bank tellers' windows, tens of billions have fled our country." With a spontaneity that deserves admiration, the young Moroccan bourgeoisie has been able to adopt the paternal and vaguely ogrelike tone of the ruling classes in the face of worker agitation. At the same time, it has thrown aside the mask of national unity at the moment when it was most needed; the Moroccan workers are in no hurry to take up their role in the nationalist drama once more, to judge from the number of exhortations to "calm" and the appeals to "maturity" with which they are graced daily. Even if President Bekkai no longer accepts the strikes "cheerfully," it is by no means certain that the tenderness that the workers have for him will preserve him from further woes.

The economic crisis comes as no surprise. The French still own 90 percent of private investments in the Moroccan economy. It is clear that since the return of the sultan (for the most farsighted, even since his exile), the profits drawn from this capital have not been reinvested: they disappeared to Tangiers, France, and Switzerland, or they were used for speculative ends, or they were even purely and simply hoarded. On the other hand, the French government suspended its financial aid until the signing of conventions giving it sufficient guarantees. Now the Moroccan budget is evidently in deficit: the metropolitan contribution alone allowed it to be just about balanced at the time of the Protectorate. Moreover, the peasants, having shown their tax collectors the door in the person of the *caids*,[2] demonstrate a regrettable tendency to ignore Rabat's fiscal administration. How to balance the budget? asks the very orthodox Bekkai government. Its solution: tax electricity and gasoline.

Just as Napoleon III "lost his revolutionary wits [*sel*] by taxing salt [*sel*]" so too Bekkai loses his nationalist essence by taxing gasoline [*l'essence*]. Since trucks are the mode of transportation in Morocco, a 68 percent tax on gasoline and the tax on electricity are enough to double consumer prices. The capacity of the domestic market, already remarkably weak, shrinks a little further. The small firms close; the unemployed—more than 100,000 in the region of Casablanca alone—begin to besiege the municipalities. The workers who are employed strike in order to obtain wage increases. This is when the strict Bekkai raises his voice in order to demand "orderly work, peace, and the security of property and persons." Failing this, he threatens to resign, along with his coalition ministry.

At any rate, the ministerial coalition has already been effectively dissolved, like the National Front in the countryside. The Bekkai government was made up of an artful balance of Istiqlal, PDI [Democratic Party of Independence], and independent ministers. Since everyone is "independent" in one way or another, and since the labels continue to serve to identify individuals (because the programs of each party—that is to say, of each "personality"—remain prudently evasive) and since secularism, interventionism, monarchism, and republicanism, "Westernism" and "Easternism," have already changed camps several times, it would be too risky to describe the parties in the government in terms of their social orientation. However, the crisis, as we have said, reveals their true faces a little more each day: the majority of the ministers, Istiqlal, PDI, or independent, are dyed-in-the-wool liberals. This includes those bloodthirsty terrorists—such as Balafrej, who so conveniently calmed the fears of the international capital sheltered in Tangiers—that the French Residence has tended to put into solitary confinement over the past few years. This majority is flanked on its right by a few representatives of the Arab *caids* (the few who are not too compromised with the French) led by the *caid* Lyoussi, former minister of the interior, currently minister of state and promoter of the antiparty cause in the mountains and in the south. Finally, Bouabid (Istiqlal) represents, on the left, the faction of the party that controls the Moroccan Trade Union Movement: he is the "progressive" of the team. This colossus moves along, tripping over its own feet, under His Majesty's leadership.

Credit must be granted to the monarch's perspicacity in that this singular hodgepodge reflects the social reality of Morocco pretty accurately. The combined development[3] of this country effectively juxtaposes a precapitalist rural society (with its tribal organization almost entirely intact, thanks to the care of the French administration) with the nucleus of a capitalist economy sowing the seeds of a modern proletariat in the ports, in the mines, and in a few factories. Roughly, the concrete problem for the Moroccan bourgeoisie consists in destroying the Arab aristocracy without letting itself be devoured by the workers. It must struggle on the two fronts, and the reproach it makes to Bekkai through the voice of the Istiqlal is that he struggles only on one front, against the workers. In fact, the agrarian aristocracy has already taken the offensive under Lyoussi's leadership, with the help (disavowed but objectively effective) of certain colonialist groups and the official support of Abd el-Krim; here again, a singular collaboration that will no doubt enlighten the Moroccan workers. If the Arab *caids* go on the attack (under the royal banner, as they should, like everyone else), it is because they are particularly threatened not only by the present situation, but by historical development itself.

The birth of the Moroccan nation means in effect the death of the lords of the hinterland [*bled*]. These aristocrats, whose title to nobility often does not go back any further than to Lyautey, underwent a slow death at the hands of the very people who had raised them to power. Imperialist penetration objectively implied the condemnation to death of the very tribal and patriarchal organization that the imperialist administration had subjectively maintained. The ever more artificial preservation of traditional social structures constrained the fellahs (two-thirds of the Moroccan population) to a catastrophic agrarian practice: lands divided in the extreme by the customs of inheritance, limited use of water according to the ancestral rites, tools as tragically pathetic as their landholdings, exhaustion of the land by repeated subsistence crops, and so forth. This picturesque "Berber" civilization, which, in the absence of any "Berbers," was of interest only to the Arab aristocracy, not only killed the peasants like flies, not only filled the shanty-towns with an immense proletariat in rags, it also prevented the development of the urban economy, precipitated the crisis, and made the agricultural barons, who profited from this state of things, still more intolerable to the peasantry. There was no domestic market, and there still isn't one: the countryside "lives," if one may put it that way, almost on the margins of the monetary economy. Imperialism accepted this situation: it speculated on the sale of lands, of buildings, on adjudications, on changes, it shot or deported the malcontents. But breaking the deadlock of the French political apparatus required nothing less than the unleashing of the force of the exasperated peasants by the Moroccan bourgeoisie. The Istiqlal penetrated the countryside by exploiting this anger, accelerating the deterioration of the tribal community and its replacement by the nationalist, or at least dynastic, ideal. There are 600,000 members of the UTM [Moroccan Workers' Union]: half are rural, proof of this transformation. Another proof: many tribes expelled their lords. The king sent new lords to rule them in the name of the nation. But these were sometimes the same individuals after a facelift, and at any rate they had to put an end to the "disorder," so they persecuted the rural cells of the Istiqlal, opening undeclared hostilities. What would the peasants do?

Lyoussi prepares his response: what they have always done, that is, what their *caids* always made them do—take up arms and enter the cities in order to impose the will of the hinterland, that is to say, of their lords. This Juin of independent Morocco launches "his" peasants against the cities of the bourgeois and the workers, in order to impose on the king the monarchy he desires, a feudal state.

A wasted effort, at least if our view of the situation in the countryside is correct. For even if the peasants are incapable of organizing their force themselves, their aspirations push them in a direction that is contrary to the one that Lyoussi wants to impose on them. The peasants will do nothing on their own, save banditry, but one cannot make them do just anything. In reality, the question of the democratic revolution is asked, if not in their heads (this is unlikely) at least in their deeds.

And here we return to the old issue of permanent revolution: this revolution whose preconditions arose in the countryside, and that should allow the bourgeoisie to constitute the domestic market it requires in order to consolidate itself; is the bourgeoisie itself incapable of making it, as Trotsky thought? In struggling on the two fronts, is the Moroccan bourgeoisie destined to failure? Is it true that "for backward countries the road to democracy passes through the dictatorship of the proletariat"?

Without wanting to resolve the question in general, one can at least show that in this case it is a false problem. The Moroccan proletariat is absolutely not ready to construct its own dictatorship. It is numerous, of course, but assessing revolutionary forces is not a matter of bookkeeping. Bookkeeping is not what counts. What counts is that the proletariat does not have a clear consciousness of its own objectives or of its capacities. This working class is not socialist and has not yet produced an avant-garde. It has barely begun to disentangle itself from the nationalist rags in which the Moroccan bourgeoi sie disguised it during the resistance. Indeed, the workers did not wait for Bekkai's reprimand to notice that a Moroccan owner faced with a strike differed little from a French owner. Certainly, the Istiqlal leaders tried to persist in the "nation against nation" line, to divert the workers' fight against the *présence française*, the French army, the French borders, the French police; yet it is still the case that the dissatisfaction of the *medinas* is directed against *all* tight-fisted employers, against *all* speculators, against *all* cops. This said, the 200,000 to 300,000 workers scattered throughout Moroccan cities are not, however, concentrated in large firms where the direct contact of each individual with the whole would be constant. In fact, the discussions are carried out in the Istiqlal cells, and the exchanges are always controlled, oriented by the Istiqlal leaders—the same ones the workers find again in the trade union: for the UTM is to the Istiqlal what the CGT is to the French Communist party. What's more, the owner of the small company where they work, for the most part, is himself Istiqlal, has resistance credentials, knows how to talk, disarms them. In these conditions, the development of class consciousness is powerfully hindered by the class that does not want a consciousness. This is why the bourgeoisie "of the left" can develop this line: we will carry out industrialization together against the *caids*, the colonists, and the right wingers.

Is this possible? If workers' dictatorship is impossible, does the same apply to the bourgeois dictatorship? The program currently developed by the bourgeois "left" calls for nothing less than a Jacobin dictatorship. All traces of imperialism—army, police, administration, and so forth—must be liquidated; the Algerian struggle must be entirely supported; the domestic enemy (colonialists and feudal bosses) must be destroyed, expropriated, and its goods redistributed. The realization of this program requires a unified leadership, which the Istiqlal claims to offer, but it is not a very strong one on account of its internal heterogeneity. Does this line provide the means to finance industrialization? Certainly not. Allal el Fassi estimates that the Five-Year Plan can be secured with 600 billion francs. On their side, the liberals think that 200 billion a year is needed. Where to find the funds? It is possible that France will lend 30 billion once the conventions have been signed. For the rest, offers of help will not be lacking, in the East and the West. But what guarantees will capital require in exchange? The "right" is ready to slow down the struggle against the feudal lords and imperialism in order to appease backers: but then it condemns itself as a merely local bourgeoisie. This is something that the "left" understands well, which is why it wants on the contrary to show the moneylenders a strong Moroccan bourgeoisie, that is, to pursue the nationalist struggle first of all. But it would have to draw support from the peasantry, to shape it, to radicalize it; and it is aware of the risks of such an operation. Did not Allal el Fassi recently declare, "Today we are in the countryside in the presence of a force similar in all points to the Chinese force"? Doubtless he only wanted to make the right-wingers and the liberals tremble a little, but he probably succeeded in frightening himself, to judge from the recent softening of his attitude concerning the problem of the ministry. It is because the bourgeoisie would itself fall by the wayside along the road to a peasant revolution: it is too tied to the landed aristocracy. And, at any rate, it would rather not find in the countryside the means of forming a rural bourgeoisie; a peasant revolution is not a matter of sharing out farms, but rather of collectivizing them.

Nothing further remains to the Moroccan bourgeoisie than to unify itself around a centrist program implying: (1) slowing down and then blocking the course of revolution in the countryside under the control of the sultan's administrators, possibly with the backing of the old underground fighters during the transition period; (2) appeasing the workers' opposition through a moderate reformism; and (3) setting in motion a plan of investment whose major lines have already been proposed to the sultan by Moroccan businessmen and for which Anglo-Saxon capital will provide the necessary nourishment. The palace has practiced this centrism systematically since the return of Mohammed ben Youssef. As his son says, the sultan "is the only person who can resolve these problems, for he is above all political tendencies."

The alibi of the *caids* against the bourgeoisie, the alibi of the imperialists against the peasants and the workers, the alibi of the imperialists against the Moroccan laborers, but the idol of the peasants, this polymorphic Moroccan de Gaulle has not yet succeeded in developing his role for the workers: he lacks the plebeian demagoguery of a Thorez that would actually get them to roll up their sleeves. But, on the other hand, there will soon be plenty of miniature Moroccan Thorezes to do the job: already the Stalinists have entered individually into the UTM, have decided to stick there at all costs. They will soon cry "Long live the king!" by way of a dialectic.

In Tunis, which is a future Rabat, Bourguiba had power over the center for a long time. Once Ben Amar's coalition government, a prefiguration of Bekkai's, had proved its incapacity, Bourguiba entered into the arena and did his centrist act, expelling the ultras and putting down social agitation. The French press applauds, and *L'Express* makes him its "man of the week." "The Tunisian government guarantees the preservation of the goods and private enterprises of French property owners," notes Article 29 of the economic convention. By the following articles, the same government refrains from tampering with the legal system regulating land or with French or mostly French companies. And Bourguiba, very reassuring, confirms: "It is not a question of extending agrarian reform to the big companies" (*France-Observateur*, August 30, 1956). The commercial exchanges guarantee preferential treatment for French products entering Tunisia. That's definitely what they call a "valid interlocutor."

But half of the workers are entirely unemployed. In order to stop the pillage, Bourguiba has bread distributed in place of land. The consequences are well known: capital must be found. Bourguiba prefers French capital. Why? Because this uncertain, braggart, and cowardly Mediterranean capitalism is the least dangerous of the international lenders. But above all because this same capitalism encounters several setbacks in Algeria that are, in part, Bourguiba's setbacks, too. The small calculation of this great man is in effect to interpose himself between the FLN and Guy Mollet in order to implant Bourguibism in Algeria: he knows very well that prolonging the Algerian struggle diminishes the mediocre prospects of an already rather weak liberal bourgeoisie grabbing power. These prospects increased a little when Ferrat Abbas rallied to the FLN: the professionals of nationalism were perhaps going to dismantle the military and political apparatus formed in the underground forces. Bourguiba immediately recognized this qualified representative as his double. However, the internal struggles are not over yet in the FLN. It is not clear who will carry the day. But Bourguiba knows that in shortening the fighting he improves the prospects of Abbas and his peers along with his own prospects.

Arbiter of a conciliatory conference, not only would he have won his first diplomatic victory and spread his prestige all the way to Rabat, not only could he speak more strongly in order to obtain better financial conditions from Paris and elsewhere, but he would end up with Algerian and French weaponry, he would obtain the departure of the French troops stationed in Tunisia, and above all he would make the Algerian underground resistance fighters give way. They would hang their weapons back on the rack, which would greatly relieve our mediator.

Why? Because the Algerian underground forces did not forget that at the moment when they formed themselves, the Néo-Destour on its side abandoned the armed struggle for negotiation. One remembers Ben Bella's phrase: "The vigilance of the combatants will nip Bourguibism in the bud in Algeria." It is now Bourguiba's vigilance that would very much like to kill what he calls "extremism" in Algeria. To bring two parties to negotiate is to bring to the fore the men who know how to speak, the intelligentsia, globetrotters for the cause. Emigration returns control of the domestic resistance to these men, outflanking the cadres of the military organization.

But what is the basis of the conflict between Bourguiba and the Algerian cadres of the FLN? A clash of personalities? Certainly, but what else is there at stake? In order to judge, one must put oneself in the situation prior to November 1, 1954: the procrastination of the MTLD leadership and the conflicts between Messali and the "centrists" had convinced some of the rank and file that the established leadership was incapable of seeing the national struggle through to a conclusion. For a long time, Bourguiba was the hated symbol of conciliatory leadership for these elements, who trained the cadres of the underground forces. Perhaps Bourguiba no longer has exactly this meaning in their eyes, now that he has won "independence." But at any rate, the reconciliation of the FLN's men with the former nationalist leadership can only be achieved through the integration of those leaders into the Frontist organization, as Abbas showed in falling in behind the Front.

Does this hostility have a social basis? There is no doubt that the equivalents of Balafrej or Bourguiba, members of the classical liberal bourgeoisie, had lost the leadership of Algeria by the end of 1954.

Bourguiba wants to give that leadership back to the Algerian bourgeoisie: it is true that the moment of French exhaustion, which will favor this, is drawing near. But this little runt of a bourgeoisie, the outdated product of the period of direct administration, does not represent a social force. If Bourguiba fails, he could end up with several hundred kilometers of common borders with an unpalatable regime, namely, a politicomilitary apparatus that will carry out a few spectacular acts of nationalization and a rather more headstrong agrarian reform than that practiced in Tunisia. This regime would be much more capable than the lifeless Destour government of carrying the masses along by demagogy, because it would give the masses the feeling, both illusory and authentic, of participating directly in the struggle for "independence." There is no reason to doubt that Nasser's example will not be contagious when the objective conditions of this "solution" are provided. The Destour would then fear suffering the fate of the Egyptian Wafd.

I do not want to say that tomorrow Ben Bella will be Algeria's Nasser. I only want to say that the question of the nature of power hangs in the balance in Algeria in a way that it never did in Tunisia or Morocco, that the transformation of the class struggle through the consolidation of a military regime would be capable of reactivating this very struggle in the neighboring countries, that such is the fear that motivates the ultracentrist and entirely conciliatory policies that Bourguiba is presently carrying out.

Meanwhile, he Westernizes the Tunisian family, school, and constitution, while the workers begin to expect that one might de-Westernize capital a little. But the Néo-Destour will not bother with capital any more than the Istiqlal. And the UTM will no more radicalize itself than the UGTT did: its reformism is only the social face of Bourguibism.

Half measures, reconciliation, reforms: as soon as the class struggle emerges from the nationalist swamp in the "backward" countries, new ruling classes seek to stick it back there once more. But they cannot hinder their very efforts from demystifying the workers little by little and leading them finally to envisage the struggle in the light of their own interests.

27

A New Phase in the Algerian Question

(1957)

Despite the French delegate's opposition, the United
Nations General Assembly puts the Algerian question on
the agenda.
*   The French and the English withdraw from Port Said.*
*   On January 28, 1957, the FLN [Algerian National*
Liberation Front] orders a general strike.

Here I simply want to take stock of a situation that is developing very rapidly by emphasizing the striking results produced by the developing contradictions of the Algerian situation over the past year.[1]

In the International Sphere

The Algerian problem was internationalized *in fact* and *as a problem* during
the last UN debate and the vote on the final resolution. Thus, the French
bourgeoisie could not completely stifle the noise made by the boots of half a
million of its soldiers in search of "a handful of terrorists." But the FLN
[Algerian National Liberation Front] did not obtain the condemnation of
France. This failure—all relative, for it is correct to think that the Front does
not want UN mediation—is as much due to the USSR as to the United
States.

Soviet "Moderation"

The position of the Soviet bloc on the Algerian question remains unchanged
for the time being: it explains the persistent inactivity of the French Communist party in the metropolitan sphere. The Soviets want to keep Algeria as
much as possible in the sphere of French economic, political, and cultural
domination, in order to improve the prospects of the Algerian branch of the
French Communist party. Moscow and the Central Committee of Paris have

not yet differed on these points: rapprochement with the SFIO, reluctance to support the Algerian armed resistance since November 1954, systematic sabotage of the struggle against the war in Algeria within the French working class (all the non-Stalinist militants who tried to organize this struggle ran up against the maneuvers of the local secretaries).

But as the Algerian conflict intensifies, the Algerian communists have undergone still more repression, which produces the effect of linking them with the nationalists, hardly the effect envisaged by those who carry out the repression. The French Communist party certainly watches repression work for it without displeasure: the death and torture inflicted on the Algerian militants assure the Algerian Communist party a place in the martyrology of the future Algerian Republic, and the wavering, opportunist, and adventurist line it currently follows leaves open the way to a reversal of policy, if the conflict of the blocs flares up again on an international scale and if the Communist party passes into resolute opposition in France.

Consequently, the tactics of the Communist party and of Moscow are dictated by international relations, current moderation being able to give way at any time to an energetic resumption of propaganda against the "dirty war."

American "Support"

The French "left" seemed disappointed with the support provided by the United States to Pineau: it seemed to hope that the Suez "blunders" would be penalized by the Americans in the UN. Apparently, nothing of the kind occurred. This is because the disintegration of the Western block since Suez had reached the limit of what was permissible. The apparent contradictions between French and American interests in the Middle East had to be stifled, and American diplomacy gave "loyal" support to the French delegation. But it is already certain that this shameless rescue was bought at the cost of a French promise to find a quick solution.

Now that the division is almost completed in Asia, the Middle East and Africa as a whole appear more and more to American imperialism as an extremely important stake in the struggle for world domination. American imperialism seems set upon taking the place of Franco-English imperialism wherever the latter does not manage to abandon the old forms of colonial domination, in the new structures imposed by recently emancipated nations. Such is the case in Algeria. It is superfluous to enumerate all the political, economic, strategic, and diplomatic advantages Yankee capitalism thinks it can draw from the political "independence" of the North African countries.

Consequently, the support given by the United States to France during the UN debate ought to be interpreted more as a respite than as a victory of the *thèse française*. The means of United States pressure on France, in a moment when it is threatened with financial, economic, and social crisis, are sufficient for the prospect of a settlement of the Algerian question to begin to appear.

Insofar as it joins in the process of the political emancipation of the countries of the Middle East and Africa, and insofar as its outcome directly or indirectly determines access to the African market, the Algerian conflict begins to assume an international significance that it did not have in the beginning. It seems that the more and more pressing greed of competing imperialisms ought to have led French capitalism, in one way or another and through many contradictions, to seek actively the outcome most beneficial to its own interests. This task, overwhelming enough given the abilities of present or future French governments, is nonetheless facilitated by an appreciable modification of the Algerian situation itself.

In the Algerian Sphere

Occuring in one year, this change seems to be characterized by the deepening and the acceleration of the process of national unification. This new element seems to favor the preconditions for a future settlement. It is advisable to view the progress of the national movement among the urban classes and in the countryside separately.

The FLN and the Urban Classes

Significance of the Strike. The strike at the end of January expressed the massive adherence of the different Muslim urban classes to the nationalist idea. It touched, on the one hand, all the wage earners (domestics, blue- and white-collar workers in the private and public sectors, functionaries, teachers, etc.) and, on the other hand, the shopkeepers and artisans—consequently, the quasi totality of the Muslim population of the cities. The deployment of the forces of repression was such (the expeditionary corps back from Suez surrounded Algiers) that the adherence of these social categories to the national liberation movement could only show itself negatively by the pure and simple abandonment of all collective life. The wage earners and the shopkeepers broke this minimum of solidarity that, *in fact*, links people, even within a torn society, and that extends, *in fact*, the gesture of a baker, a dock worker, or an administrator to the status of a social activity. Thus the repressive apparatus was, at the beginning of the strike, *isolated* from social reality; it appeared as a massive organization but nevertheless as lacking weight. In abandoning their function, the Muslim workers performed (on a lesser scale, but in the same way as the Hungarian workers) the most radical critique of the state there is. They concretely revealed its abstraction.

But a dictator without a popular arm to twist resembles a paranoiac. The repressive apparatus, abandoned by social reality, reconstructed the scenario of an imaginary "reality": one by one, with trucks loaded with machine guns and blaring Arab music (the supreme psychological ruse of our specialists of the Muslim soul), they went to drive workers, schoolchildren, petty officials, primary-school teachers out of their homes. They put them in their place. Then the proconsul came down from the palace, walked a few paces surrounded by guards in the rue Michelet, and had the goodness to judge this scenario convincing.

The Resistance and the Shopkeepers. But let us leave the little king to his logical delirium. In reality, from now on the Front appears to be present in the commercial petite bourgeoisie under the form of the Union générale des commerçants algériens [Algerian shopkeepers' union], and in the working class thanks to the Algerian trade union movement. The strike demonstrated the scope and the efficacy of the Frontists' penetration work within these two classes that, even a year ago, were relatively marginalized in what was principally a peasant movement.

The Front's consolidation among the shopkeepers should be explicable in terms of this class's complete lack of organization, until now the defenseless prey of the right-wing masters of the Algerian chambers of commerce who monopolize the wholesale trade and to the little racists of the Algerian Poujadist movement, lovers of pogroms. It seems that the excesses of the European wholesale trade, perpetrated by the Poujadist shopkeepers, have unleashed an antimonopolist and nationalistic reflex among the Muslim (and sometimes Jewish) shopkeepers.

Penetration into the Working Class. Nationalist penetration into the working class is a new fact. Of course, Messali's MTLD was a nationalist movement essentially based on the working class, principally the migrants in France. But it had never managed to produce a precise analysis of Algerian Muslim society: starting from the observation that the Muslim bourgeoisie and middle class had not developed, and that there "exists a vast and very extensive backdrop: the masses," it entitled itself "mass party" after having concluded that "in reality there are no distinct social classes in Algeria" and that, from the social viewpoint, "the country taken as a whole does not display class antagonism" (second MTLD National Congress, April 1953). This assessment, somewhat amazing and no doubt explicable in terms of the situation of the movement before the beginning of the armed struggle, made the MTLD into a monolithic and doctrineless organization, incapable, for example, of proposing any agrarian reform to the peasants.

In an inverse movement, the Front, which seems aware of the objectives specific to different social classes, seeks to coordinate and control the action of each one of them through unions (workers, shopkeepers, students). It was in the framework of this strategy that the UGTA [workers' union] first saw the light of day. The latest strike seems to show that it practically eliminated the CGT [French trade union] as a workers' organization with a grip on the Muslim masses in Algeria. The CGT was characterized by a European union leadership that at times lapsed into paternalism and that was always subject to the fluctuations of the French organization as a result of the preeminence within it of an aristocracy of workers (railway workers and functionaries) that was at times fascistic, and thanks to the limitation of its objective to wage claims, though with a few fairly crude Stalinist maneuvers thrown in. The new central organization seeks, on the contrary, to draw support from the agricultural workers, dock workers, and miners and to mobilize them in view of clearly nationalist as well as social objectives. It overtly claims the same role for itself as the Tunisian UFT or the Moroccan UT [workers' union] during the struggle for independence in both those countries. The Front thus seeks to support the struggle of the peasant battalions of the ALN [Algerian National Liberation Army] by means of the social struggle of the workers' organizations and to extend the sabotage of the colonial economy from the farms to workshops, mines, and ports.

If we consider the conditions of absolute secrecy imposed by repression on this development of the Frontist undertaking, we can only conclude that in one year it has made very appreciable progress. The Front has incorporated new social classes into the national struggle; it has increased the number of organizers; it has disseminated its ideology right into the ranks of manual and intellectual laborers and shopkeepers; it has won over the cities that had previously been isolated from all contact with the peasant resistance by the army. The crystallization of the formation of the nation has thus appreciably accelerated, while the training of the staff of the future administration of the nation has continued.

The FLN Apparatus

This last feature, which is parallel to the one that we just examined, constitutes another aspect of the deepening of the process of nation formation.

Even a year ago, the relatively extreme weakness of the Muslim petite bourgeoisie appreciably separated the Algerian situation from that of Morocco or Tunisia. The leadership of the underground forces was not yet sufficiently technically or socially consolidated to be able to guarantee a cease-fire or a "reasonable" agrarian reform to any French negotiators. The armed struggle in particular was still largely a dispersed and relatively spontaneous guerrilla affair; it mobilized the reserves of anger of the miserable and unemployed peasants to local ends. It was not a matter of a "jacquerie"[2] that could be put down by force; rather, it always appeared to be part of an irreversible process. But the organization directing the armed struggle and the social content of the underground forces were both still extremely fluid, strictly subordinated to the local conditions and without coordinated political objectives.

Military Consolidation. Now, however, all the facts that can be determined, in spite of the censorship of Algiers, reveal considerable progress in the military and political organization of the Algerian resistance. The ALN has extended its operational field across the entire territory of Algeria; it has organized its structure of military command into provinces, zones, regions, sectors; each military territory seems entrusted to a leadership tightly controlled by the politicians; military ranks have been instituted along with a system of remuneration. To this nucleus of full-time soldiers there have been added partisans who take up arms or return to civilian life according to the requirements and the prospects of the local situation. It seems, therefore, that the systematization accomplished by the forces of repression has been accompanied, or one should perhaps say preceded, by the systematization carried out by the Algerian resistance.

Political and Administrative Consolidation. A taking up of political and administrative authority consolidates this military implantation. The political commissioners establish select committees in the villages charged with organizing the Frontist cells. The watchword is this: the armed struggle is all important; the objective is the politicizing of the countryside on the ideological basis of national independence and agrarian reform (land redistribution). This political penetration tends to take the form of a working administration, coexisting with or replacing the French administration. The success of this takeover seems proved by the dissolution of all old administrative structures, from the Algerian Assembly to the official *djemaas* by way of the mixed communes: the small faction of feudal lords and Muslim bourgeoisie that still collaborated with the French administration a year ago have been physically and politically eliminated, in such a way that the power of a prefect's decrees does not seem to exceed the range of his escort's submachine guns. The divorcing of the administrative apparatus from social reality, which was so striking in the cities during the latest strike, seems almost always to be the case in the countryside. It seems that the aim of the Front is already to constitute "popular assemblies" in all the villages, embryos of future town councils over which it would maintain tight control by monopolizing the presidency of these assemblies. The conditions of secrecy in which these new steps are being taken are extremely favorable to an effective infiltration.

The Function of the Middle Classes in this Consolidation. It is obvious that this work of setting up a military, political, and administrative apparatus throughout Algerian territory required the Front to control the most economically well off and culturally most developed Muslim classes. The desertion of the universities, the high schools, and the junior schools by the student population (which, as in all the colonized countries, makes up a significant percentage of the total population) made available a large number of young intellectuals; they constituted a precious resource for the Front, first because their level of education is much higher than that of the peasant masses, next because their very youth makes them absolutely unmoved by the seductions of collaboration with the French administration. On the other hand, the middle class of Muslim shopkeepers, most of whom rallied to the resistance, fund it whatever happens (funds that must be added to the taxes levied from the European farmers and property owners).

Characteristics Peculiar to the Front. The support of the weak commercial and intellectual middle class for the nationalist movement, which is explained by the fact that this class cannot develop within the colonial structure, has led to the setting up of an unusual politicomilitary apparatus. This apparatus is characterized by the training of the peasant masses (fellahs, tenant farmers, and agricultural workers) at the hands of the most enlightened and the most entrapped elements of a numerically very weak petit bourgeois strata. These elements bring with them their specific psychology: on the one hand, "rationalism," a taste for organization, a belief in the importance of the cadres, and a tendency to centralism; on the other, populism, a sincere dedication to the cause of the miserable masses, and an authentic sense of participation in their ordeal. This psychology expresses itself both negatively and positively at the level of its nationalist ideology.

Negatively first, in that the great majority of this social group are absolutely devoid of religious fanaticism and reactionary pan-Arabism: They were educated in the French schools and know Descartes better than the Koran (nothing is here for praise or blame). They do not want to destroy either peasant religiosity or the "brotherhoods"; they are ready to take religion into account but only in terms of a progressive appropriation of the "totalitarian" character of Islamic practice. They are no less ready to struggle against the Muslim clerics, who have sold out to the French administration, and they sometimes pride themselves already on knowing not to spare the clerics' lives, even in the mosques.

The Frontist ideology displays this psychology in its positive aspects as well: it is revolutionary in its own historical context, which means bourgeois in ours; it wants to share the lands because it cannot for the time being imagine any other solution to agrarian poverty; it wants to achieve political democracy because it cannot imagine that the "people" might find a way to express its will other than in the institutional framework that French legalism taught it.

Consequently, the "poverty" of the Frontist program is a poverty for us; it is not a poverty in itself, and it is above all not the manifestation of a conscious Machiavellianism that would deliberately entertain vagueness concerning its ultimate intentions the better to impose its "solution" later on.

However, compared to this ideology full of good intentions and devoid of positive analysis (but can one ask the bourgeoisie to make the critical analysis of the bourgeois revolution?), the most extreme intransigence arises with regard to the organization's discipline: a rigorous exclusivism with respect to political representation, a centralism that is only barely democratic concerning the circulation of information and instructions.

As far as exclusivism is concerned, it is a result of the historic situation of the Algerian parties before November 1954: it put an end to the Algerian Communist party's game of switching sides, to the wait and see policy of the MTLD and the UDMA, to the inaction of the *ulémas*.[3] The Front now became, in fact, the only apparatus capable of regrouping the militants who had left the old groupings and of incorporating many individuals outside the organizations. At this point, its line is that of the single party, and the armed struggle, along with the need for secrecy, favors this exclusivism.

As for centralism, it came out of the very conditions of the struggle: the Front was at first a military organization; the subordination of all its activity to the need to support the National Liberation Army and the partisans brought with it the necessity of a single and all-powerful leadership. For more than two years, this leadership has not been controlled by the masses; the masses, on the contrary, have been influenced by its propaganda and its actions. To this must be added the fact that the cadres stemming from the petite bourgeoisie who have incorporated themselves into the Front over the past year will only, because of a level of education that sets them apart from the peasants, accentuate the tendency to unbridled centralism.

Now this apparatus, *single* and *centralized*, is pushed by the logic of development to root itself more and more solidly in the countryside and in the cities, and to control more and more narrowly the totality of Muslim society. It will tend henceforth to take in hand the administration of the country. That means that *the Front is already preparing itself for the role of the ad-*

ministrative stratum of Algerian society and that it is objectively working to bring about a confusion between the present organization and the future state.

It is still too early to know whether, once the conflict is ended, the apparatus will incorporate itself and wither away in a "democratic" kind of state or whether, on the contrary, it will swallow up the state to bring about in the end a new example of the "strong regimes" produced in young nations politically emancipated from colonialist tutelage. At any rate, the problem is already posed in the facts.

Prospects. The profound internal modification of the resistance that we have just described transforms the overall significance of the Algerian conflict. From now on, the Frontist organization constitutes for the French government an indisputable interlocutor capable of imposing a cease-fire in all areas, capable of slowing down if necessary the peasant movement of land redistribution: in short, capable of safeguarding the interests and the lives of the Europeans during a transitional phase. It is only by crude trickery that the powers that be in Paris and Algiers could claim to be carrying out a mere police operation in Algeria. Even if the form of the conflict is apparently little changed, its content has toppled: it is no longer a matter of liquidating bandits or of pacifying wayward populations, but of scoring points with an eye to the eventual negotiations; such is the direction of the fighting that from now on *imposes itself*, willy-nilly, on both camps. One must moreover note in passing the idiocy of the double bind in which the present French government has left itself: either it pursues the war, which accelerates the rise of the Front to power, or it fulfills its declared intentions, and the nature of the control exercised by the Front over the masses assures the latter success in the event of free elections.

If, finally, the international causes that we invoked earlier, which militate in favor of a settlement of the question, are taken into account, it seems possible to conclude that the Algerian affair has entered into a new phase whose import is the end of the armed conflict.

This judgment does not mean that we should expect an armistice in the near future. First of all, it is impossible to give sufficient weight to the lack of intelligence from which the French bourgeoisie has suffered since the end of the last world war, in particular with regard to the administration of its colonial interests. It has labored so assiduously at its own downfall that one would be disinclined to believe that history is a rational process, were it not that one knows that even the insanity of a class henceforth no less dominated than dominant remains rational. It can carry on sending draftees to their deaths for a while longer, the better to put Ben Bella in power in Algiers. Or again, the peculiar characteristics of the Frontists' organization

and ideology, either their exclusivism and centralism or their embryonic social program and "radical" nationalism, which are matters for "solution,"
might scare off the French leaders. They might not give up hope of suppress-
ing or alleviating them through a war of attrition or by feints (straw men,
etc.). The moment of reckoning would then be put off until later.

One cannot deny the existence of these and other hindrances to a cease-
fire. But in the last instance, they can only deepen the process of the formation of the Algerian nation and bring about, through multiple contradictions, the birth of an authority that will have the power to stop the conflict.

28

Algerian Contradictions Exposed

(1958)

On November 6, 1957, Felix Gaillard becomes president of the Council of Ministers. On January 11, 1958, near the Tunisian border, a French unit is heavily engaged by a detachment of the ALN. On February 8, Sakhiet Sisi Youssef, a Tunisian frontier village, is destroyed by a French air raid.

The Sakhiet massacre has brought into broad daylight the fact that the multiple internal contradictions of the Algerian situation have grown considerably deeper since last summer.

On the one hand, power structures have changed within the National Liberation Front following the recapture of the cities by the French army and police: the link between the resistance and the Europeans, which had been maintained up to that point by the fence-sitting Muslim bourgeoisie and French "liberals" in Algiers, has been broken. Consequently, the bourgeois political-military apparatus of the Front has devoted all its efforts to the consolidation of the peasant army. During this phase, all Bourguibist overtures have become impossible, both because the French government, intoxicated by its "successes," is not interested in negotiation and because the young peasantry that has swelled the ranks of the ALN constitutes a deeply intransigent political force. Sakhiet is, in this first sense, the explicit manifestation of the failure of Bourguibism, in Algeria as much as in Tunisia. Thus it marks the victory of the political strategy characteristic of a social group that requires close analyses because it both reveals changes in the internal power structures of the Maghreb nationalist movements and at the same time announces the class structure of these young nations.

On the other hand, on the French side, the recapture of the Algerian cities has brought about a complete union between the army and colonial society while at the same time subordinating the Algiers government to the army. The military effort, but above all the extent of repression required for recapture, involved muzzling the opposition in France. This muzzling was made easier by the fact that such opposition is entirely formal, because the organizations from which it might be expected (mainly the SFIO and the Communist party) directly or indirectly participate in the repression in Algeria. We must admit, however, that the French working class has not, in all honesty, fought against the war in Algeria in the past two years. Here we face a difficult situation that is irrefutable in that it is a reality, a situation that obliges revolutionary thought to rethink its analysis of the colonial question from the beginning if it wishes to be able to both describe and change reality.

In this article I want above all to emphasize this fact, at the risk of shocking those on the "left" for whom active solidarity between the proletariat and the colonialized remains the sacred cow of the schema of permanent revolution. When concepts or schemas are refuted by historical reality over a period of forty years, the task of revolutionaries is to discard them without remorse and to replace them with others that make an effective struggle possible. From this point of view, with the intention of making a first contribution to the complete revision of the question of colonialism, I emphasize here what seems to me to be the key to the current situation created by the war in Algeria, namely the *burying* of class antagonisms in colonial society.

This interpretation does not mean that it is advisable either to abandon the concept of class (on the grounds that there should not be classes in Algeria, as the Messalists used to claim) or even to support the existing FLN unconditionally. It is necessary, however, to show how and why a bourgeois leadership (the FLN) can successfully mobilize all the Algerian classes in the struggle for independence. That is to say, it is necessary to show that the significance of this aim can temporarily mask class objectives in the minds of Algerian workers, and to show the reasons why this nationalist ideology has acquired such power. For if it is true that nationalist ideology only *masks* real antagonisms — antagonisms that are already apparent in the present power structure within the FLN — which we will try to find out in the analysis that follows, to have broken down the colonial nationalist movement into its basic elements is not to have done with analyzing it. The ideology that animates the nationalist movement, even if in the final analysis it is composite, is lived as a unanimous response to a situation unanimously felt by all Algerians (just as, for their part, all the Europeans of Algeria unanimously feel and respond to their situation, despite the internal antagonisms that actually set them at odds).

In other words, the nationalist ideology (like the colonialist ideology that is its counterpart) is not a mere fiction that the clever among us can denounce as a mystification fabricated by the Algerian nationalist bourgeoisie for its own ends. On the contrary, to deny this ideology the status of an effectively lived reality would be fictive. This is something we admit when we attack economism or sociologism, which are content to dismiss the issue of independence with a smile as an abstraction: let such analysts put themselves to the test of reality, and let them try to advocate the slogan "class against class" in the present Algerian situation! We have to get rid of a certain kind of patronizing Marxism: an ideology has no less *reality* (even and above all if it is *false*) than the objective relations to which this Marxism wants to reduce it. First of all, I want to accord Algerian nationalist ideology the full weight of reality. In a subsequent article I will seek to show how this ideological reality inscribes itself within the contradictory dynamic of colonial society.

Deepening of the Contradictions in Algeria

Algeria is already no longer "French," first in that French policy in Algeria from now on is made in Algiers, not in Paris, and also in that Algiers holds less authority than ever over the real Algeria.

Let us first examine this second point; it is the motor of the whole dynamic. In the fall of 1957, after months of fierce repression, the FLN found itself constrained to abandon urban agitation almost entirely; a strike like that at the end of January 1957 had become impossible. The strata that had participated in the action in the cities (primary schoolteachers, shopkeepers, workers and employees) had been decimated by the police and the army; thrown into the prisons and the camps, tortured to death or guillotined, the men of the underground networks had for the most part disappeared from the political struggle. The "liberals" themselves, those without a party, and the Europeans in general, were all condemned to silence by threat or exile and found themselves forced to abandon the hope that they had been able to entertain, during the double game of Molletism, of serving as intermediaries between the resistance and the repressive forces. Their disappearance from the political map coincided with the rise of the right to power in France. The FLN could no longer even show itself through terrorism as a form of political presence and protest. Crushed by a vast police and military apparatus that enjoyed the active support of the European population,[1] isolated from the few Europeans who wanted to keep in contact with them, convinced that all contact was from now on destined to failure, the Front then directed all its efforts toward the underground forces.

Eighty-five percent of the Europeans live in the cities. In turning to the countryside, the FLN necessarily broke with the Europeans. The rupture between the communities, already ancient and profound, became still worse. The guerrilla, peasant figure par excellence, took the lead over the secrecy of the *medinas*. The consolidation of the Army of Liberation seemed to the Executive and Coordinating Committee to be their immediate task, first for reasons of domestic and international propaganda (the UN session was drawing near), next because the considerable influx of recruits made the formation of political and military cadres an urgent task. The increase in their numbers over the preceding year,[2] evident despite the far right's cries of victory, showed that the FLN's setback in the cities did not mean that it had lost contact with the Muslim masses. On the contrary, the FLN had pursued the work of political and administrative penetration that I described on an earlier occasion[3] to the point at which the ALN's troops gradually lost their initial character as irregular formations: conscription henceforth draws on all young Algerians between eighteen and twenty-five; the local officials of the popular assemblies round them up and hand them over to military officials who escort them into Tunisia or into the zones abandoned by the French army. There the young recruits receive a military and political training in the camps and are completely kitted out before leaving to take their turn in the combat zones. This organization, the effects of which are undeniable, obviously requires the active participation of the entire Algerian peasantry.

The mass of the Algerian combatants is therefore made up of young peasants with an average age of around twenty; this social and demographic composition is obviously essential for anyone who wants to understand the combativeness of the ALN troops and the leadership of their fighting. As colonial peasants first of all, these men have nothing to lose in the struggle because they had nothing before undertaking it: in 1952, 70 percent of the Muslim enterprises were judged to be economically nonviable; they became still more so as a result of the fighting and the repression, which rendered many farms unusable (as is shown by the very appreciable slowing down of the return to the lands, especially in the east of Algeria). And, on the other hand, these totally expropriated peasants were born in 1938: they were seven, the age of reason, when the Foreign Legion "mopped up" the Sétif plateau and lesser Kabylie; fourteen when Messali was deported to Niort; sixteen when the CRUA launched the offensive on the night of November 1, 1954. Their contact with the French administration did not even take place through the usual educational channels, because only 2 percent of the Algerian population (117,000 children) were educated in 1950. For them, what is France but the rural sheriffs [garde champêtre], the police, the troops? "Of France, they only know a single face, that of the 'enemy' whom they confront, who shoots, wounds, and kills," writes R. Uboldi. It will soon be four years since they last saw an unarmed Frenchman. The feeling of undergoing a foreign occupation, the conviction that the French soldiers defend a usurped power, finally the certainty that this power is already no longer in a condition to effectively administer a people who rebel against it—this aggregate of ideas and forces that makes up the nationalist ideology—can only accelerate among the young peasants, and hence among the base of the ALN. The process of alienation from all that is French can only add to their indifference to French problems and unhook the dynamic of their struggle even further from a consideration of power structure in France.

The intransigent positions taken by the FLN in articles in *El Moujahid* and in the declarations of its spokesmen in Tunis and Washington forcefully express this pressure of the fighting base and its ideological opposition to the military and political apparatus. Several journalists have testified to it. The commandant of the first battalion of the Eastern Base confided to R. Uboldi: "Those under twenty are the most intransigent. For my part, I certainly do not have much sympathy for the enemy I am fighting. But I know another face of France: Voltaire, Montaigne, the Rights of Man, the Commune, Sartre, Camus—in a word, the best there is of the enemy." Visibly, the tension between the ALN cadres and soldiers now expresses both an age difference and a class antagonism. So, despite the tenderness that the Algerian intellectuals who constitute part of the political and military armature of the Front feel for French culture, the Frontist apparatus found itself forced to demonstrate in very harsh terms its dissatisfaction with its "natural" political partner, the French "left." I will return to this point, but I should point out at once that this breach certainly expresses a change within the internal power structure of the Algerian resistance, which results in turn from the present military situation.

By an inverse but complementary process, the conditions in which the [French] army regained control of the principal cities of Algeria aggravated the rupture between the government of Algiers and that of Paris. The liquidation of the clandestine networks had required the use of shock troops, the active participation of the European population in the civilian militias, the suppression of the last juridical hindrances to searches, arrests, detections, interrogations, condemnations, and executions. The occupation of Algiers by paratroopers for several months and the official delegation of full powers to their commander in fact constituted a new political situation; all the urgent decisions become from now on the concern of the military authority, which seemed by virtue of this fact to hold sovereignty in the cities.

In reality, the situation was completely different; from the ever closer collaboration between the armed forces and the civil and police administration that they maintained there necessarily issued an unusual coalescence of the attitudes proper to each of the two parties: the mentality of revenge of those defeated in Indochina and Suez and the far-right colonialist traditions of the General Government. And this ensemble exercised an ever stronger pressure on the political leadership of Algeria, on Lacoste and his immediate entourage. This same extremist spirit, which, as we will see, is not the sole property of the great colonists and which always eroded the good intentions of the guardians of republican power in Algiers to the point where none of them could ever change anything in Algeria, though Algeria had changed all of them, then completely took over the minister for Algeria. Lacoste identifies himself totally with the *Français d'Algérie*: "plebianism," shooting his mouth off, "flag waving," secessionist blackmail, banging his fist on the table, bragging. He demands, he obtains. But no one is fooled: it is not Lacoste who has power in Algiers; it is Algiers that has power over Lacoste.

Algiers, however, is not even the military command. It is a military command under attack from the population that it delivered from terrorism. Assailed in the street, to the point that one saw the paratroops turn against the Europeans. Assailed above all by the spokesman of the *Français d'Algérie*, the leaders of the militia, the newspaper editors, the mayors, the presidents of veterans' associations, the leaders of the patriotic students, and so on—all of which organizations have representatives, or "friends" who are in their debt, throughout the administrative and repressive apparatus of Algeria. And what is the social significance of these associations? They represent the quasi totality of the Europeans of Algeria, *a mixture of all classes*.

It is therefore indeed *Algérie française* that governs Algiers—at the same time that Paris governs it—through the medium of the organizations, the police, the administration, the army, and finally the minister. It was not Mollet who intercepted Ben Bella, but it was not even Lacoste; it was not Gaillard who ordered the Sakhiet raid, but it was not Lacoste, either, nor even probably Chaban-Delmas. The power of the extremists established itself uniformly in the Algerian cities; the army reconstituted it, but it penetrated the army itself. However much it is made up of city dwellers, the army henceforth expresses the only *Algérie française*, it is its faithful reflection, and *Algérie française* takes pleasure in it.

In fact, there is already no longer an *Algérie française*, in that "France" is no longer present in any form in Algeria: in the countryside, there is an FLN administration; in the cities, there is an extremist administration. Paris is present nowhere.

Deepening of the Contradictions in France

But France is saturated by Algeria through every pore.

World opinion was rudely awakened to this fact in the most obvious fashion after Sakhiet: the entire world knew, and Washington knew, that Gaillard covered up for a military and political operation that he had not chosen and that he no doubt considered inopportune. The motives of this young premier are too clear to deserve extensive analysis: a keen taste for power and an ambition worthy of another age have no importance here except insofar as they constrain him to espouse the cause of the parliamentary majority uncomplainingly. And this majority is made up of the right, along with the socialists. The latter, thanks to Mollet's well-tried voice, discovered that this right wing is the most stupid in the world. But they did not divorce for all that, stupidity not being statutory grounds for divorce in the SFIO, and since every left gets the right wing it deserves. After all, if the right reigns in France, it is thanks to the tomato throwers of February 6, 1956; behind Duchet, it is the patriots of Algiers who begin to implant their slogans, their people, their organizations, their journals, their reasons, and their insanity in the everyday life of the country. The atmosphere of Algeria is beginning to weigh upon French political life: there arises a figure who is half para-trooper, half socialist party member, the disguised warrior with the gloved hand, the abundant cockades, the muscled and ostentatious style, the ner-vous tone (but also with a fondness for the cops and a preference for middle-class streets) of true-blooded French and emergent fascists.

These grotesque creatures come to us from Algiers, which is the one place in the world where the decay of the French colonial empire, embodied in the very troops that camp there, is most felt as a matter of life or death. But from Algeria there also return the men who fought this war whether they wanted to or not, who are not grotesque, but even more disturbing. They also have experienced the powerful corrosive force that colonial society re-lentlessly exercises over all its inhabitants when it reaches the breaking point, unleashed from all restraints by the eruption of its contradictions into broad daylight. The youth of all French social classes do in effect live in Al-gerian society itself during their stay in Algeria. As I have said, the army into which they are incorporated reflects this society. It extends its fundamental function to the point of obviousness and absurdity, namely, that of suppress-ing the humanity of the "wog" [crouille]. The decay of democratic values such as respect for the person, equality, and so on is made easier by their lack of a solid grounding in class society (where the most casual glance may find them violated daily) and also by the campaign carried on by the bour-geois press for almost four years in order to legitimate this war. Above all, the efficiency of military training, which is after all only a more intensive form of colonialism, more than makes up for the relative "brevity" of a twenty-month tour of duty in Algeria in compounding this process. It is su-perfluous to continue: whether one reads the accounts of the draftees, the Muller file, Une demi-campagne, or even Mothé's text here,[4] one already has all the documents necessary to analyze and reconstitute the ideological decay produced by the pressure of Algerian society on the draftees.

Finally, the fact remains that this permeability to the colonialist atmo-sphere, which is the only important victory that the chauvinist right has won in this war, is only possible thanks to the inertia of the French workers with regard to the Algerian question. This is the fundamental fact that allows the isolation of the FLN, the recapture of the Algerian cities by the extremists, the bombing of Sakhiet, the spread of fascistic demonstrations in France, and the aggravation of the policelike arbitrariness of the government. Everyone knows that if the spontaneous movement of the past two years of draftees refusing to serve had not been either directly opposed by the parties and the organizations "of the left" or left to wither away because of their maneuvers, none of this would have happened. But since that time, the workers have never directly demonstrated, through unambiguous actions, their solidarity with the Algerians' struggle. Why?

One can invoke obvious reasons: the SFIO and the Communist party did everything in order to prevent a clarification of the Algerian problem when these refusals to go occurred, and to exhaust the combativeness of the workers. The SFIO's motives are clear and do not deserve much attention. The Communist party's line is more wavering, and we will come back to it later on. But, at any rate, to explain the passivity of the working class solely in terms of the dilatory character of the Communist party's and the CGT's maneuvers is simply to state precisely what needs to be explained; it is to admit that the French workers were not really ready to fight on this terrain.[5] These same workers showed elsewhere during this period that they were quite prepared to press their claims as far as their own objectives were concerned. No doubt these movements were sporadic, of course they constantly ran up against the basic need for an organization capable of throwing off the union yoke, and doubtless they have not yet resolved this problem. It is not a matter of underestimating the inhibition that the workers feel and that they express daily before the immensity of the tasks that they must confront as soon as they seek to move in a direction different than one mapped out for them by the union leadership. From this point of view, the struggle against the war in Algeria ought to encounter the same crushing difficulties, the same diversionary maneuvers, the same interunion cartels as all the protest struggles have encountered for years. It is the case, however, that over the past two years workshops and offices, factories, groups of factories (Saint-Nazaire, etc.), and entire sectors of the economy (banks) have entered into struggles, sometimes short and bloody, sometimes long and resolute, struggles for wages and working conditions, but they have never gone on strike against the war in Algeria. One cannot just put this down to a general absence of combativeness; it must be noted that solidarity with the struggle of the Algerian people is not intensely enough felt by the French workers to incline them to exercise pressure on "their" organizations sufficient to make those organizations commit themselves resolutely to the struggle against the war. On this point one may make an absolutely general observation that exceeds the confines of the Algerian problem: when the independence of Vietnam, Tunisia, or Morocco was at stake, the French working class also did not actively struggle in order to aid the colonized peoples to reject the yoke of French imperialism. When the Mau-Mau rose up against British colonization, did the English workers intervene on their side in the struggle? And did the Dutch workers support the Indonesian movement? It must indeed be noted that solidarity between the proletariat of the old capitalist nations and the liberation movements of the young colonized nations does not appear spontaneously, because the European workers do not have an active awareness of the shared goals of the colonial nationalist struggle and of the class struggle; because the classic schema of this convergence remains abstract for them; because, finally, what remains concrete for the French workers is the cousin or the friend killed in Algeria, the gun that was given to them during their few months there in order to save their own skins, the assassination attempts in their neighborhoods, which are full of North Africans, and above all the difficulty of fraternizing even in the factory with workers separated from them by an entire culture.

Algeria and the "Left"

The situation is currently such that the Algerian war is a war that does not seem to concern the French proletariat. It follows that the few intellectuals who feel that this war is their affair are isolated amid the general indifference, and that they cannot find in the dynamic of a nonexistent workers' struggle the teachings, the incitements to thought, and finally the concepts that would allow them to grasp accurately the historical meaning of the Algerian struggle and more generally of the liberation movement in colonized countries. Analyses of the Algerian issue, and the positions issuing from it, remain fruitless because these theories are elaborated in isolation from any practice. Of course, the leaders and the intellectuals of the organizations of the "left" are not hard pressed to continue to stick the old labels [*appellations contrôlées*] of the reformist or revolutionary tradition of thought on the colonial question to the FLN fighting, but it happens that these appellations have not been controlled by reality for forty years.

Roused by the accusations of "inaptitude for (colonialist) combat," of "inability to master the combination of problems faced in this country," of "opportunism and chauvinism" made by the FLN against the "democratic and anticolonialist left" in its press organs, this "left" makes urgent appeals to the political realism of the Frontists, anxiously inquires about their sectarianism, urges them to make its task easier. Doubtless in this way the "left" manifests both its "political sense," its sense of "responsibility," and a reformism that is hardly any less limp [*mol*] than Mollet's. Above all, however, the "left" justifies the very opinion that the Front has of it and still more its inability to situate the Algerian resistance correctly in a historical schema.

This explains the "left's" unceasing advocacy of its solution: something like a negotiation, as quickly as possible. This also explains the role that the "left" has set aside for itself: pressuring both sides so as to lead them to an agreement. Now, it is obvious that neither this goal nor this procedure has the slightest revolutionary character: "immediate negotiation" had some meaning in the conditions in which the Russian revolution found itself at Brest Litovsk, for example, but what political sense would there have been to a roundtable of Yugoslavian underground fighters and German generals in 1942? The FLN's situation is no doubt different, but this does not necessarily justify the *defeatism* that the French left urges upon it. Everyone admits that a pure and simple military defeat of the ALN is out of the question. So this "left" offers it a political defeat! It is because the "left" places itself above the fray, because it claims to incarnate "the general interest," that it wishes to put an end to the massacre. We do not doubt the purity of these motives, but in the final analysis they actually seek to make the Algerian resistance accept a totally corrupt compromise with Algiers, that is, with the extremists, a compromise that the Algerian resistance knows it will not be long in regretting. The various left-wing appeals for moderation, the "put yourselves in our place" heard by the underground forces, resonate with the hollow sound of the cracked old class traitor's bell.

Yet this same "left" does not make the same arguments to the French bourgeoisie, which might at least convince the FLN of the authenticity of the left's internationalist zeal. In fact, the "left" tells the bourgeoisie ad nauseam that France's grandeur suffers in the pursuit of this war, that France's prestige abroad is collapsing, that the interest of France, properly understood, requires negotiation, that one cannot safeguard France's legitimate interests in Algiers and in the Sahara by continuing to fight, and so forth. What is more chauvinistic, finally, than this rhetoric? Its constant compromises with the spokespersons of enlightened capitalism show clearly that, in fact, the left bends over backward to take the interests of French capital into account, while it has never managed to take the interest of the colonial proletariat for itself and in itself as the *sole legitimate reference point* that should ground its position. The fear of the right, or of censure, cannot constitute a sufficient alibi; the truth is completely different.

The [Trotskyist] International Communist Party (PCI), for its part, occupies a position on the left that clearly distinguishes it and that is based upon an extensive application of the theory of the permanent revolution to the Algerian problem. Since the Algerian People's Party (PPA), which grew out of the Etoile nord-africaine, unquestionably had a worker base in France and a peasant base in Algeria, and since the MTLD leaders who rallied to the FLN leaned toward participation in the Algerian municipal governments on the eve of the insurrection, the PCI concluded that the FLN is reformist and the Algerian Nationalist Movement (MNA) (which had its origins among Messali's supporters) is revolutionary. Finally, since the PCI learned from *Permanent Revolution* that a colonial bourgeoisie is incapable of achieving independence through its own efforts and that a proletarian revolution must supervene to extend the democratic revolution so that bourgeois objectives compatible with socialism can also be realized, the PCI concludes that it is good politics to support Messali, that is to say, the proletarian revolution. When the FLN's "sectarianism" and the conciliatory spirit of the Messalist declarations appear to contradict this interpretation, the Trotskyists explain that in reality the Frontists' intransigence with regard to their objective—independence—has no purpose other than to forbid the presence of the MNA in future negotiation and thus to nip in the bud the prospects for revolutionary development in the Algeria of tomorrow. Thus the murders perpetrated by the Frontists on the Messalist militants can be explained. The Algerian bourgeoisie seeks to profit from terrorism, a weapon alien to the working-class tradition, in order physically to destroy the avant-garde of its proletariat. The PCI paradoxically concludes therefore that the only authentic revolutionary attitude consists in struggling for "a cease-fire, the convocation of a roundtable conference bringing together representatives of all political and religious persuasions, of all Algerian ethnic groups, and the organization of free elections under the control of international authorities" (*La Vérité*, February 6, 1958).

This is a stupefying example of the degree of false abstraction that a political reflection can attain when it is steeped in dogmatism. First of all, the very core of this position is false: the schema of the permanent revolution is absolutely inapplicable to North Africa.[6] It is based on the assumption of a combined development of colonial society completely different from that which can be found in the countries of the Maghreb. "In the Russian revolution," writes Trotsky, "the industrial proletariat *took possession of the very ground* on which the semiproletarian democracy of the craftsmen and sansculottes at the end of the eighteenth century was based. . . . Foreign capital . . . will gather around it the army of the industrial proletariat, without leaving the artisan class the time to emerge and develop. As a result of this state of things, at the moment of the bourgeois revolution, *an industrial proletariat of an extremely elevated social order will find itself the principal force in the cities*" (Intervention at the London Congress, 1907; my italics). Before generalizing the schema, it would be advisable to assure oneself that capitalist penetration in North Africa and particularly in Algeria took the same form as in Russia during its imperialist period and that it produced the same effects there. In fact, everything indicates the contrary.

It is therefore ridiculous to imagine the MNA, heir of the MTLD and the PPA, as the revolutionary avant-garde of the Algerian proletariat, with Messali as its Lenin. Let the editors of *La Vérité* therefore reread the report of the second National Congress of the MTLD (April 1953); they will not find one single phrase that authorizes this interpretation. What they will find instead in the final resolution is the principle of "economic prosperity and social justice," which is declared achievable by virtue of "the creation of a veritable national economy, the reorganization of agriculture in the interest of the Algerians, especially through agrarian reform . . . , the equitable distribution of the national income in order to attain social justice and union freedom." Meanwhile, this same congress "assures Messali of its unshakable attachment to the ideal he represents." Decidedly, the MTLD was not, and the MNA is not, Algerian bolshevism, simply because there cannot be Algerian bolshevism in the present state of industrial development. Just because 400,000 North African workers work in French factories and building sites, they do not constitute a proletarian avant-garde. Such an analysis ignores the fact that here they are émigrés, that they are not integrated, and cannot integrate themselves, into the French working class, that they always return *home*, transformed no doubt by the life in the factory, but above all confirmed in their Algerian vocation. Finally, even if all of this were not the case, it would still be true that these 400,000 workers are not even at the site of the struggle. Yet a revolutionary push in the direction of socialism, if it is to take place within the bourgeois revolutionary movement itself, requires that the armed proletariat participate directly in the struggle and stand ready to defeat the counteroffensive of bourgeois nationalism on the spot. What permanent revolution can there be when the working class is separated from its bourgeoisie by 1,350 kilometers of land and sea?

Let me make it clear that this does not mean that the FLN incarnates the Algerian proletariat more fully. The FLN is a national front, that is, a "sacred union" of peasants, workers, employees, and petit bourgeois, with a bourgeois leadership. Its CCE is its Committee of Public Safety,[7] all things being equal: it exercises an energetic dictatorship over the ensemble of the Algerian classes, a dictatorship that does not shrink from the use of terror. In order to explain the murder of Messalist union leader Ahmed Bekhat by the Front, there is no need to go looking for the pernicious influence of Stalinism infiltrating the Frontist leadership: the hypothesis is worthy at best of the intelligence of our Algerian minister and his moderate cronies. There is no collusion between the FLN and the Communist party, be it French or Algerian.

On the contrary, the softness of the Communist party on the Algerian question is now legendary, on the right as much as on the left. The official line is to justify this attitude from the perspective of a popular front. It seems

likely that the Stalinist leadership has sufficiently lost its capacity for political analysis to allow one to suspect that it hoped for nothing less than to
outflank Mollet "through the base." It is in any case certain that it never
gave up hoping to infiltrate the state, as the SFIO manages to do. In general,
people tend to ascribe it another intention as well: as an outpost of Moscow
on the banks of the western Mediterranean, it prefers to aid French imperialism to maintain itself in Algeria for good or ill (the worse it goes, the better
for the Communist party, provided that the French presence is maintained)
than to see it replaced by American imperialism. As Léon Feix has already
put it, in September 1947: "The independence of Algeria would constitute
at once a trap and a consolidation of the bases on which imperialism rests."[8]
And it is evidently not by accident that after Sakhiet, Moscow only managed
to sigh to the Arabs: "And with American arms as well . . . " Of course, the
theoretical line of the Communist party on the Algerian question has now
inclined toward independence, but only recently and under pressure from
the progressive French bourgeoisie who seriously risked ridiculing it completely by proposing an Algerian state, while it persisted in seeing in the
French union "the sole possibility for the overseas peoples to march to the
conquest of freedom and democracy" (Léon Feix, 1947). In *practice*, nothing has changed, and the Communist party contents itself simply with occasionally relaunching a "campaign for peace in Algeria" by means of
down-at-heel front organizations and in the ultraprogressive form of petition signing.

This attitude was not born yesterday. In 1936, the Communist party violently attacked the Messalists; it denounced them as allies of the fascist colonists. The Muslim Congress of January 1937 (there was not yet an Algerian
Communist party) in Algiers expelled the members of the Etoile nord-africaine, who sang the hymn of independence, from the room; finally, it "allowed" the Etoile to be dissolved by Blum without comment. In this tactic
one recognizes the necessary consequence of a policy of systematic collaboration with social democrats and the bourgeoisie "of the left." One should
also note that this is an expression of the Stalinist policy of absorbing foreign peoples into metropolitan Communist parties. At that time, the Communist party could still hope to seize power in Paris, so there was no question of letting Algiers escape. But if one digs further back in the history of
the relations between the Communist party and Algeria, one notes that at
the Congress of the International in 1921, that is, long before Stalinism was
born, the PCF's delegate for Algeria already took a stand against all Algerian
nationalism. In 1922, after Moscow's appeal for the liberation of Algeria
and Tunisia, the section of Sidi-bel-Abbès, the first to have joined the Third
International, attacked it root and branch: "The project for an uprising of
the Algerian Muslim masses [is] a dangerous folly for which the Algerian

federations of the Communist party, who have, first and foremost, a Marxist awareness of the situation, do not wish to be responsible before the tribunal of communist history." At the time of the May 8, 1948, uprising, the men of the Algerian Communist party sided with the forces of order to participate in the repression. Marty had no trouble in recognizing, at the Congress of March 1946, that the PCA appeared to the Algerians "as a non-Algerian party." Beside the constant compromises that the PCF has always sought "on the left" (that is, on the side of reformism and the progressive bourgeoisie), the fundamental attitude of the Stalinist militants of Algeria toward the nationalist movement always expressed, overwhelmingly and *up until 1955*, their adherence to colonial society. This characteristic and constant reaction, added to the tactics of the PCF, contributed in no small way to obscuring the metropolitan "left's" assessment of Algerian nationalism.

Nation and Class in Algeria

It is true that in itself the Algerian struggle has not found a manifest class content in the formulation given to it by the Front. Is it because the Front, insofar as it is made up of a bourgeois leadership, *wants* to stifle this class content? No doubt. But it is also because it *can*. And if the French left in this case can so easily lose its Marxism, or whatever else it uses as a substitute, it is because the peculiarity of Algerian colonial society lies in the fact that class borders there are deeply buried under *national* borders. It is in a completely *abstract* way, that is, exclusively *economistic*, that one can speak of *a* proletariat, *a* middle class, *a* bourgeoisie in Algeria. If there is *a* peasantry, it is because it is entirely and exclusively Algerian, and it is this class that evidently constitutes the social base of the national movement, at the same time that it is the clearest expression of the radical expropriation that Algerian workers undergo as Algerians. We will analyze its historical movement and its objectives later on. But it is not, by definition, at the level of the peasantry that the linking of classes despite national antagonisms can occur because it is obviously among the peasantry, the only exclusively Algerian class, that national consciousness can find its most favorable terrain. No European in Algeria shares the fellah's lot, none of them is exploited in the same way: the fellah's position with regard to the relations of production is specifically Algerian. The problem begins when the position of the Algerians and Europeans among the relations of production seems the same and each side identifies itself in terms of its respective nationality rather than on the basis of this position.

In reality, if one leaves aside the most notable servants of the French administration, the "professional yes-men," as their fellow citizens themselves call them (*caids, aghas, bachaghas*, presidents of Muslim veterans organizations, etc.), then no Algerian bourgeois, even if he marries a French woman, even if he apes French manners to perfection, can be admitted to European society. And there is not one of them who has not in the course of his life suffered, under one form or another, an unforgettable humiliation. No European employer or shopkeeper lives in the same building or even the same quarter as the Algerian shopkeeper or employee. The European workers, finally, do not fraternize with their Algerian comrades. This is first of all because they don't live together. Bab-il-Oued is not far from the Casbah, but the police cordon that surrounds the Arab city isolates it from the European working-class neighborhood. Second, they do not fraternize because there is a hierarchy of labor by virtue of which the more qualified European worker is assured the most remunerative and least discredited tasks, because even if Europeans and Algerians work in the same workshop or on the same building site, the team or site leader is necessarily European. And, finally, because even in the unions and the workers' organizations, whatever the efforts of the CGT since 1948, the colonial hierarchy is mirrored to the point that the Algerian "leaders" of these organizations look like straw men and, when all is said and done, like counterparts of the yes-men "on the left." We cannot impugn the good faith, the real desire to break this colonial curse, or the courage of the militants of the organizations. But their failure expresses, sometimes tragically, the impossible situation that they faced before the insurrection: the task of reconstituting class solidarity within a society founded on its suppression. In fact, the immense majority of the Algerian workers remained outside these organizations and came together only inside the sole party that, despite (or perhaps because of) its defects, allowed these workers to fraternize without a second thought, that is, that prefigured a truly Algerian community.

There is no other way to understand why the European population of Algeria, with its small number of wealthy colonists (owing to the concentration of landed property), in which workers and employees form a majority that is itself exploited, has not dissociated itself from extreme right wing policy but has instead given it overwhelming support. Nor can the success of the insurrection itself be understood, an insurrection called for by a few activists who were sick of their leaders' inaction, which would not have been able to extend and consolidate itself as it did had not the Algerian masses felt that the struggle was well founded. This breach was so extensive that no Algerian struggle could expect to draw support from the massive solidarity of the European workers. Lastly, one cannot understand the FLN's present "sectarianism" when it affirms that "every French soldier in Algeria is an enemy soldier" whose "relations with Algeria are based on force" unless one hears in this intransigence, which perhaps shocks the delicate ears of the French "left" (which is often paternalistic and *always treacherous* toward the Algerian people), the direct expression of the split that runs through and tears apart *all* the classes of Algerian society.

If the solidarity of the French in Algeria has never been seriously disrupted to the point where social forces could have taken up class positions, this means that in all their actions the *Français d'Algérie* (even if they were wage earners just as exploited as the Algerians) could not think of themselves except as Frenchmen occupying Algeria. And then it must be said clearly: the Algerian nation that constituted itself despite them could only affirm itself against them. There is in this hostility no mystique of the holy war, no resurgent barbarianism, but a people (and we intentionally employ this not very Marxist concept), that is to say, an amalgam of antagonistic social strata. This people is thrown back upon the consciousness of that elementary solidarity without which there would not even be a society, with the awareness that it must form a total organism in which the development of intrinsic contradictions presupposes the complementarity of those elements that contradict each other. Colonization both creates the conditions of this complementarity and blocks its development; the consciousness of being expropriated from oneself can therefore only be nationalistic.

Let us go further: the nationalist struggle, in the very forms in which it is carried out by the FLN, is not only liberating for the Algerian workers. It is only through its victories that the European workers of Algeria can be saved from the rottenness of colonial society and consciousness: in an independent Algeria, under whatever form, class relations will emerge from the swamp in which the present relations of domination have mired them. This does not mean that the new ruling class or the state apparatus of this Algeria should set to work at once to put the workers in their place: rather, all the workers will be united, Algerians and Europeans, to carry forward the class struggle.

With the Sakhiet massacre, one can say that the break between the two communities has been widened more than ever: Algiers makes its war independently of Paris, and pushes Paris to carry out its war. But the FLN has also won its most resounding victory over Bourguibism. Paris and Bourguiba represented, at least in principle, mediating forces between the right-wing extremists and the nationalists. The centrist policy[9] that Bourguiba implemented in Tunis in order to stifle the social contradictions of the young republic now stands as if struck by lightning. Meanwhile, the ALN imperceptibly takes possession of Tunisian territory, and Frontist ideology (which the Young Turks of *L'Action* echo in the Tunisian press) works its way into Tunisian masses exasperated by unemployment. The French colonists of Tunisia close ranks behind the president. Fifteen to twenty thousand Algerian combatants in Tunisia wait at attention for the French troops to leave, while Bourguiba only has half as many troops available. "The vigilance of the combatants," wrote Ben Bella three years ago, "will nip Bourguibism in Algeria in the bud." The blind logic of the right-wing extremists risks destroying it in full flower in Tunisia, where the classically bourgeois leadership is not strong enough to long withstand the growing hostility of the working classes supported by the dynamism of the Frontists. The struggle that Sakhiet has thus brought to light is one over the nature of power in North Africa tomorrow. But that is a problem that requires a longer study.

29

The "Counterrevolutionary" War, Colonial Society, and de Gaulle

(1958)

On March 27, 1958, the French government orders La question, *in which Henri Alleg describes his "interrogation" in Algiers at the hands of the French military, to be seized. Pierre Vidal-Naquet publishes* L'affaire Audin.

On May 13, 1958, the "pieds-noirs" revolt, and the Committee of Public Safety (CSP) is constituted under the presidency of General Massu.[1] On May 15, de Gaulle declares himself "ready to take over the helm of the Republic." On May 16 and 17, the National Assembly passes the declaration of a state of emergency. On June 1, it invests de Gaulle as head of the government with full powers.

The military totalitarianism that has revealed itself during the Algiers coup is the direct product of the "counterrevolutionary"[2] war in colonial society. There is no question of theorizing it here. I only want to (1) identify it as an *authentic totalitarianism*, unlike the movements that the Communist party or the left irrelevantly denounce as "fascist" at every turn; and (2) situate its position and identify its importance among recent events in Algeria.

What were the forces present in the Algiers coup? What is the dynamic of their development?

Two components of the Algerian situation played practically no role at all:
—The FLN did not intervene as an element directly engaged in the struggle: it is a year since it last controlled Algiers. In a sense, however, the whole affair was organized for its benefit, no less than for that of Paris.
—"Republican power" already no longer existed either in Algiers or in the cities, which had been taken in hand once more by the [French] army. It was expelled a year ago, along with the FLN: in order to destroy the Frontist networks, it was necessary to destroy legality. Full military power was es-

214

tablished on the basis of this double destruction. The actual occupation of the Ministry of Algeria and of the prefectures was thus a symbol, rather than a "revolutionary" initiative. On this level, the Algiers coup provides no new element; it brings to light a latent process that began a year ago, through which the armed forces came to hold total power.

But what does "military power" mean? The army, which actually holds power in Algiers, will claim that the army is simply a tool rather than a social force in itself. A tool at the service of which social force, then? It is in this respect that the Algiers coup reveals a new fact: the presence of the seeds of an authentically totalitarian organization in the army. We earlier claimed that the army "henceforth expresses the only *Algérie française*, it is its faithful reflection."[3] This view needs to be corrected: the relation of the military to the extreme right is not one of simple subordination. The extreme right can only exist politically for as long as the army holds back the FLN. Power is thus divided between the armed forces and the extreme right, producing an unstable political situation whose resolution will certainly involve the subordination of one group to the other.

But this assessment of the army and its position in Algerian colonial society is still too cursory. On the one hand, the army is no longer simply an instrument to be handled at will by whoever controls it. The process that brought it to power in Algerian society is in large measure beyond the control not only of the French bourgeoisie, who can only record this process by giving Salan the full powers that he already has, but even that of the extreme right, who were not a little surprised by the big display of "fraternization" staged by the army in the Forum on May 16.[4] And, on the other hand, the French army in Algeria does not *currently* constitute a homogeneous political force: not all the soldiers have the same goals.

We will restrict ourselves to the elucidation of these two aspects of the situation because they allow an understanding both of what occurred in Algiers and of the current prospects.

First of all, the army currently has a tendency toward making itself into an autonomous force. It is not a social force, it is true. Yet it is an organized apparatus, and this apparatus can, in certain conditions, exercise power, if not on its own account at least with a certain independence from the class for whose ultimate benefit it exercises power. In Algeria, the following conditions made this possible: the impotence of the French bourgeoisie and its traditional political personnel in the face of the FLN led the bourgeoisie to relinquish its control over the military command; complementarily, this giving up of authority was made necessary by the nature of the Front's military activities.

The military command, above all at the executive level, has finally grasped the nature of this war: strategically and tactically, it is identical to the one fought by the Viet Minh at the beginning of the war in Indochina. Tactics of harassment, of ambushes, of engagements restricted to advantageous situations, of vanishing in the face of "crackdowns"; a political-military strategy of setting up an apparatus for the administration of society, sometimes secretly, sometimes openly, an apparatus capable of shifting between covert and overt operations according to the military situation: "The army is in the people as a fish is in water."

The paratrooper officers know Mao Tse-tung's principle because they experienced it in Vietnam, no less than the one-time French subalterns who have now become Algerian colonels. A "revolutionary" offensive requires a "counterrevolutionary" riposte, they say. The paratroopers' objective is then no longer the defeat of the ALN (a task they know to be interminable because they have understood that there is no purely military victory in this kind of fighting and that the liberation army would always spring up once more from its ashes), but the defeat of the Algerian people itself. Two solutions are offered: either exterminate this people (which is not politically possible on a large scale and which above all is contradictory: an Algerian society without Algerians is like a bourgeois society without workers) or win over this people, by all means possible.

The army is thus engaged in a *political* struggle, which is the real game being played under cover of the staff bulletins. The myth of the "rebellion" must be chucked out along with that of legality: there is no question of the army's remaining a police force at the disposition of the prefects to put down the revolt of a few outlaws against the government of France. The army knows that its planes and its machine guns are not decisive arms against the Frontist machine; it needs the registry office documents, the land registry, the police dossiers, control of transportation, surveillance and maintenance of roads and railroads, permanent contact with the Algerians—in short, all the means of administrative management. Furthermore, the army must give this administration a real authority, install itself in the *mechtas*, live in the villages, run schools and hospitals, obtain and distribute seed, protect the harvest, organize the markets and the post office, settle local disagreements. Military "reorganization" thus becomes a kind of complete social administration that appears most obviously in the cities in the subdivision of neighborhoods into sectors, of blocks and buildings into subsectors, in the urban administrative sections, in some areas of the countryside in the special administrative sections. All possible means are used to carry out this implantation: denunciations from informers recruited among the Frontists who capitulated under torture, from among the pimps and the prostitutes of the Casbahs, the paternalism of the old officials of the Indigenous Affairs office, the missionary spirit of certain young officers of Saint-Cyr,[5] and so forth. Thus the army takes over functions that are ever more formally homologous with those that the Front used to carry out, although they are carried out to quite contrary ends. The army becomes more and more an *organism of administration* of society itself. Its practice tends toward totalitarianism.

This is the experience that crystallizes among the nucleus of the paratroop officers. They have direct and ancient experience of this kind of social rather than military war; they do not hide their admiration for their adversary; they want to model themselves after him. "We have in the sector of Algiers-Sahel," said Godard on May 22, "one organization of Europeans and another of Muslims. They were, moreover, copied from the organization of the FLN. The first functions as the mechanism for urban protection, the second as the mechanism for organizing the Muslim populations."[6] At this point, these officers encounter the contradiction that forces them to choose: either maintain obedience to the bourgeoisie, the class that employs them, or choose totalitarian subversion. And this is where the army splits apart.

The army does not constitute a homogeneous political force. For the paratroop officers, it is obvious that the successful conduct of the Algerian war requires the mobilization of the whole French nation. Mobilized militarily, of course, because the forces presently engaged are not yet numerous enough to successfully achieve the total administration of Algerian society that this totalitarian nucleus offers to perform. But also mobilized economically, because the officers and their civilian advisers are well aware that the crushing military apparatus they demand in order to pursue the war will lead in the short run to an economic crisis that presupposed the muzzling of the French workers. And finally mobilized ideologically, because the military apparatus can do nothing without the active participation of all the classes of the nation in the war. This mobilization was carried out without difficulty among the European society of Algeria, because that society understands its relations with the Algerians as quasi-totalitarian. But the social basis of the army lies in France: therefore France must be mobilized.

These prospects are *authentically totalitarian* if one understands *totalitarian* to refer to a political structure where a strongly hierarchized and centralized politicomilitary apparatus monopolizes social power and consequently manages the whole of society. There is no doubt that this military nucleus we are talking about has clearly set itself such an objective.

But it is no less certain that a faction that is currently more powerful hesitates in the face of totalitarian subversion and confines itself to Gaullism. It thus chooses to obey the discipline of the ruling class, with the condition that the latter discipline itself. Its Gaullist convictions are antiparty and antiparliamentarian, but they are not totalitarian; de Gaulle represents for it the imposition of discipline on all the factions of the bourgeois class and on the workers, and if this wing of the army supports de Gaulle, it is not in order for him to impose a totalitarian apparatus on the bourgeoisie, it is, on the contrary, in order for him to give it back its power and for that bourgeoisie, through him, to give the army both clear orders and the means of executing them. This wing of the army also supports de Gaulle because he seems in its eyes to be the only person capable of putting an end to the Algerian conflict under "honorable" conditions for the army, that is, different from those of Dien Bien Phu or Port Said.

There are therefore within the army in Algeria itself, not to mention the army stationed in France, two substantially different political forces; they have temporarily come together on a Gaullist platform, but this platform represents a minimal program for the paratrooper core, while the authentically Gaullist wing bases its entire doctrine on it.

The initiative of occupying the Government General building (GG) and of the formation of the Committee of Public Safety, on May 13, did not come from the army, but from the leaders of the groups and networks that had been constituted within the European population of Algeria over the past three years and that have multiplied over the past year with the support of the military command, because they served its project of taking the whole of society in hand: the group Union et fraternité française" (Poujadist), the group and network Union nationale pour l'Algérie française (the rich colonists), the group Combattants de l'Union française (Biaggi), the group Union générale des étudiants (Lagaillarde), and the Association générale des élèves des lycées et collèges d'Algérie (Rouzeau), and so forth. To these must be added certain professional associations (chambers of commerce, chambers of agriculture, certain syndicates), the provincial clubs (Corsica, etc.), and the veterans' associations. The web of these organizations thus effectively involves all age categories and all social classes. This intense politicization draws support from fear of the "poor whites," who make up the large majority of the Europeans in Algeria, but it takes its directives from L'Echo d'Alger, an organ of the colonists. Its objective is quite simple: the total destruction of the FLN, the return to the status quo, and the entire preservation of colonial society.

May 13 was "made" by these groups, warned by Lacoste that a "Dien Bien Phu diplomacy" was brewing in Paris. Lagaillarde took the GG; Trinquier's men, recalled from the Tunisian border, let it happen. The Comité de 13 mai was thus made up of two forces: the military totalitarian nucleus and the colonialist organizations. From its birth, the comité was therefore politically heterogenous. It is, in effect, impossible to fuse the totalitarian objectives of the paratroop officers and the colonialist objectives of the Algiers organizations. The latter were spontaneously led to a war of extermination against all the Algerians who did not choose to remain "wogs" [*bougnoules*], while the officers were resolved to use the social power given to them by their infiltration of the Algerian urban and suburban strata so as to slow down the separation of the two communities and reintegrate them under its authority. Their disagreement therefore bore on actual Algerian politics, that is, on the attitude taken toward colonial society: the Algiers organizations wanted a classic repressive war, and the officers sought a "counterrevolutionary" kind of victory, which implied the "integration" of the Algerians. But they came to terms provisionally against Pflimlin, while the bulk of the army hedged its bets and began to maneuver with its traditional opportunism between Paris, the extreme right, and the paratroopers.

The next day, May 14, a new force entered the *comité*, a force that would stifle these contradictions without resolving them, and that would offer the *comité* the prospect of political development in the metropole. This was the Gaullist wing of the Union pour le salut et le renouveau de l'Algérie française [USRAF], represented by Delbecque and Neuwirth. Essentially an apparatus stemming from the old secret police of free France and the RPF [Gaullist party] shock troops, USRAF brings together "pure" Gaullists (Soustelle) and the men of the Vichy bourgeoisie (Morice, Sérigny). It had only recently taken root in Algeria, but it was established from the day that Soustelle consented to work with the capital of Sérigny and the colonists. On the other hand, it had rapidly penetrated among the Gaullist military cadres thanks to the complicity of ministers like Chaban-Delmas. Delbecque and Neuwirth could therefore offer the three forces present—the paratroops, the extreme right, and the army—the same objective: the seizing of power by de Gaulle.

But the extreme right is not at all Gaullist: they know de Gaulle to be hostile to the Algerian status quo and are not far from considering him a dangerous huckster [*bradeur*]. To undermine their resistance, Delbecque then gets support from the military apparatus, which mobilizes the Casbah, and presents the extreme right with an accomplished "miracle": the Algerians want to be integrated into Gaullist France! It is May 16.

General amazement, and particularly of the *Français d'Algérie*, who, understanding nothing of the masquerade, feel, however, that the return to the status quo is temporarily undermined. The extreme right wingers take the blow, saving themselves for the sabotage of the integration that the Gaullists want to impose on them. Meanwhile, the latter score points: on the 17th, Soustelle arrives in Algiers; on the 19th, de Gaulle publicly supports the movement; on the 22nd, Salan cries "Vive de Gaulle!" in the Forum; on the

24th, Corsica wakes up Gaullist without knowing it; on the 29th, the Parliament capitulates.

This is a victory for the civil and military Gaullists, opening the prospect of a "strong" and bourgeois state. But neither the totalitarian aims of the paratroop colonels nor the colonialist aims of the Algiers organizations can find satisfaction in it. For the former, de Gaulle is a stage, a Néguib for whom Massu will be the Nasser, as they put it; for the latter, de Gaulle is a hostage, like his predecessors at Matignon[7]—and all the more since de Gaulle has come to power through centrist routes, after beginning by mobilizing the workers.

The forces currently present in Algiers are still at odds: an army that is presently still largely Gaullist; a totalitarian core that does not have the capacity to extend "fraternization" beyond the Algerian strata that are isolated from all contact with the FLN, but that seeks to organize in France the mobilization of all classes under the tricolor; extreme right-wing organizations that, unable to cut themselves off from the army, have swallowed the bitter pill of the project of integration but are ready to support the paratroop officers in their totalitarian program so as to cut short what they believe de Gaulle's Algerian policy to be; and, finally, the FLN, whose political-military potential is intact, its force, the peasantry, not having been seriously reached by the "counterrevolutionary" strategy, and whose diplomatic potential will soon be reconstituted by de Gaulle's very impotence.

The only immediate problem concerning the relations of these different forces is therefore this: will the army remain Gaullist? Will de Gaulle take control of the totalitarian core within it, and will he oblige it to make the colonialist organizations give in? Or, on the contrary, will the army's totalitarian experience in Algeria continue to develop into a consciousness and an organization? The answer to this question finally lies with the class struggle in France.

30

The Social Content of the Algerian Struggle

(1959)

De Gaulle, on June 4, 1958, at the Forum of Algiers: "I have got the message." On September 19 the provisional government of the Republic of Algeria (GPRA) is formed under the leadership of Ferhat Abbas. On September 28 the new French Constitution is approved in a referendum, gaining 79.35 percent of the vote in France, 95 percent in Algeria. On October 3 the "Constantine Plan" is proposed to aid Algerian development. On October 5 de Gaulle proposes a "warrior's peace" to the "rebels." On December 19 he replaces Salan with Challe and Delouvrier. On December 21 he is elected president of the Fifth Republic.

On September 16, 1959, de Gaulle announces that the Algerians have the right to self-determination through a referendum. On September 28 the GPRA declares itself ready to begin preliminary talks. On November 10, de Gaulle makes an appeal to the "leaders of the uprising" to discuss an end to the conflict. On November 20 the GPRA appoints for this purpose the four "historic leaders" [Ben Bella, Aït Ahmed, Boudiaf, Mohammed Khider] who have been imprisoned in France since October 1956.

Over the past year, the power structure in Algeria has changed radically. On the one hand, capitalism has reconstituted its domination over its Algerian sector and over the military apparatus that this sector had sought to direct according to its own interests. But, on the other hand, this success has not yet allowed it to provide a solution for the Algerian question that is in conformity with its overall interests, beginning with peace. The resistance has not dispersed; it has not capitulated. It is, more than ever, the interlocutor whose response is awaited.

Meanwhile, the war has continued, bringing to light the intensity of the revolutionary process of which it is the expression. After a brief inventory of groups for whom May 13, 1958, represented a common victory, I will concentrate on the revolutionary content of the Algerian crisis and disentangle its social and historical meaning today.

An Internal Reorganization of Imperialism

One of the elements that had previously occupied the foreground of the Algerian scene was suppressed and almost eliminated as a determining force: the extreme right. . . . [1]

What still resists de Gaulle in the army is not the army itself; it is Algerian society. What may properly be called the "opposition of the captains" to de Gaulle's Algerian politics does not express some kind of conflict between the apex of an apparatus and its executive branch but the real contradiction between present Algerian society and the intentions of French capitalism. The entire social administration in which the subaltern officers are employed willy-nilly by the very nature of the Algerian war is apparently irreconcilable with the instructions that these officers receive from the top. This was obvious at the time of the referendum and elections in Algeria. At that time, it was apparent that de Gaulle was seeking to isolate a politically intermediary petit bourgeois and bourgeois stratum among the Algerians that would be capable of serving as a counterweight to the FLN. But it is no less evident that the army (that is, the subaltern officers charged with actually carrying out the pacification), was not in a position to carry out this policy to its conclusion. The army as a whole had accepted that it could not apply such a policy: what can the order to "develop the local elites" mean for a captain charged with running a Kablye *douar*? [2] A good part of these elites belongs to the underground forces; the rest either dig in their heels and have to be forced to collaborate, or collaborate openly with the military authority. In both these latter cases, the success of the policy requires "protection" from the army against ALN reprisals, which means the consolidation of the administrative power of the captain. Consequently, having liquidated the most visionary but least solid resistances when Paris retook control of Algiers, de Gaulle's government encountered, in the figure of the "captains," the very substance of the problem, the object of the conflict in person, namely, the question of how to manage present-day Algeria. The problem of the army is no longer that of a conspiracy or a plot, it is that of a society. [3]

From this quick examination of the two large forces that were until recently united in Algeria against the Fourth Republic, we can see that over the past year Gaullist policy has put together some of the tactical conditions for an Algerian settlement, in the sense that it has freed French imperialism from certain internal contradictions that hindered its approach to the problem. The depoliticizing of the Europeans and the military means the reintegration of the French Algerian sector into the bosom of imperialism. That was a preliminary condition for any serious attempt at resolving the problem.[4] But it is evident that the problem is not yet solved, either in its appearance or in its essence, as the "opposition of the captains" has made us realize. The problem appears as 60,000 to 80,000 men who will not disarm; its essence is that Algerian society continues to escape all organization, that it lives in a kind of fluid institutional milieu.

Persistence of the Revolutionary Situation

The fact that the slightest reduction in the strength of the military presence is enough to weaken the French administrative apparatus, requiring draft deferments to be canceled, proves that the war is still going on, more violently than ever. If pacification means the set of operations that make the reconstitution of a *nonmilitary* society possible, no progress has been made in pacification. The most simple social activities are still out of the question in Algeria without the protection of half a million French troops.

As one of the generals put it, chasing away the bandits is not enough, we have to *stay*. It is a secret to no one that not even the smallest Algerian locality could last long, as presently organized, after the withdrawal of French troops. This fact means that the institutions that in principle ought to govern affairs in Algeria have lost all social reality; they function only within the range of a submachine gun. From a sociological point of view, and taking into account the nature of the Algerian war, the fact that the war continues is nothing other than the fact of the permanent maladjustment of social reality to the models of organization in which it has been dressed up over the past five years.

Not one of the legal costumes in which Algerian society has been fitted out, neither assimilation, nor "Algerian personality," nor integration, nor the "chosen place," has been able to clothe it; de Gaulle implicitly admitted this in offering a choice among three kinds of status. But this formal impossibility only reveals, in the legal sphere, a remarkable sociological situation: if French imperialism has not to this day managed to provide this society with any other mode of organization than that of terror, it is because no institution can currently respond satisfactorily to the needs of the Algerians. This is either because the behavior of the Algerians is such that the preceding social order is no longer appropriate to their conduct, or because their behavior has not yet managed to stabilize itself into a set of customs that would form a new order. One can summarize this situation by saying that Algerian society is destructured.

The Revolutionary Situation

When the CRUA [Comité révolutionnaire d'unité et d'action] opened hostilities, one could have believed that the MTLD [Mouvement pour le triomphe des libertés démocratiques] activists were continuing by violence what Messali, that is to say, Ferhat Abbas, had begun with words. When all is said and done, war was "the continuation of politics by other means."[5] Yet even if this description, drawn from the most classic reflection on war, applies extremely accurately to the imperialist conflicts of the twentieth century, it in no way conforms to the reality of any anticolonialist war. When a colonized people abandons the arms of criticism for armed criticism, it does not stop at changing strategy. It destroys, immediately and on its own account, the society in which it lived, in the sense that its rebellion annihilates the social relations constitutive of that colonial society. These relations only exist to the extent that they are tolerated by the persons who live there. From the moment when people act collectively outside the colonial framework, produce behavior that does not find a place within the traditional relations between individuals and between groups, then the whole structure of the society is, by virtue of this single fact, out of joint. The models of behavior proper to different classes and social categories, models that allowed each individual to behave in an appropriate way and to respond to typical social situations, become immediately outmoded because corresponding situations no longer present themselves.

In this way, within the family, relations between old and young, men and women, children and parents, are profoundly altered. The authority the father exercises over his son does not survive the son's political activity, his departure for the underground forces; the young man takes the initiative with or without his father's consent, and that alone is enough to prove that the situation as it is lived by the son not only contradicts his traditional subordination to paternal authority but also overcomes it. In a family structure that remains very patriarchal, the deed is already remarkable. But it is still more so when it is the daughters who escape the tutelage of their parents. No doubt the Muslim bourgeois women of Algiers had begun to "liberate" themselves before 1954; but even in this class (the one most influenced by capitalist civilization), if one showed one's legs, one still did not unveil one's face. Showing one's legs and veiling the face is, when all is said and done, a faithful enough image of what "our" civilization means by women's liberation. Nowadays, the participation of women in political and military activity is attested to by the sentencing of the Frontist militants, among whom Djemila Bouhired became an example for all of Algeria.

In another sphere, that of culture, the behavior implied by the present war completely escapes the traditions of colonial Algeria. Around 1950, schooling touched barely 7 percent of rural Muslim children; this meant an illiteracy rate (in French) of 93 percent among the young peasantry. The Koran schools gave them an idea of written Arabic, which is about as useful as Latin for a French person. The poor peasants from this period are currently in the underground forces. It is difficult to imagine that they can take on certain tasks there without at least knowing how to read, and perhaps how to write. In learning these elementary techniques, they perform, implicitly or explicitly, a critique of both the miserly distribution of French culture and the uselessness of Muslim culture in their actual lives. In struggling against oppression, they regain possession of the most basic instruments of thought, which colonial Algeria had kept from them for generations. The revolutionary content of this new relation to culture is so obvious that the French command has had to respond to it by multiplying improvised schools. No doubt, the education of the underground fighters remains as rudimentary as that of the "protected" populations, and is limited to the future cadres. But the fact that these cadres can be drawn from the mass of peasants is in itself an absolute contradiction of the subaltern functions that colonization had reserved for the fellahs. Just as illiteracy was the direct cultural expression of the prohibition of all initiative that kept rural labor oppressed, so too the development of initiative and responsibility in the underground forces leads inevitably to the learning of written language.

As far as religious, economic, or sexual values are concerned, one can show that in all the categories of everyday activity, present-day Algeria, as it is actively engaged in the war, breaks with the modes of behavior out of which the combination of local tradition, Islam, and colonization had forged the "basic Algerian personality."

Thus one can say that a revolutionary situation exists when people no longer live according to the formally dominant institutions, and such is indeed the case in Algeria. This is not to say that the revolution has been made: the revolution presupposes that those who break with traditional social relations in this way will carry their critique to its conclusion and go on to destroy the class that dominated society by means of these relations, so as finally to institute new social relations. However, the open and durable rupture of a class or of an ensemble of classes with the structure of society necessarily has revolutionary significance.

Persistence of This Situation

In Algeria, this situation not only manifestly exists but also has an *intensity* and a *duration* whose combination can put us on the track of the real sociological content of the war for Algeria.

The duration of the revolutionary situation is well known: we are now entering the sixth year of war. Five years ago, the revolutionary direction of the insurrection was hidden enough to fuel fears that the actions of the night of November 1 were a simple flash in the pan of an adventurist or perhaps provocative character, in any case without a future. During this first phase, the numerical weakness of the fellahs, the artificial way in which operations had been initiated, the apparent lack of political preparation, and above all the recourse to terrorism seemed effectively to indicate that battle had not been joined on the terrain of society itself and that the groups of the CRUA, isolated from an apparently inert population, would not bring to an end the institutions they had judged irreformable and that they sought from now on to destroy by violence. If one compares the present state of relations between the units of the ALN and the population with what it was at the end of 1954, one can measure their closeness by the density of police control that the armed forces set in motion to prevent it.[6] The support of the Algerian population for the FLN cause cannot be denied if one hopes to explain how half a million troops cannot manage to annihilate 80,000 rebels.[7] This failure of repression implies a widening of the social basis of the rebellion over a five-year period such that it has completely lost its initial character and has developed into revolutionary activity.

The *intensity* of this situation is no less remarkable than its duration. At all times and in all places, abstention from social activity constitutes the elementary form of resistance to the organization of society, the refusal of its models of behavior. One observes it in all class societies among the workers: even though they are confined to carrying out tasks, they are constantly enjoined to participate in the organization of these tasks. They oppose these requests, which soon turn to the use of force; they adopt an attitude of withdrawal and of irresponsibility that calls into question the very model of the relations of labor that are imposed on them and that is ultimately directed against any society founded on that model. Duplicity, laziness, ill will, the tendency to steal—the smallest faults of which one hears the colonials accuse the indigenes—express at different levels this same unique refusal to take part in their own exploitation. Correlatively, the hatred those of French stock direct at the Arabs translates their own impotence to make them cooperate and their anxiety at the way in which Algerian "passivity" constantly dismisses the social order that the French wish to impose upon them. Racism is born of this. The Algerian has never showed himself to be a "good boy," has never appeared cooperative; his behavior has never completely taken the edge off this barb aimed against exploitation, against the very structure of the society imposed on him, and his withdrawal into himself has in this respect been no less formidable than the explosions of violence that have shaken the history of French Algeria. The Europeans have never forgotten, then, that despite the appearances they have wanted to give it, their colonial society does not hold.

Of course, had not social relations, prior to the beginning of the rebellion, grown so tense as to render a rupture constantly possible, the revolutionary situation could not have arisen out of terrorist action. Before 1954, no political movement controlled by the Europeans had been capable of correctly judging this level of tension, and even the "centrist" leaders of the MTLD did not suspect its intensity, since they hesitated for some time before going over to the activists. This is to say that the activists, closer to the peasant masses alongside whom many of them lived in illegality, understood better than anyone else the critical content of the fellahs' attitude.[8]

But withdrawal into oneself, the impenetrability of the Muslim world to European constraint, only constituted one premise of the revolutionary situation. This form of resistance does not yet constitute a dialectical negation of the society against which it is directed, because it does not manage to overcome the social relations to which it opposes itself. It is only a first moment that calls for its replacement by a new form of struggle. The organization presupposed by such a struggle cannot be born (as the failure of Abbas's and Messali's movements proves) in "legality," in an institutional system founded precisely on the annihilation of all Algerian initiative. The shortcomings of the nationalist bourgeoisie are here at fault; we will return to this later. The absence of strong nuclei of an industrial proletariat has the same effect. As for the peasantry, it cannot find the means to move positively beyond this form of resistance either in its working conditions or in its way of life. Algerian society was organized, in the most complete sense of the word, in order to prevent its contradictions from coming to a head.

The characteristics of the 1954 insurrection proceed from this. The handful of men who touched off the armed struggle introduced, without any transition, a direct and open violence where just one week previously there had not seemed to be the least trace of struggle. In reality, the mechanism of the contradictions came unjammed, and the underground forces offered the peasants, the workers, and the intellectuals the means of positively expressing their refusal of Algerian society. We will return later to the social significance of the solution given to the contradictions of that society by the CRUA. But opening fire was enough to demonstrate that Algeria no longer existed as a French colony. A colony is a society. When the colonized take up arms, they are already no longer colonized, and colonial society as such disappears.

Signs of This Situation

The *signs* of this dislocation of society, which are just so many symptoms of the revolutionary situation, are innumerable. The successive strikes that affected workers and employees, shopkeepers, teachers, and students in the winter of 1956-57 brought the attitude of withdrawal described above into broad daylight, giving it a collective basis and solemnity. There was no doubt that these strikes could be defeated by force. But they were successful in that their defeat had required the besieging of Algiers by an entire army, since their goal was to show that henceforth that minimum of cooperation required for Algerian society to exist and function could only be squeezed out of the Algerians by violence.

But there is no end to the path of violence. At the limit, at least one soldier would be required to control each Algerian. Since dominant conditions in France, past and present, prohibited this totalitarian solution, entire patches of Algerian territory came to escape repression, that is to say, the administration of violence. What the French command called "exclusion zones" in reality excluded its own troops. The Aurès, the Kabylies, the Collo peninsula, the Ouarsenis, and the border regions all detached themselves from colonial Algeria. Of course one could not seriously imagine that these regions were impregnable. Recent operations have shown that companies of paratroopers and legionnaires can circulate in the rebel bastions and even set up outposts there. But here again it is doubtful if the real plan of the General Staff of the rebellion has ever been to liberate Algerian territory in this way. Apart from the evident strategic usefulness of these zones for the grouping of ALN units, for their fitting out, training, and furloughs, the fundamental function of these bases is also to teach the lesson that France is no longer capable of managing all of Algerian society according to colonialist norms.

This is still more the case in the zones where military occupation legitimates the fiction of an unchanged Algeria. The density of police control alone bears witness against the role it is supposed to play. The displacement, not to say the deportation, of hundreds of thousands of peasants (in reality women, the old, and children), their concentration in villages subject to the continual surveillance of the troops and to chronic betrayal by informers, the mopping up of deserted regions and the destruction of abandoned villages, the growing indifference of the military to the administration of all the affairs of the peasant collectivity — all furnish abundant proof of the inability of the French to administer Algeria, rather than of their ability to do so. This is not administration, it is treating a population like cattle. No doubt this genre of relations is implicit in every society in which some people perform tasks while others manage. The latter always attempt by every possible means to hide from the workers the fact that they have been transformed into mere objects, because the situation can only continue on the condition that the workers accept it. But here those who perform tasks are *manifestly* manipulated like things; the very intensity of the means used against the revolutionary situation that is tearing Algerian society apart contradictorily reveals the intensity of that situation.

There are, lastly, the ALN units themselves. Their number is difficult to estimate, first because no one, on either side, has any interest in furnishing exact information, and second because it is hard to define what constitutes a combatant in a war of this kind.[9] But an initial fact stands out: the ALN has not encountered any problems in recruitment over the past five years, despite the predictions (hypocritical or ignorant?) of the French command. The basis of this recruitment is the peasantry. The Algerian fellahs suffer from chronic underemployment; ten years ago partial employment afflicted half the rural population in all of North Africa, and the proportion is certainly higher today for Algeria alone, where many farms cannot be cultivated because of the military operations. To admit the hypothesis that the métier of arms has become a more remunerative profession than working the land for the young fellahs is to recognize once more (at the price of a singular ignorance of the real feelings of the underground fighter) the fundamental fact that the institutions according to which work ought to be carried out (that is, the relations of production) have become absolutely incapable of assuring production. Were it just poverty that swelled the ranks of the rebel units, that alone would be a sufficient justification of their revolutionary character. The abandonment of the land *en masse* by the young peasants is a refusal to continue to live as their parents lived; it is a break with colonial Algeria.

But so narrowly economic an interpretation misses the essential meaning of the constancy of rebel strength for years. Armed struggle is a qualitatively different form of resistance from those we have just listed: other forms of resistance *result* from it. In the existence of the underground forces and their permanence, the prior relation between the Algerian problem and the exploited is reversed: it is no longer the problem the Algerians face, it is the Algerians who face up to the problem of their exploitation, and this simple fact totally alters the situation. Previously, when any government, even the French "left" itself, broached the Algerian question, it implicitly adopted the position that it was necessary to solve the problem *for* the Algerians, which meant sometimes in their interest, and always in their stead.[10] Anyone active in the organizations "of the left" in Algeria before 1954 cannot be ignorant of the fact that paternalism, the very same relationship of dependence they sought in principle to destroy, persisted in barely veiled form between European militants and Algerian militants. Of course, posing the problem for the Algerians in this way made it insoluble, because the essential content of the problem was nothing other than the universal form of social relations in Algeria, namely, dependence itself.

Armed struggle broke the spell. The Algerians, in fighting, no longer call for reforms, no longer demand to be given schools, hospitals, factories; they force imperialism to relinquish its ascendancy, they go on the offensive, and therein lies the literally revolutionary content of their action. Algerian society ceased to be a society of dependence from the moment when the "sub-humans" it oppressed demonstrated concretely that they were not debtors, and that they were prepared to die for this. One cannot understand the anguish of the Europeans in the face of the resistance unless one situates it within the framework of the reassuring paternalism that they sought to practice. The radical critique of the myth according to which the Algerians were created in order to obey, to execute orders, and eventually to be executed already blasted from the barrels of the shotguns of the first underground forces. Imagine the stupor of the true-blooded French! It was no longer their world put to the test; it was, precisely, their world turned upside down.

The Middle Classes and the Social Vacuum

But if it is true that the revolutionary situation, through its duration and its intensity, manifests the destruction of fundamental social relations in Algeria, one can, on the basis of this same intensity and this same duration, argue that the situation has not matured. One fact stands out: no one has emerged victorious from five years of fighting, neither the forces of repression nor the ALN. In the sociological sphere this fact assuredly means, as we have pointed out, that imperialism's army had not managed to consolidate any lasting form of social relations in Algerian reality; but the duration of the war also implies that the Provisional Government of the Algerian Republic (GPRA) had not caused a new society, in conformity with its goals, to rise from the ashes of colonial Algeria. In examining the Algerian situation from this angle, I want to get at the class content expressed by this double failure.

The Bourgeoisie Does Not Control Frontist Strategy

The evolution of the ALN's strategy and tactics over the past five years furnishes a first indication in this respect if one admits with Trotsky that "an army generally mirrors the society it serves."[11] At first made up of guerrillas centered around a few illegal political circles in the regions traditionally most hostile to colonization, the CRUA network was constructed little by little between these nuclei along lines dictated by the exigencies of provisioning and by the political and military potential for taking root. The more the network tightened, the more the combat groups hid themselves deep within the Algerian population, the more the problems of recruitment and survival were simplified.

This process, evident in the countryside and the cities, reached its culminating point at the end of 1956 and the beginning of 1957. Then, the FLN's administrative hold on the rural communes and the Arab quarters of the cities made it into something like an antistate already skeletally present in an Algerian society still provisionally subject to French oppression. At that time, it was possible to wonder whether the Front might transform itself into a politicomilitary apparatus immediately capable of taking over, after victory, the administration of independent Algerian society. The combats, in which the ALN usually had the initiative, began to take the form of battles engaged in accordance with the rules of the military academy: the structure of the ALN hierarchized itself, ranks appeared, the units became larger and larger, the cultural command distributed pay. The dominant fact of this phase, namely, the massive incorporation of the bourgeois and petit bourgeois strata into the ranks of the resistance, was reflected in the ALN's organization and tactics by the growing importance of the cadres and the increased subordination of the infantrymen. The Algerian army appeared to prefigure the organization of a future society in which the bourgeoisie would not fail to subjugate the peasantry.

But it would have been premature at that time to want to identify the social nature of the Frontist leadership distinctly. First because this process of increasing structure remained only a tendency and because it was contradicted by the fact that the units owed their safety above all to the support of the rural population, who obliged the cadres to preserve the permanent motifs of rural dissatisfaction as part of their ideology, and to maintain respect for the peasant elements (whose representatives they claimed to be) in the structure of their command. Second, because this structuring of the ALN and the Front itself could be interpreted as either the expression of the rise to power of the Algerian bourgeoisie or the incorporation of elements of this bourgeoisie into an already solidly constituted politicomilitary apparatus. It was not yet possible, at this stage in the development of the Algerian revolution, to specify whether the Front had already acquired the capacity to absorb the elements of the bourgeoisie that rallied to it and to constitute an embryonic bureaucracy from among these elements and those emanating from the Organisation spéciale [OS]—or whether, on the contrary, the Algerian bourgeoisie had sufficient gravity to impose a policy on the Front that would be in its own interests.[12]

The development of events should have allowed this uncertainty to be resolved. During the summer of 1957, at the same time as Paris's authority over the fighting of the war collapsed, the block constituted by the right-wing colonists and the armed forces in Algiers imposed its own methods of struggle. The forces of repression were reorganized, their military strength swelled, the police networks multiplied, and their methods intensified. Arms were distributed to the European population and it was organized into self-defense groups, while the form taken by the fighting in the mountains worked against the ALN units from now on: although equal in structure and tactics, their equipment could not rival that of the imperialist shock troops.

In the fall of the same year, the FLN lost the battle of Algiers, and in the principal cities its organization was hunted down by the paratroops and the police. The Front then turned its efforts to the breakup of its units, now too top-heavy to maintain their advantage in open combats with elite, well-trained, and powerfully equipped French regiments. Up to the beginning of 1958, the forces of repression retook the initiative, forcing the rebel units to split up and thus accelerating the process of reconstructing the guerrilla struggle. The French command, which had a free hand politically and knew it had regained the initiative in the conduct of operations, sought to destroy the rebel bases. The bombing of the Tunisian village of Sakhiet shifted the world's attention to Paris's irresponsibility in Algerian affairs and opened the political crisis in France. The contradictions internal to imperialism had by then reached their breaking point, and they passed into the forefront of the Algerian scene. During this whole crisis, the eyes of the forces were turned much more toward Paris than toward the Algerian hinterland.

The FLN, a little weakened, if not by the "fraternizations" of May 16 at least by de Gaulle's coming to power, could on the other hand profit from the relative respite lent by the settling of accounts between Paris and Algiers to reshape its military organization and its strategy. Large military formations were resolutely abandoned, as was open combat. When military encounters became official again, in the summer of 1958, it was apparent that the ALN units had regained their initial fluidity and had adopted the tactics of harassment and ambush proper to guerrillas. Instead of pursuing, alongside Salan, a relatively stable military control that immobilized a heavy fraction of its forces, Challe set himself the task of constituting units as mobile as those of his adversary, while he gave the police a role that was more administrative than military.[13]

It might have seemed after autumn 1958 that, helped by the lassitude of the fellahs, the fifth year of war would come to mean the collapse of the armed resistance. Only small groups of three to ten men crossed the mountains, and they only engaged in combat in the most favorable conditions. Already Juin proclaimed the war "virtually terminated."[14] Excepting the fact that a war is always virtually terminated, even before it begins, this was a complete misinterpretation of the nature of the Algerian problem that confused political analysis with a military General Staff meeting. Let us drop this issue. What matters here is the following observation: there has not been, since 1954, any constant rate of stratification that might have transformed a few dispersed guerrillas into larger, hierarchized, and centralized units. Or at least this process of stratification came to a halt toward the end of 1957, and then reversed itself.

The significance of this situation in the political sphere was that it tended to restore political weight within the Frontist leadership to the leaders of the underground forces, a political weight they had lost by virtue of their previous successes. As the resistance fell back onto its strictly peasant base, it revealed at the same time the true makeup of the social forces that were in the Front. As the ALN had accumulated successes, the Front had exercised an attraction over the bourgeois elements, consecrated by its coming to support Ferhat Abbas. At that point it was tempting to consider the FLN as the organ that the local bourgeoisie would use both to control the peasants and to open negotiations with imperialism from a position of strength. One could in this sense invoke the Tunisian precedent, where it was above all the underground forces who allowed Bourguiba to open the talks that led to autonomy.

But when de Gaulle's offers were rejected in December 1958, this proved that the bourgeois faction of the GPRA had not been able to impose a Bourguibist orientation on the resistance as a whole. The peasant leaders and the surviving outlaws of the OS had demanded the recognition of the GPRA as the Algerian government as a precondition to any negotiations, which is to say, the recognition of their own presence in all subsequent political phases. The GPRA's refusal to come to Paris to have its wayward behavior pardoned meant in reality that the members of the organization refused to give the liberal bourgeoisie a free hand in negotiations in which they could only be the losers. As soon as they laid down their arms, the members of the resistance would lose all real social force. They were kindly requested to return to their families to tell stories of their exploits, while the same bourgeoisie whose impotence had motivated the recourse to violence would occupy privileged positions offered to it by de Gaulle in an Algeria confederated to France. In rejecting the Gaullist maneuver—showing the white flag to the underground forces and unrolling the red carpet in Paris—by which imperialism sought to split the Front and to choose "natural" interlocutors within it, the GPRA not only safeguarded its unity, it gave proof that the extreme right wing policy carried out in Algeria, and in particular the attempt to crush the ALN militarily, had reinforced the position of the politicomilitary cadres of the armed rebellion at the expense of its liberal-bourgeois facade. The armed peasantry was still the only really determining force, a force that despite the attempts of bourgeois elements to reap the profits of its fighting was in sole control of the organization. This rejection by the GPRA also showed a relative but assured independence in relation to the methods advocated by Bourguiba and employed by the liberal bourgeoisie.

Such an interpretation, moreover, is confirmed by the very origins of the Front. Not only did the initiative for its creation not originate among the political representatives of the Algerian middle class, not only had attempts at the constitution of an anticolonialist Front remained fruitless in the years 1950–52, it was only thanks to the destruction of the UDMA [Union démocratique du Manifeste algerien] and the MTLD that the union of the nationalist forces was accomplished in November 1954. The UDMA, traditional expression of the bourgeoisie desirous of participating in the administration of colonial Algeria, had disappeared from the political scene long before Abbas, its leader, came over to the Front. The MTLD, subsequently converted into the Algerian National Movement, lasted longer than the UDMA only because of its foothold among Algerian workers in France. However, the ever more conciliatory orientation that Messali imposed upon the MTLD, combined with the influence of the real successes of the Front in Algeria upon its militants, eventually caused the MTLD to break up. In Tunisia, to put an end to this analogy, the underground forces that arose after the massive police operations at the end of 1951 did not weaken the Néo-Destour in the least; on the contrary, they allowed this bourgeois organization to consolidate and to extend its foothold among the rural masses, and no social force ever managed to come between the group leaders and the Destourian officials.

An examination of the relations of the Front with the "brother countries" of the Maghreb provides further evidence of the particular social character of the rebel leadership in comparison with the bourgeois nationalist movements. The interests that the Moroccan and Tunisian bourgeoisie hope to protect while settling their disputes with imperialism predispose them to conciliatory methods. The perspective of the propertied ruling class adopted by these bourgeoisies finds the war in Algeria and the intransigence of the GPRA to be a permanent obstacle to its own consolidation, not only in its diplomatic relations with France but also internally, thanks to the constant pressure exercised on public opinion in the two countries by the FLN. The pressure of masses of Algerian refugees and of important ALN military bases in fact allows Frontist agitators to propagandize actively among the Tunisian and Moroccan masses who populate the border regions. It is possibly the case that certain zones are directly administered by the cadres of the GPRA; the GPRA extends its influence over the political life of neighboring countries by means of political groups such as the old editorial team at L'Action, of which Bourguiba had to rid himself, or the PDI in Morocco. Collaboration between ALN units and groups of the Armée de libération marocaine in the south evades the iron fist of the Cherifian government. If the real influence that Tunis and Rabat exercise over the Front is much less strong than the Front's audience among the Tunisian and Moroccan people, this is because the two Maghrebi bourgeoisies cannot find liberal elements among the Frontist leaders who might effectively impose "Bourguibist" orders.

One could find many more signs of the relatively weak role played by the Algerian bourgeoisie in the national movement over the past five years and more. I will examine the reasons for this later. However, it is important to emphasize the immediate implications of this weakness, which can be summarized as follows: if the revolutionary situation of the past five years has not yet developed in the form that could have been reasonably predicted, namely, as a sharing of power and profits between an Algerian ruling stratum and imperialism, this is first because imperialism has not managed to regain control of its Algerian branch, but it is above all because Algerian social reality could not provide representatives of a bourgeoisie to serve as interlocutors, a class that could at the same time present its own interests as those of all Algerian classes and show those interests to be immediately compatible with those of imperialism. There is an absolutely direct relation between the duration and intensity of the revolutionary situation and the fact that no social category capable of advancing its candidacy for the leadership of Algerian society existed at the beginning of the struggle. In other words, the elements of the bourgeoisie were still too marginal to the structure of society to be able to make changes in that society that could have brought the crisis to an end quickly.

An Aborted Bourgeoisie

The schema that Algeria offers is, from the viewpoint of the colonial question, the opposite of the traditional model. Here the political weakness of the colonial bourgeoisie does not proceed from the combination of its interests with those of imperialism in the form of sharing the profits of colonial labor; on the contrary, the Algerian bourgeoisie has been systematically excluded from the social positions where the sharing out of surplus value is decided. Its political weakness results from its economic and social weakness. It is this that requires explanation.

On the fringes of of the precapitalist empires, which Marx called "oriental despotisms," there was always a marginal mercantile bourgeoisie whose function was to trade in the unconsumed surplus product of peasant labor to the profit of the bureaucracies.[15] This stratum of merchants can be found in China and in the Indies, in the Muslim East, and still further away in Byzantium and even in pharaonic Egypt. Its presence is not fortuitous: it allowed the state to realize the surplus value present in the production seized from the peasantry over which it held an exclusive monopoly. A petit bourgeois artisan class that specialized in the production of luxury items destined for purchase by the bureaucratic strata existed alongside this mercantile bourgeoisie. The petite bourgeoisie of the bazaars and even the mercantile bourgeoisie remained inevitably subordinated to the bureaucracy because that bureaucracy was the only outlet for their goods, owing to its exclusive appropriation of the riches produced by the villagers. The prosperity of these classes was therefore dependent on the degree of domination that the imperial functionaries managed to impose on the rural workers.

In Muslim Algeria, this structure was never present in a pure form. Society was never really dominated by the Ottoman bureaucracy. That bureaucracy did not even have a direct foothold in Algeria; all it did was make the domination of Tunisian pirates in Algiers and along the coasts official in the sixteenth century. The Turkish administrators "camped" in the country. They did not constitute a class in Algeria that might have destroyed the essentially tribal social relations that existed before their arrival in order to impose their own models of social organization. The real extent of their power did not exceed one day's march by their Janissaries, and their administration looked very much like pillage. The merchants who commercialized the product of the tax or *razzia* did not form an economically stable and socially distinct stratum that might ensure the regular functioning of social relations. For centuries, the principal source of revenue was piracy, actively encouraged by the pashas of Algiers. The characteristic traits of the Algerian ruling strata at this time were thus parasitism (not only with respect to the Algerian population, but also in relation to Mediterranean commerce) and a tendency to complete identification of the mercantile bourgeoisie and the bureaucrats of Algiers.

When the French disembarked in Algiers, rural Algerian society had kept its pre-Ottoman organization almost intact. The tribes of farmers and nomads who populated the interior were effectively outside the control of the administration in Algiers. A section of the Turkish bureaucracy had begun to detach itself from the administration and to develop itself into a feudal oligarchy by appropriating the means of production and defense into private hands. For their part, certain familial or tribal leaders had directly seized the collective patrimony. Meanwhile, dominant social relations retained the form of a free community collectively exploiting agriculture and shepherding. The Algiers bureaucracy for its part appeared to be in total decay. It had become a kind of organized pillage operating by piracy in the north and through mercenary raids on the tribal territories in the south. The mercantile bourgeoisie both armed the pirate ships and pocketed most of the profits earned from ransoms and speculated on the harvest stolen from the peasants. It thus linked up with the debris of the bureaucracy to form the ruling mafia that held Algiers in corruption and terror. The consolidation of the

European states after 1815 dealt a decisive blow to the Barbary pirates and ruined Algiers. At this point, Bourmont's army came to take the place of the Janissaries.

The petit bourgeois class of artisans and shopkeepers that somehow survived in preimperialist Algeria would find itself condemned to vegetate by the nature of the French occupation of Algeria. The social nature of the groups favorable to the occupation of Algiers in 1830 (essentially commercial companies) and the perspective they imposed for a long time, until financial capital became involved in speculation on farms, show that it was at first just a question of monopolizing the commercial routes of the western Mediterranean by eliminating the Barbary Coast pirates. But as land was seized and cultivated, the companies established in Algiers monopolized the ever more profitable commerce in the exportation of agricultural produce. The small Muslim and Jewish shopkeepers with their limited capital found themselves restricted to internal commerce, which was necessarily weak owing to the poverty of the peasants or to money lending at usurious rates of interest, the sole recourse of the debt-ridden peasant farmers. As for the Algerian artisans, they could no longer find a clientele either among peasant families reduced to the most minimal conditions of existence or among a French population that preferred objects imported from the metropole. The possibilities for expansion of the middle classes after the decomposition of the former mercantile bourgeoisie were therefore limited to their most simple expression.

In the other Muslim countries, and in general in almost all the countries it appropriated, imperialism used a procedure much less costly, financially and politically, than straightforward expropriation. Drawing support from the class in power at the time of its penetration, generally the agrarian oligarchy, imperialism attempted to continue to provide that class with the prerogatives of a ruling stratum—a state, a currency, a national language—contenting itself with shadowing each "indigenous" administrative department with a corresponding European department. This implantation offered the possibility of finding work in the administrative apparatus itself to a part of the middle class in the colonized countries. The rural, artisan, and commercial petite bourgeoisie, weakened from generation to generation by the growing concentration of riches in the hands of imperialism, could send its sons to school and to the university for them to become officers, professors, customs officers, postal workers, railwaymen, and so forth. Of course, the prospect of a reclassification of the unemployed middle classes within the state apparatus encountered short-term difficulties because both imperialist exploitation and the population of these classes grew at a faster rate than the administrative apparatus itself. But the process of concentrating the contradictions stemming from the development of imperialism in the colonized countries within this administrative apparatus made the state itself into the weak point of colonial society. For the crisis that affected the middle classes and the local peasantry necessarily affected the personnel, originating from these classes, who populated the offices, the barracks, the colleges, and so on. Imperialism had no intention of offering the remedy of a welfare state, indefinitely maintained, to a society that it was in the process of destroying. The saturation of the state apparatus brought the crisis of the middle classes to its apex: ever more savage competition, generalized corruption, ever more radical contempt for the ruling class associated with imperialism. At this point the state offers, by its very structure, an organism that favors the expression of this profound dissatisfaction and accelerates its transformation into political activity; hence the determining role of the army in the Egyptian, Syrian, Iraqi, and other revolutions.

In Algeria, none of this occurred. The direct appropriation of lands and trade by imperialism was accompanied by the occupation of all administrative departments by Europeans. The social origin of the personnel of the state apparatus was not, moreover, substantially different from its Egyptian or Iraqi equivalent: the "poor whites" who carry out subaltern functions are in large part the descendants of former colonists who had been expropriated by the companies. But the competition for the bureaucratic positions was unequal: the Muslim unemployed were handicapped by the use of French as the official language, by a whole system of behavior foreign to their cultural habits, and finally by the racial barrier. The percentage of Algerians employed in the administration remained remarkably small. Thus the Algerian middle classes were condemned by their very suffocation to liberal careers, which explains the large numbers of Algerian students in law, medicine, pharmacy, and so forth and also the massive emigration. In both cases, and especially when they are combined, the Algerians were ground under and their nationalism, if it ever existed, could hardly exceed the stage of declarations of intention.

It is an uncontested fact that in colonized countries nationalism is the ultimate response of the population to the profound *desocialization* produced by imperialism. It is reasonable to suppose that direct occupation, as was the case in Algeria, desocializes still more radically than appropriation by "intermediates." Once all its institutions had been annihilated, the Algerian population experienced with particular intensity the problem of reconstructing a new social life, a mode of cooperation that takes as its basis the very state to which it has been reduced by the impact of colonialism and that therefore can no longer have recourse to a preimperialist model. Now, the nation constitutes the general type of response to this problem: it offers a mode of both coexistence and solidarity, and it espouses the very framework given to the colonized country by imperialism. The nation unites people who have been ground down together, if not in the same fashion, by colonialism. It unites them independently of their tribal, village, or religious communities.

Still, in order for nationalist ideology to develop and spread as a solution to the colonial situation, social classes, with an experience or at least a vision of the whole of the society subjected to imperialist oppression, have to be able to provide a universal formulation and common objectives for all the particular dissatisfactions, all the isolated revolts. This role is in general assumed by the elements expelled from the former middle classes and regrouped in the very state apparatus that imperialism employs to maintain its control over society. In Algeria, this condition was lacking. What else could explain how Abbas could say in 1936, "If I could find the Algerian nation, I would be a nationalist, and I would not blush from it as from a crime. . . . I will not die for the Algerian fatherland, because this fatherland does not exist. I could not find it. I interrogated history, I interrogated the living and the dead; I visited the cemeteries; no one spoke to me of it. . . . No one elsewhere seriously believes in our nationalism"?[16] What else could explain the fact that the Etoile, founded by Messali among the most politicized group of Algerian migrant workers in France, was *nord-africain* before being Algerian?

There is no need to go on: when the first shots rang out in the Casbahs in November 1954, the men of the OS had behind them neither a middle class still solidly inserted in the relations of production nor a state apparatus capable of being turned against imperialism and collaborationist elements. The nationalist ideology that burst into the light of day did not have, so to speak, specific sociological support, and it was not only a political void that they had to fill, but a social void. Speaking politically, the Front was not the pure and simple transposition of a preexisting nationalist *organization* into the universe of violence; it was, on the contrary, the violent means of making this organization exist.[17] But socially speaking, there was no *class* affected by nationalism to the point of taking up arms; rather these armed groups crystallized among themselves a nationalism that the situation of the Algerian bourgeoisie had prevented from finding its proper expression. Thus everything took place as if the middle classes, insufficiently developed to be capable of effectively incarnating an idea of the nation that could serve as a response to the crisis of Algerian society, had been replaced in this role by an organization based directly on the peasant masses. Hence the form taken by the national-democratic struggle in Algeria, hence the intensity, the slowness of the revolutionary process, the length of the war. It remains to be explained where this apparatus came from, who these men were, how their undertaking came to be the only effective response to the Algerian situation.

The Formation of the Bureaucratic Embryo

One can, in a sense, summarize everything that has just been said about both the revolutionary process itself and its class content in the following way: the Algerian national struggle could only develop in the shape of an underground resistance. These facts contain in themselves the revolutionary significance and the social import of the struggle. Its revolutionary significance, because the men who gathered in the underground forces consciously and almost geographically abandoned their traditional society in order to take up arms against it. The underground resistance is the society they want, distinct from the society they no longer want, and already present in it. This break with everyday life indicates the depth of the social crisis: since Algerian society offers no legal possibility for its own transformation, one must place oneself outside the law in order to modify it.

But the class significance of the underground resistance is much richer. The social basis of the underground forces is by definition the peasantry. If it is true that the present cadres of the FLN are largely elements stemming from the middle classes, which makes the underground forces the point of junction of the Jacobin bourgeoisie with the peasants, the same was not the case for the initiators of the movement. The role played by the outlaws of the MTLD requires some elucidation. This will furnish the proof of a real difference in social nature between the cadres of the FLN and the actual bourgeoisie.

Uprooting, Emigration, Proletarianization

Unlike the UDMA, a movement of notables, the political cadres of the old Algerian People's Party, which had become the MTLD after it was banned, came from the Algerian peasantry exiled in the workshops, the mines, and the building sites of France. If the Etoile nord-africaine was founded in Paris, this was not only because repression there was less fierce for the Algerians than in Algeria, but primarily because the consciousness of their activity and their need for solidarity was made more acute by their contact with the inhabitants of the metropole. A nationalist sentiment, still vague because it encompassed all the Maghrebis as opposed to the Europeans, was born of exile itself. On the other hand, the conditions of industrial labor and the close contacts that they maintained with workers' organizations taught these peasants who had been chased from their villages by imperialist oppression the reasons for their lot and the forms of organization they had to set up in order to transform it.

It is well known that the Algerians come to work in France for a few years and then return in large numbers to Algeria. Algerian emigration has therefore played the role of a school for cadres in the organization of the nationalist movement over the years. Thousands of Algerian peasants were born into the class struggle in the factories of Nanterre, in the mines of the north, on the dams. The metropolitan industrial universe played, in relation to the development of class antagonism in Algeria, a role parallel to that which the state apparatus played in Egypt or Iraq. In the Near East, as we said, this apparatus, by gathering together the debris of the middle classes ruined by imperialism, allowed these dispersed, individualized elements to become aware of the common nature of their lot and to seek a collective solution for it, once the crisis came to affect the functionaries themselves. In Algeria, what remained of the traditional local apparatus was annihilated, and the machinery that imperialism put in its place was practically closed to the Algerians. Hence two fundamental consequences: the crisis the middle classes underwent could not find a solution in officialdom, and their specific weight in society diminished at the same time that the population increased. On the other hand, the peasants could not find a safeguard for traditional institutions in the preservation of a local state, and thus they took the blow of imperialism in its full force. Imperialism not only stole their lands and their livelihood, it also stripped them of their way of life and their reasons to live. Thus, the debris of the classes dislocated by colonization could not seek refuge from and organize against exploitation within the colonial state apparatus itself. Rather, it was in the factories of France that peasants driven out by famine flourished and where they discovered the means of transforming their condition.

In what would come to be the bastions of the insurrection—Kabylies, Aurès, Nementchas, Ouarsenis—the peasants' contact with colonization was completely episodic. There were no large European properties, and the fellahs were not day laborers but free peasants. On the contrary, there were zones into which the peasantry had been pushed back a long time ago, while colonization took possession of the rich lands of the coastal plains and the valleys. As a result of this, the Kabyle villages, some of which are separated from any road by sixty kilometers of dirt tracks, lived in such a way that the relation between their own poverty and colonization did not appear immediately in the conditions of their work. On the other hand, in the rich lands, the peasantry was essentially proletarian: the lands were monopolized, and some of the peasants were employed as rented labor force in European cultivation, while the rest went into the city to make up the unemployed poor that populate the suburbs. Among this peasantry, which was in permanent contact with the colonial situation, certain conditions for the development of a social and political consciousness were no doubt present. But they were constantly stifled by the crushing competition imposed on the workers by the scarcity of employment: those who have work do nothing that might deprive them of it; those who do not have work are reduced by poverty to an absolutely asocial and apolitical view of things. The lumpenproletariat was never a revolutionary class.

To sum up, in the isolated zones as in those of colonial occupation, the peasant masses could not find, although for different reasons, a social and political solution to the situation in which colonization had placed them. Among the impoverished mountain dwellers, the idea that adversity did not originate in nature but in the social conditions resulting from a century of colonization could not arise spontaneously. It would have implied a view of the peasantry that each individual village could not have; it supposed a historical perspective profoundly foreign to the cyclic repetition characteristic of peasant labor. In the agricultural proletariat, the permanent threat of layoffs hindered attempts to constitute organizations of struggle. Finally, among the starving classes of the shantytowns, when it came to any class perspective, a specific attitude of destitution developed, showing itself in lack of foresight, absenteeism, and galloping population levels and definitively expressing the very essence of destitution: the lack of a future. This is why the peasantry as a whole expressed its critique of society through elementary forms of resistance, such as withdrawal into oneself or a return to the old superstitions, that contained no potential for a positive escape from its condition.

On the contrary, transplanted into the French factory, the Kabyle peasants came into contact in a real-life situation with conditions of exploitation that were bluntly exposed by the very organization of the workshops. The unemployed of the plains and the shantytowns found themselves brutally reintegrated into a socioeconomic unity that was as structured as their mode of life in Algeria had been "amorphous." For some, industrial experience taught them to unmask the exploiter behind the supposed "necessities" of assembly-line work; for others it provided a sense of belonging to a collectivity. And for all of them, the direct experience of class antagonism in an industrialized country was *at the same time* the experience both of the capitalist organization of exploitation and of workers' organizations' resistance to exploitation. The learning of forms of struggle inside and outside the factory rapidly bore fruit. The close contacts of North African workers with the CGT [French communist trade union] and the Communist party before 1936 resulted in the transformation of a good number of these uprooted peasants into active militants, inheritors of the proletarian traditions, that is to say, already corrupted by the bureaucratized forms that the Communist International imposed on the worker organization of the class struggle.

One might have thought that, through the sharing of industrial and political experience with the French workers, most of these Algerian workers would end up incorporating themselves into the metropolitan proletariat. Yet even those who settled in France continued to live separately, and the proportion of those who returned to Algeria was always high. Daniel Mothé has explained why assimilation into the French working class did not occur.[18] The reasons he gives do not hold only for the period that he describes, during the armed struggle in Algeria. Even before the insurrection, Algerian workers were not able to integrate themselves into the French working class. Their relations with each other remain stamped by their precapitalist communitarian traditions and provide considerable resistance to the pulverization and automatization caused by industrial capitalist society.

To this social difference was added, at the time of the Popular Front, a definitive political divorce. Before 1936, the Etoile was in close contact with the Communist party. During the year 1936, Messali's men joined in all the mass demonstrations and participated in the strikes; in the month of August, Messali publicly unveiled a program in Algiers in which the objective of independence was given priority. But at the end of the year, the Communist party completely reversed its position on Algerian nationalism: in the factories and bistros of the suburbs, on the podiums of the congresses, the Stalinists accused the Messalist movement of wanting secession and, consequently, of complying with the most reactionary colonists. Thus they aggravated cultural differences, insinuated chauvinism and anti-Arab racism all the way into worker consciousness, finally pushing the Algerian movement to seek support from right-wing organizations like the PSF (which would steal its new name of Algerian People's Party [PPA] from the Etoile). In January 1937, the isolation that the Stalinist campaign imposed upon the Algerians allowed Blum to dissolve the Etoile, without provoking anything on the part of the Communist party other than a few platonic criticisms.

The Algerians thus took the measure of the "proletarian" character of the Popular Front well before the French working class itself did. It was nothing more than a coalition of the radical bourgeoisie, reformism, and Stalinism, carried along by a powerful push from the masses, and destined to divert the latter from their revolutionary objectives. The case of Algeria constituted a true test of the real political content of this coalition; the measures taken by the government and known as the Blum-Violette project, in suggesting the pure and simple assimilation of "enlightened" Algerians into the French bourgeoisie, aimed to consolidate imperialism in Algeria. This was indeed how the Algerian workers understood it: they were completely demystified about both Stalinism and reformism in colonial matters. It was from this date that the Algerian movement gave up concerted action with the French "workers' " parties and that the brightest of its militants began to understand that they could count only on themselves to put an end to colonialist exploitation in Algeria. They were certainly not surprised that the MRP-SFIO-PC government ordered or tolerated the massacre of the Constantinois in 1945, nor that on this occasion the militants of the Algerian Communist party, at least individually, lent a hand in the repression.

Cultural difference on the one hand, and the political breach with French Stalinism and reformism on the other, resulted in placing nationalism in the forefront of PPA ideology, and in returning the Algerian struggle to the terrain of Algeria itself. But in relation to the social composition of Algeria, where the peasant mass had to confront the elementary problem of its basic biological needs twenty-four hours a day, and where the liberal elements, because of their weakness, remained constantly tempted by assimilation and collaboration, the political meaning of the experiences of the Algerian workers in France could certainly only be understood by themselves and by the most advanced elements of the local proletariat. The latter still remained in large part in quasi-artisan conditions of labor, restricted to the least qualified tasks and in any case little inclined to risk the unemployment that the employers promised in the event of agitation; this proletariat was, finally, numerically weak.

The militants back from the metropole and the slim local avant-garde thus formed a peculiar political catalyst in a colonial Algeria where they could not act, even though they were the indirect result of one of colonial Algeria's major contradictions. Isolated by their worker experience and political consciousness from the large peasant mass in which they had their origins, deprived of all development on the proletarian side by the weakness of industrialization, conscious of the powerlessness of the "enlightened," these men could not hope to obtain an audience in their country that would permit them to engage openly in political struggle against the colonial administration. On the contrary, their relative isolation allowed that administration to stop them, to intern them, to deport them, to ban them from staying in Algeria with total impunity. The prospects of legal political development therefore seemed completely blocked, and the project of constituting a solid clandestine organization to be used as seemed fit, below the official framework of the MTLD, was born of both the political impasse and the desire to save the most active militants from being decimated by repression. Thus the passage to undercover operations may have taken on, in the years between 1946 and 1950, the primary sense of a defensive parry; but the growing number of outlaws and the crisis undergone by French imperialism from the 1950s on would open the prospect of a fully offensive action to the underground cadres.

The violence of the repression that fell upon on the MTLD contradictorily reinforced the elements dedicated to the Organisation spéciale, that is,
dedicated to the establishment of an armed apparatus. In general, the repression reinforced the underground members of the party at the expense of the
politicians who had been previously placed in the forefront of the political
scene by the legalistic direction taken at the time of attempts to form a common front with the UDMA. In 1954, the failure of the policy of unity with
Abbas and of participation in the elections (that is to say, in the communal
administrations) that had been advocated by the central organs of the party
was manifest, at the moment when Tunisia and Morocco openly started the
struggle for independence and when imperialism was suffering its most bitter defeat in Indochina. Strongly inspired by the precedent of the Viet Minh,
with which certain of them had direct contacts and which they recognized as
an organization close to their own, and directly boosted by the Egyptian revolution, the men of the Organisation spéciale thought that the moment had
come to move into open attack, even at the price of a break with Messali.

Their linkup with the peasantry on the basis of the underground forces
would prove relatively easy, and this for two reasons: in the mountains,
many outlaws lived for years in close contact with the peasants and had
worked on them politically; on the other hand, the very formation of underground forces coincided with one of the endemic forms of peasant resistance to colonial exploitation.

Among the rural classes corroded by imperialism, one always observes
what is commonly called banditry as a chronic condition. When the fellah is
crushed by debt, when he knows himself destined for prison for having violated legal provisions of which he understands nothing and that he experiences only as the brutal constraint of the gendarme or the rural police, he
takes down his gun and rejoins those who hold the mountains. These "high-
waymen" are the immediate and immemorial products of the exploitation
endured by the peasants. It is useless to look toward the spiritual heritage of
the Arab tribes or the congenital bellicosity of the Muslim soul in order to
understand them. These are hypotheses at once too crude and too light, refuted by the observation of any other peasantry placed in the same conditions of exploitation.

It is perfectly accurate to say, as the high-minded press emphasized at the
time in tones of virtuous indignation, that there were "bandits" in the underground forces. The only thing that can make anyone indignant in this affair, apart from the hypocrisy or the stupidity of the press, is that a society
could, in the middle of the twentieth century, impose living and working
conditions on the rural workers such that they could respond to them only
with the behavioral patterns of their ancestors of the fourth century.

It is evident that this banditry did not have a conscious political direction any more than the storms of the *jacqueries* that blew right up against the gates of Algerian cities over the centuries. The simple fact that the bandits were at times obliged to attack peasants in order to survive suffices to show, if there were need, that the activity of these outlaws was not directed by any attempt at a solution to the agrarian question at the scale of the peasantry as a class.

But the symbiosis of the peasants in revolt with the outlaw cadres of the PPA would radically transform the political significance of fellaghism. By integrating men who had risen up against the crisis of the peasantry into the rebel apparatus, the cadres linked this crisis, until then felt primarily at the village level, to that of society as a whole. They thus resituated the worker in the Algerian collectivity and put his history back into the history of Algeria. They opened the eyes of a peasantry condemned to the horizon of the *douar* or shantytown to the overall perspective of political emancipation. The peasants' will to struggle thus found its continuation and the occasion of its transformation in the radical form given to political action by the cadres of the MTLD. The peasantry, incapable as a class of constructing a solution to the problem of its own exploitation, found, in the ideology and the practice that the outlaws inspired in it, a platform capable of crystallizing its combativeness and of giving universal value to its struggle.

Gestation of an Aborted Bureaucracy

One can now understand the exact relations of the *fellagha* cadres with the Algerian bourgeoisie and peasantry. The methods of struggle developed by the underground forces exercised over the middle classes both the attraction of effectiveness and the repulsion for violence that every owner of property, even a small one, feels. The middle classes could not manage, because of their specific situation, to move beyond a completely unrealistic liberalism in relation to the concrete Algerian problem. The young intellectuals, who had nothing much to lose, not even a career blocked in advance, were most quickly won over, and they were the first to incorporate themselves into the Frontist apparatus. The artisans and the shopkeepers took a more prudent stance, sympathizing openly when the Front's success offered them the hope of substantial advantages in an Algerian republic where their activity would not be bridled by imperialism, but withdrawing into neutrality (that is to say, into collaboration with the forces of repression) when the violence of those repressive forces inclined them to preserve what they had. All that the Front managed to extract from them was their money (in some small way their essence, after all). It is in any case clear that the military and political cadres of the rebellion are ideologically and politically distinct from the petite bourgeoisie. The initial nucleus had peasant origins and working-class experiences that already sufficed to separate its mentality completely from that of the keeper of a small shop or an artisan: fundamentally, the outlaws were people who had nothing to lose, whether as expropriated peasants or industrial ex-wage earners, and the line that separates them from the bourgeoisie is the one between those who have (even to a very small extent) and those who have not the means to work. Their view of the economy and society is qualitatively different; their emancipation in relation to the private ownership of produced wealth is not reducible to the religion of money, the religion of the petit bourgeois. This sociological divergence is combined with the kind of contempt that the clandestine regulars, hunted down for years and trained in armed hand-to-hand combat, could not fail to feel for a class whose most extreme ambition was always, until the insurrection, to be assimilated into the French petite bourgeoisie. The FLN's men surely consider, and not without reason, that this attitude on the part of the "enlightened" has nothing to do with the permanent humiliation of the peasant masses for decades.

The cadres are therefore not politically petit bourgeois, even if a section of the intelligentsia has been incorporated into the Frontist apparatus. Does this mean that their objectives are those of the peasantry? There is no doubt that the ALN is a peasant army; but a "peasant army" contains social contradictions. The fact that many of its cadres, perhaps even the majority nowadays, come directly from the rural classes does not mean that this army does not contain anyway an antagonism between peasant objectives and the objectives set by the Front as an apparatus. Let us recall several symptoms. If the extermination of the Messalist underground forces could be explained by the more and more ambiguous attitude of the MNA [Algerian National Movement] and by the use the French command intended to make of Bellounis's troops, there is nevertheless no question that the peasants of the ALN should not have attacked without hesitation peasants who had like them taken arms and whose will to anti-imperialist struggle was no less indubitable than their own. The spontaneous attitude of the soldiers in this case should have been one of fraternization, even while the Frontist apparatus systematically pursued its program of the total liquidation of Messalism. The discipline demanded by the Front appeared in this connection as a discipline imposed from the outside, and one does not risk much in supposing that violent discussions in the *katibas* set the cadres and the peasants at odds, followed occasionally by deaths. In the same sense, the peasants could not have taken a benevolent view of the fact that the privileges of money saved the properties of the rich colonists and the companies so that the ALN saboteur groups kept to the small and isolated farms. Here again, the larger political perspectives invoked by the political commissaries could have little impact on the sons of the fellahs, who were highly conscious that large proprietors had ruined their fathers much more than the poorer colonists, with whom, on the contrary, they felt a certain kind of community. Nationalism itself met with some suspicion among peasants too accustomed to promises not to sift them through the sieve of peasant wisdom. That the apparatus had not placed the agrarian question at the head of its agenda, that it had not untiringly repeated that the essential problem was that of the redistribution of lands and consequently of expropriation, could not leave the fellahs indifferent. It is, of course, of no importance to them whether Abbas replaces Delouvrier in Algiers, if the lands do not change hands in the countryside. They are told that Abbas will industrialize and that the overflow of rural manpower will find work in the factories. But Delouvrier also says that he is going to industrialize; and the fellah knows very well that it will take a long time for industrial employment to take up the slack of rural unemployment. In sum, there were already signs (those we mentioned and plenty of others) of an antagonism in the relations between cadres and peasants that bears finally on the overall meaning it is appropriate to give to political action and that reveals, in a still sketchy but already identifiable way, a *class* conflict.

An examination of the contradictory relations that tie the members of the Frontist apparatus to petit bourgeois elements and to the working masses proves in effect that the full-time cadres stemming from the former MTLD group and multiplied by the war itself do not faithfully represent either the middle classes or the proletariat or the peasantry, and that in fact they constitute a distinct state apparatus for the classes that they bring together (for differing reasons) in the common struggle. This peculiar class does not so much incarnate the political interests of any particular category in Algerian society as sum up the whole of Algerian society with itself: the history of its formation is nothing other than the unfolding of all the contradictions of Algeria. In the beginning, there is the absence of a bourgeois and petit bourgeois nationalism strong enough to crystallize the malaise of all the Algerian classes around the idea of independence. Next, the birth of the nationalist movement among the émigré workers in France expresses one of the fundamental contradictions created in the colony by imperialism: the formidable erosion of the peasantry is not balanced by a complementary industrialization. The peasants do become industrial workers, but only in France. The Algerian political movement thus once more draws on the French and the world labor movement at the moment that it exposes the Stalinist gangrene for the first time in the West. The impossibility of finding a solution to colonial exploitation and repression, either for the local middle classes or for the parties of the French left, keeps a nucleus of "professional nationalists" isolated for an entire phase. They will eventually find, in the crisis that weakens imperialism in Indochina, Egypt, Tunisia, and Morocco, the occasion to break out of this isolation through open violence.

The form of their struggle and its length, which I have called the intensity and the duration of the revolutionary situation, can be explained if one conceives of it on the basis of this sociohistoric content. No Algerian social stratum had the power to put an end to the war, prematurely from the viewpoint of the cadres, by entering into talks with French imperialism. On the contrary, the war was conducted in a way that transformed the nucleus of underground fighters into the elements of an apparatus, then fleshed out this apparatus itself at the expense of the social strata that suffered the colonial situation most severely. Many peasant youths left their villages in order to swell the ranks of the ALN and became politicomilitary officials; on their side, the intellectuals left the university or the legal system in order to transform themselves into political commissaries or foreign delegates, breaking all material ties with their class of origin. The Front, by on the one hand drawing the basis of its forces from the peasantry and on the other hand eroding the intellectual petite bourgeoisie, began to fill the social void of which we have spoken. Thus the organizational apparatus tended by its function in the war, and thanks to the duration of this war, to constitute itself into a distinct class. What had in the beginning been a political bureaucracy in the classic sense, that is, a set of individuals occupying hierarchical roles within a party, began to become a bureaucracy in the sociological sense, that is, a social stratum stemming from the profound decay of previous social classes and offering solutions that none of these classes could envisage.

The fact that this bureaucracy did not arise from the process of production itself, but out of the process of destruction that is war, changes absolutely nothing about its class nature, because at the same time this destruction directly expresses the inability of colonial Algeria to guarantee the productive process within the framework of former relations. Destruction here is only the form taken by the contradiction between the productive forces and the relations of production, and we already know, after all, that violence is an economic category. It is understandable that this violence should eventually give the form of a bureaucracy to the class developing among the underground forces, because the totality of relations between the members of this class is nothing other than and nothing more than the totality of relations among the cadres of the politicomilitary apparatus, constituted precisely for the war: salaried, hierarchical, administering in common the destruction of traditional Algeria, as perhaps tomorrow they will administer in common the construction of the Algerian republic.

The process that is going on within a revolutionary situation that is now five years old is the formation of a new class. The totality of the givens that compose this situation necessarily makes this class into a bureaucracy.

But in order for an Algerian bureaucracy to consolidate itself as a class, it would first be necessary for the revolutionary situation that keeps open the social vacuum in which it takes its place to continue long enough for the bureaucratic apparatus to be able to incorporate significant sections of the peasantry and the middle classes into itself. To this end, it would be necessary for the war to continue, and this does not depend on it alone, but also on imperialism, among other factors. Once this first hypothesis is admitted, it would still be necessary that the apparatus win a decisive military victory, on the order of Dien Bien Phu, from imperialism. Only then would the bureaucracy have acquired the capacity to eliminate its political competition, the French bourgeoisie, and to take in hand the reorganization of the country without compromise.[19]

Yet it is evident that the weight of French imperialism on Algerian society is much too heavy for these two hypotheses to be able to be reasonably retained. Given that the one-tenth of the population who control half of Algerian production[20] certainly think of themselves as belonging to the metropole, given that two-fifths of the land, which is more than half of the agricultural production, belongs to the French, given a Saharan mineral reserve that promises billions in profit, none of this will be abandoned, above all when imperialism emerges consolidated from the crisis to which the rebel has indirectly subjected it. On the other hand, all of this can be negotiated, and surely will be negotiated, because whether we like it or not, the Gaullist regime, if it wants to stabilize the Algerian situation even provisionally and to abort the process of bureaucratization, will have to take into account the fact that, over the past five years, some very serious candidates for the leadership of Algerian affairs have appeared.

In orienting itself in this direction, de Gaulle's declaration, however inflexible its tone, tried to locate (either within the Front or outside it) an interlocutor ready to negotiate a sharing of wealth and power with imperialism. And the response of the GPRA means that the bureaucrats of the apparatus are now ready to engage in preliminary talks within a democratic-nationalist perspective. In this present state of things, that is, if no serious reversal intervenes in the relations between de Gaulle and the European population of Algeria, this is the most likely prospect.

The political and social meaning is very clear: *the same crushing weight* of imperialism that produced the void in which the new class began to constitute itself now forbids it to develop completely. Since 1957, the Frontist cadres have been well aware that they both cannot be defeated and cannot win; for its part, the French military command has acquired the same certainty. This equilibrium cannot be broken from the inside. It will indeed have to be resolved by a compromise between the two sides. Whatever the duration, the form, and the content of this compromise, its result will be, at least during a transitory phase, that the bureaucracy will not be able to continue to consolidate itself as it did thanks to the war. The single fact that there is a compromise means in effect that it will have to accept (for example, in the shape of elections) a new type of relationship with the Algerian population. Of course, we should have no illusions about the acual democratic character of these elections, but beyond the liberal playacting, the problem posed will be that of the real rooting of the politicomilitary cadres among the peasant classes who will be decisive by virtue of their numbers.

What remains certain in the meantime is that the war in Algeria offers us a supplementary example of the formation of the bureaucracy in a colonial country (with the specific feature that here the class in question has not for the time being reached full development), but also that the emancipatory struggle in the countries under colonial tutelage, in that it requires the entry of the masses onto the political stage, is the bearer of a revolutionary meaning that is important to emphasize. We are well aware that the perspectives offered to the Algerian revolution (as to all colonial revolutions) are not and cannot be those of socialism, and we do not support the Algerian movement because it will end up by modernizing social relations in a backward country. On this account, it would be necessary to applaud the Chinese bureaucracy, that is, an "intelligent" imperialism, if it is true (as we think) that no "objective necessity" prevents it from carrying out decolonization itself (as one sees in black Africa).

But what no ruling class, local or metropolitan, can achieve, or even desire, is that the colonial workers intervene *themselves, practically and directly*, in the transformation of their society, that they break off, effectively, without asking permission from anyone, the relations that crushed them, and that they provide an example of socialist activity personified to all the exploited and the exploiters: the recovery of social humanity by its own efforts. In particular, the Algerian peasants, workers, and intellectuals will no longer be able to forget (and this is of immense importance for the future of their country) that they, during these years, mastered their lot, desired their fate, and that therefore *it may be possible* that mankind may have the fate it desires.

31

The State and Politics in the France of 1960

(1960)

Barricades in Algiers from January 24 to February 1. Proclamation of a state of siege. On February 2, special powers are passed by the government for a year. The Jeanson network is dismantled on February 24, and its members are judged and sentenced in September and October.[1] On September 6, the Manifesto of 121[2] proclaims the right to insubordination.

M. de Sérigny[3] nibbling Ben Bella's crusts in the Santé prison, M. Thorez calling on the people to defend the general's republic against the "fascist agitators of disorder," the employers and Matignon encouraging the workers to take an hour of strike holiday without loss of productivity bonuses: in the face of this apparent inversion of all political indicators, a traveler who had left France in May 1959 would believe he was dreaming. Only one constant factor would allow him to feel at home: the attitude of the immense majority of this country, as always spectatorial.

What was called "political life" not so long ago was the fact that a significant fraction of the population took initiatives relative to the problems of society, participated in political meetings and spoke at them, displayed solutions it believed just, and in this way challenged the establishment and, if it couldn't overthrow it, at least shook up its plans. Yet, with the exception of Algeria (where such a political life, even if it is in decline, appeared in January among the Europeans, and where it manifests itself every day without fail in the shape of the armed activity of the Algerians themselves), France is politically dead.

It is in relation to this fact that the phraseology of the "left" appeared, during the January crisis, as completely anachronistic; it is this fact of which the revolutionaries (no less isolated than the organizations, though for other reasons) ought to become aware, on which they ought to reflect, from which they ought to draw new ways of thinking, new ways of acting, if they intend to become the thought that human reality is in search of, as Marx put it.

Gaullism and Modern Capitalism

The Algerian crisis had been the immediate occasion for de Gaulle's accession to power in May 1958, but the new republic in reality had to untie the inextricable complex of problems that the Fourth Republic had allowed to knot together over thirteen years. All these problems could be formulated in one sole question: was the French bourgeoisie capable of initiating the changes necessitated by the modern capitalist world, in France and beyond?[4] By its very existence, this world constituted an ensemble of challenges to the structure and functioning of French society, whether it was conceived as an economic totality or as a state or as the metropole of a colonial empire.

The Fourth Republic had manifestly failed to make the necessary changes. An incoherent economic policy alternated between modern investment decisions and laws supporting the most backward productive sectors. The restoration of prewar parliamentarianism allowed different sectors of the bourgeoisie and petite bourgeoisie to make their particular interests prevail one after another and reduced the executive to nothing more than the stake in a struggle between various pressure groups. Finally, the situation created in the old empire by the immense liberation movement that stirred up colonial peoples throughout the world did not evoke any collective response in Paris. But the reflexes of colonialist repression, which led in the long run to disastrous surrenders, alternated with sporadic attempts to find more flexible forms of imperialist domination than the old colonial link. . . . [5]

The May 1958 crisis was therefore the result of a conspiracy. It was the whole crisis of French capitalism that erupted in it, and it was immediately clear that it could not be resolved like the "crises" of the Fourth Republic. This time, the question Who governs in France? was posed explicitly and in such a way as to interest not only professional politicians, but in fact all social classes, beginning with the proletariat. This was not a cabinet crisis; it was at least a crisis of the regime, at most a crisis of society as a whole.

It was at least a crisis of the regime in that, in any case, the Fourth Republic's mode of government, or of nongovernment, appeared inevitably doomed. At most a crisis of society, if capitalism could not manage to both develop and gain acceptance from the whole of society for a new regime, a regime capable of putting things in order, that is, strong enough to solve the most pressing problems (public finances, the franc, foreign trade, Algeria), a regime stable enough to begin to free the economy from the most serious obstacles to its development.

It is true that the political disorganization of the proletariat, resulting from several decades of compromises made by the Communist party and SFIO [the French International] with the bourgeois parties, gave rise to the "hope" that a serious crisis could be avoided. On the other hand, the adversary that big capital had to defeat immediately was not the working class, but the bloc of the colonels and the extreme right. But domination by this bloc, even temporary, risked leading the whole of society into a much more profound crisis than a simple crisis of regime.

The forces that openly attacked the Fourth Republic obviously only sought to impose a state in France that would serve the interests of the European colonial class of Algeria. These interests were completely incompatible with those of French imperialism as a whole. It is evident, for example, that major French capitalism could not envisage for a second the economic integration of Algeria into the metropole: that would amount to giving up ten or twenty years of normal expansion in order to end up a half century later with the whole country from Dunkirk to Tamanrasset at a still greater distance from the modern capitalist countries — not to mention what integration would have implied in the realm of domestic and international politics.

But what big capitalism could do, and what it did, was make use of the dynamism of the May 1958 insurrection in order to rid itself of the regime blocking its development in France and, once the new power had been consolidated, to rid itself of the very forces that had allowed the first phase of the operation. It thus remained master of the terrain without a serious crisis that might have called the domination of capitalism over French society into question having occurred. On the other hand, it brought about the "strong state" demanded by the army and the extreme right, while at the same time confiscating that state for itself.

In reality, the two phases were telescoped into each other, both because the project of big capitalism was not as immediately explicit as it seems in hindsight and because even had it been absolutely premeditated it would have been necessary to espouse the cause of its provisional accomplices for a short while. The current of May 13 thus swept up contradictory elements, defenders of *Algérie française* along with more or less innocent tools of modern capitalism. But, above all, this internal contradiction continues in the Gaullist state itself and explains both the essential ambiguity of its political (and oratorical) style and the permanent crisis that inhabits it. On the one hand, it cannot be denied that the diverse measures taken by this state with regard to the most urgent problems inherited from the Fourth Republic converge into one sole and identical meaning: to make the interests of big capital predominate in the domestic economy and in foreign trade as well as in relations with the colonies and Algeria. On the other hand, however, this significance could only be revealed very slowly. Each of these measures is matched or is followed by a concession to the adversary that it aims to suppress; the power of big capital can only consolidate itself little by little in maneuvering its accomplices, just as the Gaullists of May 14 manipulated the men of May 13 in Algiers. In large part, the aborted crises that ended in the resignation of the ministers representing the French bourgeoisie of Algeria or the most backward sectors of the metropole expressed nothing other than the carrying out of a settlement of accounts between the partners of May 13.

That is to say, in this respect the Fifth Republic already shares certain essential features of the Fourth. Of course, the subordination of the particular interests of this or that sector of the dominant classes to those of big capital is much more explicitly pursued than in the preceding regimes; but the resistance of these sectors has not disappeared, and de Gaulle's power has not ceased to employ trickery to put an end to it.

We will return to the precarious character of this power. First, it is advisable to emphasize the fact that dominates all the others: the whole operation could only succeed provided that a massive intervention of the workers, proposing a revolutionary solution to the problems of society as a whole, did not cause the "response" to the crisis planned by the ruling circles to fail, and did not enlarge the crisis to its real dimensions. Now, this intervention did not occur. By an apparent paradox, while the crisis openly expressed the incapacity of French capitalism to manage society, the proletariat left capitalism at leisure to resolve the crisis in its best interests. What is more, the proletariat helped in the process, first by its abstention, then by its vote in the referendum.

De Gaulle was only possible because he was available to the French bourgeoisie to contain the crisis within the limits of its legality, that is, to turn it into a simple crisis internal to the ruling sphere, and not a crisis *of* the ruling sphere as such. The power of the Fifth Republic was constituted and the power of the bourgeoisie was reconstituted because the workers did not attempt, during those few days when the decayed state ended up in the streets, to take it over, to destroy it and to impose their solution. They did not even dream, as a class, of such a solution and setting it into motion, and finally did not seriously contest—that is, through their actions—capitalism's capacity to settle this crisis.

This *depoliticization* of the exploited classes (and of this exploited class, the industrial proletariat, whose working and living conditions always created the avant-garde of the worker movement) was thus the foundation of de Gaulle's regime, but it is also its permanent atmosphere, and this is what the January crisis showed anew. This is the fundamental fact of this period, and on two accounts: first because (as we just said) an analysis of the Fifth Republic that omitted the depoliticization out of which it arose and in which it maintains itself could not understand either its genesis or its present life; second because for revolutionary critique and organization such a depoliticization constitutes a kind of challenge, almost a refutation: how, in effect, is one to persevere in the socialist project if it appears that this project no longer exists among the proletariat, at least in its *political* form? That is the question that de Gaulle's France puts to us, and it would be contrary to the task of the revolutionaries to avoid it by imposing outdated political categories on this world, by applying a political practice to it that does not correspond to reality.

We have always affirmed[6] that in the absence of a massive intervention of the workers, French capitalism is capable of carrying out a transition to the structure required by the modern world; it is moreover a kind of tautology, if one admits that the only obstacle that makes a ruling class absolutely incapable of continuing to manage the ensemble of the society on its own account consists precisely in the revolutionary initiative of the masses.[7]

Of course, this adaptation of French capitalism does not happen smoothly; it encounters obstacles within the the propertied classes themselves that come from the very structure of French society, these same obstacles that delayed as much as possible the necessary collective reorganization. But one can propose this idea by way of an overall assessment: however violent the resistance opposed by one section or another of the petite or middle bourgeoisie to the reorganization of the state, of the economy, of relations with the colonies, none had the power to make it fail irreversibly. This reorganization is not, in effect, a merely formal operation, like the arranging of a closet or the putting in order of a dossier; it has a social and political content; it means that big capital intends from now on to make *its* interests predominate over those of the petite and middle bourgeoisie.

Now, one does not risk much in prophesying that big capital will emerge victorious from this test of strength, within the limits imposed on it by its own interests, of course. It suffices to take stock of the means possessed by its adversaries and to analyze the problems that French society must resolve in the coming decade if it wants to continue to exist as a capitalist society that matters, in order to predict the final success of the "recovery" set in motion by big capital, that is to say, a still greater centralization of capital, the ever more complete domination of "organizers," the proletarianization of the former middle classes, and so forth.

In this sense, the present system, even if it is precarious in its political form, has an irreversible importance as the instrument of a deep transformation in French society. Even if de Gaulle were to disappear tomorrow, even if a "military power" established itself in France, the profound change that is taking place in this society would not be stopped. The disorder of the Fourth Republic did not hinder it, and the offensive of the Algerian colonial class, the most retrograde class in the country, which objectively sought the preservation at all costs not only of Algeria, but also of "daddy's" France, only succeeded finally in drawing big capital closer to direct political power. If it is true, as we will see, that de Gaulle's regime is extremely precarious, it is also true that the transformation of the very bases of French society, of which it is the instrument, is durable and decisive.

The first precondition for the recovery of French capitalism was political, and paradoxically it is perhaps still the least satisfied. In effect, the bourgeoisie had first to endow itself with the statist political instrument that would allow it to impose on all classes the appropriate measures for freeing society from the impasse of the Fourth Republic. This instrument had to fulfill two functions and, consequently, to take on two forms: on the one hand, to free the government from the control that the parties and the pressure groups had previously exercised over it, and therefore to incarnate itself in a "strong" power; on the other hand, to create a political organization, a mass party, capable of maintaining the contact between the ruling power and the whole of the population, capable of controlling it, and of obtaining from it finally the indispensable simulacrum of its support for government policy. We shall see later on why neither one of these forms could be achieved by Gaullism, and consequently why its political situation remains precarious.

But in the absence of this perfect instrument of domination, the Fifth Republic nonetheless profits from the political crisis in which it originated. Parliamentarianism and the parties have come out of that crisis completely discredited. De Gaulle can therefore find a pretext in the profound distaste felt by the whole of the population, including the working class, for the regime of the parties, in order to assign a purely figurative role to Parliament and to leave the parties to pursue their henceforth harmless games there with complete irresponsibility. The referendum shows that de Gaulle was not wrong in betting on general contempt for the political forms and forces of the Fourth Republic. Constitutionally at least, he has a free hand. The new Constitution in effect endows the state apparatus with a "strong" structure, that is, sufficiently centralized and hierarchical for its organs to become in principle relatively inaccessible to impulses other than those that come from the top.

In fact, this structure is really strong only insofar as the pressure groups do not continue to divert certain branches of the state apparatus in their own interests. Otherwise, it is evident that directives from the top cannot have repercussions at the executive level, and one is presented with (which is the case) the paradox of a power whose form is strong and whose effectiveness is very weak. The pressure that interest groups, and particularly *Algérie française*, exercised through Parliament has apparently been eliminated, but in reality it is only displaced; from now on it works directly in certain departments of the administration and in the most important executive branches (army, police, information). This contradictory situation results, as has been noted, from the very conditions in which de Gaulle came to power: the ultra faction, which carried him to leadership, had all the leisure, during the summer of 1958, to place its people in certain essential posts, and thus it acquired the ability to delay the implementation of measures decided at the top, or to neutralize them on the ground. If one adds to this that the branches so colonized are principally the army and the police, that the ground is Algeria, that the confusion of the state instrument and Algerian society is almost total there and has lasted for years, one can understand that the Algerian lobby found things made singularly easy.

Consequently, the present regime can only satisfy the requirement of a strong state formally, so to speak. In a sense, that is the defect it inherits from the preceding regime: the habits of unpunished disobedience in the army, the police, the administration (of Algeria above all), added to the pressures that come from the most backward sectors of society, are not easy to overcome, above all when one came to power thanks to them. But, more deeply, this precariousness of the state, so visible at the time of the January 1960 crisis, expresses more than a political heritage: it carries the real heterogeneity of the dominant class into the very structure of the administrative apparatus. It is because there are considerable inequalities of development in French capitalism—and, consequently, in sections of the bourgeoisie whose interests are radically at odds—that the instrument of bourgeois domination in this case continues to be the object of attempts at permanent seizure. A stable state presupposes at least a homogeneous dominant class. At present, the French bourgeoisie could deliberately sacrifice its particular interests to its interests as dominant class only if the working masses exercised a really threatening pressure on the political institutions that it imposes on them. But as long as the proletariat as a whole will not intervene, and as long as big capital has not, in the long term, destroyed the fundamental bases of the most retrograde strata of the bourgeoisie, the problem of the state will remain at issue. This problem is a kind of circle: the bourgeois state in France will never be "strong" while the bourgeoisie remains divided among profoundly contrary interests on most of the problems that it faces. But overcoming this division and leading the ensemble of this country's structures to modern forms coinciding with the interests of big capital requires a strong state.

This objective difficulty was only shifted by de Gaulle's accession to power, not removed. The Constitution was completely tailored to the size of the president, not worked out with a view to a durable stabilization of political institutions so as to make them relatively independent of the person of the head of state. In pushing de Gaulle to power, in giving him practically total power, big capital evidently resolved the most urgent problem posed to it by the insurrection of May; but it did not respond and could not respond to the fundamental problem of the form that its interests should give the state apparatus in the long term. Because of this, the question of de Gaulle's longevity remains a troubling question for the ruling class.

Should one say that the same is true in Germany, in the United States? This would be at once accurate and inaccurate. It is true that in all the countries of modern capitalism, the subordination of all economic and social activities to an apparatus of political administration endows it with considerable powers and that centralization within the state apparatus itself makes its leader into the symbol of the stability of the society as a whole: that is why he always appears irreplaceable, that is why the leader's cardiac arrest or senility troubles the ruling classes. But, at the same time, these regimes are equipped to avoid an excessive interregnum: they have the parties. After a fairly long gestation, to judge by the average age of their offspring, these enormous machines end by vomiting from their entrails the fully prepared successors of the great man in power. The "competence" of these successors is beyond doubt, because it has been tried over long years of purgatory within the party bureaucracy. The transmission of power thus takes place smoothly after the disappearance of the head of state or government.

But the parties have another, still more important, function in these regimes, and we discover here the second failure encountered by Gaullism with regard to the political problem.

On the political terrain, the ruling class confronts the same contradiction as in production: on the one hand, it monopolizes the functions of administration and decision, it completely excludes the worker from them; but, on the other hand, it needs the participation of the same people that it manages, even if only in order to know what they are, what they do and can do, what they want and do not want to do. Without a minimum of information, the bourgeoisie (or the bureaucracy) completely loses control of real society, its decisions remain a dead letter. In the political domain, this contradiction finds its expression and its "solution" at the same time in the functioning of the parties, such as it exists in Great Britain, in the United States, in West Germany, and so forth. These parties fill exactly the same double function as the unions in the firm. On the one hand, they have their roots in real society thanks to their base, and they express this society's opinions despite all the deformations imposed by their bureaucratic structure. But, on the other hand, and above all, the party represents an irreplaceable instrument of control over the population. Thanks to its propaganda organs and its militants, it can orient opinion in a direction that is appropriate to the conjuncture; thanks to its structure, it can capture and channel dissatisfactions. Finally, when the party is in power, its hierarchy incorporates itself from top to bottom into the state hierarchy, which assures the latter the effectiveness that ideological discipline or, more simply, careerism, gives.

The competition of two large parties allows the dominant class, in safeguarding the trappings of democracy, always to have a "spare state" in reserve; furthermore, the party of the "left" obliges the bourgeoisie in power to preserve its class discipline, while, inversely, the opposition party's structuring as a quasi state (shadow cabinet) extracts all revolutionary content from the left. The parties are thus a kind of double of the state and at the same time probes that it pushes into the population in order to overcome its isolation in relation to society.

Now, the Gaullist authority does not possess these instruments. The very conditions in which big capital seized power in France required the pushing aside of all the parties, too compromised in the decay of the preceding regime, too numerous to produce uncontested candidates for the presidency. Big capital took power against the parties or at least despite them, and it appears condemned to govern for a long time without them. Despite the shared wishes of Mollet and Duchet, the evolution of the political spectrum toward a bipartisan structure appears highly improbable, at least in the foreseeable future.

For its part, the UNR [Gaullist party of the Fifth Republic] is not a party in the sense just mentioned but a movement whose internal institutions do not make of it a quasi state, and whose ideological and social composition forbids it from even playing the role of an intermediary between the authorities and the country: from this last point of view, the UNR is a heterogenous pack of local notables, where the men of big capital are placed side by side with the small reactionary owners. It would not know how to free Gaullism from its ambiguity; it incarnates it.

One has difficulty seeing, in these conditions, how the state will be able to put up with this lamentable political situation. In the short term, the split between the parties and power continues to deteriorate; technicians, high functionaries, and other "organization men" have come, one after the other, to replace the fallen "political" ministers. But such a solution, if it does not hamper the functioning of the state in the present period, in no way resolves the problem of the relations between power and society.

The contradiction that weighs on the political "solution" that big capital has tried to give to the crisis of May 1958 necessarily recurs in other domains. But not everywhere equally: where the bourgeois adversaries of big capital cannot oppose a serious resistance to it, the general line of the latter's policy affirms itself clearly: when, on the contrary, the terrain in dispute is already occupied by these adversaries, this line bends, beats around the bush; power comes to terms, at least momentarily.

In December 1958, having obtained the double acquiescence the nation gave him in the referendum and in the elections, de Gaulle sets out "his" economic program. Essentially, this program consists in taking a cut from the purchasing power of wage earners on the order of 15 to 18 percent, directly by restrictive measures (freezing salaries, slowing down of consumption), indirectly by devaluation. The reduction of domestic consumption that follows, added to the reduction in the exchange value of the franc, allows a much more important part of the national product to be devoted to export, that is, to the acquisition of strong currencies. In a few months, the balance of foreign trade is reestablished and the currency stock reconstituted; from spring 1959, the normal rhythm of expansion begins again, and, at the beginning of 1960, the employers can envisage, if social tension becomes a little too high here or there, the possibility of proportionally loosening their stranglehold on the wage earners.

These measures are welcomed by the ensemble of the bourgeoisie, and for good reason: in making the workers pay for their carelessness, they resolve the problem of financial stabilization in the most "elegant" way. But the tidy equilibrium thus obtained is not sufficient. It is not enough to clean up the finances of the state or of foreign trade by aggravating exploitation; in the long run, one must undertake the rationalization of the most backward sectors of the French economy. Now, as we have just seen, attempts to put pressure on agricultural prices—even very limited ones—immediately provoke violent reactions from the peasant mass, for whom there is more at issue there than a haggling over its level of revenue. In the problem of the production cost of agricultural products, nothing less than the problem of the small rural property is posed: in relation to an "American" kind of economy, the French system of land ownership and its methods of cultivation are completely outdated. The peasant malaise can only get worse. The same holds for distribution.

Of course the middle classes who find themselves doomed over the long term do not have sufficient strength to block this process; but they at least have enough inertia to jam, slow down, or ride out its unfolding. It is clear that big business capital will for some time have to make concessions to this section of the active population if it does not want to alienate it; and it cannot afford to alienate it because of its enormous relative volume, the heritage of a century of conservative social policy. The extinction of shopkeepers, of artisans, of the peasants of the Midi and the West is thus not going to happen tomorrow, and French capitalism, however modern it may become in the wage-earning sector, will keep for some time yet the specific feature that a third of the active population works in financial and technical conditions identical to those of 1860. Therein lies the source of considerable difficulties, be they only those resulting from the noncompetitive character in for-

eign markets of the products manufactured under these conditions. The re-
laxation of trade restrictions by the most advanced sector of production will
for some time have to accept import quotas on many products that are in
competition with those of French agriculture and small industry.

De Gaulle and Algeria

As for the problem of the relationship with the colonies, the Constitution
already indicated that big business capital was going to try to resolve it
through loosening the colonial link, that is, was going to break as much as
possible with the exclusive tradition of violent and pointless repression. Further political development in Africa soon showed the effectiveness of this solution; the granting of a large measure of autonomy (that is, of independence) allowed a privileged local class, whose essential interests coincide
with those of imperialism and that takes on the task of channeling or re-
pressing the forces unleashed among the African masses by political emancipation, to consolidate itself on the spot.

On this point, the Gaullist enterprise did not come up against any really
organized adversary. But the litmus test, the problem where "one had hopes
of de Gaulle," the problem from which Gaullism had arisen, remained the
Algerian problem. No group inside the French bourgeoisie had known how
to provide itself with propaganda organs capable of intoxicating public
opinion, none had directly seized possession of a large proportion of the
civil administration and almost the entirety of the military apparatus, none
had defied the central authority, as had the colonial class of Algeria.

For these reasons, it proved extremely difficult to enforce a policy in conformity with the interests of big business capital. Throughout the summer of
1958, de Gaulle beats around the bush, maneuvers, does not come out either
in favor of or against *Algérie française*. After the September constitutional
referendum and the November elections, the first measures appear that tend
to give Paris back its domination over the Algerian sector. The order given to
the officers to resign from the Committees for Public Safety and the recall or
reassignment of several superior officers manifest an intention to return the
army to its executive function. Then de Gaulle's declarations seek to set in
motion little by little a kind of third way, which would be neither that of the
extreme right nor that of the GPRA [provisional Algerian government], but
rather that of big business capital, of an association that would at the same
time safeguard the essential elements of French imperialism's interests in Algeria and allow the nationalist leaders to win their case regarding participation in the affairs of the country.[8] In doing this, de Gaulle went much further
than any president of the Council of the Fourth Republic; through him,

large metropolitan capital tried for the first time to define a policy in line with its fundamental interests.

Meanwhile, the insurrection of January 24, 1960, should have shown that de Gaulle's adversaries had not given up. Beforehand, it was already evident that the directives emanating from the Elysée continued to be translated into the language of *Algérie française* on the other side of the Mediterranean: the superior officers, the generals, and other marshals continued to make clear their own opinions on the declarations of the president; the instructions Delouvrier had received when taking up his post almost remained a dead letter; the legate-general himself appeared to give way in his turn to the irresistible Algiers atmosphere; the "patriotic organizations" and the extreme right wing groups openly declared their hostility to the policy outlined by Paris and threatened to oppose its application with arms.

All the difficulties of the regime seemed incarnate in the January crisis as those of the Fourth Republic were in May 1958. Pinay's departure (orchestrated in the Algerian manner by the extreme right wing of the independents) and the peasant agitation more or less dictated by the corporatists lent consistency to the hypothesis of an offensive by certain sections of the bourgeoisie against de Gaulle's policy. The uprising of the Europeans of Algiers threw out an explicit challenge from the Algerian lobby. The hesitation of the military command and the civil authority over several days finally seemed to affect the very texture of the Gaullist state. The whole ensemble allowed one to imagine a repetition of May 13.

However, notable differences soon appeared between May 1958 and January 1960 in the very style of the insurrection and in its development, differences that are explained finally by the new political situation constituted by this regime.

First, the Europeans who intervened effectively in the street were much less numerous and much less active than on May 13. In 1958, there were 100,000 persons in the Forum; in 1960, there were 15,000 in the center of Algiers during business hours, and not more than 1,000 permanent insurgents in total. In 1958, the movement had spread like wildfire through all the cities (thanks to the complicity of the army and the administration); in 1960, it affects the center of Algiers for eight hours, the center of Oran for three days, the war memorials of four or five cities for several hours. In 1958, the entirety of the administrative structure of Algeria entered into insurrection; in 1960, the insurgents manage to control no vital organ of Algerian society, they *retrench*.

Is this to say that the January insurrection is the creation of a few conspirators? If it had been so, it would not have lasted two hours, above all after the shooting. In fact, the men who made the insurrection possible were not Lagaillarde, Ortiz, and so on but the European blue- and white-collar workers, postal workers, railwaymen who really *rose up* against what they believe to be the destiny that the solution of an "association" that de Gaulle wants to impose holds for them. They believe, in effect (and they are no doubt correct; the example of Tunisia and Morocco proves it), that such an association will oblige them to share their jobs with the Algerians, and that thus many of them will be obliged to expatriate themselves, to come to France to find work. Transposed on Algerian soil, that is, with the whole colonialist content inherent in their situation, the problem the "poor whites" encounter in Gaullist policy is, when all is said and done, the same problem as that of the peasants, the artisans, the shopkeepers of the metropole. To change Algeria into a "modern country" is to put an end to the "privileges" of race (not, of course, to the privileges of money), just as to change France is to put an end to the "privileges" of tradition. The rationalization of the capitalist world aims at the disappearance, not of the Bourgeauds, but the overseers of Bab-il-Oued, not of the Boussacs, but the farmers of the Moriban. The fear of these classes who feel themselves condemned and who know themselves to be defenseless is perfectly justified, even if the political reactions in which it is released are perfectly aberrant.

It is still the case that these reactions, we said, did not have in January 1960 the intensity they possessed in May 1958. There was an appreciable drop in tension in the Europeans' combativeness. It certainly must be linked to the reinforcement of power in France, which made an effective popular pressure on the orientation of the affairs more problematic and improbable for the *Français d'Algérie* as for the *Français de France*. Concretely, in Algiers, that meant that the rallying of the army to the insurrection appeared much less easy than a year and a half previously.

It cannot be disputed that in effect the army as a whole was run in an appreciably more "loyal" way with respect to Paris than on May 13. No doubt, the troops that were placed in contact with the insurgents, when the gendarmes and the mobile guards had been withdrawn, treated them indulgently; but this fraternization became impossible when the paratroop division that had belonged to Massu had in its turn been replaced by domestic units. Over the period of more than two years that this division was stationed in Algiers, many Algiers men had joined its ranks, and many men and officers had married Algiers women. The interpenetration of the army and the European community was exemplified in this case in an extreme and unique fashion.

But the most decisive sign of the rediscovered "loyalism" of the forces is the abstention of the Algerians throughout the entire insurrection, for this abstention was in reality that of the SAU and SAS officers [who commanded Algerians in the French army] of Algiers and its suburbs; these same officers had, in 1958, mobilized "their Muslims" in the Forum to put on a show for both Paris and the extreme right, demonstrating to Paris that all of Algeria was against it, demonstrating to the extreme right that they could not hope for the return to the colonial status quo, and indicating finally a Gaullist solution to the insurrection at the time.

In opposing the attempts of the 1960 insurgents who sought to recommence the "Franco-Muslim fraternizations," the group of captains clearly decided in favor of supporting de Gaulle's policy, and it is not excessive to see in their attitude the most significant fact of the crisis. As for the situation in Algeria, it indicates in effect that these officers, each of whom, as one knows, is "worth" the strength of thousands of Arabs voices, seem ready, in the event of a referendum, to exert pressure in the direction desired by de Gaulle, that is, for association. Thence proceeds the talk of a "Muslim thaw," thence the hurry to unleash a third force in favor of speedy regional elections. No doubt this orientation remains embryonic for the time being and can only come to fulfillment if the problem of relations with the GPRA, notably in the preelectoral phase, is positively resolved. But it nevertheless indicates an essential modification in the attitude of the section of the army that is finally the most important, the one that is occupied in the administration of Algerian society.

It is an error (which we never made here, even if we somewhat overestimated the retaking in hand of the army by Paris) to conceive of the army of Algeria, that is, the cadres in active service, as being endowed with a stable ideology, essentially fascist, and resolved only to enforce orders compatible with this ideology — not to mention those elements of the military, above all the oldest, who are officials mainly concerned with returning to a "normal" home life. The spirit of the officers most actively engaged in the colonial war cannot be reduced to a fascism or a "Francoism" of any kind. It is certain that they constitute perhaps the most politicized part of the country, in that they experience in the most immediate (in their everyday lives), most intense (their lives are at risk), and most persistent (since 1946) way the crisis of the regime that they obeyed for twelve years before bringing it down, the crisis of a society that they do not see as preferable to that of their adversaries, the crisis finally of the Western values taught to them by tradition and whose fragility they feel in the face of the enormous momentum of the colonial masses against the West. It is in this army that has for fourteen years defended an empire that it knows to be lost as such, defended a "civilization" whose real significance it could judge from its exported form through contacts with the colonists of Madagascar, of Indochina, of Morocco and Tunisia, and lastly of Algeria. Finally, it is in this army that the contradictions of modern capitalist society are lived, if not thought, more intensely than in any other section of the bourgeoisie.

It would be surprising if the army, having carried out essentially political tasks for years, were not politicized, that is, it would be surprising if it continued to "do its duty" blindly, without ever asking where it is. For even if "do your duty" means something in the traditional exercise of the military métier, on a battlefield faced with persons who on their side obey the same imperative, it loses all meaning when the lieutenant and his forty men, left in the center of a Moi or Kabyle village, receive the order to "pacify" it. The problem is then no longer to hold or die, but to find a way to give some content to the "pacification." Now, if this task is taken seriously, it inevitably means the reconstruction of a social community, integrating the soldiers and the peasants in relations that are as harmonious as possible. If therefore the military cadres as a whole harbor an ideology, it is neither fascist nor "Francoist," but "administrative": the officer imagines his task as a task of putting all social activities back on track, and he knows that this is not possible without the participation of the peasant community, nor, furthermore, without *his* participation in the peasant community.

These aspects became more pronounced in the Algerian war because, more than any other, it is a social war. De Gaulle had to try to restore to the army a minimum of confidence in his actions by exorcising the specter of a departure with arms and baggage that would have wiped out at a stroke years devoted to the reconstitution of an Algerian society. Hence the appeasements contained in his January 29 declaration and reinforced at the time of his trip at the beginning of March.

But no amount of appeasement can overcome the essential absurdity in which this administrative activity is steeped. As managers, it is true that officers tend to assimilate into the communities for which they are responsible. But this assimilation is of course impossible: first, administrative regulations concerning assignments, changes, promotions, and so forth, do not leave them in their villages for very long, which already shows that merely belonging to the military apparatus is incompatible with the task of administration. Second, and above all, their administrative ideology remains a *class* ideology. For them it is not a matter of participating equally in the reconstruction of society by following the project that the Algerians develop for themselves, but finally of imposing, under fraternal or paternal guise, a model of society as much in conformity with the interests of French capitalism as possible. And they must themselves be conscious of this fact, because they know and observe daily that the most active elements (the very force that obliged Algerian society to pose the problem of its organization anew) are not in the villages, but in the mountains, bearing arms against the village; they also know, however, that no social reconstruction is possible without these elements. The absurdity of the military task in Algeria is that it wants at the same time to manage Algeria *with* the Algerians and *without* them (not to say *against* them). There is not an SAS or SAU officer who is not aware of this, and there is no "taking in hand," even with an iron fist, that can prevent it.

For this absurdity is nothing other than the very absurdity of capitalist society transposed onto the terrain of Algeria, where violence brings it fully to light: in the factory, as well, the employers try to make the workers participate in the organization of their work but only within the framework of methods and objectives defined by the employers themselves, that is, without ever letting the workers actually manage. In this respect, the Algerian war is exemplary because it crystallizes and strips bare *the* most fundamental contradiction of the capitalist world, the only one that is truly insoluble *within* the system itself. French society, even if it were to be endowed with a state still "stronger" than de Gaulle's, would not know how to fill the gaping void hollowed out in military ideology by the crisis in that society over the past fifteen years (what pious souls call the "malaise ◆ the army" and the phraseologues of the left its "fascism").

Therein lies an objective limit to the success of de Gaulle's policy in Algeria. That is not to say that the Algerian war will last forever, but only that de Gaulle must find a solution to the impasse in which the army is caught if he wants to be able to put an end to the war without his state being seriously shaken. The modification that we said earlier could be detected in the spirits of the SAS and SAU officers will perhaps give him the means of getting out of this impasse, if they will henceforth accept working within the perspective of self-determination. That is not to say that the intrinsic absurdity of their task will be done away with, because all in all they will be asked to manage until the time when it will be preferable not to manage any longer, but for de Gaulle as for the employers, the problem is not that of knowing whether the absurdity will really disappear, it is that of knowing whether one can act as if it did not exist.

Finally, and if one does not take the fundamental contradictions inherent in the class structure of society into account, the immediate result of the Algiers insurrection appears to be the defeat of the European bourgeoisie of Algeria in the face of French capitalism. The relative isolation of the activists in relation to the demoralized population at large, along with the resigned obedience of the military cadres, allowed those in authority in Paris to decapitate the organizations of the extreme right and to displace the most compromised officers, thus at the same time consolidating its hold on the military and administrative apparatus of Algeria and breaking down, or at least seriously splitting up, a major obstacle to its policy.

The Transformation of Everyday Life

The barricades of Algiers were, like Lagaillarde's beard, anachronistic. But the appeals to antifascist vigilance that resounded in France at the end of January were hardly less so. If it is correct that an endemic fascism raged in Algeria because of the particular structure of this society, it is no less so that there is no fascism imaginable in France today, nor in any other modern capitalist country.

In order for fascism to arise and spread, it is first necessary that a profound crisis call into question the capacity of capitalism to govern society as a whole, and particularly its economy, as was the case following the 1929 crisis. Next it is necessary that a significant segment of the proletariat that violently suffers this crisis no longer has the force to develop a revolutionary and socialist response and accepts the solution that big business capital offers it through the intervention of the fascist organizations. There is no fascism without a radical and open crisis of all the traditional institutions of capitalist society, nor indeed without the almost physical elimination of the political and union organizations the working class had previously provided itself.

Now the French economy is currently "bursting with health."[9] There is no need to be a cynical banker to understand this. It is enough to look at the unemployment figures,[10] the balance of exports and imports,[11] the speed of expansion in industrial production,[12] or any other indicator: it is impossible to imagine what aberration might lead so "prosperous" a capitalism to offer itself the expensive and risky luxury of fascism. Furthermore, there is no question of eliminating the workers' organizations, but rather of their growing participation, over the past ten years, in economic responsibilities, at least at the company level. This is an inescapable necessity for modern capitalism. To diagnose fascism in these conditions is the effect of paranoia.

And it is true that, apart from their dated little plots, organizations (like the Communist party, the UGS, and the PSA) that have called for the formation of antifascist committees do suffer from an ideological archaism close to psychosis. No doubt the phantom of fascism served them as a pretext for soliciting common actions, that is to say, cartel formations, from one another (which in any case will remain on paper); perhaps they could dream of "outflanking de Gaulle" in their defense of his republic. But whatever they may have dreamed or wished, they showed above all, on the occasion of the Algiers insurrection, their complete inability to rethink the political problem of the modern society or of the society on the way to modernization in which they find themselves. They do nothing but chew over the old slogan of the union of the left; they would almost be thankful if fascism existed because at least it is a situation with which they are *already* familiar, for which they already have tactics prepared. The fact that these tactics have always failed matters little: at bottom, they cried fascism in order to bring it to life and, at the same time, to give life to themselves. This is no longer politics; it is the hypermemory of the dying.

The total indifference of the population to its appeals revealed the confirmed decay of the ideology of the left as did the open hostility or disillusioned irony with which the workers greeted the "strike" for which the unions and the bosses called with one voice.

If either the unions or the bosses hoped to politicize the workers in one direction or another, on the occasion of the Algiers insurrection, it must be agreed that they completely failed. The persistent repulsion that the proletariat as a whole feels when faced by "politics" could not be overcome despite the ingredient of fascism. The proletariat no more stirred in January 1960 than in May 1958. To tell the truth, for what, to what ends, might it have stirred? There was no question of its defending de Gaulle: the workers had directly experienced the class meaning of power, through the reduction of their standard of living and through the acceleration of working practices in the firms. Yet what did the organizations propose to them? Safeguarding the Gaullist order, that is, their own exploitation. Evidently, no political perspective could be outlined by the organizations of the "left," which deserve no further critical attention.[13]

But this distaste for worn-out organizations is not enough to characterize the attitude of the proletariat toward politics. This distaste seems to extend to the political sphere itself. The working class, if it is still capable of fighting, and hard, at the company level, is not producing new stable organizations in which not only its protest program but its communist project might crystallize. The idea of a global and radical transformation of society seems absent from the present attitude of the workers, along with the idea that collective action can bring about this transformation. The spread of this depoliticization greatly exceeds implicit criticism of the parties and the unions.

We must search for the true reasons for this, decide to open our eyes, to identify the immense transformation in the everyday life of the working class (which has been going on in the bowels of our society for the past ten years) in which this depoliticization inscribes itself, to give it its full historic and social significance and to draw from it the political conclusions that must serve as a guide to our action. We can only hope to provide a sketch of this task in what follows.

The health with which the French economy is "bursting" implies first of all a more rapid use of its labor force for workers, both blue and white collar. The present rhythm of expansion supposes in effect an increased productivity, even taking into account the entry of the younger generation into production. The "rationalization" that the employers impose almost every-where on the proletariat operates according to completely different processes from one location to another, sometimes employing brutal Tay-lorism, sometimes using the police methods borrowed from Ford, sometimes adopting the most modern techniques drawn from industrial psychology and sociology, but always with the machine itself as an objective constraint imposing rhythms and gestures. But all these processes converge into a single project, which is the increased alienation of the workers in their labor, the more and more subtle disruption of their traditional means of struggle against exploitation, their more radical expropriation from any initiative, their ever more visible degradation into the simple appendix of a manage-ment that is itself ever more invisible. The exteriority of workers in relation to what they do thus continues to deepen, and correlatively their activity ap-pears more clearly than in the past as a simple moment in the circulation of capital: on the one hand, work has now become for the majority of wage earners time wasted in gestures stripped of all interest and all real meaning; on the other hand, the money received in exchange for this time does not seem to result from this time itself in any thinkable way. The relation that exists between the eight hours passed figuring on a cash register the price of the objects that the clients of a supermarket present when leaving the store and the 30,000 or 35,000 francs [$60 to $70 at 1960 rates] that are given the employee in exchange for these eight hours is felt as absolutely arbitrary. That means that even the pecuniary stimulant, this final reason behind the whole organization of capitalist society, has lost all effectiveness, not as a stimulant, of course, but as the expression of a real hierarchy in the value of different kinds of work.

There is thus at once a more complete incorporation of the workers into the working sphere (and this is what we mean by emphasizing that the workers feel themselves to be merely a phase in the capitalist process) and a more complete exteriority of labor in relation to the workers. The rhythms are more rapid, the working practices are more oppressive, the harassments of control are more petty — and at the same time the content of what one does is more indifferent. The tensions that result from this situation are thus different from those produced by work of a more technically simple nature. The new working practices require higher and poorly remunerated profes-sional qualifications, and these tensions are released in strikes and demon-strations decided on the job, which tend to hold firm, to be directed as much at local working conditions as at wages, and which are usually rewarded with success. Even in France, where the breakup of the organizations of struggle has been significant, such workers' actions now appear frequently; they are common currency in countries like Great Britain and the United

States where "rationalization" is more advanced. But these strikes do not spread, given the lack of organizations with suitable structures and ideologies.

The "compensation" for this alienation (but need it be said that this alienation does not allow, cannot allow any "compensation," and that the very idea of "compensation" is a product of the capitalist philosophy of the permanent possibility of a cash equivalent?) is provided by modern capitalism, and is beginning to be provided in France, in the form of a more elevated standard of living. Part of the product is or can be given back to the workers, not because the employers become philanthropists, but because this payoff is finally indispensable for enlarging the capacities of the "market" as production rises, and consequently for increasing the purchasing power of wage earners.[14]

Does this "compensation," which causes the foolish to claim that the working class is becoming middle class, mean more freedom of consumption? On the contrary. There would be no end to an enumeration of the techniques that capitalism employs in order to be able to regulate consumption in such a way as to preserve the harmony of its system: the destruction of products through consumption currently attracts almost as much attention (market surveys, motivational research, consumption inquiries, etc.) as does their manufacture. And these studies do not aim only to adjust production to needs, they aim no less at constantly refitting needs to production (from both a qualitative and a quantitative viewpoint). This is to say that capitalism tries to incorporate the dynamic of needs ever more strictly within its global economic dynamic: this incorporation operates both in the form of prediction, henceforth indispensable to the functioning of the system, and in the form of a control effectively adjusting needs to production possibilities.

Thus an increased alienation in needs is added to alienation in the labor process. The needs we feel are less and less our needs, more and more anonymous needs, and the infallible symptom of this alienation is that the satisfaction of these needs does not procure a real pleasure. Many activities of consumption, on the contrary, become chores.[15]

But this behavior coincides perfectly with the functioning of the modern capitalist economy: it assures the full use of the labor force without its being necessary to employ constraint—by means of the simple self-determination of that force—and at the same time, it guarantees the full use of purchasing power. Thus the labor force is more and more caught up in the exclusive use of its capacity by the employers, and so it is that variable capital from now on incarnates itself in almost the entirety of the labor force available in society.

In the same sense, one of the notable results of economic expansion lies in the fact that social categories previously untouched by "modern life" are proletarianized. That is, they are not impoverished, but abstracted from their traditional mode of working and consuming and subjected to the increased alienation we just described: this is the case for the peasants, particularly the young; this is the case for the shopkeepers and artisans. This movement sooner or later implies a homogenization of ways of living in France, which would already be appreciable from a comparison of the pattern of consumption of a contemporary peasant family with what it was twenty years ago.

But modern capitalism does not only overthrow habits of working and consuming, it profoundly transforms all human relations, that is, everyday life itself. The remoteness of the home in relation to the workplace (it would take too long here to examine the origin of this phenomenon) brings about a considerable extension of the time taken in commuting, that is, in indirect relation to production. Correlatively, the time devoted to familial life or private life in general is appreciably reduced, and new tensions in the relations between men and women, between parents and children evidently follow. These relations are more and more abbreviated, it is more and more difficult to share experiences, the familial community as such tends to pulverize itself, and the old idea according to which it is proper to "raise a family" loses all content when husband and wife see each other for two hours a day from 6:00 to 8:00 p.m. (if there is no television), when the children are taken care of by the school, the canteen, homework, holiday camp. One of the fundamental values of traditional society crumbles away; the effect is that workers no longer find a relatively stable human milieu outside their work in which they can escape from the obsession with production — that they grasp themselves instead as isolated, that is, abandoned *individuals* — and that they lose, with the family, a goal in the conduct of everyday life.

More generally, a kind of anonymous human relation, which corresponds to the pulverization of the communities of the previous period, tends to develop: for example, the old neighborhood community, so important in the proletarian life of the nineteenth century, is broken up in the new dormitory suburbs where the occupants of the same building no longer know one another. The destruction of the stable familial and perifamilial entourage affects fundamental emotional attitudes. In the past, it was in this milieu that the choice of partners (friends, sexual partners) was traditionally carried out; today, this choice functions with ever greater difficulty. On the other hand, the fact that mixed labor becomes the rule favors the multiplication of precarious sexual and affective experiences and stabilizes a form of behavior consisting of *trying out* the other and oneself. This precariousness, when it concerns sexual relations, no doubt explains the French woman's attitude of anxiety, taking into account the prohibition of birth control, as well as her reaction in the direction of security: for her, marriage offers above all the sense of a defense against anxiety, it takes place in conditions that make her sexual success problematic.

From all of this there results an increased relativization of human relations: individuals are immersed in a society that they endure rather than understand, not because it is unbounded, but because its overall meaning, the thing that guaranteed the tissue of values out of which everyday life was made, has disappeared, along with the feeling that it is possible to reconstitute this meaning. Whence proceeds cynicism in political matters, if politics is indeed the activity through which persons intend collectively to transform the meaning of their lives, whence proceeds the apparent indifference to and the real anxiety concerning the problems that overshadow the field of everyday life.

This overall attitude manifests itself particularly among the young (whose relative importance in France is considerable given the age pyramid). They are less inclined (and indeed less able) than anyone else to oppose the good conscience and the bad faith of political or sociological "explanations" borrowed from the previous period to this general crisis; the fraction of working and student youth that is politically organized is extremely weak. Their nonpoliticization is simply the general form taken by their nonadhesion to social values. Society such as it exists is incapable of offering the young the least reason to live, and it is only on this basis that one can understand the style common to the kids in black leather and the "hoodlums," the aesthetic of violence.

One finds oneself faced with an overall situation for which it would be superficial to want to impute responsibility to a particular factor. In gestation in France, but already constituted in other countries, this society is in its fundamental features neither the effect of a simple internal transformation of capitalism nor the unique result of the degeneration of workers' organizations, nor is it the sign of the extinction of the communist project in the proletariat.

One must not lose sight of the fact that the transformation of capitalism that led it to modify profoundly the relations in which exploitation takes place itself results from the workers' struggle. Through its wars and its "peaces," its "prosperities" and its recessions, the real history of capitalism is the history of a dominant class constrained by the proletariat constantly to revise the ensemble of its modes of domination. The workers have fought for a shorter working week, for security in production, for insurance, for wages, for vacations, for allocations, for administration; and the bourgeoisie, for a century, has not ceased to retreat, to make concessions. It has always tried to take them back, when the occasion has presented itself, when the working class was beaten down and divided. The workers had to begin the struggle again in order to regain what they had lost and in order to overcome the new forms that the employers had given to exploitation. In a sense, the whole history of mechanization (if one excepts the relatively autonomous development of science and technology), the whole history of the forms of constraint in the factory and the office from the twelve-hour day to "human relations,"[16] the whole history of political and juridical institutions, is only the succession of the results of the conflict between the communist project stirring up society and the exploitative function imposing its structure on it. These results are essentially unstable, they are never anything other than precarious compromises continually made between the two forces when they can no longer carry on the struggle further.

But this fundamental conflict, which animates all of capitalist society, contains a much more important significance if one places oneself within the workers' movement itself. In these everyday struggles as in its large-scale battles, the proletariat constantly encounters the opposition of institutions and organizations that it created, that it nourished, and that have become weapons in the hands of its adversary. The political or protest organizations with which it provided itself in order to put an end to exploitation, the institutions that were created out of its victories, are left in the sphere of the ruling class by the ebbing of the tide; they have been incorporated as so many organs of the functioning of class society, and in order to carry on its struggle, the proletariat has not only to undo the stranglehold of exploitation, it must furthermore unmask, denounce, and destroy its own works. Everything that is institutionalized in a class society becomes a class institution. All activity in the past tense becomes a passivity, not through some kind of curse, some kind of burden that weighs on mankind, but simply because the ruling class assimilates it, makes it into *its* institution, turns it against those same ones who have acted and weighs them down with it. That is its function as an exploiting and alienating class: to place humanity in the past tense, in the passive mood.

This process of ruling-class takeover of the organizations and institutions whose meaning was originally proletarian attains its height in contemporary capitalism. More than ever, the bosses assimilate the forms of struggle, of resistance, that belong to the humanity they exploit and use these forms as intermediaries between themselves and the workers. Wage increases become the means of enlarging the market and of avoiding the old crises, the "frank" (face to face)[17] discussions between employers and wage earners allow the leadership to inform itself about worker opinion and to control it, employers responsibility for vacations allows them to enforce even the modes of workers' leisure, the extension of schooling makes possible the diffusion of a completely mystifying culture, the ruling class's claim to resolve the problem of housing for the workers provides it with the means of controlling even the use of familial space. The unions are on the road to integration in the hierarchy of the factory and the office, the "workers' " parties are on the road to integration in the sphere of the bourgeois state. No doubt the process is less complete than in some countries of modern capitalism such as the United States, Sweden, or Germany; no doubt there are still specific obstacles in France (essentially the nature of the Communist party) opposed to the complete incorporation of the former workers' organizations into the institutions of the society of exploitation. But the phenomenon does not differ qualitatively between France and these countries.

It is in this political vacuum, older than Gaullism, that the Gaullist state has been able to institute itself. And it maintains this vacuum. The concrete conditions of everyday life that are given to the workers are not the causes of depoliticization, any more than depoliticization is *their* cause, but there is a social totality that is present and expresses itself in each of its parts: in the forms of the exploitation of labor and in the forms of consumption, in the cooperation of the "workers' " leaderships with the class state and in the indifference of the workers toward these leaderships, in the pulverization of individuals, and in the brief and resolute struggles they carry on sporadically in the firms.

The workers no longer give life to their organizations through their struggles (the organizations detach themselves from them — become bureaucracies — incorporate themselves into the structure of class society — the ruling class tries to use them as intermediaries — the proletariat withdraws itself from them even more — the bourgeoisie increases its exploitation) but through the organizations and the institutions that had produced the proletariat, in underhanded forms. One can read this sequence in either direction — there is no absolute beginning, there is totalization. Muffled totalitarianism is this control by the leaders of the whole wage-earning population in all its activities, which takes place thanks to the organizations that the proletariat had imposed through its former struggles.

It is thus proletarian political life itself that is alienated, that is displaced from its own class in hybrid organisms (in that their genesis is worker and their function bourgeois or bureaucratic), that is seized by the ruling class. The very idea of a global political project is immediately neutralized in the workers' own heads. Incredulity, lassitude, and irony keep an exploited class in step much more effectively than open violence.

Assuredly, the proletariat was always worked upon from the inside by the ideology of class society, and the essential element of this work was always to convince it that it was not itself *a class*, that it was not this communist project. It would be a pleasant simplification, and an enormous political error, to conceive of proletarian political life as a pure development toward socialism, as a project never contested in itself by the fact of its existence in class society. But in the preceding period an important section of the workers organized themselves against the assault of the dominant ideology, banded together, counterattacked, and through this very counterattack broke the "spell" of the mystification for themselves and for everybody. Today, there are no signs of the birth and explicit organization of this activity of contestation of class society: the proletariat is no longer present in society as manifest political will. This is not to say that the communist project has been annihilated and that the dominant class has succeeded for all time in its task of reifying the workers. On the contrary, the inability of the ruling class to offer the society that it claims to govern a direction, a sense, values, reasons for doing and being what this society is and does has never been clearer, never has its incapacity to ground a really social life broken into the open as completely as today. This is what we tried to sketch out, very briefly, a while ago. More than a century ago, it is true that the proletariat was not the object of "a particular tort, but of a tort in itself."[18] But the problem posed by this profound erosion of activities and ideals is precisely that of how to know *how, by what means* the revolutionary project can henceforth express itself, organize itself, fight.

A certain idea of politics dies in this society. Certainly, neither the "democratization of the regime," called for by unemployed politicians, nor the creation of a "large unified socialist party" (which will only regroup the refuse of the "left") can give life to this idea. Such notions lack perspective, are minuscule in relation to the real dimensions of the crisis. It is now time for revolutionaries to measure up to the revolution to be made.

32

Gaullism and Algeria

(1961)

> *De Gaulle on March 5, 1960: "an Algerian Algeria." On*
> *November 4: "an Algerian republic." On April 11, 1961:*
> *"a sovereign Algerian state."*
> *On June 10, 1960, Si Salah comes to the Elysée Palace.*[1]
> *On June 14, de Gaulle calls for negotiation. From June 25*
> *to 29, Franco-Algerian discussions begin at Melun. They*
> *break off abruptly.*
> *December 1960: the Algerians demonstrate en masse in*
> *favor of the FLN in all the cities.*

Insofar as "politics" is a theatrical production, the French stage has not changed its program over the past year. The president presides, the French carry on the business at hand.

But in relation to the problems that de Gaulle's rule had to solve, the French situation has appreciably changed: the failures that have accumulated over a few months weigh more and more heavily against the regime.

Finally, at another level, the most important one, the one at which the question Who makes history? is continually posed, a profound shift in positions has occurred. Like all Western imperialisms, more even than any other, the French state has not only given way, piling concessions on concessions in the face of the immense uprising of the peoples under its governance, but in this struggle it has also completely lost its monopoly on initiative.

It is the war in Algeria that has opened up communications between these three levels—that of official policy, that of the problems of capitalism, that of the class struggle—but it takes different meanings in each of them. It is a stable element of the stage set on which the political drama plays itself out. Yet the war is also the most bitter failure, and the hardest to disguise, in the most extremely urgent task that the Fifth Republic had to accomplish. Lastly, it is already six years since the war changed its character: the unanswered challenge thrown out by a handful of fellahs to one of the world's leading capitalisms now becomes an episode, one of the last, one of the bloodiest, one of the most exemplary, but an episode in the irreversible history of decolonization.

For some months, the covering in which imperialism has enveloped the world has been fraying, worn out in some places, pierced in others. The struggles engaged in on the one hand by Korean, Japanese, and Turkish students and on the other hand by the Cuban and Algerian revolutions do not have an identical social content, nor consequently is the defeat suffered by Western capitalism in these different countries of the same importance. But there is defeat everywhere. And above all, the positive group significance of these movements breaks out openly: those who have been *objects* in world politics, in the history of humanity—these peoples who did not exist except by virtue of their strategic situation, their mineral resources, or the picturesque quality of their artists—have achieved subjectivity. They say "we"; they disrupt the calculations of the chancellery; they constrain the "great powers" to rethink, dismantle, and reformulate their tactics once more at top speed; they undertake a formidable struggle for control of the United Nations.

Autonomy has already been the true meaning of the Algerians' struggle for years: they were victorious as soon as they took their fate into their own hands, along with their weapons. In the present context, this struggle thus has an exemplary significance: all of Asia, all of Africa, all of Latin America recognize themselves in it, despite all ideological divergences. This war gathers to itself and exacerbates the thrust of these peoples not only against Western domination, but more profoundly against the monopolization of "humanity" by Europe.

Previously, the Algerians' struggle remained relatively isolated. De Gaulle was assured of a kind of monopoly over the settlement of the question. On the other hand, the détente between the two blocs incited Khrushchev to treat Paris gently in an attempt to breach NATO unity. Lastly, the African countries were still too few and too dependent on France to be able to support the GPRA [provisional Algerian government], which could only find an eventual opening through the impotent Arab League. All these elements tended to keep the problem, if not Algeria itself, in the sphere of French policymaking.

From now on, Algeria is no longer a French problem. Paris had already admitted this verbally by agreeing to the principle of self-determination. But apart from the speechmaking, and despite de Gaulle's intentions, reality has confirmed that the problem eludes French capitalism: the breakdown of the Melun talks and the emptiness of the conference of September 5 attest to this new situation.

Two implications of this observation should be emphasized. The breakdown of talks has been presented uniquely as the doing of the Elysée Palace, of its intransigence. But if relations were broken off, it was also because the GPRA did not want to capitulate, because the Algerians had not been conquered, because the degree of the masses' participation in the struggle remained as high as ever. After January 24 and the round of "stay-at-homes" [*popotes*], de Gaulle definitely intended to use his victory over the extreme right in order to negotiate, but in such a way as not to multiply the "anxieties" of the military (which he had observed on the spot), that is to say, by obtaining the equivalent of a military surrender from the ALN. This strategy was supposed to find an understanding partner in the Algerian petite bourgeoisie. It was a false calculation on two counts.

First, the Frontist leadership resisted this attempt at division by strengthening its unity. Thus it has been proved that not only are the Algerian petit bourgeois elements (the "liberals") devoid of any autonomous force, any power to win over the masses, but also that even within the Front members originating from this class had been completely absorbed so as not to form a genuinely distinct political tendency. This is an extremely important fact, because it means that in independent Algeria the bourgeoisie will probably not hold power in Western "democratic" forms. It is moreover clear that this prospect depends upon the capacity of French capitalism to come to a compromise with the GPRA. One can then understand the desperate attempt made by Bourguiba to help out de Gaulle and to give life to the "liberal" faction of the Front, for example, in forming a unified government by means of which the Tunisian bourgeoisie could bring its full weight to bear on the Algerian bureaucracy. Whatever the fate of this project is, it is a safe bet that the maneuver will fail: Bourguiba's prestige does not match up to the revolutionary potential that the FLN holds for the North African masses.

Second, the "worries" of the army cannot be so easily calmed. A long time has passed since the army was an instrument dedicated to its official purpose of disarming rebels. Even if it had achieved a military victory, which is not the case and which would have absolutely no meaning in this instance, it would nonetheless have remained a social force managing or claiming to manage the Algerian countryside and suburbs. In particular, a military surrender by the resistance would not be enough for it if the Front must subsequently be recognized by Paris as an official political force and given the right, by way of the ballot box, to stake a claim to govern Algerian affairs.

The longer the war continues, the more Algeria becomes, in the eyes of the army, the test of its own role, the justification of its existence. Displacing the officers of Algeria is not at all a simple strategic problem of troop deployment, it is a social problem, that of the replacement of the administrative class, which is to say, the major problem of a crisis. De Gaulle has not until now had the power to resolve this problem, but it is also clear that this situation weighs heavily on the actions and on the perspectives of the regime in France.

Along with the persistence of the war come the defeats encountered by the Gaullist state in all directions. Of course economic growth continues, only slowed down by the reduction of foreign markets and the threat of recession in the United States: in this sphere, the French bourgeoisie only encounters "technical" difficulties, in the sense that it possesses the means to resolve them; one can anticipate, moreover, that the unions will support wage claims, claims whose satisfaction would permit, when all is said and done, a reinvigoration of the productive sectors that have been most affected.

But the large tasks of the "rationalization" of social structures have not even been begun: they barely exist in the form of a project in the files of the Rueff-Armand Committee.[2] Decisive measures are yet to be taken either on the agricultural question or with regard to distribution. The program and the people exist, and if one examines the propositions made by the afore-mentioned committee, one will have confirmation of the assessment of Gaullism as an expression of big capital's attempt to rationalize its domina-tion over society. But what slows down this attempt is the impossibility of putting into place new political structures that might amount to such a ra-tionalization.

Let us leave aside foreign policy where there has been a general failure in European as well as in Atlantic or global affairs. In the domestic sphere, the possibility of Gaullism rested on the benevolent neutrality of the population as a whole—lacking a strongly constructed party that would have allowed him to inform himself about public opinion and to act accordingly, de Gaulle could base his power only on an atmosphere. But this atmosphere itself only existed conditionally [*sous bénéfice d'inventaire*] in public opin-ion. Today it is easy to draw up an inventory [*inventaire*] of this atmosphere: young soldiers continue to leave for Algeria, purchasing power has dropped since 1958, the margin between production costs and retail prices is still as wide, and it is less and less possible to express oneself.

As a result of this, the breach between state power and the country has widened. Parliament's function has been reduced to nothing; the govern-ment itself has been literally doubled by a system of commissions staffed by de Gaulle's personal advisers; no party has managed to fill the void that lies between the Elysée Palace and the population as a whole. The only means the state possesses is sorcery, but nowadays that only works on the old Bre-tons.

Thus, the longer a solution to the different problems posed to French cap-italism is delayed, in particular as the war of Algeria continues, the more the different tendencies that French capitalism had tried to win over or neutralize resume their centrifugal movement. There are a thousand political expressions of this agonizing struggle, which it would be tedious to enumerate. The same contradictions that undermined the Fourth Republic and that Gaullism had blocked are coming back to life; but this is still not yet the most important matter.

The great majority of workers have remained passive since May 13: the solution of the war of Algeria seemed to them to be too much for them. The actions undertaken by the proletariat here and there since the beginning of this year have remained essentially protest struggles in their aims and forms. The only truly significant fact in this country over the past year is that a section of its youth, still weak, primarily intellectual, but also working, has undertaken to resolve for itself the situation in which the war in Algeria has placed it.

For itself because, taken literally and in its origins, the refusal of military service by a few draftees cannot in itself constitute a solution or a sketch of a solution to the war, nor an exemplary political activity; what the draft dodger refuses is *his* participation in the war. But it would be more than hypocritical to be indignant at such an individualism: if the Communist party and the noncommunist left had not for six years driven the young to despair by opposing only pious wishes and votes of confidence in the army to the sending of troops to Algeria, insubordination would doubtless not seem like a solution.

But if it is true that the current of refusal has its origins in the stagnation of the parties, in the degeneration of the proletarian traditions of internationalist solidarity and anticolonialism, it cannot be reduced to a set of sporadic acts of despair. That would be a failure to recognize that the reporting of these acts has aroused a new public concern with the question of Algeria, the war, and the institutions. One cannot but note that as a result of these individual decisions, a rather large segment of youth has started to consider its relation to the war of Algeria as something other than a detestable inevitability. Future draftees ponder what course to follow; students' discussions are obsessed with this problem. The intellectuals' declaration and the trial of the Jeanson network have given this attitude a new publicity along with a larger significance: one sees peaceable novelists and honest clerks of the state publicly acknowledge that, when all is said and done, military duty is not an unquestionable obligation and that in fighting against the French army the Algerians are struggling for freedom. In the Cherche-Midi trial, the accused and their defenders have reopened the dossier on torture by calling on several witnesses whom the prosecution itself cannot impeach, thus declaring and justifying their practical solidarity with the Algerians.[3] The measures of repression immediately taken by the government obviously revive the affair: protests multiply and even sectors of public opinion that had until then remained silent take up positions on the issue.

All this is certainly not revolution. Insofar as this movement will not reach the working masses, were it only in the form of the participation of a minority of employees and workers, the challenge it poses will touch only the most obvious forms of oppression and exploitation. The workers represent an immense force because a total challenge to society is inscribed in their condition. This force can be aroused by the initiatives of the young, by the appeals of the intellectuals, on the condition that the workers do not content themselves with waiting for instructions to come from on high, but in their turn take up the initiative in the action.

For, as I remarked, the important feature is that a section of French youth has attempted to solve its problem *on its own*. For years the young have been condemned to the following choice: either play with the rattle offered by the parties under the name of politics or completely lose interest. In any case, they ended up leaving for the war, which is to say that their fate did not change, whether or not they were political. Their current refusal of this choice turns out to be the most effective policy because after this everything starts to shift, including the organizations most respectful of legality.

There is evidently a profound affinity between the concrete decision to refuse the war, minoritarian and isolated though it is, and the wider movement of decolonization that makes the initiative change hands on the global scale. In both cases, established powers, traditions, values, and behaviors so deeply rooted that they passed as natural are all contested, refuted by simple acts. Of course, when it is the Cuban or Algerian peasants, workers, and intellectuals who carry out this upheaval, it is a revolution because in the end there is no longer any power other than that which issues from their force. When it is the Korean or Turkish students, it is a revolt, which a liberal bourgeoisie or the army can take over for its own benefit. When it is one-thousandth of the French draft, it is only a hint, the echo of these revolts, of these revolutions in a modern country overwhelmed by the "good life." But this statistical nothing disrupts all the positions.

Since the autumn, the situation in France has begun to change in an important regard: the people's attitude toward the war in Algeria. De Gaulle's press conference of September 5, in which he appeared to be completely divorced from all reality; the movement of insurrection; the Jeanson network trial and the facts for which it provided judicial confirmation through the testimony under oath of high officials confirming torture in Algeria; the Manifesto of the 121 and the sanctions taken against its signatories—all these events played the role of catalysts of an awakening of public opinion that had been developing since spring.

This awakening is still limited to a relatively small section of the population; it is especially strong among the students. This explains why it was the national students' union that took the initiative of a public demonstration "for negotiated peace in Algeria." It is certain, in particular, that in the working class the will to act against the continuation of the war remains weak. This is the reason why the improbable maneuvers of the Communist party were relatively successful in their attempt to sabotage the demonstration. The number of demonstrators on October 27 was small for a city like Paris, and few workers participated in it. But the Communist party suffered a bitter defeat among the students: hardly more than two hundred communist students agreed to dissociate themselves from their comrades and meet peacefully at the Sorbonne, while the others went to be beaten up by the police. This shows that the split between Thorez's old bureaucratic apparatus and young people will only get deeper.

This does not preclude the October 27 demonstration from having marked a real step forward, and on several accounts. Taking into account the diversionary maneuvers of the Communist party and the CGT [French communist trade union], taking into account also the inevitability of fighting with the police, the gathering of fifteen thousand demonstrators is in no way negligible; and their number made the several hundred fascist counterdemonstrators look ridiculous in comparison. An important proportion of the participants showed that, for them, to demonstrate was to demonstrate and not to disperse peacefully after having heard uplifting speeches.

The best thing about the demonstration, in other words, is that it took place, that for the first time in years a section of the population and especially of the youth showed its unwillingness to continue to accept passively the fate offered to it by the government. Its weakest point was its political content. The demonstrators cried "Peace in Algeria," "Down with the war," "Stop the torture," "Negotiation." Almost no one called for the independence of Algeria; no one called into question the regime responsible for the war.

No doubt this beginning of mass activity against the war in Algeria played a role in the shift evident between de Gaulle's declarations on September 5 and his speech on November 4. It came on top of a multiplication and acceleration of the signs of an irreversible deterioration in the situation of French imperialism. The failure at Melun, far from weakening the FLN, had reinforced the Algerians' will to struggle and destroyed any remaining illusions concerning de Gaulle. The Chinese and Russian promises of assistance to the FLN threaten to materialize in the near future. This prospect incites other Western powers, and especially the Americans, to increase their pressure on the French government in order to obtain a speedy resolution of the Algerian problem. Finally, the chimerical character of de Gaulle's attempt, whether serious or not, to arouse an Algerian "third force" was resoundingly demonstrated; barely had they assembled when the "commissions of the elected" (chosen, as one knows, by the administration) began to call for negotiations with the FLN, while elected Muslim members in the UNR [Gaullists] did the same.

The speech of November 4 both reflects the new reverse imposed on French imperialism by all these factors and at the same time creates a new situation. The new overtures aiming at negotiations with the FLN, barely a few weeks after the idea of a "new Melun" had been categorically rejected, is not the most important thing. The most important thing is that French imperialism, through de Gaulle's intervention, after self-determination and *Algérie algérienne*, has explicitly recognized that Algeria will be independent, and cannot do more than express the wish and the hope that the future Algerian Republic will maintain "ties with France." The bridges have henceforth been burned. There is no possible turning back.

The discourse creates a new situation in the international sphere: it may well be that it will calm down the next discussions in the United Nations, but it is from now on officially recognized that Algeria is not a French domestic affair. In France itself, it first of all makes clear to everyone's eyes the absurdity of continuing the war. It constitutes on the other hand and above all a formal demand to the activist elements of the army to submit or to rebel openly.

This, of course, does not mean that the speech of November 4, nor even the referendum planned for the beginning of 1961, resolves the Algerian problem. In order to get out of its present situation, the government in Paris must first impose its will on the army of Algeria; it must then come to terms with the FLN. One knows that these two requirements are in conflict.

It is not a matter here of playing the prophet. But already, certain points are settled.

First, all Bao-Daism is out of the question in Algeria.[4] There is no section of the bourgeoisie or the Muslim cadres that is disposed, like Bao-Dai in Indochina, to play the role of an "independent" government and to take political responsibility for the war against the FLN. The Muslim *Gaullist* deputies themselves call for negotiation. This shows that there can only be an "Algerian republic" with the FLN.

Second, a new regime (resulting, for example, from a coup d'état by the extreme right wing section of the army) that would try to turn back the clock in relation to de Gaulle's government would encounter not only an immense and probably active opposition in France itself, but also the total hostility of the outside world and would almost certainly have to face up to a combined Russian-American intervention to stop the war. The result of its coming to power would certainly be to *accelerate* the independence of Algeria. This shows that an attempt by the extreme right to seize power is highly improbable, a successful attempt even more unlikely.

Third, the projected referendum reveals the paradoxical situation in which French capitalism finds itself. With its army and its state apparatus infiltrated by groups that oppose official policy and openly sabotage it, it is obliged to call on "the people" against its own instruments of power. The government has to prove its legitimacy anew, after having ridiculed the Parliament, which should have been the source of that legitimacy. This shows that the problem of how capitalist political institutions are to function normally has not been resolved by the Fifth Republic.

But, once again, for those who oppose the war and recognize in the Algerian people's struggle for their independence a just and positive struggle, the question is not one of speculating on what de Gaulle can or cannot do. What de Gaulle "has done" up to now, he has only done under the constraint of the invincible resistance of the Algerians; and also, in a sadly infinitely smaller measure, under the constraint of the beginnings of an active opposition to the war that is developing in France. A rapid end to the war and, furthermore, the true content of Algerian independence will be a function of the development of this opposition. The weaker French imperialism is at home, the less it will be able to try to impose, through peace, its exploitative interests on the Algerian people. Opinion must be enlightened in France, not only about torture and the atrocities of the war (or about its inconveniences for the French) but above all about the real content of the Algerians' struggle—a political content, but also an economic, social, and human one. Opposition to the war must be demonstrated actively in the universities and the factories. The masses must impose the only solution to the war: the unconditional independence of Algeria.

33

Algeria: Seven Years After

(1962)

> *In July 1961, the Tunisians attack the French garrison of
> Bizerta. The National Council of the Algerian Revolution
> (CNRA) meeting in Tripoli in August names Ben Khedda as
> president of the GPRA [Provisional Government of the
> Algerian Republic]. In September, de Gaulle agrees to
> include the question of the status of the Sahara in the
> negotiations.*
>
> *On October 17, 1961, the Algerians demonstrate in the
> streets of Paris, peacefully and without arms: several
> hundred dead. On December 19, an anti-OAS [the extreme
> right wing French Secret Army Organization] demonstration
> in Paris: a hundred injured.*

Never, in the seven years during which the Algerians have fought against
French imperialism, has French imperialism gone so far in making concessions, at least verbal ones. Seven years ago it seemed impossible that a
French government would ever recognize the independence of the departments of Algeria and the sovereignty of an Algerian government over the Saharan "territories." In order to obtain this recognition, it took a million
dead, a million deported into concentration camps, hundreds of thousands
of émigrés in Tunisia and Morocco, tens of thousands of militants and non-
militants arrested, tortured, interned, liquidated.[1] By these means de Gaulle
has discovered that *his* interest lies in abandoning Algeria. Has the cause
therefore been understood?

In no way. De Gaulle really wants to leave, but first he demands to be
thanked: assuredly a peculiarity of character, but one that suffices to hold
up the talks aimed at "disengagement." This is, however, not the essential
element. The military and civil administration cannot withdraw from Algeria in the way that one gets off a train. Its relative autonomy has existed for
a long time, as have its administrative functions. Its withdrawal therefore

presupposes its adherence to de Gaulle's doctrine. And next, were this condition fulfilled, it would still be necessary to think about "disengaging" the Europeans of Algeria, too, whose autonomy and implantation date back more than a hundred years.

Imperialism is not only an interest of de Gaulle: it is also the apparatus that colonization has used and uses to crush a people over a period of one hundred and thirty years and its revolt for seven years. Imperialism is also the European population that capitalism has installed in this country, endowed with privileges of all kinds, which has retained the mentality of another age. Imperialism is not only the balance of its present interests, it is what presently remains of its past interests, of which it cannot rid itself.

All the compromises can indeed be agreed on with the FLN [Algerian National Liberation Front]; not a single one of them can be realized if Paris does not have the means to impose it on the army and on the Europeans of Algeria.

First, the army has not been won over by Gaullism: Paris has obliged it, day after day, to give up its "successes." Gaullism, for the army, is this insidious defeat, whose meaning it is beginning to realize, and that demoralizes it. The results it had been able to obtain in the military sphere were annulled by the ceasing of offensive operations last spring and by the transfer of two shock divisions back to France; domestically, the ALN [Algerian National Liberation Army] was able to reconstitute its groups in all the areas where police control and the mobile commandos had forced it to disperse. Even at the eastern and western cordons the situation changed: one may assume that the GPRA seized the occasion offered by the Tunisian attack on Bizerta to arrange for heavy matériel to be stocked in Tunisia and Morocco.[2]

In the political sphere, the order to disperse the "concentrated" populations interrupted the contact of the army with the peasant masses. The formerly forbidden zones are now under the sole command of the Frontist administration. The administrative functions of French posts have taken a back seat to police and defense matters.

The various resistances, and finally the April 1961 putsch, arose from this situation, that of an apparatus constrained to abandon its function without any compensation: neither that of having accomplished its task, nor that of having to adapt itself to a new task. But the failure of Challe's attempt caused the army to lose its hope of modifying Gaullist politics by remaining in a state of semiloyalty.[3] The sabotage and the open resistance to the draft taught the cadres not only about general opinion in France, but also that they would not have the troops in place required for a military coup d'état.

No doubt a faction among the officers and petty officers finds a solution in participating in the actions of the OAS. But it can only be weak in the units, where offensive activity is impossible because of the draft: above all, the activist cadres desert, which shows that the army is not the OAS. One conspires more easily in the General Staffs, but it is without real importance.

In the majority, the forces wait: they cannot be Gaullists, and they consider that an autonomous initiative from the army is destined to failure; finally, they do not want to link their fate to that of the OAS activists. They content themselves therefore with carrying out routine operations without hoping to defeat the ALN; they oppose and will oppose a certain degree of inertia to any initiative from Paris. In particular, it is out of the question that the army can be heavily engaged in the repression of the OAS and more generally in an operation to bring the Europeans of Algeria to heel. Nor indeed can one imagine the army collaborating with the battalions of the ALN to maintain order in a transition period. Paris is sufficiently aware of this to have tried to create an Algerian "police force" for the latter purpose. Likewise, to control the Europeans, Paris draws almost exclusively on the gendarmes and the riot police.

The civil representatives of the French state apparatus in Algeria seem no less disenchanted. The absence of precise orders and the loss of contact with the Algerian population have deprived them of both the aim of their mission and the means to carry it out. In the police, each clique avenges its dead: the extreme right wingers continue the struggle against the FLN; the "republican" commissars who are still alive try to hunt down the OAS. The prefectoral or municipal administration, isolated in a few old colonial villages deserted by the Europeans, lets the Front's propagandists and revenue collectors operate almost openly; the Muslim mayors and subprefects consult the nationalist organization on local policy. On the other hand, in certain urban quarters, under pressure from the French colonists, the administration closes its eyes to lynchings, its men pay taxes to the OAS and let them be paid, kangaroo courts replace the legal system for criminal and even civil affairs. For their part, the economic services record not only the stagnation of the Constantine plan, but also a general paralysis that causes the exodus of profits and capital, the exile of a part of the European population and the hoarding that results from anxiety.[4]

The French state apparatus in Algeria as a whole presents the appearance of an organization shrinking on the spot, leaving behind it two communities that polarize ever more energetically around their respective organizations.

The extremist officers drew negative conclusions from April 1961: the army cannot be the instrument of the policy of *Algérie française*; Challe's kind of semilegal activity is impossible. They therefore positively organized the only force opposed to both the Algerian liberation struggle and the Gaullist policy of disengagement: the Europeans. They have set about building an illegal counterrevolutionary apparatus out of this group. Former extreme right wing organizations were broken down into compartmentalized action groups and absorbed into a single hierarchy. Operations of intimidation, intoxication, and terrorism were directed against hesitant Europeans and the administration. For the street demonstrations, the young and the students were organized into commandos and trained. Funds are collected in the same way as by the FLN. Channels exist to handle deserters and important individuals. This organization crystallizes the lessons that the military cadres have drawn from their experience in the war of repression on the colonial front over the past fifteen years, and for the first time the organization finds favorable terrain among a population predisposed on all counts to support it.

The OAS therefore constitutes a serious obstacle to de Gaulle's policy. It tends to usurp the official administration in the cities where Europeans are numerous. It manages to keep many military and civil cadres sitting on the fence. Infiltrated into the police and military apparatus, the OAS blunts any attempts to suppress it.

Nevertheless, the activists have no prospects of taking the *offensive*. An *Algérie française* government would have the support of the whole European population, but would not be able to maintain itself after secession. The problem therefore remains, as the failure of the April putsch showed, one of liaison with the metropole. The army's current attitude makes a military coup impossible, as we have seen. It remains to be seen whether the difficulties encountered by the regime in France can serve as the springboard for a more or less covert action on the part of the OAS.

Until it manages to extend its influence to the metropole in this way, the OAS holds a defensive trump card in Algeria: it can use, and it already uses, the blackmail tactic of threatening a confrontation between the communities, a "blood bath," a "Congolization" of Algeria. Rightly or wrongly, it can thus hope to participate as a third party in the negotiations over the future of the country, or at least to influence them and to lay the groundwork for its domination in the areas where Europeans may regroup in the future.

But the prospects glimpsed by the parties at hand, like the hypotheses one can construct about them, remain subordinate to the orientation that the Front intends to impose on the Algerians' struggle. The GPRA seems in effect to hold the key to the situation, depending on whether it will support de Gaulle against the OAS or whether it will attack all expressions of imperialism indifferently, be they peripheral or central.

The GPRA could lend tactical support to the policy of withdrawal by launching its own secret organization against the OAS, and it could also lend political support by reaching an accord with Paris on the transition period as quickly as possible. Do not de Gaulle and the GPRA have a common adversary in the OAS? But that is an absurd hypothesis: its apparent logic ignores the coherence of the reasons and passions at work. To be brief, the Algerians are struggling to free themselves from imperialism, and imperialism, even as a new order, remains for them a situation of dependence more or less maintained by 50,000 soldiers, by camps, prisons, deportations, imprisonments, interrogations, and, in the last instance, by Paris. In comparison with this, the OAS seems all the more like a caricature of provocation. Moreover, the FLN has no tactical interest in really weakening the activists, that is, in reinforcing de Gaulle, until he makes irreversible concessions regarding independence, sovereignty over the Sahara, the fate of the Europeans, the organization of the transition period, and his own representative status.

We cannot therefore expect cooperation between the ALN and a distinct "Algerian force," let alone the French army, before these concessions provide the guarantee that French imperialism will abandon Algeria for good. Meanwhile, the struggle will continue. It is even probable that it will intensify, at least in Algeria, where, as we have noted, the military situation favors the Algerian combatants even more than before, and where the implantation of the militants in the cities seems stronger than ever.

This is not to say that the GPRA refuses to negotiate; on the contrary, it can hope to gain concessions from the present weakness of Gaullism and from the fact that the Front is the only force capable of really opposing the activists. But it will enter the negotiations with its intransigence on principles intact. It is no longer the supplicant.[5]

This orientation shows how much the insurrection has been transformed, since 1954, in two complementary and antagonistic directions. Its popular base has been enlarged from year to year, and its program has been enriched by the experience gained in the struggle and by the contribution of the new social groups and new generations. The small clandestine nuclei of the beginning have become a formal hierarchical apparatus that reaches into all the activities of the Algerian population but that, because of its structure, can only weakly disseminate these changes. There have indeed been signs of this transformation for years; the most recent, even if it is not the most important by a long way, is the replacement of Abbas by Ben Khedda as president of the GPRA.

We have already explained the massive entry of the new Algerian generation into the political struggle proper and the tension that this necessarily caused between the "new wave" and the leadership. In renewing the staff of the GPRA, its leaders wanted to reply to this relative independence of their base as much as to the failure of the Evian and Lugrin negotiations. Ben Khedda is certainly not a new man nor the incarnation of the Algerian younger generation. But Abbas was a classic bourgeois politician who had come belatedly to the movement, while the new president is an organization man par excellence. He has occupied positions of responsibility in the Front ever since its creation. His experience is that of a "professional revolutionary." His ideology, which allows him to combine Islamic references with a bow to the "socialist" countries, seems completely eclectic. Finally, his promotion was probably the result of a struggle between factions within the GPRA and even the CNRA.

But all these particularities are so many signs of a single reaction: confronted with the failure of the negotiations, with the dynamism of the young Algerians of the cities, with the hesitation of the unions (notably in the French Federation), the Frontist apparatus replied by reinforcing itself, by eliminating the members it had not trained entirely itself, by according first place to a man in whom it could incarnate itself without reservation. Ben Khedda's eclecticism confirms this interpretation: it faithfully expresses the FLN's ideological uncertainty, but it was also an indispensable condition for obtaining a majority among the members of the CNRA and the GPRA. The factional struggles, at times political and at times personal, can presently only differentiate themselves through compromises. Eclecticism is the ideological transcription of practical compromise.

One can therefore expect that the radical requirements latent in the young generation and the "Marxisant" tendencies of the unions will not yet have a chance to express themselves through the present leadership. This leadership is going to reinforce the unity of the apparatus by simplifying and controlling internal relations. It will reinstitute its authority everywhere, in particular in the French Union Federation and the union and student organizations, it will train and more closely supervise the Algerian population by multiplying its agitators and propagandists, it will equip the ALN in exile with heavy matériel and turn it into the nucleus of a regular army, and it will tighten links with other anticolonial movements.

What this orientation means is that the consolidation of the apparatus destined to train and supervise the masses during the next stage, the stage of the construction of a new Algerian society, ought to be undertaken without delay and given the same level of importance as the struggle for national liberation. The elimination of the nationalist bourgeoisie is thus assured. The latter needed a rapid compromise with imperialism in order to establish its authority and to restrict the struggle to a strictly nationalist framework, just as imperialism needed this bourgeoisie in order to reach a compromise: this course of events is now impossible. This is not to say that Ben Khedda is Mao Tse-tung—but it only takes a Fidel Castro to make imperialism retreat. From this point of view, the question of knowing who, from among the bourgeoisie or the local bureaucracy, will finally take over the leadership of the struggle is already settled. But what remains to be resolved is the question of the training and supervision of the masses, that is, of the reinforcement of the bureaucracy in relation to the most dynamic groups of the population.

The strengthening of the apparatus is not an independent fact: on the contrary, it is the translation of more intensive activity and stronger pressure from the Algerian masses. This translation is a betrayal of the masses in that it transposes their strength into the language of the bureaucracy. If it was necessary to reinforce the apparatus, this is because it was weakening, not in relation to the struggle against imperialism, but in relation to the developing experience and political, social, and historical consciousness among all classes of the population, among workers, women, and the young. The repression and replies to the repression have been the matter of everyday life for the past seven years: the questions that arise in this life and the responses that can be given them are likewise the object of everyday reflection. There are now no Algerians who do not have views on all the problems of their society, who do not have more or less obscurely in their heads and almost in their flesh a certain image of the society that ought to be constructed, simply because the duration and the intensity of the struggle have forced extensive experience upon them.

This upheaval in traditional consciousness and this accumulation of experiences, including that of modern production for the Algerians who worked in France, together constitute a difficult fact for the leaders of tomorrow to master. By reinforcing the apparatus, the latter seek (even if they are not conscious of this) to channel the living forces of the future society while the liberation struggle allows them to require and obtain almost unconditional support; this will doubtless prove less easy during the next stage. Thus the class struggle in independent Algeria is prefigured, even before imperialism has released its grip.

34

Algeria Evacuated

(1963)

On February 8, 1962, a new anti-OAS [Secret Army
Organization] demonstration in Paris: nine dead at the
Charonne Métro station. On March 18, 1962, the Evian
agreement is reached; on the 19th, a cease-fire in Algeria.
The OAS gives the order for strike action. On March 23,
the OAS opens fire on the forces of order. On March 26,
the shooting of the rue d'Isly.

On April 8, the Evian agreement is approved in a
referendum by 90.7 percent of the vote. On the 14th, Debré
resigns and Pompidou becomes prime minister. On the
20th, Salan is arrested in Algiers.

On July 1, a referendum is held in Algeria on
independence. Independence is proclaimed on July 3. The
GPRA [Provisional Government of the Algerian Republic]
enters Algiers.

The analysis that follows does not aim to define a revolutionary policy in
Algeria. The question of this country's fate can no longer be and has not yet
been asked in this way. *No longer*, because the momentum that animated
the masses in the course of the nationalist struggle is now gone; no revolution took place. *Not yet*, because the problems that assail the workers,
which the present leadership's policy is incapable of resolving, will end by
making conditions ripe for a new intervention by the masses; the revolution
remains to be made.

The present task is this: to engage once more in a reading of the events
that have marked the first months of independence, to unravel their meaning, to chase away the thick clouds of all kinds in which the Algerian question remains enveloped, to aid the revolutionary nucleus to see clearly both
the chances that the coming crisis will offer it and the limitations that that
crisis will oppose to it.

The picture that Algeria offers after independence is, one will see, re-markable in one respect: political life has become foreign to the population of the cities and the countryside. This attitude is thrown into even sharper relief in that during the years of the liberation struggle, the participation of the peasants, the workers, the students, the women, and the young not only never failed, but went so far as to produce the demonstrations of December 1960 and deepened so as to overthrow traditional social relations. Indepen-dence broke this immense agitation. Politics flowed back into the organiza-tions or what remained of them. While the factions struggled for power, the phantom of unemployment and famine already haunted the people of the countryside and the cities.

But the most pressing questions of everyday life were not asked in the course of the battles over power in which the cliques engaged. The leaders ignored the masses' problems, and the masses did not understand the lead-ers' problems. It was only when the problem of work and bread posed itself urgently, at plowing time and at the end of the vacations, that the connec-tion was reestablished between the preoccupations of the masses and those of the leadership. At the same time, the incoherence of the policy followed by the Benbellaist leadership began to be apparent to the workers as well as to the leadership itself. The true Algerian question emerged, but it found the masses unprepared and distrustful.[1]

Disenchanted Independence

They expected a revolution; they got a country in collapse. In the political vacuum that was established along with independence, the FLN [Algerian National Liberation Front] leadership exploded into pieces. Joy at the end of the war and the ferment of liberation faded away: the masses were immo-bilized. When they intervened, it was in order to make the leaders under-stand that they had had enough of their disputes.

Here is the situation in the summer of 1962; the people of the cities and the countryside wanted to be led. There was no leader, because there was no leadership.

The Colonial Apparatus Vanishes

Everything that the peasants had simply called "France" for over seven years had disappeared in all its visible forms. The European farms were deserted, the screens lowered on the French shops, the owners gone, the soldiers con-fined to barracks, the teachers on vacation, the honky-tonks silent, and the OAS bastions abandoned. It was the great separation after one hundred and thirty years of cohabitation. The French who remained did not give orders;

they waited, and at times they collaborated. There was no more master for this enslaved people to hate.

If decolonization was such a shock, it was because the two adversaries who had held the forefront on the stage over the past few months departed in tandem. The government repatriated the draft soldiers, the officials, whether suspect or loyal, the legionnaires, and the paratroopers pell-mell. The OAS sent its colonels and its millions on fishing boats and tourist planes. Barely awakened from the racist dream, the poor European population stood in three-day lines at the ports and the airports. Paris had hastened to shield its units from the climate of the colonial war and to inspire the cadres with raisons d'être less archaic than "smash the wog" or "smash the head of state." As for the *pieds-noirs* [French colonists], their presence, at least in certain cities, had so taken the form of racketeering and villainous murder, lockout, the refusal to treat and resupply, the imprisonment of the Arabs in ghettos, that they had every reason to fear the worst when their victims became their compatriots.

There was no question of the colonial apparatus being able, as it had been elsewhere, to participate in the construction of the new regime or that the transfer of power might happen without discontinuity. The attempt at cooperation made by the most conciliatory factions of the European bourgeoisie and the nationalist leadership in the persons of Chevallier and Farès had no immediate continuation. The provisional executive was reduced to nothing in a few days: it had only owed what little power it had to the reticent cooperation of a few French officials.

In this respect, independence seemed to mean the failure of the European bourgeoisie, the only one existing in the country. Completely disqualified by its incapacity to establish a compromise with the nationalists, it now found itself constrained to leave the local administration, after having protected it from all other influence than its own for decades. It could not patronize the new power. Systematic sabotage of independence, however, left it some cards: destruction of public buildings and administrative equipment, withdrawal of technicians, and the closing of the firms ought to bring the new regime to its knees. If the regime wanted to give life to the country, then let it guarantee order and security; in other words, let the workers get back to work. The *pied-noir* bourgeoisie, defeated in its support for the OAS, was not defeated as the master of the Algerian economy. It was just that its somewhat murky political past forced it to stand aside for a short time. It went on vacation.

The National Apparatus Corrodes

One could have hoped or feared that the shell abandoned by the French administration would the very next day be occupied unchanged by the nationalist apparatus. The power vacuum showed on the contrary that the FLN had been able to construct only the embryo of a state during the liberation struggle, and that no force organized at the national level was capable of administering it at a moment's notice. Thus the crises of colonial Algeria appeared once more: the absence of a ruling class, the political cowardice of the nationalist leaders, the pettiness of the objectives offered to the masses and accepted by them despite the unceasing growth in the intensity of their actions and their initiative over the past seven years—all the features of a country stifled in its development.

Stifled first of all by the relentless repression that the politicoadministrative organization and the ALN [Algerian National Liberation Army] had suffered for years. In the military sphere, units reduced to skeletal proportions resembled guerrilla groups more than regular formations. In the regions abandoned by the French troops, the underground forces were dispersed; in the others, where, on the contrary, the concentration of opposing forces was much more significant, the battle had become too unequal.

Yet for years, with an exemplary energy, the masses had kept on producing the militants and the combatants required by the domestic resistance from within their ranks. In 1961-62, the underground fighters were perhaps not much more numerous nor better equipped than those of 1955-56; but in the meantime the movement had conquered all of Algeria, and the days of December 1960 had provided the proof that the insurrectional action of a minority had turned into a mass movement. The most combative youth no longer rushed to the underground forces, which were losing their importance: they were kept busy by organizational tasks in the cities and the villages.

But the revolutionary momentum expressed in this change was not kept up. First of all, the repression came down still more heavily. Mobile commando units swept the countryside, and the police and the army went through the cities with a fine-tooth comb. There was a veritable slaughter among the émigrés in France, who provided the movement with a number of its best-trained cadres, during the course of the years 1960-61. The rhythm of the replacement of officials augmented. It is difficult to consolidate an organization if its officials disappear after a few months. The FLN apparatus also became more and more foreign to the Algerian masses.

On the other hand, the nationalist leadership had reacted to the agitation of the urban population at the end of 1960 by asking it to calm down rather than by proposing a political and social program offering intermediary objectives that would give it a practical direction. Ben Khedda's accession to the presidency of the GPRA, at the same time as it resulted from a compromise between the factions of the CNRA [National Council of the Algerian

Revolution], showed that the Front relied on the moderation and diplomatic talent of its leaders rather than on the agitation of the masses for independence. Politics regained its customary authority: guerrillas and the demonstrations only served as backup arguments for the negotiations. The fear of being overwhelmed thus became the major concern of the leadership in exile. The training personnel received orders to instill calm and discipline. When the Algerians demonstrated in 1961, it was inside an organizational cordon that kept them to heel. The only role allotted to the militants was containment, not explanation and development.

With the negotiations came the truce, the return of the dispersed and exiled peasants. The villages were devastated, the farms dilapidated, the herds decimated. The prewar problem, that of work, posed itself even more overwhelmingly before the war had ended: everything was lacking, save for mouths to feed. In the cities, the situation created by the sabotages of the right-wing French terrorists and the complicity of the armed forces was untenable: foodstuffs, medicine, and the means of work remained under the control of the OAS. Gnawed by hunger, overwhelmed by poverty, the population retreated. It let itself be convinced that nothing could be done before the departure of the French if all was not to be lost. If tendencies to go further, to reopen and to start up abandoned firms, showed themselves here and there in the cities, it was only at a minimal level; they were swiftly repressed in the name of respect for the Evian accords. As for the peasants, for the most part illiterate and without a political tradition, they tried to go back to work without waiting any longer, with or without the aid of the local ALN. On the whole, the order to respect the Europeans' property was observed.

Meanwhile, the relations between the population and the organization were transformed. The combatants and the militants no longer incarnated the protection and the hope needed by the people of the cities and the countryside in order to resist. They were no longer any help in the face of the problems of hunger and work. In the large cities especially, the workers and the young were conscious that they had seized victory from imperialism with their cries, their flags, and their disarmed mass much more than the ALN had with its guns. Moreover, the political degeneration of FLN cells and ALN sections accelerated under pressure from the influx of last-minute resistance fighters and the unemployed. In a few weeks, the incarnation of the insurrection of a people became the garbage dump of a crisis. Discipline and revolutionary idealism gave way to interfering haughtiness and privilege. At the same time as their importance diminished among the population, the local leaders were the object of contrary appeals emanating from the factions who, in search of power, gleaned a semblance of representativeness from the domestic resistance. They gained an extra authority from on high to supplement the authority from below that they had come to lack. This renewal, which they owed to circumstances at the summit, ended up separating the officials from the civilians. Within a few days, Algeria was covered with autonomous and competing "baronies," which were no more than the letter of the revolution abandoned by the spirit.

The base imagined itself still able to appeal to the summit about the abuses of the intermediary cadres. But when the conflict broke out at the top between Ben Khedda and the General Staff of the ALN, it became clear to all that the apparatus built to struggle against French oppression had neither doctrinal homogeneity nor organic unity and that it could not play the role the population expected of it—that of a guide in the construction of the new society. Under the decorous title of the "reconversion of the organization," as it was called in ruling circles, the problem that awaited its solution at the end of the war was not only the form of the future state but also the social nature of independent Algeria. The fact that this problem had been left hanging during the liberation struggle largely motivated the masses' withdrawal into a state of uncertainty, the galloping sclerosis of the local apparatuses, and finally the decomposition of the nationalist leadership itself.

Many words have been spoken here and there on the subject of the "revolution," destined sometimes to flatter the despoiled peasants and sometimes to flatter the property owners, here capitalism and there the workers, now the Islamic tradition and now modern culture, in such a way that this revolution was stuffed with contrary hopes. But this ideological eclecticism[2] faithfully expressed the social inconsistency of the nationalist movement. The historical significance of such a movement generally coincides with the interests of the local bourgeoisie. In Algeria, direct colonization had blocked the economic development and political expression of this class, to the point that it had not been able either to collaborate with the French administration and bourgeoisie or to take the lead in the liberation struggle and indicate objectives for that struggle in conformity with its interests. Its attempts at conciliation rejected, it had rallied to the insurrection. In the offices of Tunis, the wise leaders of the UDMA and the centralists of the MTLD kept close to the plebeians imbued with populism who came from the peasantry or the poor petite bourgeoisie, the renegade workers of the Algerian Communist party, the *ulémas* [Muslim clerics]. Independence was the greatest common denominator among the classes and the tendencies that made up this amalgam because the peasants expropriated by the colonists and the French companies, the workers exploited by a French owner, the shopkeepers ruined by the French commercial firms, the intellectuals bullied by the French university and culture could recognize themselves in it.

The weight of colonization had compressed the class configuration of Algeria to the point of making it unrecognizable. The block in which otherwise antagonistic classes merged could not give expression to their respective interests. It was forbidden, under pain of breaking up, to take Algeria's real problems into consideration and to respond to them. The apparatus itself could not develop either its doctrine or its organization independently of the classes of which it was composed: the conditions for bureaucratic development did not exist. The Algerian Communist party had been too tied to the French presence in its structure as well as in its positions for it to be able to stamp the nationalist movement with the Stalinist imprint. The global policy of Khrushchevism was no more suitable for this purpose. Finally, even if it had not been able to claim the independence of the country in its own name because of its weak development, the Algerian bourgeoisie had nevertheless not been eliminated from the scene after its unhappy experience. The FLN did not confront an Algerian Chiang Kai-shek: no such person existed. It confronted imperialism directly. The result of this situation was a situation favorable to the bourgeois elements of the Front: a military victory was impossible; a compromise accord with Paris was inevitable; the moderation of politicians like Farès or Abbas was such that it might reassure the French interests in Algeria. In sum, the compromise between nationalism and imperialism could still give rise to an authentic national bourgeoisie: it would get the patriotic heritage from one side and capital from the other. For evident political reasons, the operation could not be carried out either overtly or in the short term. It was advisable to delay the moment for irreversible decisions concerning the nature of society after independence. Meanwhile, opportunism took root.[3]

Thus, for some years, no program more precise than that of Soummam was developed, and the Evian compromise was discussed without any principle in mind other than national unity and territorial integrity. Paris obtained complete satisfaction on the only point that was essential to it: the fate of the capital invested in Algeria.

The Masses Wait

Independence did not signal new activity from the masses. Having sacrificed their last sheep to the green and white flag, they simply waited. But, in the course of the crisis, their refusal to intervene changed its meaning. The leaders who returned from exile were at first acclaimed on all sides with the same fervor, without distinction between tendencies. When they came to blows over them, entire families of villagers even sat down between the "lines," opposing their peaceful presence to the war of the cliques. The will for unity resisted the ruptures at the top. Tired of violence, the population refused to engage itself in a struggle whose meaning it did not understand. This naïveté tinged with greatness was imposing. Those on high started to fear lest the base cease to trust them. But as the crisis continued with the prospect of restarting the economy becoming distant, with unemployment, insecurity, and hunger becoming worse, this patience became impatient. In many regions the cadres achieved the tour de force of making their domination as hated as that of the forces of repression. When it became the instrument with which the latecomers to the ANP gave themselves apartments, cars, and other privileges, the submachine gun of the *djoundi* [holy warriors] was discredited. People wanted peace, bread, and work. They saw no relation between the conflicts that set the leaders against one another and these simple objectives; they saw very well, on the other hand, the relation of these struggles to careerism and favoritism.

Good sentiments and bad were both pandered to by all the cliques in an attempt to build support for themselves. Each of the groups placed its creatures in the administrative positions abandoned by the French, without concern for competence. Confusion gummed up the works of what remained of the state. Opportunists wormed their way into the commandos. The accusations of complicity with imperialism, of counterrevolution, of personal ambition, flew in every sense above the heads of the Algerians, who were unable to deal with them. These acts of verbal (and at times physical) violence lacked any political basis, and shock soon gave way to exasperation: "If they are what they say, then let them all go!" In Algiers, the most politically conscious minority ended up demonstrating, in the face of opposition from the authorities, with cries of "We're fed up [*baraket*]." The enthusiasm of the liberation cooled. Formal meetings replaced the packed and boisterous gatherings of the early days, with head counts in order to determine whether one was more popular than one's opponents. The population became a clientele, politics a stage production. When the band finally came to an agreement on the way to consult the public, the public—whom they mocked by giving them banners carrying the inscription "Long live the people!"—was too busy trying to survive to be conscious of the honor done to it by such consultation. It chose the representatives that were chosen for it. Abbas, in proclaiming the democratic and popular republic, shed a tear for a long-frustrated ambition. There were 2 million unemployed.

It was "with the masses totally indifferent, preoccupied by matters of another order"[4] that the question of power was settled. This is the essential fact that dominates all the events that have occurred in Algeria since independence. Lethargy takes the place of the fervor that had stirred all ranks of the population over the last years of the liberation struggle. Autonomous actions were limited: a few occupations of vacant properties, a few demonstrations whose spontaneity cannot easily be distinguished from the interests of the cliques. Moreover, these demonstrations were always of a limited character: a refusal to intervene in the conflicts at the top, protests against unemployment, against the lack of purges, against the abandonment of the old resistance fighters and of the victims of the repression.

Motifs such as the exhaustion consequent upon years of war and oppression, the shattering of the nationalist organization, and economic collapse seem to make the withdrawal of the masses understandable. They remain, however, circumstantial; some of them, particularly the disintegration of the organizations of struggle, ought to be considered as the signs rather than the preconditions of this withdrawal.

The composite character of what has been called the masses is a less momentary element. There are peasants, workers, the middle class, each group traversed by the conflict between generations, by a more or less strong adherence to the traditional culture, by the nature of needs, by language. The overwhelming majority of the Algerian people is peasant, but what is this peasantry?

Is it the seasonal or occasional landless peasant, or the average fellah (property owner)? The agricultural worker or the farmer? What community of interests unites the small farmer of the coastal plains and the wage earner of the large domains of the Sétifois? What common experience of exploitation can the day laborer grape pickers and the small Kabyle farmer engaged in mixed cultivation share? Geography, past history, and colonization pulverized Algerian rural society into sectors among which everything differs, from cultural practices to institutions and even language. Then class antagonisms are embroidered onto the particolored costume that makes up the *bled* (hinterland), class antagonisms that are more or less distinct according to the degree of capitalist penetration into the countryside (it is dominant in the colonized flatlands), or according to the persistence of an Algerian feudal class (as in the high plains of the Constantinois or the Oranais), or according to the degree of survival of tribal or village communities (in Kabylie, in the Aurès).[5]

Contrary to what happened in many of the countries of black Africa, colonization did not always leave the traditional communities intact, communities whose structures and institutions are far from homogeneous across the whole of Algerian territory. But, on the other hand, agrarian capitalism did not, as in Cuba, subject all rural workers to uniform exploitation so as to create an agricultural proletariat lent unity and a determining social weight by its living and working conditions.

The liberation struggle had countered the dispersal of the peasants, of the whole of society. Nationalist sentiment, nourished by humiliation and anger, had driven all Algerians to construct, for themselves as well as for others, for each aspect of their everyday lives, a model of society, a model of the Algerian to set against the colonialist model. The repression failed because the consciousness of the people contained an alternative to the repression: independence. Fervor, participation in the struggle, demonstrations, and unfailing pressure directed against French oppression by all social strata were all signs that this self-image could no longer be stolen from the spirit and the life of the masses. This was their unity. Whatever creativity, individual courage, and usable institutions could be found in traditional communities and in colonial society itself were put to the service of this image. The insurrection, which could not win any military victory, had gained this far more decisive success in allowing all individuals to live with themselves, whether as young or as old, as man or as woman, as peasant or as worker, as Kabyle or as Arab. All of Algeria flooded out through the breach that the armed struggle had opened in the wall of the ghetto in which colonization had enclosed it. To the image of the "wog" the insurrection opposed that of the *djoundi*, which the population echoed, fulfilled, enriched, endlessly transformed. The struggle acted as therapy; it delivered Algeria from the image of itself that the French had introduced into its life. There were many signs that the Algerians sought to destroy not so much the French as the "wogs" into which they themselves had been transformed by the French. The pursuit of independence consisted in delivering oneself from the colonial nightmare. It could not be more intense than during the struggle, when the masses broke and trampled their own caricature underfoot.

When the other independence, political independence, was obtained, it dissolved the social glue that held all these fragments together. What held all these lives together was lost like a wadi in the sand. There were no longer any "wogs" to kill; there were Algerians who had to be given life. Each social category retakes its place in society, each individual attempts to return to his or her niche. The problem of helping Algerians to live is conceived and solved in terms of an individual or a small collectivity, a village, a family, a quarter. No consciousness can span the whole of society so as to pose the question of what that society is for itself. The unemployed person wants work; the woman wants bread for her son; the combatant wants to be honored for having fought; the student wants books and professors; the worker wants a salary; the peasant wants seeds; the shopkeeper wants to restart business. No one, no political group, no social class is able to build and propagate a new image of Algeria that Algeria might desire as it had desired independence. It was certainly useless to expect the peasants to take the initiative in such a new development. We will return to this later. The bourgeoisie for its part did not have the economic, social, political, and ideological consistency required to grasp the social problem as a whole and impose its solutions with the assent or the acceptance of large sections of the population. The proletariat, even if it is relatively important in this underdeveloped country, did not manage to become conscious of exploitation as the fundamental fact of its and the whole society's existence, nor could it distinguish its own gains from those of the other classes.

The inability of the workers to build an autonomous political organization and ideology is the other side of the agitation that marked the years of the war. It is the sign that the problem posed in colonial Algeria was not that of socialism defined as a movement toward the classless society. If all the social strata, all the economic categories, all the communities of language and culture could be mixed together in the crucible of the liberation struggle, it was precisely because the choice was not between being proletarian or free but between being "wog" or Algerian. The Algerian worker participated in the war, he made the contribution that he owed as part of Algeria in revolt, he never felt that his class held the answer to all the problems of society after independence. And doubtless he was not wrong: the problem of development in the world of 1962 is not the problem of socialism. The absence or the fragility of proletarian consciousness can properly be blamed on the terrorism directed since 1956 against the MNA [Algerian National Movement] and the USTA [Algerian workers' trade union] by the Frontist leadership, which broke up the community of émigré workers, or even on the French Communist party's break with the Messalist organization dating back to 1936. All these facts illustrate rather than explain the political and ideological weakness of the Algerian proletariat. The truth is that the Algerians could solve the problem they set themselves: that of being Algerians. But the workers could not set themselves the problem they were unable to solve: that of putting an end to exploitation.

The masses left the stage at the moment when "politics" entered it. A group of men, borrowing some of the recent energy of the passion for independence, attempted to provide *for* the Algerians (intended for them, but in their place) some goals and some means around which they might unite once more. But when the masses are missing from the construction of a society, the result of this difficult process of construction is only the simulacrum of a state.

Building the State[6]

. . .

The State and the Bourgeoisie

The political and state apparatus thus began to crystallize toward the end of summer 1962. What is its significance? Ben Bella's state is suspended in the void; it seeks its social basis. It cannot find it in either a bourgeoisie en-

dowed with political traditions and economic, technical, and social competence or in a bureaucracy capable of compensating for its own incompetence
as a ruling class by ideological cohesion, party discipline, and enthusiasm. It
is for this reason that the reconstruction of society began backwards, by the
construction of the state from the top down. The task this state encounters
at present is that of creating its "cadres," that is, the ruling class on which it
will lean and of which it will be the expression.

As I have said, the politicomilitary bureaucracy that led the war of liberation scattered on the day after independence. The only bourgeoisie in the
strict and decisive sense (a bourgeoisie that possesses the means of production) was the European bourgeoisie, which was politically eliminated along
with the most right-wing elements of the nationalist movement. The political offensive launched by Chevallier and Farès since 1962 has failed: it
clashed head-on with nationalist feeling. The fraction of the GPRA that had
signed the Evian accords could go along with a second and more cunning
attempt at reintegrating the *pied-noir* bourgeoisie into the Algerian nation.
But this time the offensive did not have time to develop, despite its simplicity, because of the disarray of the French colonists and their suspicions concerning the future of Benkheddism. The Benbellists counterattacked and
overcame it. Does this spell the end for the bourgeoisie?

The European bourgeoisie had begun to withdraw from Algeria before
July 1, and even before the signing of the Evian accords. During the summer,
the withdrawal has become more pronounced. This means its disappearance
as a political force. But the goods it possesses are not purely and simply
abandoned. During the last years of the war, Algerian farmers and managers, profiting from the absence of the property owners and from the absence
of control, pocketed the land revenues; lands, buildings, and small firms
were repurchased by the weak Algerian middle class. Speculation allowed it
to enlarge its nest egg pretty quickly. The volume of the transactions sky-
rocketed when the final negotiations began and when it became evident that
Paris had decided to recognize independence. From March onward, the
pieds-noirs' panic gave the richest peasants and shopkeepers the occasion to
strike an advantageous bargain on full ownership, management, or renting
of European enterprises and firms. They speculated on anything; the economic crisis paralleled the political crisis to favor speculation. When, in the
autumn, the lands will need to be plowed, it will be clear that the transfer of
the agricultural enterprises to Algerians has some significance; the same for
housing. While the fight for political power goes on, the Algerian bureaucracy fattens itself.

The administrators installed by the provisional executive protected this
operation at the same time as they played their part in it. The prefects, the
subprefects, the cabinet leaders, the inspectors, the members of the special

delegations, originating from either the French administration or the FLN apparatus, were paid for their complicity. The disappearance of all central control, along with the inactivity of the masses, made the matter easy. The corruption of the civil servants went along with this enrichment of notables and businessmen. They sabotaged the purges and favored the invasion of the administrations by their cronies. The new bourgeoisie proliferated in the bosom of the state.

It had no real social force, no ideology, no political perspective; it was nothing more than the association of the bandits and tight-fisted employers of nascent Algeria. But it could find an ally on the side of its natural protector, French capitalism. The decree issued by the provisional executive on August 24, 1962, ordered the requisitioning of abandoned firms by the prefects, the nomination by the same authority of administrator-managers "chosen from among the specialists" who were to take the place and the functions of the absent owners, and lastly the restitution of the firms and profits to the property owners as soon as they demonstrated a desire to recommence their activity. Measures with a double entry: the Europeans kept all their rights, which French capitalism could only view with benevolence; meanwhile, revenue fell into the hands of the prefects and the Algerian "specialists," that is, into the hands of the new bourgeoisie. This was the hope of an economic collaboration between the nouveaux riches and imperialism. Thus imperialism found a new bridgehead in the country among the speculators in the administration. Venality, when it is introduced into the very instruments of power, is not a mediocre ally when it needs only to be bought off.

When Ben Bella settled in Algiers, the embryonic state of which he assumed the leadership was the parasites' point of crystallization: it was the classic situation of newly independent countries. There was no choice: he had to either govern with this corrupt apparatus or give up. Compromises were inevitable with the members of the middle and the petite bourgeoisie who had been enriched in the space of a few months by the exodus of the Europeans and who had patrons installed in the administration. The most urgent question, that of the lands and the property left by the *pied-noir* bourgeoisie and taken over by the nouveaux riches, would remain pending for some time. Would the buyers manage to legitimate the transactions of the spring and summer, or would the government turn against them? Through this question, which dominated the end of the summer (August– September 1962), the social content of the new state was placed at issue.

The bourgeoisie could in any case find a means of allaying some of its fears in the Tripoli program, under which the land, but not the means of production, ought to belong to those who work it.[7] This sufficiently eliminates the prospect of any collectivization of industrial firms and does not exclude mid-sized rural property, which tends to be directly farmed by the owner. The program's silence with regard to workers' problems and the cautious nature of its references to the proletariat were equally reassuring. Ben Bella has made no declarations to counter this silence and caution. The president of the Democratic and Popular Republic even refused to appease the journalist from *Unità*—who objected that only the industrial proletariat could make up the revolutionary avant-garde—with the few stock phrases that would have satisfied her. He replied that, after all, "in the highly industrialized countries powerful masses of workers have not been able to impose revolutionary change."[8] The activity of the Political Bureau toward the workers is no less eloquent than its silences: the bureau brutally dismisses the UGTA's offers, it publicly discredits the Fédération de France, made up mainly of proletarians, it discourages—without daring to block them directly—the attempts made by certain local leaders of the agricultural workers' union to organize the management of the abandoned enterprises,[9] it refuses credit to the workers' committee that had taken over a metallurgical enterprise in Algiers.[10] On the contrary, the authorities keep on begging property owners to reopen the firms and the farms, they delay instrumentation of the decree issued by the executive at its request, fixing October 8 as the time after which requisition of these properties can be announced. In Arzew, Ben Bella charms the representatives of the financial groups and industrial firms come from France, Great Britain, and the United States: "Nothing can be built on hatred," he bluntly tells them. "The condition for our development is the reestablishment of security. I insist on it. Let us turn the page and help one another. In two or three weeks, Algeria will be an oasis of peace."[11]

All this in no way hinders the same Ben Bella from responding quite clearly to *L'Unita* that "the political prospects for Algeria" are "socialism." It is true that he immediately corrects himself: "an Algerian socialism." This new variety of socialism has the original features of considering the working class as incapable of radically transforming society, of excluding workers' demands from its program, and of seeking its social base among the petite bourgeoisie and the peasantry.

The artisans and the small shopkeepers certainly owe the attention devoted to them in the Tripoli program to the fact that they represent a force of social stabilization, and to their money rather than to the blows that time and again smashed the shutters of their boutiques. If the trade ministry has been entrusted to a Mozabite, Mohammed Khobzi, this is because the community to which he belongs, which controls most domestic retail transactions, had sheltered its capital in Germany. The new state desperately needed that capital to relieve the payment difficulties that were paralyzing trade and driving the administration to the brink of disaster.

The State and the Peasants

Meanwhile, the base that the new power claims for itself is elsewhere: "The peasant population is the decisive force on which we rely. . . . The poor peasants are without any doubt the base element of the revolutionary transformation. The revolutionary mass is fundamentally peasant."[12] And in order to found the theory of the revolution in the countryside, Ben Bella will seek celebrated antecedents: "The Cuban revolution took shape on foundations of this kind: an armed peasant mass seeking independence and agrarian reform"—or unexpected ones: "Czarist Russia was also an agricultural country."[13]

The importance of the peasants in the liberation struggle was immense. Not only are they the large mass of the Algerian people, but their problems incarnated and incarnate the whole social problem of this country: the need for land, bread, work, a new culture. In other "dependent countries," in Africa, in the Near East, capitalism's domination came to terms with precapitalist structures rather than destroying them; the local feudal lords cooperated with the European companies; investment remained tightly restricted to the needs of the capitalist firms and to the speculative operations of the landed aristocracy; in the interior, the peasants continued, though more oppressed than in the past, to till the soil with their age-old tools. Traditional culture was not shattered from top to bottom; it did not have to revolt in order to rediscover or discover a new social basis, an acceptable image of itself, or meaningful social relations. The rural world was not caught up in revolutionary ferment because capitalism had not initiated any new practices there.

In Algeria, direct colonization took 3 million hectares of farms and forests from the peasants in the space of a hundred years. A modern, mechanized capitalist sector and a low level of employment left most of the expropriated farm laborers without work. Demographic explosion increased unemployment. The destruction of the artisan class and of small village commerce, along with the fact that the peasants were obliged to buy their few indispensable commodities at monopoly prices, ruined the subsistence economy. The insignificance of industrial development and technical training, along with European settlement, prevented the rural unemployed from finding employment in the nonagricultural sector. At the same time as imperialism stripped the peasants of their ancient means of living, it refused them any new ones. The European invasion combined the models of the conquest of the American continent from the sixteenth to the eighteenth centuries and of the imperialism of the 1880s in its form and its consequences. The worker is chased from the land but is forbidden to become a wage earner.

In the long term, the peasants are constrained to either revolt or succumb. This is not an economic choice; it would be superficial to account for the 1954 revolt as the effect of a bad harvest. The war that began at that time was not a *jacquerie*. Little by little, the peasants increased not only the numbers of the underground forces, but also their meaning. The fighting was a reconquest of their native land. The *djebel* becomes the homeland once more. The earth and the people conspire. In wanting to be Algerian, the peasants retake possession of the country, of themselves. This reconquest occurs on the scale of the despoliation that had occurred: the traditional institutions, the community of family, village, and language are all poured into the crucible of the struggle, they are an instrument or a dimension of it, but nothing more, because they cannot on their own provide an adequate riposte to a French aggression that had created the hollow negative of a nation. It is not a matter of restoring civilization in its precapitalist state, but of installing material and social relations acceptable to everyone. These are symbolized in general by the theme of an independent Algeria.[14]

This has not meant, however, that the political content of the peasant movement has become any more distinct. Not only has the question of society, of its organization, of the state not been explicitly asked, but the preliminary and essential question of the relation between the masses and the organization remains unasked. Indeed, even the question of the real significance of the reconquest of the country by the peasants and the question of the appropriation of the lands by the rural masses have failed to emerge as a problem for these masses to resolve. Herein lies the great paradox of the Algerian revolution: a profoundly disintegrated rural society rises up in the face of its own crisis and yet does not produce the ideas or the actions that might overcome it. When the Congolese peasants returned to their tribal communities once the Belgians had been chased out, that had a meaning because those communities had preserved what belonged to them. When fellahs without land, without work, with their lives and their reasons for living shattered by an age-old expropriation, simply come to a halt when their expropriators leave and expect the solution to their problem to come from a nonexistent power, this is at first glance inexplicable. The entire world, starting with the Algerians themselves, has managed to remain stupefied by it.

To understand this hiatus, one can turn to the diversity of regional situations and the limits they impose on social consciousness. Neither the minds nor the actions of the poor peasants who work the slopes of the Kabyle or Chaouia country contain the prospect of a profound agrarian transformation. Attached by tradition to family smallholdings, concerned to defend their granaries, they have little to gain from land redistribution when there is no new land left to be conquered on the mountain. Of course, the cultivation of olive and fig trees can be improved, the soil can be improved by embankments and plantations, animal husbandry can be rationalized; but what could popular cooperatives do without the help of agronomists and rural inspectors? The archaic peasants cannot find the ends and means of a profitable agriculture within themselves. At any rate, the solution of the peasant crisis in these regions consists in the installation of processing industries (textile, foodstuffs) that can use the local hydroelectric equipment and that offer a high level of employment relative to the capital invested. But, here again, the peasants' fate is not in their own hands.

If one turns to the population of laborers, the *khammès* and the sharecroppers who cultivate the arable lands, the agrarian revolution seems capable of taking a completely different direction. Limitations on the size of landholdings and the constitution of production and sales cooperatives with the necessary tools, along with the introduction of new crops to alternate with cereals, allow the hope of a greatly improved yield per hectare and of increased employment. But the obstacle encountered by the peasantry on this route is its own attitude to the land and to work. For example, the fact that the *khamessat* could survive while giving the peasant only a fifth of the yield was due to the practical obligation by which the property owner is held responsible for the subsistence of the worker and his family in bad years as in good ones. In a rural economy continually threatened by scarcity, where monetary circulation is extremely weak, the debt-ridden peasant may well prefer payment in kind, miserable but assured, to a salary that is problematic and difficult to exchange.[15] Traditional values weigh in the same direction: the capacity to dominate nature and the attractions of economic growth have no place there. Social relations are not the product of a logic of interest, which is born only with mercantilism, but of an ethics governed by traditional rights and duties.

Institutions and geographic and historical conditions are the obstacles to a peasant movement that might seek to do anything more than claim independence, that might seek to realize independence by practically reorganizing the relationship of the fellah to the land. All that is certainly true, but it was already true during the liberation struggle. Why can the motifs of disunity and defeat still be invoked now, even though the guerrilla war has overcome them? Why did the peasant unity that arose during the struggle for independence not continue in the struggle for land and for the new society? It is true that the peasantry is not a revolutionary class in the sense that the conditions of its work and its life do not provide it with the fundamental experiences of exploitation and alienation in the raw, unencumbered by traditional forms of ownership, of individualism, of the village community, or religion, and do not constrain it to provide a total response to the total conflict that the proletariat experiences. But in the case of Algeria, this is not even the case: one cannot say that the peasant movement did not encounter the question of society; quite simply, the movement did not ask that question, and it failed to provide an alternative, even hesitantly, to what existed—at least once independence had been won.

If the unity of the peasants did not survive the struggle, even in the form of a bureaucracy, it is because they did not win their victory on the ground. Power could not take on a concrete form in the eyes of the peasants as the incarnation of a new society on the move, as a force endowed with a physical existence, constituting itself, consolidating itself, spreading along with the guerrilla who repulses the adversary, comes down from the mountains, approaches the cities. No anticapital, no capital of anticolonial Algeria, arose among the rural masses, drawing on them and expressing their aspirations, posing and resolving all the problem arising out of the insurrection as its authority spread to the very borders of the country. The political unity of the movement remained foreign to the social diversity of the country. The rural population was not able to crystallize its needs, to enact its transformation and its positive revolution, around a state on the move within it.

The idea of a peasant army, of a power remaining in touch with the countryside because of the needs of the war and those of the revolution, helping the masses to carry out the revolution by attending to the war, did indeed exist in the ALN. Fanon had tried to theorize it[16] in a confused way, without giving it its true dimensions, which are strategic as well as political. Traces of this theorization can be found in the Tripoli program. But the idea had only a nostalgic existence because the ALN was not this state on the move, but was made up of either hunted guerrillas inside the country or battalions immobilized in exile. The peasants never saw the new power take shape, they did not see the land change hands, they were not invited to form cooperatives to take over the management of enterprises, of water, of seed, under the protection of the fighters. For them, no start was made on the reconstruction of the villages, the repair of roads and bridges, the reestablishment of communications, the rebuilding of the schools under the guidance of revolutionary officials. They could not seize hold of their country. It remained the stake in a struggle between adversaries, the object of a redoubled destruction, an undecided affair, offering its paths, its shelters, its peaks, and its nights now to the one and now to the other.

Thus a concrete alternative to the power of the French was required for the peasants to be able to go further than national resistance. In the last years of the war, this alternative had even less consistency than in 1956–57. The territorial battle had been won by the troops of repression since 1958. The population displacement, which affected almost 2 million peasants, made it quite clear to them that there was no Algerian power capable of standing up to French troops on the spot, even if the concentration camps provided a veritable breeding ground for nationalist propaganda. The General Staff was abroad. The revolutionary war was lost. The fact that from the end of 1960 the national movement won over the cities and erupted there in mass demonstrations certainly took on an immense political importance. New social strata in their turn recognized the free Algerian as the only acceptable image of their future. The youth of the cities entered into the revolution. But, at the same time, the revolution abandoned the *bled*, and only the war remained there. It is true that in any case the fate of the countryside is not decided in the countryside, that even if they wanted to, the Algerian peasants could not create textile workshops or food processing factories, invent agronomists, produce the agricultural implements and seeds out of their heads (all those things without which there can be no agrarian revolution). Lastly, the extension of the movement to the urban classes, because it meant that the workers and the young in their turn posed the problems of society collectively, marked an indispensable stage in the consolidation of the revolution and allowed an effective response to the rural crisis to be envisaged. But this urban movement that spread the content of the struggle to all of the institutions of colonial society hid[17] the defeat of the peasant movement insofar as it was an attempt to establish a force among the rural masses. The city had no echo in the countryside; it took over from the countryside once it had been bled dry. The transformation of the armed struggle into a political struggle was paradoxically both a strategic victory and a political defeat: militarily, the situation that confronted the French General Staff in the cities at the end of 1960 was worse than the one that reigned on the eve of the battle of Algiers, and it had to start all over again; politically, from the viewpoint of the FLN leadership, the splitting of society between cities and countryside was not repaired. The peasantry became Algeria's burden once more, the principal theme of its crisis. The repression had borne too heavily on them for them to become an active component.

When Ben Bella took power, the "revolution by the peasantry" could no longer be the revolution of the peasantry. Its invocation could mean nothing more than that a state constructed far away from the peasants—far from the whole population—was going to busy itself with reform. Ben Bella's policy preserved only the most jarring themes of what authentic expression of peasant struggle and aspirations Fanon had been able to achieve in his descriptions. On the pretext that "Europe is springing leaks everywhere,"[18] an expurgated version of Islamic culture should be rebuilt. On the pretext that the proletariat of the developed countries did not make the revolution, Ben Bella intends to unleash the communist capacities of the primitive peasantry and to center revolutionary strategy on a Third World International. On the pretext that the workers of the underdeveloped countries are privileged (that is to say, made middle class) in relation to the peasants, he seeks to keep their organizations on a leash. When returned to the context of the

Algerian political situation at the end of the summer 1962, these half-truths — it is true that Western "culture" is no longer a culture, that the revolutionary workers' movement is nonexistent in the developed countries, that alongside the pitiful income of the Algerian peasant the salary of the public transport worker of Algiers or the metalworker of Sochaux is the product of another world and can appear as a privilege — these half-truths serve all the more as an ideological cover for the powerlessness of the government, and possibly even as a cover for the bourgeois offensive that is taking shape in the shelter of the governmental apparatus.

Although Ben Bella may try to present himself as a peasant leader, the relation of his government to the rural masses is formal, plebiscitary. This state cannot express the peasant aspirations that have been killed off. Rather, it tries to dictate them. The question of the political content and the social basis of the new power was not answered in early autumn. On the other hand, the question of the social composition of the administrations was resolved little by little. There, the nouveaux riches abound. Simultaneously, the offensive by monopolists with regard to farms and buildings (the ancient passions of underdeveloped countries) continues. In these conditions, the realization of the agrarian objectives defined by the Tripoli program becomes difficult: how could an apparatus supported by the enriched peasants and the new bourgeoisie enforce the reallocation of land to cooperatives or state farms? Even a moderate program, like the project of giving the peasant collectives the farms left vacant by the Europeans, becomes unrealizable if these farms have been monopolized by Algerians under the protection of the local authorities. In a few months, the crisis that disrupted an entire society has been reduced to the dimensions of the problem of abandoned properties. The masses' loss of energy occurs in direct proportion to this process. Furthermore, this last problem is linked to that of French aid.

French aid constitutes a test that ought to allow the new government to sort out its orientation and to reveal its social significance. The use that will be made of French aid may in effect reveal the intention and the capacity of the Algerian government to put an end to the process that is disrupting society and that is at the origin of the crisis. Whatever it is at its birth, Ben Bella's state can still find its raison d'être if it manages to impose on society and on itself the measures necessary to overcome unemployment.

Unemployment, considered as the most obvious and the most tragic expression of the crisis, is not just one fact among others but the result of the domination of French capitalism in the country.

A Process of Dislocation

French colonization involved the whole of Algerian society in a contradictory process. On the one hand, the appropriation of the farms and their exploitation for profit created an agrarian capitalist sector in the middle of the traditional economy. At the same time, a labor force newly "liberated" from earlier relations of production found itself free to become wage earners; the capital invested in agriculture reaped a surplus value sufficient to allow a normal rate of accumulation. Thus the conditions for the passage of the Algerian economy and society to the stage of capitalist relations of production were fulfilled. But the subordination of the capitalist sector to the French metropolitan system prevented it from pursuing its development toward a complete liquidation of previously existing relations and the consolidation of an Algerian capitalism. In return, the embryonic, almost exclusively agrarian, character of Algerian capitalism forced it to function as a simple economic appendix to French imperialism.

In Western countries, the organic complement to the introduction of capitalist relations in the countryside (the appropriation of the land by the landlords and the proletarization of the peasants) was the development of manufacturing industry. The farmers, sharecroppers, and tenant farmers, chased from the fields, rushed toward the cities, where accumulated capital could, in buying their labor force, provide them with employment. Of course, there is no question of painting a glowing portrait of the development of capitalism in this country: it presupposed, on the contrary, not only that the peasants were reduced to famine, but also that the new industrial proletarians were subjected without defense to the working conditions and the salary that the employers dictated to them. Meanwhile, the process as a whole implied the destruction of precapitalist relations and of the construction of new relations: capital seized hold of the entire society.

Algeria presents a social structure that bears witness to the fact that the introduction of capitalist relations into the country followed the same pattern as in the West in its major outlines: expulsion of the rural workers, constitution of large landholdings, "liberation" of a considerable mass of the labor force. This ought to have been followed by a passage to wage earning as the dominant form of the relations of production. In fact, the figures show more than half a million agricultural workers, plus 400,000 migrant workers in France and 200,000 to 250,000 Algerian wage earners in industry, trade, and public services in Algeria. In total, more than a million workers, totally dispossessed of the means of production, that is to say, either proletarianized or proletarianizable. For a colonial country, this is a significant proportion of the active population.

Meanwhile, evolution toward a fully capitalist social structure did not occur. Algerian capitalists send almost half of their profits out of the country and speculate with or unproductively consume the other half, so that three-fifths of the total investment is financed by the French state. In 1953, it was estimated that 40 percent of private savings left Algeria annually;[19] only half were reinvested on the spot. The state financed 60 percent of the 121 billion francs invested in that year. Public financing created few jobs because it was directed to the infrastructure: of 48 billion in net investment in 1953, 22 billion were devoted to hydraulics, to protection against and repair of soil erosion, to Algerian Electricity and Gas, to the Algerian railroads, to the postal and telecommunications services and the road system. Social and administrative investment (26 billion in the same year), even if it creates employment, in no way augments productive capacity. Private economic investment is essentially directed toward trade and construction. The rare attempts made to create local manufacturing and processing industries met with open hostility from French interests.

On the other hand, the presence of European settlers resulted in closing down any possibilities of employment offered to unemployed Algerians. The concentration of landholdings chased the lesser colonists toward the cities. Its Western mentality, its European culture, and its superior qualifications made this work force preferable to the illiterate peasants. In the building trade, on the docks, in the mines, the Algerians obtained only the most undesirable jobs. Even today, Algerian nonagricultural wage earners form only 22 percent of the active Algerian population.

Finally, even when it takes place, proletarianization is never complete in a colonial country. Many workers classed as "agricultural workers" are only temporary wage earners who get taken on for the day or for the season during periods of high agricultural activity. As for the "real" wage earners, estimated at 170,000 permanent workers, they are subject to the rule of the "colonial wage" according to which monetary income is in principle only a "complement" to the resources of the peasant family; they are entitled neither to family benefits nor to social security, for example. This overlapping of the wage-earning sector and the traditional sector, through the intermediary of the family or the village, prevents any clear identification of the proportion of the active population that is integrated into the circulation of capital. This situation is brutally apparent in the case of migrant workers in France whose salaries support entire villages in Kabylie.

Capitalist "Aid"

Under the pretext of helping independent Algeria to develop, the Evian accords exacted a double obligation: to respect the interests of capitalism as it was present in the country before July 1, 1962,[20] and to observe the rhythm of growth planned for by the French experts in the last years of colonization.[21] The two constraints are cleverly combined. The capital invested, notably in agriculture, serves as collateral for the capital to be invested: if you seize the lands from French ownership, you will compensate them out of the sum of our aid.[22] In return, the growth rate predicted by the development plan,[23] whose renewal the accords stipulate, assumes as a hypothesis a practically unchanged agrarian situation:[24] land ownership being what it is, here is what we can do to create employment. Imperialism agrees to aid the country, but on the basis of its colonial structure: such is the sense of the accords.

It is evidently a non-sense. The first question posed in Algeria is that of work. The only answer would be the massive transfer of half of the unemployed of the active rural population into the secondary and tertiary sectors. These have therefore to absorb not only urban unemployment, but also agricultural underemployment. Now the Ten Year Plan predicts that the number of days worked in the countryside will rise from 150 million at the beginning of the period (1959) to 177 million at the end (1968) for an unchanged active rural population of 2,693,000 persons. Assuming that 265 working days per year constitute full employment, this plan provides for full-time employment for only 668,000 persons at the end of the period. More than 2 million agricultural workers would thus remain unemployed.[25] The Constantine Plan ends up with the same result.[26] The creation of jobs in nonagricultural sectors is conceived in such a way that the question of peasant unemployment will remain pending.

Keeping to the secondary and tertiary sectors, the main subjects of the plans for investment, the same attitude appears yet again. The lack of a qualified work force is one of the sources of the bottleneck familiar to the specialists of underdevelopment. In 1955-56, the technical education and professional training of adults produced 6,700 to 6,800 qualified workers, from the OS [Special Organization] to technicians. According to the model employed by the Ten Year Plan, 20,000 would have been needed in 1959 for there to have been 55,000 by 1970,[27] the figure required by the development of the nonagricultural sectors. The Ten Year Plan, however, makes no provision for the financing of this technical program: implicitly, qualified labor remains the monopoly of the European immigrants.

Thus there is to be a lack of employment in the countryside and a lack of qualifications in the city. This situation expresses the dislocation of Algerian society in the realm of employment: rural overpopulation resulting from the theft of the lands, urban underemployment resulting from European settlement. In envisaging no modification in this state of things, the Evian accords perpetuate the evil from which the country suffers. As for investments, examination of their source and their breakdown fully verifies this assessment.

To assure an average annual growth of 5 percent in average revenue over a ten-year period, taking into account a demographic increase of 2.5 percent per year, around 5,000 billion francs must be invested over the period,[28] of which 4,000 billion should be in new construction. The Ten Year Plan predicts that around half of the financing will be supplied by Algerian funds, the other half by funds "of external origin." Almost the whole of the Algerian capital would come from private savings; the foreign funds would be in large part public and semipublic. Of the total, 16 percent will go to the primary sector, 51 percent to the secondary, 19 percent to the tertiary, 14 percent to housing. The essentially foreign public-sector funds would primarily finance the investments in agriculture, infrastructure, and housing, the private funds of foreign origin being entirely devoted to the petroleum sector. As for private Algerian capital, it will be divided above all among three main sectors: agriculture, housing, and trade. Investment in various manufacturing and processing industries does not make up 7 percent of the total of planned investments.[29] At the end of the period, the current account balance should be in deficit by 164 billion francs, which results from the increase of imports consequent upon the development of production. This deficit is to be almost entirely covered by loans to the Algerian treasury from the French treasury (150 billion francs). The movement of private capital should for its part have a profitable balance of only 10 billion francs.

The first article of the "Déclaration de principes relative à la coopération économique et financière" repeats the main themes of this set of investments. This means that (1) private savings of Algerian origin continue to be directed into traditionally favored sectors, as is the case in all underdeveloped countries: investment in lands, housing, and commerce does not contribute at all to the overthrow of the colonial structure; (2) foreign private capital is devoted to the exploitation of Saharan mineral resources and provides only small profits for the country;[30] and (3) industrialization is essentially the responsibility of the French state; as before, it consists in the provision of infrastructure and housing rather than actual industrial installations. Essentially, capitalist investment therefore follows the same lines as in the past. The only modifications consist, on the one hand, in a quantitative increase in aid and, on the other hand, in an expansion in private savings of local origin, that is, the prospect of the constitution of an Algerian bourgeoisie, whose investments are, however, envisaged as purely speculative. It should be added that by Article 3 of the Déclaration économique," imperialism reserves the right to keep an eye on the "full effectiveness of the aid and its allocation to the objects for which it was granted."

It will hardly be surprising if in these conditions the question of employment will no more be resolved in the city than in the countryside. The Ten Year Plan provides for more than a doubling of nonagricultural full-time employment. Meanwhile, taking demographic growth into account, there will remain 140,000 underemployed at the end of the period (versus

200,000 figured at the beginning) and this despite the fact that the emigration of the active population ought to more than double during this period.

The figures we quoted are only interesting to the extent that they reveal, if such a revelation is necessary, the attitude taken by imperialism in the face of the problem of Algeria's development. Certain paragraphs of the Evian accords tried to preserve some room to maneuver for the Algerian government, to allow compromises on certain aspects of financial aid, to look toward subsequent discussions over agreements on the handing over of some responsibilities. The direction taken by this "cooperation" will at best remain what is laid down in the very watermark of the Ten Year Plan: a late contribution by imperialism to the smooth formation of an Algerian bourgeoisie. Furthermore, it must be added that since 1958 the situation has grown still worse: new destruction has resulted from the intensification of the military operations; the OAS has sabotaged part of the social, administrative, and cultural infrastructure; the departure of four-fifths of the French population has deprived the country of its technicians and its qualified workers; the reduction in military strength stationed in the country has slowed down the influx of capital destined to finance their administrative and private expenses.

Of course new investments have been made, in conformity with the Constantine Plan. But the extreme caution of private investors, Algerians as much as foreigners, has kept these investments very much below predicted levels. A significant part of the sums invested was devoted to the current expenses of metropolitan administration, especially military, in Algeria. This money evidently created neither wealth nor employment. In total, the plan was a failure because it was a political paradox: capitalism could not engage in the construction of a bourgeois Algeria until it had obtained guarantees from the nationalist leaders concerning invested wealth and the transfer of capital and profits. The Evian compromise was destined to present the future Algerian government with a fait accompli: the potential local bourgeoisie was granted financial assistance, some satisfaction of self-esteem, a few economic advantages, and guarantees against a possible uprising by the masses in exchange for which it conceded economic and political advantages to the petroleum producers, to the armed forces, to the colonists, to companies of all kinds. Such was the basis for the sketchy bourgeois offensive at the end of the summer and the beginning of the autumn of 1962.

A Society Absent from Itself

Ripples on the Surface

But just as it has failed to be a peasant state, the Benbellist state has not yet become a bourgeois state. The events of autumn show this. When the time for plowing had arrived, and the winter approached, the question of farms, work, and hunger was asked before the government had taken any collective action on the subject. In the Constantinois and certain regions of the Oranie, big farms were occupied, and management committees were elected in the villages. The work and its product were divided among the unemployed fellahs. On the plateau of the Sétifois, it even reached the point of requisitioning, in the presence of the property owner, farms considered by the peasants to be insufficiently cultivated.

The plowing campaign announced by the government unleashed the movement. Officially, it was limited to soliciting the loan of their agricultural materials from the European colonists and rich Algerian farmers, once their own plowing was done. On October 8, the ministers and regional authorities met at the Oran prefecture to launch the operation in the region. The president of the National Office of Vacant Properties expressed the position of the ruling circles as follows: "No enterprise will be restarted without prior study. At any rate, we still envisage the eventual return of property owners, for the right to property remains intact, and the rules that are being prepared will determine under what conditions a firm will be able to continue its activity." At the same meeting, the director of agriculture and forests specified that this campaign meant, as far as equipment was concerned, "an amicable mobilization of underused tractors."[31] Peasant good sense stretched the interpretation of these rules here and there: they put the tractors into service without waiting for permission from the property owners and, if permission was refused, the machines tended to catch fire.

This movement should not mislead us, however: its claims remain elementary. The peasants want work and bread. They plowed the abandoned land, in the large arable plateaus of the east and the west and in the regions where intensive colonization was most concentrated, like Boufarik, but the movement was still not widespread. In any case, the management committees did not extend their activities further. And even in these regions, their initiatives remained timid. Very soon they encountered needs they could not fulfill by themselves: spare parts, construction material for the rehabilitation of homes, cash advances. The local authorities were thus able to block the peasants' initiatives immediately if necessary.

Nonetheless, peasant hostility to the transfer of French cultivations to the Algerian bourgeoisie, and to all speculative activities in general, obliged the government to decree on October 17 the "freezing" of vacant agricultural properties, the annulment of contracts signed after July 1, 1962, and of the acts of sale or rent concluded abroad. On October 20, *Le Monde* still entitled its special correspondent's dispatch "The Landless Fellahs Wait for the Agrarian Reform Announced by the Government." But, on October 23, it announced that "the plowing campaign will permit a temporary relief of the fellahs' poverty and will calm their impatience." The next day, the government agreed to the proposals made by the FLN cadres at their national conference October 15 to 20: its decree forbade transactions with regard to *all* property and movable goods and the institution of management committees in the vacant agricultural firms. Finally, on October 25, this last measure was extended to *all* the abandoned enterprises: industrial, artisan, mining, commercial.

The timid initiative of a few peasants sufficed to shift the situation. The state was fragile and uncertain enough to be unbalanced by a weak push. At the same time, Ben Bella seized the chance offered by the campaigns to take his distance from the monopolists. In annulling all property deals since independence, he tried to halt the formation of the new bourgeoisie. By instituting management committees for all the vacant properties, even in the firms where there had been no spontaneous movement, he tried to create a "collectivized" public sector that would be removed from the bourgeois, but also from the workers if perchance they wanted to take a step further. The October decrees specified in effect that the committees were only permitted in the case of vacant properties, that they had to obtain the agreement of the prefect, that the property owner's rights were not called into question, and that in the case of the latter's return, management and the profits were to be shared between the owner and the workers.

These limited measures gave the French government the pretext to react in the name of the Evian accords. On the occasion of the incident of the RTF [French television and radio] of Algiers, it recalled its ambassador for consultations. Rumor has it that, taking everything into account, "French goodwill could not be as great as it would have been if almost all the Europeans had remained in Algeria."[32] This warning drew its force from the fact that it was issued at the time when Washington, after Ben Bella's visit to Cuba, postponed its discussions with Algiers on the subject of American aid sine die. To tell the truth, de Gaulle is quite ready to seize the chance to get out of his responsibilities toward Algeria: Germany has replaced Algeria not only on the front page of the dailies, but also in first place among France's clients.[33] The French will easily give up on Mascara wine. As for petroleum, the companies have the means to defend it. Finally, the strategic interest of the country has become nonexistent in the epoch of intercontinental missiles. It is only considerations of political opportunism, whether national or international, that prohibit abandonment. But they allow neglect.

Is the Algerian government constrained to choose between the peasants and capital? Not at all. It continues its winding course. Its president calls Castro "comrade" after having, the day before, dined at Kennedy's table, declares in the same breath that he does not want multiple parties in Algeria but that he doesn't want just one either, and, without "calling into question" the Evian accords, wishes, however, to "modify" them.[34]

There would be no end to a list of the contradictions encountered in the application of the Tripoli program: Giving the land to the peasants without touching French property. Compensating for expropriations and developing the nonagricultural sector. Obtaining the financial assistance of a primarily rural capitalism and bringing about an agrarian revolution. Putting an end to the dislocation of the economy by asking for capital from imperialism, which had caused the dislocation. Mobilizing the masses for a collectivized revolution and not causing the bourgeoisie any trouble. Seeking the support of the most traditionalist sectors in Islamic and Arabic matters while having to take radical measures concerning education and perhaps birth control. Erecting customs barriers against France and continuing to sell it wine at special prices.

But none of these contradictions can reach a critical level as long as the peasants, the workers, the youth of the cities—the categories that participated most actively in the struggle of liberation—do not call into question, when one or another of these contradictions occurs, the orientation or the absence of orientation that Ben Bella's power signifies.

From the viewpoint of classical political categories, Benbellism is impossible. Simplifying it to make it fit these categories, it would define itself by the following policy: leaving capitalism (actual French and potential Algerian) free rein in the industrial and commercial sectors, and giving satisfaction to the peasants by setting up agricultural cooperatives and state farms wherever they are technically desirable by redistributing farms elsewhere.[35] But at the level of this strategy, the contradiction already appears that had to make it impossible: the integrity of the excolonial domain is used as a criterion for the supply of capitalist aid. Yet the constitution of a semi-"collectivized" or "collectivized" sector through the sharing of the large farms among the peasants requires reparations, and Paris will garnish the compensation due to the property owners from the aid promised in Algiers.

An analysis at the deeper level of social attitudes or structures encounters the same structural impossibility: French aid would remain untouched even if it served more for speculation on land, buildings, or trade than for the financing of productive investments. The new Algerian bourgeoisie does not have or will not have any more social consistency, economic capacity, or responsibility in relation to the country than any other African bourgeoisie; the mercantile precapitalist tradition does not disappear of its own accord in three months.

Always from the same viewpoint, one could say that these contradictions can be suppressed and these impossibilities removed by a strong political apparatus: by a party that would be the mouthpiece and the ear of the leadership among the masses and consequently capable of agitating them as a bogeyman to scare French capitalism and oblige the latter to give up all or part of the compensation, and also capable of training and restraining them so that their initiatives would not scare away investors; by a state that imposes an economic and social discipline on the new bourgeoisie and a long "austerity" on the workers, a state that would have no pity on its own servants; by an ideology in which each social stratum could find the means of accepting its lot in a working society.

Depth of the Crisis

But we have to wake up from this dream. These would be the prospects — that of the reinforcement of political apparatuses, that of bureaucratization — if the contradictions of which we spoke above tore apart not only three accountants and ten leaders in Algiers but also the very flesh of society, if the problems posed by work, land, school, and financing provoked collective responses among those who are their victims (the unemployed, the peasants, the workers, the young), provoked as complete a consciousness as possible of the crisis of this society and a group response to this crisis. Then the problems of Algeria would move beyond ministerial files, they would pass on to the only terrain on which they could receive a real solution, the terrain of the social struggle, and they would take shape as dramatic alternatives: for or against the poor peasants, for or against French capitalism, for or against the *ulémas*, for or against the monopolists, for or against the FLN party. A political apparatus can only reinforce itself by remaining at this level because it responds to a need present in society or in certain classes, because objectives arise in people's minds and actions are sketched out spontaneously. If, despite the efforts made by Mohammed Khider and Rabah Bitat, the construction of the cells and federations of the new party failed during the autumn of 1962, it was because a mass organization cannot be built without the masses, from the top down and out of nothing.

This is not to say that the development of class struggle would make things clear and that the attitude to take would be dictated by the unambiguous content of the adverse camps. Not only does the class struggle never offer pure situations, so to speak — in Algeria, the class struggle could not take place right away on the only terrain where ambiguity is reduced to a minimum, that of exploitation. The problem posed to the country, the content of its crisis, is not that of socialism. The word may well be on the pens or the lips of the leaders, but its spirit does not breathe among the masses, and it cannot because the present social crisis is not the result of the incapacity of capitalism to assure the development of the country, in the fullest sense of the word: not just that of production and revenue, but also of social relations, personality, and culture. On the contrary, the crisis is the result of the failed development of capitalism itself as positive human domination of elementary needs: to work, to eat, not to die of hunger and sickness. Even when the crisis took shape in Algerian society, the response that could be provided remained ambiguous; for it is not true that to struggle against the poverty left as a heritage to the Algerian people by the imperialism of the colonial epoch is to struggle against all exploitation.

The truth is that development is one thing and socialism another. In the present conditions of the world domination of capitalism under the Russian bureaucratic form or under the Western imperialist form, a once dependent country can only begin to reverse the mechanism of underdevelopment by a massive investment in labor. This means, at least for "overpopulated" countries like Algeria, that the unemployed labor force is used to the maximum; it also means that the greatest part of the supplementary product is not redistributed but reinvested in production — which means overall, for workers, peasants, and employees, additional work without a notable improvement in living conditions. In taking power in an underdeveloped country that achieves independence, the native bourgeoisie or bureaucracy is expected to satisfy the elementary aspirations of the masses. This involves destroying the social and economic basis of underdevelopment (inequalities of development that, in all the sectors of activity, result from imperialist penetration) so as to divide work and its product among the workers as best it can. From this strict point of view, the real difference between the domination of the bourgeoisie and that of the bureaucracy is that the first does not carry out capital accumulation and does not transform society (each of these incapacities accounts for the other), while the second manages to do this for good or ill.[36] It is still the case that development is theoretically and practically achievable, even in a single country. All it takes is to understand development as the more or less complete suppression of the inequalities inherited from the preceding era and the more or less rapid increase of productive capacities. This function can be assumed by a bureaucratic or bourgeois-bureaucratic authority.

But, once again, such an authority can only constitute itself on the basis of a real social crisis, on the basis of action by the rural and urban masses in search of a solution. No choice is necessary if its options are not actually embodied at the level of social turmoil by several opposing classes (and finally by two opposing classes), each offering the response that it is able and willing to give to the crisis. The situation in Algeria is for the time being distinctly different from this. The question is not to know which side to take — for that there would have to be sides — it is a matter of peering into the fog of the present situation to see what forces, with what goals and what means, may emerge.

Of course, there are signs that this search is not hopeless, that the Algerian population is not purely and simply absent from its problems.

The peasants shook off their lethargy somewhat at the time of the autumn plowing. The dissatisfaction of the city workers, even if it never reached the point of direct action, nevertheless sufficed to stiffen the UGTA [Algerian General Union of Workers] against the offensive launched against it by the authorities: not only were local officials reelected, but the union as a whole staked its claim to autonomy from the government. In the same way, the students of the UGEMA [students' union] adopted a critical attitude toward the authorities. The "constructive opposition" of the Aït Ahmed tendency (which enjoyed a certain influence among the young) and that of the Algerian Communist party, though essentially opportunist, nevertheless obliged the authorities to come to terms with an important sector of public opinion. The militants who gathered behind Boudiaf in the PRS [socialist revolutionary path] are doubtless only a handful of adventurist bureaucrats mixed with the most conscious workers. Even if the ideology expressed in the tracts and declarations[37] of this party hardly lends itself to critique, there is no assurance that it is really shared, discussed, and elaborated by its members; its composite and embryonic character makes it impossible to analyze the party fully in the absence of further information. Nonetheless, the creation of this group has a symbolic value. Other signs of activity could be noted — for example, the immense popularity of the Cuban revolution among the city dwellers or the banners saying "No to salaries of 500,000" that were unfurled at the November 1 festivals under the eyes of the deputies suspected of wanting to pay themselves such salaries. The peasants, the employees, the students, and the workers continue to look for a solution to everyday difficulties. Even if many of the unemployed, having run out of options, leave to find work abroad, the consciousness that only a general reorientation can provide the solution in question exists. A link is established between the lack of work and the image of the Cuban revolution, between the race for seats or the bourgeois offensive over land ownership and the idea of what the construction of a popular state or the probity of a prefect should be — and the difference makes itself felt in many minds.

But these signs, if they suffice to make the activity of a revolutionary avant-garde in this country possible and legitimate, do not indicate a latent orientation among the masses, which this avant-garde might attempt to free, specify, and diffuse. The signs of dissatisfaction are one thing, those of aspiration another. The first are easily apparent in the fact that the Algerians, be they peasants or workers, young or old, men or women, have not only failed to take any important initiative for months, but also respond only weakly if at all to the appeals of the leaders, whether those of the opposition or those in power. However, the *need* for change would have to appear for one to be able to say "That's where Algeria is headed."

A collectivity can be incapable of measuring up to its problems in two ways. In the first case, one group differentiates itself from the collectivity and dominates it as a class, as the social embodiment of that society's impotence to understand and guide itself and at the same time as the instrument of response to the social crisis. This group then imposes its goals, creates its means of coercion, installs its conception of human society. In the second case, the weakness of society cannot embody itself in a ruling group, and imagination fails to measure up to the social crisis at the same time that no material force exists, in the productive or political apparatus, that can serve to unify social diversity. The political categories we apply to the first kind of situation cannot be applied to the second. A state without social basis, a power without power, a party without cadres, ideology, and organization, leaders without leadership—all become possible in this case. To try to assign class motifs to such a politics, to decode its acts and its declarations with the key borrowed from a political universe where conflicts and their consciousness have become institutional, is to perform an abstraction.

That is not to say that Ben Bella can do whatever he wants, that anything is possible, and that the history of Algeria has no meaning. The situation is quite the contrary: Ben Bella can do almost nothing, the field of the possible is minuscule, and if Algeria has no meaning for itself at this time, this is the result of a failure to grasp that meaning rather than of the fact that Algeria is meaningless. Thus the minimum that has to be done to cure unemployment cannot be done with the help of the capitalist on the spot (as was already explained), nor with the help of the unemployed workers in the cities and the countryside, because they cannot see a solution and lack the means to solve their own problem collectively. In these conditions, Ben Bella leaves the question of work to settle itself through the massive emigration of the unemployed to France.[38] Thanks to the hiring of an important section of the Algerian work force, French capitalism remains what it was before independence: the beneficiary of the crisis that its domination has provoked in Algeria. At the limit, this kind of government policy means that nothing has happened since 1954 and that summer 1962 was only a slightly more prolonged vacation. One could perform the same demonstration for the question of schooling or that of technical training. In the absence of a living alternative model among the masses, in the absence of any reply to a crisis that touches every element of society, the old structures cannot be fully liquidated; on the contrary, they return to life because they guarantee the functioning of the society, even if on the most minimal level.

Algeria cannot remain without a response to its problems indefinitely. To say this is not to pronounce an eternal truth. First, it is not an eternal truth that a society cannot, for years, remain fallow: if nothing comes to trouble the minimal functioning assured by the fragile state at its head, there is no need for a crisis to break out from which a class might emerge to take over leadership. But above all, Algeria is not a society without history whose structures and culture are in momentary disarray (a century-long moment), it is not a society that could return to its precolonial condition.

Capitalism has disintegrated Algeria's traditional communities, starved and exiled its peasants, created a proletariat of emigrants, stifled the petite bourgeoisie and the bourgeoisie. If no class could provide a response to the crisis evoked by this destruction, it is because there was no fully established class, with a social function, an economic role, political instruments, and a conception of history and society. Of course, none of these features is ever completely distinct in a class; the transfusion of ways of life, ways of thinking, and interests continues between one class and another, even in the most developed societies. But in Algeria the major poles of society were not sufficiently differentiated for the bourgeoisie to lose its exclusive desire for property and domesticity, for the workers to be cut off from their villages and find out about the condition of the proletarian with no turning back. Still less was it possible for the peasants—the most rebellious survivors of the precapitalist epoch even in Europe—to be reclassified, according to the alternatives imposed on them by farming for profit, as either rich farmers or agricultural workers. All these categories exist, it is true, but in an embryonic state, and seven years of war were not enough for another society to develop in the womb of the old colonial society. If the infant bureaucracy represented by the FLN during these years was stillborn, it was, as I said, because it was a social composite: on the one hand, none of the strata that were represented there had the necessary consistency to take sole possession of the apparatus and direct it toward its own solution; on the other hand, the conflict between the Algerian classes had not reached a point of such intensity that the apparatus itself was able to and forced to bypass them to stifle their antagonisms and to build a model of the future society that would be accepted by all, whether they liked it or not. In particular, the fact that "communism" could not root itself deeply in the Algerian proletariat and that consequently a consciousness of the social crisis and the capacity to remedy it through the bureaucratic process (of which the Communist party was elsewhere the instrument) were impossible here is a supplementary sign of the relative lack of differentiation in society. The Algerian workers and peasants did not resist Stalinism on the basis of an antibureaucratic critique, but because they had not had to suffer the relentless offensive of a national bourgeoisie and because the crisis had not demonstrated the incapacity of this bourgeoisie to respond to society's problems.

Capitalism did not reorganize a new society, but it did disorganize the old one. It is unnecessary to reemphasize the intensity of the disintegration to which it subjected precapitalist institutions. But it is important to draw the following conclusion: the Algerians were expelled from their traditional universe; they could not seek shelter there from the present crisis. And this not only for economic or demographic reasons (subsistence agriculture can no longer feed the population), but for reasons that touch on all the forms of social life: the set of needs, behavior, and values that formed a culture a hundred years ago and that regulated work, familial relations, and the use of everyday objects—the traditional representation of the relations between humans and the world—all became outmoded, at least in the eyes of the social category most detached from tradition by its age and its way of life, the young people of the cities, be they workers, employees, schoolteachers, lycéens, students, or unemployed. The ferment of the revolution to come must be looked for among them; it is they who from now on feel most intensely the insufficiency of all the existing rags of traditional culture or the debris of the colonial past as responses to the whole set of problems that are now posed. In December 1960, this same youth, by defying the submachine guns of the French troops, literally carried off victory. The force of the movement that raised them then, its demonstrated capacity for autonomous initiative, its resolution, its very abnegation, show it to be the milieu par excellence where the consciousness of and the desire for another Algeria can be born.

This country is still not the dwelling place of those who inhabit it; it remains to be conquered. *Some crises* may shake it, may provoke famine, unemployment, misery, despair. But none of them will be decisive, and none will bring a response to *the crisis* from which Algeria suffers, until a social class or a strongly organized and implanted section of society builds a model of new social relations and makes everyone accept it.

Notes

Foreword

1. Karl Marx, *The Eighteenth Brumaire of Louis Bonaparte* (New York: International Publishers, 1984), p. 3.

2. As many indigenous Marxists in colonial struggles have argued, an appeal to the "astatic mode of production" is not sufficient to explain the multiple contradictions between anticolonial nationalism and the economistic thesis of class struggle as the sole motor of history. Nationalism, as Lyotard shows in Algeria, moves across class divisions in complex ways and causes the merely ideological (national consciousness) to act as a determining force in and upon history.

3. A more detailed theorization is provided in Lyotard's *L'enthousiasme: Critique kantienne de l'histoire* (Paris: Galilée, 1986).

4. See also chapter 31, "The State and Politics in the France of 1960."

5. Stanley Aronowitz, in *The Politics of Identity* (New York: Routledge, 1991), provides an excellent account of this process in the United States.

6. In the sense that Deleuze and Guattari speak of the minor in *Kafka: Toward a Minor Literature*, trans. Dana Polan (Minneapolis: University of Minnesota Press, 1986).

7. For a detailed analysis of the distinction between a politics of justice and a politics of truth, see Bill Readings, *Introducing Lyotard: Art and Politics* (New York and London: Routledge, 1991).

8. J.-F. Lyotard and J.-L. Thébaud, *Just Gaming*, trans. Wlad Godzich (Minneapolis: University of Minnesota Press, 1985).

9. Immanuel Kant, "An Answer to the Question: 'What Is Enlightenment?' " in *Political Writings* (2nd edition), ed. Hans Reiss, trans. H. B. Nisbet (Cambridge: Cambridge University Press, 1991), p. 54.

10. The tendency to identify the proletariat as the unconscious of history appears in some of the essays in *Dérive à partir de Marx et Freud* (Paris: Christian Bourgois, 1973). Dangerously Manichean, it assumes a Hegelian understanding of history as a rational process and merely opposes the direction of that process.

11. Some feminisms, one should perhaps say. Other feminisms have of course proposed a separate women's identity or an undifferentiated bisexualism as resolutions to the enigma of sexual difference. On this see Lyotard's "One thing at stake in women's struggles" in *The Lyotard Reader*, ed. Andrew Benjamin, trans. Deborah J. Clarke with Winifred Woodhull and John Mowitt (Oxford: Basil Blackwell, 1989).

1. Tomb of the Intellectual

1. *Le Monde*, July 16, 1983.

2. The Differend

1. [For a more heroic account of the electoral struggle of the socialists, see R. W. Johnson, *The Long March of the French Left* (New York: St. Martin's, 1981). — Trans.]

2. [Chirac, mayor of Paris, has been François Mitterrand's right-wing rival for the presidency (along with ex-president Valéry Giscard d'Estaing) for over a decade now. His hour has not yet come. — Trans.]

3. [This point is elaborated by Lyotard in *The Differend: Phrases in Dispute*, trans. Georges Van Den Abbeele (Minneapolis: University of Minnesota Press, 1988), sections 12 and 13 (pp. 9–10). — Trans.]

3. For a Cultural Nonpolicy

1. *Le Nouvel Observateur* asked in a questionnaire what attitude each of those addressed [Lyotard and others] was going to take, as an intellectual, in the face of the socialist power and its cultural politics. In particular, would he actively and personally take part in it? The designated space and the time prohibited answers worthy of the name, but they sufficed to question the "facts" evoked and invoked in the questions of the weekly magazine.

2. *Conseil supérieur des corps universitaires*, which at the time decided on careers in higher education.

4. New Technologies

1. Such was the formulation of the subject in the program of the seminar organized by the CEP [Public Education Council] and IRIS [Institute for Research in Computer Science] during the first semester of 1982.

2. [I have preserved the term "Idea" (capitalized), though Lyotard's Kantian account of the regulatory absolute (which exceeds the concept) has often been translated as "ideal." I avoid "ideal" so as to forestall a too-ready accusation of "idealism." — Trans.]

3. Here I mean by idea a concept of reason that exceeds the limits of our experience. One cannot present examples or cases of it, but only analogues. These are almost what the decision makers call models. They are always debatable. They give rise to dialectical arguments, to rhetorical undertakings of persuasion (including propaganda), to studies (including this seminar), to tests (of an experimental character).

4. It is useless to describe in detail the interactions between the four domains. These interactions were constituted into a hierarchy during the nineteenth and twentieth centuries (Keynes is the symbolic name of these interactions).

5. Only an ignoramus would try to "answer" this question.

5. Wittgenstein "After"

1. [The philosophers of the Enlightenment. — Trans.]

7. A Svelte Appendix to the Postmodern Question

1. A modest contribution to the "postmodernity" dossier that *Babylone* was preparing.
2. [See "Philosophy and Painting in the Age of their Experimentation: Contribution to an Idea of Postmodernity," in *The Lyotard Reader*, ed. Andrew Benjamin (Oxford: Basil Blackwell, 1989), for a detailed reading of Diderot by Lyotard. —Trans.]
3. [A reference to the thought of the group Socialism or Barbarism. —Trans.]
4. [Literally "slenderness." —Trans.]

8. Dead Letter

1. [In the sense of the Latin *sensus communis*, the understanding of community that comes with a common understanding. The French does not have the implication of "common sense" as "received wisdom" or "moderation" that the term does in English. —Trans.]
2. [*Faculty* is capitalized here to indicate the institutional grouping: the Faculty of Arts and Letters, which is assigned the task of attending to "culture" in the French university system. —Trans.]
3. Psychoanalytic speech would seem to be an exception to this rule: doesn't it provide a cure? But to cure is not to find a meaning for activities that were intrinsically contradictory, it is the destructuring and the restructuring of the subject's manner of being-there. It is a revolution: in this respect psychoanalysis is an exception from anthropological interventions. Culture is people.

9. Preamble to a Charter

1. [According to this plan, proposed in 1966, tertiary education was to be split between two-year vocational degrees and four-year degrees. This involved an effective reduction in the number of university places. —Trans.]
2. [A reference to the strategy of *détournement* practiced by the Situationist International under the leadership of Guy Debord. See "Detournement as Negation and Prelude" in *Situationist International Anthology*, ed. and trans. Ken Knabb (Berkeley: Bureau of Public Secrets, 1981), which defines *détournement* as "the reuse of preexisting artistic elements in a new ensemble" (p. 55). —Trans.]
3. [Lyotard is punning on the faculty of letters and the faculty of human sciences. —Trans.]

10. Nanterre, Here, Now

1. [The teacher unions for instructors, high school teachers, and university teachers. The University of Paris campus at Nanterre, opened in 1964, was the focal point of student political activity and the home of the March 22 movement, named to commemorate the student occupation of the administration building in protest at the arrest of six members of the National Vietnam Committee on March 22, 1968. —Trans.]
2. The passages in italics are provided by a group of students.
3. [Money-Commodity-Commodity-Money: Marx's algorithm for capitalist exchange, sometimes also rendered M-C-M. Marx's point is that, far from money being the neutral medium of exchange (Commodity-Money-Commodity), the capitalist marketplace replaces use value with exchange value as the ruling form of value. —Trans.]
4. [An allusion to Lenin's pamphlet of the same title. —Trans.]

5. [M. Francés's statement:] *Before taking the decision to open the campus to the police, the members of the council must clearly imagine how this measure will be translated in deeds. The police authorities will not be content to station one or two agents on the paths. Several police cars will certainly be sent. The effect of this presence will certainly be disastrous, will unleash violences greater than those that we just heard listed. It is also beyond doubt that this presence alone will make a good number of students from several elements presently isolated, who indulge in plundering, stick together.*

I am thus hostile to opening the campus to the police. Another solution has been proposed: checking ID cards at the entrance to the campus. It seems to me to be the only opportune solution, despite the difficulties in enforcing it.

6. [Edgar Faure, de Gaulle's education minister.—Trans.]

7. [The Committee for Democratic Reform, a noncommunist group of teachers committed to reforming the university system.—Trans.]

8. [Unité d'enseignement et de recherche (UER): an administrative grouping within the French university system, equivalent to a department.—Trans.]

9. [Georges Séguy and Eugène Descamps, leaders of, respectively, the Communist Trade Union (CGT) and the more conservative CFDT (Confédération française démocratique du travail).—Trans.]

10. [Lyotard notes the irony that the French term for continuous assessment is "contrôle continu."—Trans.]

11. [Flins-sur-Seine is a major automobile manufacturing town. The Renault factory there was the scene of a major strike in 1968, about which Jean-Pierre Thou made the film *Oser lutter, oser vaincre (Dare to Struggle, Dare to Win)*. The CGT film in question is Paul Seban's *La CGT en Mai.*—Trans.]

12. [Alain Geismar, president of the university teachers' union (SNE Sup).—Trans.]

11. March 23

1. [See note 1 to "Nanterre, Hère, Now" (chapter 10) on the movement of March 22.—Trans.]

2. [The French is preserved here to underline the allusion to situationism, particularly to Debord's *The Society of Spectacle. Mise en spectacle* means the dramatization of social activity as spectacle.—Trans.]

3. [Led by Pannekoek, to whom Lyotard refers in chapter 24 of this volume.—Trans.]

4. [The remarks on "bound energy" that follow rely explicitly on Freud's use of the term in his account of the functioning of the psychic processes.—Trans.]

5. [The two Freudian drives, eros and thanatos.—Trans.]

6. Daniel Singer, *Prelude to Revolution* (New York: Hill and Wang, 1970), p. 32.

7. [In the sense of rhetorical figures. The opposition of discourse to figure is treated at length by Lyotard in *Discours, figure* (Paris: Klincksieck, 1971).—Trans.]

13. Endurance and the Profession

1. [Prisoners who during an escape attempt turned against guards who had previously aided them.—Trans.]

14. *Ersiegerungen*

1. [A portmanteau word, made up of the name of the college (Siegen) at which Lyotard was teaching the seminar he describes and the German *Ersetzung*, meaning repayment. Thus, *Ersiegerungen* would mean something like "the repayment of debts at Siegen."—Trans.]

2. [*Outre mur*, literally "beyond a wall," plays on *outremer*, meaning "lapis lazuli" or "ultramarine" and *outre-mer*, "overseas."—Trans.]

3. [Public sphere (an allusion to Habermas's essay on this topic).—Trans.]

4. [Uncanny (an allusion to Freud's essay on this topic).—Trans.]

5. [Literally, "the message is its contents."—Trans.]

6. [In English in the original.—Trans.]

15. Born in 1925

1. [Poetic theory that insists upon the ritual or sonorous materiality of language, with particular reference to the early Situationist International. Lyotard's specific reference is to the latter.—Trans.]

2. [A children's library, widely published in France, aimed at children between ten and fifteen years old.—Trans.]

3. [Title of a collection of poems by Francis Ponge, literally "the bias of/for things."—Trans.]

4. Sartre, *Situations I* (Paris: Gallimard, 1947), p. 288.

16. A Podium without a Podium

1. [The program, for all its implications of a podium for free speech, imposed the following conditions, all of which participate in a certain metaphysics of the present speaking voice: Programs must be taped live, without use of montage techniques, and must not use any inserted film clips except for the occasional still. The entire program must be filmed in not more than three sessions. Only one retake of each sequence is allowed. In light of these conditions, Lyotard's refusal of the authentic direct voice of the intellectual takes on a particular significance.—Trans.]

2. [See *Just Gaming* and *The Differend* for such a demonstration.—Trans.]

17. *Oikos*

1. [This essay was originally written in English and French, with German headings in the "Answers to Questions" section. Some stylistic modifications have been made in those parts written in English in the interests of clarity, but no attempt has been made to efface the singularity of Lyotard's English usage.—Trans.]

2. The accumulation of facts and in particular of numbers in Holger Strohm's discourse is a very old form of persuasion. This has an effect of stupefaction on the hearers, and it belongs to the rhetoric of persuasion. You can look at the very frequent presence of scientists on television, which has exactly the same function: properly speaking, not to inform but to stupefy the public; the public is very eager for stupefaction. Personally, I consider the use of these facts to be a matter of rhetoric.

3. [*Zurückgezogene* means "the withdrawn," *Abgeschiedene* "the secluded."—Trans.]

4. [A reference to Lyotard's book *Economie libidinale*.—Trans.]

18. The General Line (for Gilles Deleuze)

1. Nina Berberova, *Le roseau révolté*, translated from the Russian by Luba Jergenson (Arles: Actes Sud, 1988).

19. The Wall, the Gulf and the Sun: A Fable

1. [The talk was delivered in Germany. This essay was originally written in English; I have made a few minor grammatical modifications in the text. — Trans.]

20. German Guilt

1. [*The Question of Guilt*, available in English as Karl Jaspers, *The Question of German Guilt*, trans. E. B. Ashton (New York: Dial, 1947). — Trans.]
2. [Life in a mask. — Trans.]
3. M. Dufrenne and P. Ricoeur, *Karl Jaspers et la philosophie de l'existence* (Paris: Seuil, 1947).

21. *Heidegger and "the jews"*: A Conference in Vienna and Freiburg

1. [These paragraphs and the long quotation that follows are drawn from *Heidegger and "the jews."* I reproduce here the translation by Andreas Michel and Mark Roberts (University of Minnesota Press, 1990). David Carroll's excellent introduction to that volume provides a good commentary. — Trans.]
2. [The organization responsible for the rounding up and deportation of Jews in the East. — Trans.]
3. [Lower-case *being* here translates *étant* (Heidegger's *seiend*) as opposed to *être*, which is translated as *Being* (Heidegger's *Sein*). The distinction is between beings and Being in general, between the ontic and the ontological. — Trans.]

22. The Grip *(Mainmise)*

1. [Literally, "takes back the hand," in the sense of the English "take over the helm," with a play on *manchot* as "one-handed" or "one-armed." — Trans.]
2. [Latin *se-ducere*, to lead away from oneself. — Trans.]
3. [The original says "principle," which would seem to be a misprint. — Trans.]
4. [The theologically well-informed "you" addressed here and elsewhere is that of the readers of *Autre Temps*, a journal of "social Christianity." — Trans.]
5. [The Kapos were trusties in Nazi concentration camps (often German communists, imprisoned since before the war). — Trans.]
6. [The word *liance* brings an echo of "alliance" or "covenant" to the notion of tying in the sense of binding. I have had recourse to the ambiguity of "bond" and "bind" in order to translate it. — Trans.]

23. Europe, the Jews, and the Book

1. [Leader of the left-wing French Popular Front in the 1930s. — Trans.]

24. The Name of Algeria

1. [For an account of the journal *Socialisme ou Barbarie*, see Cornelius Castoriadis's "General Introduction" to his *Political and Social Writings* (2 vol.), ed. and trans. David Ames Curtis (Minneapolis: University of Minnesota Press, 1988).—Trans.]

2. [Lyotard here alludes to Lenin's pamphlet "Imperialism, the Highest Stage of Capitalism," published in 1917. See V. I. Lenin, *Selected Writings*, vol. 1 (Moscow: Progress Publishers, 1977), pp. 634–731.—Trans.]

3. [The POUM, or Parti ouvrier d'unification marxiste (Marxist United Workers' Party) was the grouping that united noncommunist left-wing forces, usually anarchist, on the Republican side during the Spanish Civil War.—Trans.]

4. [Amadeo Bordiga (1889–1970) was one of the founders of the Italian Communist party.—Trans.]

5. [Lyotard here alludes to the form of attention prescribed by Freud for the analyst during a session of psychoanalysis.—Trans.]

6. [Lyotard here alludes to the dictum of Chairman Mao that the Communist party should be in the workers' movement like "a fish in water."—Trans.]

7. [The mountain range of central Algeria.—Trans.]

8. [An industrial suburb of Paris.—Trans.]

9. [A city in northeastern Algeria.—Trans.]

10. [The title of the book in which chapters 24 through 34 originally appeared.—Trans.]

11. [Mohammed Ramdani was responsible for editing and introducing the volume *La guerre des Algériens*.—Trans.]

25. The Situation in North Africa

1. The clampdown on Cap Bon (January 28–February 1, 1952) constitutes the repressive phase that leads from riots to the development of an underground resistance. This schema is almost identical for the three countries, although at different times.

2. [The Istiqlal, or PDI, was the Moroccan party of independence struggle, the Néo-Destour the party of Tunisian independence, led by Bourguiba.—Trans.]

3. In 1941, 60.6 percent of imports came from France, 63 percent of exports went there. In 1938, France carried out 16 percent of its total trade with North Africa (figures calculated according to Despois, *L'Afrique du Nord*, 482–84).

4. Figure calculated according to *Problèmes économiques* 336 (June 1954).

5. Old francs.

6. Figures cited by Sauvy, *L'Express*, February 26, 1955.

7. In 1951, out of 8 billion in private investments in Morocco, 4.5 billion went to the former versus 2.6 billion to the latter. *Problèmes économiques* 300 (September 1953).

8. Vialas, "Le paysannat algérien," *Notes et études documentaires*, no. 1626.

9. The largest part of Algerian and Tunisian exports consists of agricultural materials; mineral products make up a quarter of the value of Moroccan exports and half of Tunisian exports.

10. Figures taken from Dresch in *L'industrialisation de l'AFN*, 224–28.

11. Dumont, *L'Algérie dans l'impasse*, 49. Hence proceeds the role of usury in the process of expropriation.

12. For Algeria alone, 600,000 families, or 3 million to 3.5 million persons.

13. For Algeria, 700,000 families, or 3.5 million to 4 million persons.

14. In 1946, Wisner estimated the proportion of the industrial and mining (semiagricultural) proletariat in the active population at 2 percent. Dumont, *L'Algérie dans l'impasse*, 27.

15. In Algeria, 100,000 agricultural workers in 25,000 concerns. All the preceding figures are taken from Vialas, "Le paysannat algérien."

16. In 1883, each inhabitant possessed five quintals of grains (feed grains included). In 1952, this figure was two quintals (Dumont, *L'Algérie dans l'impasse*, p. 55).

17. *Notes et études documentaires*, no. 1963 (December 1954).

18. Profit rates of several mining and agricultural companies in Tunisia in 1950: Djebel M'dilla, 30.45 percent; Djebel Djerissa, 45. 68 percent; Djebel Mallonj, 74.22 percent; Fermes françaises, 66.25 percent. Adapted from *Notes et études documentaires*, no. 1553 (1952), cited in *Bulletin d'informations coloniales*, October 15, 1954: p. 6.

19. [Etoile nord-africaine, or Star of North Africa, was one of the primary independence organizations among Algerian migrant workers in France. Founded in 1926, it formed the basis for the MTLD.—Trans.]

20. [Messali Hadj was leader of Etoile nord-africaine from 1926 onward and a founder of the PPA. In 1947, he founded the MTLD, which later split into the MNA and the FLN.—Trans.]

26. The North African Bourgeoisie

1. The article that follows was written before the latest events that have just disrupted the barely established relations between Tunisia, Morocco, and France. It sheds light on the situation in which the arrest of the FLN leaders occurred. In one sense, the new wave of nationalism can allow the social problems that confronted the Moroccan and Tunisian governments to assume only secondary importance. But in another sense, and no doubt this aspect of the situation is not more important than the first, the fragile political edifice erected by Bourguiba and the sultan finds itself considerably weakened. Their "centrist" orientation is called into question under the pressure of the unbelievable offensive launched by the French government. (*Socialisme ou Barbarie*)

2. [*Caid*, from the Arabic *qa'id* (chief), was the name given to indigenous local magistrates in North Africa under French colonial rule. The term may also more generally refer to feudal lords.—Trans.]

3. [A reference to Trotsky's theory of uneven and combined development, usually invoked to explain the peculiarities of the Russian Revolution.—Trans.]

27. A New Phase in the Algerian Question

1. This article was already written when the second edition of *L'Etincelle* came out, distributed in 8,000 copies. There is little to be said about it. As usual, the fundamental analyses are put off until later, and the driving forces behind the bulletin seem especially concerned to prove their loyalism. Let us cite a phrase that summarizes the situation: "We know that dozens of comrades, discouraged and on the point of leaving the party, regained confidence and hope thanks to our initiative. It is a significant first result. We, the 'liquidators,' already act as a catalyst of life and renewal for the party."

On the other hand, on February 15, *L'Express* published a text emanating from an "oppositional group," distinct from that of *L'Etincelle*. There one finds a whimsical enough analysis of the diverse "tendencies" in the PCF [French Communist party] and a programmatic definition of socialism that discourages criticism, among others: "The socialism we want to realize is not identical to the present system of the Soviet Union. It ought to seek to combine the collective ownership of the essential means of production with an economic and political democracy in which this social ownership would not be an abstraction, but a reality perceptible to the consciousness of the members of the collectivity taken individually."

2. [A peasant revolt. The original jacquerie, like the English Peasant Revolt, occurred in the late fourteenth century, after the Black Death. It was bloodily put down by royal troops.—Trans.]

3. [*Uléma* or *ouléma*: a doctor of Muslim law, both a jurist and a theologian.—Trans.]

28. Algerian Contradictions Exposed

1. In the cities with a strong Muslim majority (Constantine, etc.), the FLN was not defeated; this proves the role played by the Europeans in the repression.

2. Official estimates: in February 1957, 20,000 fellahs; in February 1958, 35,000. Estimates of R. Uboldi (*Les Temps Modernes*, December 1957): 100,000 regular troops and 300,000 partisans.

3. See "A New Phase in the Algerian Question" [chapter 27].

4. D. Mothé, "Les ouvriers français et les Nord-Africains," *Socialisme ou Barbarie* 21.

5. This is what Mothé's article, which we have already cited, shows. Its conclusion of course imputes responsibility for the workers' passivity on the Algerian question to the French Communist party, but the whole first part shows that this passivity rests on a much more profound separation, which is of a properly sociological order.

6. See "The North African Bourgeoisie" [chapter 26].

7. [The Committee of Public Safety was the radical ruling body in revolutionary France from 1793 to 1795, charged with accelerating the executive process.—Trans.]

8. Cited by C.-A. Julien, *L'Afrique du Nord en marche*, p. 133.

9. See "The North African Bourgeoisie" [chapter 26].

29. The "Counterrevolutionary" War, Colonial Society, and De Gaulle

1. ["Pieds-noirs" is a derogatory nickname for the colonial French of Algeria, with a tone and field of reference roughly equivalent to "white trash."—Trans.]

2. We are taking this expression in the sense given in Massu's confidential breviary *Contre-révolution, stratégie et tactique*.

3. [Chapter 28, "Algerian Contradictions Exposed."—Trans.]

4. [General Salan was one of the four generals later involved in the 1961 putsch. In 1958 he was given the charge of maintaining the French Republic's authority in Algeria.—Trans.]

5. [Saint-Cyr is the elite French military training school, the equivalent of West Point in the United States or Sandhurst in England.—Trans.]

6. *Le Monde*, May 30, 1958.

7. [Matignon is the official residence of the French prime minister.—Trans.]

30. The Social Content of the Algerian Struggle

1. [A detailed tactical account of maneuvers by right-wing groups, de Gaulle, and the army is omitted here.—Trans.]

2. [A *douar* is a rural administrative district. The word originates from the Arabic name for a nomadic encampment.—Trans.]

3. The journalists of the left and elsewhere, in continuing to wonder about plots hatched in the upper echelons of the army and aimed at de Gaulle, give a good indication of their com-

prehension of the problem. According to them, May 13 was never anything other than a military putsch. Do they hope that the current regime will perish at the hands of its own troops? That would give one pause for thought about the confidence the "left" has in its own activity. In any case, this would be to leave out the fact that the current regime marks a consolidation of the capitalist state, which henceforth renders conspiracies generally ineffective.

4. [See "The 'Counterrevolutionary' War, Colonial Society and de Gaulle," (chapter 29). — Trans.]

5. [An allusion to Clausewitz's dictum that diplomacy is the continuation of war by other means. — Trans.]

6. This police control is what de Gaulle calls "the wide and profound contact [of the army] with the population," which he says had never before been made. He makes this one of the achievements of the pacification. But, put back into real history, these "contacts" are a failure: they bear witness to, on the one hand, the previous lack of administration — that is, the exteriority of the Algerian state apparatus to the rural masses in particular — and, on the other hand, the present necessity of closely surrounding the population in order to safeguard the fiction of an *Algérie française*.

7. Over the past year, if one believes the communiqués of the General Staff, the French troops have eliminated six hundred combatants per week, destroyed hundreds of munitions dumps, recovered thousands of weapons, dismantled many networks, obtained massive results, and so on — and provided the strongest refutation of all this themselves by each week finding new combatants to put out of action, new munitions dumps to destroy, and so on. Six hundred *fellaghas* lost per week makes 30,000 per year, that is, the strength of the ALN officially recognized by Algiers. Consequently, either the figures are false (and it is certain that the six hundred victims are not all soldiers and that the ALN has many more than 30,000 men) or the ALN is capable of mending its losses as fast as it undergoes them. Or, finally, which is most likely, the two hypotheses are correct together: the total strength is indeed higher than 30,000, one baptizes every dead Algerian a "fellagha," and the ability of the ALN units to regroup remains intact.

8. This was true above all of the regions where this tension had already reached a brutal breaking point: thus the 1945 massacres in the Constantinois and the Sétif regions remained present in everyone's memory. We will return to this later on.

9. The rebel organization distinguishes between the Moudjahidines, regular combatants, and the Moussebilines, temporary partisans. One can conceive of intermediate states. Algiers figures the rebel strength at 30,000, sometimes 40,000. Yazid spoke in Monrovia of 120,000 combatants. If one keeps the figure of 80,000 *fellaghas*, that admits a one to six ratio between regular underground fighters and the army of repression, which seems to me to justify the absence of military successes on both sides. A higher ratio would give an appreciable advantage to the rebellion: this was the case before 1956. And inversely, the one to six ratio was that which the German generals, in 1949, judged necessary to set defenders and assailants *at parity*, according to their experience on the Russian front. See Ph. Guillaume, "La guerre et notre époque," *Socialisme ou Barbarie* 3, p. 11.

10. J. Baulin in his book *Face au nationalisme arabe* cites this commentary of a collaborator with *Le Monde*: "To claim to buy off a nationalist movement is still OK; but to hope to get it at a discount . . . " (pp. 125–26). This exactly defines the extent of the subtlety of the "left" and the "intelligent bourgeoisie" in the Algerian question: set the price. It is moreover one of the remedies advocated by Baulin himself in the Arab question with the exception that he presents it openly as capitalism's only coherent strategy.

11. Trotsky, *History of the Russian Revolution*, vol 1. (Ann Arbor: University of Michigan Press, 1957), pp. 251–52.

12. See "A New Phase in the Algerian Question" [chapter 27].

13. [General Challe, chief of the French armed forces in Algeria since 1958, was one of the leaders of the putsch of April 1961, an anti-independence insurrection that united the extreme right and the French army in Algiers against de Gaulle. — Trans.]

14. [General Alphonse Juin was the French military governor of Morocco prior to independence. — Trans.]

15 To apply the notion of a bureaucracy to the really dominant class in Oriental societies and, more particularly, to that class that, in the guise of the Ottoman Empire, dominated the whole Near Eastern world from the Danube to the Persian Gulf, from Aden to the Maghreb, for more than three centuries does not arise from an acute form of generalizing bureaucratophobia, but rather allows one to establish the characteristics of the development of the Oriental world without tampering with history as the Stalinist historians do. Analysis shows, in effect, that the predominant relations of production in these societies belong to the order of slavery, in that the extraction of surplus value occurs under the *manifest* form of taxes in work [*corvées*] and in kind (levies on the products of labor). Yet the relations of production are not of a feudal order, because the class that appropriates the surplus value is not made up of lords who *privately* possess the means of production. The form of property is completely different from that which one sees in the Western Middle Ages: the land and the waters — that is, the essential elements of the means of production in these predominantly steppe regions given the low level of development of the forces of production — are the formal *property* of the sovereign; their *disposition*, that is, the social reality of property, belongs in fact to his functionaries. The *role* of this class of functionaries in the productive process clearly emerges in the perfect example of ancient Egypt: the extension of crops into the Nile valley required the full use of periodic floods; but the construction of embankments and rudimentary dams, the cutting of canals and reservoirs, the regulation of flow in the irrigated zones, the synchronization of the maneuvering of the gates, the prediction of the high-water levels in the different points of the valley, the immense labor by which humankind took possession of all of fertile Egypt could not be accomplished by scattered peasant communities. Once the zones that could be cultivated by means of local irrigation had been developed, the structure of dispersed villages or even of separate fiefdoms constituted an objective obstacle to the development of the productive forces. Bringing new lands under cultivation required the control of the whole valley from Aswan to the Delta — that is, the incorporation of all the workers into a centralized state.

16. *L'Entente*, February 23, 1936; quoted by C.-A. Julien, *L'Afrique du Nord en marche*, p. 110.

17. "The ideological unification of the Algerian people around the principle of the Algerian nation has already been achieved. Actual unification, unification through action, will continue to be our principal objective because we are convinced that it is the effective means of bringing oppressive imperialism to an end." These words, from an editorial in *El Maghrib el Arabi* [the French-language newspaper of the MTLD] of January 16, 1948, express this situation accurately. The editorial adds, "We are extremely worried by certain developments," alluding to the difficulty of achieving unity of action with bourgeois elements.

18. Daniel Mothé, "Les ouvriers français et les Nord-Africains," *Socialisme ou Barbarie* 21, pp. 146 ff.

19. Such was no doubt the perspective of Ramdane, the former official for Algiers.

20. Algeria's overall annual income was in 1955 thought to be 537 billion francs (on the basis of figures given by Peyrega). The total income in the hands of Muslim Algerians could be calculated at 271 billion, according to the Maspétiol report in 1953. The *Français d'Algérie* thus received appreciably half the overall production.

31. The State and Politics in the France of 1960

1. [The Jeanson network was a French clandestine organization—named after its leader—that sheltered deserters from the French army of Algeria and supported the independence movement.—Trans.]

2. [A declaration signed by 121 noncommunist French intellectuals affirming the right to refuse the draft.—Trans.]

3. [De Sérigny was a prominent right winger, editor of the newspaper *L'Echo d'Alger*, involved in the anti-independence insurrection of 1958.—Trans.]

4. See the collection of articles on "La crise française et le gaullisme" in *Socialisme ou Barbarie* 25 (July–August 1958).

5. [A summary of economic statistics detailing the crisis of the Fourth Republic is omitted here.—Trans.]

6. See Chaulieu, "Perspectives de la crise française."

7. See P. Chaulieu, "Sur la dynamique du capitalisme," *Socialisme ou Barbarie* 12 (August–September 1953).

8. See "The Social Content of the Algerian Struggle" [chapter 30].

9. *L'Express*, February 4, 1960.

10. At its height, in February 1959, registered unemployment was less than 1 percent of the labor force, and it has since declined.

11. In deficit by $1,020 million in 1956, by $1,080 million in 1957, and by $480 million in 1958, this balance showed in 1959 a surplus of exports over imports of $516 million.

12. In the fourth quarter of 1959, the index of industrial production was 11 percent higher than that of the fourth quarter of 1958.

13. See "Bilan," *Socialisme ou Barbarie*, November–December 1958.

14. Which is not to say that it happens always or automatically.

15. See D. Mothé, "Les ouvriers et la culture," *Socialisme ou Barbarie* 30 (April–May 1960).

16. [In English in original.—Trans.]

17. [An ironic allusion to the language of Stalinist communiqués, which tend to speak of "frank and comradely discussions" attendant upon the imposition of central policy.—Trans.]

18. [The analysis of this phrase of Karl Marx's is conducted at length by Lyotard in "A Memorial for Marxism," appended to *Peregrinations* (New York: Columbia University Press, 1988).—Trans.]

32. Gaullism and Algeria

1. [Ahmed Ben Salah, Tunisian secretary of state for finance.—Trans.]

2. [Committee on the economic development of France.—Trans.]

3. [A trial of deserters and draft evaders in which the fact of French army torture of Algerian prisoners (especially by paratroopers) was adduced as a defense for the refusal to serve.—Trans.]

4. [Crowned emperor of Vietnam in 1925, Bao Dai abdicated in 1945 in favor of Ho Chi Minh's Vietminh forces. He was recalled in 1948 by the French in order to serve as a figurehead in the war against the Vietminh. He was officially deposed in 1955 in an American-controlled referendum, which replaced him with Prime Minister Diem.—Trans.]

33. Algeria: Seven Years After

1. Among a population of 9 million Algerians. This would mean for present-day France 5 million dead, 5 million deported, several million émigrés, and more than a million interned.
2. The French post of Sakhiet was evacuated at the beginning of October.
3. [The Challe putsch or generals' putsch of April 1961 was led by four generals: Challe, Salan, Zeller, and Jouhaud. This protest against Gaullist government policy by a coalition of extreme right wingers and army members fell apart after four days.—Trans.]
4. [The Constantine plan was the French plan for the economic development of Algeria passed by de Gaulle.—Trans.]
5. Tunis is again calling for the participation of Ben Bella and his comrades in the negotiations: this would be equivalent to a de facto recognition of the GPRA.

34. Algeria Evacuated

1. See "The Social Content of the Algerian Struggle" [chapter 30].
2. A striking image of which can be found in *La révolution algérienne par les textes*, ed. André Mandouze (Paris: Maspéro, 1961).
3. "One can in large part say that from August 1956 on, the FLN ceased to be a unitary organism and became a coalition, precisely a 'Front'; the former members of the MTLD and the UDMA, the Ulémas then penetrate into the ruling organizations without truly renouncing their individuality. It is from 1956 on that the present 'Front,' this magma, constitutes itself" (interview with M. Boudiaf, *Le Monde*, November 2, 1962).
4. Interview with M. Boudiaf, *Le Monde*, September 7, 1962.
5. See R. Gendarme, *L'économie de l'Algérie* (Paris: Armand Colin, 1959), pp. 189–237; P. Bourdieu, *The Algerians* (Boston: Beacon Press, 1962) [orig.: *Sociologie de l'Algérie* (Paris: Presses Universitaires de France, 1958)], passim. In the first edition of his book, Bourdieu emphasized above all the cultural differences prior to colonization, notably the disdain for agricultural tasks that the Arab-speaking regions had inherited from their nomadic ancestors. He says, for example: "This type of economy [of the Arab-speaking countries], where farming by the owner is rare and despised, where those who possess some wealth neglect work to taste the refinements of society-life, where agricultural work therefore always presupposes the cooperation of two parties, the property owner and the *khammès*, differs profoundly from that noted in the Berber countries" (77).
6. [A detailed description of political maneuvers within the Algerian independence movement, leading to Ben Bella's accession to leadership, is omitted here.—Trans.]
7. The Tripoli program was edited by the Internationalist Communist party (PCI), with a preface dated September 22, 1962, and a commentary by M. Pable, "Impressions et problèmes de la révolution algérienne." Another edition of the program was published at the same time by the "revolutionary tendency of the PCF (French Communist party)," with a preface signed "Le Communiste" and dated October 1, 1962. The text itself is identical in the two editions. The content of the preface of the PCI edition is summed up in this sentence: "The Algerian revolution henceforth possesses a program, adopted unanimously in Tripoli, which, if it is applied, will make Algeria into a society belonging to the Algerian masses of peasants and workers, and will make the Algerian State into a workers' State building a socialist society." The content of the "Communiste" preface is summed up thus: "The Political Bureau of the FLN and the General Staff of the ALN . . . represent, whether one likes it or not, the most revolutionary and also the most important forces, the most solid in their anticolonialist stance." [Note moved from original location—Trans.]
8. *L'Unità*, August 13, 1962.

9. "Comment 2,300 fellahs de Boufarik ont jeté les bases de la réforme agraire," *Alger Républicain*, October 17 and 18, 1962. According to this report, the idea of a management committee for the vacant farms dates from June, that is, from before independence.

10. According to information given, without guarantees, by our correspondent in Algiers.

11. Ben Bella's declaration at Arzew, September 15, 1962.

12. *L'Unità*, August 13, 1962.

13. Ibid.

14. Fanon develops this point with a certain intemperance, in *L'an V de la révolution algérienne* (Paris: Maspéro, 1959).

15. P. Bourdieu points out in *The Algerians* (pp. 78–79) that the agricultural workers at times call for the advantages of the *khamessat*: payment in kind, advances.

16. *The Wretched of the Earth*.

17. And hid us from ourselves.

18. J.-P. Sartre, preface to *The Wretched of the Earth* (New York: Grove, 1968), p. 27.

19. *Rapport du groupe d'études des relations financières entre la metropole et l'Algérie* (Maspétial report): Algiers, 1953), pp. 154–56 and 191.

20. "Déclarations de principes relative à la coopération économique et financière," Articles 12 and 13, *Journal officiel*, no. 62–63, March 1962.

21. Ibid., Articles 1 and 3.

22. That is, you will not be aided at all, since the compensation for the expropriated lands will exhaust the total amount of aid.

23. The Constantine Plan (October 4, 1958), whose model had been established, essentially, by the minister of Algeria in March 1958, in the report entitled *Perspectives décennales de développement économique de l'Algérie*, Algiers (Ten Year Plan).

24. Contrary to the *Perspectives*, however, the Constantine Plan provided for the distribution of 2,500 hectares of new lands to the "Muslims"—a matter of stabilizing the situation in the countryside by forming a rural petite bourgeoisie. See on this subject A. Gorz, "Gaullisme et néo-gaullisme," *Les Temps Modernes*, no. 179, March 1961.

25. Gendarme, *L'economie de l'Agérie*, pp. 290–310.

26. Gorz, "Gaullisme et néo-gaullisme," p. 1157.

27. Gendarme, *L'economie de l'Algérie*, pp. 305–10.

28. In old francs. The Constantine Plan likewise projected an investment of 2,000 billion for five years.

29. The figures of the Constantine plan are appreciably the same, reduced for a period of five years.

30. However, item two of the preamble to the "Déclarations de principes sur la coopération pour la mise en valeur des richesses du sous-sol du Sahara" substitutes Algeria for France as concessionary. In the same direction, item four of the same declaration limits the rights of the concession holder in relation to the "needs of Algerian domestic consumption and of local refining activities."

31. *Alger Républicain*, October 9, 1962.

32. *Le Monde*, October 27, 1962.

33. For decades, Algeria was France's principal client. In 1962, the Federal Republic of Germany purchased 5,407 million new francs' worth of French goods, Algeria 4,375 million (*La Vie Française*, February 23, 1962).

34. *Le Monde*, October 17 and 18 and November 6, 1962.

35. On November 10, 1962, Ben Bella says to the peasants of the Sétifois: "We want to create a truly popular socialist and democratic society"; he has the Ministry of Agriculture set up state farms in the Kabylie (see *Le Monde*, November 11, 12, and 16). On the 20th, he reassures the bourgeoisie: "There is one sector that is vital for our country: the public sector, but

there will also be a semipublic sector and a private sector. Even in the socialist countries, there exist private sectors that are at times important. There is talk of nationalizations, of draconian measures: there is no question of that. Let the firms that exist resume their activity as quickly as possible" (*Le Monde*, November 21, 1962).

36. This traditional contrast has exceptions and will have them more and more to the degree that the opposition between bureaucratic society of the Russian kind and bourgeois society of the Western kind will become blurred. What determines the capacity of a ruling class to carry out the transformation of an underdeveloped country is in particular its ability to break the commercial monopolies of the international firms and the privileges of the landed aristocracy and the local parasitic bourgeoisies and, consequently, to control the breakdown of foreign aid. The process of bureaucratization that society and the state are undergoing in the West increasingly provides capitalism with the political and economic means to bypass the particular interests of specific groups and to constrain the local bourgeoisie, confronted by the "communist peril," to make a serious effort to transform the country. Under pressure from the United States, Chiang Kai-shek forced the landlords of Formosa to reinvest their profits in the industrial sector; this was also Peron's policy in Argentina. On the other side, to the degree that needs in Russian society develop according to the capitalist model, particularly as a regular increase in the standard of living comes to be required, the ideological link that tied the Soviet Union to the bureaucracies of the underdeveloped countries begins to come undone, and Soviet aid begins to be given in exchange for complete subordination to the policy of peaceful coexistence.

37. See *La Voie Communiste*, October 1962; *Le Monde*, September 23-24 and November 16, 1962. For its part, *Azione Communista*, in its edition of October 8, 1962, announces that a group (called Spartacus) of the "new forces who are inspired by the fundamental principles of communism" is at work among the Algerian migrant workers. Spartacus "identifies the FLN, presently in power with Ben Bella, as a military and administrative caste that has taken the place of the old domination to exercise the same functions with the support of the French bourgeoisie." Spartacus's manifesto declares, according to the same source: "Peace in Algeria, far from introducing a revolutionary development of the conflict and permitting a first step toward social revolution, is only a diplomatic and military agreement between the French bourgeoisie, the French colonists, and the bureaucrats of Cairo and Tunis to set a common price for Saharan petroleum and the labor power of the Algerian masses."

38. On the French side, "the balance of arrivals and departures for September leaves an excess of 15,726 and in October 244,355. The average monthly balance had been only + 1,963 and + 3,564 in 1961." One can savor in passing the humane style of this declaration by the French minister of labor (September 14, 1962).

Index

Compiled by Robin Jackson

Jean-François Lyotard is professor of philosophy at the Collège International de Philosophie in Paris, professor of French and Italian at the University of California at Irvine, and the author of numerous works. Minnesota has published his *Postmodern Condition: A Report on Knowledge* (1984), *The Differend: Phrases in Dispute* (1989), *Heidegger and "the jews"* (1990), and *The Postmodern Explained: Correspondence 1982–1985* (1993).

Bill Readings is associate professor of comparative literature at the University of Montreal. He is the author of *Introducing Lyotard* (1991).

Kevin Paul Geiman is an assistant professor of philosophy at Valparaiso (Indiana) University.